Books by Malachi Martin

THE SCRIBAL CHARACTER OF THE DEAD SEA SCROLLS
THE PILGRIM (under the pseudonym Michael Serafian)
THE ENCOUNTER
THREE POPES AND THE CARDINAL
JESUS NOW
THE NEW CASTLE
HOSTAGE TO THE DEVIL
THE FINAL CONCLAVE
KING OF KINGS (a novel)
THE DECLINE AND FALL OF THE ROMAN CHURCH
THERE IS STILL LOVE
RICH CHURCH, POOR CHURCH
VATICAN (a novel)
THE JESUITS
THE KEYS OF THIS BLOOD

A TOUCHSTONE BOOK

Published by Simon & Schuster

New York   London

Toronto   Sydney

Tokyo   Singapore

Malachi Martin

The Keys of This Blood

The Struggle for
World Dominion
Between Pope John Paul II,
Mikhail Gorbachev,
and the Capitalist West

TOUCHSTONE

Rockefeller Center
1230 Avenue of the Americas
New York, New York, 10020

Library of Congress Cataloging in Publication Data
Martin, Malachi.
The Keys of This Blood: The Struggle for World Dominion
Between Pope John Paul II, Mikhail Gorbachev, and the
Capitalist West/Malachi Martin.
p.   cm.
Includes index.
1. John Paul II, Pope, 1920– . 2. Gorbachev, Mikhail
Sergeyevich, 1931– . 3. Catholic Church and World
Politics. 4. World Politics—1985–1995. I. Title.
BX1368.5.M37   1990
909.82′8—dc20   90-42369
CIP
ISBN: 0-671-69174-0
ISBN: 0-671-74723-1 Pbk.

For the Immaculate Heart

Contents

II. THE GEOPOLITICS OF FAITH

CODA: THE PROTOCOL OF SALVATION

The Servant of the Grand Design

Willing or not, ready or not, we are all involved in an all-out, no-holds-barred, three-way global competition. Most of us are not competitors, however. We are the stakes. For the competition is about who will establish the first one-world system of government that has ever existed in the society of nations. It is about who will hold and wield the dual power of authority and control over each of us as individuals and over all of us together as a community; over the entire six billion people expected by demographers to inhabit the earth by early in the third millennium.

The competition is all-out because, now that it has started, there is no way it can be reversed or called off.

No holds are barred because, once the competition has been decided, the world and all that's in it—our way of life as individuals and as citizens of the nations; our families and our jobs; our trade and commerce and money; our educational systems and our religions and our cultures; even the badges of our national identity, which most of us have always taken for granted—all will have been powerfully and radically altered forever. No one can be exempted from its effects. No sector of our lives will remain untouched.

The competition began and continues as a three-way affair because that is the number of rivals with sufficient resources to establish and maintain a new world order.

Nobody who is acquainted with the plans of these three rivals has any doubt but that only one of them can win. Each expects the other two to be overwhelmed and swallowed up in the coming maelstrom of change. That being the case, it would appear inescapable that their competition will end up as a confrontation.

As to the time factor involved, those of us who are under seventy will see at least the basic structures of the new world government installed. Those of us under forty will surely live under its legislative, executive and judiciary authority and control. Indeed, the three rivals themselves —and many more besides as time goes on—speak about this new world order not as something around a distant corner of time, but as something that is imminent. As a system that will be introduced and installed in our midst by the end of this final decade of the second millennium.

What these competitors are talking about, then, is the most profound and widespread modification of international, national and local life that the world has seen in a thousand years. And the competition they are engaged in can be described simply enough as the millennium endgame.

Ten years before this competition became manifest to the world at large, the man who was destined to become the first, the most unexpected and, for some at least, the most unwelcome competitor of all in this millennium endgame spoke openly about what he saw down the road even then.

Toward the end of an extended visit to America in 1976, an obscure Polish archbishop from Krakow by the name of Karol Wojtyla stood before an audience in New York City and made one of the most prophetic speeches ever given.

"We are now standing in the face of the greatest historical confrontation humanity has gone through," he said, ". . . a test of two thousand years of culture and Christian civilization, with all of its consequences for human dignity, individual rights and the rights of nations." But, he chided his listeners on that September day, "wide circles of American society and wide circles of the Christian community do not realize this fully. . . ."

Perhaps the world was still too immersed in the old system of nation-states, and in all the old international balance-of-power arrangements, to hear what Wojtyla was saying. Or perhaps Wojtyla himself was reckoned as no more than an isolated figure hailing from an isolated country that had long since been pointedly written out of the global power equation. Or perhaps, after the industrial slaughter of millions of human beings in two world wars and in 180 local wars, and after the endless terrors of nuclear brinkmanship that have marked the progress of the twentieth century, the feeling was simply that one confrontation more or less wasn't going to make much difference.

Whatever the reason, it would seem that no one who heard or later read what Karol Wojtyla said that day had any idea that he was pointing to a competition he already saw on the horizon: a competition between the world's only three internationally based power structures for truly global hegemony.

. . .

An isolated figure Karol Wojtyla may have been in the fall of 1976—at least for many Westerners. But two years later, in October of 1978, when he emerged from the Sistine Chapel in Rome as Pope John Paul II, the 263rd successor to Peter the Apostle, he was himself the head of the most extensive and deeply experienced of the three global powers that would, within a short time, set about ending the nation system of world politics that has defined human society for over a thousand years.

It is not too much to say, in fact, that the chosen purpose of John Paul's pontificate—the engine that drives his papal grand policy and that determines his day-to-day, year-by-year strategies—is to be the victor in that competition, now well under way. For the fact is that the stakes John Paul has placed in the arena of geopolitical contention include everything—himself; his papal persona; the age-old Petrine Office he now embodies; and his entire Church Universal, both as an institutional organization unparalleled in the world and as a body of believers united by a bond of mystical communion.

The other two contenders in the arena of this "greatest historical confrontation humanity has gone through" are no mean adversaries. Rather, they are the leaders of the two most deeply entrenched secular powers, who stand, in a collective sense, on their record as the authors and the primary actors in the period of history that has been so much the worst of times that the best face we can put on it is to say that we were not swallowed up in the apocalypse of World War III—as if that were the best man could do for his fellowman.

The first of those two powers, the Soviet Union, is now led by John Paul's most interesting adversary and a fellow Slav. Mikhail Sergeyevich Gorbachev was as unexpected and unpredicted a leader in the new world arena as Karol Wojtyla himself. A husky man still in his prime, hailing from the obscure industrial town of Privolnoye in the southwest of Russia, Gorbachev is now what he was groomed to be: Master of the Leninist-Marxist Party-State whose power and standing in the community of nations was built upon seventy years of physical and spiritual fratricide carried out in the name of a purely sociopolitical vision and a thoroughly this-worldly ideology.

The final contender in the competition for the new world order is not a single individual leader of a single institution or territory. It is a group of men who are united as one in power, mind and will for the purpose of achieving a single common goal: to be victorious in the competition for the new global hegemony.

While the acknowledged public leader and spokesman for this group is the current American president, the contenders who compose this assemblage of individuals are Americans and Europeans who, taken together, represent every nation of the Western democratic alliance.

Unremittingly globalist in their vision and their activities, these individuals operate from two principal bases of power. The first is the power base of finance, industry and technology. Entrepreneurial in their occupations, the men in this phalanx qualify themselves, and are often referred to by others, as Transnationalist in their outlook. What they mean by the term "Transnationalist" is that they intend to, and increasingly do, exercise their entrepreneurship on a worldwide basis. Leaping over all the barriers of language, race, ideology, creed, color and nationalism, they view the world with some justification as their oyster; and the twin pearls of great price that they seek are global development and the good life for all.

Members of the second phalanx of this group of globalist contenders —Internationalists, as they are frequently called—bring with them invaluable experience in government, in intergovernmental relationships, and in the rarefied art of international politics. Their bent is toward the development of new and ever wider interrelationships between the governments of the world. Their aim is to foster increasing cooperation on an international basis—and to do that by maintaining the peace, at the same time they accomplish what war has rarely achieved: the breakdown of all the old natural and artificial barriers between nations.

In the current competition to establish and head a one-world government, Transnationalists and Internationalists can be said for all practical purposes to act as one; to constitute one main contender. The Genuine Globalists of the West. Both groups are products par excellence of the system of democratic capitalism. Both are so closely intertwined in their membership that individuals move easily and with great effect from an Internationalist to a Transnationalist role and back again. And not least important in the all-encompassing confrontation that is under way, both groups share the same philosophy about human life and its ultimate meaning—a philosophy that appears, in the surprised view of some observers, to be closer to Mikhail Gorbachev's than to Pope John Paul's.

There is one great similarity shared by all three of these geopolitical competitors. Each one has in mind a particular grand design for one-world governance. In fact, each of them talks now in nearly the same terms Karol Wojtyla used in his American visit in 1976. They all give speeches about an end to the nation system of our passing civilization.

Their geopolitical competition is about which of the three will form, dominate and run the world system that will replace the decaying nation system.

There is at least one other similarity among these groups that is worthy of note, primarily because it leads to misunderstanding and confusion. And that is the language each group uses to present its case to the world.

All three contenders use more or less the same agreeable terms when propagandizing their individual designs for the new world order. All three declare that man and his needs are to be the measure of what those individual designs will accomplish. All three speak of individual freedom and man's liberation from want and hunger; of his natural dignity; of his individual, social, political and cultural rights; of the good life to which each individual has a fundamental right.

Beneath the similarity of language, however, there lies a vast difference in meaning and intent; and greatly dissimilar track records of accomplishment.

The individual in Gorbachev's new world order will be someone whose needs and rights are determined by the monopolar government of Leninist Marxism. Indeed, all individual rights and freedom and dignity are to be measured by the needs of the Party to remain supreme and permanent.

In the new world order of the Wise Men of the West—the most powerful of the Genuine Globalists—the rights and freedoms of the individual would be based on positive law: that is, on laws passed by a majority of those who will be entitled to vote on the various levels of the new system of governmental administration and local organization. Ultimate rule, however, will be far removed from the ordinary individual.

The primary difficulty for Pope John Paul II in both of these models for the new world order is that neither of them is rooted in the moral laws of human behavior revealed by God through the teaching of Christ, as proposed by Christ's Church. He is adamant on one capital point: No system will ensure and guarantee the rights and freedoms of the individual if it is not based on those laws. This is the backbone principle of the new world order envisaged by the Pontiff.

Similarities of public rhetoric, therefore, do more to mask than clarify the profound differences between the contenders, and the profoundly different consequences for us all of the grand design each one proposes for the arrangement of our human affairs.

The three are contenders for the same prize; but they are not working in the vacuum of a never-never land. No one of them expects the others to change. Mr. Gorbachev knows that his Western competitors will not renounce their fundamental democratic egalitarianism or cease to be capitalists.

The capitalists, meanwhile, know Gorbachev is a hard-core, convinced Leninist; his goal is the Marxist "Workers' Paradise"—however he may now configure that fearsome Utopia.

Similarly, neither of these contenders expects Pope John Paul to renounce his Christian optic on the world of man or cease to be Roman Catholic in his geopolitical strategy.

Indeed, so definitive is the cleavage and distinction among the three that each realizes only one of them can ultimately be the victor in the millennium endgame.

When he spoke in 1976 of "a test of two thousand years of culture and Christian civilization," Karol Wojtyla was as aware as any human being could be that the pre-Gorbachev Soviets of the East and the Globalists of the West remained frozen in their political, economic and military stalemate.

Never mind that the Leninist-Marxist empire of the East was slowly deteriorating to the point of falling in on itself in shattered ruins.

Never mind that the West was bound to its treadmill of democratic egalitarianism, hard put to maintain its position but without any forward movement possible.

Never mind that countless nations were caught in the grinding maw of the East-West stalemate. Some countries in the West, and most in the Third World, paid the price of helpless pawns. They found themselves caught up in surrogate wars; in hopeless famine and want; in plots to destabilize the governments and economies of countries and of entire regions. Even imprisonment of whole nations was not too much to bear.

In the teeth of all that, leaders of East and West remained stubbornly engaged in the ancient exercise of international politics reduced to its grossest terms—the maintenance of the status quo through constant interplay between the threat and the use of raw power.

That unacceptable and untenable world condition was one that Karol Wojtyla knew intimately. By the time he was elected Pope, he had worked for nearly thirty years beside the tough and canny Cardinal Stefan Wyszynski of Warsaw, a man who earned his stripes as the "Fox of Europe" by planning and executing the only geopolitical strategy—the only successful strategy—ever carried out by an Eastern satellite nation against the Soviet Union.

All during those years, the two Churchmen—the Cardinal and the future Pope—already thought and worked in terms of what Wyszynski called the "three *Internationales*." That was the classical term he used to talk about geopolitical contenders for true world power.

There exist on this earth, Wyszynski used to say, only three *Internationales*. The "Golden *Internationale*" was his shorthand term for the financial powers of the world—the Transnationalist and Internationalist globalist leaders of the West.

The "Red *Internationale*" was, of course, the Leninist-Marxist Party-State of the Soviet Union, with which he and Wojtyla and their compatriots had such long and painfully intimate experience.

The third geopolitical contender—the Roman Catholic Church; the "Black *Internationale*"—was destined in Wyszynski's view to be the ultimate victor in any contention with those rivals.

Surely such a thought seemed outlandish to much of the world—including much of the Roman Catholic hierarchy in the Vatican and elsewhere. Nonetheless, it was a view that Karol Wojtyla not only shared. It was one that he had helped to prove against the Soviets and that he now carried into the papacy itself.

According to the outlook Wojtyla brought to the office and the role of Supreme Pontiff of the Roman Church, it was unthinkable that the Marxist East and the capitalist West should continue to determine the international scheme of things. It was intolerable that the world should be frozen in the humanly unprofitable and largely dehumanizing stalemate of ideological contention, coupled with permissive connivance that marked all the dealings between those two forces, with no exit in sight.

In a move that was so totally unexpected at that moment in time that it was misread by most of the world—but a move that was characteristic in its display of his independence of both East and West—Pope John Paul embarked without delay on his papal gamble to force the hand of geopolitical change.

In the late spring of 1979, he made an official visit as newly elected Roman Pope to his Soviet-run homeland of Poland. There, he demonstrated for the masters of Leninism and capitalism alike that the national situations that obtained in the Soviet satellites, and the international status quo that obtained in the world as a whole, were outclassed and transcended by certain issues of a truly geopolitical nature. Issues that he defined again and again in terms based solely and solidly on Roman Catholic principles, while Soviet tanks and arms rumbled and rattled helplessly all around him.

It is a measure of the frozen mentalities of that time that few in the

West understood the enormous leap John Paul accomplished in that first of his many papal travels. Most observers took it as the return of a religious leader to his beloved Poland; as an emotional but otherwise unremarkable apostolic visit, complete with sermons and ceremonies and excited, weeping throngs.

One commentator, however, writing in the German newspaper *Frankfurter Zeitung*, not only read the papal achievement accurately but read the papal intent as well: "A new factor has been added to the presently accepted formula of international contention. It is a Slavic Pope. The imbalance in our thinking has been unobtrusively but decisively and, as it were, overnight corrected by the emergence of John Paul. For his persona has refocused international attention away from the two extremes, East and West, and on the actual center of change, *Mitteleuropa*, the central bloc of Europe's nations."

Presciently as well as by planned design, the Pontiff's first step into the geopolitical arena was eastward into Poland, the underbelly of the Soviet Union. In John Paul's geopolitical analysis, Europe from the Atlantic to the Urals is a giant seesaw of power. Europe from the Baltic to the Adriatic Sea is the center of that power. The Holy Father's battle was to control that center.

World commentary and opinion aside, therefore, the point of John Paul's foray into Poland was not merely that he was a religious leader. The point was that he was more. He was a geopolitical pope. He was a Slav who had come from a nation that had always viewed its own role and its fate within a geopolitical framework—within the large picture of world forces. Now he had served notice that he intended to take up and effectively exercise once more the international role that had been central to the tradition of Rome, and to the very mandate Catholics maintain was conferred by Christ upon Peter and upon each of his successors.

For fifteen hundred years and more, Rome had kept as strong a hand as possible in each local community around the wide world. Still, because what might be advantageous for one locale might be detrimental for another, it had always been an essential practice for Rome to make its major decisions on the premise that the good of the geocommunity must take precedence over all local advantages. International politics might be driven and regulated according to the benefit to be derived by certain groups or nations at the cost of others. But geopolitics properly conducted must serve the absolute needs of the whole society of nations.

By and large, and admitting some exceptions, that had been the Roman view until two hundred years of inactivity had been imposed on the papacy by the major secular powers of the world. By and large, that had been the Polish view, as well, until some two hundred years of official nonexistence had been imposed on the Poles as a nation by those same powers.

It was the first distinguishing mark of John Paul's career as Pontiff that he had thrown off the straitjacket of papal inactivity in major world affairs.

On his trip to Poland in 1979, barely eight months after his election, he signaled the opening of the millennium endgame. He became the first of the three players to enter the new geopolitical arena.

Karol Wojtyla's mentor, Cardinal Wyszynski of Warsaw, used to say that "certain historical developments are willed by the Lord of History, and they shall take place. About many other—mostly minor—developments, that same Lord is willing." He allows men the free will to choose between various options, and he will go along with those choices; for, in the end, all human choices will be co-opted as grist into God's mill, which grinds slowly but always grinds exceedingly fine."

From that unfashionable point of view, it was not to be wondered that suddenly, and without any of the laborious worldwide politicking that normally attends such matters, Karol Wojtyla was placed at the head of the world's only existing and fully operating georeligious institution: the universal organization of his Roman Catholic Church.

From that point of view, in fact, it was Karol Wojtyla's destiny, as Pope John Paul II, to be the first world leader to take up a central position in the geopolitical arena of the society of nations in the twentieth century. For not only did his unexpected supremacy of leadership of the Roman Church immediately put him within the machinery of geopolitics. His bent of mind, his training as a priest in Nazi Poland and in Rome, and his work as a member of the Catholic hierarchy in Stalinist Poland all provided him with the noblest weapons tested against the most abject sociopolitical systems the world had yet devised. He was one of a relatively few individuals in a position of great power in the world who had already been prepared for what was to come.

Though in one sense his new life as Roman Pontiff was a very public one, another dimension of that life gave John Paul a certain invaluable immunity from suspicious and prying eyes. That white robe and skullcap, that Fisherman's Ring on his index finger, the panoply of papal liturgy, the appanage of pontifical life, all meant that the rank and file of world leaders, as well as most observers and commentators, would see him almost exclusively as a religious leader.

There were· some early advantages for John Paul in that immunity. For one thing, his remarkable new vantage point was like a one-way geopolitical window at which he could stand, at least for a time, relatively unobserved himself and essentially undisturbed. With all the incomparable information of the papal office at his disposal, he could suddenly train his vision with extraordinary accuracy on the whole human scene. He could sift through all of those historical developments Wyszynski had mused about. He could examine them in terms of what would work geopolitically, and what would be pointless. He could form an accurate picture of the few—the very few—inevitable trends and forces in the world that were slowly and surely, if still covertly, affecting the lives and fortunes of nations as the world headed into the 1980s.

More, he could clearly discern all the players—the champions of those inevitable forces—as they emerged and came to the fore in the confrontation of the millennium endgame. Even before the competition had begun, he could predict from where the true competitors would have to come. In general terms, he could outline where they would stand and in what direction they would plan to move. Finally, once all of the individuals who would be in true and serious contention were in place—once all the players had names and faces, as well as ideologies and agendas that were clear—he thought he could simply put the final pieces together.

By examining the vision each contender held concerning the supreme realities governing human life, and by paying careful attention to the designs they fashioned and pursued in the practical world, he did form a clear enough idea of the brand of geopolitics they would attempt to command, and of the new world order they would attempt to create.

All in all, then, Karol Wojtyla was in a privileged position, from which he could form the most accurate advance picture possible of the millennium endgame arena. He could assess the lay of the land; sort out the primary forces of history likely to be at work in the competition; look in the right direction to find the likely champions of those major forces; and reckon what might be their chances for success.

A second advantage for Pope John Paul in the peculiar papal immunity he enjoyed was that the champions he expected to enter the endgame arena did not expect him to be a contender. They failed to read him in the same geopolitical terms he applied to them. He was not seen as a threat even in those political, cultural and financial circles outside the Roman Church where there has always been an abiding fear of "caesaro-papism." A fear that implied an ugly suspicion of totalitarian and anti-democratic ambition in any pope, whoever he might be. The ancient but still entertained fear that if any Roman pope had his way, he would damage or abolish democratic freedoms—above all, the freedom to think, to experiment and to develop politically. There seemed to be no fear of John Paul as a potential Caesar.

In point of fact, however, John Paul's ambition went very far. As far as his view of himself as the servant of God who would slowly prepare all men and women, in their earthly condition, for eternal salvation in the Heaven of God's glory. For many minds, the combination of such transcendent aims with the worldly-wise discernment of a canny geopolitician would have been an unacceptable shock.

As it was, however—and well before globalism was even added to the lexicon of high government officials and powerful corporate CEOs around the world; well before the world was treated to the spectacle of Mikhail Gorbachev as supreme public impresario of dazzling changes in the world's political landscape; well before the globalist trends now taken for granted were apparent to most of the world's leaders—this Slavic Pope had a certain leisure to scan the society of nations, with a new eye toward a purpose that is as old as the papacy itself. With an eye that was not merely international, but truly global. And with a purpose to lay his papal plans in concert with those few and very certain developments Cardinal Wyszynski had spoken of as "willed by the Lord of History." In concert with those trends that were already moving the whole society of mankind the way the stars move across the heavens—according to the awesome inevitability of the unbreakable will of God.

As clearly as if they had been color-keyed features marked on a contour map, Pope John Paul recognized the inevitabilities of late-twentieth-century geopolitics already flowing like irresistible rivers across the world's landscape in the fall of 1978.

The inability of the United States to maintain its former world hegemony was undeniable in its clarity. Just as clear was the similar inability of the Soviet Union to hold all the unnatural members of its ungainly body in its close embrace. Those two factors alone made it necessary to take a fresh reading of the efforts to form a new "Europe." A different alignment of power would inevitably supersede the old Western alliance that had been put together for the purpose of offsetting the Soviet threat.

Then there was the question of the People's Republic of China (PRC). Neither the Soviet East nor the democratic West could afford to ignore China's importance; but neither had found the key to unlock its door.

True, the Soviet Union was engaged with the PRC in a carefully

planned and executed international tango—the Soviet Union's Leonid
Brezhnev showed the softer face of negotiation toward democratic egalitarianism, while China stood as the threatening giant of hard-line Leninist Marxism to stampede the West into Brezhnev's corral.

The democratic alliance was interested in Brezhnev's dance of détente, all right. To some degree, it was gulled; and to some degree, it
found its own interests were served in cooperating with some of Brezhnev's proposals—the Helsinki Accords of 1975, for example, and the
START negotiations.

However, the West was not beating a defensive path to Moscow's door.
On the contrary, the Western democracies seemed more interested in
beating their own path to Beijing. Using its best weapon—entrepreneurship—the West embarked on a campaign to alter the ideology of the East
and Far East with a flood of managerial and technological know-how,
and with the vision if not the reality of a rising tide of the good things of
capitalist life.

Interestingly enough from the point of view of fomenting geopolitical
change in the near term, all this activity focused on China had a greater
effect on the relationship between the USSR and the West nations, than
on the leadership of the PRC. For if China intended to remain essentially
closed, then, at least in the opening phases of the millennium endgame,
central Europe would remain what it had always been—the indispensable springboard for geopolitical power.

There was one more geopolitical inevitability that John Paul faced as
he entered on his pontificate in 1978. And while it directly affected all of
Europe and all of the Americas, as well as the whole of the Soviet empire,
it was of no deep concern to any geopolitical contender except the Polish
Pope. The reality in all the territories of the world that were once thoroughly Christian was that even the last vestiges of Christianity's moral
rules for human living and behavior were being drowned by the increasing prevalence of a "human ethic" or "value system" in the management
and direction of all public and most individual matters. For all his adult
life, Karol Wojtyla had lived in a world dominated by such ethics and
value systems. Poland had been buried alive for two hundred years by
such ethics and value systems. There was not a doubt in Pope John Paul's
mind about what lay in store for the world in such an un-Godly climate.

In the broadest outlines, that was essentially the state of affairs when
John Paul made his decision to travel to Poland in 1979. If God was with
him, he would use his own homeland—the historical *plaque tournante*
of Central Europe—to disrupt the unacceptable status quo of the postwar years. That much accomplished, trickles of innovation and experi-

mentation would be the first sign that the floodgates of geopolitical change would crank slowly open.

Though certain Western leaders—Jean Monnet was but one among many—had for some decades been keen on a rather restricted idea of a commercially united Europe, it was in fact the Soviet Union that was the first and most deeply impressed by John Paul's 1979 challenge in Poland. Given the internal conditions of the USSR, that was not altogether surprising.

The following year, the Kremlin masters of Leninist Marxism responded to the papal challenge by giving the green light to the accords between Poland's shipyard workers in Gdansk and the Stalinist government in Warsaw. From those accords came the birth of the urban Solidarity trade union, followed shortly by the rural Solidarity union. It was the first trickle of innovation; the first experimental breach of the Iron Curtain.

Though that experiment failed—less, it must be said, from Soviet recalcitrance than from Western connivance and fear at the loss of a cheap labor source—John Paul knew that the issue of geopolitical innovation was joined now in the minds of Moscow. The matter only awaited a wider application by a Soviet leadership increasingly desperate for a new alignment of forces.

The motive impelling Moscow's interest in John Paul's challenge was not innovation for its own sake, of course. The engine driving their interest was their dilemma—becoming more urgent month by month—of how to relieve the tensions threatening the USSR with economic implosion, without destroying the Soviet drive toward ultimate proletarian victory throughout the world.

In one of those interesting coincidences that often attend the great forces of history, Mikhail Gorbachev ascended to the Soviet central hierarchy of power in the same year that Karol Wojtyla became Pope. In 1978, under the personal direction of Moscow's baleful General Secretary, former KGB chief Yuri Andropov, Gorbachev was named Secretary of Soviet Agriculture and Secretary of the Central Committee (CC) of the Communist Party of the Soviet Union (CPSU).

As the intimate and most trusted protégé of two supreme Soviet leaders —Andropov and his immediate successor, Konstantin Chernenko—the young Gorbachev dealt directly and from the highest vantage of power with the USSR's economic stagnation, its industrial ineptitude, its sociopolitical backwardness and its technological deficiency. By the time a fully seasoned Gorbachev emerged in 1985 as General Secretary of the CPSU and supreme leader of the Soviet apparatus and empire, he had a clear understanding of the internal ills plaguing the Soviet Union and threatening the Leninist-Marxist world revolution.

For Pope John Paul, the most interesting thing about Mikhail Gorbachev as General Secretary was that he did not respond to those potentially lethal ills of the USSR as any of his predecessors had done. He did not ignore the problems, for example, as Khrushchev had done in his unimaginative and doctrinaire confidence that the West was on its last legs and would collapse under the weight of its own corruption. Nor did he continue Moscow's economically insane buildup of military superiority, as Brezhnev had done, preparing to take the West by storm if desperation led in that direction.

Instead, Gorbachev began to make the kinds of moves that marked him at once in John Paul's power ledger as the geopolitical champion of the East: the kinds of moves one geopolitician would expect of another. For in entirely new ways, the new Soviet leader began to activate the true and so far untapped geopolitical potential of the Soviet Party-State —the only other global apparatus that was already in place worldwide and that could be got up and running with relative ease as a rival to John Paul's Roman Catholic georeligious institution.

It quickly became apparent to Vatican analysts that Gorbachev read the problems of the Soviet Union as intimately related to the three areas outside the USSR that were already the object of John Paul's geopolitical focus.

On one flank, Gorbachev was faced with the fact that Western Europe, with West Germany as its heart, promised soon to become a community of 300 million people with enormous economic power.

On a second flank, the People's Republic of China not only outstripped the USSR demographically, with a population of 1.5 billion, but was more than likely to do so technologically and economically, as well, if the Soviet Union remained economically stagnant.

Finally, a still-prosperous United States, with its own stepped-up military clout, had renewed the stigma of international unacceptability against the Soviet Union. President Ronald Reagan's often repeated "evil empire" epithet lay like an international shroud over every Soviet move.

This was not the way to reach the Leninist geopolitical goal. As the second true geopolitician to enter the arena of the millennium endgame, therefore, Mikhail Gorbachev began a brand-new world agenda. Clamoring for attention, throwing off scintillating sparks of geopolitical dynamism and sheer tactical genius, he established himself on every level that mattered as progenitor and public hero of a new outlook for the nations.

At one level, he conducted a personal public relations campaign that must have made Madison Avenue blush with envy. He wooed and won his two most adamant and conservative enemies among the leaders of the West, Ronald Reagan and England's Margaret Thatcher. He wooed and won the United Nations with a bravura performance whose substance was drowned in the emotional tide of acceptance he created. In successive and indefatigable travels, he wooed and won vast populations in America, West Germany, England, France and Italy, leaving behind him a truly global tide of Gorbi-mania.

At another level, meanwhile—at the level of the mechanics of geopolitical innovation—by 1989, within four years of his ascendancy to leadership in the Soviet Union, Gorbachev had accomplished what no Soviet leader before him had ever thought to do, and would probably not have believed possible. He had forced the West into a complete, 180-degree reversal of its seventy-year policy toward the USSR. He forced the "Group of Seven" European nations to hold a seminal meeting precisely to deal with his presence and proposals on the world stage; and then he literally hijacked their meeting without even setting foot out of Moscow. And finally, he forced major meetings of the European nations in June and October 1990, to deal with unheard-of questions. Questions absolutely vital to the solution of the problems of the USSR and to the success of Leninist Marxism. Questions such as the integration of Eastern Europe, and even of some parts of the Soviet Union itself, into the new European power equation supposedly to take shape from 1992 onward.

Every move Gorbachev made underlined for John Paul the Soviet leader's complete understanding of European power as the first springboard of his geopolitical vision; his understanding that such power lay in a Europe that would run from the Atlantic to the Urals; and his understanding that the hinge of that power lies, as it always has, in the area of Central Europe from the Adriatic to the Baltic seas.

In 1989, in a chessman's move remarkable for its theatricality and its boldness, and redolent with the confidence of a master of the game, Gorbachev began what appeared to be the "liberation" of his Eastern European satellites. Thereby, in a single stroke, he accomplished a world of good for his cause.

He banished the "evil empire" image from international sight. He removed an unbearable economic incubus from the outer carcass of the USSR and placed it on the West instead. And not least, he successfully transformed himself and his supreme leadership of the Soviet Union into the sine qua non of the foreign policies of the Western nations. Mr. Gorbachev had to be helped in every way. He must not be put at the

mercy of the "conservative hard-liners" in the Kremlin. No truthful criticism must be risked of his cruel suppression of nationalism in the unwilling Soviet republics of Armenia, Georgia and Azerbaijan, for
example; nor of his brutality with the Baltic States of Lithuania, Latvia
and Estonia. Even his flagrant violations of the U.S.-Soviet INF missile
treaty, never before off limits for comment and complaint, were passed
over in deafening official silence.

The attitude toward Gorbachev by the opening of the final decade of
the millennium was neatly, even lyrically, summed up in a letter from a
respected American professor of political science, published in *The New
York Times* on April 27, 1990. "Mr. Gorbachev has probably made
greater contributions to the wellbeing of humankind than any other
political figure in history," wrote Professor Reo M. Christenson of Miami
University in Ohio. ". . . ending the cold war, reversing the arms race,
liberating Eastern Europe, introducing democratic and economic reforms in the Soviet Union as rapidly as feasible, withdrawing from Afghanistan and from most of the Soviet international mischief-making of
recent decades, and changing the political atmosphere for the better
constitute unparalleled achievements. I can think of no statesman in
history to have done so much."

Gorbachev's greatest triumph can only be described as a phenomenal
victory in the opening phase of the millennium endgame. For, by the
early days of 1990, not only scholars and commentators but virtually
every political and entrepreneurial leader of the West, on both sides of
the Atlantic, was not only contemplating but talking and planning about
Mikhail Gorbachev's proposal for a new "European" community, comprising some 800 million people and stretching westward from the train
yards of Vladivostok to the sun-drenched beaches of California.

Whatever geopolitical fate might ultimately await Gorbachevism, Gorbachev had indeed taken up John Paul's Poland challenge with gusto.
He had done more than crank open the floodgates of geopolitical change.
He had created a new mind in the West. Or, more precisely, he had got
the West to adopt his mind and cater to his needs. He had successfully
included the Soviet Union in the very entrails of the economic life and
machinery of the new world aborning. From now on, Gorbachevism—
and Wojtylism—will be potent factors activating the society of nations,
even if either or both leaders should leave the human scene or be toppled
from positions of supreme leadership.

As the Pope he is, John Paul would typically pray that one day Mikhail
Gorbachev will enter the house of God that Peter built—not because as

a Leninist he covets the Roman Church as the geopolitical power tool it is; and not because he needs the cooperation of the Pontiff as a fellow Slav and a geopolitical equal; but as a prayerful penitent. Gorbachev was baptized as an infant, after all; and he was a churchgoing believer in his boyhood. Perhaps it is not too much to hope that the Soviet leader is not totally impervious to the grace of his erstwhile faith.

As the geopolitician he is, however, John Paul would just as typically not let such prayers and hopes, deeply genuine though they are, cloud or replace his crystal-clear understanding of the design Mikhail Gorbachev has formed for the new world order: the design he and his associates in the Soviet Party-State are fully confident they will install as victors in this "greatest historical confrontation humanity has gone through."

There is no mystery for John Paul about Gorbachev's design. It is the late-twentieth-century version of Lenin's old "Workers' Paradise," but intelligently purged of the crudities and stupidities that marred Lenin's vision. Lenin's definition of the Proletarian Revolution, for example, has been expanded to encompass something much wider than the masses of workers. The new Leninist Revolution will liberate all people from slavery to the meaninglessness of daily life, including the meaninglessness formerly characteristic of Marxism. It will share common ground with capitalists in the solution of world problems. And it will do all that unremittingly and pointedly for man's sake only. Man will take credit for it all in the certainty that man himself is the creator of all things good and pleasant.

At the geopolitical level, the Gorbachevist design for a new world order envisages a condition in which all national governments as we now know them will cease to exist. There is to be one central governing hub located in Moscow and dominated exclusively by the Communist Party of the World (CPW). Governing structures in the various nations will be peopled with appointees of the CPW, and will be reproductions of the CPW in structure, though not in power.

All military and security matters will be in the hands of the CPW and its surrogates throughout the nations. The geo-economy of the new world order, meanwhile, will incorporate all the practical lessons Communists have learned from the market economies of the Western democracies; but it will preserve the centralizing principle of Leninist Marxism.

The CPW will also take charge of the cultural value system of the new world order. Religion will be banned. But because the spirit in man requires a specific nourishment to which the organized religions catered in the past, such catering will continue as a matter of practical necessity.

However, it will ensure that the bone and marrow of the new value system are constructed not of God's worth and God's qualities, but exclusively of human worth and human qualities.

To this end, the education of each individual must be a womb-to-tomb affair. On the one hand, there must be constant and lifelong revision and reinforcement of the individual's grasp of pure Leninism, with its emphasis on that individual's total dependency on the overall directorate of the CPW. On the other hand, a parallel educational effort will filter out all ideas about civil and political rights that presently cluster around capitalist democracy—most notably, the notion that there are certain inalienable rights of the citizen that are superior to the needs of the CPW.

Pope John Paul is aware that such a reading of Gorbachev's geopolitical vision for the new world order runs counter to the hopeful rhetoric current in the West. Rhetoric content for the moment to purr that democracy has won its long battle with Leninist Marxism at last; that Gorbachev has seen the light at the top of the capitalist hill and is making his way bravely up that slope.

Nevertheless, the reality as John Paul sees it appears to weigh in another direction. Mikhail Gorbachev has said straight out to the world that he is a Leninist, and a Leninist he will remain. In almost those very words, in fact, Gorbachev told the Moscow cadres of the CPSU in November of 1989, "I am a Leninist, devoted to achieving the goals of Leninism and the worldwide Leninist association of all workers under the banner of Marxism." Pope John Paul has learned from long experience when to take a Soviet leader at his word.

Moreover, Gorbachev does have the global machinery of the Leninist structure available to carry out his design; and he has the fuel of an abiding geo-ideology that is shared by countless millions of men and women the world over.

And finally, even among the world population that may not share or care about the Leninist-Marxist ideal, the materialist view of human life that has become so rampant has already shown itself to be entirely compatible in important ways with Gorbachev's classical Leninism, refurbished as it is in the light of historical events subsequent to Lenin's time.

On the other side of the coin, meanwhile, two principal weaknesses dog Gorbachev's every move. First, he stands or falls depending on the support of the KBG; the support of the Red Army Central Command Corps within the supersecret Soviet Defense Council of the USSR; and the support of the Central Committee of the CPSU. All three are Leninist to the core. He has to make sure that his Leninist credentials remain spotless and unsullied. For without that troika, Gorbachev's chariot of geopolitical conquest would be immobilized. He would be finished.

And second, he cannot with any degree of impunity jettison the centralized authority of the Party-State. Shorn of that authority, the USSR has no further reason to exist. Yet Gorbachev must, if he is to succeed in the endgame, build a workable bridge between that centralizing organization and the Western-style market economy without which his *perestroika* will never get off the ground.

Both weaknesses provoke one torturing question for him: How far is too far? How far can he go in "liberating" the satellites and the dissident republics of the Party-State without violating the strategic requirements of that Party-State? How far can he liberalize the economy of the USSR without its de facto conversion into a capitalist system, so repugnant to his Leninist supporters?

From Pope John Paul's point of view, however, the greatest weakness of the Gorbachevist design for the new world order lies in its denial of God's existence; in its bedrock cultivation of man as completely and solely a creature of nature and of the CPW. Any design based on such a principle is both unacceptable and unworkable, the Pope maintains, for one and the same reason. It is a cruel denial of man's highest aspirations. It is a violation of man's deepest instinct—to worship God; and of his deepest desire—to live forever, never to die.

"The claim to build a world without God," the Pope stated bluntly in Czechoslovakia during his visit in April of 1990, "has been shown to be an illusion. . . . Such a hope has already revealed itself as a tragic Utopia . . . for man is unable to be happy if the transcendent relationship with God is excluded."

On the face of it, the champions of Western capitalism—the Transnationalists and Internationalists of America and Europe—appear to be far and away the most effective and powerful architects of a new world order, for the simple reason that their power base rests on the indispensable pillars of money and technology.

Given their background and their history, these Globalists of the West have developed a totally different design from Gorbachev's, both for establishing a new world order and, once it is in place, for nourishing and developing it. Their plan is to broaden the scope of what they do so well; to exploit democratic capitalism and democratic egalitarianism to the full. The new world order, they say, will develop organically from

the fundamental idea of a nation-state democracy into a geopolitical
system of world regulation.

The father of this version of the new world order is to be the interdependence of nations. Its mother is to be that peculiarly modern
process called international development. It is to be midwifed by the
entrepreneur, the banker, the technocrat, the scientist and, ultimately,
the lawyer. It is to be born between the printed sheets of compacts and
agreements; joint ventures and mergers; contracts and covenants and
international treaties signed and countersigned by the political bureaucrat, and sealed with the stamp of united nations.

It is a tribute to the geopolitical skill of Mikhail Gorbachev that there
is an almost perfect coincidence between the framework he has chosen
as his method of approximating his geopolitical goals and the framework
adopted by President Bush and Secretary of State James A. Baker III as
the public leaders and spokesmen for the Transnationalist-Internation-
alist Globalists of the West. They express that framework in terms of
three concentric spheres of international unity: the European Economic
Community; Greater Europe, composed of the Western European
states, the former Eastern satellites of the Soviet Union and the USSR
itself; and finally, both of those welded geopolitically with the United
States.

Again, as Gorbachev has done, the most influential leaders of this
Globalist group, the Wise Men of the West, have taken account of the
main sources of disequilibrium that must be addressed before their globalist design for a new world order can be stabilized. The ominous threat
of an isolated People's Republic of China could be the spoiler and must
therefore be offset and diverted. The role of West Germany—already
powerful and now to be reunified with its eastern half—must be regulated in order to quell the fears of the Soviets and of most Western
Europeans concerning any renascence of German imperialism. And—
tribute of tributes—Mikhail Gorbachev must be aided so that he will be
able with impunity to reform the economico-political structure of the
Soviet Union.

If these main sources of disequilibrium can be taken care of, then—
given the time—this third contender group in the millennium endgame
sees itself within reach of a geopolitical structure. Indeed, the Globalists
already see themselves in the very midst of an orderly transition—an
organic evolution—from the divisive nation-state politics of yesterday to
a new world order. More, they see the whole process as in the nature of
a logical consequence. Their presumption is that the old internationalism, allied with the new capitalist-based transnationalism, will carry dem-

ocratic egalitarianism to a geopolitical level. They presume, in short, that the new world order will be a logical consequence of yesterday's mode of democratic politics.

With that facile transition already visibly under way around the world, the Western Globalists don't feel they are jumping the gun by much when they speak of the final prize to come. Just over the horizon, they say, still out of sight but firmly presumed to be there waiting for us all, stretch the smiling upland meadows of plenty for all; and not far beyond that lie the rolling plains of man's continuing perfectibility.

There is no doubt in John Paul's mind that the Western Globalists are true and powerful contenders in the millennium endgame; or that they are already determining certain contours and aspects of our global life. But that is not to deny specific and practical weaknesses of an important kind in the West's position.

Of the three principal contenders in the struggle to form a new world order, the Western capitalists are the only ones who must still form a truly geopolitical structure. The most serious question they face, therefore, is whether there can in fact be an organic evolution of the democratic egalitarianism of the capitalist camp into a geopolitical mode.

In this vein, surely it was the recent democratic evolution in Eastern Europe that prompted Francis Fukuyama, a Harvard-trained official in the American State Department, to argue categorically that there can be no organic evolution of democratic egalitarianism into anything further of its own kind. To argue, in fact, that there is no evolution of political thought possible beyond the idea of liberal democracy.

So adamant is Mr. Fukuyama that his persuasion amounts to nothing less than an interdict. A serious argument taken seriously that human thought in the matter of democratic government has reached the outer limit. A serious argument that, if history can be defined not as a series of events, but as the living force of new ideas incarnated in political institutions adequate to vehicle those ideas, then the history of democratic egalitarianism is at an end.

The fundamental idea of democracy—government of, for and by the people, with its ancillary institutions guaranteeing both continuity in government and fundamental rights on the personal and civic levels of life—is inviolable in its structural elements. Take away any element—the right to vote, say; or the right of free association—and the entire structure loses its integrity. Tip the balance in favor of one institutional arm—executive over legislative, or legislative over judicial—and the orderly system is jiggered. Adopt only one proviso of democracy—take the right of free association again—or even three or four, and as Mr. Gorbachev is presently learning the hard way, you will not have anything resembling the democratic egalitarianism of the United States or Great Britain.

The fact of the matter is, however, that any geopolitical structure worthy of the name would necessitate an entirely different regime of rights and duties. In a truly one-world order, it would not be possible to regulate an election of high officials in the same manner as democratic egalitarianism requires. General referenda would also be impossible.

So obvious has this difficulty been—and for far longer than Mr. Fukuyama has been on the scene—that warning scenarios have long since been prepared in the democratic capitalist camp itself. Scenarios that show in considerable detail just how and why, in the transition to a world order, the various processes of democracy would have to be shouldered by select groups, themselves picked by other select groups.

It takes little imagination to see that such a situation is not likely to lead to egalitarianism, democratic or otherwise. Nor is it likely to lead to wide rolling plains and smiling upland meadows of popular contentment.

Even if the most dour assessments of the globalist structure that is likely to come out of the capitalist design are correct, that is not the only weakness faced by the West. Intent as they are on winning the competition, the Western democracies tend to conceal from themselves two additional problems that are paramount in John Paul's assessment of their likelihood of success.

The first is the problem of time. There is not at the present moment a geopolitical structure—or even the model for such a structure—native to democratic egalitarianism or born from its own specific sociopolitical principles. Quite apart from the stark Fukuyama interdict, which indicates that such an elaboration of democratic egalitarianism is now impossible, there does not seem to be any leeway of time available for the champions of Western democracy to attempt such an elaboration. The speed and urgency of events, together with the ongoing geopolitical readiness of Gorbachevism, afford no leisure for cautious experimentation. A new world order is all but upon us, demanding a geopolitical structure in the immediate here and now.

The second is the problem of morality: of a moral base as the necessary mooring for any system of government, whether national or global. In and of itself, capitalism does not have, nor does it require for its specific functioning, any moral precept or code of morality. What currently passes for such a moral base is nothing more than moral exigency; pressing needs calling for immediate action are responded to on a situation-by-situation basis.

Speaking at Prague Castle on April 21, 1990, John Paul was pointed in his warning to the newly liberated Czechoslovaks that in getting rid of Communism, they should not replace it with "the secularism, indifference, hedonistic consumerism, practical materialism, and also the formal atheism that plague the West."

Already John Paul sees that the exigencies forced by Gorbachev and Gorbachevism upon the Western democracies can and do evoke from them the same brand of ruthlessness and incompassion that the Soviets have long displayed as a daily behaviorism. He has already seen, for example, the United States' attitude to the rape and genocide of Tibet; to the cruel oppression of democracy in Myanmar (formerly Burma) and in the PRC; to the Indonesian genocide of the East Timorese; and to the war of extermination Syria's Hafez Assad has waged against Christian communities in his land.

It is sufficiently evident, therefore, at least to Pope John Paul, that as Mikhail Gorbachev elaborates his ideological position within the new architecture of Europe, the main trends of the new global society begin to take on the color of Gorbachev's Leninist-Marxist design.

Put another way, it is sufficiently evident that, if Gorbachev's greatest geopolitical triumph to date has been the creation of a new mind in the West that is compatible with his great Leninist design for the new world order, then the corollary weakness for the capitalists' design lies in the fact that the Western Globalists think they are in charge of the forces of change.

Admittedly, there is little quarrel between Gorbachev and the capitalists about the need they both see to fill our bellies with fresh food, and our minds with fresh knowledge, and our world with fresh air and water.

The difficulty comes, however, with the Leninist proviso embedded within Gorbachevism that we must never more repeat the famous cry of the German philosopher Martin Heidegger: "I know that only God can save us."

Even granting Western Globalists the necessary time to achieve their one-world design, therefore, the questions of structure and moral underpinning lead Pope John Paul, with many others, to anticipate the total effect of the Western Globalist model on the society of nations.

Good intentions notwithstanding, one can foresee the demise of democratic egalitarianism as we have known it. One can predict the rise of massive bureaucracies to govern every phase of civic development. One can expect the insertion of the statist element in all phases of private life, and the slow elimination of compassion; of good taste; of the wild hope-fulness that has made mankind venturesome in this cosmos; and finally of truth itself as the basic rule of the human mind in its quest for knowl-edge.

Unfortunately for us all, the basic lesson is not quickly learned that on this new globalist plane, once a geopolitical structure is established, pow-erful forces take over that are difficult to change. As Czechoslovakia's new leader, Vaclav Havel, has already observed, "In organizational de-crees, it is truly difficult to find that God who is the only one who can save us."

The contemporary world over which Pope John Paul casts his wide-sweeping gaze is not a tidy place. It is cluttered with all manner of groups, large and small, able to command greater or lesser publicity, all making their own globalist claims.

Well before Karol Wojtyla took up his own position in the geopolitical arena as Pope, in fact, many such groups had already claimed a place on the world stage. Some were inspired by the creation of the United Na-tions. Others who disliked that institution proposed their own form of globalism. Still other groups, ancient and modern, elaborated extensive plans in the name of some religious belief or philosophy about human life.

Common to all of these aspiring globalist contenders is the fact that, of themselves, they lack even the most basic tools for practical geopolit-ical contention. They have neither an extensive, articulated organization nor even the means to network all the nations, much less the power to entrain the world in the globalist way of life of their choice.

Some of these groups have simply decided to wait out their own geo-political impotence in the belief that someday they will somehow achieve a global status and capacity commensurate with their ambitions.

Of principal interest to John Paul in terms of their present influence, however, are certain more venturesome groups, who plan to piggyback a ride to global status and supremacy by straddling any vehicle that appears to be headed in their direction.

Such in particular are the thousands of New Agers in our midst. And such, too, are the so-called Mega-Religionists—those who are per-suaded, and who work to persuade us all, that all religions of the world are fusing into one globe-spanning mega-religion of mankind.

The members and spokesmen of both of these groups wax poetic about their vision. In their imagined grand design, the new world order will be one great Temple of Human Understanding. The truly global home of all nations will still resound with the languages of every race and tribe; but they will all be harmonized into one. Their Temple of Human Understanding will be roofed over with the all-inclusive allegiance to the common good. Its walls will be decorated with the icons of the new values—peacefulness; healthfulness; respect for Earth and environmental devotion. But over all, there will be the great icon of Understanding. What divinity exists will be accepted as incarnate in man; divinity of, for and by—and only within—mankind. All other shapes and concepts of divinity will melt—are already melting; fusing gently and irresistibly into the Understanding of mankind's own inherent and godly power to fashion its own destiny.

The chief interest of these groups for Pope John Paul is that they spend their days leeching off of the geopolitical power of others. Intent upon predisposing as many minds as possible to the task of achieving heaven on earth, they have developed infiltration to a high art. Chameleon-like, they are to be found basking at the height of power everywhere in the West—in Transnationalist boardrooms and Internationalist bureaucracies; in the hierarchies of the Roman, Orthodox and other Christian churches; in major Jewish and Islamic enclaves already dedicated to the total Westernization of culture and civilization.

Neither New Agers nor Mega-Religionists are any less helpless finally than the many globalist pretenders crowding at the edges of the arena where the millennium endgame has already developed into a game of power—power understood, power possessed and power exercised.

Beset by delusions of grandeur and illusions of a favorable geopolitical future for themselves, New Agers and Mega-Religionists not only lack a geostructure. They must go a-begging for bits of georeligion and pieces of geo-ideology; and they are totally bereft of a realistic and rounded geo-mind-set.

The important effect of these globalist dreamers in the geopolitical contest is the weight they add to the forces already intent upon disposing the world toward the idea of an earthly Utopia and away from any knowledge of the transcendent truth of a loving God who, as John Paul is convinced, has a very different design in store than any they are able to imagine.

Among the primary contenders dominating the economic and political moves to form and control the new world order, Pope John Paul stands apart in several ways.

He is, first, the only one of the three whose vision of the grand design for that world order has undergone an abrupt revision of the most major kind. And he is the only one who has, from the first moment of his assumption of power, faced a concerted effort from within his own organization—indeed, on the part of some of the most powerfully placed members of his hierarchy—to wrest his entire georeligious and geopolitical structure from his control as Pontiff. An entrenched effort to take the Keys from Peter, and to divide the spoils of power that lie uniquely within his authority.

By contrast, and for all of Mikhail Gorbachev's genius as an innovative and imaginative geopolitician, the Soviet leader is heir to a mentality and an organization that remain committed to Leninist ideology and goals, however they are to be achieved. And, for all of his difficulties as he tries to steer the Soviet Union into the river of Western European progress—avoiding shipwreck on the rock of Stalinist hard-lining as best he can, while maneuvering around the hard place of implosion and disintegration of the Leninist system—he has never been at the mercy of forces within his own house that clamor for an end result any different from the one he himself is after. Neither the problems Gorbachev faces, nor the bold and unprecedented means he has adopted to overcome those problems, provide John Paul with realistic and persuasive evidence that Gorbachev's vision for the ultimate grand design is at odds either with Lenin's seminal vision or with the aims of the most powerful elements of his own Party. The quarrel in the USSR is not over the end to be desired, but over the means to achieve that end.

The Wise Men of the West likewise proceed in the same hope they have always shared that their animating spirit will be sufficient to propagate democratic egalitarianism into a coherent geopolitical structure, and never mind the nay-sayers. They are as one in their intent to give the lie to the medieval maxim "Hope is a good companion, but a bad guide." Even the fact that they have been forced by Gorbachev into a deep revision of their earlier plans is not in itself a revolutionary change; for it has been true more often than not over the past seventy years that Soviet leadership has been the active agent in international affairs and that the West has made hay out of its role as a powerful reactive agent. There may be as many opinions in the West as there are in the Soviet Union about which path to follow in any specific situation. But about the end result that is desired and sought, there is no bedrock disunity. In that sense at least, the West is not a house that is irreparably divided.

. . .

When John Paul started into the millennium endgame—when he initiated it—all of his moves were tied to his clear but decidedly long-range
vision that he could supersede the plans of both East and West; and,
further, that he could leaven and finally supplant those superpower plans
with some system that would tie the condition of the whole world no
longer to the success barometers in Moscow and Washington but to the
legitimate and absolute needs of the whole of mankind.

Even had any of the world leaders in 1978 and 1979 known what John
Paul had in mind in their regard, none of them would have ventured a
guess that the Middle European hotbed of nineteenth-century politics
and wars would become the actual arena of the late-twentieth-century
contest for world hegemony. For, to all intents and purposes, those
leaders accepted the Iron Curtain as a permanent element of international life; as a kind of reliable center they could count on as they moved
forward with their contentious agendas.

It was expected by most that the United States, Western Europe and
Japan would continue as the trilateral giants of their camp. It was expected by those giants themselves that, over time, they would be able to
weave and extend a net of profound change in the conditions of life
around the world. It was expected that, over time, such profound change
would lead to the creation of a geopolitical house in which the society of
nations would live happily ever after. It was expected further that, over
time, as the West built the sinews of a new world on the foundations of
its technological, commercial and developmental prowess, it would simultaneously wear down the Soviet Union by the same means.

John Paul's program was intent upon sweeping all such plans aside.
The suffering caused by the East-West divide was too intense—too urgent and too widespread—to be acceptable as the permanent center or
the reliable element in anybody's plans. He came to the papacy, therefore, certain in the knowledge that the old order had to go.

Moreover, the Holy Father's own certainty that the locus of change
must lie within Eastern Europe was not mere whim or contrariness or
personal will. It was not even luck or untutored intuition. It was based
on the careful penetration of what the West had long regarded as the
Soviet enigma. It was rooted in the facts of hard-nosed intelligence; facts
he analyzed without the impediment of an ideology rooted in the motives
of profit or seduced by the siren song of raw power.

Pope John Paul was not surprised, therefore, by his early victory in
Poland in 1979. Nor was he surprised that it was not the West, but the
Soviet Union—the constant catalyst of twentieth-century affairs—that
saw its advantage in shifting the locus of significant activity away from

the agenda that had been fixed by the trilateral allies for their own advantage, and toward Eastern Europe, where the USSR needed early solutions to grave problems.

First, as he planned it then, he would introduce step-by-step and carefully balanced alterations in the sociocultural forces already deeply at work in Poland, not as a governmental entity but as a nation of people. His aim was to provide a model the Soviet Union could follow to ease the mounting pressures besetting the Politburos in Warsaw and Moscow; and to do that without spooking them in the areas of their military security and political dominance in that key sector of Eastern Europe.

With that delicate purpose in mind, and with the on-site cooperation of Cardinal Wyszynski and his Polish hierarchy, who were already past masters at such activity, the first instrument the Pope fomented—Solidarity—was devised purely and simply as a model of sociocultural liberty. Pointedly, he did not demand or want for it a political role; nor did he envision for it any action that would precipitate a Soviet-inspired security or military backlash.

The sociocultural model in and of itself was not an original idea. It traced back at least as far as the argument set out by Thomas Aquinas seven hundred years ago to the effect that the two seminal and ineradicable loves of any individual human being are the love of God and the love of one's native country; and, further, that these can live and flourish only within the framework of a religious nationalism.

The greatest significance of Solidarity, therefore, was to be its function as a modern laboratory of sociocultural liberty rooted entirely and sufficiently in religious nationalism. If it was totally successful, it would be an important new ingredient introduced into the dough of international affairs that would produce a slow leavening of the materialist mind dominating East and West alike.

Even without total success, however, Solidarity would be an unbloody battleground for a choice John Paul was certain would have to be made. A choice, on the one hand, for the sociocultural religious nationalism vindicated in Poland by the Pontiff's mentor, Stefan Cardinal Wyszynski, and championed in the Soviet Union itself first by Aleksandr Solzhenitsyn and more recently by Igor Shafarevich. Or, conversely, a choice for the opposing sociopolitical model personified in the Soviet Union mainly by Andrei Sakharov and in Poland by the two well-known activists Adam Michnik and Jacek Kuron: a model totally based on the Western ideal of democratic egalitarianism.

To some degree, then, Solidarity was the first international arena in which John Paul's early idea—his early vision, if you will, of religious nationalism as the vehicle for sociocultural freedom—made its debut in the hostile territory of the Soviet Union, and at the same time went head-to-head with the basic premise of the capitalist superpower.

Solidarity alone would not do the trick, of course. The melting of the Soviet iceberg of materialist, anti-Church and anti-God intransigence would, as John Paul saw the matter in 1979, be an intricate affair of papal policy that he would begin. But it would continue into another pontificate after he himself had joined his predecessors in the papal crypt beneath the altar of St. Peter's Basilica.

While time was thus not the primary factor for the Pope in those early years of his reign, still he wasted not a moment in setting the broader lines of his new policy with respect to the USSR. And the manner in which he proceeded was instructive concerning his whole approach to Vatican politics.

The policy toward the Soviet Union initiated in 1959–60 by Pope John XXIII, and subsequently elaborated from 1963 to 1978 into the well-known *Ostpolitik* of the Vatican under Pope Paul VI, presented a practical problem for John Paul. For, at its heart, it was the same policy of containment that the Western powers had adopted toward the USSR of Joseph Stalin in the forties and that they had followed ever since. Its essence was to contain Soviet aggression; to react to Soviet moves; and to wait for some favorable evolution within the Soviet system.

Whatever the results of such an *Ostpolitik* for capitalist democracy, it was a barren policy for religion and for the Church. It promised only silent martyrdom amid the slow erosion of all religious tradition by the steady pressures of a professional antireligion. It was a seemingly perpetual tunnel with no light at the end, filled merely with the ever-encroaching darkness of spreading godlessness.

Nonetheless, Pope John Paul made it clear that he would not abrogate the policies of his predecessors. Practically speaking, it would have been difficult and even counterproductive to do so in any case, for diplomatic protocols with some Eastern European countries had already been signed, and others were in train.

The solution for John Paul lay in the fact that there was nothing in the Vatican's *Ostpolitik*, and nothing in the Vatican protocols, to keep him from attempting an end run around the Soviet Party-State. In precisely such a move, the new Holy Father set about building closer and ever closer ties with the Russian Orthodox Church and with Eastern Orthodoxy in general.

This papal end run included certain overt moves—John Paul visited the Greek Orthodox center in Istanbul, for example; and he received and openly favored visits to the Vatican by Orthodox prelates. But there were also constant covert moves originating in Poland and radiating into western parts of the USSR, moves that fostered a common religious bond between Eastern European Roman Catholics and Russian Orthodox communities.

Later historians with access to records unavailable today will document the successes of John Paul's end-run policies and their basic premise. Suffice it to say now that, in spite of the official prostitution of the Russian Orthodox Church to the ideological policies of the Party-State, John Paul's efforts nourished within that Church a genuinely Christian core of prelates and people eager once and for all to reenter the mainstream of European Christianity as vindicated by papal Rome; and eager as well to renounce the role, accepted once upon a time by Russian Orthodox Church authorities, as servants of the Soviet Party-State in the fomentation of worldwide revolution.

By the opening of the eighties, about half of the Orthodox prelates were already secretly prepared, if the opportunity were afforded, to place themselves under the ecclesial unity of the Roman Pope. A sociocultural leavening had been produced within the Russian Orthodox Church. While the Vatican's official *Ostpolitik* remained undisturbed, a deep cultural change was being effected covertly within the body of Russian Orthodox believers that could lead in the long run—as all deep cultural changes do—to sociopolitical change.

Yet another factor the Pope reckoned as working for his new policy of stirring up change in the Soviet Union was the information revolution taking place worldwide. Launched in the West, and already producing a global invasion of practical knowledge into the business of international linkage and development, this was not a factor under John Paul's control. But it could only work hand in glove with the sociocultural change so essential for his stategy in the Soviet Union. For the information revolution would inevitably mean the dawning of the factual truth about things on the minds of Soviet citizens. Factual truth about past history, for one thing; and about present economic and social conditions in the world. The kind of truth that would help free those citizens from the darksome toils of the Big Lie foisted on them by the Party-State.

John Paul achieved some remarkable successes in the dynamic pursuit of his independent policies to sow the seeds of sociocultural change in the geopolitical soil of the East. Indeed, his assault on the Soviet monolith was key to the 1989 liberation of the Eastern European states. And by 1990—almost overnight, as it seemed to the inattentive—whole blocs of Russian believers voted themselves and their church property back into the Roman Catholic fold.

Nevertheless, this was not a pope for halfhearted ventures, nor for half an international policy. His end run around Soviet officialdom was not a religious gambit, but a geopolitical strategy, and it was therefore joined to a twin policy toward the West. His concern, in other words, was not only to produce a change in the policies of what Cardinal Wyszynski had always called the Red *Internationale* of the USSR. At least as much of his attention, and a great deal more of his physical energy, was devoted to a change in the increasingly materialist, anti-Church and anti-God stance of the Golden *Internationale* of the Western capitalist nations.

It was significant in that regard that the Solidarity experiment with which the Pontiff was so deeply involved in his Polish homeland would quickly fire the popular imagination, and the deep concern of all truly democratic minds, in the Western nations. But the deepest and broadest effects of John Paul's policies were produced in the West as a direct consequence of his crisscrossing lines of world travel. By those travels he achieved a high international profile; he made his ideas current coinage among world leaders; and in countries that were battlegrounds between East and West, he was able to juxtapose those ideas persuasively with Leninist-Marxist ideas. Within a brief time, it became so clear that Pope John Paul had taken his due place among the nations' leaders that—after over a hundred years of an attitude that passed for a policy, an attitude regarded by some as "Hands off this political hot potato"—even the United States reestablished formal diplomatic relations between Washington and the Vatican.

At the same time he was making such geopolitical headway, however—and despite urgent advice from some of his most trusted and certainly his most loyal advisers, as well as a mounting cry of anguish from ordinary believers who were subjected to extraordinary displays of un-Catholicity among bishops, clergy and religious around the world—the Pontiff neglected almost totally what many argued was his primary problem and responsibility. He put off indefinitely any attempt to reform his own Church, or even to arrest the accelerating deterioration of its universal integrity.

The surprising thing was that this was not negligence in office occasioned by the heat of his geopolitical agenda. As in the case of his choice not to abrogate the Vatican's formal *Ostpolitik*, it was a conscious decision on the Pontiff's part. As early as 1980, in fact, John Paul was frank in declaring that a reform of his rapidly deteriorating Church—or even an attempt to arrest that deterioration—was an impossibility at that stage of his pontificate. In his gradation of papal values, the geopolitics of power took precedence over the geopolitics of faith. Reform of his churchly institution would be vehicled on the global change he was pursuing with such intelligence and vigor.

That was essentially the agenda and the climate in Pope John Paul II's Vatican for the first two and a half years of his pontificate. As revolutionary as his geopolitical vision was, it was keyed to and gridded upon nothing more astounding than an educated understanding of human affairs. Like the Wise Men of the West, in a certain sense he took time for granted. He remained comfortable in the persuasion that the shift from the old internationalism to a more truly geopolitical globalism would be a gradual affair: that it would come on the long finger of slow and laborious historical changes. He presumed that as the gradual changes he was sowing within the geopolitics of power would bear more and more fruit, so too the preeminence of the geopolitics of faith would emerge.

Nothing short of the rudest shock of ultimate reality—of life and death and the inescapable will of God—would change that mind-set.

At a certain moment on May 13, 1981, during an open-air papal audience in St. Peter's Square, in the presence of some 75,000 people and before the eyes of an estimated 11 million television viewers, Pope John Paul spied a little girl wearing a small picture of Christ's mother as Our Lady of Fatima. Just as he bent from his slow-moving "popemobile" in a spontaneous gesture toward the child, hired assassin Mehmet Ali Agca squeezed off two bullets, aimed precisely where his head had been. As two pilgrims fell wounded to the ground, two more shots rang out, and this time John Paul's blood stained his white papal cassock.

Robust though he was, it took six months of painful convalescence for the Pope to recover. During that time he had the strength and the nobility of soul to receive in private audience the sorrowing mother of his Turkish assassin-designate. Motivated by the love of Christ, and by that ancient principle of powerful men to "know thine enemy," he also went to see Ali Agca in his prison cell. In quasi-confessional intimacy, John Paul talked with the man who knew the enemy who had commissioned so grisly a desecration.

The attempted assassination of John Paul shocked the world as a planned act of high sacrilege. In its immediate intent, however, that most vile act had no religious significance. For it was an act committed against the Pope not as a religious leader but as a geopolitician well along on the highroad of success. The wrath that had boiled up in homicidal anger, and that by the remotest and most covert control had guided the actions of Ali Agca on that day, was the wrath of important hegemonic interests separated from St. Peter's Square by huge distances of land and water. Interests unwilling to see this Pope reintroduce the Holy See as an independent and uncontrollable force in international affairs.

Already John Paul's successes in Poland had jiggered alliances presumed to have been inviolable. As he had widened the ambit of his attention and his energies, he had consistently shown himself to be a leader capable of carrying out his intention to shape events, and to determine the success or failure of secular policies for the new world order. He had not opened the new game of nations by chance, as some had originally thought. He was not some papal Alice who had carelessly fallen down a geopolitical rabbit hole and then wondered where he had landed. He was a purposeful contender for power, who cast a shadow that already blocked the light of success from the eyes of some with diametrically opposed plans for the geopolitical future of the society of nations. Better, then, to cut that shadow down to the abject shades of death in the noonday glare of the Italian sun.

Given the fact that the attempt to murder him was itself a badge of his geopolitical success, there was no earthly reason to expect John Paul to change his vision of the new world order or his agenda to influence it. It was not lost on him, however, that the attempt on his life had taken place on May 13. Or that a series of very curious supernatural events— events of intimate interest to the papacy—had begun on May 13, 1917, in the obscure Portuguese hamlet of Fatima, and had ended there on October 13 of the same year with a miracle centered on the Virgin Mary and her apparent power to control the sun in spectacular ways. Nor, finally, was it lost on him that, but for the picture of the Virgin of Fatima pinned to the blouse of a little girl, his skull would have been shattered by the first bullets out of Ali Agca's gun.

Given such circumstances, it would have been a stony papal heart indeed that could have refused to reexamine the compelling events that had taken place at Fatima over five months, from spring to fall, in 1917.

Like most Catholics the world over, Karol Wojtyla had been acquainted for as long as he could remember with most of the facts about Fatima. The Virgin Mary had appeared several times to three peasant children; she had confided to them certain admonitions and instructions, including a detailed set of instructions and predictions that were in-

tended for papal action at a certain time in the future; and she had ended
her visits in October with a miracle that recalled for many the Bible verse
that tells of a "Woman Clothed with the Sun, and giving birth to a Son
who will rule the Nations with a scepter of iron."

Once elected Pope in 1978, John Paul had become privy to the papal
instructions and predictions Mary had entrusted in confidence to the
children at Fatima. That part of her message dealt with matters of trib-
ulation for the Roman Catholic institutional organization, and with the
troubled future of mankind in general.

Like his two predecessors, John XXIII and Paul VI, Pope John Paul
had long since accepted the authenticity of the Fatima events of 1917.
In fact, he had been rooted and reared in a certain special intimacy Poles
have always cultivated with Mary as the mother of God; and his papal
motto reflected his personal and public dedication to her. Still, as those
same predecessors had done, John Paul had always taken the papal instructions and predictions of Fatima as a matter for the future. "This
matter," John XXIII had written of Fatima in 1960, "does not concern
Our time." This matter, Pope John Paul had concluded in 1978, does
not concern my pontificate. Based on the facts available, it seemed a
legitimate judgment call at the time.

Now, however—after what were arguably the very pointed events that
had taken place in St. Peter's Square; after exhaustive examination of
the documents and living witnesses and participants connected with the
Fatima events themselves; and after nothing less than a personal communication from Heaven during his long convalescence—John Paul was
all but forced to face the full meaning of Stefan Cardinal Wyszynski's
familiar maxim that "certain events are willed by the Lord of History,
and they shall take place."

More, he came face-to-face with the realization that, far from pointing
to some distant future time, the contents of the now famous Fatima
message—and, specifically, the secret contents directed to papal attention—amounted to a geopolitical agenda attached to an immediate timetable.

Gone was the Pope's agenda in which Central Europe figured as the
primary springboard for lasting geopolitical change, or as the strategic
base from which he could slowly interact with and leaven the policies of
East and West alike to satisfy the patient demands of God's justice. Instead, there was now no doubt in John Paul's mind that Heaven's agenda
had located the catalyst of geopolitical change in Russia.

Gone, too, was the Pope's presumed time frame involving a leisurely
and relatively peaceful evolution from the traditional system of sovereign

and interacting nation-states to a veritable new world order. Instead, there was now no doubt in John Paul's mind that in Heaven's agenda, all would be thrown into the cauldron of human judgment gone awry; of human evil sanctioned by men as normal; of unparalleled natural catastrophes, and catastrophes caused by the panic of once regnant power brokers scrambling to retain some semblance of their once secure hegemonies, and for their own very survival.

When Pope John Paul had left the Apostolic Palace to greet and bless the people in St. Peter's Square that May 13 of 1981, he had done so as the leading practitioner of the geopolitics of power. By the time he took up his full papal schedule again six months later, his entire papal strategy had been raised to the level upon which the "Lord of History" arranges the geopolitics of faith.

This is not to say, however, that he was out of the millennium endgame; or that Fatima had done what Ali Agca's bullets could not—removed him as a leader to be reckoned with in the contention for power in the new world order.

On the contrary, it would seem that all through history, Heaven's mandates appear to involve the servants of its designs more deeply and more confidently than ever in the major affairs of the world. In its essence, in fact, Fatima became for John Paul something like the famed Heavenly mandate and guarantee of success proffered to Constantine on the eve of his battle at the Milvian Bridge. Suddenly, Constantine had seen the Sign of the Cross appear in the sky, accompanied by the Latin words *In hoc signo vinces.* "In this sign you will conquer." Improbable as it was, Constantine took that sign as anything but unrealistic or unworldly. He took it as a guarantee. With miraculous confidence, he not only conquered at the Milvian Bridge but proceeded to conquer his entire world, transforming it into what became the new civilization of Christianity.

True, Pope John Paul was not a sword-toting conqueror; and at Fatima, Mary hadn't exactly said, "In this sign you will conquer." But she had given a mandate that was every bit as clear. And as a consequence, in the light of what he now understood his situation to be, the millennium endgame became as important and as urgent for John Paul as the international situation had become for Constantine in his time.

With stunning clarity, the Pope now knew that there was even less time left than he had thought for the old adversarial juxtaposition of East and West that still held sway in 1981 across the face of Europe and the wide world.

Moreover, he knew with equal clarity that his careful and detailed assessment of the contemporary geopolitics of power was correct, but that its significance lay in the fact that the game of power itself would be played out in a totally different manner than he had previously expected.

And finally, he knew that he could not be less involved than before in the millennium endgame. Rather, with supreme personal confidence, and with a tranquillity that would confound many of his adversaries, he would plunge his pontificate with ever greater energy into the game of nations that would soon enough engulf the entire world, before spending itself like raging waters poured out on cement.

If the Pontiff's understanding of Heaven's geopolitical agenda for our time—his outlook and expectations for the near term of history—seems too stark and unsettling to fit today's common superstition that God is incapable of anything but acceptance of man on man's own terms, John Paul knows something about man's own terms. He knows from long and bitter personal experience that the raw exercise of the geopolitics of power inflicts far deeper hurt and barrenness in suffering and death than the God of Love would wreak on his children through the geopolitics of faith. He knows that the greatest divine punishment would be like balm compared to the inhumanity and ruthlessness of such a godless society as either Leninist Marxism or democratic capitalism is capable of generating.

And if, to the modern mind of his competitors in the millennium endgame, John Paul's finalized geopolitical stance seems too deeply based on transcendental matters, too dependent on invisible reality and on "the substance of things to come," that is a problem that time and events have already taken care of. For, within a scant four years of the change in John Paul's geopolitical outlook, thrust so brusquely upon him between the spring and the fall of 1981, Mikhail Gorbachev emerged from the heartland of Russia, right on schedule, as the agent of un-imagined and unimaginable change in the old world order. Suddenly, nothing—not even the Kremlin fortress in Moscow itself—seemed permanent. Suddenly, the whole world was expectant.

Clearly, the new agenda—Heaven's agenda; the Grand Design of God for the new world order—had begun. And Pope John Paul would stride now in the arena of the millennium endgame as something more than a geopolitical giant of his age. He was, and remains, the serene and confident Servant of the Grand Design.

While Pope John Paul engages himself in the totally new agenda for a totally new world order, there is one area crucial to his success where his early policies have not changed at all. Anybody who examines the Pontiff's governance of his Roman Catholic institutional organization since 1978 must come away stunned at the deterioration that began during the fifteen-year reign of Pope Paul VI, and that the present Pope has neither reversed nor arrested.

Whatever may have been his grave policy decision in this matter, and while nobody in his right mind would assess John Paul as anything but a thoroughly Catholic soul and an intensely professional pope, the conclusion is inescapable that there has been no reliable sign from his papal office that a reform of his Church has even been seriously mounted.

The overall result of that policy for the Roman Church has been profound. But in one key area—the area of papal privilege, and of the papal power embodied in the sacred symbol of the Petrine Keys—the policy has been disastrous. For it has enabled those in the Church bent on an antipapal agenda—the anti-Church within the Church—to arrive within touching distance of their main objective; namely, the effective elimination of papal power itself as an operative factor in the administration of the Roman Catholic structure and in the life of the Roman Catholic institution.

This policy decision of John Paul's is the more puzzling because, while it bears directly on the obvious fragmentation of the Church Universal, if there is one aspect of that Church upon which this Pope lays continual emphasis, it is unity. The fact remains, however, that because he has steadfastly refused to discipline his bishops, he has no means to resist the planned ways in which many of those bishops, through such regional bureaucratic organizations as the National Catholic Conference of Bishops in the United States, for example, and the European Conference of Bishops—to name just two among many—have in effect deprived bishops as individuals of their consecrated power to govern their individual dioceses.

The result is something that has never before existed in the Roman Church. An anonymous and impersonal force has been created, centered in the regional Bishops' Conferences around the world, which has now begun to exercise its own power in contravention of papal power.

So far has this situation progressed already that—even though their actions often imply and sometimes condone deep departures from the traditional teaching and the moral laws of the Roman Catholic Church —such regional intra-Church groups are consistent in claiming both autonomy for themselves and special discernment concerning doctrine and morals in their separate regions.

It is true that this victory of in-Church papal enemies is only a de facto affair; that nowhere and by no explicit statement has Pope John Paul formally renounced his Petrine power. But that is cold comfort for those who find his huge gamble with the Petrine Office the most frightening element of John Paul's papal policy. It is all very well, warn some papal advisers, that the Pope refuses to bless the work of those intent upon shattering the Rock of Peter. But the effective catalyst here is the Pontiff's abstention from exercising his papal power in matters critical to Church governance. And, the warning continues, unless the Pope begins to extirpate those who are silently and covertly sapping the foundations of papal privilege and power upon which his Church rests, then into the bargain he might just as well give his blessing to the anti-Church.

That may be an extreme sentiment, especially for men who do remain faithful, and who do accord to John Paul the deference due him as Pope; but it is a sentiment that is understandable. For while the Pope tarries, his in-Church enemies—those who are sworn to rid the earth of the papacy as a centralized governing institution—use this strange and unsettling policy of John Paul's as a comfortable highway leading to their own ultimate victory. Day by day, these papal advisers and advocates see the desuetude and obsolescence of the papacy more fully confirmed as a fact of life. In that situation, and as human affairs go, they foresee that the bulk of Roman Catholics can more and more easily be induced to look upon Rome much as they look upon St. Paul's of London—as a venerable institution with its classic dome and whispering gallery, housing invaluable memories of the past but having no practical bearing on their faith or their lives. And in that situation, these advisers expect that the bulk of Roman Catholics can be ever more easily persuaded to accept the papacy itself as the office of a somewhat influential and honorific Catholic bishop who happens to live in Rome, and who will be as revered as the Dalai Lama—and just about as powerful.

Those among Pope John Paul's advisers who are most urgently and deeply concerned about what some call this "self-slaughter" of the Roman papacy do remain confident in Christ's promise that its destruction will not be completed; that even the Gates of Hell itself will not prevail against the Church Jesus founded upon Peter as its Rock. But, as Lord Nelson commented after a cannonball came too close for comfort at the battle of Trafalgar, it looks to be "a damn near thing."

In the serenity of his own convictions concerning Heaven's agenda for the nations, meanwhile, it is reasonable to think that John Paul himself fully expects that as Pope he will one day in the not distant future be hailed by the generality of his contemporaries in much the same terms as Czechoslovakia's President Havel used to welcome him to Prague on April 21, 1990.

After the Pontiff, following his now familiar custom, stepped off the papal plane and kissed the ground, Havel told the world that "the Messenger of Love comes today into a country devastated by the ideology of hatred. . . . The Living Symbol of civilization comes into a country devastated by the rule of the uncivilized. . . . I have the honor to be a witness when its soil is being kissed by the Apostle of Spirituality."

To all who are presently skeptical about the acceptance on a universal scale of such a role for this or any Roman pope, John Paul might well respond, with Havel, that "I do not know whether I know what a miracle is. . . . Nevertheless, I dare say I am a party to a miracle now." And indeed, to an extent John Paul would be justified in making such a response. For, five years before—even five months before—no one would have imagined such a papal visit possible. As he said that day to his Czechoslovak hosts, "Almighty God can make the impossible possible, can change all human hearts, through the queenship of Jesus' mother, Mary."

Nevertheless, it would appear that now, as in 1980, John Paul has judged that he still can find no way to reform his rapidly deteriorating Church structure; that he cannot make an end run around the anti-Church, as he did so successfully in regard to the Vatican's established policy of *Ostpolitik*.

Meanwhile, the threat to the power and authority of the Petrine Office has become so critical that, at least in the view of faithful and important Churchmen who are themselves as steeped as he is in practical and hard-nosed experience, somewhere down the slope of papal desuetude and obsolescence John Paul will have to issue what will amount to his Protocol of Salvation. They foresee a day of confrontation when Pope John Paul will stand in front of friends and enemies and recite the words with which Jesus once confronted Simon Peter as the chosen head of his Church, to reassure him that his own weakness would not end in the destruction of that Church: "Simon, Simon, Satan has set out to make you like useless chaff he can blow away. But I have prayed for you that your faith not be extinguished. So, in time, you will return to the true faith. And you will correct your ways. And then you will reinstill faith in your brothers."

That day may come suddenly, out of the blue. It may come too late to salvage and restore the faith of millions who have been disillusioned, or to revive the faith of other millions of Roman Catholic apostates. It seems probable, as things are going, that it will come after most who still retain fidelity to the Pope, to the papacy and to the traditional dogmas and faith of universal Roman Catholicism have been shut out of places of Catholic worship that will, for the most part, be fully occupied by those who retain no such fidelity.

When that day does arrive, surely not all of John Paul's friends, nor most of his enemies, will accept the Holy Father's Protocol of Salvation. Surely, many will walk away from him and his papacy forever. But those who submit and remain will no longer be troubled by the ambitions and the meretricious promises of the many among them who would be little popes. Nor will they be blinded and shriveled by the subsequent glory of the Woman Clothed with the Sun.

I

The Geopolitics of Power

Part One

———

The Arena

1. "Everything Must Change!"

On October 14, 1978, a new era began for the Roman Catholic Church and its nearly one billion adherents around the world. And with it, the curtains were raised on the first act of the global competition that would end a thousand years of history as completely as if a nuclear war had been fought. A drama that would leave no regions or nations or individuals as they had been before. A drama that is now well under way and is already determining the very way of life that in every place every nation will live for generations to come.

On that October day, the cardinals of the Roman Catholic Church assembled in the Vatican from around the world for the second time in barely two months. Only in August, they had elected Cardinal Albino Luciani of Venice as Pope John Paul I. Still in shock at the sudden— some said suspicious—death of the man now sadly called the "September Pope," they had convened to settle on a new man from among their contentious and divided ranks who could lead this unique two-thousand-year-old global institution at a time when it seemed in immediate danger of painful self-destruction.

Before and after any papal Conclave, discretion is normally the watchword for every Cardinal Elector. But, on this day, Joseph Cardinal Malula of Zaire did not care who in St. Peter's Square might hear his views about what kind of pope the Church must have. A stocky, well-built man with brilliant eyes and expressive mouth, Malula gestured at the Vatican buildings all around him, then struck a sharp blow against one of Bernini's columns with the flat of his hand. "All that imperial paraphernalia," he declared, "all that! Everything must change!"

At 6:18 P.M. on the second day of Conclave, fifty-eight-year-old Karol Cardinal Wojtyla of Krakow emerged on the eighth ballot as the new

Pope. Malula reportedly let out a discreet but audible whoop. He had his wish.

In fact, he now had something more complex and far-reaching than perhaps even he had bargained for. Suddenly, and without anything like an explanatory statement, there broke upon the Roman and the international scene the figure of a Pope who was about to shatter every mold. A Pope who was anything but imperial and who was not about to be isolated—at least, not in the sense Joseph Malula had meant.

From the first moment of his papal election, publicity figured, as an unusual dimension even for a Pope, in the pontificate of John Paul II. The most avid public attention seemed to fall upon him like a cloak that had been made to his measure. It was a cloak he would wear with startling and unremitting purpose.

At the outset, it all seemed a natural enough consequence of the curiosity one could expect to surround a new Pope. The immediate and seemingly insatiable hunger for details, whether accurate or not, was only to be expected, the more so given the exceptional nature of this choice for the papal throne. Between the time of his election in Conclave and his formal investiture as Pope, early publicity had to feed on what was easily available concerning Wojtyla's life in Poland. Even so, there was a peculiar shape to many of the stories. Things seemed in hindsight to have marked the young Polish bishop as a man of special destiny.

Take, for example, the solar eclipse on May 18, 1920, the day Wojtyla was born. Did not that confirm the supposedly ancient prophecy that the 264th Pope—for so he was—would be born under the sign of *labor solis* (the classical expression for a solar eclipse)? Was not destiny also written in the death of three important people in Wojtyla's life: his mother, when he was nine; his elder brother, when Karol was twelve; his father, when his son and namesake was twenty-three? After all, another old legend had it that a triple death signified a triple crown. And that, in turn, was applied to the triple tiara traditionally used to invest new popes with the universal authority of Peter.

Never mind that John Paul would refuse to wear that ancient gem-studded symbol of his churchly power and temporal influence. Destiny is destiny; and until the new Pope had time to settle in and provide fresh news, the legend that linked death and power made good copy.

Not all the early stories in that brief waiting time were of such a Gothic nature, however. For one thing, there was a lot about Karol Wojtyla that did not fit the popular idea of the papal mold; but it always made for avid reading. Like the still-beloved John XXIII, always remembered as "the good Pope John," there was nothing of the patrician about John Paul II.

His early life proved him to be a man familiar with both the common and the heroic struggle of people everywhere.

On the more common side of the publicity ledger, much was written about the fact that he had been born in an obscure—some said drab— little town named Wadowice, a place of about 9,000 souls, 170 miles south of Warsaw in the foothills of the Beskids mountain range. A good deal of media time was given to the fact that he had spent his earliest years growing up in an unremarkable two-room apartment. Story after story spotlighted the three years the young Wojtyla had spent as a worker in the Zabrzowek Quarry and in the Belgian-owned Solvay Chemical Works, where he was a boiler-room helper.

Less commonplace were the stories that focused on Wojtyla's close association with the mysterious tailor-mystic Jan Tyranowski; on his skill as a soccer goalie; on his love of music and his talent as an amateur guitarist; on his membership in the Rapsodyczny Theater of Krakow, where he specialized in poetry reading.

Not one, but two, bona fide underground experiences made for a dramatic edge in the early publicity. Much attention was given to Wojtyla's association during World War II with the Polish underground team that supposedly helped obtain one of the first Nazi V-2 rockets to be smuggled out of occupied Poland and over to wartime London. And at least as much was made of his life as an underground novice in the now famous "conspiratorial seminary" set up under the noses of the German occupation forces by the Polish cardinal Adam Sapieha, Archbishop of Krakow.

Even destiny and drama and war stories were not the whole of it, though. A modest amount of research, and a good bit of help from Vatican sources who already knew the huge changes the new Pontiff had in store, quickly uncovered a series of "firsts" in Wojtyla's life, dating back to 1946, when he had become the first Polish priest ever to be ordained after a mere four years' study. Then, in 1958, he had become the youngest auxiliary bishop in Polish history. In 1964, he became the youngest archbishop in the history of the diocese of Krakow. Again, in 1967, he became the youngest cardinal Poland has ever had. And now, in 1978, he had become the first Polish Pope in history, and the first non-Italian Pope in four hundred years.

It appears now with hindsight that it was during this waiting time, even before his formal investiture as Pope, that the contradictions about John Paul and his intentions began to surface, and with them, some serious concerns in the wider world of government and global commerce.

On October 21, five days after his election and a full week before the ceremonial papal coronation, John Paul held a press conference for two thousand journalists in the Vatican. On the same day he addressed 125 members of the Vatican diplomatic corps representing over one hundred countries. If such a practice was not unusual in itself, the message on both occasions was certainly new in the all-encompassing international framework that was sketched out. "It is not our business," he said, "to judge the actions of government. . . . But there is no way the dignity and the rights of all men and every human individual can be served unless that dignity and those rights are seen as founded on the life, death and resurrection of Christ. . . .

"The Church seeks no privileges for herself," he went on, "but we do desire a dialogue with the nations." Even though the Church's diplomatic relations with so many countries "do not necessarily imply the approval of one or another regime—that is not our business." Nevertheless, the Pontiff went on in a sort of summary preview of the scope of his interests, "we have an appreciation of the positive temporal values, a willingness for dialogue with those who are legitimately charged with the common good of society, and an understanding of their role, which is often difficult."

Clearly, this Pope portended more than a soft and appealing personal style in his pontificate; he was pointing early and with startling frankness to a new road of papal internationalism. But what—or whose—positive temporal values did he have in mind? And who among temporal leaders did he include among those "legitimately charged with the common good of society"? More pointedly, some began to wonder, who was excluded?

If those questions were not raised in public, they were surely raised in more than one political chancery and boardroom around the world.

Then there was the matter of his ceremonial coronation. Actually, it was not a coronation at all, for he refused to have the papal tiara placed on his head as the symbol that he was now, among other things and in the language of the ceremonial, "the Father of Princes and Kings."

That refusal was not entirely new in itself. His immediate predecessor, the "September Pope," had been the first to break with that ancient custom. Was John Paul II's behavior a sign of defiance? A sign that he had no fear of the fate of the "September Pope"? Perhaps. Was it a soothing democratic gesture after his unsettling policy speeches of a few days before? Surely, there were those who hoped as much.

Popes rarely explain such ceremonial behavior. In his own break with papal custom, however, John Paul gave the most public explanation imaginable. To all those gathered around him in St. Peter's, and to the estimated billion or so people around the world watching on television, the Pontiff gave a glimpse of his mind as Pope, and a look at the vigorous papal policies that would soon prove so troublesome to so many.

"This is not a time," he said, "to return to a ceremony and to an object" —the tiara itself—"that is wrongly considered to be a symbol of temporal power of the Pope."

Very soon, his actions and overt policies would illustrate over and over again the meaning of his words: John Paul's firm belief that neither tiara nor the power symbolized by such a thing was an adequate expression of the divine claim he did indeed have to exercise spiritual authority and moral primacy over all those who wield such temporal power in our lives.

About the scope of that authority and primacy he tried to leave as little doubt as possible, that October day. Speaking successively in ten languages, he gave to the world a message that was explicit and direct. "Open wide the doors of Christ. To his saving power open the boundaries of states, economic and political systems, the vast fields of culture and civilization and development. Do not be afraid. . . . I want your support in this, my mission."

There were those in very high places who understood and winced at the global reach John Paul seemed ready to make his own as Pope. Some powerful leaders at the helm of those states whose boundaries the Pope wanted open to him would not be entirely happy to oblige. Hard-driving leaders of economic and political systems he referred to, with their own plans for development well along in the "vast fields of culture and civilization," would not willingly open those fields to this Pope or any other. And not least among those who took the point, and winced, were some among the highest of John Paul's own clergy, in and out of the Vatican.

John Paul anticipated those reactions, and later learned about them in some detail. What seemed more remarkable was the seeming lack of interest demonstrated by the media around the world in what was a stunning glimpse into the heart of the new papacy. Still, if he was worried about either the international concern or the seeming indifference in the media, he gave no sign of it.

Instead, shortly after his election, John Paul gave yet another clear notice of how sweeping he intended his policies to be.

His intention, he said, was "to start anew on the road of history and of the Church, to start with the help of God and with the help of man."

Lest anyone mistake his mind on the subject of temporal power, or perhaps in answer to a worried complaint or two, the new Pontiff addressed the same point again at his first papal Mass. With St. Peter's filled to the last seat by many of the leaders he most intended to reach, he declared: "We have no intentions of political interference, nor of interfering in the working out of temporal affairs. . . . It is not our business to judge the actions of governments."

Fevered diplomatic brows were not soothed, however. The unasked question in many minds was obvious: "But Your Holiness *does* intend to insert yourself into our temporal affairs—to cross our political and cultural and economic boundaries. But if not as a wielder of temporal power yourself, in what guise, then, Holiness?"

Apparently, the media at large could still find no way to zero in on what the new Pope might have meant by such statements. Or perhaps they found it dull copy after the death-and-destiny stories of just a few weeks before. Whatever the reason, publicity continued to focus its ever-present lenses on an entire landscape of trivia still to be mined. Everything was grist for the mill, from the fact that he was the tallest of the twentieth-century Popes to the fact that he was the first Pope to wear long trousers under his papal robes, and the first to be an accomplished skier. Even his impressive academic achievements were judged to be better copy than his open notice to the world of what could be expected from him as head of the only power in the world whose organization, institutions and personnel, as well as its authority, crossed all the borders and all the cultures and all the civilizations he had targeted without benefit of tiara in St. Peter's Basilica.

As if to spare the world the boredom of endless stories that were appearing in the media about such things as his three doctorates, in philosophy, theology and phenomenology; or about his ten published books, including drama and poetry; or about his university lecturing, John Paul launched into activities that were the dream of reporters and editors and proved themselves to be sources of fresh material. Stories not of the past, but the present. Stories not of opaque policies they couldn't explain, but of people with faces they could photograph.

Even here, John Paul's activities and gestures began to speak loudly of a new papal approach. Before October's end, he had granted a $375 bonus and a five-day vacation—from the first to the fifth of November—to all Vatican workers.

More significantly, he began to shoulder aside the idea that the Pope must dwell within the tranquil golden amber of the Vatican. The idea, so detested by Cardinal Malula, that the Holy Father did not come to see you or your surroundings. The idea that the most you might see of him if you went to Rome would be at public blessings in the luminous Roman airs. There was to be no such constricted, hidden life for John Paul.

For one thing, he refused the traditional use of the papal "We" and "Us" and "Our." "I," he said, in referring to himself in every context and conversation; and "me" and "my," just like everyone else.

Moreover, he popped up everywhere, as if Rome were Krakow and Italy were Poland and he had never left his home or his people. In quick order, he visited the towns of Assisi and Siena. He inspected the papal summer residence at Castel Gandolfo. He worshiped at the mountain shrine of La Mentorella. He traveled to see one ailing bishop and one ailing cardinal in Roman hospitals.

Far from being questioned or criticized, such spontaneous and rapid-fire visibility—undertaken, moreover, with an obvious zest and personal energy—was welcomed by the media and delighted the public. Italians —and Romans in particular—who, for centuries before this, had invented the very Italian concept of *l'uomo* in order to characterize the exclusive flair and personal style of an individual, took this extraordinary Pope as their very own.

They loved his public apologies for the few mistakes he made when addressing them in Italian. They loved his obvious delight in their children. They found his independence of mind concerning ancient customs so much like their own attitudes. Quickly they began calling him *il nostro polacco*—our Pole. But even this gave way to "Papa Wojtyla": just as Paul VI had been Papa Montini for them; and John XXIII had been Papa Roncalli; and Pius XII had been Papa Pacelli. Pole by birth, he was now Roman by adoption. Papa Wojtyla was *theirs*.

Whenever he walked in St. Peter's Square, crowds literally mobbed him. In fact, so close were their encounters with him that he often returned to his apartments minus several buttons from his papal robe and with some dozen lipstick marks on his white papal sleeves.

When he went to take possession of the ancient papal church, the Basilica of St. John Lateran, tens of thousands left their shops and offices and homes all along the way to cheer him, to kiss his hand, to ask his blessing. When he took a helicopter to reach the mountain shrine of La Mentorella, he found crowds of men and women who had already scaled that difficult height and were waiting there to greet him.

The delight of the Italian press in all this papal activity was infectious, at least for a while. Many a newspaper in other lands seemed to echo the benign and favorable tone taken by *The New York Times* in its lead editorial of November 11. "A man," said the *Times* of Pope John Paul, "who knows himself to be in charge, beholden to no nation or faction, strong without being rigid."

For the moment, Archbishop Rembert Weakland of Milwaukee could find few Churchmen who could comfort him publicly for having rushed too soon to tell the world that "the Italian people were deeply hurt by the election of a Pole as Pope."

Papa Wojtyla's personal innovative style within the Vatican itself did spark a few complaints of unpapal behavior. The ever-alert paparazzi, with their zoom lenses ever at the ready, caught excellent shots of John Paul jogging in the Vatican gardens at 4:30 in the afternoon. *Il jogging papale*—the papal jogging—as his clockwork habit was quickly dubbed, was readily taken by lighthearted Romans to fix the time of their after- noon rendezvous.

When John Paul ordered a 40-by-82-foot swimming pool to be dug at Castel Gandolfo, there were some reproaches about the expense. The Pontiff countered that "a new Conclave would be much more expen- sive." The deft and smiling implication that even a pope might succumb because of a lack of adequate exercise added an easy personal tone to the publicity that no one had expected, and that few could match.

As the weeks went on, there seemed to be so much to write about this Pope that was so new, and often so downright entertaining, that no amount of copy seemed to satisfy an ever-mounting curiosity about the uncommon common man who had come to the papacy. Even his work schedule proved to be good copy. His eighteen-hour day caused much rolling heavenward of Italian eyes. The world learned that he was up at 5:00 A.M. That he had a working breakfast, a working lunch, a working dinner, always with guests and always with plenty of documents. That he went late to his bed.

Among those government leaders who were far more interested in John Paul's policies than his publicity were the leaders in the countries of Eastern Europe and their Soviet masters in Moscow. By late October, their worries in particular were raised to a new level by the first orches- trated rumors and speculation—spread by word of mouth and by author- itative media articles fed from within the Vatican itself—that this new Pope was going to visit Poland.

In later years, the world became accustomed to the idea of John Paul II popping up in the most unexpected places as easily as he had gone to Assisi and Siena and La Mentorella. But in October and November of 1978, the very thought of a visit to Poland was a bombshell. Preposterous, said some; foolhardy and pointless, said others.

Nevertheless, it was officially confirmed: John Paul's Vatican was "talk- ing with Warsaw." And while it might turn out to be foolhardy, it was anything but pointless. It was the clearest indication of what John Paul regarded, and still regards, as the essential hub of his vision of the new "road of history and of the Church."

Warsaw was not the only bombshell John Paul lobbed, as he went rapidly about installing the new spirit of his papacy. By means of his papal style, and taking the mantle of publicity that fell so easily and so usefully around him as an instrument—one of several—he began a series of truly unsettling meetings within the Vatican.

On November 18, he received the dissident French Archbishop Marcel Lefebvre. Lefebvre had been hit with a severe ecclesiastical Roman sanction in 1976, and had been banned from the papal presence. But here he was, as large as life, spending fully two hours in a private and cordial talk with the new Pope. The message was clear for all those who hated the "retrogressive and destructive conservatism" Lefebvre represented for them. And John Paul was serving notice that he was Pope for all Catholics.

The Pontiff's reception at the Vatican of Donald Coggan, Archbishop of Canterbury and the spiritual head of all Anglicans, spread the net still wider. Coggan was the second Archbishop of Canterbury ever to be received by a reigning pope since the sixteenth century. John Paul's message was clear for all those who hated the liberal, breakaway independence Protestants represented for them: Even those Rome holds to be long-standing heretics remain open to the influence and leadership of the Pope, whose primacy they once rejected.

It quickly became clear as well that John Paul would not confine his message, his influence or his leadership to ecclesiastical matters. Those who had begun to worry that His Holiness intended to insert himself into their temporal affairs were apparently right to do so.

Toward the end of November, the Pope met with four black liberation leaders from sub-Saharan Africa: Oliver Tambo, President of South Africa's African National Congress (ANC). George Silundika of Rhodesia's Zimbabwe Patriotic Front (ZPF) together with ZPF Secretary of Social Services and Transport Kumbirai Kanyan. And Sam Silundika of the Southwest African People's Organization (SWAPO).

It was hardly lost on some who were entrenched in power in and out of the Vatican that John Paul had pointedly and early in his reign decided to meet some of the most powerful challengers to all vested power—including his own. The question in such minds was: How far was this Pope going to go? The rainbow of startling possibilities they began to see was just beginning to form over their heads. One answer to the question "How far?" was given by John Paul himself. He gave it on December 8, a feast day in honor of the Virgin Mary, to whom he had dedicated his papacy.

There has grown up in Rome a papal custom observed each year on this day commemorating the Immaculate Conception of the Virgin

Mother of God. The Pope proceeds sedately by automobile to the Piazza
di Spagna, where the statue of the Virgin stands atop a graceful column.
He places a basket of roses from the papal gardens at the base of the
column. He gives his solemn papal blessings to the crowds in attendance.
And then he returns to the Vatican as sedately as he came.

Not so John Paul.

First, he interrupted the drive to the Virgin's statue with a stop in the
Via Condotti—Rome's version of posh and trendy Rodeo Drive in Bev-
erly Hills—to accept a chalice presented to him as a gift from the Via
Condotti merchants. Then, after going on to the Piazza di Spagna and
placing the basket of roses at the base of the column, he preceded his
papal blessing with a discourse so sweeping and so inconsistent with
modern precedent that many there seemed not merely unwilling but
literally unable to comprehend it.

He spoke that day of how he viewed human history: "The entire history
of man is in fact pervaded by a tremendous struggle against the force of
evil in the world. . . . This Pope desires to commit the Church in a
special way to Mary in whom the stupendous and total victory of good
over evil, of love over hate, of grace over sin, is achieved. . . ."

He announced that day his new principle of religion: for all Christians,
yes, but for all mankind as well. "This Pope commits himself to her
[Mary], and to all those whom he serves, and all those who serve him.
He commits the Roman Church to her as the token and principle of all
the churches in the world in their universal unity."

So there it was. His thrust would truly be universal. He really would
stake a modern-day claim to that universality that had always been asserted by the Church he now headed. Perhaps because no pope had ever
spoken of "a universal unity" shared by all the churches of Christianity,
the idea was unintelligible for Roman Catholic Churchmen as well as for
the leaders of other churches.

Rome's Communist newspaper, L'Unità—the name means unity, but
not the brand John Paul had in mind—was quicker off the mark when it
came to a clear understanding of the political consequences of such
"universal unity" on the lips and as the policy and driving force of a
Roman Catholic pope. Such a "universal unity," L'Unità warned, over
which this Roman Pope would obviously claim primacy, clearly implied
"an interference in the internal affairs of the USSR whose Russian Orthodox Church belongs to no pope."

L'Unità seemed almost alone, however, in its trenchant willingness to
look John Paul and his policy straight in the eye. As Christmas 1978
approached, many newspapers appeared content to concentrate on an-

other sort of papal first in John Paul's Vatican: an all-Polish Christmas feast was described in succulent detail. The barszcz; the small stuffed pastries called pierogi; the roast pork; the cabbage and kielbasa and cake: all received lighthearted and sometimes hilarious attention.

With the turn of the new year, 1979, John Paul began in earnest to flesh out his early statement about starting "anew on the road of history and of the Church." In initiatives that were highly visible and depended solely on him for their success and effect, his earlier references to the role of his papacy within the scope of international affairs became a central focus of his most public activity.

On January 9, John Paul's personal representative, Antonio Cardinal Samore of the Vatican's Secretariat of State, succeeded in a dicey bit of international diplomacy at which even the Queen's government in England had failed. At issue was a question of war and peace between two of South America's most important countries, Argentina and Chile. Those two had fought bloody wars before, and were seemingly willing to go at it again—this time over the possession of the three islands, Nueva, Picton and Lennox, in the strategically important Beagle Channel.

After what amounted to extensive shuttle diplomacy that took him back and forth between the capital cities of Buenos Aires and Santiago de Chile, Samore at last persuaded the two governments to send their negotiators to the neutral grounds of nearby Montevideo, Uruguay. There, under Samore's guidance, foreign ministers Carlos W. Pastor of Argentina and Hernan Cubillos of Chile signed an agreement pledging both countries to demilitarize the disputed area, and to submit to binding arbitration that would be conducted by John Paul's papal envoys.

What stood out as the fascinating element in this Latin American venture were two things. First, that John Paul was willing to commit himself and his prestige in an international arena at the very outset of his pontificate. And second, that without politicking of any kind, but solely because of the religious and psychological prestige of John Paul and his Vatican, two nations backed off from political claims so intense and so laden with history and emotion that war had seemed the inevitable recourse.

On January 24, John Paul dramatically underscored the worldwide ambit he had in mind for exactly that type of apolitical intervention by his unconventional papacy. He met that day in the Vatican with the Soviet foreign minister, Andrei Gromyko. The Pontiff spent nearly two hours in private face-to-face discussion in fluent Russian with the man the Soviets had nicknamed the "Icy Survivor."

Western diplomats who had dealt with Gromyko had always been impressed—sometimes frightened—by the cluster of talents he had displayed in negotiations, and by his near-miraculous political agility in surviving nearly forty years of Soviet intrigue and other vagaries of Kremlin life. John Paul, too, was impressed. In answer to a query about what he thought of Gromyko in comparison to all the other diplomats who had dutifully trooped through his private study in the first months of his pontificate, the Pope was undiplomatically candid: "He's the only horse shod on all four feet."

Of more concern for Western governments, perhaps, was Gromyko's interest in Pope John Paul. Gromyko rarely spent that amount of time with any individual statesman. The question in embassies and cabinet rooms and chanceries was: What on earth had they discussed for two hours, this unpredictable Roman Pope and this wiliest of Soviet diplomats? Beyond Gromyko's reference to John Paul after their meeting as "a man with a worldview," the Soviet gave no hint of what had passed between the two of them. Characteristically, it was the Pope, sometime later, who spoke frankly with reporters.

"I welcome any criticism from Communist officials," John Paul said, adding that he and Gromyko had discussed "the prospects for world peace."

Far from satisfying the questions, the Pope's remarks raised concern in certain government and diplomatic quarters to a higher pitch. Why on earth would Gromyko discuss matters of "world peace"—matters, in other words, that were exclusively of a political and geopolitical nature —with this Pope who hailed from the Polish backwater? For that matter, why would the Pope of Rome discuss them with this Soviet man?

It was still January of 1979 when, with such questions hanging in the air of international diplomacy, John Paul gave the surest sign that he would not merely set a grand new papal tone for others to pick up. He would not merely say what was to be done by means traditionally used by popes and then leave it to his hierarchy and the faithful to get it done.

That signal was John Paul's first trip to Mexico, widely covered by the media, from January 25 to 30. That trip did begin to reveal something about what the world beyond the Vatican and Rome could expect from the reign of John Paul II. But it demonstrated again that commentators were not prepared for so radical a change as was even then under way, and certainly not for one so quick in coming.

Already well behind the new pace and the new course being set by the Pontiff, the eighteen hundred reporters and commentators assigned to cover this papal trip assumed that the Pope wanted simply to counteract the spread of Marxism—a recognized target of Vatican and Roman

Catholic opposition, after all—among his clergy and people in that part of the world.

It was admittedly difficult for those covering the trip not to be beguiled by what seemed to be this Pope's public relations instincts, already in full swing during the ten-and-a-half-hour flight from Rome across the Atlantic. Passing over the Azores, John Paul sent his blessing by radio to the Portuguese living there. Flying over the island of Puerto Rico, he chatted with President Jimmy Carter by radio.

Not even his opening words—"I am come as a traveler of peace and hope"—spoken during a one-day stopover (January 25–26) in Santo Domingo, were seen as pointing to the new role this Pope had chosen for himself.*

It was only to be expected, after all, that he would present himself at this gateway to the Americas as the embodiment of five hundred years of Christianity in the Western Hemisphere. Referring to the fact that Santo Domingo was the selfsame Hispaniola where Columbus had first set foot in 1493, John Paul offered the reminder that "here the first Mass was celebrated, the first cross was placed."

However, speaking later to a quarter of a million people gathered in Santo Domingo's Plaza de Independencia, the Pope began to speak, not of some self-satisfied continuation of old ways, but of something like a revolution for which he wanted to prepare as many as would listen to him. "The present period of human history requires a revived dimension of faith, in order to communicate to today's people the perennial message of Christ adapted to the realistic conditions of life."

Later, in the Cathedral of Santa María la Menor, the oldest cathedral in the Americas, built of limestone blocks in the early 1500s, John Paul carried the point further and again applied its pressure to more than his own Roman Catholics. "All Christians," he declared, "and all peoples must commit themselves to construct a more just, humane and habitable world, which does not close itself in, but which opens itself to God."

This combination of traditional religious devotion to the Mass and to the Cross of Christ, on the one hand, and allusions to sweeping geopolitical intentions, on the other, had much the same effect in the world press as John Paul's December 8 commitment to "universal unity." Even seasoned observers were simply not able to take it in.

Things went much the same way in Mexico. Commentators and reporters expected the Pope to talk with his bishops. And they expected his remarks about Marxism and religion. A pope is supposed to do that sort of thing.

But now, perhaps, they had even come to expect the same freewheel-

ing personal spontaneity that had so endeared John Paul to the people
of Italy. And sure enough, everyone loved the exotic touch in his meetings with the Indians and *campesinos* in Monterrey and Guadalajara. He
kissed babies and embraced invalids, led crowds amiably in their spontaneous chant, as enthusiastic as for some home-game football match:
"Papa! Papa! Rah-rah-rah!" He joined happy crowds in singing a popular
Mexican song. He donned all the hats he was offered—a peasant's straw
sombrero, a broad-brimmed ranchero's hat, a feathered Indian head-
dress. He joined eighty thousand in singing Beethoven's "Ode to Joy."

Given that beguiling dimension of John Paul's performance, most
journalists gave the world a folkloric, if not folksy, view of John Paul's
entire stay in Mexico. They did, of course, report the Pontiff's conversation of nearly two hours with Mexico's President López Portillo, who,
though born a Catholic, described himself as "a Hegelian." And they
reported that López Portillo took the Holy Father to visit the President's
mother and sister in the private chapel of their home.

The significance of those visits was another matter, however. Nobody
raised publicly the interesting question as to why López Portillo, as president of constitutionally anti-Catholic and anticlerical Mexico, should
have anything of substance to discuss for nearly two hours with this
greatest of Catholic clerics. Or why López Portillo should have taken the
personal trouble of escorting the Pope to what amounted to an audience
for his mother and sister in a private chapel. At its most serious, the
Mexican trip was taken as an exceptional and even overdramatic gesture
by His Holiness; and López Portillo's behavior was taken as equally exceptional.

Still, offstage and away from the glare of the press, there were again
those who were becoming alarmed over the Pope's ability to command
and sustain a high level of world attention for far longer than had been
foreseen.

Once back in the Vatican, John Paul was unperturbed by any carping
criticisms that did begin to surface. He continued his pontificate with the
same personal touch that was so natural to him. On February 24, 1979,
in fulfillment of a spontaneous promise he had made to Vittoria Ianni,
the daughter of a Roman street cleaner, John Paul solemnized that
young woman's marriage to Mario Maltese, a Roman electrical worker.
And he continued to step farther along that "new road" he had proclaimed for himself and his Church.

On March 8, he received a delegation of thirty Shintoists, together
with their High Priest, a man called Nizo, from the famous Ise Shrine in
Japan. No pope had ever done such a thing. Within the Vatican—a place

of venerable protocol and strict emphasis on religious priority—this extraordinary papal gesture was alarming to just about everyone. Here, without doubt, was an unexpected change in the rules everyone—friend and enemy alike—had thought they understood. The gesture was so extraordinary, in fact, that in Japan—which pays little even in the way of lip service to the religious side of Rome—and even in religious quarters elsewhere long noted for denunciation of Rome's traditional claim to religious exclusivity, eyebrows began to knit in puzzlement. They, too, had thought they knew the rules.

That same month of March saw the publication, with John Paul's permission, of a book of his poetry in Britain, another land not altogether easy in its ecclesiastical relations with the Holy See. In Italy, meanwhile, a translation was prepared of a two-act play that Papa Wojtyla had written in much earlier days, *The Goldsmith's Shop,* and it was broadcast over Italian radio.

As such a welter of papal interest and activity piled up for all the world to see, opinions about him in the media became almost schizophrenic in their confusion. At one extreme, there were emotional expressions of admiration for the versatility of his character. At the other, there was at least a growing distrust for what appeared to many to be his unpredictability. What there was not, was any publicly expressed understanding or analysis of John Paul's actions in the light of his own early, continuing and exceptionally clear announcements about his intentions. What made that lack of understanding more remarkable was the fact that John Paul was so insistent in his message and that phrases and sentences were turning up as "quotable quotes"—but as virtually no more than that—in Italian and foreign news coverage.

"The Church wishes to stay free with regard to competing systems. . . ." "The inexorable paradox of atheistic humanism . . . the drama of men deprived of an essential dimension of their being, denying him his search for the infinite. . . ." "Market forces alone should not determine the price of goods. . . ." "We must clarify and resolve the problem of a more adequate and more effective institutional framework of worldwide solidarity . . . human solidarity within each country and between countries. . . ." "The fundamental question of the just price and the just contract. . . ." "The process [of remuneration for work done] cannot simply be left to . . . the dominant influence of small groups. . . ."

Finally, by dint of repetition, as John Paul's conversations, addresses, discourses—even his off-the-cuff remarks—became more and more widely reproduced, the reaction to him began to take on a more cohesive aspect. Early on, one English writer had taken it upon himself to dismiss this Pontiff as merely a Polish bishop elected Pope by "the ingrown minds of superannuated cardinals, and let loose on the complicated world of today."

Increasingly, however, many of his own Churchmen, as well as many in government and power around the world, began to share Andrei Gromyko's far different assessment of the "Polish bishop" as "a man with a worldview."

In reality, as some began to think, this was a man with a perspective so new and a goal so vast that it was far beyond the imagining of a whole array of political and financial leaders who had thought themselves immune in their separate and protected strongholds.

Meanwhile, the public at large appeared to have no such concerns. John Paul's personal appeal for ordinary men and women grew visibly from day to day. The crowds that came from nearby and from around the world to catch even a glimpse of him in the Vatican became so great and so unmanageable that the Pope ordered his regular Wednesday general audience to be shifted from the already vast space inside St. Peter's Basilica to the still vaster square outside his door.

John Paul chose his first Easter as Pope to clarify as deeply and as pointedly as it was possible to do the thoughts and considerations that lay at the heart of all his actions: everything from his marriage of a street cleaner's daughter and an electrical worker, to his meetings with Marxists and Shintoists in the Vatican, to his visit to Mexico, to his coming visit to Poland, already confirmed for the coming June, and the scores of papal trips still in store to every corner of the world.

In a 24,000-word document known, as papal documents generally are, by its now famous first words, *Redemptor Hominis*, John Paul displayed a depth of thought and consideration coupled with a message that was characteristically simple and startling.

No human activity escapes the religious dimension, he said; but especially important are the activities that constitute the sociopolitical life of men and women wherever they reside. Indeed, the note that dominated and animated that encyclical document was John Paul's insistence that the hard, intractable problems of the world—hunger, violation of human dignity and human rights, war and violence, economic oppression, political persecution—any and all of these can be solved only by acceptance and implementation of the message of Christ's revelation announced by the papacy and the Roman Catholic Church.

With the delivery of that encyclical, Pope John Paul seemed to mark a turning point. From that time forward, he did not go out of his way to explain his mind further than he had already done. He did not pause to smooth the ruffled feathers of those who felt he was clearly poaching now on the preserves of others. It was as though he no longer considered it productive to try endlessly to correct wrong impressions, or to widen views narrower than his own.

If there were those who could or would not understand that, even in his simplest statements, he was saying something entirely new, they at least were learning that they were listening to a Pope who had taken it upon himself to break ancient customs. If few could yet know that he had arrived in Rome with a mind already filled with a new and wider and hitherto unimagined role for the successor to Peter, John Paul himself could not afford to wait for the rest to catch up with him. Friends and critics and all interested parties alike could read his Easter encyclical letter. And they could read his actions.

If there were many, whether of good will or ill, whether opposed to Rome or devoted to it, who couldn't deal with the papacy turned inside out by John Paul's innovations, he could only promise much more of the same. And if, finally, as often happens with the greatest of the world's events, the real confrontation John Paul said was already taking place had escaped public notice, then time and great events would make everything clear even to those most unwilling to acknowledge it.

2. Nobody's Pope

If the secular reaction to Pope John Paul II in the early days of his reign was strewn with misunderstanding, concern and confusion, it has to be said that most of those within the Roman Catholic Church itself were still more astonished and baffled.

Here, however, the consternation centered around the bare fact, visible to everyone everywhere, that John Paul's Church was in shambles.

And the confusion centered around the fact that this Pope's conscious decision, unbelievably enough, was to refuse to halt the process of decay.

For the faithful in his Church, and arguably for the millions who had left it in pain and dismay during the long pontificate of Pope Paul VI, John Paul was more than an ordinary public figure, more than a man, more even than a religious leader. For them, he had become the personal representative of God on earth. His was the ultimate voice of authority about how the world should be governed by men. He was the court of last resort for all human doubts. He was supposed to fix the Church. Or at least to run it.

It was all very well for John Paul to stride forward as a pope whose mind was filled with a new and wider and hitherto unimagined role for a successor to Peter, the Great Fisherman. It was all very well for him to attend, as some said even then, to a strange and alien light that only he could see, but that certainly seemed to illumine his actions as he touched the rarely reached acme of worldly exposure and recognition. But what about touching power within the Church itself? There seemed to be plenty of worldly leaders, the complaint went. But what about John Paul's irreplaceable role as Peter?

For those who treasured the amber-encased papacy that John Paul had already put behind him forever, it was too much by far to see a pope who allowed himself to be touched and greeted and addressed and, yes, even rebutted by millions of ordinary men and women. That he had already been appropriated in some sense by millions of very different people, baptized and unbaptized, and that he obviously intended to travel the world in order to continue that overdemocratic process, shattered the fragile mold within which large numbers were convinced the papacy—the real and Catholic papacy—must ever remain.

That wasn't to say, however, that there weren't plenty of Roman Catholics and others besides on the other side of the fence; people to whom the shambles of John Paul's Church were a welcome sight; people who would have been more than content to see the papacy remain sealed away from the rough-and-tumble of the world's scramble toward its future. In such quarters as these, the strong desire to see the Pope mind his Churchly business was not sparked by deep faith. Rather, the hope was simply that the papacy would truly wither to nothing; that it would no longer be a central unifying factor of universal Catholic life.

For these people, who not only nourished that hope but had, many of them, labored daily for the death of the papacy as the unifying force of Catholicism, John Paul threatened a dream. They found his behavior and his appeal so distressful, in fact, and so maddening, that some in this group could not keep from an early and open display of their dislike for the Pontiff, and of their contempt for his highly publicized actions.

Milwaukee's Archbishop Rembert Weakland, arguably no stranger to notorious behavior, stepped far beyond the normal bounds of public comment for high Churchmen when he characterized John Paul II as "a ham actor whose speeches don't make sense unless you dramatize them."

In a tone of loftier disdain, the English Cardinal, Basil Hume, Archbishop of Westminster and onetime willing papal candidate, held John Paul up to that discreetly disguised contempt once favored by the English upper classes for the ill-bred and lowborn. After listening to the newly elected Pontiff address all his cardinals in the Consistory Hall of the Apostolic Palace, Hume complained, "I became increasingly flabbergasted and amazed at the pace it [the Pope's address] went on, especially since the weather was quite warm." The barb that no true gentleman would subject another needlessly to suffer through such a meeting when the weather was disagreeable made Hume's deeper implication clear to all who heard him: John Paul could not possibly have anything of importance to say.

Such a lack of discretion and extreme feelings aside, it was not long before just about everyone within the Roman Catholic Church had some complaint to make. And though the complaints were varied and covered a wide spectrum, all of them focused in some way on one remarkable trait of this new Pope. Wherever they might stand on the ever-widening range of action, of faith and of loyalty to the papacy; and whatever rung they might occupy in the Church's structure, from lay person to activist to priest to cardinal, the seeming tranquillity of Pope John Paul in the face of the decay that was eating at the vitals of his Church was cause for uncertainty and for downright bafflement.

From the very beginning of his pontificate, it was clear that John Paul was acutely aware of his Church's disarray. And it was equally clear that his conscious decision was to refuse to halt the process of decay.

So consistent was this mystifying attitude on John Paul's part that a somewhat later incident came to symbolize the apparent fruitlessness of any attempt to change the papal mind on that score. Early in his pontificate, one of John Paul's most invaluable allies and servitors, the powerful Joseph Cardinal Ratzinger, who heads the Congregation for the Doctrine of the Faith, underlined for the Pope just one festering source of Church decadence. The Cardinal implied that the Holy Father might profitably address himself to the problem in question.

To the surprise of all within earshot—for the exchange took place before the two had reached an entirely private area—and as if to under-line his papal refusal to bring order out of chaos, the Pope turned on Ratzinger with a sharp and open rebuke of a kind rarely seen in the Apostolic Palace.

It was not merely that the tone and the quasi-public nature of this encounter were so unusual, but that the unpapal attitude it displayed was so alarmingly consistent toward Church decay still advancing on every side.

Nevertheless, as Ratzinger and everyone present at that unpleasant moment realized, no one who knew this Pope, or who knew more about him than the trivia afloat in the press, had ever thought for a moment that the explanation of such unprecedented behavior might reasonably lie in any flaw in John Paul's own Catholicism. Even so formidable a figure as the late and supremely canny Carlo Cardinal Confalonieri—regarded by friend and foe during his long Vatican career as the very embodiment of what is genuinely Catholic and of Romanism—gave the stamp of approval to John Paul on this score. "We have a Catholic Pope!" the Cardinal exulted to newsmen on the October day of Wojtyla's papal election.

In that Cardinal's mouth, the word "Catholic" was not some merely partisan label. It was his summary of what he knew firsthand to be this Pope's profound grasp of what it means to be Catholic today. In his shorthand way, Confalonieri was saying that no one could seriously fault John Paul's credentials as theologian, philosopher or scholar, as student of history and religion, or as experienced Roman Catholic Churchman.

Nevertheless, and even though he was bombarded from East and West with detailed reports and firsthand evidence of rampant decadence and unfaith among Churchmen who were everywhere entrusted with the pastoral care of nearly a billion Catholics, John Paul refused to take any significant action.

Complaints and questions mounted. How could this Pope refuse to do anything even to slow what he acknowledged openly to some to be the steady deterioration of the institutions of his Church? How could he refuse to defend his own Petrine authority by strong exercise of it and, at the same time, keep railing at the world to pay attention to him and his "new mission"?

It did not take long for what could only be taken as John Paul's hands-off policy within his own Church to encourage some of his most signifi-cant adversaries in the struggle that did seem to interest him, the one struggle to which he was committed as Pope from the first instant of his election.

As his intimate associates knew, John Paul was aware, name by name and to his own pain, of Churchmen with front-rank power over the sinews of Church strength who were committed to his failure as defender of the Church and its traditional moral and religious teachings, and as defender of Petrine authority itself.

Yet the Pontiff's refusal, early or late, to rebut such in-Church adversaries—even to the degree that he rebutted Cardinal Ratzinger, among others of his supporters—led quickly and directly to the spread of a truly eerie state of affairs among Catholics and non-Catholics alike, the world over.

It seemed to take no time at all, for example, for an increasing and remarkably vocal array of cardinals, bishops, prominent theologians and lay people everywhere to join forces openly, as a phalanx of in-Church adversaries to John Paul and his authority. Aptly dubbed the anti-Church, this widely dispersed group was recognized by John Paul—as well as by his advisers and his adversaries—as conscious and willing collaborators of all who saw the Church, its papacy and its independent centralized governing structure as an unsuitable and ill-fitting element of modern life.

Then as now, John Paul understood that these anti-Church elements within his Church were reckoned publicly as Catholics. Then as now, however, and as John Paul understood equally well, these same anti-Church Churchmen saw every new announcement of the fledgling Pope —his every break with tradition; his every innovation; above all, his encyclical letter *The Redeemer of Men*—as an unacceptable obstacle to the personal leadership roles they fancied for themselves on the highroad of humanity toward its near-future destiny as a world society.

Not only was John Paul aware, even as the balloting went forward in the Conclave that elected him, that highly placed Churchmen in and out of the Vatican were fostering the inner decadence of Catholic faith and practice. In his inner councils soon after his election, it was clear that he took it as a sign of that decadence that, even as the worldwide Church was being split into segments, those segments themselves were dubbed and defined in political rather than religious terms. As with everything else in the world, Catholics were seen—and more important, from John Paul's point of view, they saw themselves—as standing on the Right, on the Left or in the Center in matters of supremely, but by no means exclusively, Catholic importance.

This switch in descriptive terminology was symptomatic of the inner rot. An Augustine, an Aquinas or a Pius XII would never have resorted to political categories in describing the faith of the Church. They judged

matters from a supernatural and theological viewpoint. But now the
norm for judging the behavior of Catholics in regard to their faith was
their position vis-à-vis worldly interests in the political and social marketplace.

Both the Left and the Right bristled with leaders and with constantly
networking activists about whom the Pope received reports so stunning
that many an earlier pope would have taken immediate and summary
measures against them. The Center, meanwhile, was leaderless and had
no activist network worthy of the name.

One major element of this breakup of the Church's worldwide institutions into Left, Right and Center was as clear to John Paul as to the
cleverest of his advisers. The issues splitting the Church into these politically labeled factions were many, and some of them were complex. But
all of them centered ultimately about John Paul himself, just as surely as
everything in the Church had always centered around the Pope. Everything, in other words, rotated around the teaching and legislative authority of the Pope as the sole successor to Peter and Vicar of Christ.

The Catholic Left wanted John Paul's authority to dwindle as quickly
as possible to that of any nonpartisan chairman of the board, whose
mandate, pure and simple, would be to respect and accept all opinions
and ideas. Especially the idea of human rights in and of themselves as
the ultimate value. Human rights, that is to say, defined humanistically
and without reference to inconvenient moralities based on "outmoded"
religious underpinnings.

John Paul as Bishop of Rome, said those on the Left, should wield the
same authority as any other bishop. True, he might cast a vote now and
then to break a tie. But he should lay claim to no outmoded special
dignity, respect, honor or power just because he happened to be bishop
of a venerable diocese called Rome. Indeed, the very fact that Rome was
seen as the center of Catholicism was taken by the Left as no more than
the happenstance of geography.

John Paul was not surprised, then, at the official reports and other
intelligence that showed in graphic and sometimes scandalous detail the
impatience of those on the Left within his Church for the complete
disintegration of his institutional organization in its present form; and for
the disintegration above all of the papal monarchy he now embodied.

Scholar that he is, in fact, John Paul might well have summed up the
policy of the Catholic Left with Friedrich Nietzsche's neat and nihilistic
principle: "In the world, if you see something slipping, push it."

At the other extreme, the Catholic Right, then as now, defended papal
authority as such—entrusted for the moment to John Paul—exactly as
it had always been defined and understood in Roman Catholic tradition.

In religious matters, said those on the Right, the Pope has the authority of an absolute monarch. He has not merely the power but the obligation to teach and to legislate for Catholics everywhere. In fact, his teaching in certain circumstances enjoys an infallibility that endows his papal persona with privilege. For the Right, therefore, this or any pope's power and obligation, privilege and infallibility, were issues to be reckoned with at the profoundest level.

As to Rome, its importance for the Right had and has nothing to do with happenstance. It is sacred. It is the Holy See of Rome. And the Bishop of Rome will, by that fact—the Roman Fact—be the head of Christ's Church Universal until time is no more.

No wonder, then, that the clamor on the Right would come soon enough to excoriate John Paul II for the shambles he would allow to continue in the papacy, in Rome and in the Church Universal.

At the Center, occupied by the greatest mass of Catholic men and women, then as now the most dizzying confusion and pain stretched across the entire landscape of Catholic life. No certainties buoyed the Center as they did the Right. Nor did any dreams of bold revolution energize the Center as they did the Left. Here reigned fear and doubt, discouragement, vain hope and real disappointments, moral seediness and religious inertia. Here, horror at peculiar novelties in Church ceremonial and revulsion at un-Catholic teaching by priests and bishops drove thousands upon thousands out of the Church and onto the wide plains of aimless consternation.

In the Center was none of the certainty of the Right or the Left. All questions were open again. What did it really mean to be Catholic? To be Pope? To go to Hell for all eternity? To commit a sin? To eat and drink the body and the blood of Christ? What did it mean for the Pope to be infallible? What did it mean to be celibate and, at the same time, a balanced human being? What did it mean for sexual union to be blessed by a covenant with God, and for life itself to be sacred? The doubts were legion and growing. The questions were endless and mounting. The pain extended to the deepest areas of personal and social life.

And so, even as John Paul II was striding forward as an international figure of the first order on the world scene, inside his own institutional Church no one on any side of any fence could doubt that the decay in that worldwide institution was as critical as it was obvious.

At a certain level of Vatican life and service, however, there was worry over a still more significant weakness. There were those at this level who pointed to a far greater danger to John Paul's pontificate and to his Church.

This is the level within Vatican operations at which one finds, for example, the men John Paul brought with him to the papacy, as every pope does. Here, too, one would find the "caretaker" group—the core found within any center of power—ensuring its continuity, maintaining the memories, discarding the pointless practices of a former pontificate once a new one has begun.

Neither dispersed at a papal death nor taken over by a new pope, these caretakers are servants of each of those truly isolated men who, having accepted the Ring of the Great Fisherman, comes to occupy alone the throne of Peter and to wield the Keys of that ancient Apostle's unique power.

At this level are the men who have come to know at close quarters that it is never an easy thing to be called to the public work of the Church at large. These are the men who knew the mountain to which John Paul put his shoulders when he made the decision, as he gave such clear notice at the outset of his reign, to become an active competitor on the international scene.

Like the Pontiff they served, these intimate collaborators kept their eyes, then as now, on the goal this Pope had chosen. For that very reason, among themselves, and sometimes with the Pope, they outlined the most significant weakness—the greatest danger—to John Paul's over-all policy, and to the strategies by which he pursued it from the start.

These caretakers at the core of John Paul's administration found that even before he came to Rome, this Pope had been made aware of this greatest in-Church threat to his pontificate. He already knew that the danger was so well installed that it had earned its own shorthand name within some quarters of the Vatican. The superforce, it was called.

Though John Paul knew of the organized existence of this superforce before his papal election, it was only as Pope that he was quickly forced to appreciate every menacing detail of its membership, its organization, its influence throughout the institutions of the Vatican and the world-wide Church, its single-minded intention, and the agenda by which it pursued its deadly purpose.

The superforce had taken its members from what some with a fanciful turn of mind called the specters loose in the Pope's house—that growing number of John Paul's intra-Church adversaries. But these were not just any specters. These were Churchmen of such rank and power within the Vatican and at key points of the hierarchic structure that they controlled the most vital organs and sinews of that structure, worldwide.

In two thousand years of the Roman Church's existence, there had never been anything like the superforce. Schisms, heresies, inner-Church struggles, prolonged alienation of parts of the Church from the main body, decadence of belief and morals among prelates, priests and laity, wholesale abandonment of the Roman faith by entire stretches of territory—the Catholic Church had seen and survived them all. Popes have been kidnapped, imprisoned, injured, forced into exile, murdered. For a time in the early Church, a goodly majority of bishops were heretics. At other times, in the sixteenth and nineteenth centuries, it was fashionable in Rome to be a nonbelieving cleric. But the aims and the activity of the superforce had already produced for John Paul a situation that was qualitatively different from any and all of them.

Since the day Peter came to Rome in chains as Caesar's prisoner and became the first in the long, unbroken line of men claiming to be the personal representative of Jesus, John Paul, as the 264th in that line, was the first to come to power with the knowledge that he would have to face something so calculated, so simple and so sinister as the bated intention of this superforce.

That intention was then, and remains today, the destruction of the Petrine Office and, ultimately, of the Catholic faith as it has flourished and developed over twenty centuries.

One thing this superforce does not intend is the destruction of the physical institutions of the Church—the museums, the libraries, the abbeys, the hospitals, orphanages, great cathedrals, university complexes. For, in oversimplified terms, this superforce is a sort of ecclesiastical version of a hostile corporate takeover team. Those physical institutions are the corporate plant, the hard and useful assets the takeover team seeks to control.

For these corporate raiders of the Church, the Pope meanwhile—not to mention the Trinity, the saints, the Virgin and the whole immemorial paraphernalia of traditional Catholicism—represents the last vestiges of the prior management, the "old group" that is to be replaced by the "new."

The agenda of the superforce—for, as in any hostile takeover attempt, there was and is an ordered agenda—was already well along its way in 1978. Twenty-five years along its way. Thus, by the time John Paul came to the papacy, the ever-increasing control of the superforce over the visible organs of Church strength had already guaranteed it a number of advantages.

Just how important those advantages were is easily seen by means of two basic facts faced by John Paul, and by those who were loyal to him and to the papacy.

The first was that no pope had been able to dislodge or control this superforce, or to exorcise its destructive purpose. Instead, the tide had gone so much the other way that within a very short time, John Paul II would see that he controlled no more than two of his own Vatican ministries, and even in those two cases, there would be, by the end of the 1980s, increasing evidence that his control was being effectively loosened.

More palpable for John Paul—but already a deep problem for his weak-willed predecessor Paul VI, who had been blindsided by the superforce, as by so many things—the second dire fact for the new Pope was a direct consequence of the first. With the channels of instruction, discipline and command so deeply affected by so many cleverly devised choke points, John Paul was faced with his own increasing papal impotence. As far as the superforce was concerned, he could travel, he could preach and exhort and command. But unless he could find some way to free up those choke points, such activity would be of no great avail. Slowly but surely, in a deadly circular progress, the Petrine Office would be nullified and excluded from contention by nonexercise. It would fall into disuse, in other words, because it would no longer work. And it would no longer work because its use was being steadily prevented. Papal instructions ordering "Tridentine" Masses to be allowed in each diocese would be "interpreted" to mean that such Masses would be said only if the bishops wished—the opposite of John Paul's intentions. John Paul's encyclical letters were called "personal meditations of the Pontiff," not papal teachings.

The purpose and the agenda of this superforce were clear enough to John Paul. But what about the motive? What was this superforce after, should its adherents be successful in their hostile takeover attempt? And aside from the fact that many of them were cardinals, bishops, priests, prominent theologians and influential Catholic lay people, what characterized the members of this superforce?

According to those who even then opposed it as best they could on a daily basis, the partisans of this anti-Church-within-the-Church were, for the most part, as they are today, individuals who had for a variety of reasons exchanged their Catholic faith for another, more to their liking.

More serious than that, however, was the fact that a certain number among them—and virtually all of these were, as they are today, in ecclesiastically high places—had thrown their weight on the side of those outside the Roman Church who recognized in the papacy, and in the centralized governing structure beneath it, the global force that stood then as now between today and all the tomorrows of a brave new world.

The heart and essence of the struggle between John Paul and the superforce was clear to both sides. It concerned, then as today, the building of a new and global society whose outlines were even then emerging. The superforce consisted of visionaries who, along with John Paul's adversaries in the secular world outside the Church, had long since thrown themselves into a tug-of-war for control of that global society.

Supreme realist that he was, John Paul knew in greater detail than most just how far along his competitors already were in breaking down, reorganizing and then reassembling the working structures of economic, political and cultural life everywhere. In such a context, there could be no illusions on any side that control of the unique, world-encompassing structures of the Universal Roman Catholic Church would be anything but a major prize in the battle for total geopolitical and georeligious preeminence in the new society.

So far had the situation gone by the time John Paul came to power that many who were both close and loyal to John Paul—those who knew at least as well as he what he was up against in this superforce competing with him for control of his Church—began to clamor at him as insistently as everyone else in the Church. Many complained that a course of action radically different from the one he had taken was open to John Paul. Another course of action was not merely possible, they insisted, but absolutely essential if the Church and the papacy were to survive such a global, deeply entrenched and dedicated assault from within.

This inner core of papal advisers lost little time, then, in laying before John Paul a clear if forbidding set of alternatives. And in turn, each set of alternatives was attached to a dizzying expanse of possible consequences, both for the Church and for the world at large. His Holiness would, he was told in the most respectful terms, have to make early and unequivocal decisions under at least five headings.

He must choose, these advisers said, between the remains of what was even then called the "Old Church" and the increasingly predominant "New Church."

He must choose just as urgently either for the exclusive claims of the Roman Catholic tradition as the one true Church of Christ, or for the egalitarian ecumenism of non-Catholic and "new" Catholic alike. If he opted for the first, the danger would be that in defending the faith as it had been defended for two thousand years, his isolation would only grow greater. If he chose the second, the danger would be the end of the Roman Catholic institutional organization and, with that, any ability to defend or teach that faith with authority.

Third, he would have to make a long-awaited papal decision between the two dominant superpowers, each courting him as assiduously as they

had John XXIII and Paul VI, and each with its important array of surrogates and enemies. For like it or not, the secular and religious worlds
were divided into "East" and "West," and as surely as the sun rose over
the one and set over the other, the deeper causes of that division could
not be reconciled even within the ambit of a pope claiming universal
authority.

His fourth choice was made urgent by another sort of division. He
must choose between the age-old formula of Peter with his all-powerful
Keys of authority, and the new democratizing independence that was
fast splintering the Church Universal into as many divisions as might
care to claim autonomy—units calling themselves the "American
Church," the "French Church," the "German Church," "woman-
church," the "homosexual church," the "Liberation Church," and so
on.

Finally, there was the choice that had been deferred by John XXIII
and by Paul VI, the choice that the "September Pope," John Paul I, did
not live long enough to address. Urged immediately upon John Paul II
was the choice between pointed and brooding admonitions of recent
private revelations, and the perennial Christian hopefulness in the salvation offered by a loving and merciful God.

The pressure on John Paul to make these five basic decisions was
heightened by the shrill laments of a broader array of advisers about the
dreadful state of things in Rome and the world. Men who were normally
calm and levelheaded had become convinced, and made every effort to
convince the new Pope, that like it or not, his recent predecessor, Paul
VI, had been right. "The Church is engaged in autodestruction," Paul
VI had said; and so said these advisers. "The smoke of Satan has entered
the very sanctuary," Paul VI had warned; and so warned these advisers.

To be sure, there was immediate and heavy counterpressure to such
voices. An already powerful if not yet preponderent majority, headed by
the superforce that controlled so many of the choke points in the
Church's governing structures at Rome and abroad, scoffed at the Cas-
sandras who whined at the Pope with such alarmist views. No such shrill
laments were heard from this quarter. Rather, these were men bent on
co-opting the new Pope, courting his blessing and favor for the furtherance of their ideas about what the Church should be: about "redefining
the Church's mission," in the more recent words of one American cardinal, and about what the papacy should become.

It was not lost on John Paul—more experienced and worldly-wise by
far than he was given credit for by either side—that the largest group of
all, the rank-and-file Catholics the world around, made no clamor. Per-

haps they were not organized into blocs or pressure groups. Perhaps they did not guess how they would themselves soon be blindsided by events, as Paul VI had been. Whatever the reason, these millions for whose allegiance the fight was on in earnest had no voice in the din. Nor could most of its members have known then, any more than they do now, what choices to urge upon Pope John Paul.

In any event, one has to think it would not have mattered. One voice more or less on any side of any fence would not have deepened John Paul's understanding. For, in point of fact, before he came to the papacy, John Paul already knew the urgent issues that would be thrust at him for decision, just as he knew what each of those groups stood for.

It would not have mattered, moreover, because to everybody's chagrin and confusion, no one—not the most intimate and trusted among his advisers—succeeded in swaying John Paul, any more than the hapless Cardinal Ratzinger succeeded in doing a few years later.

True, the Pope resisted the might-and-main efforts of the superforce to have him transform the papacy. But then, he also refused to exercise the authority that is the living heart of the papacy, in order to redress— or at least to arrest—the deterioration of his Church. And he steadfastly refused to address head-on that fateful series of options so urgently pressed upon him by his intimate advisers.

Instead, as John Paul set course on a pontificate that was to be longer and more influential than many in history, he presented to one and all the crowning contradiction and the greatest enigma. To adversaries and supporters alike, to superforce and loyalists, to the powerful in the secular world and to ordinary, faithful Catholics in their hundreds of millions, to everyone, in fact, John Paul appeared not merely calm as the debris of his Church and of his power piled high about the Throne of Peter; he seemed totally unconcerned. "Imperturbable" was the word many used to describe him. With a tinge of envy, perhaps, some of his counterparts in this-worldly power spoke privately even of some towering dimension that seemed to grow stronger in John Paul, even as the Church and his own power appeared to grow weaker.

For better or for worse, what lay at the heart of that towering dimension was John Paul's vision of the near future that so many would have given so much to fathom. A vision of his own about the way our human affairs would go in the not distant future.

From the moment John Paul answered "yes" to the ritual Conclave question "Will you accept the papacy?" asked of him in 1978, he placed everything that had been entrusted to him as Pope on the line in his decision to enter that same grand-scale, winner-take-all competition in which the superforce and the anti-Church had long since thrown their weight on the side of his adversaries. He had no illusions going in. He knew he was a late comer. And though in reality there was nothing in history to compare with this competition, he knew that, as with any rivalry as deep and as global as the one under way, he was going to be only one of many, many players. And he knew one more thing: Not all of the players were yet in the game by 1978. He would not, he was sure, be the only newcomer. As for the stakes, they had to include even the essentials of the Roman Church, because those essentials had to be— indeed, already were—a prime target of those who were arrayed against him and of the player or players he still expected to take the field on the opposite side.

John Paul understood that, in their varied ways, his adversaries were all visionaries of that society they planned as the first truly geopolitical system of secular and government life: not a system that would stop at merely international or even transnational institutions; but a truly universal system whose institutions they were still groping to devise. Therein lay the importance of the institutions of John Paul's Church: and therein lay the importance of the superforce control over those institutions. For the Church was very nearly unique in the true universality of its own borderless systems and institutions. It was unique as a georeligious and a geopolitical force.

The competition, then, was not a tug-of-war to decide whether in fact there would be a global society. Every major player in the competition understood that John Paul's competitors were even then well along in their work of reorganizing and reassembling the economic, political and cultural resources of the world. Everyone who was a major player understood that structures were already being built that would soon enough include the world's every nation and race, its every culture and subgroup. John Paul knew that neither he nor anyone else could reverse that momentum.

For John Paul and the handful of truly major players he faced, therefore, that was merely the arena in which his real competition would have to take place. For the few who were engaged in this struggle at or near the height of power where John Paul was determined to engage in it, it was a given that the real competition had to be far more profound than would ever be apparent in the merely visible rush of change and innovation. It had to be nothing less than a fight to capture the minds—to direct the very impetus of will—of men and women everywhere, at the unique moment when all the structures of civilization, including those of John Paul's Church, were being transformed into the framework that would not only house the new global society but shape everything about it.

Within that unprecedented context, those closest to John Paul knew that he had, and still does have, his own unwavering vision of the way human affairs will develop and climax. He knows—or is persuaded that he knows—what the ultimately resulting system will be, should he lose this gargantuan gamble of his.

In other words, John Paul has a clear vision of our near-future world. And his reading of what that world will be is at serious odds with that of his dedicated adversaries.

All of the Pontiff's papal actions, and his inaction as well, were and still are dictated by that vision. Moreover, everything he did, even in the earliest days of his pontificate, was undertaken according to a timetable linked to that vision.

This papal timetable was, and remains, as unprecedented in its way as so much else in John Paul's pontificate. It is a timetable synchronized with the galloping historical developments of our present era. And yet, it was never defined or set out in days or weeks or years. John Paul never saw himself or his adversaries in the world's supercompetition in a race against time, as might be the case in some more banal struggle. He was always certain that he would have all the necessary time of this world at his disposal, just as he always knew that his competitors were equally confident that time was on their side.

For whatever comfort it might be, John Paul's vision did not, nor does it now, encompass bloody events in terms of bodies and lives. He did not, nor does he now, see the competition into which he had plunged in terms of wars and military weapons. He saw it, and sees it now, in terms of mind-destroying and soul-consuming clashes of irreconcilable human-isms ranged against himself and one another. Nevertheless, John Paul knew that the tension between himself and his adversaries would be no less fierce for the absence of crude weapons and invasion dates. A histo-rian and realist, the Pope knew that victory in any war—and certainly in this war—is made possible above all by the spirit of the combatants.

From John Paul's point of view, then, and in the calculations of his competitors, the stakes were too high for lukewarm spirits or halfhearted efforts. Hence, he refused to break out in distraught laments and would allow himself only a few angry reproaches. Hence, too, he would refuse to lash out in a policy of harsh repression or sanctions. Despite constant urgings from every quarter, he would declare no wars of any expected kind on anyone.

For the many who believed then, and who may still believe, that this so public Pope was what they saw and no more, it was an irony that, while his efforts in the arena of papal foreign policy quickly evened up some of the odds against him, the enemies of his Church were scoring just as heavily through John Paul's own failure to control his Church from within.

Meanwhile, for those of his enemies who understood, as they still understand, that there is much more to John Paul and to his pontificate than meets the inexperienced eye, worry rapidly replaced any sense of irony. No one of his enemies, and no combination of them who were in the arena at that moment, were able to match the international stature John Paul so quickly and skillfully made his own. Nor would they try; in this quarter, discretion was still the better part of valor. Nevertheless, if this Pope could not be beaten on what his adversaries regarded as their turf, perhaps he could not be beaten at all.

Of course, there was another side to that coin. The critical question even among the Pope's staunchest supporters was: How far could John Paul advance without a vibrant and papally unified Church behind him? Papal serenity was all very fine; but how far could the shambles be allowed to go? How far would be too far? Or—and this was always the ultimate fear for some who had John Paul's ear and for an ever-increasing number who did not—was it to be that the Church under this Pope would become invisible, reduced to some sad and tattered modern equivalent of the Church of the ancient catacombs?

Even in the context of his great competition, therefore, there were always those who warned the Pope that if he didn't address the decay and disarray in his own papal backyard, he could gamble his whole position right out the window. Now more than ever, this argument went, leaders are powerful only insofar as they stand at the apex of a powerful institution or organization. Obvious examples were cited again and again over time to sway John Paul's mind. The power of the American presidency, he was reminded, rises or declines in our time with the power and hegemony of the United States as military and economic centerpiece of the Western alliance. Later, the more somber example of Ferdinand Marcos was brought to bear. For when Marcos lost control of his political machine and of the Philippine Army officer corps, his fate was sealed.

Except that they had lately become more unforgiving and inexorable, the essentials of that equation of power had not changed since the rise of the Egyptian pharaohs six thousand years ago. However grand one's past, anyone whose hand slips for a moment from the levers of power finds himself the next moment to be the pawn in someone else's game. That was the warning to John Paul.

Despite this cyclone of questions and lethal arguments that swirled around himself and his papacy, however, this young and stubborn Pope John Paul II remained the steady-as-you-go Vicar of Christ for whom everything—no matter how important it might appear to others—was and would remain secondary to his central perspective and preoccupation: the progress and outcome of the international, winner-take-all competition.

In the arena where that competition would be fought, government reports from around the world were already beginning to take account of the wide-ranging mind of this Pontiff, and of the accuracy of his judgments, which, even before his election in October of 1978, were somehow based on deep and exact intelligence. And as if to give the lie to the dire warnings of what happened to men like Marcos, who lose everything when they lose their visible power base, John Paul was perceived to hold in his hand such real power, in spite of the tatters of his institutional Church, that many of the players arrayed against him in his supercompetition felt themselves impelled to seek him out for the respect and legitimacy he alone seemed able to confer on them, and on their causes.

Great power brokers who had no use for what they regarded as his outmoded faith or his Petrine privilege—but who certainly coveted his institutions and his universal authority—quickly began to seek even the briefest meetings with John Paul II. Like rival guerrilla leaders who learn to stop shooting at the enemy long enough for a good photo opportunity, current and rising and declining political leaders of every stripe trooped to Rome. International and transnational money managers came and went. Professional technocrats and humanists who busied themselves with the nuts and bolts of the new internationalism joined the crowd. For in spite of their back teeth, John Paul had to be recognized as the X factor who had entered the millennium endgame they had thought they had all but sewed up.

With each of those encounters—no matter how contradictory or bizarre they might seem to some—it became clear to his adversaries that, by a long shot, this Pope was not, as some were suggesting in apparent frustration and lusty irreverence, just some Polish bishop who had stumbled in from the Soviet satellite Gulag of Poland, locked away in its nineteenth-century Marxism, and then lost his way in the world of the twentieth century. Instead, many recalled those terse words of assessment the Soviet foreign minister, Andrei Gromyko, had given after the first of his several meetings with the new Pope: "a man with a worldview."

Nevertheless, and even if the world competition had to be the driving force of his pontificate, there still remained all those urgent and painful questions of the Catholic faithful themselves. Even though he was so busy about so many things, was there still not some way John Paul could attend to the upheaval in the Church that was tossing the faithful about like so many millions of rag dolls? With so wide a spectrum within the Church from Right to Left, and with so deep a hunger at the Center for some measure of comfort—the smallest measure would do, perhaps—could John Paul not find the opportunity to satisfy *somebody*?

Certainly, there were those who expected—who demanded—that he try.

John Paul did not even try. Instead, this very public man in the white robe stood as though he were the prophet Habakkuk standing on his watch, waiting for the appointed time to roll around, waiting upon the vision that would surely come, the vision that would not tarry and that would not disappoint when it dawned around him.

Yet soon, very soon, in his pontificate, and vision or no, this Pope who had been hailed as a man of firsts and as marked by destiny from birth was seen by the faithful adherents of his Church as the ultimate enigma: the first successor to Peter the Apostle destined to be everyone's guest, but nobody's Pope.

3. Into the Arena: Poland

The hard-faced men of the Soviet surrogate regime in the Poland of 1979 needed no help from press or commentators to make up their minds about Karol Wojtyla. Scratch the surface of government sentiment about him, and you would hear such descriptions as "stormy petrel," "trouble-maker," "dangerous," "unpredictable."

Their history of difficulties with Wojtyla reached back through his years as protégé of Poland's Primate, Stefan Cardinal Wyszynski of War-saw. The "Fox of Europe" had for nearly forty years successfully outwitted the plots of Russian commissars, Nazi Gauleiters and Polish Stalinists. He had groomed the younger man carefully to follow in his steps.

Wojtyla had been an apt and eager pupil. Most recently, the Polish government had suffered him as the thorny Cardinal Archbishop of Krakow. Even as recently as September of 1978, not long before he was summoned to Rome for the second papal Conclave in as many months, Wojtyla had written and circulated throughout Poland a pastoral letter in which he had not merely denounced state censorship, but declared that "freedom of information is the proper climate for the full development of a people, and without freedom all progress dies."

The effect of that letter on the people was still causing trouble for the Warsaw government, when a friendly warning arrived from Rome on October 16, 1978, the second day of the Conclave, that Karol Wojtyla was heading for election as Pope. The Politburo of the Communist Party of Poland (CPP) lost no time gathering for an emergency meeting. It was urgent that the leaders agree on an official government stance in the face of this most unwelcome news.

The wisest course, it was decided, would be to issue a calm, anodyne statement congratulating this son of Poland on his high honor and confidently predicting that his papal election would contribute to fraternal harmony and world peace: "The election of Cardinal Wojtyla to be the next Pope can lead to cooperation between the two ideologies, Marxism and Christianity." That, it was hoped in official Warsaw, would be that.

In Rome, however, it proved to be the beginning. No sooner was Wojtyla invested as Pope John Paul II than the first trial balloons were floated in the press indicating that he was thinking of a papal trip to Poland. A few chats between well-placed acquaintances—between a member of the Vatican's Secretariat of State and a Polish Embassy official in Rome, perhaps—nudged the proposal more firmly toward Warsaw.

May of 1979 soon emerged in such conversations as John Paul's target date. The idea was to commemorate the nine hundredth anniversary of the martyrdom of St. Stanislaw at the hands of the tyrant King Boleslaw the Bold, who consequently lost his crown and kingdom.

The unofficial Vatican proposal was nightmarish for the Warsaw regime. In Polish eyes, Stanislaw was the dissident par excellence, the prime symbol of Polish resistance against a chauvinist and ultimately unsuccessful government. Unless the CPP wished to risk riots and strikes that might well shut down the whole country, it would not do to have millions of Poles listening to a typical Wojtyla speech on such a day.

As its reply, the CPP managed to get several Eastern European diplomats in Rome to point out to their counterparts in the Vatican Secretariat of State that any papal visit to Poland now—by which they meant the next five years or so—would be unwise. As to May of 1979, that would be impossible. To emphasize the point, the Warsaw government did something remarkably offensive: They censored John Paul's 1978 Christmas message to Polish Catholics, pointedly excising from it all reference to St. Stanislaw.

The nightmare refused to evaporate, however. Instead, it walked into the presidential palace in Warsaw in the person of Karol Wojtyla's old mentor, the now aging but always redoubtable Cardinal Wyszynski. With an icily superior demeanor, and his demonstrated ability to command the emotions and the actions of millions of citizens, Wyszynski froze Polish President Henryk Jablonski into a corner. For the sake of peace, and very likely his job, Jablonski conceded the possibility of a papal trip in, let us say, perhaps, a year or two.

"*Nie! Tego roku, Ekscelencjo.*" The Cardinal reportedly remained icily firm. "No! This year, Excellency."

When Jablonski replied with a tentative query as to what date Wyszynski had in mind, the Cardinal had outmaneuvered the President. The papal trip was on. It remained only to fix those pesky dates—the Cardinal had June in his pocket before he left—and to set the itinerary.

The Communist leaders abhorred the discussions that followed between John Paul's advance men and the government watchdogs. The CPP tried to dictate the length of the Pontiff's stay, what he would discuss, what sort of reception he would be accorded, the cities he would visit. "The Pope can't go everywhere he likes," came one stiff negotiating rejoinder from Cults Minister Kazimierz Kakol. But having given the first crucial inch, they found that fiat was no longer a trump card for them. They were forced into negotiation.

No, the Pope could not visit the Katowice and Piekary Ślaskie coalfields just because he once worked in a quarry. No, there would be no state holiday so that schoolchildren and workers could greet the Pope. Yes, His Holiness would be officially received at the airport upon his arrival. Yes, President Jablonski would sit down in a private meeting with John Paul. No a thousand times to any papal visit to the church he had built at Nowa Huta in the teeth of the government's armed opposition. Well, all right then, a visit to the Nowa Huta suburbs would be tolerated, and a few further side trips would be worked out. But emphatically no, there would be no official government "invitation." Having been outmaneuvered was one thing. Allowing the government's nose to be publicly rubbed in it was another.

Putting the best face on a bad situation, the government finally agreed on a plan to be offered to John Paul. The Pope's representatives had named several places the Holy Father wished to visit. The government would divide the country into four parts. Each quadrant would be centered around a principal city John Paul insisted be included. There would be Warsaw, of course, as the capital where the Pope would arrive, and where he would have his reception and his meeting with President Jablonski. There would be Gniezno, the official See of Poland's Cardinal Primate and a place of abiding religious and historical significance. The third quadrant would center around Częstochowa, the site of Poland's great Marian shrine of Jasna Góra. Finally, Krakow, where John Paul himself had until recently been such a troublesome cardinal archbishop, would be the center of the fourth quadrant.

Citizens would be allowed to travel only within the quadrant where they lived in order to see Papa Wojtyla. The forty thousand Soviet garrison troops would be confined to barracks for the duration of the papal visit; but in their place, special mobile units of "security agents" would be trucked into each city.

The side trips that would be allowed, it was finally determined, would include the Pope's hometown of Wadowice and the Nazi death camps. But Nowa Huta's little church still got an emphatic thumbs down.

It was specifically decided that none of the wives of government officials would attend any reception. Presumably, the danger was too great that some might be overcome with emotion at the Holy Father's presence and kneel to kiss his ring.

Back and forth the discussions and the emissaries flew between Rome and Warsaw. When just about everything was in place except Moscow's approval, one Vatican official summed up the tone and the mood of the negotiations: "It has been a fight from start to finish. The [Polish] authorities are terrified."

Speculation inevitably arose in some quarters that Moscow's relatively quick approval of the plan—surprising to some, and surely disappointing to officials in Warsaw—may have owed something to the long meeting a few months before between John Paul II and Andrei Gromyko. "This papal visit is a Polish bit of nonsense," Soviet Party Chief Leonid Brezhnev reportedly grumbled. "Let them take care of it. But no accidents!"

Though it had been agreed that no official invitation would be forthcoming, Warsaw had insisted on making the first official announcement. It did so on March 2, 1979. His Holiness the Pope would come for a nine-day "pilgrimage" to Poland. The dates agreed were June 2 to June 11. Two hours later, a Radio Vatican broadcast followed with the same news, as arranged.

"This is not a religious or state visit." Chauvinist editor Mieczyslaw

Rakowski was quick to make clear the official CPP stance in an editorial published in the government organ, *Polityka*. "He [John Paul] is a Pole coming to his home country, and we will welcome him as a Pole. . . . We believe the papal visit will strengthen unity in Poland."

This pair of announcements set the stage for a sort of split-screen drama, entirely new to current world politics, that would be played out in Poland's streets and squares and conference rooms, a drama that would be ever so carefully monitored as a test case by John Paul's adversaries and friends in the arena of geopolitical contention.

The Polish regime was one prime actor in the drama. It had been forced by Rome into a perilous tightrope situation. Since the Party's beginnings after World War II as representative of a rabidly Stalinist Soviet regime, its history in Poland had been dismal. Its members had been consistently anti-Catholic and anti-papal. In 1948, seven hundred Catholic priests had been jailed. In 1953, Stefan Cardinal Wyszynski had been "deposed" and imprisoned. At least once, a plan to do away with Karol Cardinal Wojtyla had been contemplated.

The tally on the secular side of things was no better. The economy of Poland was in ruins. The infrastructure was aging and broken down. Production was sagging. The country's debt to foreign banks ran well over $25 billion. The Communist regime existed in Poland only because of those forty thousand Soviet troops quartered in the eastern part of the country. At its maximum, the CPP itself counted a mere 2.5 million members out of a population of 35 million. After thirty-five years of total control over all means of production and all that was produced, and over education and the media, the brute fact was that in Poland, the special constituency of any Communist Party—the workers—was totally alienated from Communism in general and from this Communist regime in particular. And the brute fact was, further, that workers and nearly everybody else had remained firmly devoted to the Church.

Now the Warsaw Politburo was faced with the reality that it had been forced by Wyszynski and Wojtyla—two powerful adversaries they had thought to destroy—to receive one of them as Pope and as honored guest. To deny John Paul's visit would have been seen as imposing further government oppression; and any such signal would have had two likely consequences. Further financial bailouts from the West would become a much more difficult proposition. And further unrest at home would become much more likely. Either one of those consequences could bring on the military investment of Poland by the Soviets.

Yet by acquiescing in the papal visit, the government leaders were not by any means clear of those same risks. They well knew from experience that John Paul could not be prevented from disseminating direct challenges, in person and over the airwaves, to vast crowds of Poles and to the world. Oh, they would do their best. They would delay and misroute busloads of pilgrims. They would beat "disorderly" Catholics now and again. They would grumble over the airwaves and arrange for third-party criticisms in the international media. But they knew they could neither totally predict John Paul's actions nor totally control the public response to his presence for nine days.

Already rejected by the people they ruled and nominally represented, the CPP could not tolerate an open show of the Party's weakness or of popular unrest. Whatever happened, they would have to act out the pretense that the visit was yet another triumph of the proletarian regime of the Polish People's Republic, and then pick up the pieces as best they could.

On the other side of this split-screen drama, John Paul was about to make an extraordinary entrance, bringing with him to what seemed this unlikeliest of places a deep and compelling challenge to the status quo of the world order.

By contrast to the position of the Polish regime in this affair, it was true that in a certain sense John Paul was leading from strength in coming to Poland to make this first test of everything essential to his pontificate, as he planned it even then. He knew this country—its people, its leaders, its problems, its astonishing strengths—not only as one of its sons but as one of its heroes. In the negotiations just completed for his pilgrimage, he had demonstrated again his ability to use that knowledge to his advantage.

Nevertheless, the risks for the Pope were greater in some ways than those faced by the CPP. If he had his way, the Communist Party in Poland would be playing out an endgame of sorts. At the same time, however, the entire future of his own papal policy would stand or fall on this testing ground of Poland.

Success for John Paul would mean a tacit acceptance by a variety of players—not all of them visible onstage—of a long-range challenge that he would offer on the basis of the apparently fragile strength of the papacy. A challenge not to his Polish Catholics, but certainly to the Communist Party in Poland, to the Soviet system itself and, further, to the entrenched powers of the world beyond Eastern Europe that had tied certain vital interests of their own to Poland's deplorable condition. As no other man alive, John Paul saw himself at this one moment in a position to show up the limits of the Soviet system on the very ground it occupied, and to show the way to a different path—a different direction —for politics and policies.

Still, success for John Paul did not mean that Poland was to establish its freedom by leaving the Soviet system. Rather, the role he saw for Poland was messianic, in the sense that it would—if he succeeded—become the very leaven that would change the Soviet system itself. And not only in Warsaw, but at its heart.

And if he failed? Despite the obviously decayed system of Soviet Communism, both the task John Paul had set for himself and his risk of failure seemed monumental to those advisers privy to his aims. Perhaps he was leading from strength by coming first to Poland. But there were dangers enough to match the advantages. He would have his own tightrope to walk.

For one thing, John Paul could not afford an uprising in Poland any more than could his unwilling hosts. He was about to come home to 35 million Poles who in their majority would rise up if he said to rise up, who would respond to his every emotion. Yet if he allowed his presence to become a signal for riots and revolt, then what was meant to be the beginning of a long, patient and dangerous road would instead be the end for all his plans. He would at the very least be branded as an American lackey. He would certainly be seen as a bull let loose in the china shop of Cold War tensions. Just as certainly, his delicate probe at the Soviet Union, already under way in various East European countries, would be doomed. He would introduce no challenge, no new spirit, no leaven, in Poland or anywhere else. He would, in fact, be unwelcome in the world; and plans already on the drawing board of his mind for future variations of this Poland card he was about to play would be worse than useless. He would have no choice but to slink back to Rome to rethink his entire papacy.

There could be no loss of control, therefore. However emotional this homecoming might be for him—and how could it be otherwise?—there could be no bowing to short-term ego satisfactions, no empty triumphalism, no isolated moments of inflammatory mistakes.

Never in any future trip would John Paul have the same breathless sense of opening a door and stepping into the unknown. No subsequent papal action of his would involve so lethal a gamble.

As the date drew near for this split-screen drama of the Polish Party and the Polish Pope to begin, those who settled in to watch with interest included some in Western capitals who regarded the whole venture as unwarranted papal meddling in the politics of a very sensitive area—and in the profits they reaped from it. There were others, in the Soviet-dominated East, who had already decided this Polish Pope had feet too big even for the sandals of the Great Fisherman. And there were those in John Paul's own Vatican who fervently wished this entire episode would quickly end, and that there would be no more of its kind to follow from this venturesome Pope.

At 10:05 on Saturday morning, June 2, as Pope John Paul's all-white Alitalia 727 jet transport touched down at Okecie, Warsaw's military airport, bells in every church, monastery and convent throughout Poland's eleven thousand cities, towns and villages rang in joyous welcome. A smiling John Paul II stepped from the plane to the shouts and cheers of twenty thousand people from the Warsaw quadrant who had been allowed to approach the landing site.

Every unsmiling member of the formal reception committee watched as the Pope knelt and kissed the ground of Poland. Was this a kiss of love from a returning son? Or was it an embrace of the land and its people by a Pope claiming possession of both?

No hint of an answer came from John Paul as he rose, squared his shoulders and for some seconds looked each government official in the eyes. For, to be sure, every official worthy of the name was there: CPP Chief Edward Gierek; President Henryk Jablonski; Prime Minister Piotr Jaroszewicz; *Polityka*'s editor, Mieczyslaw Rakowski; CPP Secretary Stanislaw Kania; Cults Minister Kazimierz Kakol; some three or four more. They all had to be there; for no one or two or three would have come without the whole contingent.

Standing to one side in a delegation of black-robed Churchmen was the slightly built, sharp-eyed Stefan Cardinal Wyszynski. He exchanged an unsmiling glance with the younger man, once his protégé, now his Pope. By now, the Cardinal and the Church in Poland had prepared things as well as could be done. Advance copies of John Paul's speeches had been widely distributed. Stewards from local parishes all over the country had been organized and instructed by Catholic groups to help keep things calm. On this morning, Wyszynski's shining blue eyes gave the only hint of his satisfaction at this, his latest triumph, of his affection for Karol Wojtyla, of his hope for this venture that had earned the derision of one Polish official as "a piece of papal mania."

Standing between his old enemy, Party Chief Gierek, and his old friend, Cardinal Wyszynski, Pope John Paul viewed the march-past of the goose-stepping honor guard. He listened to the solemn playing of the Vatican anthem. He heard the familiar words of the Polish anthem: ". . . while we live, who still believe in Poland's ancestral faith. . . ." He heard the formal words of welcome from his hosts.

When John Paul's turn at the microphone came, there was an imme-

diate contrast to the civil but frigid official welcome. With appealing
reference to the Polish anthem's refrain, the Pontiff exulted that "a Pole
coming today from the land of Italy to the land of Poland is received on
the threshold of his pilgrimage with those words which we have always
used to express the nation's unflagging will to live." Every Pole who heard
him—officials and citizens alike—understood his meaning. Poland's "ancestral faith," he was saying, is the heart of its people. Without faith as a
living presence, the people die and there is no Poland.

The response from the crowd was like a tidal wave sweeping outward
from Okecie Airport. Whether or not they had actually heard his remarks
at his arrival or read an advance copy of his speech, his very presence
was meaning enough. An estimated 290,000 cheering, weeping, chanting, praying Poles scattered flowers in the path of the Pontiff's motorcade; they waved a forest of papal and Polish flags and displayed brightly
colored banners.

His Communist hosts, on the other hand, were enraged from the start.
They were not to be fooled by the Pope's official references to his visit
over the past weeks as a pilgrimage. "What is Mr. Karol Wojtyla, head of
a superstitious church, doing in our socialist Poland?" one Warsaw newspaper would scream in its editorial headline the following day.

"Mr. Wojtyla" gave them reason enough for concern from the outset.
In the heart of Warsaw on this first day of his pilgrimage, John Paul
began to speak with the voice of insistent and unambiguous truth that
would remain the same for the next nine days. There was, first of all, the
official reception—as agreed, no wives were present—in Henryk Jablonski's presidential home, the Belvedere Palace. Jablonski, Gierek and their
colleagues heard unwelcome facts wrapped in John Paul's gentle language. Facts about Poland, and about military and political alliances.
The acceptability and validity of such alliances, John Paul declared,
depended totally on whether they led to more well-being and prosperity
for the participant state—Poland. Ideology, he said, was not acceptable
as a criterion for a good alliance.

As his speech went on, no one could mistake the Christianity of his
message, or the anti-Communism of his proposals. "The exclusion of
Christ from history," he said, referring to the Soviet habit of omitting
from the record what they did not like, "is an act of sin against man. . . .
Without Christ, it is impossible to understand the history of Poland, the
history of the people who have passed through or are passing through
this land"—a subtle reference both to the occupying Soviets and their
quisling Polish supporters. "These are just passersby," Wojtyla was saying, "like so many others who thought to enslave Poland."

After so bold a start, John Paul went on that day to say Mass for over 200,000 Poles who jammed into Warsaw's historic Victory Square. In response to his appearance, his voice and his message of hope, a spirit of pandemonium began to surface, lapping outward from the center to the farthest edges of the great crowd. A great chant—a kind of hunger cry on behalf of millions—rose up: "We want God! We want God! We want God!"

"It was like the sort of throaty growl that raises goose bumps on you," wrote one Western newsman. "That crowd was taking on the single emotion of the classic 'street mob.'"

It would have been an easy matter for John Paul to let emotions run. Or worse, to whip them to fever heat and set the people loose on Henryk Jablonski's presidential palace and on CPP headquarters. How impressive that might have been for a moment; how dramatic for the world's press. If John Paul was tempted in that direction for a fraction of a second, it was not apparent. Instead, the Pontiff went on with his address, calming the crowd with his own calm words, his gestures, his presence.

There was no doubt that the deadly game the government had feared and expected had begun. They seemed to be up for it, however. The catcalls and high-pitched protests of the officially controlled media began in earnest on June 3, the day following John Paul's arrival. "This visit," warned Bogdan Bogin, minister for religious affairs, "may have a harmful effect. . . . How dare this self-styled Slavic Pope appeal to the people of Eastern Europe over the heads of the Party leaders? A critical error on his part!" That same day, a commentator on Moscow television suggested darkly that "Church leaders are trying to use this event [the papal visit] for antistate purposes."

One Eastern European diplomat speaking to an American colleague suggested that Poland was in quite the same position as the United States. Referring to John Paul's insistence on Slavic Christianity, the Communist official warned, "This Pope is not saying these things because the spirit moves him. These are calculated statements designed to pose a direct challenge to governments that no modern nation—especially you Americans with your separation of church and state—could tolerate."

Even as the June 3 Warsaw editorials sounded the first exasperated denouncements of Pope, papacy and pilgrimage, John Paul was already in Gniezno, the headquarters city of the second quadrant of his visit. This spot was not only the official See—though no longer the actual residence—of Poland's Cardinal Primate; it was also a place redolent for Poles with ancestral pride of race, a place of Polish roots and a focus of

Polish national folklore: the "nest of the Polish white eagle"—Poland's symbol.

Official anger notwithstanding, the Pontiff did not abandon his religious theme. Rather, he widened its focus. Had the government censored St. Stanislaw from his Christmas message? Well, then, at Gniezno he would preach about St. Adalbert, apostle of the whole Slav race. More, he would use that apostle to promote the spiritual unity of all Europe, with Poland as its geographical center.

His challenge to the Soviet empire could not have been clearer, broader or more insistent: All Eastern European Communist governments should allow freedom of conscience, individual rights, individual possession of private property, open elections and national independence. And he emphasized, in an equally trenchant challenge to the West, that "there can be no just Europe without the independence of Poland marked on its map."

Such enormous challenges—already sounded in Warsaw as a theme —rose into a fully scored symphony in Gniezno. But played as they were with a moderation of tone and language, they made the government's high-pitched countercampaign seem lurid by contrast. The Pope indulged in no anger or shouting or sarcasm. He didn't even joke, as Poles are wont to do, about Communism's ridiculous claims and mythical success stories. Always he sounded the lightsome note at just the right moment. He taught his Poles to sing again, and to hope again for better and greater things, and for yet a while longer to be patient.

June 4 was the day John Paul arrived at Jasna Góra, the deeply popular mountain shrine to Mary, at the monastery of Częstochowa. It was the third day of his pilgrimage, and would mark the first dangerous confrontation with the government since the Victory Square face-off in Warsaw.

The heartfelt and enormously enthusiastic response the Pope generated from the people everywhere had increased with every speech— almost with every wave of his hand to the crowds that lined the streets and pressed forward as he passed to and from official meetings and Masses and other gatherings. He was fast transforming his pilgrimage into a kind of trick mirror in which were reflected all the details of the Polish regime's complete lack of popular support. With that high visibility that he had already cultivated so well, and with the international media following each step, John Paul forced the world's gaze upon the drab, grim, dilapidated, run-down, oppressed condition of this nation under the control of its Soviet-supported keepers.

By the time John Paul actually arrived at the mountain shrine of Jasna Góra, therefore, it may have been that the huge crowds amounting to almost a million people gathered around the shrine caused the local officials to be a little trigger-happy. In any case, John Paul delivered an unmistakable, stinging indictment of Marxism; and he made the Polish regime a special target for its 1976 refusal to permit Pope Paul VI to visit Poland.

So effective were his words, and so immediate was the screaming, shouting assent of the vast crowd gathered on the Częstochowa hillside, that the government authorities panicked. Dozens of army tanks rattled their way toward the monastery and cordoned off the entire mountain.

It was a public indignity the government might have spared itself. The local parish stewards, who had long since been prepared for such situations, were scattered throughout the crowd and on the job as always. But it was a seemingly relaxed Pope John Paul, steady in his intention not to lose control of things, who defused the crisis.

With barely a glance down the hillside in the direction of the tanks, he spoke into the microphone. "I am sure," he joked in an easy, familiar tone, "that there are people out there who are already having a hard time taking this Slavic Pope!"

The crowd loved it. Not only did they know the government had played the wrong card and been trumped; they knew they had been part of it. A big part. Just like old times at Nowa Huta!

John Paul was halfway through his homeland pilgrimage, heading for his scheduled June 7 arrival at his former diocese of Krakow, near Poland's border with Czechoslovakia; and for his June 7 visit to his boyhood home of Wadowice, a few miles southeast of Krakow. Still the Party labored mightily to blunt the effect of his presence and his insistent message. "We have been surprised," said one disingenuous spokesman for CPP Chief Edward Gierek, "by the political nature of many of the Pope's statements."

"The solution for the Karol Wojtyla problem," Ukrainian Communist Party Chief M. Vladimir Shcherbitsky chimed in from across the Soviet border, "must lie in a renewed and more vigorous propaganda in favor of atheism in the Soviet Union and its 'fraternal socialist societies.' "

John Paul's rejoinder to these and similar messages was never long in coming. Yet no matter what measures the government took, the Pontiff never stepped over the danger line. He knew well how to stage his actions for maximum effect. He knew he could count on his Poles and on the organizing work that had been done before his arrival.

Krakow had been home to Karol Wojtyla; his visit here was a return to a virtual landscape of personal emotions. He visited with the silver-haired Helena Szczepanska, now eighty-nine, who had looked after him as a nine-year-old boy following his mother's death. "He is just like the 'Lolek' I cared for as a child," she said, referring to the Pontiff by his childhood name, as though nothing much had changed. He saw Maria Morda, who had been his housekeeper during the sixteen trying years he had put in here as priest, bishop and cardinal. He visited Wolski Woods, a fifteen-minute drive from the center of Krakow, where he had often walked alone for hours, praying and pondering. He even got his pilot to wander off course a bit in midflight so that he could glimpse the Tatra Mountains, where he used to ski and contemplate the grandeur of God in nature.

In the flood of memories and reunions, was John Paul reminded of how alone he was now in Rome? Of how unsustained he was, as a rising world figure, by the old familiar faces and sights and sounds? If so, he allowed none of it to tell in his public behavior even here.

At Krakow University, students packed eagerly into St. Anne's Church and heard rousing words of hope from John Paul. "The whole world is open to you in all fields," he urged. He echoed again the meaning of the Polish anthem, as he had done on his arrival in Warsaw. "You must be strong with love, which is stronger than death."

By agreement with the authorities, the Pope was not allowed to visit Silesia, the nearby sector of coalfields and industry. No matter. The Silesians came to the Pope instead. They poured into Krakow in huge numbers and, along with what seemed like the whole population of the Krakow quadrant, overflowed the Pontiff's open-air Mass in the city square, where again he preached a militant, pan-Slavic Christianity.

His appeal was answered with enormous zest by the crowds. "Father!" the cry went up from the Czechoslovak pilgrims. "Come! Awaken us in Czechoslovakia!"

The answer from the authorities, largely predictable by now, was as ham-handed as ever. Seventy-five truckloads of Mobile Guards surrounded the area, only to be jeered noisily and continually, even while some in crowd were attacked and pummeled by government security men.

Still John Paul would not back away from the unforgiving edge of danger. His remaining three days were packed with yet more emotion-charged encounters, some of a most personal kind. Hour by hour, it seemed, he was able to demonstrate how hollow, how possessive, how inimical and how jittery was the regime that gripped the Slavic states.

June 8 found the Pontiff in the town of Nowy Targ, a site nearer still to the Czechoslovak border. At a place called Blonie Krakowskie—a large grassland area in the shadow of Mount Kosciuszko, itself named to honor

Poland's most famous freedom fighter against Russian imperialism—the Pope delivered another rousing pan-Slavic speech to a multitude of Poles, Czechs, Hungarians and East Germans. His message again was laced with the themes of human rights and the right of all individual nations to be independent.

The same day, he made what he termed "a pilgrimage to the heart of cruelty"—the Nazi death camps of Birkenau and Oświęcim. It was at the latter, known in the West as Auschwitz, that, aides later said, John Paul experienced an onrush of emotions that could have unbalanced his entire performance. He celebrated Mass. He placed a wreath of flowers at the Wall of Death, where Nazi jailers had whipped and clubbed and shot their prisoners to death. He made a visit to Cell Block 11, and to one dungeon in particular, where prisoner No. 16670—a Franciscan priest named Maximilian Kolbe—had been starved and then injected by his impatient captors with a lethal dose of phenol into his heart.

"How far can cruelty go?" John Paul murmured audibly at the door of Kolbe's dungeon. To his aides, his anger at this moment was open and visible for the first time during his exhausting pilgrimage; it was an anger that transcended all the past grisly work of the Nazis, and spilled over in a wave of emotion against the extermination being carried out right then throughout the entire Soviet Gulag system. The Pope confided not long after to close and trusted personal associates that he wanted to say then and there, "Communism is the same evil as Nazism—only the face is different!" He was on the verge of saying, "The Gulag here among us is the same as the one in Hitler's day. Is it not time—high time!—that we disinfect our Motherland, Poland, and all of God's holy world, of this institutionalized evil!"

Had he said any of that, of course, all constraints would have been off. He had raised public emotions to such a pitch that his own self-control was the only sure safeguard against a wildfire of insurrection. It would have been a release for him, and for millions whose emotions were tuned to his own. And, as at Warsaw or at Czestochowa, it would have been the failure of all his plans.

It cost him a deep personal toll to keep his silence; but keep it he did. A couple of years later, he did make his statement, but in a different way, open only to him and his Church. He raised Maximilian Kolbe to sainthood.

Ironically, the June 9 papal visit to the suburbs of Nowa Huta, feared and resisted with such tenacity by the Party leaders in the early negotiations, turned out to be an interlude of relative peace compared to the prior days. The mood of the crowds was like his—gently and strangely triumphant. They had jointly beaten the regime. They were alive; the regime was already half dead. This was the spirit abroad at that moment.

The night of June 9, however, his last in Poland, was a different matter. A very tired Pope John Paul addressed a crowd of ten thousand people gathered outside the Cardinal's residence, where he was staying. High emotions were evident in the songs and chants and cheers that filled the night air. The people were unwilling to let their Papa Wojtyla go. He finally did leave the balcony to get a few hours of much needed rest; but even then the crowd did not disperse.

Lying in his bed, John Paul listened to songs he had so often sung himself. He heard thousands of voices rise one more time in a solemn chorus of the Polish anthem, "Poland Is Ours Forever!" At a certain moment, as if some cue had been given, silence became the frame for a young voice chanting over a hand-held microphone. The words had been set down over a hundred years before, in 1846, by Julius Slowacki, Poland's greatest poet:

> We need strength
> To lift this world of God's.
> Thus here comes a Slavic Pope,
> A brother of the people!
> And already he pours
> Balms of the world on our bosoms,
> And the angels' chorus
> Sweeps his throne with flowers. . . .

This was no common moment of affection and symbolic embrace. For John Paul, it was an experience of deep personal temptation. In the very intimacy of the emotion between himself and the men and women who were so loath to see him go lay the possibility that he could take this crowd to the highest pitch of danger. For them, he *was* that pseudo-messianic "Slavic Pope" of Slowacki's verse. How quickly would any spark—whether from him, or from the crowd, or from the ever-present and always heavy-handed government authorities—have converted that crowd into a rambunctious, rampaging street mob.

John Paul gave up any idea of sleep. He rose from bed, put on his white cassock and went out again to the balcony. His voice cracked more with emotion than with weariness; but there was a nicely tuned edge of humor, too, as he pretended to scold: "Who's making all that noise?"

A wave of laughter rose up from the crowd; then a hush again as John Paul spoke to them—embraced them—for a little while longer. At last, though, the moment came to give his solemn blessing to them all, and to retire for the second time.

This time, the crowd slowly dispersed. John Paul had not lessened their passion. He had contained it and molded it and channeled it in such a way that, with himself as its very symbol, it would do its work far beyond this June night, and for long after he had gone. It was for this, at least in part, that he had come. It was for this, at least in part, that he would make many more visits to many other places.

The last big public event of John Paul's homeland stay was the open-air Mass with which he ended his pilgrimage to Krakow. A million people were there. When Mass was over, however, the ordeal for the government had still not quite ended.

Together with Poland's foreign minister and a few other dignitaries, President Henryk Jablonski and CPP Chief Edward Gierek had traveled to Krakow Airport for the ritual send-off. They had to cool their heels for an extra half hour, however. Tearful crowds slowed the progress of John Paul's motorcade, as the people said farewell to this ebullient figure of a man who had preached faith and encouragement and hope to them; had laughed and wept and sung with them; had chided and reproached their oppressors; and had dared to become the first man in thirty-five years to speak the truth publicly and insistently.

When at last the Pontiff did arrive at the airport, many of the details of the official leave-taking seemed on the surface very like the Warsaw welcome nine days before. There was the same martial music; troops were reviewed; officials spoke. But everyone there felt how completely the atmosphere had changed.

Nearly every step this traveling, teaching Pope had taken had been strewn with flowers from Poland's fields and gardens. He had managed to push the noses of President Jablonski and the other CPP officials into the cold reality of Polish life. Every illusion the CPP had sought for so long to foster about its hold and command over Polish hearts and minds had been shattered forever during John Paul's brief time there.

To adapt a description Gabriel García Márquez used in *The Autumn of the Patriarch*, the CPP had been brought without surprise to the ignominious fate of commanding without power, of being exalted without glory, of being obeyed without authority, of living without love. John Paul had made it all so obvious.

After reviewing the honor guard of mountaineer troops, John Paul stepped to the microphone for his final address. He spoke to the eleven thousand people who crowded around the edges of the tarmac, and to the millions throughout Poland and its neighboring countries who crowded around their radios.

"The visit of the Pope to Poland," he said, speaking of himself in the third person, as he rarely did, "is certainly an unprecedented event, not only in this century, but also in the entire millennium of Christian life in Poland—especially as it is the visit of a Polish Pope, who has the sacrosanct right to share the sentiments of his own nation. . . ." Sentiments, he did not need to add, that would remain a living presence for years to come. Hundreds of thousands of tapes had already been recorded of his speeches; and they would multiply still more, circulate still further, to be heard not only in Poland but in all the "nations of silence" where John Paul had staged his incredible witness, and had called forth the lesson of history before the eyes of the world.

Turning to Party Chief Edward Gierek, John Paul held out an infinitely careful hand to him and his Politburo companions: "The unprecedented event [of this papal visit] is undoubtedly an act of courage both on the part of those who gave the invitation"—he smiled at Gierek— "and on the part of the person who was invited. However, in our times, such an act of courage is necessary . . . just as once Simon Peter needed the courage to journey from Galilee to Rome, a place unknown to him."

His remarks finished, John Paul embraced President Jablonski just long enough to whisper a blessing to be conveyed to his wife. He gave his papal blessing to the weeping crowds near the tarmac. Then he knelt down once more and kissed the ground. "Farewell, Poland." He said the words softly, but those nearest could hear "Farewell, my Motherland."

As his plane bore him away, veering south toward the Alps and Rome, John Paul left the Polish surrogates of the USSR and the Soviets themselves to deal with a future he had thrust upon them in terms he alone had chosen.

The Polish regime had been founded on bedrock opposition to everything the Pope stood for. It had seen itself entirely dependent on its Muscovite masters for its survival and progress. Now, however, a Polish bishop once written off as a provincial intellectual had lit up the entrance to a different landscape.

To be sure, the old familiar mad dogs of hate, mistrust, and inhuman cruelty had not been magically chained or tamed. The rage of some at the mere presence of "this bumbling prelate masquerading as one of us," as Romania's foreign minister complained of the Pope on radio, did not die at the Pontiff's leaving. If anything, the desire grew in some quarters to see John Paul fail significantly, so that internationally he could be blamed for ineptitude and clumsiness; labeled as a disturber of the delicate status quo; uncovered as an interloping cleric poaching on the preserve of politics and superpower ideology.

For a while, Warsaw would put on the same old public face of the triumphant "People's Republic." Even before John Paul's departure, Polish Foreign Ministry spokesman Stefan Staniszewski had declared the papal visit "a complete success. We are very pleased with it," he insisted. "We are happy that the Pope is so broadly and warmly greeted. We are not surprised, and not embarrassed by this fact. He is a great Pole, an unusual, outstanding personality. He is a great humanist."

Others continued the refrain in the wake of the papal pilgrimage. "The government," said one, typically, "found much to agree with in Pope John Paul's words, especially his affirmation of the dignity of the worker and his labor."

In a certain sense, these were brave words, coming as they did from dedicated Communist spokesmen. For they could not be Polish and fail to know what John Paul claimed to know. And they could not but fear in some corner of the mind that the Pope's claim on the people, and his claims in their behalf, might one day be vindicated.

In fact, that very possibility seemed to set itself out in bold relief when no less a leader than Edward Gierek admitted to a questioning Western newsman that there was no ready answer to John Paul's pointed rebuke that "in an age of disclosure, and an age of vast exchange of information, it is difficult to understand and accept that any Pole, any Slav, cannot be informed and free to inquire."

Jerzy Turowicz, a Polish commentator in the U.S.A., was among the first to turn the official questions around. And in doing so, he raised an amazing new agenda that John Paul had made it possible to think about in the heart of the Gulag: "How do you deal with so much hope, so much new self-confidence, all this new feeling of involvement and freedom?"

For most Western observers, and for the nervous Polish government, Moscow's reaction of forbearance during and after the Pope's visit to Poland was unexpected and puzzling. There had been some sniping, and even a salvo or two from the Soviets, of course. To John Paul's stunningly open and persistent challenges to classic Marxism, however, some far more explosive and decisive reaction should have been forthcoming.

It was not that the Soviets had paid no attention. On the contrary, Leonid Brezhnev was not the only Soviet official who had received hourly bulletins as the papal visit had progressed. John Paul's remorseless probing of his adversaries' central weakness had been followed speech by speech.

"Europe," Moscow had heard John Paul say, "which, despite its present and long-lasting divisions and regimes, ideologies, economic and political systems, cannot cease to seek its fundamental unity, must turn to Christianity. . . . Despite the different traditions that exist in the territory of Europe between the eastern and western parts, there lives in each the same Christianity. Christianity must commit itself anew to the formation of the spiritual unity of Europe."

If those words jangled in some ears like the death knell for a failing and decrepit Marxism, Moscow gave no bellicose sign that it heard the same toll.

"The state," John Paul had gone still further, "must always be subsidiary and subservient to the full sovereignty of the nation." According to such reasoning, the Warsaw Pact and the Comecon economic organization should no longer exist, for their sole purpose was to provide logistical support for the Soviets in what Stalin had once contemptuously called "the Soviet back garden."

There was no pretending that this Pope's words were not heard far beyond Poland; that they were not heard by millions in Czechoslovakia, Hungary, Bulgaria, Yugoslavia; in Lithuania, the Ukraine, Armenia and all the captive republics of the USSR. There was no pretending they had not been heard even in Cuba and Nicaragua, half a world away.

What was it about John Paul that allowed him such liberty of speech? Why did Moscow suffer such flagrant violations of the first and cardinal rule of the Gulag system that declares, Thou shalt allow no man to speak freely to my people?

It was unheard of for Moscow to bear such a protracted, flagrantly public challenge. Had John Paul somehow managed to capture the cautious ear of at least some aging members of the Marxist-Leninist old guard, and of at least some of the younger men nearing the brink of power? Was it at least interesting for some Soviet leaders that John Paul's seemingly inflammatory but truly controlled performance had brought on no mob scenes, no riots, not even so much as a strike or a workers' slowdown? The system remained in place, even though its failures had been made clear.

It had been made equally clear, however, and on a worldwide stage, that one way or another, change was inevitable. If the leaven of change from within was the gift John Paul had intended to bear to Eastern Europe, then given a little time and patient kneading, perhaps the dough would rise even in Moscow.

While Warsaw and Moscow and the rest of the "socialist brothers" of the Soviet satellite empire reckoned up the tally of John Paul's visit to Poland, so did the Pope and his close advisers in Rome and in Warsaw.

There was no pretense among any of them—John Paul included—that even as monarchic head of Vatican City State and of the Roman Catholic Church, Karol Wojtyla could claim the kind of power profile shared among the usual brokers of clout in world affairs.

True, his Church had something in excess of 907 million nominal adherents—about 18 percent of the present world population. He had 483,488 priests and about 3,000 increasingly rambunctious bishops serving some 211,156 parishes, which formed the world's 1,920 dioceses and 513 archdioceses. His institutional organization included an infrastructure of schools, universities, research institutes, medical and social science centers, hospitals, convents, churches, cathedrals, chapels, monasteries, religious centers, embassies, legations, archives, libraries, museums, newspapers, magazines, publishing houses, radio and television stations. True, too, he controlled his own Vatican Bank, with its team of international advisers who administered an extensive portfolio of the Holy See's holdings and investments in virtually every sector of the world's commercial and industrial activity.

In spite of all that, however, John Paul knew that in terms of diplomatic power he was seen as an anomaly among traditional world leaders. Most of the 116 full-fledged embassies on Vatican Hill are, in the internationally recognized formula, accredited to the "Holy See." In practical terms, Karol Wojtyla, as Pope John Paul II, is that Holy See. Neither his institutional organization nor his investment portfolio—and certainly not religious reverence or agreement with the Pope on moral matters or political ideals—dictates the necessity of maintaining those diplomatic missions, but simply hardheaded realism.

Most of those diplomatic stations are run by decidedly non-Catholic and often predominantly non-Christian states. Not all of them by far are benign either to religion in general or to Roman Catholicism in particular. Yet while all of them, from major nations to pint-sized principalities even smaller than the Vatican, are host to John Paul's reciprocal diplomatic representatives, even the weakest national government in the most primitive of nations can, at least physically, cripple local sections of his worldwide organization.

In fact, at the very moment of his visit to Poland, several had taken it into their heads to do just that. And in doing so, they had demonstrated that as world leader, if that was what he claimed to be, John Paul had no military alliances to protect him or his interests. He had no economic or industrial punch to use as a retaliatory threat. He had no preponderance in international law or in the assemblies of nations to hold his attackers to account. He could not even call upon any preeminent scientific or academic prowess that would command the respect of Poland's Communists, or any other regime for that matter.

Nevertheless, it was not lost on Moscow or on Warsaw that he had not gone to Poland as a weak supplicant asking for favors. Pilgrim though he might call himself, he had carried no beggar's bowl, had waited upon no alms or contributions or official indulgence.

Instead, once he had stepped off his papal plane, everything he had done had spoken volubly and dramatically of a peculiar kind of power. He had behaved everywhere as if he was possessed of, or heralded, a force to be reckoned with, a force his peers in government could neither ignore nor maltreat with impunity. This they seemed to sense.

For Warsaw and for its neighbors on every side, John Paul had demonstrated that the very papal persona of Karol Wojtyla embodied the unshakable Roman Catholic persuasion that the papacy, older by far than any secular government, and certainly more durable than the Marxist "revolution" of 1917, would be alive and vibrant long after the "Polish experiment" was reduced to a few pages of recorded history.

No doubt some Poles may and do choose to become atheistic Marxists and anticlerical Communists. But in the presence of Peter's 263rd successor, and in the face of the total intertwining of Roman Catholicism with Polish nationalism, such Poles in particular fall victim to what Lord Acton cleverly called the "millennia jealousy"—the deep and helpless frustration of those who had thought to face and outlast such millennial force as John Paul represented, but who see all too clearly that they have no realistic chance of making it around the next curve of history's road.

In Poland, John Paul had successfully staked out his first strong claim to be heard as a judging voice, and not merely in an ecclesiastical setting —in a papal letter or a sermon from a church pulpit. He had entered the arena of public and civil and political affairs in a segment of the world claimed as the turf of superpower. He had held up in despicable detail the total lack of justice and popular support of that regime. He had exposed the local Communist leadership as not merely unloved, but as inconsequential. More important for his adversaries, East and West, this seemingly unpapal Pope had redefined power in unexpected, irresistible terms; and then he had taken that power in his two hands and marched off with it.

In the aftermath of the drama that had been played out, it was neither in Warsaw nor Moscow nor the Vatican, but primarily among Western commentators and observers, that the peculiarly Slavic ironies, and the sometimes almost mystic overtones of the give-and-take that had passed between John Paul and his reluctant hosts, remained puzzling for some time. A few Western reports and commentaries did contrast the Pontiff's reception as head of state with his proclaimed role as pilgrim. But they seemed unable to reconcile the two. Perhaps *The New York Times* summarized as well as anyone the early Western assessment of the strange endeavors of this unconventional Pope at this stage in his pontificate: "The visit of John Paul to Poland does not threaten the political order of the nation or of Eastern Europe." If only the *Times* editorialist could have had a crystal ball for 1989.

Not for much longer, surmised John Paul's advisers among themselves, would the real successes of the papal visit to Poland be dimmed, either by Western misunderstanding or by the faint praises of Polish government spokesmen conceding to the Pontiff the puny stature of an "outstanding personality . . . a great humanist."

For the Roman assessment of John Paul's pilgrimage to Poland was this: Without a single armored division at his command—a factor that would always emphasize his power for some, and throw doubt upon it for others—John Paul had taken on not merely a national regime but an international system of government. He had violated with impunity all the taboos imposed by a rigid dictatorship of Big Brother. He had opened the first effective challenge to the political order of the Soviet satellite system, and of the Soviet Union itself. Just as he had said he would in his earliest speeches after his papal election, he had indeed called for the beginnings of "a new order" in Central Europe, and in the international, political and economic order enlaced with it.

He had, in short, within eight months of his election as Pope, made his first entry into the high-stakes competition to which he had committed his papacy. And he had emerged from it with the stature of an international figure.

"I am a giver," John Paul once said of himself. "I touch forces that expand the mind."

It was true. Some special magnetism that had been apparent even in his earliest days in the papacy seemed to follow him everywhere. As Pope, he had been heard calling for Poland's free integration not only into a free Europe but into an integrated world.

His voice was that of a Polish bishop become Roman Pope. But, if he had his way, the message was of one who would be regarded by increasing millions in many lands over decades to come as the patriarch of that integration.

4. The Visible Man

Pope John Paul's foray into Poland was deeply successful in several ways. It had been performed with such precision that, with no crude revolutionary onslaught upon the political and security systems in place, the Pontiff had nonetheless forced powerful and appealing alternatives into the forefront of the arena. Not only had Poland and the entire Eastern bloc been compelled to look those alternatives straight in the eye. The Western bloc, which had long acquiesced for its own benefit in the status quo, was forced to face those alternatives as well. That could only have profound and lasting consequences on every side.

Equally important was the fact that, for millions upon millions of people, John Paul had given those powerful and appealing alternatives a human face. The face of Christ's Vicar on Earth.

Nevertheless, and though the drumbeat of publicity that attended his every step in Poland had been all but deafening, it proved difficult in their own din for the hordes of journalists and commentators to catch up with the mind-set of this Pope. It sometimes seemed to John Paul's aides that the press was watching a bravura performance whose substance remained a mystery for them.

Right enough, a certain dramatic slant came through in the Polish coverage. But the most that came from that was the portrait of an exiled and now powerfully placed son of *Polonia Sacra* who had returned for a high noon face-off, a personal challenge Vatican-style, with the Soviet-controlled persecution that had blanketed Karol Wojtyla's homeland for nearly thirty-five years.

Even at the most favorable level, and as John Paul's travels multiplied far beyond Poland and far beyond 1979, they were understood and presented in the media for as long as possible, and commented upon by experts, as no more than pastoral visits by a caring Pope to troubled parts of his Church. The wider and deeper confrontation John Paul had in mind seemed stubbornly to escape the torrent of public reportage and expert commentary.

Perhaps there was a tinge of wishful thinking in such commentary, or perhaps some other powerful force drove it along its own lines. In any case, memories seemed very short. It had not been so long since Cardinal Malula stood like a symbolic spokesman for the world, a prophet of sorts, in St. Peter's Square that October day in 1978 and demanded that "Everything must change!" Yet now that the change had truly begun— now that there was no longer to be a Pope echoing the familiar tones and behavior of his predecessors who had been content or constrained to wait upon history—everyone seemed to reject the idea as unintelligible or indigestible or invisible.

This mentality was to pursue John Paul for years. In September 1989, 1.1 million young people—in their quasi totality ranging in age between sixteen and twenty-five—came of their own accord to greet John Paul at St. James de Compostela in Spain. No television or radio networks, no government agency, no international PR company promoted the visit. There was no television coverage of that huge gathering. Why not?

It was as if it was too difficult—and for some, within and outside the Church, too unwelcome—to recognize that in John Paul II they were not dealing with anything like a traditional papal mind. And they were certainly not dealing, as some appeared determined to think, with a provincial cleric at play in a worldwide ecclesiastical maze.

What they were dealing with was a pope who had come to the papacy already fitted with a supremely innovative mind. A man who had been schooled by long experience, and by such tough and wily Polish Church-men as Cardinal Sapieha and Cardinal Wyszynski, at a unique, subtle, unremitting and successful confrontation with brute power. They were dealing with a pope who had emerged from the crucible called Poland, where religious reality and moral justice had survived centuries of daily warfare with every changing face of oppression. They were dealing with a man whose intent was to leave behind all that was done and over in the papacy, the Church and the world, and take with him as many as he could, to span the quantum leap to a fast-approaching new world order.

The time finally did have to come, of course, for a different range of reactions to set in.

It began to be noted that, though John Paul's trips multiplied, there remained an unexplainable absence of any changes such as might have been expected, though dreaded, if the Pope's intent and motive had to do with pastoral reform. After a public humiliation accompanied by sacrilege in Sandinista Nicaragua in 1983, after being insolently insulted during his American visit—and with the connivance of the American bishops—after he was burned in effigy and had his "popemobile" spattered with excrement by Dutch Catholics in 1986, there were no witch hunts, no vindictive appointments, no retaliatory actions. In strict law, he should have reacted punitively. He bore an office, and his was the duty to defend its rights and prerogatives. He did nothing.

Then, too, there was the curious fact that, as John Paul ranged ever more widely throughout the world, he was obviously throwing a far wider net than was needed for his Roman Catholics. He spoke not only with them and not only with Christians.

One day it would be five resident swamis in Los Angeles, and on another it would be animist priests in Togoland. Or maybe it would be Buddhists in Thailand; Parsis and Hindus and Muslims and Jains in India; or Protestants in South Carolina; or Humanists in Switzerland; or the Anglican Royal Family in England. This Pope clearly showed that he wanted to meet them all, talk with them, pray over and with them, bless and be liked by them.

If such papal behavior was strange, the reaction of some of the most interested commentators was at least as strange. To be sure, the publicity tone changed; but understanding did not deepen. The general approach seemed not so much to explain the extraordinary—for such papal behavior as this was nothing if not extraordinary—but to explain it away as a new act in a sort of continuing papal road show.

"This Pope," commented one U.S. writer, "is tremendously at home with crowds."

An Irish editorial commented on the Pontiff's "natural flair" for "the public relations gesture."

The Times of London summed up its view of John Paul's visit to France in 1980 as though it were covering some costly civic parade. "On the whole," said the Times, "the Pope was well received. But it is to be doubted that the outlay of expenses will be justified very soon."

Some accused John Paul of traveling to escape a Vatican bureaucracy they were certain he found unbearable, and of being a bad administrator incapable of governing his Church. "We have, in fact, a simple Polish Bishop," commented one highly placed Roman official, "who remains merely a Bishop at heart and who craves simple, pastoral work. He's not papal timber."

Others saw a kind of perverse triumphalism of retrenchment and defeat in the papal travels. "The Pope," declared one American Protestant scholar in a global masterpiece of backhanded praise, "is well aware that, in the next century, Catholicism will survive only in Third World countries. Catholicism has always flourished only in poor populations of low educational quality. The sophisticated West can take Catholicism's narrowness no longer. The Pope realizes that."

On the whole, then, the general feeling seemed to set in, at a very acceptable level of reporting, that Pope John Paul was simply doing what he did best. You might pick a fight over whether he was escaping from the burden of day-to-day governance of his Church, or over the crueler accusation that he was doing the only thing he was capable of doing. Such quibbling aside, however, it was taken as modern gospel that John Paul II was neither more nor less than a public relations genius. If he could only skip some of his more puritanical and narrow opinions—especially the ones on morality—he could be expected to do no great damage to anyone. In fact, it was generally conceded, in some instances he might even be a rather effective ambassador of good will.

As time went on, it was only natural that some papal sources within the Vatican did show a certain exasperation with such insistently naive interpretations of the Pontiff's motives and intent on his travels. It seemed to these observers and participants that commentators and reporters had not paid sufficient attention even to their own early stories about Wojtyla's record of "firsts," or about Wojtyla as a man marked for a special destiny, or about what he had accomplished as priest and bishop in Poland.

Still, Rome is a persevering and patient place. It was felt that, even without rereading the early press, and without extensive papal interviews either, a simple review of John Paul's achievements would soon force recognition that, by his travels alone, in a true and benign sense, this Pope was turning the papacy inside out.

Besides, argued some of John Paul's aides, in all fairness it was not surprising that public and private understanding lagged far behind the reality of what John Paul was really about in undertaking his trips. The mere fact that he was becoming a sort of papal Marco Polo was in itself a revolution that took some getting used to.

After all, as these partisans of patience reminded their Vatican colleagues, the Roman Catholic Pope had always been someone who resided and presided in Rome. Even for Romans, he had always been permanently "*there*," never in the "*here*" of our ordinary lives. He had been perpetually separated from "*here*" by flanks of cardinals and prelates. He had been housed in hush and secrecy. A precious few might gain access to a semiprivate audience, where they would listen to the

Pope speak from a throne surrounded by severe-faced chamberlains and exotically dressed guards. People who were very special might have their picture taken with the Holy Father and kiss his ring. A very few—usually important people in their own right, the kind who lived in a *"there"* somewhere else—might actually meet deep in the mysterious recesses of the Vatican's Apostolic Palace for a conversation with the Pope.

The ancient ecclesiastical reason for this most Catholic attitude had always seemed simple and clear and willingly accepted. It was true that, as a point of sacred physical origin, the mother church of all Christianity was in Jerusalem. But it was also true that, under the Holy Spirit's inspiration, Christianity had long ago renounced all freehold lease on those places made holy by Christ's earthly presence as a mortal man. In the primary Christian optic, it was on one of Rome's seven hills—on *mons vaticanus*, Vatican Hill—that God had staked a perpetual claim to 110 acres for the precise geographical and spiritual center of his visible Church as sole source of blessing and salvation.

And so had Rome been held in all the long heyday of Catholicism as the universal religion in all of Europe. From Galway Bay in Ireland to the Ural Mountains of pre-Soviet and even Soviet Russia, and from Archangel in the Arctic Circle to the Congo River in Africa, this Rome was held to be the truest center of the universe.

Even when the Americas and Asia and Oceania hove into sight of Christian eyes, Rome remained the center. And the European countries ringed nearest around it came to be seen as the Christian heartland in an expanding world.

For the first seventeen hundred years of the papacy, then, and in a very real sense, it could fairly be said that the Pope was Rome, and Rome was the Pope. It wasn't exactly that no pope ever traveled outside Rome. But it was true that no pope ever traveled over the high seas. Never beyond that Christian heartland, in fact. Not even in forced exile.

It was true, as well, and just as significant, that whatever papal travels there were had always had a pointedly clear and totally ecclesiastical objective. A special council of bishops, perhaps; a royal coronation; a political meeting; a visit to a particularly venerable shrine.

The few exceptions only served to prove the rule. The instance of Julius II riding out in the full regalia of a knight at arms to fight his own battles, in the literal, hand-to-hand sense of the term, was something Catholics preferred to forget as most unpapal behavior. Even when the papacy was transferred to Avignon in southern France—allegedly for security reasons that encompassed sixty-nine years and six pontificates— the popes stayed put at Avignon. The principle, if not the site, remained the same. They still were "Roman popes."

In the nineteenth century, there were two exceptions to this tradition. Pius VI and Pius VII left Rome, but only because they were kidnapped by French governments and imprisoned on French soil. Even then the reason was arguably—and perhaps doubly—ecclesiastical. And while Pius VI died in his imprisonment, Pius VII made it back to Rome as soon as he was allowed by his captors.

Moreover, staying in Rome has not always been an easy matter. Leaving aside the early martyr popes, who included Peter himself, as late as 1870 Pius IX suffered the loss of all papal territory in Italy—a swath of some 16,000 square miles—to the infant Italian state. In retaliation, Pius declared himself a "prisoner of the Vatican." He not only refused to leave the complex of buildings on Vatican Hill; he would not so much as set foot on the front balcony of St. Peter's Basilica to give his blessing to the crowds in the square below.

This historic resolve was perpetuated by every pope after Pius IX until, in 1929, the Italian government made honorable amends, indemnifying the Vatican of Pius XI for its earlier losses with an undisclosed sum of money and certain concessions of privilege in the social, economic and political life of the country.

No sense of wanderlust invaded the papacy even then, however. Rather, popes simply and most naturally reverted to the ancient pattern. Neither the summer retreats of Pius XII to Castel Gandolfo, for example, nor his compassionate succoring of the wounded in the streets of Rome in the midst of at least one of the twenty Allied bombings during World War II, were seen by him or anyone else as exceptions.

In a similar manner, John XXIII's rare forays out of the Vatican—a pilgrimage to the holy shrine of Loreto, a visit with the convicts in Regina Coeli, Rome's central prison—were wholly and traditionally ecclesiastical in nature.

Paul VI did break one mold: He was the first to travel overseas. But it was almost a technical change that did not alter the basic pattern; for his intent and his every action on those trips were entirely governed by the ancient ecclesiastical tradition. From the papal point of view, in fact, the travels of Paul VI were not to cities or to nations at all. They were to a shrine here, to a devotional exercise there, to an international organization elsewhere.

To effect a reconciliation between Catholics and Greek Orthodox Christians, for example, he went to the Holy Land and to Turkey. It was for Eucharistic celebrations that he went to Uganda, India, Colombia, the Philippines and Australia. Even his stopovers in Iran, Indonesia, Samoa, Hong Kong and Sri Lanka were taken as what they were— necessary stepping-stones along an ecclesiastical journey. A major speech—a highlight in Paul VI's life—took him to the United Nations headquarters in New York. It was to honor the Virgin Mary that he went to Portugal's famous shrine at Fatima. Though there was the appearance of innovation, in other words, and though he occasionally adopted the description of himself as the "Pilgrim Pope," Paul VI set no new pattern, at least in this area of papal tradition and observance.

When seen against the backdrop of so long, so consistent and compelling a record of papal travel, the more patient members of John Paul's inner council argued that it was fair to expect a certain resistance to change; to expect a lag time for understanding to catch up even with John Paul's traveling ways, not to mention his remarkable outlook on the world he was coming to know so intimately.

Moreover, it was pointed out, for anyone who understood the very nature of the Vatican, it would not do for long to argue that John Paul was just a publicity seeker or craved simple pastoral work. It made no sense to argue that a proven media magnate such as John Paul would not bother to set foot out of the Vatican, if all he wanted was a high publicity profile. Or that the two to three million visitors who came to the Vatican each year would not serve even the deepest pastoral urge to press the flesh.

In point of fact, the Vatican has long been the one place in the world where nothing is treated as off limits by the most intricate, ever-watchful, sometimes irreverently curious and incompassionate network of global communications. The Vatican has always been what one veteran hand described as "a place where every corridor is a whispering gallery and every office an echo chamber." The eighteenth-century French diplomat Joseph de Maistre doubted "that even the Holy Spirit could fly through it without being buffeted by the winds of gossip and the stentorian breathing of secrets." And things had not changed a bit two hundred years later when Frank Shakespeare, posted as United States ambassador to the Holy See, observed that "the Vatican is unrivaled as a listening post."

Within that atmosphere, a swarm of international journalists, reporters and commentators—not to mention embassy and consular officers whose business it is to monitor this Pope and his Vatican—spend entire careers wiring themselves into vast networks of "confidential" Vatican sources.

On top of that, it is an open secret—especially since the 1981 attempt on the Pope's life—that not only the Italian secret services but at least three other governments participate in the most minute monitoring of John Paul: his comings and goings; his staff; his food; his clothes; who reaches him by letter and by phone, and whom he reaches; who sees him and why and for how long and what transpires between them. Always someone is watching, someone is listening, someone is probing and noting and reporting.

It is well understood by all, moreover, that no matter who is involved in any Vatican conversation or discussion, and no matter at what level of importance or secrecy, or what the subject at hand may be, matters finally turn to what the Pope may think about this, or what he may or may not do or say about that. Finally, in other words, whether he is personally present or not, the Pope is at the center of every confidence, every informal chat, every speculation and rumor.

In short, if John Paul were to be dismissed as merely a master of public relations, then by the same inexorable logic it had to be admitted that in the Vatican itself he had the ideal bureaucratic weapon for making news. He needed only to stir any pot of speculation with the papal stick of rumor to make headlines whenever he might choose. If all he wanted was publicity, why bother to log hundreds of thousands of miles in scores of supremely exhausting papal trips to something approaching a hundred countries to get it?

Within the arena of global competition where lay the real reason for John Paul's gargantuan travel agenda, there were a certain number of leaders who did begin to understand in a general way that they were watching and listening to a pope who was saying and doing things that were entirely new. But even they were unable to span the quantum leap between the traditional papal mind as they had always known it and the mind of this once Polish Pope.

To be sure, he had come out of provincial Krakow. In the words of one doorman there who had known him for years, Papa Wojtyla "had left . . . for Rome with an overnight bag, a toothbrush and a couple of bread rolls to eat." Perhaps so. But quickly enough he seemed to have been transformed by the papacy. And now he was returning the favor. That much, at least, seemed clear.

Nevertheless, even his adversaries in the geopolitical arena—men who saw themselves as the very embodiment of a bright and totally new future for the world—displayed in John Paul's regard all the parochialism of which they habitually accused so many others. Like the skeptical Nathanael who asked on first hearing about Jesus, "Can any good come out of Nazareth?" such papal critics wondered, "Can any good come at the hands of an archbishop from provincial Krakow in retrograde Poland, who fancies for himself certain worldwide and internationalist aims?"

Lurking beneath the surface of such doubts, however, was the dawning realization for some that, fitted for combat or not, John Paul regarded their competition, and had entered into it, as the most important struggle of our age. And there was the dawning realization, as well, that he had entered it over their heads by thrusting himself and the papacy he embodied into the forefront of the transnational mind that was being formed so swiftly and surely among his contemporaries.

"Holy Father," John Paul was asked toward the end of a private audience for visiting dignitaries in 1983, "can we expect Your Holiness to undertake many more of these papal visits to different parts of the world?"

John Paul replied with candor. "Until as many men and women and children as I can reach have seen the face and heard the voice of Christ's Vicar; for I am their Pope, and this is what the Blessed Mother wishes her Son's Vicar to do."

That was anything but the voice of someone seeking publicity as an escape, or a high international profile because he enjoyed the razzle-dazzle. It sounded the authentic tones of a man led by a commanding vision and intent upon a definite goal.

The trouble was that the more John Paul traveled in the world and the more he spoke to leaders and citizens in the countries and the cities and the wide places in the road where they lived, the more he seemed to be taken in some quarters as a living, traveling enigma. And as surely as nature abhors a vacuum, so do leaders in political, economic and social power abhor an enigma loose in their territory.

Even among John Paul's more observant and careful adversaries, some seemed truly at a loss to know what it was this Pope saw abroad in their world that was so dire as to have plunged him into what many in his own Church were criticizing as a perilous course, and possibly the most disastrous one any pope had ever set for himself. The most careful watch on this most public of popes, and the most searching analyses of his moves, did not seem to reveal to John Paul's secular adversaries—or to most of his allies—what lay behind the vast array of odd and seemingly contradictory aspects of his behavior as world leader, or as Vicar of Christ.

On the contrary, nothing of what could be seen from the outside seemed to serve anything in John Paul's pontificate that could be identified as a cohesive grand policy. No consistent strategies seemed visible. At least, not unless you could label as a strategy the sort of papal conduct for which any subordinate in an earlier papacy would have been condemned and punished.

And yet, because strategy is always the very fuel with which great wars are driven forward, so immense a blind spot having to do with papal strategy was regarded as a crisis of intelligence by more than a few.

Public coverage and pettier critics notwithstanding, there could be no doubt that—far from seeking publicity or running from administrative burdens—John Paul was deeply conscious of his innovations. For, slowly but surely, as those innovations multiplied with his travels over the decade of the 1980s, John Paul was building for himself as Pope an unrivaled personal status as the most visible and well-known human being of the twentieth century. Not only was he seen in the flesh by hundreds of millions of people in the so-called civilized world; he was seen as well by men and women in the unlikeliest backwaters one could imagine. Alone —and certainly with no help from anti-Church or superforce—this Holy Father was making his very own a truly central spot on the world stage.

Of course, anti-Church adherents and superforce members had their own considerable publicity arsenal; and they were not bashful about using it. The well-founded rumor, the well-timed leak, the word from a well-placed "unnamed source": all these had been efficient weapons over twenty-five years of effort to separate the Pope from the traditional means of the governance of his Church. However—and owing in some part to those innovations that drove everyone so crazy—this Pope became the centerpiece even of the interest generated by the anti-Church. More often than not, the publicity that came as a result of their efforts centered around John Paul. Admittedly, that fact was always incidental to the main goal of the anti-Church publicity seekers. But it was nonetheless a fact, and a concrete result.

In their bafflement about him, a few world leaders of the less careful variety sometimes underestimated the enigmatic John Paul, or even counted him out as a player in the rush of world events. One such leader, a Western head of state noted in the Vatican more for his cynicism than for his wisdom, made the mistake of going in like a lion for a private and "frank" discussion with His Holiness. When he came out, he was not merely defanged; he seemed at once both incredulous and rueful that he had not been forewarned. "There is something else here," he commented about John Paul. "He is more than they said, and more than he seems to be. Surely! He is more than that."

Not long ago, the story of a different sort of encounter made the rounds at a certain level of gossip on the world stage where John Paul had chosen to stride as no pope before him.

The year 1988 was the one thousandth anniversary of the birth of Christianity in the Ukraine. Mikhail Gorbachev—fairly recently and still only partially emergent from the time warp that is the Soviet Union— decided to appropriate this millennial anniversary; to claim it as a banner of *glasnost*; and, by means of a propaganda event to which he gave the meaningless name "Moscow Celebration Service," to co-opt it as a Soviet achievement.

To this "Celebration" Gorbachev invited just about every living religious leader from just about every Christian church. In his by now well-known take-charge manner, the Soviet Chairman jumped in with both feet tied in one shoe, communicating an invitation through intermediaries to John Paul II: Would His Holiness care to join the many other prelates who would on this occasion dutifully trundle off to Moscow in search of reconciliation?

Back to Gorbachev, again through intermediaries, went the response of His Holiness, who had made plain in many ways his awareness that despite its seventy-year relegation to the catacombs of the Soviet system, religion had never left the mainstream of Soviet life. His Holiness, the reply informed Gorbachev, would accept the invitation on condition that, on the same occasion, the Pontiff would be equally welcome to visit his Catholics in Lithuania.

Gorbachev categorically refused. How could he do otherwise? A papal visit would only stir up new troubles—might set fire to the dry tinder of Lithuanian nationalism, for example. It might even ignite the smoldering resentment of fifty million very Christian-minded Ukrainians, who were already angry at having their once-in-a-thousand-years anniversary filched from them by a Russian who was a professional atheist in their eyes.

In response to Gorbachev's refusal of his request, His Holiness declined to appear in Moscow, adding that he would, of course, send the General Secretary a written message with a lower-level papal delegation to the "Celebration."

Surprised, confused and offended by such an uncompromising rebuff of an offer he had thought would be irresistible for a Roman Pope, Gorbachev belatedly looked for a reading of this stubborn Pole. For him as for all Russians, Poles have always been either overlords or serfs. Which was this Karol Wojtyla? What better man to consult for the answer than General Wojciech Jaruzelski, Moscow's man in Poland, a Pole himself and a Catholic, a man who had stood toe-to-toe with John Paul on more than one occasion in recent years?

As gossip had it, Jaruzelski's reading was unsettling for the Soviet leader. Gorbachev, the Polish general said, had already made two mistakes. The first was to have invited the Pope in the first place. The second, once the invitation had been made, was to have refused the Pontiff's condition.

"Why mistakes?" Gorbachev is said to have asked. "He's just a figure-head."

"That's what we thought when he arrived in Krakow, back in 1978."

"Ah!" Gorbachev apparently drew an obvious conclusion. "You know his game."

"That's just it." The Polish general confused the matter still further. "We don't."

"So?" Gorbachev was getting nowhere.

"So." Jaruzelski made the political point that had already become so obvious to so many. "He's dangerous. If you go along with him; if you oppose him; if you have any truck with him. *Wóz albo przewáz*. It's Hobson's choice."

"Yes," Gorbachev is said to have agreed. "That's dangerous."

John Paul had made his point. Gorbachev was learning the lesson many a leader was taking to heart. And when the "Moscow Celebration Service" did take place, the General Secretary doubtless took cold comfort from the words of Archbishop Runcie of Canterbury: "Under Mr. Gorbachev, religion has entered the mainstream of Soviet life."

The late Franz Josef Strauss of West Germany best expressed the view of John Paul that began to take hold at last among the wiser of the world's more experienced "huskies." "For all we know," said Strauss, "he seems to follow one vision, have one supergoal in view, to which all these diverse interests of the nations are tending, each in its own separate way."

And that was the nub. Try as they might, neither Strauss in his wisdom nor his peers on the world stage were able to fathom what that supergoal of John Paul's might be. In their efforts to understand what in the world this Pope was doing, they were always stopped short by the sight of a Church filled to capacity with decay and disobedience, left untended, and by strange contradictions in John Paul's own behavior. It almost seemed as though, in the Pope's hands, bafflement had taken on the dimensions of a weapon in this modern warfare he was engaged in. And it almost seemed he was deploying confusion the way a general deploys armies.

Take even the most visible level of John Paul's activities as an example. The level of his many and varied travels. Even here, deep and troubling uncertainties could not be resolved.

Surely he had something more in view than such specifically religious problems as, say, the spread of Liberation Theology that was so deadly for Catholic faith and dogma? But what? How were his adversaries in the global competition to deal with a politician—even if he was a pope— who stood face-to-face one day with one or another of the power-thirsty generals and totalitarian strongmen in Haiti, Chile, Guatemala or Uruguay, and on another day confused the pattern by an official visit to

Benin in West Africa—to take but one possible case in point—where he addressed a cheering crowd of thousands as he stood beneath a gigantic banner that exhorted, "God Bless Our Marxist Revolution and John Paul II!"?

On another level, what sense could anyone, East or West, make of this Pope's staggeringly patient policy that emerged, even after his Polish trip, toward the Soviet Union and its Eastern European satellites?

What glimpse into his hidden strategy could be gleaned from John Paul's hands-on/hands-off attitude toward authoritarian governments in Latin America?

Who could make head or tail of his versatile and ever-adaptive treatment of Communist China, on one side of the world? Or his steady input into the gathering forces of a united Europe, set to emerge in 1992 on the other side of the world?

What gave him the ability, on the one hand, to escape a head-on collision with the international Jewish organizations that lobbied for an opportunistic papal recognition of the State of Israel; and, on the other hand, to avoid any close identification with the Arab Mideast cause without being branded as its enemy?

And on the broadest level of the geopolitical competition under way, how were the shifting, crumbling and realigning secular power centers to understand a visionary—even if he was a pope—who spoke about a future condition of the nations that would be free of socialism and Marxism but equally free of the baneful "superdevelopment" John Paul had taken to criticizing so roundly and pointedly as the curse of democratic capitalism?

These were but some of the bafflements that were so important for John Paul's secular rivals in the grand-scale competition. But in place of any answers, there remained only an abiding and uneasy sense that, if there was, as Franz Josef Strauss had said, "a single-track purposefulness in all this Pope is doing," and if he did "follow one vision . . . have one supergoal in view," no one might be able to figure it all out in time to make any use of the information.

5. The Keys of This Blood

In truth, Karol Wojtyla was not transformed by the papacy. Rather, he was practically tailored for the roles of priest and bishop within a Poland that was a microcosm of the troubled twentieth-century world around it, as well as for the role of Pope within the Church whose divinely mandated obligation was to be a source of eternal salvation within that world, come what may.

As a young cleric in the late forties and quickly as a bishop, in that Poland he was heir to a very specific ecclesiastical tradition. Preceding him and molding that tradition, men like Cardinals Stefan Wyszynski and Adam Sapieha insisted that the Church not flee to catacombs. It had to be everywhere in Polish life and society, even in the teeth of brutal repression. Nor had that Church made any of the compromises so disastrous to the Church in the United States, Latin America and Western Europe. Wojtyla inherited a thoroughly Roman Catholic tradition, unadulterated and vibrant.

Besides, the Church in Poland, in its thousand-year history, had developed an outlook that was genuinely global; and this globalism was faithfully reproduced in its political institutions, which, though serving Polish nationalism, were imbued with a genuinely geopolitical sense. This, too, he inherited.

The great difference between the Karol Wojtyla who entered the papal Conclave on October 14, 1978, and the man who emerged from it two days later was that he had walked in as Archbishop of Krakow, and had walked out as Bishop of Rome. He had become the 263rd successor to Simon Peter the Apostle, monarchic head of Vatican City State, religious leader of some 900 million Roman Catholics spread over virtually every nation of the five continents. He held in his hand the ancient Keys of Peter. He now possessed a georeligious power and a geopolitical role to play.

Now he was the sole legitimate head of the only georeligion the world has ever known—a living, active, multicultural, multinational, multiracial institutional organization, an institution structured so that the local and national norms of its members could be accommodated in harmony and union with the global aims of the universal organization now confided exclusively to Wojtyla's leadership and care.

Moreover, he emerged from the Conclave as the personal embodiment of the global political entity known as the "Holy See." In that capacity, he was accepted immediately—and, in a certain sense, as more than a peer—in the rambunctious world of international politics and diplomacy with which the Vatican is inextricably linked.

Hardly a day passes in that political world without some incident, large or small, that underscores the constant and intimate intertwining of the georeligion John Paul came to head with the geopolitical nature of the world arena. And each such incident, large or small, links the Roman Pontiff himself to the international life and political activity in what has come to be regarded as the secular world.

Even the briefest glance at a pair of such incidents from recent history is sufficient to illustrate how interesting a match had been made in Conclave between the papacy and the Pope who had learned so well at the feet of Sapieha and Wyszynski.

In the early 1940s, when young Wojtyla and his Poland were deeply and tragically caught in the connivances of Nazi Germany and Soviet Russia, and in the weak-kneed policies of Western governments, Archbishop Amleto Cicognani was posted to Washington, D.C., as Pope Pius XII's Apostolic Delegate in the United States.

During his service at that post, Cicognani struck up a friendship of sorts with Maksim Maksimovich Litvinov, the best-loved and most large-minded Soviet ambassador the Kremlin has ever sent to Washington. Litvinov served there for three years, from 1941 to 1943.

It was an unlikely friendship, perhaps, given the committed and unremitting atheism of the Soviet Union and the equally committed and unremitting condemnation of the Soviets by every Roman Pope since Pius X. But Litvinov had a genius for friendship, and an exceptional gift for conversation. He talked with everyone and anyone, and many of his public and private pronouncements are still repeated by some in Washington today who are unaware of Litvinov as their author. A Polish Jew born in 1876 in Bialystok—that eastern portion of Poland occupied at the time by Czarist Russia—Litvinov had spent his professional life in the Soviet government's Commission for Foreign Affairs.

No one in Washington ever doubted his devotion as Joseph Stalin's representative in those three crucial years of World War II. But his closest Washington associates always felt that Litvinov the Jew had Litvinov the Soviet representative under strict control; that he always had his eyes fixed on the larger picture—on basic human values—as he surveyed the world scene. In fact, even after he retired, in 1946, Litvinov maintained his foreign contacts and collaborated, sometimes, through quite unofficial channels, with Vatican personnel and others in the West —especially when humanitarian causes were involved.

In those war years, the perennial topic that surfaced in the private chats between Litvinov and Archbishop Cicognani was that diehard opposition of the Church under Pius XII against having anything to do with Stalin, with Stalinism, with Leninist Marxism, or with the Soviet regime. Soviet strategy at that critical moment was directed toward securing some softening of Pius's position. The geopolitical purpose of this Soviet effort was to galvanize the war effort against Hitler's Germany, which was still far from beaten. To gain even the neutrality of the Holy See and its representatives throughout the world would be an improvement and a help.

So important was Pius XII's stance considered by all sides in the war that several countries had joined the Soviets in bringing immense pressures to bear on the Pope's administration to let up on its official opposition to the "Soviet ally." Even New York's doughty and conservative Francis Cardinal Spellman, though always a great supporter of Pius XII, was one of a fair number of powerful papal representatives who joined the international pressure group. Using as pretext his position as Chaplain General of the U.S. Armed Forces, Spellman undertook a worldwide tour of the Catholic hierarchy to lobby for the temporary softening of official Catholic horror of Stalin and Stalinist Russia. "Hitler has to be beaten, one way or another," the American Cardinal would say in his own defense. The line was his own version of Winston Churchill's more famous defense of Britain's alliance with the Soviet Union against Hitler: "Any stick is good enough to beat a dog, when you've got to beat him."

It was in that internationally charged atmosphere, and in one conversation in particular, that the topic of Pius's intransigence toward Stalin surfaced yet again between Amleto Cicognani and Maksim Litvinov.

To the Soviet ambassador's reasoned arguments, Cicognani finally replied that Generalissimo Stalin—for so he was called during the war— once saved from annihilation, would very likely consign every Catholic priest, prelate and nun to a one-way cattle-car trip to Siberian death camps, just as he had disposed of some four million independent Ukrain-

ian farm owners. "We know all about the kulaks," Cicognani said in
pointed reference to that slaughter.

"Oh, no, Excellency!" Litvinov engaged in no shallow denials. Instead,
he pointed to that all-important geopolitical power bound up with the
Holy See. "The Generalissimo knows you people are not kulaks. Enemies of socialism, yes; that he knows. But he also knows your terrain is
the world of nations, not some godforsaken acres in the Soviet hinterland."

A little more than two decades later, in a different part of the "world
of nations" that even Stalin understood to be papal terrain, another,
smaller war erupted. Again, though Stalin and Litvinov had departed the
scene, Soviet influence was present. And again the unique geopolitical
status and capability of the Holy See became crucial.

On April 24–25, 1965, in the tiny island nation of the Dominican
Republic, rebellious army units under Colonel Francisco Caamaño
Deñó seized part of the capital city, Santo Domingo. He distributed large
quantities of arms indiscriminately to the populace at large, and demanded that ousted president Juan Bosch be reinstated in office. Bosch
had been deposed in 1963 by the military, who correctly suspected him
of being under Communist influence.

Under the command of General Antonio Imbert Barreras, meanwhile,
military forces loyal to the current Dominican government established
control in the parts of the capital not occupied by Caamaño, and in the
surrounding countryside.

To no one's surprise, it was rapidly established that Caamaño's rebels
included an important Communist element and that the hidden hand of
the KGB had been at work. The Santo Domingo uprising was therefore
quickly seen to be a crisis of international importance. It had implications for the whole hemisphere, in fact. The United States was in no
mood at the time to allow another Cuba, or another shredding of the
Monroe Doctrine.

As quickly as possible, the United States landed a large force in the
island nation, and established a security zone dividing the Imbert forces
from Caamaño's rebel troops in Santo Domingo. By May, the Organization of American States (OAS) integrated the U.S. forces into an inter-
American peace force commanded by a Brazilian general and composed
of personnel from Brazil, Nicaragua, Honduras, Paraguay and Costa
Rica.

The American public in particular, still mindful of the disaster at the
Bay of Pigs and of the Cuban missile crisis, watched as the explosive
Dominican situation unfolded in graphic press coverage. Striking and

dramatic photos focused their attention increasingly on the strong frame of a man clad in the white summer cassock of a Roman Catholic cleric, a lone figure striding back and forth across the dangerous no-man's-land that separated the two armed camps.

That man was Archbishop Luigi Raimondi, Pope John XXIII's Apostolic Delegate to Mexico. With his broad forehead, sharp eyes behind spectacles, Roman nose and determined chin, Raimondi was the very embodiment of a man who was not so much immune to passions as able to place them in a larger context, and then to make that context compelling for all concerned.

Raimondi had been requested by the OAS authorities, and accepted by the Caamaño command as well, as an agreeable negotiator in the protracted truce efforts.

During those hot and trying months of negotiation that extended from the end of April to the end of August, one Santo Domingo newspaper editorialized on the choice of the Apostolic Delegate as the man for the job. And in doing so, it enlarged significantly on the point that Soviet Ambassador Litvinov had made to Archbishop Cicognani nearly twenty-five years before.

"Who could pass with immunity from one side to the other? Who could be trusted to take no side between rebels and authority, between Communist and capitalist, between foreigners and Dominicans? Only someone delegated by the one man on earth who is only on the side of God, the Heavenly Father of rebel and authority, of Communist and capitalist, of foreigner and Dominican. Only such a man as the Holy Father, and only his official representatives, have the Heavenly Father's mind and love for all mankind; for only they serve all mankind as one family, and have the capacity to tend it as one family."

The insight of that editorial into the mandate and the capacity of the Holy See, and the confidence it expressed in the Pope's personal representative, were both on target. Raimondi's negotiations led to the end of the military standoff by August 31, and to regularized elections and the final withdrawal of all foreign troops from Santo Domingo by September of the following year.

Both the Cicognani and Raimondi incidents, and the Dominican editorial as well, combine to put a tooth in one more story—less well documented but much repeated in the years following World War II—that linked the Soviet Union, Great Britain and the Holy See.

Britain's Prime Minister Churchill, the story went, was urging on Stalin the importance of that very policy that Litvinov and so many others did in fact take up: As allies, Churchill reportedly argued, the British and

Soviets ought to try somehow to co-opt Pope Pius into the war effort. In caustic contempt, Stalin is supposed to have replied, "How many divisions can the Pope supply us?"

As the story continued, after the war Churchill recounted the exchange to Pius XII. Rather than insist upon the obvious—on the fact that, despite his open contempt, Stalin had mustered world pressure in an effort to gain Vatican support—Pius is said to have replied, "Tell my son Joseph that he will meet my divisions in eternity."

Whether that story is accurate in all or any of its details, it points up a great deal about the power that was later placed in John Paul's hands when he accepted the papacy. Any world leader who discounts the eternal revelations on which papal power claims to be based flirts with problems. But, at the same time, any world leader who takes the Roman Pontiff as possessing only the spiritual weapons of the unseen world and the afterlife with which to deal in practical, this-worldly matters is making a strategic error of great proportions.

By definition, the problem faced by Stalin and the Allied nations in the 1940s, and the one faced in 1965 in Santo Domingo, were geopolitical. The common good of a wide community of nations was involved. And, as the Dominican editorial observed, only an institution with truly geopolitical capability—the capacity and the mandate to serve and tend "all mankind as one family"—can truly serve the greater good of the wider community of nations.

However unpalatable the idea may have become to much of the world in latter days, Karol Wojtyla was one man who came to the papacy with a full understanding and a sophisticated appreciation of the geopolitical power of the Holy See. And, an idea more unpalatable still, that geopolitical power was understood by him as generated by and inseparable from the georeligious power claimed at the very dawn of Christianity by its first preachers, the Apostles.

Christianity started off in the early thirties of the first century professing to tell all mankind about the divine revelations made for them all by Jesus Christ. "Go forth and teach all men, baptizing them in the name of the Father, the Son and the Holy Spirit," Jesus commanded his Apostles. That, backed up by his giving the Keys of salvation on this earth and in God's Heaven to Simon Peter, alone and personally, was the last great and well-remembered instruction Jesus gave his Apostles before he disappeared from human sight.

It took almost two thirds of its nearly two-thousand-year existence for

Christianity to achieve that georeligious status so clearly mandated by its founder. In hindsight, and even in simplified outline, it is easy to see by what painful fits and starts the Church finally developed the truly geo-religious institutional organization placed in the hands of John Paul II.

For one thing, georeligion was not to be a simple question of mere numbers or of demographic spread. What was involved was something far more difficult: the slow-moving effort to free the human expression of that original divine revelation and mandate from the powerful limitations—the anti-georeligious elements—that have particularized all the other great historical movements of mankind. Limitations that break people into groups, and that maintain each group separate from all the others. Language; local customs; ethnic traditions; racial memories; nationalistic ideals and goals; and those greatest of all limiting factors, human egotism, selfishness and greed. All had to be faced and reinterpreted and overcome in a new context.

The earliest set of great limitations that Christianity had to face was the fervent Judaism of the first Christian Apostles and disciples themselves. Jews almost to a man, it took them nearly twenty years to realize that they were not commissioned by Christ to convert the world to the Judaism in which they had been raised. Their leader, Simon Peter, had to be instructed by a special revelation that forever changed his outlook. And, even then, he had to hear and understand the arguments of the fiery Paul of Tarsus, who bluntly declared to his non-Jewish converts that "there is neither Jew nor non-Jew, there is neither slave nor free man, there is neither male nor female. For you are all one in Christ Jesus."

By A.D. 50, the matter was settled. The Christian leaders realized that, according to Jesus, they were not supposed to convert the world to a Christianized Judaism—Peter's original misunderstanding. They were to convert all men to Christianity, which had inherited all the divine promises made to Judaism's founders. Christians were the spiritual descendants, the "seed" that God promised to Abraham some two thousand years before Christ's birth. "If you belong to Christ, you are Abraham's seed," Paul wrote to the Galatians, "and, therefore, you are heirs to all that God promised Abraham." That Christian claim laid the groundwork from the beginning for an undying enmity in Jews for Christians.

The next important shift in Roman Christianity's march to georeligious status came after almost three hundred years of fierce and lethal persecutions under the iron hand of the dying Roman Empire.

Ironically enough, and portentously, this second shift began with Christianity's success at last, during the fourth to sixth centuries, in adapting itself to the framework of that same ancient Roman Empire. And a vast shift it was; for it raised Christianity from the level of a provincial and sociopolitically nondescript sect, originating in the largely unknown backwater of Palestine, to civil, public and international status.

There was a price to be paid for this huge facilitation of Christianity's preaching: Roman Christianity adopted not merely the framework but many traits of the recent Roman imperialism.

Hardly had this shift taken place than Christianity was subjected to the destructive invasions by Nordic and Asiatic barbarians, principally between the sixth and eleventh centuries. Roman Christianity ultimately tamed the invaders, however. And in Christianizing them, it extended its religion from its originally small nucleus in Mediterranean lands, until it covered all of Europe. The See of Peter—the Holy See, as people called it—was the hub of that Europe.

Out of this new population, the Church diligently formed the matrix from which came the civilization that developed all those higher civil, political, artistic and cultural values treasured today as marks of progress and civilization—justice, compassion, democracy, dignity, the rights of man, even medicine and science. A new Europe now enjoyed a unity and a verve that the ancient Roman Empire, even at its apogee, had never been able to create.

The centerpiece of it all was the man who sat on the throne of Simon Peter in that Holy See of Rome. Among the major players at the Round Table of international politics, no ruler could take command, no government could govern, no commerce could function, without the spiritual blessing and the imperial nod of the Roman Pope.

Moreover, whatever overlordship this man, the Roman Pontiff, exercised—whatever armies or fleets he commanded or could assemble; whatever binding laws he laid down governing civil, political, artistic and personal life throughout Europe—ultimately his right and claim to do so was based on his possession of Peter's Keys of supreme spiritual authority.

Alien though the thought may be for our timid modern minds—and no matter how secular the business in hand might have been, or how this-worldly the practical means adopted to deal with it; and no matter what the turmoil within the Church itself—ultimately and sincerely, the authority of those Keys was taken as guaranteed by the actual life's blood shed by Christ in his bodily sufferings and death on a Roman cross.

Catherine of Siena reflected this widely and firmly held religious conviction when in the very teeth of deep Church turmoils—the problem of two claimants, Gregory XI and Urban VI, to the See of Peter—she recounted a conversation she had during one of her many ecstatic visions.

> *God the Father:* Whose is this blood?
> *Catherine:*   The blood of Our Lord, Your divine Son.
> *God the Father:* To whom did My Son give the Keys of this blood?
> *Catherine:*   To Peter the Apostle.
> *God the Father:* Yes. And to all Peter's successors up to this day. And to all Peter's successors until the end of time. That is why the authority of these Keys will never be weakened, because the strength of this blood can never be diluted.

The men and women who were Catherine's contemporaries in the 1300s surely nodded in acquiescence at this special affirmation of their own belief in the unending validity and power of Christ's mandate to the Apostles, and to Peter as their leader.

The problems confronted by Catherine and the Church of her day were by no means the first or the last of the upheavals that tested the right and power of Peter's successors to possess those Keys. Indeed, the first truly massive defection by believers from the Petrine authority symbolized in those Keys had come some three hundred years before Catherine's day. In the year 1054, the Greek and Russian portions of Christianity severed all relationship with the Roman Pope.

But it was in the sixteenth and seventeenth centuries that the religious unity of Europe itself was shattered by the Protestant revolt against papal authority; by the high winds of sociopolitical change and economic development; and by a rising insistence that science, as the self-proclaimed and exciting engine of progress, must sever all connection with revelation.

Throughout its ancient heartland of Europe, the Roman Church was reduced steadily and drastically in its raw sociopolitical power and in its exclusive religious dominance. With stunning effectiveness, Martin Luther—himself a priest married to a former nun, Katherine von Bora—exhorted all priests and nuns to marry, and to go forth and win the whole world for Christ, leaving behind them forever "those cruikshank Roman celibates."

The surprise for everyone in this seeming new calamity for Rome was that even as the Roman Church lost whole populations through the breakup of religious unity in Europe, "those cruikshank Roman celibates" gained vast new populations in Africa, Asia and the Americas. Over the next four hundred years, armies of selfless—and, yes, celibate—

priests, nuns and religious proceeded to gather a membership of faithful adherents that no other church has ever equaled. A membership unparalleled not only in its size but in its national, racial, cultural and linguistic diversity.

Increasingly shorn of its territories, and liberated from that political imperialism borrowed like a regal but ill-fitting cloak from the ancient Romans, the Catholic Church began to display its innate georeligious capacity. It developed a diplomatic style that relied principally on moral status, not on political weight, or even on its financial clout. It developed to a high degree the Catholic sense of the papacy as the ultimate arbiter for problems and dilemmas affecting nations all over the globe. It entered public contentions—political, scientific, cultural—with no strength behind it beyond its storehouse of experience, its independent judgment, and those Keys of Christ's blood, to which more than one pope and many a "cruikshank" missionary was willing to add his own blood.

By the beginning of the twentieth century, the Roman Catholic presence was everywhere. With each decade, its membership increased still further. The centralizing authority of the Roman papacy developed more and more absolute rules tying local communities to Rome. Devotion to the papacy and ecclesiastical unity between Pope and bishops, priest and laity, was widespread and normative.

It was, in a certain true sense, a Catholic high renaissance so singular that it did not end even with the signal conclusion of the Church's once grandiose sociopolitical power base, upon which Rome had for so long thought its influence rested. In 1929, the territorial holdings of the Roman Pontiff were legally defined as a 110-acre estate called Vatican Hill, on the left bank of the Tiber River. Technically speaking, even that scrap of territorial integrity persisted only thanks to the good will of nations that, many of them, neither shared the Roman Catholic faith nor had any great love for the institutional Church that housed it.

By that time, however, even testy nations had other reasons for being at least benign in their relations with the now physically defenseless Vatican City State. Shorn of its territories, liberated from the limiting factor of its own political imperialism, the Church in and of itself was recognized as a potent force in the affairs of nations of every stripe. A force that could neither be dismissed as negligible nor commandeered at will.

Owing in no small part to the caliber of the first four popes of the twentieth century—Pius X, Benedict XIV, Pius XI and Pius XII—no one tried to identify that force with any divisive secular system, or with any single nation, or, for that matter, with any international organization. By the time Pius XII died, in October 1958—twenty years to the month before John Paul II took his own place in the Apostolic Chair—the Holy See and its Church were seen as a single, supranational entity, one that had attained a georeligious status and stature eliciting from the world a geopolitical recognition that was unique.

From the outside—from the point of view of those who hold and wield significant secular power in the world arena—the Roman Catholic Church in its unequaled maturity as a georeligious institution is analyzed in hard and practical terms. Such leaders entertain no romantic illusions. If the visions and the faith of Catherine of Siena were no more than bits of a hateful fairy tale for Joseph Stalin, the hard reality he was forced to face was that the geopolitical influence of Pius XII had to be courted in the effort to save his Soviet hide and the Allied cause in World War II.

For the secular world, there are just two facts about the Holy See that are convincing: the fact that, in his person, the Roman Pontiff is the embodiment of the Holy See; and the fact that the organization he heads came at last, and alone, to fulfill all the prerequisites of a georeligious institution. These are the tangible truths that provide the Pope in secular eyes with the unique capability to act in and for the world community—to serve and tend mankind as one family—as it gropes its own way toward the borderless international plane on which he already—and prior to anyone else—stands.

The first prerequisite for that unique, supranational capability of the Pope is that the aim of the institution he heads must be exclusively directed to the good of the international community it comprises, as a community. And in parallel fashion, the community he heads, as it is enlarged and vindicated and propagated by his institution, must itself share that supranational aim directed to the good of all.

The second prerequisite flows directly from the first. In order for the greatest good of all to be served, the institution headed by the Roman Pontiff must not be bound by anything that is merely ethnic or national or nationalistic; or by anything regionally or racially or culturally particularized. Such attributes must be accommodated, but only to the degree that they neither shatter the unity and harmony enjoyed by the supranational community, nor deflect the global aim of the universal institution.

The third prerequisite for capability on the georeligious plane is one of structure. The institution must have arms and hands and legs that carry out and reinforce its aims for the common good of the global community, in all of the many nations and situations where the parts of that community may find themselves. Like the institution itself, and like the community it serves, the organizational structures must accommodate the differences of the various parts of the community, but always within the unity, harmony and aim of the institution.

The final prerequisite for georeligious capability is authority. The institution, in its organizational structures and undertakings, must have unique authority: an authority that is centralized; an authority that is autonomous vis-à-vis all other authority on the supranational plane; an authority that carries with it such sanctions as are effective in maintaining the unity and the aims of the institution as it goes about its business of serving the greatest good of the community as a whole and in its every part.

Even shorn of its former imperial and territorial trappings—or, more probably, especially shorn of those things—the Roman Catholic institution in the twentieth century has fulfilled all of those prerequisites. And its compelling status for the secular powers of the world lies primarily in its two greatest attributes: first, its independent and religiously based moral imperative both as embodied in the faith and dogma of the Roman Church and as defended and propagated by the Roman Pope; and, second, its unrivaled position—unique among all the world's religious, ethical and political units and groupings—as a truly borderless, truly global and totally independent institution whose terrain, as Maksim Litvinov remarked so pointedly, "is the world of nations."

If the political elements essential for georeligious success were rooted in something other than the global prerequisites fulfilled by the Roman Church—in something other than universal aim, community, structure and authority—then the world would have any number of competitors to look to, and the Catholic Church would have some tough competition on the supranational plane.

If, for instance, longevity alone were enough to assure georeligious capability, then at least four religions and ethical units would surpass Rome. Judaism, Hinduism, the Zoroastrianism of the modern Parsis and Shintoism are all of older origin than the institutional organization of the Catholic Church. But each came into being within a once dominant political system; and in its essential religious traits, each is characterized by a specific racial, geographically located and culturally conditioned tradition. Moreover, for any of these systems to renounce its tradition, still rooted in those same racial and cultural characteristics, would be to abandon its soul. Yet it is just those specifics—those limiting factors— that preclude these systems from developing supranational institutions.

Among these four ancient systems, a distinction has to be made between religion—Judaism, say, or Islam—and the ancient *ethical* systems whose very beginnings and essence were defined exclusively by race and culture and localized ways of living. Over countless centuries, such systems have seemed to sing a siren song of religious "neutrality" for many with an international mind-set, but who hold religious faith to be of little or no account.

Buddhism, for example, which is fundamentally atheistic, arose under the stimulus of its legendary founder, Gautama Buddha, as a human response to the unmitigated hardship and hopelessness of Gautama's social and political surroundings in the fifth and sixth centuries before Christ. Buddhism was never a religion, and it never developed any supranational clout.

Confucianism, meanwhile, was the measured response of a mind jaded by a hollow and animistic paganism that had been outlived by a sophisticated society. Confucianism is one of the noblest human failures ever to attempt to provide a life ethic of virtue and humanly beneficial works divorced from any particular belief, pagan or otherwise.

That ethical siren song has continued with a renewed potency into the era of rationalist rejection by many of any notion of revealed truth.

The most notable ethical invention of the nineteenth century, perhaps, was the Baha'i teaching. Designed as a system of social ethics that would suit all races of mankind—would be a geo-ethic, in fact—Baha'i excluded any and all religious content. Consequently, lacking that specific energy—that aim and passionate purpose—it has remained in the status of a localized way of life followed by a restricted number of people.

In an effort to correct that fault—to borrow such passion and transplant it—some ethical systems, particularly in the twentieth century, have attempted to mingle variations of Buddhism, Confucianism and the Baha'i with Western religious contexts. Predictably, however, the bland result of such continual borrowings and adaptations and retrofits has generally been a dilution both of the ethical system and of religious belief.

On the religious side of the supranational ledger, Judaism professedly and explicitly claims to be the religion and faith of the physical descendants of Abraham. It does and always has been willing to accept converts from all other religions. It does and always has maintained the universality of its great moral laws. But, properly speaking, ethnicity is endemic to Judaism. This of itself precludes a genuine georeligious note from Judaism.

When Islam, with its special brand of religious fervor, burst upon the

Middle Eastern scene, it was nothing if not a firebrand of international aim and ambition. In its spread, however, it became an international assemblage of local communities. And though those communities were marked by a close similarity in religious faith and in principles of moral behavior, there has been no unique, central authority—a lack clearly understood by the late Ayatollah Khomeini of Iran. Furthermore, even in its heyday of European conquest, Islam has never surpassed the cultural roots of its origins. Supranational and georeligious are not terms that suit Islam.

Still, if neither age, nor experiments and adaptations, nor religious fervor are enough in themselves to provide supranational capability, what about all those breakaway creations that have derived from Catholicism itself? Cannot at least some of them be looked to for the same supranational capabilities as the Roman institution? After all, the Orthodox Russian and Greek churches did accept the ancient councils that defined the basics of Christian dogma, faith and practice. What more of a beating heart could be needed?

Here again, however, those same limiting factors first faced by Peter and the early Apostles repeatedly raised their heads. For nationalist and racial themes have rarely been absent from the religion of Eastern Christianity in all its branches.

The two patriarchal sees of Constantinople and Moscow are the focal points of churches whose Christianity is steeped by now in the racial, cultural and linguistic characteristics of Greek and Slav respectively. And each is based on its own tradition of nationalism.

In his autobiography of 1988, Archbishop Iakovos, Greek Primate of North and South America, essentially joined his voice to that of the Greek Patriarch of Constantinople when he exulted in "the Orthodox [Greek and Russian] *oikumene*"—the lands and peoples who share the Eastern Orthodox faith. On the Greek side of that Orthodox *oikumene*, however, stand no fewer than thirteen independent (or "autocephalous") churches, plus four semi-independent (or "autonomous") churches, plus two monasteries, one on the Greek island of Patmos and one in the Sinai Peninsula. As to authority, the Patriarch of Constantinople is the titular head of this assemblage of churches, but only as the "first among equals." As in any federation, decisions are reached by a vote of consensus. One code of law governs all members; but enforcement and, to a degree, even interpretation of that code is left to each individual church or monastery.

In the Russian equation, meanwhile, Pimen, the late Patriarch of Moscow, did not seem to share Archbishop Iakovos's sense of ecumenism. Instead, he joined his predecessors in that patriarchate in speaking of a stubbornly separatist view—of "Mother Russia" and of the "Holy

Church of Mother Russia" as the focus of Church unity and the locus of its community.

Once such limiting factors as land and people take on a dominant role, things seem to splinter still further. Vasken I, the eighty-year-old Supreme Patriarch and Catholicos of All Armenians—a population of about 6.5 million worldwide—declared on February 5, 1989, in New York's Cathedral of St. John the Divine, that "we [Armenians] are one people with one mother Church, with one fatherland, with one destiny and one future." That one fatherland is Armenia. And that one mother Church is not composed of Eastern Orthodoxy's *oikumene;* or even of "Mother Russia." It is specifically defined as the fourth-century cathedral at Etchmiadzin near Yerevan, the capital of Soviet Armenia.

One way or another, that separatist pattern has been repeated by the many churches and splinter sects—sometimes calculated to be nearly three thousand in number—that resulted from the sixteenth-century Protestant revolt against the papacy.

Some have achieved an impressive growth. The Anglican community, though relatively small in membership, is a worldwide organization. But it, too, remains a federation of local churches, in which membership and principles of behavior and communal action are determined by consensus. No obloquy or disrepute attaches to those who secede from these associations; and no unique authority binds the community as a single unit.

Whatever the size of their membership or the structure they employ, few of the churches that trace their existence to the Roman Church of earlier centuries have escaped a more or less continual splintering into ever-smaller communities, whose aims, institutional organizations and authority all shrink with every new branch torn from each transplanted tree.

As to other religious organizations—post-Christian revisionist groups, for example, such as Unitarians, Mormons, Christian Scientists and Jehovah's Witnesses—it would be unrealistic to speak of any of them in terms of georeligious or supranational capability. And it would be fanciful for secular leaders—not a fanciful lot—to call upon such groups to galvanize the world against armed international oppression such as Hitler represented; or to enter an East-West dispute as a credible and effective arbiter among nations.

Even such a cursory survey can leave no doubt that by 1958, as the nineteen-year reign of Pope Pius XII drew to its close, he passed on to his successors an organization recognized by his secular peers as unique in the world as a global, supranational, independent and borderless power of immense proportions.

Everywhere they might look, in fact, other wielders of power in the world arena could see the particulars of the georeligious power of the Holy See. It lay in the major Vatican Congregations, or ministries, through which the Pope governs the religious and moral life of his global community. It lay in the far-flung ecclesial network of 1,920 dioceses comprising 211,156 parishes; and in some 3,000 bishops and 483,488 priests who tend those dioceses and parishes.

The lifeblood of all these and more—of the Vatican Congregations and everything they administer—is the personal authority of the Roman Pontiff. His coat of arms—the Keys of Peter beneath the triple tiara— placed over door lintels, stamped on letterheads, carved in wall plaques, embedded in official seals, is but one ever-present and never-fading statement of the source of that personal power. The holder of those Keys authorizes a living network of representatives to speak directly for him. He dispatches his own on-the-spot spokesmen abroad to act for him in at least ninety countries.

Those spokesmen in particular are not, any one of them, members of any local hierarchy. Nor are they dependent on any other source but the Pope for funds, instruction, moral support or inspiration as they cover the world, taking in all nations and every culture and religion. These personal representatives of the Holy Father are the twentieth-century version of the net Peter was bid by Jesus "to cast out over the deep waters."

Like any secular diplomatic corps, this personal papal network is divided into ranks of some complexity. In this case, the rankings go by such names as Apostolic Delegate, Nuncio, Pro-Nuncio, Internuncio, Chargé d'Affaires, Apostolic Delegate and Envoy, and so on through a diplomatic system as intricate and complete as the most sophisticated of its secular counterparts. Thus, each rank is designed to cover a particular type of mission. And each rank, each title and each mission functions as a working, living part of a global system of government and influence whose center is the Vatican and whose embodiment is the Pope himself in his international designation as the "Holy See."

What focuses the attention of these papal representatives and guides their practical judgments is not the status of their locales as precise and individual entities. It is the status of those locales as members of the global community.

What captures the unwavering attention of the secular leaders of the world in this remarkable network of the Roman Catholic Church is precisely the fact that it places at the personal disposal of the Pope a supranational, supracontinental, supra-trade-bloc structure that is so built and oriented that if tomorrow or next week, by a sudden miracle, a one-world government were established, the Church would not have to undergo any essential structural change in order to retain its dominant position and to further its global aims.

The most important facts and details about the Roman Church from the point of view of any secular power holder, however, all come down to one point. There is a tacit agreement among the great international political and financial leaders that the very attributes that give the Holy See its georeligious power and capability provide it, as well, with everything essential for the same power and capability on the political plane. In secular eyes, the Roman Church stands alone in every practical sense —and not merely among religious and ethical structures and groups—as the first fully realized, fully practicing and totally independent geopolitical force in the current world arena. And the Pope, as the sole legitimate head of the Holy See's organizational institution and structures—as the only one who fixes the overall goal of that institution's efforts—is by definition the world's first fully fledged geopolitical leader.

Of course, the Catholic Church did not freeze in its institutional tracks when Pius XII left the scene. Immediately after his death, in fact, and long before Cardinal Malula's plaintive cry "Everything must change!" there began a series of pontificates for which there were no precedents in all the turbulent history of the Holy See. No one—friend or enemy— could have been prepared for the changes that came so suddenly with the election of Angelo Cardinal Roncalli as Pope John XXIII, in October of 1958. "Good Pope John," as people sometimes liked to call him, became the first in a line of four popes to date who have taken up a new and hitherto unheard-of papal stance.

Overtly, and in so many words, John declared that in this age, in his moment as Holy Father, the Church had decided to open itself to the world in an unprecedented way, to engage in the affairs of men in a way that was never the Church's way for all its nineteen hundred years of history.

The first prime characteristic of the new papal stance as John XXIII presented it was summed up on one word: *aggiornamento*—an "updating," in which the Church would "open its windows," would open itself up to the world in a way for which there was no parallel in the reign of any of the 261 popes who had come before.

John, in fact, was quite explicit when he spoke to the bishops assembled in St. Peter's Basilica on October 11, 1962, at the opening of his

Second Vatican Council. Formerly, he said, the Church enforced the doctrine of faith by means of sanctions and punitive methods for violations of the papacy's teaching. This was now changing, he went on. The Church had decided, as Mother of all men's souls, to rely on explanation and dialogue in order to exact obedience, along with understanding, from its children. Why this change? Because, John explained, once the Church explains to a man the error of his ways and the correct doctrine of faith for belief and moral practice, he will accept it.

John XXIII's fundamental error here was to believe in a sort of natural goodness in all men and women, a goodness of such a kind that it could *and would* prevent them from following the dictates of evil—the evil in themselves as a remnant of Original Sin, and the evil around them borne by "the world, the Devil and the flesh." It was, on the Pontiff's part, a grave misunderstanding of a sacred Church dogma, and at the same time, a piece of naïveté that is hard to understand in a man of his wide pastoral experience.

But, in fact, by that decision, John had misleadingly renounced one chief function of the Holder of the Keys of authority given him as Peter's successor. Technically, it was—perhaps all unconsciously—an act of misfeasance in high office. Practically speaking, it provided for the anti-Church and the superforce just the opening they needed to overturn the authority of Peter. If only John had lived to see how that "natural goodness" reacted to *Humanae Vitae*, the encyclical letter of his successor, Paul VI, about the inherent sinfulness of contraceptive methods! If only he could have foreseen that two thirds of the Church's bishops would, by 1975, have taken his words as a cue to them that they could cease to be authoritative pastors, cease indeed to obey papal laws and observe papal wishes!

John XXIII's application of his new principle of Church government was just as counterproductive when it was applied to the difficult relationship between the Church and the Soviet Union.

The second major characteristic of this astounding change demonstrated in a practical way just how profound its implications were for international affairs in the geopolitical arena. For suddenly, after so many years of such mighty efforts to break the Holy See's uncompromising attitude toward Leninist Marxism, the Soviet Union was dumbfounded to find itself included within the scope of personal and official papal attention.

John XXIII engaged in a personal correspondence with Soviet Party Chief Nikita Khrushchev. He received Khrushchev's son-in-law, *Izvestia* editor Aleksei Adzhubei, in the Pope's private library. And—most stunning of all after more than forty years of muscular and untempered enmity—John made an agreement with Khrushchev: In the Second Vatican Council, which the Pope had announced as the very vehicle of his Church's new opening to the world, there would be no official condemnation by the Holy See of the Soviet Union, or of its Leninist Marxism.

If the world was dazed by Pope John's words and actions, it was not unwilling to capitalize on the "windows" he opened so trustingly, or to enter as many of the geopolitical structures as it found suddenly unlocked, or to contribute to the Church's "updating" in ways John had neither foreseen nor intended.

Such problems notwithstanding, each of the three popes who have succeeded John XXIII has ratified and carried on the new and radical papal stance he introduced.

John's immediate successor, Pope Paul VI, amplified both the policy of *aggiornamento* and the new attitude toward the Soviet bloc. Grandiosely, and perhaps too loosely, Paul announced that not only were the Church's windows open but the preoccupation of the Church now was "man in all his works and ambitions to build a secure home on this earth."

As to the Leninist Marxism so freely exported by the Soviet Union, Pope Paul went so far as to inaugurate official protocol talks in view of eventual relations with the Soviet satellites of Eastern Europe; and to throw his weight behind the Soviet opposition to the American cause in Vietnam.

Brief as the next pontificate was, Paul VI's successor, Pope John Paul I, had no time to indicate what policies he had in mind concerning the Soviet Union and its satellites. But he did find time to speak of the Church "walking with man through all the highways and byways of man's pilgrimage." Clearly, he had no intention of closing those windows.

John Paul II is the fourth in this revolutionary line of popes that began barely twenty years to the month before his own election. Characteristically, he had understood everything that had come before. And he was frank about his own orientation in the selfsame direction.

John Paul's own rule of behavior concerning the opening of his Church to "man in all his works and ambitions to build a secure home on this earth" was the subject of his first encyclical letter, published at Easter 1979.

In a pointed rhetorical question, the new Pontiff asked, What ministry "has become my specific duty in this See . . . with my acceptance of my election as Bishop of Rome and Successor of the Apostle Peter"?

His answer was categoric. He would take up with new energy and purpose where the previous three popes had left off: "It falls to me not only to continue it [his predecessors' policy] but, in a certain sense, to take it up again at the same starting point. . . . I wish to express my love for the unique inheritance left to the Church by Popes John XXIII and Paul VI. . . . They represent a stage to which I wish to refer directly as a threshold from which I intend to continue."

In that encyclical letter, John Paul was already more specific than his predecessors in speaking publicly of his papal intentions. And his words were those of a leader who could be expected to initiate still more changes in his papal dealings with the world. "We are in a new season of Advent," the Pope observed, "a season of expectation. . . . We can rightly ask at this new stage: How should we continue? What should we do in order that this new advent of the Church, connected with the approaching end of the Second Millennium, bring us closer to Him whom Sacred Scripture calls 'Everlasting Father'? This is the fundamental question that a new Pope must ask himself."

Referring to his institution as "the Church that I, through John Paul I, have had entrusted to me almost immediately after him," John Paul underlined his understanding of the new papal stance that had begun with John XXIII, and his understanding of what he called "the Church's consciousness" of "that most important point of the visible world that is man," and the Church's "awareness of apostolates." And then, in his turn, John Paul pledged that this new "Church consciousness must go with universal openness."

John Paul having made himself clear on the subject of *aggiornamento*, there could be little doubt that he would regard the change of papal attitude toward the USSR as of capital importance—and one that was right up his apostolic alley. For it was, after all, a policy followed in essence by every Polish Churchman in order to assure not merely the survival of the Catholic institution in that land, but its living force in every sector of public and private life of the nation. He had no intention of letting the Eastern European policy inaugurated by John XXIII and pursued by Paul VI continue on in its sterility. That *Ostpolitik* was nothing more than a connivance with the dreadful status quo the Soviets had imposed. John Paul intended to behave as Polish Churchmen had reacted to Stalinism—actively, not connivingly.

In the light of what he said in that early encyclical, and in the light of his own background as priest and bishop in Poland, Pope John Paul's early meetings with Soviet Foreign Minister Andrei Gromyko need not have been so puzzling as they seemed to some. And the rumors that surfaced so quickly that the Pope would go to Poland need not have been so surprising. For both were signals not only that he intended to bypass the *Ostpolitik* of John XXIII and Paul VI, but that he had long since mastered the art of dealing with the rough men of the Kremlin.

Nothing of John Paul's early attitude, or his confidence, or the finesse of his understanding with respect to the Soviet Union, was altered by the advent—to use the Pope's own pointed word—of Mikhail Gorbachev on the Soviet and world scene. In April of 1989, following the news that Gorbachev planned a visit to Italy that fall, John Paul was asked by newsmen during his papal visit to Mauritania if he would receive the Soviet leader in the Vatican. The Pontiff showed no hesitation and no confrontational mentality. "I would meet him as a head of state," John Paul answered, "as the head of a system, a large state."

That John Paul meant to emphasize a political framework and a geopolitical purpose in any such meeting with Gorbachev became clear when a follow-up question speculated too boldly about a possible answering visit by the Pope to the USSR. "No!" John Paul was emphatic. "A Vatican meeting with Mr. Gorbachev should not be linked to a possible papal visit to the Soviet Union—that possibility is something else, because that is a Church matter." It was one thing for the Pope to grant an audience, as head of Vatican State, to a visiting head of state. It was quite a different matter for the Pope to visit an officially godless state that actively persecuted all believers.

Nice distinctions made by John Paul to the press in far-off lands, distinctions between the georeligious and the geopolitical power of the papacy, were all very fine. But, in Rome and elsewhere, the comparison was quickly made—gleefully by some, glumly by others—between the attitude of John Paul II and that, to take but one possible example, of Pope Pius XI toward Adolf Hitler.

When the jackbooted German dictator visited his Italian ally, Benito Mussolini, in Rome in 1938, Pius XI didn't hesitate in his response; and he made no nice distinctions. He closed all Vatican buildings, right down to the last museum; and then he retired to his villa at Castel Gandolfo, outside the city, until the "Nordic pest," to quote one man in the papal entourage, had left Rome and gone back to Germany.

But the differences between a Pius XI or a John XXIII, on the one hand, and a John Paul II, on the other, lay in their individual circumstances and in their papal policies. Pius XI's policy was "hands off." John XXIII's and Paul VI's was "open hands." Both were reactive—if not reactionary—policies. John Paul's policy, characteristically, was active, even aggressive in its own way. Neither Pius XI nor John XXIII was faced on a daily basis with organized enmity in his own household. John Paul has to live with the superforce he cannot dislodge from his Vatican, and he must reckon with the network of anti-Church partisans spread throughout the length and breadth of his Church Universal.

With both superforce and anti-Church, he must reckon as with enemies of his Petrine Office. He is aware of their intent. He has experienced their strength. But, he knows—or thinks he knows—that his main battle and objective do not lie in that direction. Rather, he and his grand papal policy are oriented outward. He does not hold up those Keys of authority in order to quell that in-house opposition. There's no point to that, for they no longer believe in the divine authority of those Keys. They firmly believe in the power and prestige of a pope as one more secular head. And they desire that power and prestige for themselves and for the obscure Master they serve.

But in the face of the geopolitical world, John Paul relies on the authority symbolized by those scarlet Keys, the "Keys of this Blood." Precisely because of his unique power and status as head of that georeligious and geopolitical colossus, the Roman Catholic Church, his analysis of his secular counterparts has to be weighed into the balance of an accurate judgment about this extraordinary Pope.

Part Two

The Lay of the Land

6. The Morality of Nations: Whatever Happened to Sinful Structures?

The competition into which Pope John Paul II has entered, and upon which he appears to have staked everything, was fired by two great booster engines of modern vintage, and largely of American invention, that have already lifted the entire world into a new orbit of human activity and values.

The first booster engine was the helter-skelter global rush to material development, a factor that never before operated among all the nations of the world simultaneously.

That first engine fired the second: a genuinely global entrepreneurship that, once ignited, has worked in steady tandem with the first to create the conditions that are propelling the world into a single geopolitical community.

The firing up of the first engine—that rush to material development—was made possible by the worldwide economic-financial hegemony of the United States in the years immediately following World War II. And the force that fired it was the celebrated technological creativity of Americans.

Once scientific technology was harnessed to American entrepreneurship, the first test orbit into the atmosphere of the good life was successfully achieved. More and better things were produced for every sector of life: for the home, the company, the city, the state, the federal government. American innovations in everything from basic home appliances to convenience and luxury goods, and from agricultural methods to military equipment—not to mention the manufacturing and management systems that were produced along the way—developed a postwar culture that very soon became the envy and the objective of other nations.

In the world of the early 1900s, such development might have remained very much indigenous to the North American continent. In the postwar world, it could not. The United States was rebuilding Europe and Japan. The American dollar anchored local currencies around the world, and whatever kind of international monetary system prevailed. The United Nations, itself headquartered in the United States, brought new nations out of their ancient cultures and into newly born but materially backward nationalisms.

"The world," said Winston Churchill in 1954—not ten years after the end of World War II—"has grown frighteningly small in compass; and astride it stands the American colossus, whose strength and girth none can match, but whose clothes we all wish to wear."

The primary purpose of the United States in its technological drive and in its entrepreneurship was economic and financial. The business of America, just as Calvin Coolidge had said in 1929, was still business— balanced budgets; bottom lines in very black ink; a sound dollar.

Such a primary drive had been at work in the U.S.A. since its founding. The culture of Americans—both as a mosaic of immigrant cultures and as a singularly American creation—grew and adapted itself to the quick transformations that changed the quality of life in the nation from 1900 onward. But it was the immense growth and progress of American industrialization, triggered by World War II and by postwar American entrepreneurship, that brought the United States uninterruptedly and without any jarring changes to the threshold of the technotronic era.

By 1960, the American "pursuit of happiness" was concretized in the attainment of the "good life." And "good" referred primarily to life made easy, leisurely and materially pleasurable. It referred to the quality of life that could be achieved with the introduction of modern technological inventions for the individual, the family, the company, the city, the state and the nation. It was much more than "two chickens in every pot and a car in every garage." There was a profound change in the moral quality of American life.

By 1960, as well—and largely because the U.S.A. was so deeply involved in the postwar rebuilding of Europe and Japan—the drive for material development had been jump-started in the nations and was sputtering to life around the world. The good life as portrayed in America became the ideal of nations, whether they were in a preindustrial condition or already possessed some degree of industrialization, great or small.

A lot of fuel was poured into the big new engines of development and entrepreneurship. Worldwide communications—principally television, news networks, and the American film industry—told underdeveloped, undeveloped and developing nations more about the good life than any government brochure. American tourism, which became an important source of annual income and increased wealth for many nations, performed the same task. The increasing importance of the United Nations, and the increasing pace of decolonization of scores of nations in Africa and Asia, emphasized the importance of economic dignity. Undeveloped and underdeveloped nations reclaimed for themselves the right to exploit their own natural resources.

In what seemed no time at all, the full tilt toward development, American style, became quasi universal. The goods of the good life nourished the urge everywhere to develop *à la Américaine*. The automobile replaced the camel in Saudi Arabia. The tea merchant posted outside Beit-El-Ajaib in Zanzibar's Stone Town offered his patrons a Kleenex with every plastic container of lemon tea. The drone of village gossip in Tralee, Ireland, was lost in the blare of "Family Feud" and "Wheel of Fortune," beamed in by satellite. The bark of Alaskan sled huskies was supplanted by the roar of snowmobiles in Prudhoe Bay. Mukluks were replaced by Mars Bars; and the sewer system in Barrow, Alaska (pop. 3,000), was heated at an annual cost of $239 million.

In the Philippines, in Calcutta, in Glasgow, householders planned wall-to-wall carpeting in Manhattan Blue. In Kuwait, refrigerators were cast in Lagoon Blue. Automobiles in Tropical Avocado purred around Panama City. The flea markets of Europe offered Navajo headbands, American Indian earth-mother ornaments in turquoise and silver, and Levi's jeans. The Cuisinart vied with the laptop computer in the annual budgets of Cairo and Malaysia.

Even in the late 1980s, when the financial hegemony of the United States had been displaced, and its military hegemony had been successfully challenged by the USSR, the good life American-style continued to be the desired end product among nations, the aim that inspired them to development. Sales of American television programming, which had reached $1 billion by 1987 and was projected at $2.3 billion by 1990, continued to bring the good life as portrayed in "Dallas" and "Falcon Crest" to a widening world of converts. In 1988, meanwhile, American movies—everything from *Rambo* to *Rain Man*—brought $1.1 billion to the United States from abroad.

By that time, the booster engines of development and entrepreneurship had fired the main engine of trilateral global dominance. The United States was joined by Western Europe and Japan in the race for the future. Just as America had had its land rush and its gold rush, so now the world had its development rush. And it was the fast track along which a new breed—pioneers of genuinely global entrepreneurship— would ride hell-for-leather. The old-fashioned American entrepreneur was replaced by a new breed on a new frontier. The new cry wasn't "Gold!" but "Economic Utopia!"

For all its momentum and power and excitement, however, there was trouble from the start in the emergent Utopia. The development produced by the new entrepreneurs was unevenly spread among the nations. At the end of the 1980s almost four fifths of the world population, though tantalized by the good life, had no share in it. From one year and one decade of superdevelopment to the next, most men and women saw no substantial improvement in their economic condition, no solid hope that the bleak landscape of their present lives would not stretch into long and grim tomorrows for their children, and for their children's children.

On the shores of the Atlantic, John Paul II himself has spoken to the golden-skinned Brazilian youths who still sport carefree on the beaches of Rio and dream of moving to one of the money meccas in the United States or Europe. And he has seen the favellas teeming with families, whose more meager dreams wash down muddy hillsides along with their tiny hovels when the rains come to Rio year after year, every year. The rich remain comfortable. Nothing changes.

In the middle of the Pacific, John Paul has seen the millionaires who flourish in the Alabang Hills and Corinthian Plaza in Metro Manila, within sight of deathly slums. He knows what it means that the Hacienda Luisita of Philippine President Corazon Aquino's family, the Cojuangcos, still dominates the serfs of Tarlac Province. He understands why revolutionaries like Father Jesús Bolweg, S.J., and his fellow priests and nuns still die in Philippine mountain fastnesses alongside Communist guerrillas. The rich remain comfortable. Nothing changes.

Among some global entrepreneurs there are signs that a certain well-founded anxiety has replaced the original mechanistic and certainly naive optimism of their vision. Even such an inward-looking and self-concentrated nation as Japan has been forced to consider how "to adapt . . . to sharing the burdens and responsibilities in the world economy," as the problem was delicately phrased in 1989 by Keiya Toyonaga, Senior Managing Director of Matsushita.

Anxiety or no, the movement toward the realization of a global community within a geopolitical framework advances along the track of the good life. Happiness is bought and sold by the new breed of global entrepreneur. But the price of entry is far from common coin.

It is upon this world that John Paul's Church, with its own supranational organization already in place, has opened its windows. It is this humanly anomalous situation—the situation in which the have-not majority of the human race is being pulled by forces beyond its control toward a destiny not of its own free choosing—that is the focus of much of the Pontiff's attention and impels his crisscross global travels, unparalleled among world leaders.

It is no surprise to the new pioneers of global development that John Paul II has made a moral appraisal of his contemporaries as people preparing—or being prepared—to become a geopolitical community. Nor can it be a surprise to those pioneers that by "moral" the Pope does not mean their own newly defined set of values measured in the goods of the good life. For all the "updating" that has gone on in his Church, the assessment John Paul makes is provided by that taproot of human morality that reaches into the very soil in which Christianity began.

When John Paul speaks to his secular peers in the world arena of development about his own moral appraisal, he does not have in mind merely local adaptations of pop jargon, or even noble-sounding phrases ringing out in the midst of fiery conflicts.

Through their spokesmen demonstrating in Beijing in April and May of 1989, the Pontiff heard the cry of hundreds of thousands of Chinese students that "democracy is as much a moral issue as a political one." And he understood the wide appeal of the students' reasoned explanation that "moral" in their context meant that "officials must be prevented from exploiting the people and the country's resources."

At about the same time, John Paul observed the controversy in Moscow over the Lenin Mausoleum in Red Square, where the mummified body of Vladimir I. Lenin has brought endless queues of viewers for over sixty-five years. "The body should be buried in the ground," contended Mark Zakharov, director of the Leninsky Komsomol Theater.

Not so, huffed Central Committee candidate Ratmir S. Babonikov. "Lingering over such issues is simply immoral . . . Zakharov's proposal is blasphemous and a sign of *glasnost* gone amok."

The Communist daily *Pravda* sounded the voice of Soviet reason, declaring that "we must not venerate the corpse of Comrade Lenin but his cause." Not to be outdone, Central Committee member Aleksei P. Myasnikor argued that "what was said by Zakharov about the most sacred thing, Lenin, is worse than incomprehensible."

Incomprehensible was the word for it. Given the ethical limits of morality to be expected among young Chinese today; and given the professional atheistic Marxism current in the Soviet Union, John Paul finds the use of such words as "moral" and "immoral" and "blasphemous" and "venerate" and "sacred" emptied of all religious understanding. They have become hollow vessels to be filled with the passions and the intentions of the moment. When the next desperate occasion arises, the same vessels will be emptied again, and filled with other passions, other fleeting intentions.

John Paul has made it clear enough that in speaking of "morality" and the "morality of nations"—for since the moment of his election as Pope, he has done so constantly in public and in private with great leaders and hopeful pretenders in the emergent geopolitical race—his meaning for those words is identical with the Christian meaning preached and vindicated by the Roman Catholic Church from its beginnings. In fact, John Paul insists that the meaning and the drive and the power of morality cannot be eradicated in the lives of men and women. For human morality itself derives from one most basic fact: Because God created man in his own image and likeness by endowing him with an indestructible principle of being—a principle of being called a soul—in all that mankind does, the important dimension is spiritual, is a thing of man's soul and its spiritual values.

That fact is so basic that it holds true for all man does, even for what he does economically and financially.

Moreover, because God created all men as one family, there is a radical unity, a unity at the base of all human activity that makes each individual his brother's keeper. On the other side of that coin of caring is the parallel fact that, because God gave the material cosmos and all things in it into the custody of the family of man, all men and women have a basic right to what they need for the sustenance of life and for their reasonable prosperity and enjoyment.

However, because God found it necessary to send his only son, Jesus of Nazareth, to sacrifice his life by dying on a Roman cross, there must be a significant condition of man's soul and being—a condition of spirit —that needs repairing and help. There must be an evil let loose among mankind that can only be thwarted by Jesus' saving power as God's Son. There must, in other words, be actions of men and women that need forgiveness through Jesus, because they offend against God's laws about the family unity of mankind, and about the right of all individuals and groups to their due share of the earth's goods.

The Christian meaning of human morality has always come from these beliefs. And from these beliefs come John Paul's moral assessments. What is morally good, says this Pope, in one voice with all the popes who have preceded him, respects those laws of God about the family unity of mankind and about individual rights. What is morally bad breaks those laws, and is called sin.

Because it was only to Simon Peter, the chief of his Apostles, and to Simon Peter's lawful successors in the Holy See, that Jesus confided the Keys of his moral authority, the Roman Catholic Church has always claimed—and, under John Paul II, claims today—to be the ultimate arbiter of what is morally good and morally bad in human actions. Those Keys, sanctified and strengthened in the blood of Jesus himself, are the symbol and the substance of John Paul's insistence upon a moral assessment of the world he travels and monitors so closely.

Among people who adapt such words as "sacred" and "blasphemy" to the problem of what to do with Lenin's corpse, there will be difficulties in accepting the moral content of the Christian vocabulary as it has always been used by the Roman Church, and as it is used by Pope John Paul everywhere he goes.

How much more difficult, then, is the fact that in the present context of the emerging global community—in the context of what the pioneers are doing economically and financially and ideologically in the family of man—John Paul is talking about something beyond the moral assessment of individuals. He is talking about structures, about the moral assessment of structures that not only have been built, but are already expanding rapidly according to a blueprint that will guarantee the mutual interdependence of nations in a global system of economics and governance.

What sort of moral critique can a Christian—pope or otherwise—make of a structure? And what sort of secular mover and shaker will listen to him if he does? After all, except in a purely metaphorical way—and probably just to feed human emotions—how can a Roman Catholic or anyone else assert that a structure is sinful? That a structure commits a sin? That a structure is guilty of a sin?

Let's face it: Even atheists know the Church teaches that sin is, first and only, personal. It involves the choice of individual will in a man or woman who freely and knowingly violates God's revealed law. In strict theological language, as anybody will tell you, there is no such thing as collective sin; the sin of a group. Much less, then, can a structure—whether formed of stones and wood, or of bureaucratic arrangements—be said to commit sin, to be sinful, to be in a state of sin.

John Paul may be the fourth in the line of revolutionary popes that began with John XXIII. But he will brook no such arguments about sinful structures. And in that, his theology is one with that of every pope who came before him. In insisting that slavery as an institution was a moral evil that would explode, the Church of the fifteenth and sixteenth centuries was making a moral assessment of a sinful structure and of the huge harm that would come from it. In insisting that Leninist-Marxist institutions constituted a moral evil that would provoke untold misery for millions of people and that should not be connived at by the West, John Paul is at one with every pope since Pius IX in the nineteenth century, who kept up steady warnings of the danger and harm such institutions would bring in their train for everybody.

World-class theologian that he is, John Paul understands more than the theological precedents of history. His "sinful structures" argument is based on unchanging solid principles; and it proceeds with inexorable logic.

As Christians and Roman Catholics, he insists, we not only can but must speak of "sinful structures" when we find that such structures are created by men and women who are inspired *uniquely* by economic, financial, political or ideological gain. For in acting out of such motives alone, the builders of such structures violate at least the First Commandment, which forbids the worship of false gods.

When money, ideology, class or technological development dictates exclusively how we behave, then we are in effect worshiping idols, just as surely as if we were to set up a golden calf in the Sinai of our world, ascribe omnipotence to it, and give it our obeisance and adoration.

In that sort of situation, at least one and probably two sinful intentions are operative: an all-consuming desire for profit; and the thirst for power. In fact, as these human attitudes and propensities are built into the structures of our society, they are not merely operative; they quickly become absolutized. They dominate our thoughts, our intentions and our actions. They become the household gods on the mantels of our structures.

The structures themselves, therefore, are rooted in the personal sins linked to the choices and the concrete acts of the individuals who design and introduce those structures, consolidate them, promote them, build their lives on them, define success in their terms, and make those structures difficult to remove.

As such structures grow stronger and spread farther, they become the source of other personal sins. They influence the behavior of increasing numbers of individuals, leading them in turn to violate God's moral law and thus to commit sin.

The originators of those structures have, in other words, introduced into the everyday world of men and women influences and obstacles that last far beyond the actions and brief life span of any individual. The structures are the vehicles of their sins, and can aptly and accurately be described as "sinful structures."

As he has traveled throughout the world, one of Pope John Paul's main purposes from the start has been to establish a positive agreement with his peers in this matter of moral values. He has sought an understanding, however rudimentary, about a specifically human value that the secular pioneers among the nations would agree is distinct from all other values, whether those values are cultural, political, ideological, economic, financial, nationalistic or sectarian.

The context of these conversations, of course, is never a pie-in-the-sky exchange of religious or philosophical views. Whether in meeting with President Ronald Reagan in Miami in September 1988, or with Captain Blaise Campaoré, dictator of Burkina Faso, in the capital, Ouagadougou, in January 1990, or with President Hissen Habré of Chad on the following day in the capital, N'Djamena, or in any of the scores of other such encounters, the context is always the growing interdependence of modern nations.

From the outset of his pontificate, John Paul has found increasing awareness among his peers about what is happening in world affairs. Though some were as articulate in their practical judgment about those affairs as John Paul, all have demonstrated at least a growing intuition about the two primary forces that are reshaping the world in the final decade of the millennium. Everyone he has spoken to agrees with the Pope at some level that there is in the making nothing less than a *world system*, determining relationships between all the nations that constitute human society.

And predictably enough, all agree with him that this world system— this newly minted and all-encompassing interdependence that is coming into existence—includes economic, political, cultural and sectarian elements.

What was less predictable for many onlookers was the success John Paul has achieved in hammering home what he is certain is the most basic fact of all: the fact that interdependence among nations must be based upon some common agreement as to moral good and moral evil in modern life. And, further, that if such common agreement cannot be reached as a working basis of globalism, then all attempts at establishing a new world order will end only in disaster.

It is true, of course, that most of the Pope's counterparts in the arena of developing global interdependence among nations do not talk about "moral values"—at least, not in those precise words. But almost anybody will talk about environmental pollution as a moral evil, and about an institution that causes pollution as a sinful structure. In the same way, there is general agreement, for instance, that to forestall and finally to prevent sub-Saharan famine would be a moral good or benefit to the whole community of nations.

Among both capitalist and Leninist internationalists, as well as in the nations pulled irresistibly along in their wake, John Paul has found many men and women of faith who do entertain some deeply rooted concept of moral good and moral evil in our lives. He has found many who recognize even that truly human life involves a moral value that they do identify as a demand of God's will, and as the only valid foundation of an ethic that is absolutely binding on all individuals, themselves included. He has talked with many more who have no explicit faith, but who nonetheless admit that the obstacles to the development of nations rest on profound "attitudes" that human beings can "decide" to regard as absolute values.

The one thing John Paul has not found in his papal travels, in fact, is any disagreement with him about the need for a binding ethic that must obligate the whole society of nations. Christian believers and crypto-believers, nonreligious believers and positive atheists—even those who have a diehard antireligious attitude and policy—all are prepared to go that far with the Pontiff.

Many differ with him about the source of any such binding ethic, and about its details. But, by and large, John Paul has found most secular leaders profess a deep respect for the great spiritual values.

If not all of his secular peers place spiritual and moral achievement at the top of their daily agenda of things to do, they have nevertheless all agreed with the Pontiff that, in the concrete and practical actions between the nations, there is a human element—a human law—in all mankind's activity that cannot be reduced to material necessity alone, or to any law of material forces.

Again, not every secular leader agrees with Pope John Paul that man was created by God for a divine destiny, and that moral primacy in human life and affairs is bound up in the matrix of eternity. Nevertheless, not one leader has expressed any doubt to John Paul that the spiritual value of man finds expression in religious and moral codes, which in turn have direct and profound effects on cultures and civilizations.

Above all, even the most cantankerous secular leaders do all agree with what everyone sees as John Paul's inescapably practical and very this-worldly proposition: Unless that mysterious element innate to every man, woman and child on earth—that element which John Paul analyzes in the unrelenting terms of morality and immorality—is defined and accepted in the new world order as the very basis of its structures and its aims and its day-to-day activities, then whatever is built by way of geopolitical structure will only lead to greater human misery.

In that unrelenting moral analysis of Pope John Paul and his expert advisers, the globalist pioneers who are his peers in the world arena fall, broadly speaking, into four principal groups.

There are the so-called Wise Men of the West, together with their Internationalist and Transnationalist associates in the Western world. This group has the longest experience in developing a specific socioeconomic policy tied to an underlying political ideal. Then there are the oil-rich Arab nations. And there are the "Asian Tigers"—Japan, South Korea and Taiwan—to whom Thailand, Singapore, Malaysia and Indonesia are already acceding as peers. And finally there is the surprise late entry: the Soviet Union of Mikhail Gorbachev, together with the full panoply of its Eastern European empire; its surrogates abroad—today, mainly Cuba, Angola, Syria and Vietnam; and its loose hangers-on, such as the Ethiopia of Mengistu Haile Mariam, Colonel Qaddafi's Libya, and Marxist Benin.

Because of Gorbachev's remarkably sophisticated approach to the new geopolitical dimension of human affairs, and because of the Soviet leader's position atop the only other geopolitical structure already built and functioning in the world, John Paul sees Gorbachev as unique among his peers in the world arena. But the Pope also understands that even Gorbachev has been constrained by concrete circumstances—mainly the grievous errors of his own predecessors and the ebullient economic-financial strength of the Internationalists and Transnationalists—to join in the current pre-geopolitical preparations.

In other words, neither Gorbachev nor his refurbished Leninist internationalism can escape what John Paul has identified as the hallmark condition of our age: our universally experienced interdependence. Gorbachev has had to enter that arena along with everybody else. At least as far as his spoken and written words go, he apparently wishes to become a peer. And, were he to disappear tomorrow from the supreme leadership of the Soviet Union, his own "opening up" of the USSR to the world—like the analogous "opening up" of John Paul's Church—has already gone so far that, with him or without him, the fact of change is irreversible.

That Gorbachev himself agrees on this point was made clear in the summer of 1989. During his visit to Paris, he was asked on July 5 if his innovative course would survive should he "disappear from the scene." Referring to himself in the third person after the manner of Genghis Khan, Napoleon Bonaparte and General de Gaulle, the General Secretary's answer was categoric and confident: "My policies do not have to be tied to Gorbachev himself."

So powerful is this global tide that even important nations, such as India, that have insisted on their "nonaligned" status either will coast with the smaller nations on the periphery of events or will ride on the backs of the dominant players, drawn irresistibly along in the contest for political, economic, financial and ideological dominance in the formation of the new world order.

Yet, as powerful as that tide is, the juncture at which the architects and builders of global development and interdependence find themselves is so critical that, whether they love him or hate him, they are all but forced to look closely at Pope John Paul's moral analysis. They examine every detail of the Pontiff's moral assessment of themselves as pioneers of human life as they expect it to be lived in the twenty-first century. They carefully inspect his moral assessment of the nations that are, without exception, being re-formed before our eyes.

They test his moral analysis of the new structures that bind us all ever more closely in a common fate. Above all, they find themselves agreeing with his principle that it is impossible to understand how to proceed from this point unless there is agreement as to how we all—as a society of nations—arrived at this point in the road. The lay of the land ahead has been determined by what the nations have effected in the land already traveled.

7. The Morality of Nations:
Rich Man, Poor Man . . .

If there were such a thing as a historical map of shame—a map colored with the terrible consequences of sinful structures of bygone days—great human atrocities inevitably produced by those structures would loom as the tallest, grimmest mountains dominating that map.

Nearest the United States in place but the most distant in time would be the pre-Columbian institutions of Latin America that regularly and by accepted law doomed tens of thousands yearly to brutal death. It is difficult for us even to imagine fifty thousand people garroted and eviscerated on the same day and in the same place. Institutionalized impoverishment of over eight million Irish during the worst centuries of English Penal Codes, Ottoman Turk attempts to liquidate all Armenians, Stalin's cool disposing of fifteen million Ukrainians, Hitler's dreadful "Final Solution" spelled out in numbers running to six million Jews, the Allied betrayal of some hundreds of thousands of Slavs back into Stalin's hands and certain murder, the liquidation of the East Timorese by the central Indonesian government—this would be a partial list of such promontories and peaks of human horror on a historical map of shame.

If there were such a thing as a contemporary map of shame—a map of shame in our world now, as it is being prepared for its geopolitical debut at the end of the second millennium—that map would be dominated by whole new mountain ranges of institutionalized exploitation. It would be dominated by structures and by systems of structures that foster, connive at or simply allow the domination of eighty percent of the world's population by the other twenty percent.

In short, that contemporary map of shame would be the graphic expression of the atrocity we have come to describe so blandly as the division of the world into North and South, which is to say, in plainer terms, the division of nations, and of populations within nations, into rich and poor. Such a map of shame might find some way to show us the homeless, the refugees and the stateless—the human throwaways of our new world—who increase in their millions year by year, region by region, nation by nation.

Such a map would surely show the enormity of the most active volcano in our midst, formed by the greater part of our human family, which can be said to go to bed hungry and wake up miserable, with no hope today, tomorrow, next year that the coagulated mass of their suffering will be diluted and reduced and finally eliminated.

It is just such a map of shame that Pope John Paul does hold up to the world in his moral assessment of the geopolitical arrangements that are setting up our future for us. In his private conversations with the architects of those arrangements, in his meetings with secular leaders, in his speeches delivered in the Vatican and around the world, in his speeches and encyclicals delivered to the faithful of his Church, Pope John Paul's constant theme is the moral and human unacceptability of this appalling mountain chain of human suffering and injustice. And his constant warning is that those mountains will either be reduced by our willingness to change or, by the very weight of their own misery, come crashing down upon all our hopes as human beings, shattering all our selfish visions of the good life, and burying in their rubble whatever peace we might have thought to fashion in our single-minded rush to development.

On the modern map of world shame that is the subject of so much of John Paul's attention, North and South do not figure as precise geographical terms. Instead, they are the global frontiers where wealth and poverty divide not only nations, but societies within nations. They are the frontiers by which most of humanity is systematically and deliberately separated from any share in the prosperity and enjoyment of life to which each of us has a basic moral claim.

Deliberately. That is the operative principle. For, in his assessment, John Paul leaves no doubt that in the North-South division of the world, the North countries—steeped for the most part by now in their preoccupation with the race to superdevelopment—are steeped as well in immoral complicity in the sinful structures that contribute to and perpetuate the sufferings in the South countries. He leaves no doubt in the mind of anyone he speaks to that the multiple structures based in the North countries—industrial, financial, monetary, fiscal, political—line the pockets of many in the North and a few in the South, while the suffering of millions is prolonged beyond endurance. By definition, those structures must be called sinful.

To the discomfort of more than a few, John Paul underlines two main characteristics of the North. The first is its advanced state of industrialization. The North countries have a head start of immense size in regional and global entrepreneurship, and a growing—almost monopolistic —participation in the recent advances of the technotronic era.

The second main characteristic of the North is financial domination. Domination in the worldwide flow, management and use of capital and of manufactured goods. This wealth provides the North, among many other things, with a capacity for extensive investment in the South countries, and a capacity to make financial loans to the South.

By contrast, John Paul defines the South in terms of a series of crippling conditions that he has seen firsthand and whose details fill hundreds of reports that reach him yearly. These are conditions that only deepen and widen the already enormous gap that separates the South from the North countries.

Illiteracy; no possibility of higher education; economic and social inability to join in building one's nation; discrimination that cuts deep ravines along religious, social, political and financial lines; denial of the right to economic initiative; inadequate housing; helter-skelter urbanization by millions as a last resort for mere survival; widespread unemployment and underemployment. This is but a partial litany of those crippling conditions—a minisurvey of the vermin endemic to the South and eating away at its vitals.

That these same conditions are becoming a plague in some areas in the North countries—even though they are still limited and usually controllable—is something John Paul takes as a preliminary tap on the shoulder of the North countries, as part of Heaven's early warning system to the North's leaders and citizens alike that institutionalized moral evil travels ever so easily back to bite the hands that feed it.

It is as obvious to the Pontiff as it is to many others that, beset by such an array of crippling conditions, the South countries cannot lift themselves by their own bootstraps out of their continuing poverty. At the same time, however, it is just as obvious that in their present ways of working, the much vaunted international trade, financial and monetary systems of the North cannot mesh and harmonize adequately with the limited possibilities of the South. That pair of basic facts is highlighted in every facet of the relationship—if it can be called that—between North and South countries.

Take, for instance, the billions of dollars in so-called foreign aid, and the billions more in profligate loans that have already been poured by the developed North countries into Africa, Asia and Latin America. What effect, the Pontiff has asked pointedly more than once, and in more than one way, can come from aid or from loans when there is lacking in the South any adequate infrastructure—physical, social, technological, educational—onto which the North's cooperation can be grafted?

The overall answer to that critical question can be written by too many millions—if they can write at all—with one word: "tragedy." But "dangerous" might not be a bad word to use either, when you glance at the total national debts among the South nations—or even if you look at some of the debts in Latin America alone.

By the end of 1988, the national debt of Brazil was $120.1 billion. The national debt of Mexico was $107.4 billion. Yet neither country has the gross national product or the sophisticated financial, industrial, economic and educational underpinnings that will keep it from being crushed by debts of that magnitude.

Or focus even briefly on the case of Bolivia and Argentina. Bolivia is one of the poorest of the poor countries of Latin America, while Argentina is one of the most developed and cosmopolitan countries in the region. But both are engulfed in the same deadly dilemma. A large chunk of Bolivia's meager national income depends on its sale of natural gas to Argentina. Bolivia depends on that income just to pay its national debt. But Argentina, racked by its own debt and by hyperinflation, has stopped all payments to Bolivia. So Bolivia in its turn has to renegotiate repayment of its debts. Yet without a bridge loan, which will carry it still deeper into debt, it cannot enter into such negotiations.

That dismal spectacle, which is not confined by any means to Bolivia and Argentina, becomes almost lurid when yet another essential question is asked. What has happened to all the billions that have been poured into the South countries? Indeed, what has happened to the domestic earnings of oil-rich Venezuela, which has a debt of $35 billion? What has happened to the domestic earnings of oil-rich Nigeria, which owes $30.5 billion?

Or take the case of Gabon. With a total output of 160,000 barrels of oil a day from its giant Rabi-Kounga onshore field, Gabon—after Nigeria and Angola—is black Africa's third-largest oil producer. Yet, with a population of a mere one million, Gabon's foreign debt in 1986 was $1.6 billion.

The culprits blamed here were depressed oil markets and the weak dollar. And no doubt about it, they are part of the story. But that leads right back to the sinful structures John Paul talks about. For the management of the dollar's value and the fixing of oil prices are both in the hands of those who could—with new and benign policies—avoid putting

Gabon's economy in jeopardy. Significantly, in fact, Rabi-Kounga is jointly owned by two groups that are a portrait in miniature of the affluence and the power of the structures of the North countries: Shell Gabon, which includes the Royal Dutch/Shell Group of the United States; and Elf Gabon, which includes Elf Aquitaine of France.

So mightily do the problems escalate in the South, and so desperate does the climate of life become, that a kind of cannibalism begins to operate. For there can be no doubt that in virtually every South country —in Brazil, in Nigeria, in the Philippines, in Venezuela—anywhere you care to look, in fact, there are successful South disciples of North policies. In each poverty-stricken place there is a moneyed class, mainly entrepreneurs and investors who have managed to plug themselves as individuals into the good life of their North counterparts. But without the systematic help of the North countries, there is no possibility that these tiny groups can build the infrastructure by which they could, even if they wished, begin to spread the benefits in any way that might begin to make a difference.

Thus, while the wealthy few in the South lead flourishing lives just the way they see it done in the North, they are as impotent as eunuchs in a bedraggled harem. They see what surrounds them; but they have no means of doing anything significant about it. And so they carry on with their isolated lives, while the poverty and general helplessness endemic to the bulk of the populations in their individual countries only increase from year to year.

Nor do the problems end even with such an awful litany. Incomprehensibly enough, blithe and cruelly misleading conclusions about the South are drawn in the North. The mistakes are honest ones, surely; and probably these are made in the hope that things are turning around— that maybe they're not so bad after all.

In March of 1989, to illustrate with one case upon which John Paul has remarked privately, a World Bank report found that in the forty-five sub-Saharan countries, agricultural production and the gross national product had risen since 1985; and that for the first time since 1970, food output in the region was expanding faster than the population. "Africa," the report concluded, "has begun a fragile but sustainable economic recovery."

Such misleading optimism was quickly and correctly blasted out of the water by the United Nations Commission for Africa. Pointing precisely to the underlying condition that makes moral mockery of such baseless predictions of "sustainable economic recovery," the U.N. Commission showed that no signs of a solid infrastructure had yet appeared in those

sub-Saharan countries. In fact, the commission painted a future of no
recovery at all, but one of "dire long-range consequences for the future
of the African people and economies."

Pope John Paul had no need of either report to tell him of the conditions he has seen for himself, in Africa and in too many other places
where he has spoken over and over again of the conditions that make
our world increasingly a place of shame.

"Is it merely a rhetorical question," the Pontiff wondered publicly in
Zambia on May 3, 1989, "to ask how many more infants and children
must die every day in Africa because resources are now being swallowed
up in debt repayment?" In the same vein, is it merely a rhetorical question to ask why the average Zambian man must be dead and buried by
the age of fifty? Are such questions, as John Paul said, no better than
rhetorical? Is anyone in the North countries listening?

Possibly not. For the developed North nations deepen the misery of
the South countries yet further by their policies of destroying or storing
surplus supplies of basic foods, instead of arranging for their allocation
to offset the waves of hunger that continually lay waste to whole populations.

In the main, what puny efforts there are to supply food to even a
fraction of the most desperate peoples are isolated at best. They are
frequently complicated by wars waged by poor South surrogates of
wealthy North powers. More often than not, those efforts are undertaken
not with surplus supplies but with special donations from average citizens. More often than not, those efforts are undertaken only after enormous pressure is brought to bear by those same average citizens. And by
comparison to the capabilities available for. the job—capabilities demonstrated and improved every day in more profitable enterprises—even
the biggest and the best of those efforts must be judged as poorly organized and inefficiently carried out.

Other structural arrangements by which the North steadily accelerates
its superdevelopment imply equally reprehensible policies and decisions.
There are the import and export arrangements that benefit elitist groups
within South countries. Favors and facilities are accorded to special-
interest lobbies. Exploitation of the South's natural resources, and regulation of prices on the world markets for raw materials, are managed in
a way that benefits the large cartels at the expense of far larger populations. Special tariff-relief arrangements benefit chiefly foreign investors.
Acquiescence is prolonged in the entire roster of fiscal deficiencies
plaguing the South countries, because it helps North countries in their
international policies with South countries—usually the ones with

strong-arm or one-man governments that are called democratic for reasons of convenience.

Governmental complicity among the North countries in the sinful structures that cause and prolong suffering in South countries becomes still more sinister, morally speaking, when yet one more aspect of activity is factored into the equation of sinful global structures.

It is a fact known not only to Pope John Paul but to all governments that companies in the United States, Germany, France and Switzerland provide governments in South countries with both materials and technology—not to mention financial "aid"—with which the "weapons of hell" are manufactured and then used primarily on the populations of other South countries.

Thus, at least forty West German companies shipped chemicals and technology to the well-known Libyan plant that is uniquely geared—to the tune of forty tons a day in production capacity—to turn out the instruments of chemical warfare. Already those weapons have been used against Iranians and elsewhere in the Middle East, as well. Because sauce for the goose is generally sauce for the gander, particularly if the sauce made money for the goose, a Swiss company has negotiated with Iran for the construction of a similar plant.

There is much more. Syria, Iraq and Iran all have been given assistance in building missiles. Both Pakistan and India have received clandestine help in providing themselves with nuclear capacity. But however long and whatever the grim particulars of such a list, the prime motive behind the activity is profit.

Structures whose primary motives are profit, power and superdevelopment—structures that outlast the life span of the individuals who planned and erected them—have become the vehicles of clearly terrible actions whose consequences are suffered on a global scale never before seen.

To a T, then, these are living, functioning embodiments of Pope John Paul's definition of sinful structures. And day by day, with the deepest complicity of the North countries, the chaff spewed out by those structures in their global harvest of superdevelopment is all that is left to the South to sustain the economies of its nations and the lives of its people.

Change and alleviation, not blame, are Pope John Paul's motive in his analyses of the world's sinful structures and in his constant and candid exhortations to other world leaders concerning the conditions they all see as well as he.

In that respect, however, perhaps the most compelling reason for John Paul's moral appraisal of the way the South fares amid all this entrepreneurial activity of North countries is that at present he sees no sign that even the most pernicious of the conditions crippling the South are the serious targets of the developed countries as they fine-tune their own expanding structures of finance, trade and industrialization.

If this state of affairs were to continue, said Kazuo Haruna, Economic Committee chairman of the Japanese corporate giant Keidanren, "it would result in what could become an irreversible and irremediable divergence in the standard of living of the populations of these two regions [the North and the South], and an eventuality of this kind would inevitably raise important ethical questions."

Whatever Mr. Haruna may have meant by "ethical questions," John Paul insists that the "eventuality" is already upon us. The few signs of acknowledgment that the problem must be addressed seem too halfhearted to promise that a genuinely professional solution for the ominous North-South gap will get under way anytime soon.

U.S. Treasury Secretary Nicholas F. Brady raised expectations in the debt-ridden South countries when, in his much publicized "Brady Plan," he proposed greater debt relief action on the part of commercial banks. But the amount of debt relief encompassed by that plan—about 20 percent—would not make a dent in the overall problem. Nothing so far proposed by the "Brady Plan," or by the International Monetary Fund and the World Bank, promises remotely to mitigate the $350 billion debt of the South. Or even to mitigate the interest payments on that debt, which are higher than the net earnings of the debtor nations. And so the misery continues.

To ask, meanwhile, as do many giant lenders of the North, why the South countries incurred such debt in the first place, if they had no hope of repaying it, is something Pope John Paul finds worse than begging the question. It is more in the nature of asking why a drowning man would grope for a lifeline if he hadn't the strength left to pull himself to safety. And it is, in any case, to ask the wrong question.

It might be more profitable in every sense to consider the shortsighted motives of North countries as they rushed to pour high-interest loans into areas that neither could prepare, nor were given significant help in preparing, those structures of finance, trade, education and industrialization without which almost any sum of money, no matter how grand the total, must be seen as no more than a doubtful and momentary life preserver.

Lest the North countries forget, meanwhile, there is still that rising hillock of trouble already extending the mountain ranges of misery into certain nations of their own region.

In May of 1989, the American Economic Association published a study that confirmed a fact that had already become starkly evident. The wealthiest 20 percent of American families increased their share of the national income from 39 percent in 1973 to 43.7 percent in 1989. In the same period, meanwhile, the share of the nation's income in the hands of the poorest 10 percent of American families sank from 5.5 percent to 4.6 percent.

American children did not fare very well either. Another report showed that in 1966, back when superdevelopment was young, some 17.6 percent of American children were living below the poverty line. In 1987, the misery figure for the young had risen to 20.6 percent.

In such numbers is portrayed the fact that the United States—the giant who jump-started the global race for superdevelopment, and has ever been its inspirational leader—now has an unexpected and unwanted new growth industry: its quasi-permanent urban and rural underclass.

There is nothing foreign to the American public in Pope John Paul's insistence that we should be morally disturbed by an economic system in which the steeply rising earnings of professional corporate managers contrast shockingly with the condition of millions of their homeless and hungry fellow citizens. It is not hard to see that the highest incomes recorded in 1988 for a handful of individual Americans—incomes of $53.9 million, $45.7 million, $40 million—grossly exceed any common sense of equity and justice. And even discounting any extremes of wealth and poverty, it is difficult to justify structures in which the average chief executive of a large American company is paid ninety-three times more money than the average factory worker, and seventy-two times more than the average schoolteacher.

Whether it is applied in the confines of the United States, or in the world at large, John Paul's moral assessment of North and South is simple and clear. In a morally adjusted economy, he insists, the rich should not get richer if the poor get poorer.

The warning that goes with the papal assessment of North and South is just as simple and just as clear. It may well be that those suffering masses we refer to so impersonally as the South will be allowed no real say—and no real participation—in the building of our near-future global community. It may be that they will continue to be herded and dragooned down a tortuous path, increasingly bereft of human dignity.

But if that is the way matters are permitted to go, then the new world community already carries within it the seeds of its early disintegration, seeds visible even now in the shooting war between desperate poverty and unlimited greed that erupts every day in the streets of cities such as Medellín and New York and Los Angeles, seeds whose harvest is more visible still in the rubble that was once Beirut.

As surely as a lethal cancer, warns Pope John Paul, the inhuman fate already afflicting millions upon millions of men and women, children and infants, must infect the entire body of humanity. It must surely produce convulsions and agonizing pain. It must surely end in our death as a civilized human community.

8. The Morality of Nations:
. . . Beggarman, Thief

Geopolitically speaking, the two greatest contenders with Pope John Paul II in the arena of the millennium endgame are at one and the same time the best of enemies and the worst of friends. And thereby hangs the tale of the division of the world in our time into East and West.

That tale of East and West has its similarities, its differences and its points of direct intersection with the wretched story of North and South. The similarities are all told in terms of human misery and suffering created, fostered and maintained by means of sinful structures; and in terms of the motives of the West nations that spurred them to connivance with all of that.

The differences lie primarily in two areas. The first is the fact that to some degree at least, conscious decisions of West leaders at crucial turning points led directly to the creation of the East as an empire and as an increasingly dominant power in human affairs at the end of the second millennium.

The second is the fact that by those conscious decisions, the West connived for far longer than was justified by any crisis, and for its own material benefit, at the wholesale theft of people's sovereignty over their own nations, their own lives and their own futures. Nations of rich and noble heritage were turned away from the banquet of freedom and development in the West and became the beggarmen of modern history, knocking at the back door of prosperity's mansion.

In Pope John Paul's moral assessment of the making of our twentieth-century world, it serves no useful purpose to characterize the mutual opposition between East and West in the economic terms that mark the North-South division so completely. On the contrary, one of the most significant things about the so-called confrontation between East and West nations is that the East has consistently been a nonrival of the West economically. In fact, the East bloc would not have survived economically—would not even be a factor in the millennium endgame now under way—had it not been for the financial, commercial and industrial subsidies supplied to it willingly and for profit by the West nations.

Yet for all its economic failure, there is no doubt in Pope John Paul's mind that the East has managed a kind of moral dominance of the West insofar as the West has been gulled into a moral equivalence with the East.

As early as April 1918, within six months of Lenin's takeover of the moribund Czarist Russia and of the emergence of the Leninist Party-State that would in 1922 become the USSR, Archbishop Achille Ratti, Apostolic Visitor at post–World War I Warsaw, sounded the alarm about Leninism that was to keep ringing in the Vatican until the mid-sixties. "The future configuration of Central and Eastern Europe is almost decided by the advent of an evil empire under the Bolsheviks in Moscow, and the bias of the three Allies. Poland is a test case. Warsaw is the focus. . . ." The bias Ratti referred to was the decision taken by Britain, France and Italy in their top-secret treaty of London in 1915 that the Holy See be excluded deliberately from any peace settlement. Ratti's commentary: "Any such settlement will be a preparation for a far worse war and the victory of that evil empire."

Those allies knew but did not want to take account of the papal moral appraisal. They wanted merely revenge. "What then was the difference between the combatants?" Ratti could have asked. "They are equivalent on the plane of morality." The backbone of John Paul's moral appraisal of East and West is precisely that: If both sides act as if God did not exist, and both act for purely materialistic motives, what moral difference can be seen between them? Surely there is a moral equivalency between them?

Achille Ratti was named Pope Pius XI in 1922. His assessment of the USSR and later of Hitlerian Germany was based on that principle of moral equivalence as the fatal flaw in the reaction of the Western powers in the face of the Nazi and the Leninist threats. Reduced to a practical rule of statecraft, that principle was: You may not proceed in the affairs of nations (or, for that matter, in the affairs of individuals) on the assumption that you are able to establish a modus vivendi with what is morally reprehensible, morally bad. This may suit your convenience and comfort, but it means that you have given a morally acceptable equivalence to the morally bad.

Inevitably, this will corrupt whatever was morally good in your initial attitude. For you will not stop at mere tolerance, a sort of live-and-let-live treatment at a safe distance. Inexorably you will be led to compromise what was morally good in your original stance.

The plaint and criticism of Pius XI was precisely that: Toleration of the USSR led to the USSR's being admitted into the comity of nations. He had the same critique to make of the treatment accorded both Hitler and Mussolini. Indeed, there is more than one reason to think that Pius XI's life was successfully terminated by a Mussolini fearful that his regime would be rocked to its foundations by a blistering attack from the Pope such as he had launched against Hitler on March 14, 1937.

But already by the time Ratti became Pope in February 1922, the early pioneers of the historic process of material gain and the increase of raw power—leaders who were to the engines of geopolitical development what Ford and the Wright brothers were to automobiles and airplanes—were subject to the consequences of their passion; to a turning away in mind and action from God's enlightening grace. Under such leadership, and in effect as a matter of policy, the great nations ceased to observe the First Commandment and worshiped freely and by consistent choice instead at the altars of the false gods of financial gain and political power.

The recognition accorded to the Soviet Union by the great nations in the early years after World War I was simply and principally rooted in the potential for increased trade. And in the beginning, it was no more than a de facto affair.

Trade, however, is always facilitated by diplomacy. And so by 1925, the great powers of the West, led by Germany and Great Britain—with the sole exception of the United States—had established full diplomatic relations with the Soviet government.

In the practical terms of profit and power, it was obvious that the United States could not afford to be odd man out. And in fact it joined the crowd in 1928 when, in the first breach of the "credit blockade" it had erected against the USSR, a contract was signed in New York between the Soviet Trading Company and General Electric.

If the West was prepared to argue, even at that early date, that in its trade and diplomatic arrangements it had done no more than acknowledge the Soviet Union as a practical fact of life in the world's changing landscape, a far greater concession, which came in 1934, left any such argument without a leg to stand on. It was in that year that the League of Nations decided to admit the Soviet Union to its membership.

With that action, an entirely new status was accorded the ruling Soviet regime. Its recognition by the West was no longer a de facto affair; it was de jure. That is, the great world powers made a clear and deliberate decision to recognize not just the practical fact of the Soviet Union's existence. They made a decision to recognize the *right* of the Soviet system to behave as it was behaving and to pursue the goals it was pursuing.

Not one of the great powers of the day didn't know that those goals included the takeover of all nations of the West, the destruction of the capitalist way of life, the liquidation of all formal religion and the abrogation of all human rights.

Moreover, everyone responsible for the acceptance of the USSR into the community of nations—for its admission by right of international law to a place of equality with all the other nations—knew that the Soviet regime was built from the word go on the pillars of official atheism; the use of persecution, prison camps, torture and mass executions; and the systematic infusion into the world of lying propaganda.

In Pope John Paul's view of history, this de jure recognition of the USSR, conceded principally for reasons of economic profit and material aggrandizement, was a policy step of the West that was based upon twin principles: acquiescence in the multiple sinful structures upon which the USSR had been built; and concession to the USSR of the right to continue on that same course.

It is Pope John Paul's argument, moreover, that everything that happened for the next fifty years was no more than the logical follow-through of that conscious policy decision of the West nations, a policy decision that conceded moral equivalence to an immoral system and that was ratified over and again as time progressed.

Of course, the principles involved were not called the principles of acquiescence and concession. In fact, they weren't really given a name at all until much later. But their outlines were so clear, and their acceptance in world affairs became so widespread, that when Pope John Paul II speaks privately, he refers to both of those principles together in appropriate shorthand as the principle of *balance*.

Whatever its name, this principle dictates that once a power emerges on the human scene, the primary judgment about its acceptability is not based on any moral—and certainly not on any religious—norms. The only judgment made concerns how aptly this new power can be integrated into the comity of nations so that international trade can be promoted, profits can be turned, and the "good life" can be continued in its upward course.

Even if the new power functions by means of sinful structures, therefore, its entry and acceptability are still not only feasible but desirable—provided only that those sinful structures do not terminate the balance necessary for the common pursuit by the other nations of those three goals of trade, profit and the development of the good life.

No source of wider trade, in other words, and no basis for the enhancement of prosperity need be excluded as long as that balance can be maintained.

Once that principle of balance had been set in place, it became a sort of lodestone of international policy, whose magnetic field was irresistible. As the decade of the thirties drew on, the same reluctance to declare the Soviet regime an outlaw among nations was shown for as long as possible in every quarter.

It was, in fact, only after most of the West nations had been literally forced at gunpoint to confront a threat to the principle of balance that came from another quarter—from Adolf Hitler's Nazi regime in Germany—that British Prime Minister Winston Churchill and American President Franklin Roosevelt each made personal agreements with Soviet dictator Joseph Stalin by which whole populations in Eastern Europe, the Baltic States and Asia were handed over to Stalin lock, stock and barrel.

"Your President," Stalin growled in 1944 to a visiting group of United States senators inquiring belatedly about his postwar plans, "has given me total and sole influence in Poland and China, and what I plan to do there is none of your business." The sorriest and most shamefaced page of Churchill's wartime memoirs, meanwhile, records how, during one of his wartime visits to Moscow, with the flourish of a pen he blithely signed away the freedom and lives of millions in the Balkan States.

It may be, as Churchill was so fond of saying, that even the Soviet stick was good enough to beat the Nazi dog. Nevertheless, within a decade of the League of Nations action in 1934, the right of the Soviet Union to continue on its singularly brutal course not only was ratified by the two most important leaders of the West nations; that right was cemented and enormously enhanced in the spoils of war.

Given the motive of Roosevelt and Churchill in this affair, it is a most savage irony that in the annals of human cruelty and deliberately planned genocide, not even the bloody record of Adolf Hitler can match the Stalinist record. For without delay, the Soviet Union imposed its totalitarian dictatorship on the hapless nations of its new empire. And without delay, it resumed by fair means and foul the pursuit of its primary goal of world hegemony—its own version of the global village.

The catastrophic proportions of the East-West division to which he had contributed in a time of desperation was best characterized by Winston Churchill himself in 1946. In Fulton, Missouri, that British statesman gave one of his most famous postwar speeches. He conjured up for the world the forbidding but accurate image of an iron curtain that had been clamped into place by the Soviets from Stettin on the Baltic Sea all the way to Trieste on the Adriatic. Europe had been divided. East and West had become the coordinates that would dominate the international life of the world and all its people for the next forty years.

Logically enough—inevitably, in fact—it was the Communist Party of the Soviet Union that usurped the role of sole leader in the East bloc. And just as inevitably, all human rights—civil, political, religious—as well as the right to organize labor unions and to exercise economic initiative, were denied or severely limited. Huge sums of money were devoted to the enrichment of the *nomenklatura*—that privileged class of bureaucrats and Party officials in the Soviet Union that was so quickly exported to each new satellite country as its new ruling class. Stockpiles of weapons ate up still more money, while the vital development needs of war-racked populations were stifled by military expenditure, by elephantine bureaucracy, and by an inefficiency that rapidly became as endemic throughout the satrap East nations as in the South nations.

Stalin, already guilty prior to World War II of the persecution, imprisonment, torture and death of some fifty million human beings, imposed the same kind of totalitarian dictatorship on the betrayed nations of the newly created East bloc.

We now have firsthand testimonies from inside the Soviet system itself about the mass arrests, deportations, tortures, imprisonments and executions that befell millions of innocent citizens in the USSR and throughout its satellite nations. In the network of labor camps; in the total censorship of the media; in the one-man totalitarian rule; in the dossiers kept on countless people; in the repressive police apparatus and the murders that continued throughout the post–World War II period; in deliberately planned genocide; in the total control of the daily life of millions—what they ate, what work they did, what they read, what they thought, how they lived and how they died—in all of that, Stalin's record is unsurpassed in recorded history.

Though there were continual cries of outrage from around the world, in the main the reaction and studied response of the West nations to this spectacle of Soviet horror that had been expanded over an entire region of the world was a refinement of its earlier principle of balance. Or more aptly, it was the codification of that principle of balance into a policy by which balance could still be maintained. And this time, it did have a name. The doctrine of "containment."

In fact, it even had an author. George F. Kennan was the West's foremost international analyst and perhaps the finest mind to appear in the West since England's Lord Acton died in 1902. Kennan was, as well, the nearest modern America has come to producing a genuinely geopolitical thinker.

In a now famous eight-thousand-word telegram dispatched from the American Embassy in Moscow to the State Department in Washington in 1946, Kennan, a junior at the embassy, proposed that the United States meet the Soviet expansionist thrust by "the adroit and vigilant application of counterforce at a series of constantly shifting geographical and political points." He discouraged any unnecessary militarizing of the conflict with the Soviets, or any reliance on nuclear weapons. Military force, in his mind, should not be the principal means of countering the Soviet Union.

The motive force of Kennan's thought was, at its base, a moral one of truly geopolitical intent. For him, the need to avoid war with the Soviets sprang from a moral imperative. All and every effort should be made to avoid such a war, because it would probably mean the total destruction of our present civilization.

At the same time, Kennan was explicit concerning what the West could or should do about the peoples now held captive in Russia and throughout the latest colonialist empire in the world's history.

Condemning the Stalinist regime as one of "unparalleled ruthlessness and jealousy," he counseled the West to become and to behave as a "benevolent foreigner," to maintain "polite neighborly relations with the Soviets, and then to leave the Russian people—encumbered neither by foreign sentimentality nor by foreign antagonism—to work out their destiny in their own particular way. . . . The benevolent foreigner, in other words, cannot help the Russian people; he can only help the Kremlin. And, conversely, he cannot harm the Kremlin; he can only harm the Russian people. That is the way the system is geared."

One admiring commentator wrote about the Kennan doctrine that it was based on "a realistic assessment of America's and Russia's respective power and interests." And true enough, if one considers "polite neighborly relations" by a "benevolent foreigner" as the means to maintain the principle of balanced development in the West; and if one considers "an assessment of Russia's power and interests" an acceptable basis for justifying moral connivance with the horrors of life in the East nations—then Kennan had indeed provided a thoroughgoing and realistic general framework within which the West could pursue its development interests with as little moral discomfort as possible.

The deep human consequences of the Kennan doctrine of containment were clarified beyond doubt, if clarification were called for, when in 1956 the people of Hungary staged a desperate uprising against the brutal police presence, starvation wages, crowded homes, empty larders and makeshift substitutes for the merest necessities of life that had been foisted upon them by Stalin. The Hungarians were convinced that the West would come to their aid. Unfortunately, they had not assessed the West's reliance on the balance-of-power principle. If Stalin wiped out the entire nation of Hungary, the West could still see its way to flourish. The nation in revolt was suppressed bloodily. In 1968, there was a repeat performance of the same scenario, this time in Czechoslovakia.

Fatally compromised from its beginning of "life with Uncle Joe," the West had entered into a spiraling bipolar relationship of antagonism over which it had only the most tenuous control. Not only had it accepted the East as a parallel power, the East had succeeded in the dream of every classical strategist: it had lured the West onto the particular terrain it had chosen for the struggle.

Inevitably East and West, each with its own forms of propaganda and indoctrination, evolved their ideological opposition into a professional military opposition of the most curious kind. Two blocs of armed forces, though suspicious and fearful of each other's plans for world domination, were each as frightened of direct conflict as of the geopolitical threat from the opposing side.

Given the elements of the Kennan doctrine of containment, the armed tension between the East nations and the West, the atmosphere of distrust and suspicion that reigned between them, and given above all the deep ideological contest between the two blocs, it was only a matter of a short time before the East-West coordinate of opposition spilled over to affect the South nations.

For one thing, the vast outlay of billions of dollars in foreign aid became a means by which West and East alike hoped to further their divergent foreign policy interests. For the East-West rivalry was global; and funds were meant to buy loyalties, not relieve endemic poverty.

The South nations in turn, in desperate need of effective, impartial and prudently administered aid from the richer developed countries of the North, found themselves overwhelmed instead by the ideological conflicts of East and West. For it was in the South nations that East and West alike found the most convenient targets for what George Kennan had called "the adroit and vigilant application of counterforce at a series of constantly shifting geographical and political points." The South nations found that they were assigned one position or another along the East-West coordinate.

More often than not, and unfortunately for the South, the inevitable results were internal conflicts and divisions, famine, cruelty, and even full-scale civil war. The South is replete with monuments to this policy, monuments with names we all know: Nicaragua, Vietnam, Laos, Cambodia, to name but a few.

Despite the fact that tragedy on an international scale became the order of the day, no concerted plan was ever thought out and put into action in order to prevent the still-widening gap between North and South—the rich and the poor—because it was the global rivalry between East and West—the beggarman and the thief—that dictated the expenditures of the West nations. In fact, over time every local government even among the East nations received its own ration from the billions of dollars in credits and aid paid out by the West nations in their continuing balancing act.

Out of this mutually accepted arrangement of association and opposition between East and West sprang one major factor in modern life—the armaments race—which has caused the nations to squander so many hundreds of billions of dollars every year that even the giants of the West became debtor nations. Had it been managed prudently and for other motives, that expenditure alone could probably have wiped out endemic hunger, disease and homelessness in all the lands of the South.

Despite so dismal a harvest, the West nations put the final cap on their systematic acquiescence in the institutionalized injustice, cruelty, hypocrisy, lies and anti-God intent of the East bloc of nations.

In the Helsinki Agreement of 1975, the entire West again, and as a bloc, officially ratified the principle of balance. The inviolate character of the Soviet empire, composed of and erected upon sinful structures, was confirmed officially and on treaty paper. All the compromises with and acquiescence in institutionalized sin—in sinful structures—were ratified with international fanfare as the global policy of the West nations. The Kennan doctrine had led to the triumph of what has been called the Brezhnev doctrine: the untouchable right of the Soviet Party-State to control its captive nations.

. . .

Such were the barest facts of association and rivalry in 1978, when Karol Wojtyla came to Rome from the Soviet East; and so they remained in essence for all the years of his reign as Pope John Paul II, until the emergence of Mikhail Gorbachev in 1985.

The East nations remained as they were, grouped around the USSR as their dominant leader and as the Party-State it had always been—a counterintelligence state in form and function. The West nations remained as they were, grouped freely if sometimes grudgingly around the United States as military umbrella, and as financial and entrepreneurial leader. And the world remained as it was, tied to the global torture rack of mutual opposition and rivalry between the two major blocs—sometimes strained almost to the snapping point, at other times less ominously stretched, but never totally released from tension.

From the beginning of his pontificate, Pope John Paul has insisted that no worthwhile moral appraisal of the East-West rivalry, and no moral appraisal of its effects on the world, may, even for a moment, consider anything like a principle of balance. Nor will a moral appraisal even remotely base itself on a winking policy of containment. For principle and policy alike were no more than acquiescence in moral evil all dressed up in the latest "go-to-meeting" clothes. Less lightheartedly expressed, they were the ropes that kept the whole world bound to the torture machines of sinful structures.

True enough, there were always differences of the deepest kind between East and West. The East system was structured politically, economically and socially according to classical Marxism, modified and adapted by the Stalinist Soviets. The West system was structured according to classical capitalism, which underwent its own modifications and adaptations. And true enough, from these totally irreconcilable ideologies flowed the political, social and economic rivalry between the two blocs of nations. Totalitarian dictatorship in the East versus capitalist democracy in the West. Absolute statism in the East versus open and free market economies in the West.

Nevertheless, for all the differences between the two sides, and no matter how deep those differences may appear to be, John Paul points to one overriding bond between East and West—one common and lethal flaw that shackles them together as bitter but not always unwilling partners. There is no element in either of these two systems that finds sinful structures morally repugnant, provided that the systems themselves can function and pursue their individual and differing goals.

It is clear to Pope John Paul that the West, never systematically deprived of its right to make free choices, will ever have a multitude of silent accusers reminding the world of those in the West who accepted the Stalinist East as a dark and contentious partner in world affairs; reminding the world of those who accepted moral equivalence with a morally evil regime. For, following this principle of moral equivalence, the connivance of the West in the sinful structures of the East laid a trail that is clearly detectable in all its horrible details.

Following the principle of moral equivalence, the West restricted the advance of its Allied troops in the closing days of World War II in order to allow the Soviets first entry into Germany, Czechoslovakia and a wide swath of additional territories.

Following this principle of moral equivalence, the whole series of sinful structures erected by Soviet leaders was permitted to clone itself throughout Eastern Europe and the Baltic states of Estonia, Latvia and Lithuania. Unjust, corrupt, dictatorial, godless structures that directly and systematically violated human dignity in individuals and nations by a denial of all human rights; structures that violated basic justice and love of fellow man, structures that inflicted hunger, poverty, social and mental deprivation, pessimism and bodily violence upon millions of men, women and children. Above all, they were structures that were officially and by explicit state policy impregnated with godlessness—with a professional denial of God's sovereignty and law.

Moreover, following the principle of moral equivalence, the United States and the main protagonists of the West under its leadership rarely looked back over their collective shoulder once they had officially signed away the lives, liberties and rights of all those millions into Soviet captivity.

Instead, steadily following that same principle, the West consented time and again to treat as a due member of the family of nations an officially godless and professionally anti-Christian, antireligious power. The West accepted the Soviets as bona fide, if admittedly troublesome, members of the international community, exchanging ambassadors, establishing cultural ties and fostering whole pyramids of commercial, industrial and financial links with the East.

By all these means, and with the principle of moral equivalence ever as guiding star, the West connived at the Big Lie that the captive nations were genuinely sovereign states, and not the unwilling captives of sinful structures that sustained themselves by harrowing a harvest of death among human beings who were never permitted a chance at sufficient sustenance for life.

As Pope and as Pole, John Paul II knows firsthand the depth and the breadth of suffering caused by such moral connivance between East and West leaders. He knows all too well that an entire generation was born that, to adapt George Kennan's powerful words, has "never known security of peace in its lifetime." An entire generation lived and died with no hope for the future.

In Poland, as John Paul has sometimes said, he and his people preserved a wistful hope and irrepressible faith in the future God would bring about, because Poles never allowed themselves to be robbed of their belief in God and in Christ as Savior, and because they never for a moment accepted the principle of moral equivalence under the self-serving guise of balance and containment, as did those who pretended that, despite the mounting human toll, the absence of a shooting war between the principal nations of East and West could pass for peace.

There will always be the ineradicable mass graves of Soviet citizens at Bykovnia near Kiev, at Kuropaty near Minsk, at Vinnitsa and Lwów and how many more sites that stretch from Archangel in the Arctic Circle all the way to Odessa on the Black Sea, and from Moscow to the Boguchany prison village in the Soviet highlands. Any attempt to justify the West's feckless de jure acceptance of the Soviet empire and the Brezhnev doctrine will forever be countered for John Paul by the mass grave of 4,443 Polish officers in Katyn Forest, by the graves of 11,000 Polish officers at the Kozielsk and Ostaszkowo internment camps, by the abandoned graves at all of the 3,500 internment stations of the Soviet Gulag system throughout the USSR and its captive nations.

Surely, too, the millions who have lived and died unknown, undefended, unrecorded, unmourned and unaccounted for constitute a bill of indictment drawn in flesh and blood against Soviet authorities. But implicated just as certainly are all those who connived and acquiesced and accepted the masters of the Soviet regime, all those who insisted on pursuing that principle of balance so convenient to the capitalist system and so dear to the hearts of leaders in the West.

Still, not by a long shot are all the accusers of East and West silent witnesses. And not by a long shot are all of them in the Soviet Union, Eastern Europe and the Baltic region. For the principle of moral equivalence worked its way right around the world. In practical geopolitical terms, it turned out that George Kennan's global strategy of "adroit and vigilant application of counterforce at a series of constantly shifting geographical and political points" meant that nations and entire regions had to become pawns caught in the crossfire of East-West opposition and hostility.

The internal conflicts, famine, cruelty and even full-scale civil wars are but some of the miseries that resulted, in such far-flung "geographical and political points" as Pakistan, Mozambique, Angola, Ethiopia, Guatemala, Nicaragua, El Salvador and Afghanistan.

How many more accusers must rise, as well, out of the no-win policies of the West in Korea and Vietnam, which took their own toll in the death of millions and in the heartbreaking misery of millions more? For John Paul, the conclusion is inescapable that the West was not anything so benign as an unreliable ally, despite the many assertions to that effect. On the contrary, under American leadership the West was the ever-faithful disciple of moral equivalence. It was dedicated to its policy of "polite neighborly relations" with the Soviets, whose surrogates joined the West in paying the price for conniving—even in war—with the Eastern masters of sinful structures.

Okinawa became another pawn of such "polite neighborly relations" between the power blocs of East and West. Okinawa was enforcedly included as the forty-seventh prefecture of Japan, despite the fact that Japan's dubious claim rested only upon its seizure of the island in 1898. But Okinawa was needed as a strategic base for Japan and the United States vis-à-vis China. So Okinawa has not been given back to its people. On the contrary, nearly twenty percent of its land is occupied by American bases.

Western interest in China figures again in Tibet, where the United States has practiced a mincing delicacy concerning the brutality of the Communist Chinese government against human rights, and particularly against religious rights. Why? Because in the struggle between the East and West blocs, the West counted China as its trump card. Surely the Tibetans who have suffered so greatly as a result would, if they could, rise as witnesses against such "polite neighborly relations." And just as surely, the more than one million homeless Tibetan refugees in India and elsewhere would join that throng of witnesses.

And then there is Lebanon, by any measure one of the most poignant examples of the hapless nations trapped in the policies of moral equivalence adopted by the West nations. For here the East-West crossfire of opposition and hostility is anything but a figure of speech. It is a way of life.

In the early spring of 1989—in one eight-week period alone—some 100,000 shells were pounded into the Christian area of Beirut by Syrian gunners, while Christian gunners lobbed another 30,000 shells on areas controlled by the Syrians. Clearly, then, as in Korea and Vietnam, both East and West have done far more than merely acquiesce in the daily suffering and decimation of Lebanon's 3.5 million civilian residents. For

Syria is the Soviet Union's Middle East surrogate, while the Christian enclave has until recently been able to look to the West for what support it could garner.

In this region, however, unlike Korea and Vietnam, the hand-in-glove nature of moral equivalence was recently made almost surprisingly clear. For after the shelling and countershelling of the bloody spring of 1989, U.S. Secretary of State James Baker and USSR Foreign Minister Eduard Shevardnadze issued a joint communiqué calling for "a national dialogue on reconciliation in Lebanon." The Arab League chimed in as well, calling for the withdrawal of all "non-Lebanese troops."

From John Paul's vantage point, it is clear that if East and West intend anything more than lip service to "reconciliation in Lebanon," they need not bother with any joint communiqués. The Soviets can simply withdraw their financial and military support, which allows the Syrians to fight at all; and the Americans can withdraw the financial aid that makes it possible for the Christians to continue their part in the continuing rain of death in Lebanon. And the Arabs, too, can withdraw their contributions—which come to more than the annual sum they pay for the expenses of the PLO, and which make it so much easier for "non-Lebanese troops" to remain in Lebanon.

Just how easy it would be to stop the fighting in Lebanon—if the great players in the East-West game of "polite neighborly relations" were of such a mind—becomes even clearer to John Paul when he looks at the far different situation in the Bekaa Valley. The Bekaa, which lies in Lebanon and well within the reach of destruction such as Beirut is undergoing, is well known as one of the most fertile spots in the world for the cultivation of the cannabis plant. Under Syrian control, the Bekaa brought in $1 billion from drug exports in 1989 alone. Such an incentive apparently commands respect that rises above all other considerations; for the Bekaa Valley is consistently and, in that area, almost uniquely preserved from harm's way.

Is it not at least instructive to ask, as John Paul does in many of his meetings with interested secular leaders, why the Bekaa has not become another of those countless "geographical and political points" where East and West alike have chosen to apply their "adroit and vigilant counterforce"? Might it not be even more to the point to ask, as the Pontiff also does, why Lebanon must be kept so consistently and so brutally within harm's way?

In such circumstances, one news reporter remarked most aptly that what amounts in effect to the silence of both East and West about Lebanon's agony is not only deafening; it is deadening.

Suffering of a different kind, meanwhile—but equally a product of the

West's connivance in the sinful structures erected by the East—befell the people of Romania within the same decade that has seen the virtual destruction of Lebanon. Like all the Communist dictators of the Soviet satellite nations of Eastern Europe, Romania's Nicolae Ceauşescu put his nation heavily in debt to the West. Between 1981 and 1989 he borrowed $11 billion, in fact. But unlike the rest of the satellite leaders, and unlike the debtor nations of the South, Ceauşescu did not look for debt relief or for a refinancing scheme that might be acceptable to the West. Instead, he repaid that $11 billion to the last cent.

More than any other world leader, perhaps, John Paul appreciates what that meant for the Romanian people. For he knows in detail that such a scheme, accepted readily by the West, added to the sufferings the Romanians already had to bear—meatless months, milkless months, uprooted villages and towns, scores of labor camps. All the omnipresent cruelty of a police state bested in its ruthlessness only by Communist Albania and by Stalin's USSR of the thirties and forties was only intensified by what must be thought of as the financial arm of the East-West "foreign policy wars."

Pope John Paul does not end his moral assessment of East and West even with such a damning global portrait of the consequences of moral equivalence. For that portrait looks out at us all through the eyes of the millions upon millions of refugees in our world, refugees whose number and whose condition of misery may have no equal in all the annals of history.

Governments count this toll in numbers—12 million refugees by the end of 1988—more than the population of entire nations. And to no one's astonishment, the largest concentrations are to be found in precisely those South nations that were assigned their places along the lethal coordinate of East-West contention: 817,000 refugees in the Sudan; 625,000 refugees in Ethiopia; 852,750 in Jordan; 600,000 in Malawi; 105,220 in Malaysia; 447,850 in the Gaza Strip; 259,850 in Syria; 165,000 in Mexico; 430,000 in Somalia; 250,000 in South Africa. The list goes on. The terrible numbers mount without relief.

For Pope John Paul, this portrait is the very face drawn by the hands of those who rule the world by means of the principle of moral equivalence. It is a portrait that looks out at the whole world from the sunken eyes of too many children he has personally encountered who are literally dying from hunger. It looks out on the world from the eyes of too many young mothers condemned with their babies to a fate of perpetual migration and want. It looks out on the world from the eyes of too many men, old far before their time, emaciated and all but lifeless, who wait only for the release of death. It looks out from the terrified eyes of too many youths who, fleeing from enforced conscription by opposing armies, run headlong instead into the homeless and hopeless deserts of life.

The Pope has seen too many of these refugees in too many lands not to realize that they are the children begotten by sinful structures. Global surrogate wars and politics and other East-West "diplomacy" has made all of this possible. But as long as the West continues its policies dictated by the principle of moral equivalence, no amount of money or of effort from any quarter will be enough to halt and reverse this starkest and still growing flood tide of human deprivation and misery.

Worse still, the West is so deeply committed to the brand of development that constantly produces such by-products of suffering, that even when Third World nations at least try to attain some degree of modern development of their own, John Paul sees their way constantly obstructed, and their efforts consistently hampered by the same moral deficiency shared for so long by East and West.

In Helsinki in May of 1989, for example, representatives of eighty countries gathered at an international forum aimed at countering the problem of chlorofluorocarbons and other chemicals eating away at the earth's ozone shield. The developing nations present pointed out that they could not develop environmentally sound alternatives by the year 2000 as the target date and at the same time maintain even their present slow pace of national development. The developed countries present balked, however, at demands by some that, for the benefit of all, an international pool of money be established to enable the poorer nations to include this critical factor in their already troubled and overburdened national agendas.

In its successful moral domination of the West nations, the East has been aided mightily by something more than its ability to lure its adversary onto its own terrain in the struggle for world domination. It was aided at least as much by the snowballing of what has accurately been called the "industry of blame."

For over forty years, the rulers of the East nations explained away their total failure to provide their populations with a decent standard of living as the exclusive result of the machinations of West nations. As part and parcel of the Big Lie that the Eastern satellite nations were sovereign states happy in their bondage, and that Marxist totalitarianism is democracy perfected, this industry of blame was foisted on East and

South alike. Anything bad in those regions—any ill fortune, including natural catastrophes—was blamed on the devilish doings of the West. Perhaps the most ludicrous and evil-minded recent example was the idea launched by the KGB that the West had deliberately scattered toxic material abroad in order to create the AIDS epidemic, first in Africa and then in the countries of the "socialist fraternity."

Just how successful the East has consistently been in its domination of this industry of blame can be seen in the degree to which many, both individuals and organizations within the West, have bought into the Soviet arguments. In what one American politician aptly named the "blame-America-first" syndrome, representative segments of the world of the West have steadily widened the scope of "freedom of expression" to include a moral distortion of the first order. Freewheeling agencies of democracies in Europe and North America have joined with increasing energy in corroding the self-knowledge of the peoples of the West nations. Every channel in the powerful communications industry has become implicated in the destruction of moral accuracy of judgment.

Thus, the West has not merely been persuaded, it has joined in persuading itself, that all our communal ills—environmental, civil, political, religious—are of its own doing.

So widespread has Pope John Paul found this attitude to be by now that he frequently encounters it as the dominant and motivating "belief system" among many of his own bishops, priests and religious in the West nations, as well as among the authorities in other churches. The United States, as the leader of the West nations, is accepted as the archvillain of international life.

However, just as John Paul roundly rejects the principles of balance and containment as the bastard children of the principle of moral equivalence, so he rejects the industry of blame as yet another bastard child of the Big Lie.

Pope John Paul II insists, as the Church always insists, that in any moral appraisal of East and West for the existence and maintenance of sinful structures, there must be a just distribution of responsibility. And he insists that this is both possible and necessary because, as he is ever mindful, sinful structures never just pop up like mushrooms in a damp forest. They are always and only brought into being and nurtured into systematic power by dedicated groups of men and women who have a goal in mind.

In this regard, in fact, the Pontiff makes an important distinction. He stresses the fact that in neither bloc of nations, East or West, did the populations at large have anything effective to say or do about the institutionalization of sinful structures in their midst. In East and West alike, it was the chief protagonists of the *systems* who were coresponsible.

It is John Paul's considered opinion and principle of action and reaction that, above all today, at the opening of the nineties, when most of the captive nations of the East are shaking off the chains that bound them so helplessly to the USSR, a moral appraisal of the nations' behavior over the past forty years is a required prelude to any sound consideration of what must now be the principle of behavior as regards both those formerly captive nations and their captor, the USSR. It will not do to deceive oneself and say that "the West has waited patiently for this [the revolt of the satellites] to take place. Our policy of containment paid off!"

Papa Wojtyla's appraisal of those North-South, East-West coordinates appears in three main judgments comprehensively answering the query: Who has been morally responsible for the creation and maintenance of those two crippling coordinates of world crisis?

As regards the North-South coordinate, he pronounced a very solemn judgment when speaking in Ouagadougou, capital of Burkina Faso (the former Upper Volta), in West Africa: "The earth is becoming sterile across an immense area, malnutrition is chronic for tens of millions of people, too many children die. Is it possible that such a need is not felt by all humanity? . . . Shouldn't the 'developed' societies ask themselves what model they present to the rest of the world, about the needs they [the developed societies] have created, and even about the origin of the riches that have become necessary for them?" The "developed" world (the North) has treated Third World nations "as clients and as debtors who are more or less solvent," but "that attitude, whether conscious or not, has already led to too many dead ends."

The remedy? One must imagine that lone white-robed figure standing on the wasting fringes of the deadly blowing sands of the Sahel, crying obstinately and authoritatively over a sea of black imploring faces in an effort to reach the ears of Europe, the United States, Japan, the "Asian Tigers," and the USSR, "In the name of justice, the Bishop of Rome, the successor to Peter, begs his brothers and sisters around the world not to scorn the hungry of this continent [Africa], not to deny them the universal right to human dignity and the security of life."

Only the Bishop of Rome, only the one man holding the Keys of divine authority guaranteed by the human blood of God made man, could even venture to brandish them in that Ouagadougou—in all the miserable Ouagadougous of the South nations.

As for the East-West coordinate of opposition and mistrust and human waste, John Paul's moral judgment can be sought in his addresses, speeches, sermons and conversations during the months of 1989 and into 1990, when the "Gorbachevist" liberation movement started.

There is no doubt in Papa Wojtyla's mind that the creation and maintenance of the Gulag empire was the work of those dedicated to establishing the Leninist "proletarian revolution" worldwide. But, entwined with that primary moral responsibility of the USSR and of all the USSR's surrogates, supporters, clients, fellow travelers, "moles" and "frontmen," there is the secondary responsibility of the capitalist West, which from the beginning and for the whole of the Leninist lifetime connived at the perpetuation of that evil system just because the West concluded that its peace, security and profits lay along that way.

John Paul's third moral judgment concerns the distribution of moral responsibility for the successful and godly conduct of the new phase of East-West relationships opened up by the dawn of Gorbachevism in the USSR and Eastern Europe.

Again, the prime moral responsibility lies on the shoulders of the Party-State: the men who ran it—the *nomenklatura*—as well as their surrogates and supporters outside the USSR. But secondary and by no means less important is the responsibility of the West. Having connived, with the Kennan doctrine of containment as the umbrella principle of action, with the "evil empire," for so long and with such dire human consequences, the West now has a moral obligation to give of itself in order to heal the grievous wound inflicted on so many millions of humanity during the lifetime of more than two generations.

Here, Papa Wojtyla tries to point out the nature of that deep wound. There is now a common illusion in the West that freedom has broken out in all the former Soviet satellites, and that with that democratic freedom will come not only democratic egalitarianism but all the virtues entertained—at least originally—by the proponents of freedom. But this is mere illusion.

The human devastation in the former members of the Gulag system lies far deeper than can be reached by a supply of dishwashers, VCRs, bank accounts, luxury foods, convenience goods, plentiful necessities, free media, free elections. The populations of those former satellites have no ideology, no set of moral principles, no ethic, no goals—other than an immediate and full participation in the "good life" as they have longingly seen it presented by Western media: the rip-roaring hedonism of J.R. in "Dallas," the meteoric acquisitions of huge dollar fortunes by Western entrepreneurs, the limitless stretches of sexuality as propounded in the flourishing pornography establishment of the West, and the politics of no higher authority than the demands of each human self.

This, as many sociologists in Europe are already beginning to remark, is a movement in those East populations that should be labeled the "no-idea movement." It is a violent reaching out for the objective—the good life—without any guiding credo, without any ideology worthy of those who ostensibly are fleeing the crass materialism and amoral godlessness of the Gulag.

Of course, as John Paul points out, each man and woman in the Gulag will answer to God for their individual actions. But over and above their individual responsibilities, they have been unwilling victims of the sinful structures at which the West connived for so long.

The West therefore has incurred a moral responsibility for a holistic healing of that deep communal wound; and, for that healing, not merely a flood of dollars and an array of joint ventures will suffice. There has to be a healing of minds, a curing of the soul's disease. John Paul is insistent: Europe—the "new Europe" eyed by East and West—"can only be built on the spiritual principles that originally made Europe possible," he told visiting "Europeans" at the end of January 1990.

In facing the changes now taking place throughout the Gulag archipelago, the West and Pope John Paul differ profoundly in the interpretation of what those changes forebode.

The general feeling abroad in the West is that the "Cold War" has ended, that Communism is bankrupt and that the changes are irreversible, even if Mikhail Gorbachev is swept aside by the internal ills of the USSR. At its most morally perceptive, this general feeling in the West glories—and rightly so—in the apparent triumph of democratic ideas, the departure of those Stalinist relics—Todor Zhivkov from Bulgaria, Erich Honecker from East Germany, János Kádár from Hungary, Milos Jakes from Czechoslovakia, Wojciech Jaruzelski from Poland.

These new initiatives apart, we are now recording a widespread impression or conviction reflected in public commentaries, by columnists, in the words of statesmen and the manifestos and declarations of particular groups—cultic, humanistic, philosophic, even religious. It is, to phrase it in ordinary words, that some important change is taking place. But further precisions are hard to come by; and many who probe the matter, seeking some further precision, end up with a rosy-hued optimism or in dithering doubt.

The impression or conviction in this matter is very fragile and volatile, just like our perception of sunlight in the autumn. Watching the sun's reflection in a frequented room, in early fall, your awareness is caught by a subtle change in the light. It is ever so slight. But it is there. You marvel at it because it seems so slight. Yet it has a clarity unnoticed for some time. Then doubt sets in: Is it because something is changing in you—a new clarity in certain matters, a shift brought about by external events and your own inner development? Or is it a change in the quality of the light that produces a change in you? For we, with all other things in our cosmos, do change. So, finally, when all is said about these changes, does a severe doubt amounting to an anxiety hover in the minds of Western onlookers of the chaotic scene.

What, in other words, people in the West are asking, is happening in this era of Gorbachevism's first impact? Is there a big change under way in the society of nations (the USSR included)? Or is it all a trick of our autumn sunlight, an illusion, therefore, a darkening of our vision? Has the society of nations been taken unconsciously captive by someone who may be the prime master in the exquisite art of political illusion on a grand scale?

There is no such doubt running through the Roman Catholic papacy and its reading of events: from Pius XI through Pius XII, John XXIII, Paul VI, up to the present holder of the Petrine Keys of authoritative teaching about the good and the bad in human affairs. Even a John XXIII, who made the first papal overtures to the USSR and was betrayed in his trust, and a Paul VI, who was totally outclassed in this confused arena of East-West relations—even they faithfully transmitted the unchanging judgment of the Roman Catholic papacy.

That is: Nothing short of a religious and moral conversion of the people of the USSR, accompanied by a similar change in the West, will solve the ever-intensifying geopolitical crisis, and allow the fierce millennium endgame to result in a peace that can be accurately called human —precisely because it will have a divine blessing.

This judgment of the ever-continuing papacy comes reinforced by the sustained memory of the papacy, which, from the beginning of the Soviet Party-State, has watched each of the Champions of Hammer and Sickle and fully comprehended what is involved in the Leninist creation. Memory of that seventy-three-year-old history from Lenin to Gorbachev is the key to accurate interpretation of present events.

Part Three

Champions of
Hammer and Sickle

9. The Hall of Heroes

In the Hall of Communism's Heroes, Karl Marx and Vladimir Ilyich Lenin are ringed around with the ranks of no mean comrades.

Karl Kautsky, for example. A follower of Marx, Kautsky did more than systematize Marx's theories. More learned as a philosopher and more authoritative about Marxism than Marx himself, Kautsky came to be known as the "pope of international socialism"—a touch of irony he and Marx might have savored! And there was Friedrich Engels, of course, who was somewhat more humanistic and certainly more practical-minded than Karl Marx, but not a whit less bitter or less bloody-minded. As a lifelong colleague of Marx and Communist activist, he helped make the penniless Marx financially viable for most of his life.

Obscure as they may now be, there were hundreds of others among the "international socialist fraternity" who would be in such a Hall of Heroes. Men such as G. V. Plekhanov and P. B. Axelrod, for example, who pinpointed the masses of workers—the proletariat—as the pivot of any successful revolution, and so set the basic lines of Lenin's thinking about a Russian birth for political Marxism.

Even before Marx, there were some dozen social theorists and active experimenters who would have their hero's niches too. Wales's Robert Owen, with his "New Harmony" foundation in Indiana, and France's Charles Fournier, with his original "Phalanx" of workers, are but two who must come quickly to mind.

Name as many more such men as you please, however, and list all their accomplishments, and still the preeminent dais must be reserved for just those two. For Karl Marx, who developed a novel way of thinking about the death and burial of all social classes in the world, except the "working class"; and for Vladimir Lenin, the fierce and resourceful activist—the one man who set out to create an international body that would bring about the actual and violent death of capitalism. The man who would entomb capitalism beneath the sun-kissed meadows of a near-future and totally this-worldly "Paradise of the Workers."

Like many others born and bred in the sterile world created by Leninist Marxism—like Aleksandr Solzhenitsyn, for example, or like Milovan Djilas of Yugoslavia—Karol Wojtyla watched the twilight shadows lengthen decade by decade over that cruel and sterile Paradise. From the start of his pontificate, therefore, John Paul had been preparing for some sweeping and possibly convulsive change that he knew was inevitable in the Soviet East. And he was certain that once it came, such a change would have its profound effects in the very foundations of the capitalist West, tied as it had been for so long with the East nations.

In his mind, therefore, Pope John Paul II has always reserved two more places of special distinction in that Hall of Communism's Heroes. It was always possible, he thought, that a virtually forgotten Sardinian by the name of Antonio Gramsci would rise from the little covert of obscurity assigned him by Lenin, to claim his own and special place as nothing less than a genius of Marxist pragmatism. The remaining place on the dais, John Paul has always thought, would be reserved for the first Soviet leader with the practical sense, the breadth of mind and the political daring to listen at long last to Antonio Gramsci.

As it has turned out, that place will probably be occupied by Mikhail Gorbachev.

Since the emergence of Gorbachev as the standard-bearer of expected and long-overdue change, John Paul has focused on certain basic points about him, and about his Gorbachevism, that provide the most accurate reading of the mind and intent of the Soviet leader, and that therefore most accurately foretell the future course of his policies.

For those who share the Pope's belief, mind and outlook, the point of greatest significance about Gorbachev is that he is the head of the only government, and leader of the only political ideology in the world and in all of recorded history, that are officially antireligious—officially based on a belief that everything about human life is material. In all its manifestations and abilities and destiny, there is nothing more to mankind beyond gross matter. That is a basic belief of the genuine Marxist. As the Pontiff knows from the deep experience of a lifetime, any claim to the contrary is put forward as pretext, and is accepted out of ignorance or connivance or wishful thinking.

For the other contenders in the geopolitical arena with these two Slavs, Pope John Paul II and President Gorbachev, meanwhile—

whether or not such contenders share the belief, mind and outlook of either one—the point of greatest significance about Mikhail Gorbachev is exactly parallel to the point of greatest significance about John Paul. For just as the Pontiff's foothold on the geopolitical plane derives from his position as the head of the world's only georeligious institution, so Gorbachev's foothold on the geopolitical plane is guaranteed him by the fact that he is titular head of the world's only existing geo-ideology—the Soviet Marxist version of Communism.

In strictly geopolitical terms, in other words, the parallel between these two leaders holds firm because of one simple and inescapable circumstance: At a critical moment in world history, each assumed an office through which he inherited an already functioning and geopolitically structured institution.

Geopolitically, it matters little that Gorbachev has but six predecessors —Lenin, Stalin, Khrushchev, Brezhnev, Andropov and Chernenko— whose lives taken together span barely more than a single century, while John Paul's 263 predecessors reach back to Simon Peter as the first to take in hand the Keys of authority as Christ's earthly Vicar.

For in the geopolitical arena, it is not age or lineage, but institutional structure and historical opportunity, that are the operative factors of overriding importance.

There are other factors about Gorbachev, and about Gorbachevism, that are of prime significance in John Paul's thinking.

For one thing, the Pope recognized in Mikhail Gorbachev a leader as deeply endowed as he is himself with an instinct for the geopolitical issue. The Soviet leader has his eyes fixed just as surely as the Pontiff does on a geopolitical goal. Each man, in fact, displays precisely those talents that facilitate his geopolitical policy and action in order to attain the goal he has in mind.

John Paul II, himself emergent from the maw of the Russian Bear, is as intimately acquainted as Gorbachev with the lineaments and the gut issues of the Soviet system. For more than one visiting representative from free-world governments who seek the Pontiff out in this matter, as in many others, he has ticked off the early highlights and pointed to the future aims of Gorbachev's innovation. "Gorbachev," he remarked to one such visitor, "is potentially as great an innovator as his founding father, Vladimir Ilyich Ulyanov, better known to you Anglo-Saxons as Lenin."

John Paul is fully convinced that the purpose of Gorbachev's innovation has everything to do with adaptation of failed Soviet structures and nothing at all to do with change of Soviet ideology. There is not the slightest doubt in the Pontiff's mind that Gorbachev understands as clearly as anyone that the non-Marxist nations are now building international structures in which eventually to house a geopolitical world. Nor can there be much question that his dramatic innovations are intended in the first instance to take full advantage of the tried-and-true formula of balance still favored by the West. The Soviet Union must establish itself quickly as an acceptable partner in the building of those new international structures. Indeed, it is fairly certain that Gorbachev will, if he can, chisel the Soviet name deeper than even Lenin might ever have dreamed into the very cornerstones of those new structures.

If Gorbachev can accomplish that much—and he appears to be well on his way—then John Paul is convinced that the USSR has a fair chance at its long-term goal: the effective and thoroughgoing domination of those same structures.

If those near- and long-term goals sound simplistic to some; or if they seem too much like the goals always nurtured and nourished by less appealing Soviet leaders of the past; or if they fall as uncomfortably on the mind as John Paul's moral assessment of the East-West division of the world, the Pope suffers no embarrassment for that. For it has been his experience that most modern leaders of nations, and most ordinary people in the West, do not realize that Mikhail Gorbachev is thoroughly soaked in the Marxism of Lenin; or that Lenin was deeply, sincerely committed to his hatred of everything about capitalism and capitalists. Only those who do not really accept that ugly fact about Soviet Leninist Marxism as a backdrop to all Gorbachev says and does, only they can blithely do business with the Soviet Union and its surrogates as if their doing so invited no danger to what they hold most dear—their fortunes, their lives and their way of life.

Not for a moment does Pope John Paul share such attitudes. On the contrary. Because he finds them unrealistic—and potentially at least as deadly as the policy of containment that housed them for so many decades—the Pope cannot even label those attitudes as hopeful.

What he emphasizes instead is a seemingly unmistakable line of heredity and evolution leading from Marx's Marxism, through Lenin's Leninism and Stalin's Stalinism, all the way up to Gorbachev and his Gorbachevism. Four different styles distinguish these four men one from the other, no doubt about it. But one common thread can be seen that unites them all—the frustrated would-be university professor who lies buried in London's Highgate Hill Cemetery, the dapper little zealot mummified beneath Red Square in Moscow, the black-toothed tyrant hidden away in the Kremlin's wall, and the current mover and shaker of our international community.

For all their many differences, these are the four great Champions of Hammer and Sickle. The four greatest visionaries who share a utopian ideal that has already left the world a misshapen place, and that would remake the whole of the human race according to a mind John Paul recognizes as filled with hatred for all that is divine in the human condition.

Leaving aside that question of personal style, the most important differences between Mikhail Gorbachev and his predecessors lie in three areas for Pope John Paul.

First, this new Soviet leader has an extraordinary grasp of the geopolitical capability of the Leninist-Marxist system he now controls. Second, he has a clear understanding of the basic errors in Lenin's thinking. And finally, he realizes that Lenin should have listened to Antonio Gramsci—the one man who got the scenario right the first time, because he had taken the measure of the West in the twentieth century as no other Marxist before or since has ever done.

For John Paul, therefore, no understanding of Mikhail Gorbachev or of his Gorbachevism will be possible in the West as long as the West leaders insist on wearing historical blinders. There will be no understanding of Gorbachev as a prime contender in the geopolitical arena, or of Gorbachevism as his intended vehicle for ultimate Soviet success in that arena, unless the West rids itself once and for all of the international pretense that has permitted it to accept the Big Lie that the Soviet Union was founded and developed as a normal nation by normal means.

It is essential, insists John Paul, to understand that the USSR was never a nation at all, in fact, but a hybrid system of structures forced upon a hundred ethnic groups and a variety of nations. It is a system of thoroughly sinful structures that gave itself a clever name, the Union of Soviet Socialist Republics, under which it has been allowed to masquerade as a normal nation in the family of nations. Moreover, it is essential to trace how all this happened; and to do so without draping the Big Lie any longer in the acceptable folds of principles of balance and policies of containment.

To understand Gorbachev and his Gorbachevism, insists Pope John Paul, understand the real and unromanticized Marx and what drove him. Understand the real Lenin together with the vision and purpose of his Leninism. Understand the successful, blood-soaked mania of Stalin. And understand the fundamentally Leninist turn that Gorbachev has given to the direction of world affairs. When all of that is digested, understand the one man who might have saved Lenin's vision from Stalin's rape.

Understand the one man whose voice Gorbachev seems to have heard as the clarion of Soviet triumph. Understand the role of Antonio Gramsci in the geopolitical endgame of our age.

If the West nations fail to do all or any of that, then, John Paul warns, they will also fail to understand Mikhail Gorbachev. They will fail to understand Gorbachevism. And they will fail to see how Gorbachev configures the future of the Soviet Union and of our coming world.

Meanwhile, and whether or not Gorbachev remains personally in power, it is a certainty, in John Paul's unblinking assessment of past and future, that this most appealing and most theatrical of Soviet leaders has triggered events that prefigure an unparalleled new course for East and West alike. And for East and West alike, there is no turning back now from a future whose roots lie deep within the ineradicable truth of Soviet history.

10. Karl Marx

Karl Heinrich Marx was born into a Jewish family at Trier, Germany, on May 5, 1818. He passed rapidly from the undigested Judaism of his childhood into a short but perfervid period of Lutheranism, to which he converted with his whole family; and during that time he wrote touching poems to Christ as his Savior.

That moment gave way to another intense period of his youth, however, as he progressed through the universities of Bonn, Berlin and Jena. At Berlin University, he indulged in a virulent form of ceremonial, confessional Satanism. Dating from that period, his youthful poems in adoration of "Oulanem"—a ritualistic name for Satan—contrast eerily with his earlier poems in homage to Christ. But the chief outward effect of his early personal Satanist attachment was to be seen in his consistently and professionally anti-God and godless outlook. Marx remained violently opposed to faith and religion for the rest of his life.

By the time he graduated from Jena, in 1841, Marx had settled upon the social condition of mankind throughout history as his field of special interest. No philosopher himself, it was not surprising that he should have looked to the philosophy of another man to supply the superstructure of his own historical and social outlook. What was extraordinary was that Marx, dedicated heart and soul to atheism, should have derived that centerpiece of his thinking from Wilhelm Friedrich Hegel, who had flourished and passed from the scene before Marx was fourteen. For Hegel had lived and died a believing Christian; and his theories about human history were steeped in his faith.

Hegel saw human history as a process through which all mankind has been advancing from the most primitive conditions of thought, culture and belief right up to the emergence of Christianity as the fullest expression of human ideals.

In essence, human progress was defined by Hegel as a process very much like a discussion between two men arguing about something in order to explain it. One man states his opinion or theory. His companion criticizes that theory, and proposes a different one. From their continuing discussion—presumably a friendly and constructive one—there emerges a third and new theory, which preserves what was true in the first two and which both men accept.

Hegel called the first theory a *thesis*. The second theory, he said, was an *antithesis*, because it opposed the first. The discussion itself he labeled a *dialectic*, from the Greek word for "conversation" or "arguing." And the theory finally accepted out of this process he called a *synthesis*.

For Hegel, that dialectic exactly marked the manner of all human progress. There was one primitive stage of human history: a thesis. Another stage appeared in opposition: an antithesis. Out of the clash between the two—the dialectic—came a third and victorious stage: the synthesis.

All human progress, said Hegel, from the most primitive condition up to the most refined, proceeded along the lines of this triple-stage dialectic toward an ultimate goal. Moreover, God himself had fixed that goal ahead of time; and so, too, had God laid out the plan of triple-stage steps by which to arrive at the goal.

That ultimate goal was the transcendence by mankind of its own finite and created nature, and the attainment of absolute knowledge of the infinite: of God.

What Hegel had worked out, in other words, was a *dialectic of spiritual transcendence*—an attempt to codify the system provided by God from the beginning, by which man was to transcend the material limits of his nature. The entire *dialectic process* was part and parcel of the destiny God had mandated for mankind to become greater than itself. Spirit inhabited matter, said Hegel, and drove mankind on through the successive triple-stage steps of history to that destiny.

By the time he appropriated Hegel's idea of the dialectic and applied it to his own thinking about the social condition of mankind throughout history, Marx was a thoroughly convinced atheist, fully persuaded there was no such thing as a soul and no such thing as spirit in man. Obviously, then, there would have to be a few adjustments here and there, if Hegel's theory was to be made suitable.

Yes, said Marx, there is a dialectic moving men through history. And, yes, that dialectic is a clash between thesis and antithesis. But while there is a series of steps leading to a goal, there is nothing transcendent about any of it.

In fact, for Marx there was nothing transcendent about mankind itself. There was no spirit and no soul. There was just this highly developed and totally material animal called man. And this animal was driven, as all matter was, not by transcendent spirit but by blind forces completely innate in matter. Powerful natural forces that mankind could not successfully resist. All was immanent to man. There was nothing in him that transcended his material condition.

In total contrast to Hegel's dialectic of spiritual forces, then, Marx constructed a dialectic of material forces. Thus was born the *dialectical materialism* of the Marxist lexicon.

As the chicken had been redefined, it was obvious that the egg would hatch a new and different beast, as well. The history of material mankind, said Marx, was a series of clashes, or dialectics, which all represented stages in what amounted to just one great clash—a kind of super-dialectic of human history that came to be called by the most famous of Marxist terms, the "class struggle." That clash was and always had been between the blind, material, irresistible forces inner to the proletariat, and the opposing forces of whatever privileged classes there might happen to be at any given historical period.

Human history itself, therefore, was written within the framework of dialectical materialism. It was the story of that clash of clashes. In Marx's reading of history, the proletarian mass of landless, moneyless, powerless workers—the thesis in Marx's redefined dialectic of material forces—constituted the structure of human society. In every set of historical arrangements that had ever existed, the proletariat was the manifestation of that same irresistible force, the dominant thesis of human history.

Throughout history, the privileged classes—the antithesis in Marxist thinking—have always imposed a "superstructure" of oppression on the proletarian "structure." Emperors had imposed their empires. Kings had imposed their kingdoms. Princes had imposed their aristocracies. Religious people and their churches had imposed their hierarchies. The bourgeoisie and the merchant class had imposed their systems of capital and land.

Marx was convinced by all he could see around him that the antithesis of his time was a spent force. The old regime of authoritarian kings was giving way to the rise of parliamentary democracy. But that circumstance itself, said Marx, was just one more passing step on the road to the true destiny of material mankind: the triumph of the proletariat as the final great human synthesis of history.

The first internationally resonant bellow of Marxism was heard in 1848, when, together with fellow socialist Friedrich Engels, Marx published *The Communist Manifesto*. It was too much for the resident "antithesis" powers of Europe, which were already badly shaken by what historians have dubbed the "year of revolutions." For Marx was feeding the fires of social upheaval with his prediction of the imminent fulfillment of mankind's irresistible destiny: the proletarian revolution that would sweep away the oppressive superstructure finally and for all time.

"Society as a whole," insisted Marx in his *Manifesto*, "is more and more splitting up into two great hostile camps, into two great classes directly facing each other: Bourgeoisie and Proletariat. . . . The workers have no country . . . and the supremacy of the Proletariat will cause the Bourgeoisie to vanish still faster."

As bellicose as such material was, it was only a foretaste of what was to come. For when Charles Darwin published his theory of evolution two years later, in 1850, Marx regarded it as far more than theory. He seized upon it as his "scientific" proof that there was no kingdom of Heaven, only the kingdom of Matter. Darwin had vindicated Marx in his rejection of Hegel's belief in the soul, in the spirit and in God as the ultimate goal of human history.

So elated was Marx at the idea that man had actually evolved from stuff and matter that, had he been of a different mind, he might have hailed Darwin as a godsend. As it was, he wrote a self-congratulatory letter, in which he hailed Darwin as the one who had accomplished for anthropology what Marx himself was accomplishing for sociology.

It might have been foreseen that Marx would find no congenial home in the continental Europe of his day. In 1843, he had married Jenny von Westphalen, with whom he remained deeply in love all his life. Circumstances never allowed him to settle his family as he would surely have liked, however. He shuttled back and forth between Germany, France and Belgium. Finally, in 1849, he migrated to London, where, as the supreme irony of his life, he eked out a sustenance for himself and his family in total dependence on the generosity of members of the capitalist class he hated so thoroughly. His own beloved Jenny was a member of that class. Horace Greeley, founder of the *New York Herald Tribune*, literally protected Marx and his family from starvation. And his friend Friedrich Engels helped out too, with his own capitalist earnings from the Manchester affiliate of his father's textile industry.

To add to Marx's trials, he lost several of his children to death, including his only son, Edgar. His greatest consolation was his love for Jenny. And his only triumph was that, by the time he joined his children in death, on March 14, 1883, Marx had established himself as the foundational theoretician of what we now call Communism.

Marx was primarily a student of social developments and a compiler of the views of others. He was saddled with the impossible desire, but not the necessary mental ability, to be a metaphysician. He was frustrated in his lifelong wish to hold a professorship at a prestigious university. In no way a doer of deeds, however, Marx kept to his books and his writing. He devoted his energies to outlining, if not exactly refining, his new process of social engineering.

Because of his virulent opposition to religion, and his quasi devotion to the scientific requirements of his day, Marx watered down his messianic persuasion that the proletariat would very soon be supremely dominant in human society. At least, he rationalized away the more mystical elements of that messianism, in order to produce a mentally satisfying synthesis of Hegelian dialectics, Darwinian evolutionary theory and the brutal facts of life in the world that lay outside the cocoon in which he came to live.

What he saw and tried to grapple with in that world were such burgeoning and hardheaded problems as the decline at one and the same time of both the ancien régime and the middle class, the start of galloping urbanization, labor relations, commodity pricing systems, the rise of colonialist empires and the inevitable politicization of the working classes by the heady leaven of nationalism.

Ignoring the fact that Darwin's theory of evolution was just that—a theory—and ignoring the fact that in any case what might be feasible anthropologically cannot be presumed to hold sociologically, Marx adapted Darwin's ideas to the social classes of his day. He asserted that a social class was definable solely in terms of its relation to the ownership, the production and the exploitation of all natural economic goods. By such reasoning, the social class with the greatest control over those material processes and goods would be the dominant class at any given stage of history. Owners, workers, entrepreneurs, politicians, aristocrats—even artists, intellectuals and religionists—were all defined exclusively in those terms.

Darwin's theory of evolution being what it was, Marx reasoned that the social classes, like all matter, must always be in a struggle with each other for survival and dominance. A struggle, in other words, for those economic goods. That much had to be so. For mankind was and would always be exclusively material; and history was and would always be exclusively materialistic.

Marx observed further that shifts in the control of economic goods do not follow a straight-line pattern. One social class gets control for a while. Then another rises, clashes with the old, dispossesses it of its control, and takes over. In imitation of Hegel, Marx continued to call that movement of history—that seesaw pattern of shifting control—a dialectic.

Unlike Hegel, of course, Marx continued to insist that the motor of this struggle was not anything outside or above or transcending the social classes themselves. Within the vast proletariat of the world, there was only that inner power, that immanent force, blind and materialistic, driving the vast basic "structure" of society—the proletariat—to overthrow and cast off the oppressive superstructure of capitalism. It was that force, in fact, that created a solidarity between all the proletariats of the world. Through the unceasing dialectic of the class struggle, that blind and material force immanent to the masses was driving them inexorably forward to the *proletarian revolution.*

Never a consistent and logical thinker, Marx waffled about some of the basic properties of this dialectic. It was true, he said sometimes, that there could be no peaceful shift of control from one class to another, no movement through a process of democratic reform and renewal. The old class is destroyed through the sacrifice and suffering of the new class. Hence the sacrosanct position and exalted function in Marxism of violent revolution. Violent revolution is as natural to mankind's totally material condition as the pangs of childbirth to a mother.

On the other hand, Marx allowed for the possibility of democratic change. He did believe that matter was eternal, but he wasn't so sure about the struggle. He left open the point, in other words, of whether or not the struggle between the classes would be unending.

Whatever the reason might have been—perhaps because he was too much of a student to indulge in poetic fanaticism, perhaps because his ideas were adaptations of the ideas of others, perhaps because he was too afflicted with painful and seemingly endless carbuncles and other physical ills to indulge in violent revolution, perhaps for all these reasons and others besides—the fact remains that Marx did not exclude peaceful change, or improvement through democratic means, as possible elements in his dialectic.

While such credulous errors and inconsistencies in abstract theorizing can be readily forgiven a pioneer such as Marx, his gross errors in analysis of the concrete data at his hand's reach are unforgivable by history. Even taking Marx on his own ground of atheism, virulent opposition to religion and deep hatred of capitalism, it is impossible to justify his unfounded assumption that between "structure" and "superstructure" everywhere, there was and can be no homogeneity—no commonality in matters cultural, religious and philosophical.

In examining the conditions of the social classes of his day, Marx unequivocally divided the society of all the nations around him into the structure of the proletariat and the superstructure of the dominant capitalist classes. He cast the entire world along the lines of his native Prussia and of Russia, a society in which the state and its apparatus were predominant and stood in opposition to a civil society that was leaderless, spineless and primitive.

True enough, in that society there was no cultural cement between the classes. There was no organic connection, no cultural relationship, no mutual loyalties, no shared commonality of daily life between the powerful and the powerless. And true enough, in that situation, if the proletariat were to rise up, it would sweep the superstructure of power away, and never look back.

Myopically, however, Marx applied this analysis to everyone. To European and North American countries. To China and Africa. To all the nations of the earth without exception. In that sense, Marxist theory, errors and all, was a geopolitical mandate.

It was all wrong, however. Wrongly based, wrongly analyzed, wrongly applied. Marx's theories were not merely colored by, but dependent upon Marx's out-of-hand rejection of man's religious striving, and of any possibility of the Heavenly Father's spirit among his children on this earth. Beyond that, his theories were spun out from the historical myopia that enveloped him in his exile's existence.

The England where he lived was still resplendent with the glory of the Raj and the appanage of a long-reigning queen whose navies laid claim to the world. It was a place where Disraeli could remark fatuously that English currency and honor were both "just as acceptable in Piccadilly as in Shanghai and, I am sure, at the Gates of Heaven." In such an atmosphere, Marx was virtually doomed to play out Kafka's nightmarish concept of a *privatdocent*, a penniless tutor living in a garret, his days filled with his own imaginings and with jealousy of the university professors who had the benefit of preferential honors, and a good living besides.

Effectively isolated by his overriding personal bias and by physical circumstance, Marx simply did not see that in Italy or Spain or Ireland or China—even in England, in fact, where he labored over his flawed worldview—there was no frontal opposition at all between his hated "superstructure" of the bourgeoisie and the basic "structure" of the proletariat. What there was instead was a considerable homogeneity between all the classes in those countries, as in most others. There was what could loosely but accurately enough be called a common philosophical culture, a common outlook concerning human life, activity and destiny.

Believing that all religion was trash and that spirit was an opiate invented by the bourgeoisie to keep the proletarian masses drugged in their serfdom, Marx was literally unable to see that between a plowman in Donegal, a count in his Venetian palazzo, a weaver in Manchester and a miner in Poland's Silesia, the selfsame spirit he rejected so roundly could blow gently, firmly, binding them all, and all their fellows, in the grace of their common Savior, Jesus Christ, and in the love of their common Father.

It can hardly be surprising, therefore, that not one of Marx's political forecasts was fulfilled in later history. His adaptations of the ideas of men such as Hegel and Darwin did not benefit from his own a priori bias. His grasp of monetary, fiscal and financial matters was as skewed and primitive as his grasp of religion. His demographic studies proved to have no practical application over time.

For religion, therefore, Marx amounted to no more than another thumb-mark of the Fallen Archangel consecrated to his own dreadful oath: "I will not serve." For politics, he was no more than a cog in the developing machine of human relations, a character thrown up by circumstances he dreamed of mastering but never understood. For human intellectualism, he was a mental flatulence; and for human culture, he was no better than Edgar Allan Poe's raven, shrieking, "Nevermore! Nevermore!" at the dawn of a new day.

Doubtless, in a much later and more tranquil age than this era of Gorbachevism, Marx's proper epitaph will be written. But in the meantime, even in this middle period of the Marxist interlude of history, there are already generations of witnesses—hundreds of millions of witnesses, living and dead—to the judgment that he would have served the world better by far had he joined his father probating wills in the courts of Trier, or peddled ties and laces on a busy city street of Königsberg.

For now, however, the bespectacled bust atop his grave at Highgate Hill Cemetery stands as a monument to perverse propaganda and puffery. It gives no hint of Karl Marx, renegade Jew, renegade Christian, halfhearted Satanist, pseudo-intellectual, whose life effort gave birth to the most antihuman ideology our world has ever known. The flowing locks, the ample beard, the bespectacled look of intense concentration are meant to convey the impression of the professor he so longed to be and of the sage he never truly was.

11. V. I. Lenin

Had Marx and his ideas not been swallowed head, tail and entrails by the political founders of world Communism in the twentieth century, beginning with Lenin, there need never have been a Marxist interlude in the progress of human society. For what Marx poured out in ink on paper, Lenin successfully institutionalized.

Lenin was as different from Marx as chalk is from cheese. True, he too borrowed all his ideas from others—chiefly from Marx and Engels. And true, he too was driven by one all-consuming goal—the worldwide proletarian revolution Marx and Engels had predicted. But, unlike Marx, Lenin was a doer of deeds of the first order. He never coveted a place of honor in a university, and he despised the "socialists of the salons."

A flawless genius when it came to organization, an utterly unscrupulous maneuverer for whom any means were acceptable for success, Lenin adapted Marx's social engineering theories holus-bolus to his own revolutionary needs. He was never saddled with any of Marx's moral scruples or intellectual waffling about the violence of that revolution. The fire that burned in Lenin's fanatical mind illumined for him a world already on the threshold of a bloody social and political upheaval on a universal scale.

Nor did Lenin pause over the question, so troubling to Marx, of whether there would ever be an end to the violent class struggle. He was convinced that once he had established the "Paradise of the Workers," the struggle would be finished forever, swallowed somehow in a self-governing Utopia.

In retrospect, it is possible to envision the mind, the character and the intentions of this man of destiny waiting and working for his day. Marx's dry discussions and the touch of poetic pretense in his forecasts contrast with the bloody realism of Lenin, whose predictions were far from idyllic. His plans all were aimed at a complete and bloody break with the past, and at the violent death and final entombment of capitalists and capitalism.

Lenin spent thirty years of his life fomenting those plans. When he did effect the break with Russia's past, he had a mere seven years in which to create the geopolitical instrument necessary for the worldwide revolution that he believed would surely follow as the hinge event of world history.

In essence, Lenin's vision was of another 1848—that "year of revolutions"—in which Marx had defiantly published his foundational *Communist Manifesto*. But this time, the institutional organizations designed and put into place by Lenin would ensure revolution on a world scale.

The one poetic touch in Lenin's otherwise abrasive mind, in fact, concerned that almost dreamlike "Workers' Paradise" he foresaw at the end of the proletarian rainbow. To find a parallel, you would have to go back to the early Hebrew prophets and their forecast of the Messianic Age. Hills flowing with must wine; fields dotted with livestock; children playing with lions and snakes; men and women, workers all, living in a "stateless" society under conditions of endless plenty, absolute justice and perpetual peace among all nations: that was the Leninist Utopia at the end of the revolution's rainbow.

On the near side of that rainbow, however, the reality Lenin foresaw and worked so feverishly to bring about was the grinding tyranny that has been witnessed by the world for seventy years and more.

Lenin began his life on April 22, 1870, as Vladimir Ilyich Ulyanov. He was born into a far different world than Karl Marx's well-groomed, urbanized, middle-class family cradled in conventional European society. According to his contemporaries, he was reared in "conditions of indescribable filth" at a place called Simbirsk—later renamed Ulyanovsk in his honor—on the Volga River, about six hundred miles southeast of Moscow.

In a youthful brush with destiny, he attended the local school directed by Fedor Kerensky, whose son, Aleksandr, would later become prime minister in the only democratic government Russia has ever known, the government that would be overthrown in 1917 by Lenin's armed coup d'état.

It was, at least partly, due to the execution of his older brother, also named Aleksandr, that Vladimir took to the idea of revolution while still in his early teens. Marx's theories and predictions about the proletarian revolution took fire in this young man, as in so many others, because a fire of undying hate already burned within him.

By the time he graduated with a law degree in 1891, Ulyanov had become an authority on Marx. And from the beginning, his vision and his intentions were geopolitical. "The victorious Communist revolution," he wrote as early as 1894, is "the historic mission of the Russian worker," who "will lead the Russian proletariat, side by side with the proletariat of all countries . . . to a victorious Communist revolution." The whole world of mankind—"all this, nothing less than this, nothing more than this"—was his focus and his intended terrain. World history, not merely Russia's story, was the deliberately chosen backdrop for his revolutionary undertaking.

Ulyanov was then twenty-four years old.

In that same year, he met another revolutionary spirit, a young woman named Nadezhda Krupskaya. When, predictably enough, he ran afoul of the Czarist authorities and was sent to Siberia, Krupskaya followed him there. The two were married in 1898 and were never separated until he died twenty-six years later. It was at about that time, too, that Ulyanov changed his name to Lenin. The new name had no meaning as a word; but as a symbol, it stood for his total break with the past.

From the time he left Siberia until he acceded to full power over Russia in 1917, Lenin was constantly on the move. He shuttled back and forth between his homeland and Germany, Switzerland and France, Belgium and England, Sweden and Austria. Always he was writing and talking. Always he was contending for primacy in the leadership of the socialist international fraternity. Always he was maneuvering and plotting, organizing his own political party, the Bolsheviks. And always he was fully persuaded that his day was just around the corner.

That day dawned in the spring of 1917.

The Russian middle class was being impoverished by taxes and by the

destructive onslaught of the Kaiser's Germany in World War I. Workers
were not being paid. The police were corrupt. Landowners had carried
rule over their serfs to terrible extremes. The Russian Orthodox Church
was a slave of the Czarist monarchy. And the monarchy itself, officially
in the hands of Czar Nicholas, was actually in the hands of his German-
born wife, Queen Alexandra, and of her adviser, the pseudoprophetic
monk Grigori E. Rasputin.

The total military defeat of Russia by the Kaiser's forces blew the lid
off the cauldron. In February and March of 1917, the long-simmering
discontent of the Russian people boiled over into the streets. Czar Nicholas abdicated in favor of his uncle, the Grand Duke Michael. But Michael, who saw the handwriting on the wall and preferred life to what he
saw written there, refused the crown.

In the vacuum, a popular government was hastily set up by the main
political parties, based on the collaboration of councils (or soviets) of
Russian workers who elected delegates to a central national assembly.
Those delegates from the soviets formed a Constituent Assembly, or
Duma, which was eventually headed by Lenin's boyhood schoolmate
Aleksandr Kerensky.

It was specifically in regard to that Constituent Assembly that Lenin
committed his first major crime against the Russian people. For seventy
years, the formation of just such a governing assembly had been the aim
of every political party in Russia. "All the best people," wrote Maxim
Gorky, "had lived for the ideal of a Constituent Assembly." Democracy
of some viable kind now had a fragile chance.

Lenin had been in Switzerland before these early volatile events took
place in his homeland. But he was quickly conveyed back to Russia in a
sealed train by the Germans, whose motives were simple and clear
enough: Lenin and his Bolsheviks would help cripple Russia. Unlike
Kerensky, Lenin was predisposed toward Germany by his affinity for the
German-born Marx, but his motives were far more interesting than that.
He had always seen a Russo-German alliance as the key to his domination of the whole of Europe. Not to put too fine a point on the matter by
any means, this was Lenin's early vision of what, in a much later day,
Mikhail Gorbachev would call "our common European home." Once
back in Russia, Lenin threw all his skills as an agent provocateur, as a
redoubtable politician and as a plotter into making this brief democratic
day fruitful for his own plans.

By November 6, his Bolsheviks—who had already formed and armed
their own military units, subverted police and government troops, and
assassinated the more dangerous of their opponents—had moved into

attack positions in the capital, Petrograd (St. Petersburg). Deputies arriving at the Tauride Palace, which was to function as parliament house, found their path blocked by Lenin's troops. By the evening of November 7, Petrograd—later renamed Leningrad—was in Bolshevik hands. Kerensky, who only narrowly escaped death, later fled Russia and eventually made his home in the United States.

Late in November, 42 million people voted in the only free elections Russians have ever been allowed. Lenin's party, the Bolsheviks, polled 24 percent of the vote. The non-Marxist Social Revolution Party emerged with a solid 58 percent. Lenin would have none of it. "We made the mistake," he said, "of promising that this talk shop [the Constituent Assembly] would open up . . . but history has not yet said a word about when we will shut it down."

Lenin quickly made up for history's lack.

Before Lenin's ring of steel closed down all hope, one soviet deputy, S. A. Sorokin, faced the Bolshevik leader with the enormity of his crime. "Now," he screamed at Lenin in public session, "when the great dream [of a truly constituent assembly of free Russians] is about to come true, you dally with the idea of a Bolshevik Paradise. You refuse to do your duty. . . . By clinging to this mad delusion, you will reap its certain fruits: starvation, tyranny, civil war and horrors which you cannot even imagine."

Sorokin's was the prophetic voice of blame not only for that first crime against the great Russian dream, but for all of Russia's subsequent ills and all its subsequent crimes against humanity. For Lenin's "mad delusion" of the violent destruction of all things past, and of absolute power in his own hands, held him fast. The smashing of the Constituent Assembly by an armed minority was purely and simply the first essential step.

Sorokin was only one of many critics. The ablest theoretician among the Bolsheviks, Lev Bronstein (he changed his name to Leon Trotsky), also disagreed with Lenin. He summed up Lenin's action in a single sentence. "The simple and open and brutal breaking up of the Constituent Assembly dealt formal democracy a blow from which it never recovered." For Trotsky, Lenin had betrayed both Russia and the Communist Party.

For Lenin, however, it made no practical difference that his cause had been trounced in the popular vote. It didn't even matter that there had been no Communist Revolution—no glorious uprising of the Russian people in a living expression of his proletarian dream. And certainly it did not matter that there had only been the unlawful and violent rape of national power by the armed bully boys of Lenin's failed Bolshevik Party. A coup would serve the purpose every bit as well in the end.

With power in his hands, there was a great deal for Lenin to do. Peace had to be concluded with European powers. The civil war between various factions within Russia had to be ended. The war had to be settled between Lenin's infant Bolshevik government and the various republics of Russia that did not want to join the Bolsheviks. The economic organization of the country had to be effected.

Over the five years that followed the Bolshevik coup, Lenin at least dominated those problems, even if he didn't solve them all. But by any standard the world might care to use, his greatest achievement by far was his creation of the worldwide institutional organization perfectly suited to the geopolitical attainment of his proletarian ideal. Into the building of that organization Lenin threw every skill he had acquired over the years: his logic, his oratory and his prestige. The ingrained traits of his character all came into play. Mercilessness and ruthlessness with his opponents. Lies. Betrayals. Deception. False promises.

Lenin moved quickly to organize his own deeply revised version of the destroyed Constituent Assembly—a pan-Russian Congress of Soviets, dominated by his Bolsheviks. Hardly had that been accomplished, than a Council of People's Commissars was drawn from the Congress and organized into a Sovnarkom, a Soviet government.

Through his Bolsheviks, Lenin exercised a keen control of the entire process of assembly, discussions and voting. To no one's surprise, therefore, he emerged as the Chairman of the Sovnarkom. He now had in his hands everything he needed by way of building blocks with which to erect the state that would be, in its very essence, the apt and ideal instrument for fomenting and managing every step of the coming worldwide proletarian revolution. The Big Lie had been born.

The constitution and makeup of any other state in his time and before him had been created, first, to render the lives of citizens secure and, second, to promote the public commonweal. That is what men for a long time had considered the aim of any state and government to be.

Lenin, however, had created the historical circumstances that allowed him to turn the entire formula on its head. The Russian people were the vanguard of a new era, and he was the vanguard of the people. The new state he intended to create was not primarily and essentially meant to function for the people. It would use the people for another and wider aim.

As early as 1901–2, in a pamphlet entitled "What Is to Be Done?" he had outlined what sort of a Russian state the proletarian revolution should produce as a transitional stage on the way to the final victory of the worldwide revolution. Russia as a people and as a government should be wholly and professionally devoted to fulfilling just two parallel roles:

the fomenting of that worldwide revolution, and the prevention of all subversion by counterrevolutionaries.

By nature and by definition, all capitalist states were counterrevolutionary, of course. This bedrock conviction supplied Lenin with a clearly defined category into which, infallibly and irrevocably, he placed every government except his own.

One and all, they were enemies of the proletarian revolution in Russia and elsewhere. One and all, they were out to betray, to spy upon, to subvert and to frustrate the proletarian revolution. One and all—by means of propaganda and, above all, by means of their intelligence services—they would bend their efforts to penetrate and honeycomb the Russian proletarian revolution with their own agents. And, one and all, the capitalist states and governments of the world continually suppressed and enslaved their own workers by means of foul propaganda; and thus they were preventing the outbreak of the revolution among the peoples of the rest of the world.

Worse still, it was not only capitalist states that were the enemy. By the very fact of being a capitalist—of making money through capitalism—any individual qualified as a spy, a saboteur, an intelligence agent of the enemy, an oppressor of the proletariat. If you had a shoe factory in Peoria, Illinois, or if you were a pork butcher in Bath, England, or if you drove your own taxi in Sydney, Australia, you qualified as a capitalist in a capitalist country. You were the enemy, and the day was almost at hand when you would be treated as such.

For Lenin, in other words, it was a foregone conclusion that the new Russia—the jealous child of the putative proletarian revolution—would have to be set up structurally and in the most practical terms as a counterintelligence state. It would have to be built to function in such a way as to prevent the penetration and subversion of the liberated Russian people by capitalist espionage, intelligence and propaganda agencies.

At the same time, the new Russia would have a sacred duty to help the proletarian revolution abroad to free itself from the suppression it was undergoing in all capitalist-dominated countries.

These were the only functioning values of the new Russian state, therefore. To counter capitalist intelligence and subversion at home. And to midwife the proletarian revolution in capitalist territory. Once those two aims were achieved, insisted Lenin, the worldwide revolution would take over, and then there would no longer be any need at all for government. The class struggle would be done and over. The people would be free.

Exactly how all that would happen, and what practical order of governance would follow, were not immediately clear. Perhaps state and government would simply fall away universally, like so many leaves in winter; or perhaps they would have to be frozen into submission, defeat and death like unwelcome armies in the Russian snows.

In light of the brutal dictatorship he actually devised, it is remarkable that Lenin truly regarded all constitutional government—including his own infant Sovnarkom—as no more than provisional. It strains credibility that he could for a moment have thought that the wholesale revolution he envisioned and planned for the world would end the class struggle for all time, would relieve the proletariat of all burdens of constitutional government, and would establish the earthly "Paradise of the Workers."

In any case, it was clear that Russia under Lenin would not be anything like an ordinary state.

For one thing, and true to the Leninist call, it would be a state totally under the control, and at the beck and call, of the dedicated Russian proletarian revolutionaries—the Bolsheviks—who were now grouped in the Leninist Communist Party (CP). The CP would be the state. The state would be the CP. The Party-State.

In the most basic and practical terms, Lenin had already done away with the state. Or at least he had made Party and State identical, coterminous with one another. So fundamental was this single factor to the house that Lenin built, that there is no understanding possible of the remarkable geopolitical structure he invented without an understanding of the total identity he forged between Party and State.

Admittedly, Lenin owed more than a bow and a doff of his hat to Marx, even in this. At the same time, like a settler building on land already pioneered and cleared for his use, Lenin imbued Marxist ideas with his own subtle thinking about the political form Marxism should take. And he brought to bear two talents Marx had lacked: a ruthless organizational ability, and long revolutionary experience. The result has rightly and accurately been called Leninist Marxism. Lenin spent the last seven years of his life, from 1917 to 1924, inventing and refining this global machine. It was and remains Lenin's bequest to the Russian people and to the wide world in general. And to Mikhail Gorbachev in particular.

In practice, Lenin carried his decision in favor of violent revolution to a fanatic and fantastic extreme. "Only force would produce social change," he wrote without equivocation.

Logically, then, his first draft of a Soviet constitution in 1917 did not provide for a legal and orderly transfer of power to the proletariat around the world, but for the global seizure of power by armed uprising. Lenin made sure that factor was a matter of bedrock law. The final and complete victory of the proletariat throughout Russia would be the irresistible signal for the workers of the world to sweep away all capitalists everywhere. Then, by Soviet law, all government would be abolished—would simply and immediately disappear from the face of the earth—and the "Workers' Paradise" would ensue.

While such a constitutional provision might resemble an unbirthday party in a proletarian wonderland, it did make clear to Lenin the exact nature of the structure he needed to build. For the first time in history, the Party—the ideological organ of political action—would become the essence and the soul of his new creation. The State would be no more than its outer body.

This new creation—the Party-State—would be the Leninist embodiment of the proletarian march through history, on the rampage against all those spies, intelligence agencies, propaganda machines and other capitalist oppressors of the world proletariat.

By definition, it followed that Lenin's first institutional priority had to be the reorganization—the re-creation, in fact—of the Communist Party. Henceforth, the CP would be composed exclusively of dedicated and professional revolutionaries, men and women virtually consecrated to Lenin's principle of armed and violent overthrow of all governments standing in the way of his worldly and worldwide Paradise. Consecration to principles was a beginning. It was essential, however, that there be a structure—one that would result in the successful creation of a Party-State; that is, a state in which Lenin's ideological Party would in every way be superior to and more powerful than any formal structure of government, because it would be the government.

To that end, Lenin organized his CP on the foundation of the dual "dictatorship"—Lenin's term—of a new organization: the Central Committee (CC) of the CP.

Though the CC would be a part of the CP, it would be so very much in the way that the heart is part of the body: that is, it would be superior to any other Party organ in crucial and specified ways.

The first crucial dictatorial role specified for the CC was in relation to the Party itself. As a practical matter, the handpicked members of the CC exercised control over the lives, the thinking and activities of all the CP's revolutionary members. Absolute and unremitting obedience to the CC was required from all. The purity of the Party in its revolutionary principles, in its proletarian goals, and in its worldwide mandate was thus guaranteed in Lenin's central revolutionary institution.

The second dictatorial role of the CC was to ensure the same degree of purity out among the proletariat at large. The obedient CP was, therefore, the only political party permitted. The proletariat would still have its soviets, or councils of workers' deputies. But all candidates for the deputy posts would be selected by the CP, which in its turn was answerable to the CC.

Lenin's arrangement was that, within clear limits, there should be "freedom of expression"—Lenin's term again—and of opinion within the CP and the proletariat. By design, however, the limits of such freedom were reached the moment the CC took a decision or declared its attitude on doctrinal or practical issues. Once that happened, everyone—CP and proletariat alike—owed blind obedience.

Lenin so organized the all-powerful Central Committee that it exercised its inward dictatorship over the Party, as well as its outward dictatorship over the proletariat, by means of three "sections" that Lenin devised for that purpose: the Secretariat, the Political Bureau, and the Organization Bureau.

The function of the second section, the Political Bureau, was to be the surveillance arm of the Party-State, to monitor and maintain ideological correctness and purity in the political structure of the Party and the State.

It fell to the third section, the Organization Bureau, to monitor the functional efficiency and excellence of the CP, of its CC, and of the entire Party-State government.

In all three sections, of course, Lenin had the first and last say as to candidacy to become a member (already an honor) and actual membership. And all three sections reckoned efficiency and excellence primarily in ideological terms. They were there as the internal organs of the CP, devised to keep it clean of contamination and vigorous in its Leninist-Marxist health.

Except for the final darkened months of his life, Lenin would use these extragovernmental structures to dominate every facet of the CP and the all-powerful CC. For what remained to him of life, he would continue to refine those structures and to stamp them with the unmistakable hallmark of genuine Leninism—an explicit and ever-haunting preoccupation with that element so vitally important in the Leninist geopolitics: the counterintelligence mission of the Party-State.

Indeed, as early as December 20, 1917, and under Lenin's inspiration and insistence, the then spanking-new Sovnarkom had already issued the protocol that first established the All-Russian Extraordinary Commission to Counteract Counter-Revolution and Sabotage. Known by one of the most famous of all Soviet acronyms, CHEKA, this department was attached structurally as the good right arm of the CC's first section, the Secretariat.

CHEKA became more than the linchpin of the Leninist structure. In a true sense, CHEKA was *the* essential structure. In its later forms—GPU, OGPU, NKVD and KGB—it would remain so, both within and outside the Soviet Union. Unchanged in its purpose, it lived through every change in Soviet government and leadership down to and including the Gorbachevism of our present day. As long as the KGB backs Gorbachev, he will last.

Headed first by a Polish ex-seminarian, Feliks Edmondovich Dzerzhinsky, CHEKA had fused within its charter and its functions all effective police powers, all state security duties and all judicial powers. It was the single most efficient expression of Lenin's concept of the new Bolshevik Russia, and of the new Bolshevik world: state security must be coterminous not with the government, but with the Party. Government security was assured, because the government was the Party's own bailiwick.

Dzerzhinsky, born in Vilna as the son of a country squire, was dismissed from the Catholic seminary at the age of seventeen. Already a Marxist, he spent twenty-two years in and out of Czarist political jails until his mentor and close friend, Lenin, freed him from prison in March 1917.

As a hardened Party member, a cold-eyed fanatic and an experienced student of espionage, torture, subversion and human psychology, Dzerzhinsky was the ideal man to create what Lenin wanted: an all-seeing, all-knowing, all-penetrating, octopus-like organization with its own rules and procedures, its own internal security measures, its political self-purging processes, its mechanism of detecting and foiling the intelligence and subversion activities of the Party-State's enemies, internal and external.

It took Lenin and Dzerzhinsky a short time to realize that the intelligence game between nations was only secondarily a matter of data gathering, of "spying" in the classical sense of the word and of ascertaining the factual condition of opponents and competitors.

As the game of nations, intelligence was and still is, as Angelo M. Codevilla wrote, the art of assessing the opponent's predilections—what he seeks and what he expects of you; and then of shaping and manipulating what he knows about you and what he expects you to do.

That subtlety of induced deception has been the essence of international intelligence since the legendary Sun Tzu, writing in China in the fourth century B.C., set out its principles in the text of *Ping Fa: The Art of War.* It is of more than passing interest that *Ping Fa* has been obligatory reading in all the military academies of the USSR and its satellites.

Under Dzerzhinsky's twisted and almost preternatural genius for such things, CHEKA developed precisely those sophisticated forms of deception, designed and refined to elicit the consent of those who are being deceived. In one of the few remarks authentically ascribed to him, this "Polish Master of Deception"—Churchill's phrase—boasted that "We get to know what a man insists is real, and we give him precisely that. We have food for everybody's taste."

The fact that as early as 1918 Lenin and Dzerzhinsky launched their first successful deception scenario—the famous "Lockhart" or "Ambassadors" plot of August 1918—reveals how deeply and sensitively the founders of the new Party-State had studied their role as leaders of an international counterintelligence state. In the twenties, there followed other successes, known to intelligence specialists as the "Trust" and "Sendikat" legends.

If, as a practical matter, the Party had intrusive designs on the totality of human life, CHEKA made those intrusive designs achievable. For, just as the Party was not limited by the government, so CHEKA was not limited by the Party. Somewhat like Frankenstein's monster, CHEKA was at least potentially stronger than its creator and would-be master.

In *Chekisty*, a particularly brilliant analysis of CHEKA, John Dziak puts the matter clearly and—given Lenin's unremitting hatred of all religion in general, and Roman Catholicism in particular—ironically, as well. Lenin, says Dziak, had established a "secular theocracy . . . in which the Party was Priesthood, served by a combination of Holy Office (Central Committee) and Temple Guard (CHEKA)."

The numbers speak eloquently in favor of that analysis, and of the ever-increasing power of the "Temple Guard." In 1917, CHEKA had 17 members. In January 1919, it had 37,000 members. By mid-1921, reorganized as GPU, it had 262,400 members. By the time Feliks Dzerzhinsky died in 1926, the troops and civilian staff of this "enforcer arm" of Lenin's creation numbered almost half a million.

It has become a kind of axiomatic shorthand among today's Westerners to talk about this Leninist creation—from CHEKA to KGB—as though it were nothing more than the so-called intelligence services commonly established by other nations as subordinate adjuncts of civil government.

Obviously, however, and by design, CHEKA was not subordinate to any government. Up until that point, Lenin's organizational victories had resulted in the unique creation of a Party-State. With his creation of

CHEKA, that Party-State became in its very essence what it has since remained: a counterintelligence state.

Given that the Party itself was the creature of Lenin's adaptation of Marxist ideology, and given Lenin's own ideal of the worldwide Workers' Paradise, it followed that the Party would have to pursue its built-in ideological millennial imperative. Its mandate, its function and its destiny were to head the worldwide proletarian revolution that would usher in the millennium of that Workers' Paradise on earth. Armed with CHEKA, Lenin's counterintelligence Party-State was ready to become the executor of history's mandate on the geopolitical plane.

Virtually all of the stunning reorganization and creation of Party structures dedicated to that single-minded purpose was well on the way to completion by 1918, when, under Lenin's guidance and at his behest, the infant Sovnarkom transformed itself by a unanimous vote of its delegates into the rawboned youth calling itself the Russian Federation of Socialist Republics (RSFR). Like Sovnarkom, the RSFR was to be but a passing instrument in the hands of the Leninist Party-State. Quickly, the RSFR adopted Lenin's 1917 draft constitution as basic law, complete with its mandate for the overthrow of capitalist regimes by violent force.

In that same year, Lenin already lamented that "our CHEKA unfortunately does not extend to America."

Seeking the first pegs on which to anchor a geopolitical network that would hasten the day of worldwide proletarian revolution, Lenin seized upon an earlier initiative of European socialists. This was the International Workingmen's Association, founded with Karl Marx's participation in London in 1864. Known as the First International, it had been succeeded by a refurbished Second International in 1889. It was at the Moscow Congress of 1919, convened to produce the Third International, that Lenin seized control and created the Communist International (the Comintern), intending it to be an international clone of his own CP. The Comintern did indeed function as that Party clone, until it was dissolved by Stalin in 1943. He did not need it anymore.

By the end of 1920 and into 1921, Lenin had in place the beginnings of a network covering Western Europe and the Americas. It began with single individuals—"moles," in latter-day jargon—placed strategically so that they could work clandestinely toward their ultimate function of promoting the revolution, now constitutionally mandated abroad by the Leninist Party-State in its drive to the millennium.

Never one to miss the full opportunities afforded by structural reorganization, Lenin took two more ingenious steps, one hard upon the other. In December 1920, he created the Foreign Department (IND) of his enforcement arm, CHEKA. Then, in 1921, he reorganized the "third section" of the Red Army into the Intelligence Directorate (RU), which he placed under the direct control of CHEKA's IND.

As night follows day, then, it followed that the secret role of RU in foreign intelligence was to be an obedient extension of Soviet domestic intelligence. That is, the aims of RU abroad were identical with CHEKA's domestic aims: first, to establish and protect the Party-State across the world as nothing more or less than a global counterintelligence state. And, second, to guard the ideological purity of the workers' revolution always and everywhere.

The means used by RU—and by its successor organization, GRU, to this day—in carrying out its assigned role was the intimate and completely clandestine interlayering of its own personnel within the diplomatic missions sent by the Party-State all over the world.

No image more exactly conveys the working ideal of this most clandestine army of the Leninist structure abroad than webs spun by a spider from its very entrails. Webs so transparent as to be invisible unless—improbably—the light of day were to shine directly upon their ever-widening embrace of individuals, governments and societies.

Complementing this invisible structure was a second one that also rode piggyback on diplomatic missions. Or, more exactly, it redefined the basic purpose of Soviet diplomatic missions to include the counterintelligence functions already enshrined in Moscow's machinery.

Under the direction and control of CHEKA, diplomatic missions—in addition to acting as funnels for the entry of RU's moles around the world—were themselves transformed into export vehicles for the Leninist ideal. Every diplomatic mission was to have the same ultimate objective as the Soviet Party-State it represented.

It was not merely logical, therefore, but unavoidable that the foreign policy of the Leninist Party-State would be conducted through its diplomatic missions on two tiers. On the overt level, the necessary diplomatic relations proper to every state were carried on in a more or less usual manner, by more or less usual personnel—ambassadors, consuls, chargés d'affaires and the general contingent of accredited individuals.

At a decidedly unusual level, meanwhile, the IND arm of CHEKA saw to the systematic inclusion of a dedicated intelligence component within the staff of every diplomatic mission around the world.

Separate and independent from the totally covert RU network—and sometimes at odds with it, though both were controlled ultimately by CHEKA—this IND diplomatic intelligence component was multidimensional. It was the chief instrument through which Moscow's policy directives were delivered to the more or less normal mission personnel. And it was Lenin's organizational insurance policy, guaranteeing that his foreign missions themselves would be kept in line.

But it was far more than a mere monitor and control sector. For this intelligence component was designed as well to carry on its officially assigned and directed program of espionage and counterintelligence abroad.

IND activity abroad wasn't as invisible as the web spun by the RU, to be sure. But it was nicely camouflaged all the same.

Under the cover of such seemingly benign front organizations as "friendship" societies, cultural organizations, labor unions, peace movements, and the like, Lenin used IND to set in place the successful model for what was to become one of the most effective official programs of daily, systematic and dedicated international espionage and counterintelligence ever devised, a program that finally embraced industry, political institutions, military matters and cultural affairs in every nation that hosted an accredited Soviet diplomatic mission.

In 1922, the RFSR transformed itself—again at Lenin's behest, and again by unanimous vote—into the fully formed adult we know as the Union of Soviet Socialist Republics (USSR). The home-based Communist Party (CP), therefore, became the Communist Party of the Soviet Union (CPSU).

By that time, in his single-minded fanaticism, and with his never-failing organizational genius, Lenin had established the interlocking domestic and international network upon which the geopolitical institution of Leninist Marxism would continue to be built. And he had established as bedrock the three most basic principles of that institution.

The first principle was that the world dictatorship of the proletariat could be established only by violent revolution, resulting in the overthrow of capitalist-based governments. The choice for violence, made irrevocably before he was twenty, was Lenin's most enduring personal thumb-mark. It stamped all of his thinking, planning and organization for the worldwide proletarian revolution. And, therefore, it determined the course of Soviet history, and that of much of the world, for most of the twentieth century.

The second bedrock Leninist principle dealt with authority and structure. The Communist Party of the Soviet Union, because of the experience it claimed in revolution, always knew best. For that reason, all non-Russian CPs were to function as local branches of the CPSU. Any CP outside Russia was to be organized along the same lines. Moreover, each foreign CP must be subject to the CPSU—to the centralized control of Lenin and his successors—both in its choice of local CC members, and in its policies.

The third Leninist principle was the basic counterintelligence dimension of Party rule. That principle would hold in the Soviet Party-State and would be extended country by country as an essential element of the proletarian Paradise.

Long after Lenin's corpse was encased in glass and granite beneath Red Square, and long after his ideal of the world as the Workers' Paradise had been betrayed, those principles would stand as the pillars upon which the Soviet geopolitical institution he made possible would be based. His firm conviction about the international—and ultimately the geopolitical—role of the USSR remained as the ineradicable hallmark of the authentic Leninist-Marxist mind.

Lenin's errors of judgment are patently clear to a later generation, and to list them does magnify one's horror at his mental provincialism; at the same time it underlines the mountain to which Mikhail Gorbachev has set his shoulder.

Relying on analyses produced by Marx in the last third of the nineteenth century—analyses already flawed in themselves and, in any case, based on data no longer valid in the twentieth century, Lenin went on to commit his gravest mistake in judgment. Led by slanted or incomplete data of his own, his perspective distorted by what amounted to wishful thinking, Lenin presumed that everywhere there was a vast downtrodden proletariat "structure." And he assumed that everywhere an utterly oppressive "superstructure" lay atop the proletariat like an incubus.

Topple that superstructure, he imagined, and—Presto!—the proletariat would rise as one world body and destroy its oppressors.

If the workers of the world did not arise in wrath, it was only because capitalism—in its agonizing death throes—had temporarily prolonged its life by expanding into colonial areas in the late nineteenth and early twentieth centuries. But he saw it collapsing with the start of World War I. With that collapse, Lenin was certain that the last alternative for the decadent capitalist systems would be spent. Soon, therefore, very soon, there would be an overwhelming wave of revolutions. They were just waiting to be sparked among the working classes everywhere—in Europe, Asia, Africa, the Americas. One supposes that such a simplistic trust in a coming wave of revolutions was at least bolstered in Lenin's mind by the visible breakup of empires, and by the economic plight of post–World War I Europe.

Having renounced all reliance on the moral and religious traditions that had made Western civilization possible in the first place, however, Lenin suffered from a poverty of alternatives. His organizational genius was undeniable. But his intellectualism was a borrowed and piecemeal thing; and it had gone barren. Like Marx before him, he was guilty of a false and subjective reading of history that left him with an appallingly skewed vision of what the future must be like. And not the least of it was his misreading from start to finish of how free-market economics would actually fare, and of how resilient was democracy as preserved in capitalist nations.

There was one quickly passing moment toward the end of his life when Lenin had within arm's reach the possibility of correcting the most fatal flaws in his Leninism. It came in the person of a relatively obscure and resourceless Sardinian by the name of Antonio Gramsci.

A convinced Marxist living in Italy at the very moment Benito Mussolini came to power, Gramsci took off for Lenin's USSR in 1922 and remained there for the last two years of Lenin's life. He absorbed all of Lenin's geopolitical vision, and all of Lenin's conviction that a force innate in mankind was driving it on toward the "Workers' Paradise."

For all that, however, Gramsci was too aware of the facts of history and of life to accept the gratuitous assumption—made in the first instance by Marx, and then accepted unquestioningly by Lenin—that human society was divided throughout the world into the two broad and simple camps defined as the oppressed "structure" of the people and the oppressive "superstructure" of capitalism.

As a well-informed historian and a well-trained objective analyst, Gramsci argued against such deceptive imaginings. He argued and wrote about a common culture that had forged a complex homogeneity among all the classes in the Western capitalist nations. He recognized it as a culture that had been seeded and brought to fruition by nearly two thousand years of religion and politics, literature and art, war and peace. There was no chasm, said Gramsci, between the proletarian masses and what Marx and Lenin called the superstructure. There was only social advantage and economic predominance.

As a realist, Gramsci knew he was knocking his Marxist head against the bulwark of Christian culture, which pointed unceasingly to something beyond man and outside man's material cosmos. Gramsci's triumph—a posthumous one, as it turned out—was that he understood how that Christian bulwark could be and would be undone; and it had nothing to do with violent revolution and the universal uprising of the proletariat. Indeed, it was a solution that would prove to be far more subtle and far more effective than anything imagined by Marx or Lenin.

Gramsci's discussions and arguments on this crucial point of Leninist violence did not earn him any great popularity among his socialist brothers in the Moscow of that time, however. By the time he left the Soviet Union, Gramsci knew the world would face two specters in the immediate future. The Fascism of Mussolini—*"il gran pappone di tutto fascismo"* (the granddaddy of all Fascists), as he later described the Italian dictator—was the first specter. The rise of Stalin in the Soviet Union was the second.

Gramsci chose to make his stand in Italy. His day in the Leninist sun would be postponed. But it would come.

While it is testimony to Lenin's driving persuasiveness, and to Feliks Dzerzhinsky's prowess at seductive deception, it is hardly to their own credit that over time—and unlike the clear-eyed Gramsci—a certain number of highly regarded intellectuals in England, France, Germany and the United States bought into Lenin's reading of history, flaws and all.

The Depression at the end of the twenties and in the thirties was the convincer for those minds. Stunted by the same poverty of historic alternatives that afflicted Lenin, and willing to believe Dzerzhinsky's sophisticated scenarios—"disinformation" was the word the Soviets finally coined—those intellectuals could conceive of no choice left for the West except Sovietization. The permanent Marxism of an Edmund Wilson, and the slavish adulation of Stalin by so many English and Americans, are explicable if not excusable in the light of an intellectualism that was less realistic than romantic, and that was easily cuckolded.

Lincoln Steffens raised the most apt and famous banner for this group. With one visit to the USSR behind him, Steffens was like a teenager in love. "I have seen the future" in the Soviet Union of Joseph Stalin, he declared with an unreserved and now manifest fatheadedness, "and it works."

It had to be admitted that the free press of the West did nothing to disabuse such fatheaded assessments. There were no Gramscis among the journalists sent by the major Western news organizations as resident correspondents to Moscow over the years. There were no news flashes alerting the world to the mass liquidation of millions of political enemies of the Leninist-Marxist proletarian revolution on its bloody path to the Marxian ideal of the Workers' Paradise. There were no protest votes at the assemblies of the old League of Nations, no diplomatic protests by Western powers, no sanctions applied by the international community. On the contrary, a steady stream of well-placed magazine and newspaper articles kept on extolling the glories of "what was going on over in Russia," as Bernard Shaw described it, "and how finally commonsense and reason are prevailing over the worn-out shibboleths of past ages." Lenin and Dzerzhinsky must have smiled in satisfaction, and Stalin must have been highly satisfied. The deception was working admirably.

12. Joseph Stalin

Symptoms of cerebral sclerosis were already manifest in Lenin by March of 1921. His physical deterioration was hastened, no doubt, by the two bullets that remained lodged in his neck and his left shoulder following an attempt on his life in 1918. Ignoring his physical decline, however— and at his most benign shunting aside all criticism, including the clever and prophetic ideas of Antonio Gramsci—Lenin worked on as hard as he could at perfecting his created instrument for violent world revolution.

On February 6, 1922, CHEKA was replaced by a new organization, the State Political Directorate (GPU). Lenin wanted to get rid of "deadwood" in the organization and to implement the lessons learned about counterintelligence not merely as a security service but as a systemic principle for the domestic and foreign functioning of the USSR Party-State.

Despite the fact that Lenin's weakened physical condition was regarded by his physicians as temporary, the need was apparent, by the time the Eleventh Party Congress assembled in Moscow in April of 1922, to appoint someone to carry on until Lenin could regain his strength and resume full control.

The temporary post of General Secretary was created. And, though it was intended as a momentary expedient, the post carried with it control over the Secretariat—the first and most powerful section of the Central

Committee of the CPSU. Control, therefore, over the entire machinery of the proletarian revolution.

The Party's choice to fill this post, aided by Lenin's vote, fell on a man who had been Lenin's close follower since shortly after the turn of the century: the forty-three-year-old Iosif Vissarionovich Dzhugashvili.

Born in Gori, Georgia, on December 21, 1879, to a sadistic shoemaker, Vissarion, and a rigidly orthodox and pious mother, Keke, Iosif was destined by Keke to be a Russian Orthodox priest. He did enter the seminary, stayed for five years, and then was dismissed for "disloyal views."

There followed a more or less murky period in which it is extremely difficult to detach later created legends from original events. Dzhugashvili was into revolution, that much is sure. He was supposedly a socialist with Marxist views. But rather compelling evidence indicates that he did function as a onetime agent for the dreaded Czarist secret security police, the Okhrana, who were hunting to the death all such revolutionaries as Lenin and his Bolsheviks.

Nothing we know about Dzhugashvili's character forbids us to draw this conclusion: He was always a man to hedge his bets until the winning horse broke from the pack. The ambiguity of his character, however, also allows us to speculate that if he did—as seems likely from the evidence—betray some of his "socialist brothers" into Okhrana dungeons and death, he did it in order to get rid of colleagues he considered to be otherwise immovable obstacles on his own path to success.

Presumably, it became clear to Dzhugashvili soon enough that the Czar and his regime were not the horses to back. For once he met Lenin at a Party conference in Tammerfors, Finland, in 1905, Dzhugashvili became his close adherent and a dedicated Marxist.

With Lenin, he attended Party Congresses in Stockholm and London. He became a specialist in raiding Czarist treasury transports to secure working funds for the Bolshevik Party. Like any good revolutionary, he underwent imprisonment and deportation. Like any clever revolutionary, he always managed to escape. Like any canny revolutionary, he never engaged in hand-to-hand combat. And over the years he steadily built up a record as a fantastically skilled organizer with a cool, calculating head, a mind tenaciously attuned to the long term, and nerves of steel.

Dzhugashvili was married three times and fathered two sons and a daughter. The day he buried his first wife, Ekaterina Svanidze, he stood beside a boyhood friend at the edge of the cemetery, and through the already blackened stumps of his teeth spat out the oath that was perhaps the most revealing commentary on his whole life to come. Defeated in his personal choice and deeply angry, he swore, "I will never again love anybody in this life."

It may be that he never did. His second wife, Nadezhda Alliluyeva, unable to withstand his hardness and hate, committed suicide. His third wife was Rosa Kaganovich, sister of Lazar Moiseyevich Kaganovich, a fellow revolutionary and one of Dzhugashvili's trusted lieutenants; they were divorced, and Rosa disappeared into total obscurity.

Even his mother seemed never to have received the slightest token of positive feeling from Dzhugashvili. Despite her son's rise to dictatorial glory, she lived all her life in poverty and obscurity. Content with her icons and medals and devotional activities, Keke died in the reassurance of her Russian Orthodox faith in Christ.

Like many of his revolutionary comrades, Dzhugashvili collected a bevy of aliases over the years—"Ivanovich," "Koba," "Comrade K," "Vassily." His earliest *klechka*, or nickname, among his comrades spoke of a chilling side to his character. "Demonschile," they called him. "Devil."

When he was thirty-four, after some eight years of outstanding Bolshevik activity, Dzhugashvili was co-opted by Lenin into the Central Committee of the CP. It was then that he changed his name once and for all to Joseph Stalin. "Man of Steel."

Having served by that time as the first editor of *Pravda*—then as now, the newspaper mouthpiece of the Party regime—and in several other important posts in the Party and its state apparatus, Stalin was increasingly privy to all the inner councils of Lenin's Bolsheviks.

By the spring of 1922, Stalin did appear to be the most capable man to put in temporary charge of the Party machinery as General Secretary. In any case, it would only be for a short while. Lenin would be back in shape and in charge again in no time, after all. But the first stroke hit Lenin on May 26, 1922. It left him with his right arm and leg partially paralyzed, and with some speech disturbance. Determined not to give in, he was back in his office by October. But on December 15, a second stroke meant that Lenin's work was effectively over.

Lenin had seen enough even in those six months, however, to draw the same conclusion as Antonio Gramsci, who soon chose to take his chances in Fascist Italy. Stalin was not to be trusted.

Matters came to a head as Lenin sided with Stalin's rivals in a Central Committee clash over economic measures. Rather than attack Lenin directly, Stalin aimed an extraordinarily abusive attack against Lenin's most visible surrogate, his ever-loyal wife, Nadezhda Krupskaya. He even went so far as to threaten to have Krupskaya tried for treason. Presumably, Stalin sought to cow Lenin through Krupskaya; but whatever his reasoning, it was a needless tactical mistake for which he paid a price.

Lenin dictated what has since been called his last will and testament —his famous "Letter to the Congress" (of Party Delegates)—in which he recommended that the Party set Stalin aside. "Comrade Stalin has concentrated boundless power in his hands," warned Lenin, "and I am not certain he can always use his power with sufficient caution."

Lenin recommended that Stalin be replaced by either of his two great rivals, one of whom Lenin pointedly praised. "Comrade Trotsky . . . is distinguished by remarkable abilities. . . . [He] is the most able person on the present Central Committee."

Lenin made a point of being present when his "Letter" was read to a plenary meeting of the Party. Stalin sat beneath the podium, a suitably miserable, repentant and unhappy look on his face. For Stalin, however, it was all theater. And for Lenin it was all over. The Man of Steel—an organizational genius in his own right—understood all the byways of the revolutionary structure he now controlled. He had locked his power center away from any tampering, even by Lenin.

Several old colleagues of Lenin, whom Stalin had already recruited to his own support, rose to lead a "boys-will-be-boys" defense of this remarkable comrade, Joseph Stalin. There did remain the matter of Stalin's inflamed attack against Krupskaya—a prematurely intemperate act that had to be normalized to satisfy Lenin's power bloc.

As Lenin had once observed, however, Comrade Stalin was not a man for petty intrigues. It cost him little to make a public apology to Krupskaya. There were more important things to attend to, and Stalin meant to get on with it. From that point on, it does not seem to have mattered what Lenin thought or wished in Stalin's regard.

Had Lenin's physicians been right—had he regained but half his strength, in fact, and lasted just two or three more years—the matter of Stalin's rise would have been disposed of, and world history might have taken a different course. But Lenin's day was spent. There remained for him only lingering hours with his beloved Nadezhda at their villa in Gorki, the honorable attention of his followers, and the smiling stare of Stalin's dark brown eyes watching every move by everyone.

If Antonio Gramsci understood at least as well as Lenin what lay in store for the Soviet Union and the proletarian revolution under Stalin, Stalin himself understood Lenin's structural invention of the supreme Party-State—including its geopolitical potential—to a fare-thee-well.

Lenin had been driven by his ideal of the world proletarian revolution, and by his goal of the Workers' Paradise. Stalin was driven by perhaps the most grasping and possessive personal ambition in the annals of great leaders. He would be master of all nations. Of all the earth, in fact. For, like it or not, Lenin's monolith—the geopolitical institutional organization he had created—now belonged to Stalin. And Stalin knew what he had to do: transform Leninist Marxism with his own ideas.

Given the shift in Stalin's intended use of that monolith, there were three basic elements that were liabilities from his point of view. Three elements that would have to be eliminated.

First, Leninist Marxism advocated inner-Party democracy. Limited as it was, that freedom of opinion and expression always supported by Lenin and his Bolsheviks within their own ranks could mean nothing but trouble for Stalin's personal rule. He wanted no one doing to him what he had done to Lenin, after all. He needed the Party apparatus to be a monolith of another sort, a body not primarily at the service of the proletariat, but completely subservient to him personally.

The second liability of the Leninist setup was that it was internationalist. Stalin had no altruism. He never indulged in messianic dreams or poetry. The "pie-in-the-sky" dimension of Leninism, even if the sky were proletarian, was so much idealistic poppycock. And, in any case, a worldwide dictatorship of the proletariat, followed by the disappearance of all government and statist control, would mean simply and clearly that Stalin himself would fade from central importance.

The third liability was that the Leninist monolith incorporated no ultimate plan to place the Soviet Party-State—and Stalin as its leader—at the forefront of nations. For that, and not some messianic promise of earthly Paradise, was the goal at the end of Stalin's proletarian rainbow. And already he was aware of disturbing information about certain foreign leaders of Communist parties in Europe—some Germans, French and Yugoslavs, for example—whose analysis of the world situation, and whose expectations in their own countries, seemed more in line with Antonio Gramsci's ideas than with Lenin's. Obviously, then, and whatever the details, there were certainly socialist ideas circulating abroad that did not square with the revised monolith Stalin now proposed to fashion.

Lenin was still alive when Stalin moved to eliminate the first Leninist liability—inner-Party democracy. It was a simple and ingenious matter of a turnabout of Lenin's priorities.

Lenin's last important structural change in his monolith, made in February 1922, had been to replace the all-powerful CHEKA with a purged GPU. In July of 1923, under Stalin's guiding hand, GPU was replaced in its turn by the United State Directorate (OGPU), whose membership was purged again—this time of Leninist Bolsheviks.

More important, the new charter of OGPU implied the reversal of Lenin's dictum that the Party was supreme. For OGPU was no longer under control of the Central Committee, and certainly not of the Party. Instead, it was placed under the direct control of the General Secretary, Joseph Stalin. And to its duties of border control and internal security was added the duty of surveillance of Party leaders themselves.

Inner-Party democracy was a dead letter.

Stalin took one more stunning step in his re-creation of the Party-State before Lenin died, a step with implications for Stalin's solution of the second liability of Leninist internationalism, as well as the third liability that would allow the Soviet Party-State to slip from world dominance, and Stalin along with it.

Lenin's constitution adopted in 1918 by the RFSR applied only to the territory encompassed by the traditional Russian heartland and Siberia. The RFSR did not include, or make constitutional provision for, the Transcaucasian Federation composed of the Ukraine, Byelorussia, Georgia, Armenia and Azerbaijan. As a practical fact, however, the Red Army was in control of those territories. Moreover, Lenin's Bolsheviks dominated all the soviets, or workers' assemblies, in those areas, as well as the Council of Soviet Commissars elected by the soviets. Structurally, in other words, the CPSU already dominated the politics and policies of those nominally "independent" regions.

It required only the expedient of rubber-stamp approval by the Central Committee on July 6, 1923, for Stalin to inhale those territories into the USSR. It was just one more proletarian victory that came without the glory of a proletarian revolution, or even the pretense of proletarian consent.

There has always been a suspicion that a slow-acting poison was the cause of Lenin's death in January of 1924, and that Stalin had Lenin's viscera removed and cremated—against the violently expressed wishes of his widow, Nadezhda Krupskaya—to avoid later forensic medical detection.

Whatever the truth may have been, Lenin was dead. The childless Krupskaya was reduced to a living cipher, and would remain so until her own death in 1939. Feliks Dzerzhinsky might have meant trouble for Stalin. As the first head of CHEKA, he was the one man who knew everybody's secrets, including Stalin's. But Dzerzhinsky's sudden death on July 20, 1926, guaranteed his silence.

Stalin now had no worthwhile opponents left.

· · ·

With that farsightedness Lenin had once so admired, Stalin now set in earnest about the job of securing the whole of the Party and the whole of the State as one monolithic body subservient completely and personally to himself.

At first, he stayed with inner-Party maneuvers—another skill Lenin had admired. Later, there were direct assassinations through paid henchmen. Finally, Stalin's Great Purges and Mock Trials of the thirties would transform Soviet society, and achieve Stalin's objective at home. His cult would be securely established. The "Miraculous Georgian," as Lenin had once called Stalin, would eliminate what dissension remained, would once and for all secure the Communist Party as the only party in the Soviet state, and would secure his own position as that Party's only leader.

At about the same time he set out on his course of securing complete power at home, the means fell into Stalin's hands to tackle the second major problem of the Leninist structure—its "altruistic" internationalism. In this area, in fact, he had the greatest ally he could want: the timing of events over which he had no control.

The proletarian revolutions that had been fomented by Lenin in China and Germany were in shambles by 1923. There had been no uprising of the proletariat in either country. In fact, the chief architect of the Leninist plan for China, Mikhail Markovich Borodin, had been brought home and garroted for his failure. And the decisive defeat of the German Communist Party in the elections of 1923 spelled failure for revolutionary success in that country. In the thirties, Stalin would make Lenin's mistake all over again in Spain, and would find out at a terrible cost that even he could not make a badly based formula for revolution pan out. On this occasion, however, he made such failure work for him.

Less than a year after Lenin's death, with the full support of his bloc on the Central Committee behind him, Stalin was able to announce that true Leninism did not insist on internationalism, after all, for this moment of history.

What it did insist upon, Stalin declared, was something he called "socialism in one country"—a phrase that came to be as renowned around the world as its portentous meaning: Soviet predominance. The Russian Revolution was "self-sufficient," Stalin announced to the CC. It needed no bolstering by socialism in other countries. The perfecting of "socialism" in the USSR (the "one country") was the quickest path to worldwide "socialism."

Stalin insisted further, and truthfully, that this was not a repudiation of the proletarian revolution. It meant simply this: The Russian Revolution was supreme; and Stalin was its supreme leader. Neither he nor the Soviet Party-State was the mere equal of anyone in the worldwide "socialist fraternity."

That much settled in the Central Committee of the CPSU—for settled it was—every trait of the Leninist brand of Soviet internationalism was eliminated from the Soviet Party's pronouncements, discussions and ideology. Only the practical matter of its complete burial around the world remained to be accomplished.

For that purpose, Stalin turned to another of Lenin's structures, the Comintern. By means of the troika of tactics at which he was so adept—parliamentary maneuvers, bribery and forceful elimination—Stalin first transformed the still weakling Comintern into an interim body through which to channel his domestic dogmas and his foreign policies. When it suited him later, he would simply eliminate the Comintern altogether. But during the twenties and thirties, Stalinist activities were extended through the refurbished Comintern to the colonies of the capitalist empires—British, Dutch, French, Portuguese.

Such moves made perfect Stalinist sense. For the proletarian fact of life now was that any Communist revolution that produced a possible rival to Stalin in the matter of total and worldwide control was unacceptable. In time, such men as Tito in Yugoslavia, Mao Zedong in China, Enver Hoxha in Albania, all became examples of what lay in store for Communist revolutionaries who refused to accept a properly subservient place within the Stalinist monolith.

Even in the interim, however, Stalin could not rely totally for his international power base on so weak an organization as the Comintern. Nor did he have to. He had the three Moscow-based networks Lenin had set in place to carry out intelligence and counterespionage abroad. Under Stalin's control, the coordination of those three Leninist networks was raised to an unprecedented level of efficiency.

It was the third of these Leninist networks—the one that covered "client" socialist states, satellite states and revolutionary movements abroad—that was Stalin's true base of international expansion.

"Wherever Soviet clone states emerge"—American analyst John Dziak's words again—"the same pattern repeats itself—whether it is Cuba or Nicaragua in Latin America, or Ethiopia or Angola in Africa, or Afghanistan or China in Asia. The first products exported to such states invariably are a Party or Party-type movement to organize and focus political power; and a state security apparatus to secure the monop-

CHAMPIONS OF HAMMER AND SICKLE

oly of that power, to organize society in an atomized manner in order to facilitate control, and to commence the search for 'enemies of the people.' . . . General impoverishment soon follows. . . . The counter-intelligence state can generate power. . . . It cannot generate economic welfare for the common good."

That is a fair description of the Stalinist version of Lenin's Workers' Paradise.

Control and authority were everywhere paramount for Stalin, no doubt about that. But by 1931, it became clear that he had to give priority to another liability—a purely domestic one—that he had inherited from Lenin.

"We are fifty or a hundred years behind the advanced countries," Stalin declared to a conference of industrial managers in that year. "We must make good this lag in ten years," he warned. "Either we do it, or they crush us." Democratic capitalism was not dying after all, it seemed.

The cost of Stalin's plan to transform the Soviet Union from a backward nation into a twentieth-century power was horrific to a degree unparalleled in human history. Stalin called that plan the Second Revolution. It was beside the point by that time that there had been no First Revolution.

Internally, Stalin transformed the society and the economy of the Soviet Union by means of two gigantic processes, which also completed the consolidation of Stalin's uncontested power in the USSR: the collectivization of agriculture; and the Stalinist reign of terror. By these two sweeping policies, Stalin aimed to eliminate every vestige of private capital. Only the state would be enriched. In turn, the state would transform the USSR into an agriculturally self-sufficient and industrially advanced world power.

The specific function of collectivization in this plan was to rid the Soviet Union of prosperous private-enterprise farmers—those same hapless kulaks whose terrible fate served as a grim warning to Archbishop Amleto Cicognani only a few years later, when Soviet Ambassador Maksim Litvinov argued for Vatican support of the USSR in World War II. Indeed, some years down the line, Stalin himself told Winston Churchill coolly that the problem of private ownership had been solved "by the use of cattle cars." Four million small landowners were packed into those cattle cars, which transported them to Siberian detention camps and quick, merciless execution.

Stalin did not mention a word to Churchill about what chronicler Robert Conquest has called the "Harvest of Sorrow"—the planned liquidation of some fifteen million Ukrainians. Nor did he bring up his fixed triple policy of terror: systematically induced famine, the use of poison gas and the creation of a vast network of death camps in Siberia, to which those who survived were deported. Conservative estimates put the total number of Stalin's victims at 25–35 million.

Stalin found ample and explicit mandate for his policy of planned genocide in the work of Marx and Engels. As far back as 1869, Engels had even provided what amounted to a grisly blueprint, and a self-serving justification, for dealing a literal death blow to the bourgeois class. "Until its complete extermination or loss of national status," wrote Engels, "this racial trash always becomes the most fanatical bearer there is of counter-revolution, and remains that. That is because its entire existence is nothing more than a protest against a great historical revolution."

Early in his career, Stalin himself had proposed genocide according to the doctrine of Marx and Engels. In his *Foundations of Leninism*, he declared that the reactionaries (against the proletarian revolution) must die, not as individuals, but as whole nations. There could be no doubt, he insisted, that "the whole of National Socialism" included the genocidal solution.

To effect his reign of terror on the scale he deemed essential, Stalin needed more than ideological justification. He had to make another significant change in the Party structure. To be sure, he never lost sight of the genius of Lenin's basic structural creation. At the same time, he never hesitated to make his own modifications—if so benign a term can be used—by which he steadily transformed the Leninist monolith into the means to secure, strengthen and guard his personal power.

When the Seventeenth Party Congress met in 1934 at Stalin's bidding, its 1,966 delegates replaced his earlier watchdog organization, OGPU, with yet another: the People's Commissariat of Internal Affairs (NKVD). At the heart of the NKVD, the delegates obediently created an elite force. The Special Sector.

At home and around the world, the NKVD inherited all the duties and privileges of OGPU. It was an army apart from the Red Army, which it monitored and controlled. It was the right arm of the Party-State. And the Party-State, with the vigilant help of the NKVD, was simply and reductively Stalin himself.

With respect to his policies of genocide, however, it was the creation of the Special Sector of the NKVD that made the great difference. For the Special Sector was not merely another watchdog of the watchdogs, another guard to keep the guards in line. Placed at the heart of the Central Committee of the CPSU, it was in effect Stalin's personal extermination force. It enabled Stalin to carry Lenin's basic revolutionary principle of violence to its most stunning level. Stalin's reign of terror could now be as extreme as it had to be.

The targets of first importance for this new extermination arm of Stalin's monolith were within the Party-State. The moment to argue that boys will be boys was over. It was time to be rid of all the old Leninist Bolsheviks from whom Stalin might expect any residual resistance to his personal control and absolute authority.

Perhaps it was ironic that the Purges and Trials that cost the lives of tens of millions of Soviets were made possible at all by the Party's creation of the NKVD and the Special Sector. If so, it was an irony so thoroughly soaked in blood that most of the Party members themselves did not live to appreciate it.

Along with the millions of Soviet citizens who were killed or imprisoned, 1,108 of the 1,966 delegates who had so obligingly brought these new Stalinist creations into existence were executed between 1936 and 1938 during Stalin's Great Purges and his three Great Public Trials. Within the Central Committee itself, 98 of its 138 members and member candidates were executed.

When the bloodletting was over for the most part, not only the NKVD but the Party and the State as well were creatures that were wholly Stalin's in membership, function and aim.

Stalin's main preoccupation outside the Soviet Union was dictated by the geopolitical vision he inherited from Marx and Lenin. In its Stalinist form, however, that vision was shorn of any notion that the Soviet Party-State, which was totally in his control now, should relinquish its intended role of geopolitical dominance in the world.

As in the Soviet Union itself, Stalin made headway around the world by means of the Leninist structures already in place and waiting for his hand—specifically, in this case, the triple network of worldwide counter-intelligence structures that had begun years before with the expansion of Feliks Dzerzhinsky's CHEKA personnel into Soviet diplomatic and cultural missions abroad. Again, as in the Soviet Union, Stalin's latest successor to CHEKA, the NKVD, made it possible for the Man of Steel to clamp his personal control on the international Soviet counterintelligence network and eventually to expand and perfect it almost without constraint.

At its height, the NKVD was composed of three-quarters of a million members distributed into fifty-three divisions and twenty-eight brigades. By the beginning of World War II—that is, within five years of the creation of the NKVD—thirty-six countries spread around the globe had well-established pro-Moscow Communist parties. Over and through them all were spread the tentacles of the NKVD. And for obvious reasons, here at least, one internationalist principle insisted upon by Lenin remained the order of the Stalinist day: Every CP outside the Soviet Union was modeled on, and entirely subject to, the CPSU, as re-vamped by Stalin. The General Secretary had the NKVD's guarantee on it.

Stalin owed another important debt to Lenin's geopolitical vision and intent. For the very centerpiece of Stalin's geopolitical strategy was that same Russo-German alliance that Lenin had always seen as the keystone of his intended domination of Europe and the world by the proletariat.

Actually, the idea that the alliance of Slav and German could domi-nate the whole of Europe and, indeed, could dominate the world was older than Lenin or Marx. It dated from before the time of Peter the Great. As solid geopolitical strategy, it was once entertained as an ideal on both sides of the river Elbe.

Because Lenin's whole purpose was geopolitical from the outset, it was to be expected almost from the moment of the Bolshevik takeover of Russia in 1917 that the idea of a Russo-German alliance as the first essential step in gaining geopolitical preeminence had to become com-mon coin in his discussions and plans with his Bolshevik Party.

The thinking was blatant in its duplicity. If it was possible to restore national virility to Germany following its depletion and humiliation dur-ing World War I, then another war at least as destructive could be engi-neered in order to reduce England and France—and Germany again, into the bargain—to a singular state of weakness. The infrastructure of all three nations would be destroyed. The capitalist rulers would be beg-gared. The proletariat would rise up—that old saw seemed never to die in the Soviet Marxist mind. And the Great Revolution would ensue at last, with the USSR—the strongest and most intact nation—as the cap-stone of the new world order.

Lenin himself had started the wheels in motion for just such a plan as early as April of 1922, just over a month before his first stroke. As he had foreseen, Germany had been worn out by the four years of the World War. It had been humiliated by foreign occupation. It had been stripped of its former colonies. And it was racked by hunger and soaring inflation. It was, in short, ripe for the picking.

On April 16, the People's Commissar for Foreign Affairs of Lenin's USSR, Georgi G. Chicherin, met with Walter Rathenau, foreign minis-ter of the German Republic, to sign the famed Treaty of Rapallo. By that treaty, Most-Favored-Nation treatment in Soviet-German relations was ensured, and the humiliated Germans were able to begin rearming themselves with guns, tanks, aircraft and poison gas—all of which had been forbidden by the conditions of the Versailles Treaty that had ended the war in 1918.

It was the start of a long and deadly game of cat and mouse. For while the Treaty of Rapallo was signed in secrecy, it was published by the Soviets the very next day, to put the bee of renewed hostilities in the bonnets of the French and English.

During the ten years from 1929 to 1939, Stalin carried on with Lenin's plan for achieving domination of Europe through Germany. And Adolf Hitler's rise to total power in Germany in 1933 provided the opening Stalin needed. His brother-in-law and intimate, Lazar M. Kaganovich, put the idea with remarkable candor in a piece he wrote for the Bolshevik newspaper *Izvestia* on January 20, 1934: "The conflict between Germany and France and England reinforces our situation in Europe. . . . We must work at deepening the divergence between the states of Europe."

Work at it Stalin did. He tried everything in his power to make a Soviet-German military pact possible and feasible. In 1935, when Hitler brazenly defied the military restrictions still mandated for Germany by the Versailles Treaty, Stalin gave a lofty lecture to England's foreign minister, Anthony Eden. "Sooner or later"—Stalin shook a verbal finger at the Britisher—"the German people must liberate themselves from the chains of Versailles. . . . I repeat, a great people such as the Germans must tear itself away from the chains of Versailles."

By the end of that year, Stalin proposed to Hitler that they sign a bilateral nonaggression pact. It was another move in the game of cat and mouse begun by Lenin over a decade before. For earlier in the year, Stalin had already signed a treaty of "mutual assistance" with France. And in any case, even as Stalin courted Hitler, Moscow gave instructions to the Communist parties in France, England and elsewhere to raise a screaming hue and cry for the need to defend democracy everywhere against German and Italian Fascism.

Clearly, the fires of war had to be stoked on both sides of the pot. If Stalin failed to make that clear by his actions, he set the verbal record straight in the summer of 1939, when he publicly declared that "we shall be unable to undertake a geopolitical plan of action unless we successfully exploit the antagonisms between the capitalist nations in order to precipitate them into armed conflict. The principal work of our Communist parties must now be to facilitate such a conflict."

Two months later, on August 23, 1939, Stalin's infamous nonaggression pact with Hitler was finally signed in Moscow. This was the pact by which, in the words of the historian N. Nekrich, the USSR "opened the door for the next world war." That was the very plan, of course. And so, at the moment of the signing, Moscow was also playing host to important military delegations from France and England.

All the ironies of the Stalinist era are bloody ones. Insofar as Hitler was an apt target for the advances of Marxist Russia, it was precisely because of his admiration for Stalin and for his proven methods of genocide. Stalin's *Foundations of Leninism*, which had argued so passionately for wholesale genocide as a legitimate tool of socialism, had been published in German translation in 1924. Soon after taking power in 1933, Hitler remarked to a confidant, Hermann Rauschning, that "the whole of National Socialism [the Nazi political philosophy] is based on Marxism."

That was not too much to say. At the very least, there can be no doubt that Hitler found the justification and the model for his ghastly "Final Solution" in the principle of genocide advocated as doctrine and policy to foment the Marxist proletarian revolution.

Truth to tell, Hitler was far from lonely, even in the West, in his admiration for the Marxist-Leninist-Stalinist doctrine of genocide. It found able and even celebrated defenders in the likes of such English literary heroes as H. G. Wells, Havelock Ellis and George Bernard Shaw, to name just a few.

Shaw even went so far as to call for the invention of "a humane gas that will kill instantly and painlessly"; and for the extermination of "useless races" on a "scientific basis." As Nazi Adolf Eichmann testified years later in his Jerusalem trial, Hitler found exactly what Shaw had called for in the Zyklon-B gas with which he snuffed out the lives of six million Jews and other "useless races."

Admiration for Stalin in the United States was a more tender sort of thing. Despite his incomparable ruthlessness, which was in full swing in the 1930s, Stalin's NKVD was so unbelievably skillful in promoting his cult that America was able to allow itself to ignore his genocidal policies the way bad manners are ignored in polite company. An article in one popular American magazine of the thirties, *Harper's Weekly*, presented but one example of the agreeable stereotype that came to be accepted in the United States: "Uncle Joe"—as President Franklin D. Roosevelt himself dubbed Stalin familiarly—that gentle bear of a man, firm, pipe-smoking, devoted to his family, and living modestly on a manager's salary, like any honest American capitalist.

Truly, as Lenin had said, Stalin was the "Miraculous Georgian."

· · ·

Stalin's entire plan for European and global conquest reposed on the success of his 1939 nonaggression pact with Hitler. But it was Hitler who was quicker on the draw by far. The German dictator's admiration for Stalin and his methods proved to be no stumbling block to betrayal. In a hatred born of envy, emulation and his own megalomania, Hitler turned on the Soviets. Nikita Khrushchev revealed twenty-five years later that, when Stalin learned of the German invasion of the Soviet Union in 1941, he suffered a nervous collapse and shouted, "All that Lenin created we have lost forever!"

There was precious little to choose between these two dictators who styled themselves as champions of the world socialist cause. But despite Stalin's fit of nerves, his day was to be a longer one than Hitler's. For once again, the Miraculous Georgian was aided by a strange combination of events over which he had no control: Hitler's maniacal mistakes. The heroism of the Russian people. And, above all, the entry of the United States into World War II.

The trouble was that the Americans as saviors turned out to be a mixed blessing for Stalin. On the one hand, they saved his hide by resupplying England, France and the USSR itself with needed military equipment and food, and by their own enormous military effort. On the other hand, however, the Americans saved Europe's hide into the bargain; and that threw a spanner into Stalin's plans for a debilitated France, England and Germany.

In fact, the United States became the most important of the historical factors of World War II on which Stalin had not counted. The presence of America, with its ebullient economy and its exclusive possession of the atomic bomb, in the heartland of Europe from 1945 onward changed the whole Leninist-Marxist equation for geopolitical dominance. The age-old dream of a Slavic-German basis for such dominance was out of the question. At least, for the foreseeable future.

Still, perhaps tomorrow would be a different sort of day. And there was no harm in working to see it.

Here, at least, the United States turned out to be particularly obliging. Franklin Roosevelt allowed himself and his Western allies to be agreeably and painlessly bamboozled out of their original purpose in going to war —the liberation of Poland and all European nations.

A cartoon-like image comes to mind of a swamp drainer so frightened by alligators snapping at his hide that he forgets why he came to the swamp in the first place. But sadly, the facts of their gross betrayal of

Eastern Europe suggests something far less comic—and far less complimentary and exculpatory—for the American and British leaders who connived at yet another nonrevolutionary victory for the Leninist-Marxist proletarian revolution. A bitterly cynical cartoon appeared in one of the last editions of Budapest's principal daily, a short time before the iron hand of Stalinism wiped out all freedom in Hungary. It showed the Eastern European nations as a maiden being swept away in the paws of a bearlike Joseph Stalin, while she cries to three uniformed men—Britain, France, and the U.S.A.: "You promised to free me from this rape . . . you promised!" Their answer: "Sorry, my dear, but we all belong to the same club."

That, in sum, was the difficulty. Already a "beloved ally," already a founding member of the United Nations Organization, already possessing treaty papers granting Stalin all power over those nations, the West lacked any moral backbone to stand up to Stalin. The best that could be done was the Kennan containment policy and the tedious, sometimes bloody, always duplicitous Cold War, splotched with Korean blood and Vietnamese blood, and unmatched in the history of nations for the number of men, women and children made the victims of man's grossest inhumanity to man.

Nor did Stalin's death, in March 1953, change any of the fundamentals on which the Party-State continued to function. The Leninist geopolitical structure animated by the Leninist geopolitical aim was handed on intact by the successors of Stalin. Constantly maintained at par was the international grid of local Communist parties modeled on the CPSU, the ever-active subversion through diplomatic missions and front organizations, the ideological presumption that everywhere it was possible to bring about the final overthrow of the capitalist "superstructure" and thus "liberate" the "proletariat."

In true Leninist style, there never was any serious effort at a skillful cultural penetration. The Soviet efforts, right up to the advent of Mikhail Gorbachev, did foment cultural relations organizations and movements. But no one in any position of leadership was ever deceived. In propaganda, the Soviets had far greater success than the West. But, in matters of substance, they failed miserably. There was never the slightest sign of a genuine proletarian uprising in any country—only the meretricious imposition of Soviet domination by deceit, assassination, threat and military investment.

Only somebody like Karol Wojtyla, in the position he occupied as Cardinal Archbishop of Krakow, in the front line of the Stalinist empire, could—among his Poles and fellow Slavs—smell the dry rot in the timber of that empire and could confidently predict back in the mid-seventies that "nothing can ensure the continuance for long of a system that is eating its own vitals."

By the time the sinister Yuri Andropov died, in February 1984, the men huddled around the Politburo table in the Kremlin were beginning to realize that time was not on their side, that the hated capitalist world was growing stronger, that a new spirit was abroad even among their captive nations within the USSR and outside its borders, and that the colossus to the east—Communist China—was developing dangerous-looking muscles. There would be a short reign by the already ailing Konstantin Ustinovich Chernenko—really an interregnum. For in their midst since 1980 there was this bustling, agile-footed Mikhail Gorbachev, already substituting for Andropov and Chernenko. His Party orthodoxy was above reproach. His administrative powers were recognized as superb. Under such headings of practical housekeeping, there were no doubts registered in his Politburo colleagues' minds.

But what about his constant harping on a restructuring of the Marxist economy? And his proposals of a new mission, an utterly new mission for the Party-State, involving an entirely new way of penetrating the already burgeoning globalism of the capitalist nations? What did he imply by the "disaggregation of useless surrogates"? The refurbishing of the governmental structure of the USSR itself? The historic ties between Germany and the Soviet Union, the Germanic peoples and the Russian peoples? Nothing, he had stated to his colleagues, in the last seventy years of the Revolution has prepared us, in terms of how we have practiced Leninism, to deal with the new globalism.

Eventually, in their hardheaded way, those colleagues would yield to the importuning passion this comparatively young man brought to their brooding discussions. They vested him with all authority over the Party-State in March 1985. But it is most probable that none of them, or not, at least, the majority of them, had ever seriously delved into the writings and theories of Antonio Gramsci. His prison notebooks and their fateful analysis of Leninism were the textbooks of their new General Secretary.

13.   Antonio Gramsci:
The Haunting of East
and West

When Pope John Paul II reckons up the major forces against him and his Church in the millennium endgame, the geopolitical strength of Soviet-led world Communism at the end of the twentieth century rests in his view on the contributions of one man, who stands second only to Marx and Lenin. The historic events that have been gathering momentum since the end of World War II, and that have reached a pitch of euphoric fever at the opening of the 1990s, have proved Antonio Gramsci the worthiest, the most farsighted and, in practical terms, the most successful of all the interpreters of Karl Marx.

Italian Communists have long recognized Gramsci as the authentic founder, theoretician and strategist of their party's unique success in the West. But that is not the basis of John Paul's judgment. Rather, the Pope counts Gramsci's greatest contributions as three. His incisive critique of classical Leninism. His stunningly successful blueprint for the reform of that Leninism, which has now swept the world. And his accurate prediction of the cardinal mistake that the Western democracies would make in their confrontation with Gramscian Communism, and with their own future.

Antonio Gramsci's contributions have outlived the man by half a century. And, though Moscow has been chary with its kudos for him, the fact remains that the political formula Gramsci devised has done much more than classical Leninism—and certainly more than Stalinism—to spread Marxism throughout the capitalist West. All that has happened both to capitalist and Communist powers since 1945—and most dramatically since 1985—has completely vindicated the judgment of this authentic Marxist genius in the Hall of Communism's Heroes.

Personally speaking, Antonio Gramsci was not the most fortunate of men. But he was probably one of the most tenacious. He was born in the village of Ales on the island of Sardinia in 1891. As the only road upward for any Sardinian is the road out, Gramsci left for mainland Italy, where he studied philosophy and history at Turin University. By 1913, he was a member of the Italian Socialist Party. In 1919, he founded a newspaper, whose name alone—*L'Ordine Nuovo*, The New Order—gave clear indication of his bent of mind and of the fact that, like Lenin, he was both a visionary and a doer of deeds.

In 1921, in association with Palmiro Togliatti, Gramsci founded the Italian Communist Party. The next year, however, the squat, broad-shouldered, lantern-jawed, forty-year-old Benito Mussolini came to power. Like a toad who had been masquerading as a prince, that onetime Italian Socialist turned into a Fascist dictator. Italy became a Fascist nation. And Gramsci took off for what he no doubt expected would be the safer haven of Lenin's USSR.

Marxist though he was, and as fully convinced as Lenin that there was a force completely inner to mankind driving it on as a whole to the Marxist ideal of the "Workers' Paradise," Gramsci was too aware of the facts of history and of life to accept other basic and gratuitous assumptions made by Marx, and accepted unquestioningly by Lenin.

For one thing, Marx and Lenin insisted that throughout the entire world, human society was divided into just two opposing camps—the broad "structure" of the great mass of people, the workers of the world; and the unjustly created "superstructure" of oppressive capitalism.

Gramsci knew otherwise. He understood the nature of Christian culture, which he saw as still vibrant and thriving in the lives of the people all around him. Not only did Christianity point unceasingly to a divine force beyond mankind—a force outside and superior to the material cosmos. Christianity was also the spiritual and intellectual patrimony held in common by the bone-poor peasants in his native Ales, the workers in Milan's factories, the professors who had taught him at Turin University, and the Pope in his Roman splendor.

Gramsci himself rejected Christianity and all its transcendent claims. He knew Mussolini was the latest in a long list of leaders who abused it. He knew the Sardinian peasants and Milanese laboring classes readily accused the upper classes of playing on it. He knew the university dons might have contempt for it. And he knew it was under attack from many sides.

Nevertheless, he knew Christian culture existed. It was far more real, in fact, than the still nonexistent proletarian revolution. Moreover, as a religion, the appeal and the power of Christianity could not be denied. For that was the force binding all the classes—peasants and workers and princes and priests and popes and all the rest besides—into a single, homogeneous culture. It was a specifically Christian culture, in which individual men and women understood that the most important things about human life transcended the material conditions in which they lived out their mortal lives.

True, in the Czarist Russia in which Lenin and Stalin had been reared, there had been an oppressive "superstructure"—the Czar, the aristocracy and the Russian Orthodox Church—which had stood in opposition to the mass of citizens. But even in such ripe conditions as that, there had been no such proletarian revolution as Marx and Lenin had predicted.

Perhaps Lenin and Stalin and the rest of the Bolshevik Party were prepared to pretend otherwise. And perhaps the rest of the world was prepared to accept their Big Lie. But Gramsci would not. For him, a coup d'état was not a revolution. And for him, the Russian masses, whom he described contemptuously as "primitive and spineless," had no importance, in any case.

Gramsci agreed that the great mass of the world's population was made up of workers. That much was just plain fact. What became clear to him, however, was that nowhere—and especially not in Christian Europe—did the workers of the world see themselves as separated from the ruling classes by an ideological chasm.

And if that was true, Gramsci argued, then Marx and Lenin had to be wrong in another of their fundamental assumptions: There would never be a glorious uprising of the proletariat. There would be no Marxist-inspired violent overthrow of the ruling "superstructure" by the working "underclasses." Because no matter how oppressed they might be, the "structure" of the working classes was defined not by their misery or their oppression but by their Christian faith and their Christian culture.

Realist that he was, Gramsci understood that he was knocking his Marxist head against that strong millennial wall—the pervasive culture with which Christianity had built, housed, defended and buttressed its faith. The Marxist insistence that everything valuable in life was within mankind—was immanent in mankind and its earthly condition—was impotent against such a bulwark.

Had Gramsci needed any concrete reassurance that his analysis of the situation, and not Lenin's, was the correct one, it came in 1923, toward the end of his exile in the Soviet Union. In that year, the proletarian revolution Lenin had expected in Germany died in the ballot box and on the streets of Berlin.

Indeed, Gramsci's critique even held true in China, where all of Lenin's careful networking for the proletarian revolution came to its own dismal end. Perhaps Mikhail Borodin took the official blame for that failure when, as the chief architect of the effort there, he was brought home and garroted. But Gramsci was convinced that neither Germany nor China nor any other country—especially any European country—fulfilled the simplistic Leninist-Marxist formula of a vast, featureless structure of the masses who perceived themselves as fundamentally different from a small, alien superstructure.

Gramsci still nourished the Leninist conviction that the final birth of the "Paradise of Workers" would take place. But he knew that the way to that peak of human happiness had to be completely different from the Leninist concept of armed and violent revolution. He knew there had to be another process.

As it happened, the failure of Lenin's efforts in Germany and China not only confirmed Gramsci in his convictions; it also meant time was running out for him in the Soviet Union. His point of view was not overly popular in Moscow in any case. It had been his misfortune to have arrived in the Soviet Union in the twilight time of Communism's "glorious genius," Lenin. Now, with Joseph Stalin in charge of the Central Committee as General Secretary of the CPSU, and with inner-Party democracy becoming an increasingly fragile and dangerous thing at best, Gramsci would probably end up in the infamous Lubyanka Prison, where he would be tortured into a confession of his deviancy and then killed.

In the circumstances, Gramsci turned his eyes back toward home. As great a foe as Mussolini and his Fascism were to Gramsci's ideals, Stalin's already impressive control of the Party machinery in Moscow would leave Gramsci with no allies in the USSR. Italy would at least be the better of two bad choices.

Once he returned, things went well enough for a short time. Gramsci was elected to the Italian Chamber of Deputies in 1924. As the head of a nineteen-man Communist faction in Italy's Parliament, however, he rapidly became a danger for Mussolini's regime. He was arrested in 1926, and in 1928 was sentenced by a Fascist court to twenty years imprisonment.

By that time, he had already converted the major Italian Communist thinkers and political leaders to his critique of classical Leninism and to his own suggested reform of that Leninism. But over and above that, in a sort of continuous paroxysm of Marxist dedication, the imprisoned Gramsci spent the next nine years of his life writing. He set down his ideas on any scraps of paper he could get his hands on. By the time he died in 1937, at the age of forty-six, and against all odds, he had produced nine volumes of material that pointed the way to achieve a Marxist world.

Gramsci did not live to witness Hitler's betrayal of Stalin and the failure of yet another plan for violent proletarian revolt. He didn't live to see the disgrace and ignominious death of his Fascist persecutor, Mussolini, at the hands of the Italian Communist partisans. Nor did he live to see even the first traces of the vindication and victory of his ideas.

Nevertheless, when the first volume of what he had written in prison was published in 1947—a full ten years after his death—the voice of the long-dead Marxist prophet became a reality for which the world at large had no ready answer. A reality that would bedevil Joseph Stalin and each of his successors until Mikhail Gorbachev, who listened at last, would finally take the hand of Gramsci's ghost and set off on the Leninist-Marxist road to the twenty-first century.

Gramsci's willingness to face the fact that the idea of a violent worldwide proletarian revolution was bankrupt from the outset allowed him to rethink and reapply the most powerful of the ideas of his Marxist predecessors. For he never broke faith with the ultimate Communist and Marxist ideal of the Workers' Paradise. He simply read without tinted glasses the basic philosophic text Marx had imbued and taken as his own. And then he put a sharp knife to what he saw as the mistakes of both Marx and Lenin.

Gramsci—intellectually a product of the Roman Catholic society of Italy—was far more advanced than either Hegel or Marx in his understanding of Christian metaphysics in general, of Thomism in particular, and of the richness of the Roman Catholic heritage. That understanding, and his own insistently practical mind, allowed him to be far more sophisticated and subtle in his interpretation of Hegel's dialectic philosophy of history than Marx had been.

A key element of Gramsci's blueprint for the global victory of Marxism rested on Hegel's distinction between what was "inner" or "immanent" to man and what man held to be outside and above him and his world—a superior force transcending the limitations of individuals and of groups, both large and small.

The immanent. The transcendent. For Gramsci, the two were un-avoidably paired and yoked. Marxism's "transcendent," said Gramsci, was the utopian ideal. But he understood that if Marxism could not touch the transcendent motivation presently accepted as real by men and women and groups in the largely Christian society that surrounded him, then Marxists could not get at what made those individuals and groups tick, what made them think and act as they did.

At the same time, however—and precisely because the immanent and the transcendent are paired—Gramsci argued that unless you can sys-tematically touch what is immanent and immediate to individuals and groups and societies in their daily lives, you cannot convince them to struggle for any transcendent.

As far as Gramsci could see, therefore, the call of Marx and Lenin to impose their "transcendent" by violent force was a futile contradiction in human logic. It was no wonder that, even in his time, the only Marxist state that existed was imposed and maintained by force and by terrorist policies that duplicated and even exceeded the worst facets of Mussolini's Fascism. If Marxism could not find a way to change that formula, it would have no future.

What was essential, insisted Gramsci, was to Marxize the inner man. Only when that was done could you successfully dangle the utopia of the "Workers' Paradise" before his eyes, to be accepted in a peaceful and humanly agreeable manner, without revolution or violence or blood-shed.

Deeply critical though he was, Gramsci still did not tamper with the most fundamental and motivating of Marx's ideas. He totally accepted the strange utopian vision that is the siren call of all true Marxists. The idea that capitalism and capitalists would be eliminated, that a classless society would come into existence, and that such a society would be the Paradise of Marx's dreams. And he was totally convinced that the mate-rial dimension of everything in the universe, including mankind, was the whole of it.

From Lenin, meanwhile, Gramsci absorbed two major and supremely practical contributions. The first was Lenin's extraordinary geopolitical vision. The second was his even more extraordinary practical invention —the Party-State as the operational core of geopolitically successful Marxism. For, in Gramsci's blueprint, Lenin's intricate international Party machinery would remain the basis for a worldwide Communist Party under the dominant control of the Central Committee of the CPSU.

In fact, Lenin's organizational creation was Marxism's ideal answer to the centrally directed global structure of the Roman Catholic Church.

What Marx and Lenin had got wrong, Gramsci said, was the part about an immediate proletarian revolution. His Italian socialist brothers could see as well as he did that, in a country such as Italy—and in Spain or France or Belgium or Austria or Latin America, for that matter—the national tradition of all the classes was virtually cosubstantial with Roman Catholicism. The idea of proletarian revolution in such a climate was impractical at best, and could be counterproductive at worst.

Even Stalinist terror methods, Gramsci predicted, could not eliminate what he called "the forces of bourgeois reaction." Instead, he warned, those reactionary forces—organized religion, the intellectual and academic establishment, capitalist and entrepreneurial circles—all would be compressed by any such repression into dense streams of tradition, resistance and resentment. They would go underground, no doubt; but they would seek converts in the Leninist structure. They would bide their time until, at the opportune moment, they would thrust to the surface, shattering Marxist unity and ripping open the seams of the Leninist structure.

Once that happened, Gramsci understood, the capitalist circles abroad would be waiting to jump into the situation and exploit it for their own gain, to the detriment of the Leninist-Marxist ideal of the ultimate Workers' Paradise.

Gramsci had a better way. A subtler blueprint for Marxist victory. After all, was not Lenin's geopolitical structure already a more brilliant creation by far for fomenting a stealthy revolution in the way people think, than it would ever be for fomenting bloody uprisings that never materialized anyway?

Use Lenin's geopolitical structure not to conquer streets and cities, argued Gramsci. Use it to conquer the mind of civil society. Use it to acquire a Marxist hegemony over the minds of the populations that must be won.

Clearly, if Gramsci was to change the common cultural outlook, the first order of business had to be to change the outward face of the Communist Party.

For starters, Marxists would have to drop all Leninist shibboleths. It wouldn't do to rant about "revolution" and "dictatorship of the proletariat" and the "Workers' Paradise." Instead, according to Gramsci, Marxists would have to exalt such ideas as "national consensus" and "national unity" and "national pacification."

Further, advised Gramsci, Marxists around the world would have to behave as the CP in Italy was already behaving. They would have to engage in the practical and normally accepted democratic processes, in lobbying and voting and the full gamut of parliamentary participation. They would have to behave in every respect the way Western democrats behave—not only accepting the existence of many political parties but forging alliances with some and friendships with others. They would have to defend pluralism, in fact.

And—heresy of all Leninist heresies—Marxists would even have to defend different types of Communist parties in different countries. The Central Committee of the CPSU would still be the operational center of world Marxism—would still direct this new style of world revolution by penetration and corruption. But no Communist Party in any country outside the Soviet Union would be a forced clone of the CPSU.

On top of all that, Marxists must imitate, perfect and expand the roles already invented by Lenin and his "intelligence expert," Feliks Dzerzhinsky, for the foreign arms of CHEKA and its successor organizations. In other words, they must join in whatever liberating causes might come to the fore in different countries and cultures as popular movements, however dissimilar those movements might initially be from Marxism or from one another. Marxists must join with women, with the poor, with those who find certain civil laws oppressive. They must adopt different tactics for different cultures and subcultures. They must never show an inappropriate face. And, in this manner, they must enter into every civil, cultural and political activity in every nation, patiently leavening them all as thoroughly as yeast leavens bread.

Even such a pervasive blueprint as that would not work in the end, however, unless Gramsci could successfully target Marxism's greatest enemy. If there was any true superstructure that had to be eliminated, it was the Christianity that had created and still pervaded Western culture in all its forms, activities and expressions. This attack must be strong everywhere, of course, but particularly in Southern Europe and Latin America, where Roman Catholicism most deeply guided the thinking and the actions of the generality of populations.

For this purpose, Gramsci felt the timing was rather good. For though Christianity appeared on the surface to be strong, it had for some time been debilitated by unceasing attacks against its teachings and its structural unity.

True to his general blueprint for action, therefore, Gramsci's idea was that Marxist action must be unitary against what he saw to be the failing remnant of Christianity. And by a unitary attack, Gramsci meant that Marxists must change the residually Christian mind. He needed to alter that mind—to turn it into its opposite in all its details—so that it would become not merely a non-Christian mind but an anti-Christian mind.

In the most practical terms, he needed to get individuals and groups in every class and station of life to think about life's problems without reference to the Christian transcendent, without reference to God and the laws of God. He needed to get them to react with antipathy and positive opposition to any introduction of Christian ideals or the Christian transcendent into the treatment and solution of the problems of modern life.

That had to be accomplished; no question about it. For Gramsci was a Marxist through and through. And the bedrock essence of Marxism—the cornerstone of the Marxist ideal of a this-worldly Paradise as the summit of human existence—is that there is nothing beyond the matter of this universe. There is nothing in existence that transcends man—his material organism within his material surroundings.

It was a fact pure and simple, therefore, that the residue of Christian transcendentalism in the world had to be replaced with genuinely Marxist immanentism.

It was also obvious that such goals, like most of Gramsci's blueprint, had to be pursued by means of a quiet and anonymous revolution. No armed and bloody uprisings would do it. No bellicose confrontations would win the day. Rather, everything must be done in the name of man's dignity and rights, and in the name of his autonomy and freedom from outside constraint. From the claims and constraints of Christianity, above all.

Accomplish that, said Gramsci, and you will have established a true and freely adopted hegemony over the civil and political thinking of every formerly Christian country. Do that, he promised, and in essence you will have Marxized the West. The final step—the Marxization of the politics of life itself—will then follow. All classes will be one class. All minds will be proletarian minds. The earthly Paradise will be achieved.

The actual implementation of Gramsci's formula for Marxist success went by fits and starts. Predictably, it seemed to Stalin—and to Stalinists everywhere—that such a program as Gramsci had laid out for his Italian socialist brothers and argued so persuasively in his writings was a threat to the most fundamental tenets of Leninism. There was only one principal Communist Party: the CPSU. And the function of all other Communist parties was to march behind the CPSU in fomenting violent proletarian revolution around the world.

Furthermore, Gramsci's formula for allowing varying forms of Communism to be conditioned by the situation in each country and, therefore, to be different from Soviet Communism ran head-on against Stalin's insistence on total personal control and preeminence.

Nevertheless, while Gramsci's basic ideas were repudiated by Moscow, they did begin to find their way into practical field operations around the world. Over time, there was a gradual, if unspoken, rapprochement between the "official" Leninist process and the process set in motion with the spread of Gramsci's ideas. Even as early as the late 1940s and early 1950s, it began to dawn on some that the stealthier process of revolution by infiltration that the dead Sardinian had bequeathed to them was exactly the means of spreading Leninist Marxism throughout the world.

Gramsci's tactical wisdom became increasingly evident in its success. The principles he had set out—especially his principle of Communism tailored to fit conditions and situations that varied from country to country—gave birth by the early fifties to what came to be called Eurocommunism.

Indeed, as his process took hold in an increasing number of countries in Western Europe, the Gramsci bug bit such Eastern satellite countries as Albania and Yugoslavia, as well; for they found in Gramsci added justification and fuel for their continuing refusal to move in lockstep in the Stalinist orbit.

Not surprisingly, Stalin's opposition to Gramsci's ghost only grew greater during those years. But, in his very opposition, Stalin proved his dead Marxist adversary correct in another of his prophecies. For Gramsci had accurately predicted the reaction of the West to any overt advance of Leninism, even as he had known it in the thirties.

The West's response to Stalin's strident official post–World War II policies of the forties was to reach for the defense of military arms and economic provision. The Marshall Plan was proposed and carried out to revive Western Europe. NATO and SEATO were created. Western nations patrolled the strategic choke points in the trade lanes of the world's oceans; and they elaborated extensively on their own counterintelligence operations. Within their own borders, meanwhile, the several Western nations began their own far-reaching welfare structures as an answer to the economic needs of their various populations.

But time ran out for Stalin at last. Despite his decades of rampaging in blood and gore—and thanks to the first beginnings of success for Gramsci's policies—by the time Stalin died, at 9:50 P.M. on March 5, 1953, Eurocommunism was an irreversible fact of life.

· · ·

In important ways, the history of East and West during the tenures of the four general secretaries who followed Stalin in the USSR—Nikita Khrushchev (1953–64), Leonid Brezhnev (1964–82), Yuri Andropov (1982–84) and Konstantin Chernenko (1984–85)—is the story of the successful haunting of both sides of the Cold War by the ghost of Antonio Gramsci.

With Stalin gone, the professional counterintelligence experts in the Party-State of the Soviet Union were the first officially to recognize the truth of Gramsci's prediction that following the Leninist and Stalinist policy of fomenting violent revolution abroad, they could not create the proletarian revolution in the minds and lives of capitalist populations. And they were the first to understand that, in Gramsci's blueprint, they had stumbled onto the counterintelligence formula par excellence. They knew he had provided the Soviets of the Kremlin with what could be described—in appropriate KGB parlance—as the most far-reaching exercise of deception ever executed by the Party-State, an exercise already perfectly fitted to the international structure Lenin had created.

Professional intelligence experts have detailed the various phases of that Soviet counterintelligence operation over the years following Stalin's death. As John Dziak sets it out, a whole new intelligence vocabulary had to be developed to cover the intricate activity inspired by Gramsci's mandate. It was, as Dziak phrases it, a stylized "Russian and Soviet operational vocabulary used in the integration of varied state security operational activities."

Even a partial lexicon of that new vocabulary is instructive: "active measures" *(aktivnyye meropriyatiya)*, "disinformation" *(dezinformatsiya)* and "military deception" *(maskirovka)* were brilliantly "combined" *(kombinatsiya)* to elicit from the West precisely the desired reactions.

Trained and field-hardened Soviet agents made sport of the West with their calculated gambles designed to elicit consent to their own deception on the part of leading political, educational, bureaucratic and editorial targets. The entire field of play was webbed with the intricacies of "provocation" *(provokatsiya)*, "penetration" *(proniknoveniye)*, "fabrication" *(fabrikatsiya)*, "diversion" *(diversiya)*, "clandestine work" *(konspiratsiya)*, deadly "wet affairs" *(mokrye dela)*, "direct action" *(aktivnyye akty)*, and by a "combination" of all those tactics and more.

Though he had predicted it all, it might have boggled even Gramsci's mind to see the degree to which governments and individuals in the Christian, capitalist West responded to his anonymous revolution with their willing consent and their downright cooperation with the Soviet purpose regarding them.

Things were helped along a good deal when, in time-honored Soviet style, Nikita Khrushchev placed the blame for the problems the world had experienced with the Soviet Party-State squarely on Stalin's head. Having come to the General Secretary's chair in 1953, Khrushchev had consolidated his power by 1956. At the Moscow Party Congress that year, he made a scathing speech in which he denounced Stalin for his unspeakable crimes, repudiated Stalin's personality cult and sent the "Miraculous Georgian" tumbling posthumously into thorough disgrace.

Within perhaps three years more, by about 1959, strategic military deception (*maskirovka*) and all the various forms of strategic political deception inspired by Gramsci's brilliantly underhanded formula were organizationally centralized in the bureaucratic processes of the Soviet Party-State.

By that time, the twenty-eight-year-old Mikhail Gorbachev, already a veteran of Komsomol, had graduated from university and come to the attention of the doctrinal guardian of the CPSU, the then all-powerful Mikhail Suslov.

Both Gorbachev and Suslov understood and valued the new Soviet preoccupation with what John Dziak calls "complex operations analogous to chess moves." The acme of counterintelligence was now seen to be—Dziak's words again—"various operational undertakings in different times and places to enhance overall operational results."

Such language may not sound romantic. But it was Gramsci's dream coming true. The unbloody penetration of the West by means of his clandestine and nonviolent Marxist revolution was on its way.

Not that it was all smooth sailing, even then. It turned out that Nikita Khrushchev was not entirely firm in his choice of Gramsci's policies over those of Stalin. It seemed to take the 1962 Cuban missile crisis to convince him once and for all that the capitalists—the Americans in this case—when pushed to the wall in open confrontation, would fight, even if to do that meant a nuclear war. Score another point for Gramsci's judgment.

While the Cuban crisis made clear that the military and economic resistance of the West to Leninist Marxism was serious and well concentrated, it was still true that the whole field of Western culture, and all the places where culture is elaborated and diffused, could not be protected. Gramsci's targets of first choice—educational facilities from grade school to university, for example, the media, political parties and structures, even the family unit—were all fat, happy and wide open to systematic and professional Marxist penetration.

By the end of the Khrushchev era, therefore, the Gramscian process had been fully integrated into the official Leninist process. Gramsci's ghost had won the political war in Moscow that Gramsci the man had lost in 1923. Next to his accurate analysis and predictions, the expectations of Lenin and Stalin appeared bumbling, and their policies seemed elephantine.

Under Leonid Brezhnev, who succeeded Khrushchev as General Secretary of the CPSU in 1964, the official thrust of modified Leninism was concentrated in two main policies. The first—total penetration of Western intelligence—presented no great difficulty for the Soviets. The second—insistence that the USSR be accepted, "warts and all" in the expression of the time, as a legally constituted and fully legitimate world power—took a little while to get under way.

The first policy was steadily advanced by the KGB in its stunningly professional counterintelligence operation, which successfully penetrated the military, scientific and industrial fields throughout the West. Western experts are only now coming to count the number of "deep" contacts—the network of dormant "moles" devised forty years before by Lenin as part and parcel of his global structure—who were activated during the 1960s. And then there were all those others who were not exactly "moles" but who had been so cleverly and deeply compromised one way or another by the KGB that their cooperation could be called in at will, like so many outstanding IOUs.

This facet of Brezhnev's intelligence policy enabled the USSR to keep pace with the West in military, scientific and space breakthroughs. But it left the masses of peoples in the West largely untouched. The second part of Brezhnev's policy—his thrust at full acceptance of the USSR by the capitalist West—addressed that problem like a steamroller. And it owed its success to the process Gramsci had authored.

That policy was given a name. The "Brezhnev doctrine," it was called. And its meaning could not have been more clear as it developed during the presidencies of Richard M. Nixon and Gerald R. Ford. The peoples and territories the USSR had acquired—whether by military conquest; or by political sabotage and subterfuge; or by reneging on its word to its World War II allies against Hitler—all of them now "belonged" to the Soviet Union. Moreover, the Soviet Union could resort to arms and invasion, if necessary, to enforce its claim to those territories. The meaning of what was politely called "détente" between East and West during the terms of Nixon and Ford was summed up precisely and accurately in that so-called Brezhnev doctrine.

In 1975, the West fully and officially acquiesced in the Soviet policy of détente. At the Conference on Security and Cooperation in Europe, thirty-five nations signed the Final Act of the Helsinki Agreements, by which the West agreed to pretend that the USSR had a legal right to all those territories and peoples it had acquired.

Not only had détente worked; it had worked on Gramsci's terms. Despite its lies, its excesses, its terrorist methods, its genocidal policies and its continuing existence as the world's only counterintelligence state, the Soviet Unon was a respectable member of the comity of nations. It was right there in black and white: As a nation that respected and observed the rights of men outlined in the United Nations Declaration of Human Rights and specified in the Helsinki pacts, the Soviets had reached the summit of international acceptability.

Following the Gramsci blueprint, however, that was hardly the end of the matter. Rather, it was more in the nature of a new beginning. For the USSR was now in a position to posture in all seriousness as a normally regulated world power, while the counterintelligence activity of the Party-State—that first arm of Brezhnev's dual policy—redoubled its operational efforts.

Clearly, the time had come to get on in deadly earnest with the Marxization of the mind of Western culture. For, following Gramsci's lead, long use of Lenin's labyrinthine geopolitical machine by the KGB had finally paid off. At Helsinki, the West had shown itself to be leavened to the point of willing cooperation in its own final conversion.

It had not been forgotten during all those years that the oldest and most formidable enemy of cultural and political Marxism was the worldwide Roman Catholic Church. Neither the Brezhnev doctrine nor détente nor Helsinki changed that.

The first opening by which the Roman Catholic Church did in fact become the most useful tool of all for the Gramscian penetration of Western culture presented itself out of the blue while Nikita Khrushchev was still running things in the Soviet Union.

In the fall of 1958, the smiling, rotund little Cardinal of Bergamesque peasant stock, Angelo Giuseppe Roncalli, was elected to the papacy as John XXIII. Within a scant three months of his election, Pope John stunned his Catholic hierarchy and the entire world with the announcement that he would convene the twenty-first ecumenical council in the two-thousand-year history of the Catholic Church. The Second Vatican Council.

With that announcement, there came a sort of undeclared truce in the deep and professional enmity long held by the Vatican and the Church against Marxism and the Soviet Union. For all the decades since Lenin's coup d'état of 1917 and right through the papacy of Pope Pius XII, the Soviet Union and its Marxism were considered and described as the enemy of Catholicism and the seedbed of anti-Christ.

During the three years of preparation for the Council that followed his initial announcement, however, Pope John reversed that policy for the first time. For one of his principal aims was to convince Nikita Khrushchev to allow two Russian Orthodox clerics from the USSR to attend his Council in Rome as observers.

The Pope's idea was much more open than Gramsci's backhanded blueprint for cultural penetration; and it was far more benign, as well. The Pontiff's idea in calling the Council together at all was that the Holy Spirit would inspire all who attended with renewed vigor of faith and renewed evangelism around the world, and he wanted to include the Soviet Union in that renewal.

Pope John paid more than one stiff price for Khrushchev's agreement to send those two Soviet clerics as observers. And one price was the opening of the first serious breach in the Catholic bulwark against Communism. For, at Khrushchev's insistence, the Pontiff secretly agreed that his upcoming Council would not issue a condemnation of Marxism and the Communist state.

Such an agreement was a huge papal concession; for precisely such condemnations had always been included as standard fare in any Vatican or Roman Catholic commentary on the world at large. And the scope of Vatican II, as the Council was quickly dubbed, was certainly intended to include the world at large.

Another price Pope John paid came as a deep disappointment to millions of faithful and expectant Catholics around the world, and came to be seen by them as another breach in the Catholic anti-Communist rampart. A powerful Church tradition had it that if, in the year 1960, the reigning Pope would perform a public act consecrating the Soviet Union to the protection of the Virgin Mary, the USSR would be converted from its official hard-core atheism, and a long period of world peace would ensue.

As it turned out, John XXIII was that Pope. But in the circumstances, he felt that to carry out such a public act would be to declare war all over again on Khrushchev's Soviet Union, branding it anew, and on an international stage, as a nest of atheists. "This step is not for our time," Pope John observed privately, and he shelved the whole proposition.

• • •

Vatican II consisted of four sessions, and spanned more than three years, from the fall of 1962 until December 1965. By the time it ended, John XXIII and Nikita Khrushchev were both dead. And the story of the Church in the following twenty-five years became the story of the secularization of Roman Catholicism.

Very soon after the first Council session convened, the breach already opened by John in his agreement with Khrushchev was widened. More than five hundred of the bishops attending—well in excess of the quorum required—proposed that the Council issue a condemnation of atheistic Communism and its Marxist ideology. The proposal was unilaterally quashed by Vatican authorities, and so never made it to the floor of the Council for a final vote.

For the most part, the other concerns of the Council, as expressed in the documents that did come to a successful vote, seemed legitimate enough to the average observer—which is to say, they appeared to be properly pastoral in intent and purpose.

In its survey of the contemporary world, for example, what could have been more pastoral than for the Council to single out the poor—and particularly the poor of the Third World—as especially deserving of attention by the Church?

The document on religious liberty did seem a little dicey to some, declaring as it did the principle that everyone should be free from any constraint in religious matters, including the choice and the practice of whatever religion one might care to select. Couldn't this be taken to mean that you need not become a Roman Catholic to be saved from Hell-fire? Many have so interpreted it. Still, the ayes had it.

Then, too, there was the curious question of ecumenism. Traditionally, the terms "ecumenism" and "ecumenical" had referred exclusively to Christians, and specifically to the matter of reunification among the separated Christian churches.

Before the end of the fourth and final session of Vatican II—presided over by Pope John's successor, Paul VI—some bishops and Vatican personnel had already adopted entirely new and innovative meanings for the idea of ecumenism. The powerful Augustin Cardinal Bea, for example, was a leading figure at the Council and a close adviser to Paul VI, as he had been to Pope John. Bea was seen as the Vatican's own spearhead in what came to be nothing less than an ecumenical revolution. The Cardinal organized "ecumenical gatherings" that included not only Roman Catholics and Protestants as usual, but Jews and Muslims as well.

In time, as was only logical, Buddhists, Shintoists, animists and a host of other non-Christian and even nonreligious groups would find a place in the poorly and broadly defined new "ecumenism."

In such various ways—sometimes open, sometimes very subtle indeed —was the breach steadily widened in what had for so long been the Catholic bulwark against Communism. By December of 1965, when the Council ended its final session, the groundwork had been laid for the key transformations in faith and in practice that were to follow in its wake.

As reigning Pope, Paul VI gave a farewell address to the departing bishops of the Council on December 5. That speech provided the broad philosophic and quasi-theological umbrella beneath which secularism within the Roman Church would be protected from the storm of protest and outrage mounted by traditional Catholics in the years following the Council.

While the Catholic faithful were protesting, that same speech was used by the heirs of Antonio Gramsci to drive a coach-and-four as handsomely as you please through the worldwide structural organization of the Roman Catholic Church.

Pope Paul VI told the departing bishops that their Church had decided to opt for man; to serve man, to help him build his home on this earth. Man with his ideas and his aims, man with his hopes and his fears, man in his difficulties and sufferings—that was the centerpiece of the Church's interest, said the Pontiff to his bishops.

So pointedly did the Pope elaborate on that theme of the Church's devotion to subserve material human interests that Gramsci himself could not have written a better papal script for the secularization of Roman Catholic institutions or for the de-Catholicization of the Roman Catholic hierarchy, clergy and faithful.

By the mid-1960s, then—with Brezhnev at the helm of the Leninist geopolitical structure, and with Paul VI at the helm of the Roman Catholic georeligious structure—it appeared that the ghost of Antonio Gramsci had all but won the day. In Moscow, his doctrine of revolution through disguised and clandestine penetration of capitalist populations had come out on top in the political wars of the Leninist-Marxist leadership. And in Rome, the Second Vatican Council had handed over the keys to the millennial faith of the Catholic Church, and to the culture that had for a thousand years been the living expression of that faith.

What happened to the Roman Catholic Church in the decades following the Second Vatican Council also happened to the majority of mainline

Protestant churches. With partial and self-serving interpretations of Pope Paul's formula as their armor, and the vague wording of the documents produced by the bishops of Vatican II as their justification, new and pointedly secularist heresies swept through Christianity.

The special attention the bishops had intended that the Church pay to the plight of the poor of the world was translated into something called the "preferential option for the poor"; and that in turn was taken as a carte blanche mandate for deep political alliances with socialists and Communists, including terrorist groups.

Paul VI's emphasis on human interest became the basis for discarding sacrifice and prayer and faith and the Sacraments of the Church as the watchwords of hope in this world. They were replaced by human solidarity, which became the aim and the centerpiece of Catholic striving.

Ecumenism was no longer an attempt to heal the heretical and schismatic rifts that over the centuries had split the one Church Christ had founded on the Rock of Simon Peter's central office. Ecumenism was a means not of genuine healing but of leveling differences of whatever kind between all Christian believers and nonbelievers. That fit nicely with the new central aim of human solidarity as the hope of mankind.

The fundamental struggle in which the Church and all Catholics were engaged was no longer the personal war between Christ as Savior and Lucifer as the Cosmic Adversary of the Most High in the quest for men's souls. The struggle was no longer on the supernatural plane at all, in fact. It was in the material circumstances of the tangible, sociopolitical here and now. It was the class struggle Marx and Lenin had propounded as the only worthwhile combat zone for humans.

Liberation was, therefore, no longer release from sin and its dire effects. It was the struggle against oppression by big capital and by the authoritarian colonialist powers of the West—particularly the United States as the archvillain of all human history.

Within five years of the end of Vatican II, by the dawn of the 1970s, the whole of Latin America was being flooded with a new theology— Liberation Theology—in which basic Marxism was smartly decked out in traditional Christian vocabulary and retooled Christian concepts. Books written mainly by co-opted Catholic priests, together with political and revolutionary action manuals, saturated the volatile area of Latin America, where over 367 million Catholics included the lowest and poorest strata of society—that ninety percent of the population which had no concrete hope of any economic betterment for themselves or their children.

Liberation Theology was a perfectly faithful exercise of Gramsci's principles. It could be launched with the corruption of a relatively few well-placed Judas goats. Yet it could be aimed at the culture and the mentality of the masses. It stripped both of any attachment to the Christian transcendent. It locked both the individual and his culture in the close embrace of a goal that was totally immanent: the class struggle for sociopolitical liberation.

Swiftly, the linchpins of Vatican and papal control were replaced by the action-oriented demands of the new theology. The most powerful religious orders of the Roman Church—Jesuits, Dominicans, Franciscans, Maryknollers—all committed themselves to Liberation Theology. In Rome and in the worldwide field of their apostolates, the policies and the actions of these religious orders became the lifeblood of the rising colossus of Liberation Theology.

Corruption of the best is the worst corruption. It was not long before a majority of diocesan bishops—not only in Latin America but in Europe and the United States, as well—were swept up in the new theology of this-worldly liberation. The entire effort was helped along by the careful and intricate networking of Catholic dioceses by a new creation: the Base Community. Essentially composed of lay Catholics, each Base Community decided how to pray, what priests to accept, what bishops—if any—would have authority, what sort of liturgy they would tolerate. All reference to traditional Catholic theology and to Rome's central authority was considered secondary, if not altogether superfluous.

The Base Communities in Latin America—riddled with Liberation Theology and openly Marxist in their political philosophy—were pronounced in their hatred of the United States. They were stubborn in their attachment to the Soviet Union. And they were fierce in their preference for violent revolution—the one non-Gramscian note in an otherwise faithful adherence to his blueprint.

The accelerating spread of both Liberation Theology and Base Communities was boosted beyond measure by several factors. But among the most important was the string of Peace and Justice Commissions—branch offices, as one might say, of the central Commission in Rome—that existed throughout the worldwide dioceses of the Roman Church. These commissions became powerful allies of Liberation Theology. Manned mostly by clerics, nuns and laity who were already convinced Marxists, they turned themselves into centers for the dissemination of the new theology. They ate up Vatican funds to pay for congresses, conventions, bureaucratic trips and a flood of printed materials—all of it aimed squarely at the reeducation of the faithful.

In the United States and Europe, meanwhile, the poor were too small in numbers, too isolated and too uninterested to serve as a primary target of Gramscian opportunity. No matter. For in both areas there were major seminaries that were already antipapal in their sentiment and antitraditional in their theology. They rapidly enshrined Liberation Theology as the new way of thinking about all the old questions. Reference to Catholic theology and to orthodox Roman teaching went out the window.

The process of secularization in the Catholic and Protestant churches progressed so rapidly and with such energy that, just as Gramsci had foreseen, it fed into other streams of anti-Church influence in the West. Those were streams that, seemingly independent of Marxist influence, advocated a materialistic interpretation of all sectors of human thought, investigation and action.

At some date toward the end of the sixties, it had already become evident to a surprisingly cohesive minority that the technical solution to the problems of overpopulation and the rising costs of living could lie only in contraception and abortion. The push was quickly mounted to count those solutions as part and parcel of basic human rights. Legislative measures had to be taken, of course, to have such measures officially declared as human rights. Accordingly, legislative approval and sanction for contraception and abortion were widely proposed throughout the West by movements other than Communist parties, movements that had become strange allies indeed.

The flood tide of secularism was not all legalistic and legislative, however. As time went on, the academic faculties of Europe and America, already proud of their position in the vanguard of liberal and forward-looking political thinking, took like ducks to the rising tide of Marxist interpretations of history, law, religion and scientific inquiry. The complexion of education in everything from genetics to sociology and psychology became decidedly, and often exclusively, materialistic.

Everything now seemed to proceed on the principle that all the puzzles of humankind and all the problems of human life had to be solved without any admixture of the transcendent. All the meaning of human life and the answer to every human hope were contained within the boundaries of the visible, tangible, material world of the here and now.

As John Paul II settled into the Apostolic Palace in Rome as successor to Paul VI and the short-lived John Paul I—by the end of the 1970s and into the early 1980s—the many and varied streams of materialist influence had already broken over their banks and flooded into the general landscape of Western culture. Everything seemed to coalesce in Gramsci's favor.

Christian-Marxist dialogues and conventions were everywhere. The influence of the unequivocally Marxist and pro-Soviet World Council of Churches went through the roof. Traditional principles of education collapsed in Catholic schools, from primary through university levels. The refusal of Western bishops to insist on obedience of the faithful to Church laws about divorce, abortion, contraception and homosexuality became the norm, not the exception. Everywhere, in fact, there was a massive lethal thrust, on Antonio Gramsci's terms, at the Catholic and Christian culture of the West nations.

By the time John Paul II came to the papacy, in fact, it was no longer even a secret that echelons of clerics in the Vatican itself had been deeply affected. Indeed, perhaps the profoundest victory of the Gramscian process was visible primarily in the mind-boggling confusion, ambiguity and fluidity that was already the hallmark of Rome's reaction to the rapid de-Catholicizing of the Church, as well as of Vatican dealings with bishops who sometimes openly declared their independence from papal authority. To a large degree, papal and Vatican control had been effectively removed from the georeligious machinery of the Roman Catholic Church.

Pope John Paul did not arrive from Poland unaware. He understood better than most what had happened to his Church in the West. He was, in fact, probably the only major non-Communist world leader who knew the contribution Antonio Gramsci had made to operational Marxism around the world, and who understood both the murky process he had advocated and the Leninist machinery in which that process was now enshrined.

Nevertheless, if John Paul had hoped that in his five papal trips to Latin America, he could put a dent in the allegiance of his clergy there to Liberation Theology, or that he could recall his bishops and his religious orders in the region to their vows of obedience, he was disappointed in those hopes. No papal exhortations in public or in private, and no directives by his Vatican, made the slightest substantial difference in the situation there.

Indeed, by 1987, the pro-Soviet and violence-prone Base Communities in Latin America alone numbered over 600,000. By comparison, there were not even 1,000 Roman Catholic dioceses in North and South America combined—and virtually all of those were at least questionable in their allegiance to Rome.

Finally, even in such countries of the Catholic heartland as Italy and

Spain, there was nothing to stand in the way of the legalization of divorce and the liberalization of all Christian-based laws and moral constraints, including the most basic and personal ones concerning family, sexuality and pornography.

Inevitably, as the 1980s progressed, non-Marxist streams of influence were increasingly and ever more rapidly affected by Gramscian penetration and cooperation. The "liberalized" culture of the West nations essentially converged with the process of mounting secularization, sharing freely and solidly in the new sacred principle that all the life, activities and hopes of mankind rested on the solid structures of this world alone.

Professionally secular systems of belief—Humanism, Mega-Religion and the grab bag of New Age, for example—forged their own not-so-strange alliances with Gramsci's heirs, rushing into the religious vacuum of formerly Christian societies. For they, too, were united in insisting on the major proposition that religion and religious faith had no function except to help all mankind to unite and be at peace within this world, in order to reach its ultimate peak of human development.

In the same decade of the eighties, a new bent of mind surfaced within virtually all of the merging secularist streams of activity in the West. Globalism.

The generality of thinking people throughout the West nations—entrepreneurs, academicians, politicians, artists, media people, industrialists, scientists—all inclined themselves toward the concept that the whole society of nations should and could be forged into a unity, into one great society, secular to the marrow of its bones, rejecting all the old religious divisiveness, spurning all of religion's old and outworn claims of otherworldly ambitions and purposes.

By the beginning of the 1990s, the Gramscian process in the West had been fused seamlessly, like molten glass, into the most important energies and impulses of the new culture prevailing in democratic capitalist societies.

Within what was still called Catholicism, the word "Roman" was frequently dropped; Roman Catholicism was not a concept that was compatible with secular globalism, after all. Within "Modern Catholicism," as it called itself, a large majority of bishops, priests, religious and laity had adopted all the traits of the new culture that surrounded them. They had ceased to be Catholic in any sense that would have been recognized by Pope John XXIII as he summoned his Second Vatican Council to "open the windows" of his Church to the world in the search for its renewal—its *aggiornamento*.

The mental deception of so many millions of Catholics by a thoroughly this-worldly, materialistic and un-Catholic persuasion was matched only by the intellectual darkening into which the cultural elites of the West had worked themselves. Gramsci's ghost had captivated them all into his "Marxist hegemony of the mind."

The transcendental had bowed to the immanent. Total materialism was freely, peacefully and agreeably adopted everywhere in the name of man's dignity and rights, in the name of man's autonomy and freedom from outside constraints. Above all, as Gramsci had planned, this was done in the name of freedom from the laws and constraints of Christianity.

To tell anyone in the West—any of the participants in the entrepreneurial activities of America and Europe, anyone in the Western media, anyone in the scientific community or in the academic faculties of colleges and universities—that all of them, along with the leading theologians and Church dignitaries the world over, had been thoroughly grounded in the basic principles of Marxism would be to elicit hoots of derision and self-righteous cries of protest. Pope John Paul's answer to such hoots and cries, however, is to point to Gramsci's ghost, which has thoroughly penetrated all of these groups with the Communist revolutionary sense of immanence.

Many who would reject this claim by John Paul point in their turn to the social democracies that flourish in the Scandinavian countries. Surely, Marxism cannot be said to flourish in such areas—not even so unbloody a brand of Marxism as Gramsci's. After all, in Sweden, in Norway, in Denmark, there has been a revulsion from the Marxist oppression of liberty. And in all of them there flourishes a large bourgeois class with no liking for Marxist economic weaknesses and no inclination to renounce either capitalism or the material comforts it brings.

John Paul's answer to any such finger-pointing is that it misses the whole subtle attack of Gramsci's ingeniously congenial process. In fact, argues the Pontiff, to make this argument is in itself to cooperate with the most central operating principle of Leninist Marxism: deception.

The Pope readily concedes that the Nordic model of social democracy in Norway, Sweden and Denmark has produced a comfortable way of life, a way of life ingrained with values of moderation, egalitarianism and social solidarity, a way of life bolstered by hefty social benefits, a way of life in which there is a virtual absence of ostentatious wealth, but in which living standards hover near the top of the international scale.

Nevertheless, as John Paul understands to his pain, the model social democracies in these countries rest upon a way of life that is in no way concerned with any value transcending the here and now. All public values are immanent. In a private conversation with one of his American counterparts, a Swedish book publisher remarked that "Sweden is a small and godless country." Pope John Paul would extend that observation with equal accuracy to Sweden's Nordic partners in social democracy.

In their efforts to join in some degree of economic unity with the Europe of 1992, meanwhile, the Nordic administrations have a tough time of it. It is hard for them to place a cap on public-sector expenses; or to step up national productivity; or to allow private enterprises a freer rein. For to do any of that would jigger the national consensus in their own countries. And this is a consensus that rests exclusively on the "value" of material comfort.

In Pope John Paul's reading, the crux of the matter in the Nordic countries is not all that different from that in the rest of the West nations, including the United States. In every case, national culture was developed on the basis of Christian beliefs and Christian moral laws. Indeed, the Pontiff argues from history, those beliefs and laws gave each nation its resiliency, its courage and its inspiration. In sum, as Gramsci realized, Christianity was both the philosophy and the lifeblood of the Western culture shared by all of the nations in question.

By the end of the 1980s, however, there was no longer even any serious talk of Christian beliefs or Christian moral laws. If they entered into the great dialogues of the day, they were reduced to "values," like any other coinage that existed for the sole purpose of being bargained away for something else.

George Orwell once wrote that "at any given moment, there is a sort of all-pervading orthodoxy—a general tacit agreement not to discuss some large and uncomfortable fact."

For John Paul's money, the "all-pervading orthodoxy" in the West in the final decade of the twentieth century is a tacit agreement not to discuss the "large and uncomfortable fact" that Western leaders and populations, in their public consensus, have abandoned the Christian philosophy of human life.

In fact, according to Pope John Paul's analysis of Western culture at the present moment, there is no philosophy of life worthy of the name. What now passes for philosophy is nothing more than a hybrid complex of fashions and vogues and impulses and theories that mold public opinion, that guide public education and that dominate artistic and literary expression throughout the West. What better scenario than that could Gramsci have written into his blueprint? It is the perfect stage for his process—long since adopted by European Marxists—to promote the growth of social democracy within the society of European nations and to occupy the spaces left vacant by the bourgeois culture itself.

With their own philosophy still in place and as inflexibly based as ever on the materialistic dialectic of Marx, Gramsci's latter-day heirs have sold the free-market West on a new prize commodity: that type of immanence which is specifically Communist.

The General Secretary of the Italian Communist Party, Achille Occhetto, gave a little demonstration in early June of 1989 of how well the Gramscian formula works. The occasion was his pious denunciation of the CP in China for ordering the People's Liberation Army (CPA) to use tanks and automatic weapons to crush the student protest on the streets of Beijing a few weeks before.

"In the East [China]," Occhetto declared without even a wink at the bloody history of Marxism, "Communism is a term that has no relation any longer to its historic origins and constitutes a political framework that is completely wrong." Then, in the great deception demanded by Gramsci's policy, Occhetto proclaimed, "There is absolutely nothing left of Communism as a unitary and organic system." To illustrate the point, in fact, Occhetto and his comrades in the Italian CP went on to organize public demonstrations of their solidarity with the doomed student-led democratic movement in China.

Occhetto's words notwithstanding, his was the perfect display of Gramsci's mandate to Marxists everywhere. Take advantage of every opportunity that presents itself, Gramsci had said. Be inflexible in the materialist dialectic of Marx. Be rigid in material philosophy and unbending in the Marxist interpretation of history. But be clever as you do it. Ally all of that with any forces that present an opening for Marxist immanentism.

Obediently, Gramscian Marxists in Europe and elsewhere fuel nationalism in Africa. But at the same time, they ally themselves with the globalism of the world's entrepreneurs and with the Europeanizers of Europe. They side with American sentiment condemning the excesses of Chinese Marxism. But they support the elements in the American Congress and administration that foster compromise with the Chinese Marxist leaders.

They join with the Christian churches in brotherly dialogue and in common humanitarian ventures. But the object is to confirm the new Christianity in its antimetaphysical and essentially atheistic pursuit of

liberation from material inconvenience, from the fear of a nuclear holocaust, from sexual restriction of any kind and, finally, from all supernatural constrictions as from all material fears. Total liberation is to
construct the long-dreamed Leninist-Marxist Utopia—that is the rule.

By just that process, authored by Antonio Gramsci more than half a
century ago within the dismal confines of Mussolini's prisons, has Western culture deprived itself of its lifeblood.

Running through the ancient arteries of once Christian lands, Pope John
Paul sees the soul-killing, watery serum of what he has called "superdevelopment," and an always nervous striving for economic soundness.
The ideal is exclusively here and now. Every aim is totally immanent to
historical man in his cities and his houses and his pleasures; in his industries and his factories; and, above all, in his banks and his money markets. This is the predeath trickle of serum that has replaced the blood of
culture in the West.

Given such a state of Western culture—including the much vaunted
Nordic models of social democracy—it might have been laughable, had
it not been so painful, for John Paul to hear the recent, almost mystical,
judgment of Krister Ahlstrom, CEO of the Finnish Employers Confederation. "Something indefinable binds Nordic countries together," pondered Ahlstrom, "as though they had an invisible force." That force,
maintains Pope John Paul, is not invisible at all. It is the force of Gramsci's success. Not only the Nordic countries but the entire West has given
birth at last to the child of Gramsci's ghost: a completely secularized
society. And in what is still called "the spirit of Vatican II," John Paul's
worldwide Roman Catholic institutional organization has been both midwife and wet nurse for that force.

Only once was there a truly serious threat to the Gramscian process. It
came, of all places, in Poland. And it followed Pope John Paul's "pilgrimage" of 1979, with its risky, dramatic and compelling challenge to the
status quo of the Communist regime in his homeland.

Bitter and sustained experience—first under post–World War II Stalinism; and then under Khrushchev and Brezhnev—had taught John Paul
one basic lesson. Stalin's brand of Leninist Marxism would brook no
tampering with the nuts and bolts of the Soviet Union's imperial hold on
Poland. Any attempt to dilute Soviet control of the Polish Armed Forces,
or of the KGB-organized security police, or the rubber-stamp Polish

parliament, would be met with the full force of the Soviet mailed fist—which was to say, with total repression, with the use of Soviet divisions stationed in Eastern Poland if necessary, and with the clampdown of even closer surveillance by the KGB itself.

The effective answer to that insistent hands-off-our-turf requirement of the Polish regime came from Cardinal Wyszynski, Primate of Poland, and mentor of Pope John Paul during his days as priest and bishop in Krakow. Wyszynski always insisted that in other Eastern satellite countries—notably in Hungary—the Church's tough and intransigent fight with the atheist puppet regimes of the USSR had met with disaster. On the other hand, neither could the Church in such countries run away from the hostile and oppressive situation that engulfed them. The Cardinal devised a third way. The Church had to cohabit Poland with the Marxist political regime, he said; but at the same time, it had to preserve its people intact in their culture.

Under Wyszynski's canny and guiding hand, the all-pervasive Catholic Church in Poland developed its own anti-Gramsci version of Gramsci's process, its own network within which Polish culture could be preserved and developed.

The underground or "flying" university, of which Pope John Paul himself was a product; underground publications and libraries; underground cultural activities and artistic pursuits—all of these efforts and countless others blanketed Poland and constituted a popular stratum of Polish culture. All of it was Church-related—devised, fomented, nourished and solidly supported under Wyszynski's guidance. And all of it was untouched by the deadening hand of Marxism.

In the months following Pope John Paul's careful but unequivocal call for change during his 1979 papal speeches in Warsaw and Gniezno and Krakow, the Solidarity movement—originally based among shipyard workers in the Baltic ports—found its way throughout Poland. It came into official existence in 1980, when the first accords were signed in the Lenin Shipyards of Gdansk.

The success and vogue of the Polish Solidarity movement added a whole new dimension to the Wyszysnki concept. Almost insensibly, a new proposition was born in many minds. It was true—and as nearly as anyone could see at the time, it was going to remain true—that Poles were forced to concede political, military and security powers to the Soviet regime in Moscow. But that regime could allow exactly the aboveground freedoms John Paul had called for in all areas of culture. In education and art and literature, to be sure, but also, and at long last, in the field of labor relations.

When just that proposition was actually made, the officials of the CP in Poland found it appealing in a number of respects. Warsaw was being badgered continually by Moscow to do something about Poland's economy, which was in shambles, and about its labor unrest, which was always ready to boil over, and about its $30 billion debt to Western creditors.

Given recognition and status, it was just possible that Solidarity could do away with the crippling strikes that bedeviled Polish industry. It might even prevent the subtle and costly "go slow" tactics used by Poland's workers, who saw reduced productivity as their only means of protest against starvation wages, food shortages, police brutality and all the other forms of governmental oppression.

It might even be that, if such a prescription could work in Poland, the Soviet Union might see in it a formula to be tried in other ailing economies of its Eastern satellite empire.

It is unlikely that the record of private conversations between the participants in the negotiations, or the cable traffic between Cardinal Wyszynski's Warsaw, Pope John Paul's Vatican and General Secretary Brezhnev's Moscow, or the few additional documents involved, will ever be laid bare to the eyes of today's historians. It does seem certain, however, that with Moscow's approval, at least a verbal agreement was finally reached between the background organizers of Solidarity and the Polish Communist regime.

It was a brilliant idea. A mixed bag of carrots and sticks for both sides. It would make any penetration of Polish culture by the Gramscian process difficult. But there would be common agreement at last to leave security and political control of Poland in the hands of the Soviet-controlled Communist Party. And it promised economic relief in at least one of the satellite countries that were draining Moscow's already strained resources.

The plan might have worked, had the agreement concerning exclusive political control by the Communist regime not been violated. But among Solidarity's organizers were members of another organization—the Committee for the Defense of the Workers, known internationally by its Polish initials: KOR. Whether by design or by tactical error, KOR managed to push Solidarity's policies and demands beyond the bounds of culture. KOR wanted a share of the regime's political power, as well; and it was not content to wait for time to ripen the possibilities.

KOR's demand was too much too soon for the Soviet Union of Leonid Brezhnev and for its surrogate regime in Poland. The agreement collapsed. The attempted assassination of Pope John Paul took place. And by December of 1981, Polish General Wojciech Jaruzelski had imposed martial law in Moscow's name. The alternative, as the General insisted in his own defense to Cardinal Wyszynski and Pope John Paul, was a direct military takeover by the Soviet Union.

In retrospect, both Moscow and Warsaw seem to have suffered a loss of nerve. In Poland, Gramsci's process had been met head-on and squarely for the first time by the dedicated use of its own tactics. And when those tactics seemed to threaten the control of Soviet Marxism within its own domain of Polish politics, all thought of Gramsci's call for the CPSU to foster different faces of Communism in different countries was lost in the panic.

What Brezhnev saw in the situation was a threat to total Soviet control in its own territory. In those unprecedented circumstances, he reverted to his Stalinist roots. He abandoned the Gramscian experiment in Poland —the first, but not the last that would surface in the satellite countries.

Even here, however, the aftermath of Brezhnev's action demonstrated still one more time the unwisdom of classical Leninism. For once again, such heavy-handed policies failed to change the way the people thought about their lives and their problems. Poles remained fundamentally Christian in tradition. Their culture, with its moral laws and civic customs, was only driven underground. True, the people were again forced to behave outwardly according to hated rules within a hated sociopolitical regime. But just as Gramsci had said, the religious transcendent— God, with his laws and his worship—continued to flourish, and to nourish enmity for what Poles everywhere saw was the alien superstructure of a Soviet Marxist dictatorship.

The dramatic Polish experiment that opened the decade of the 1980s failed. Who might have won at that moment in time—Gramsci or Wyszynski—will never be known. But the day was not far down the road when the gamble would be tried again. And when the time came, as the eighties drew to a close, the high cards were all in Soviet hands. For, despite Moscow's loss of nerve in putting Gramsci's formula to its first test within the Soviet orbit, the fundamental Marxization of the West itself had not been impeded or slowed in the least.

On the contrary, the originally Christian mind in the West nations was so far eroded already, that capitalist nations were persuading themselves that they had to be content with the conviction that the purpose and meaning of all life is life. Life rooted in loyalty to a nation. Life conducted with a maximum sense of solidarity among a society of nations. Life with a reverence for all living things, whether walking on two legs, or four legs, or no legs. Life, as onetime Marxist Milovan Djilas wrote with extreme pathos, "which is patriotic without being nationalistic, socially responsible without being socialist, and respectful of human rights and those of all creatures without calling itself Christian."

With those conditions as a backdrop in the West, the Soviet refusal of Poland's challenge to Gramsci's process in Poland became a thing of the past, a mistake of history.

Mikhail Gorbachev burst upon the world scene as the first Soviet leader big-minded enough to appraise, appreciate and fully embrace the Gramscian formula. The only Soviet leader realistic and courageous enough to commit even his own satellite territories to the dead Sardinian's plan for victory in Marxism's consistent struggle for total geopolitical predominance among the nations, and for its total acceptance in the newly de-Christianized hearts and minds of the men and women who people those nations.

One by one, the former Soviet satellites are seen as liberated from the direct control of the USSR. The Communist parties in those individual countries have been shunted off their solitary perch on the dais of government; indeed, in Hungary, the former CP has renounced even calling itself "Communist." And the Gorbachev-blessed changes are going further. Now the reunification of the "two Germanys" has his approval. No doubt, in a short time, the three Baltic States—Lithuania, Estonia, Latvia—will attain a status even more detached from the USSR than the former satellites.

In his Gramscian pattern, Gorbachev envisions a new governmental structure for the USSR itself and—unimaginable wonder of wonders!—a new status for several of the "Socialist Soviet Republics" that flesh out the USSR. Armenia, Georgia, Azerbaijan, the Ukraine will all attain a new status other than that of fully integrated "Republics" in the former "Union of Soviet Socialist Republics." The Gramscian process requires such changes. Gorbachevism implicitly endorses them. In this, as John Paul perceives, Gorbachev is being very faithful to his hard-core Leninism, while adding his own updating and correctives.

In John Paul II's reading of the geopolitical arena of the 1990s, the secularized West would seem to be custom-made for Gorbachevism. The Soviet General Secretary has made it clear that he is perfectly aware of the barrenness afflicting the bloody-minded plans of Lenin, whom *Pravda* once hailed as "the radiant genius who lights the path of mankind to Communism." Gorbachev has read his contemporary world instead, and unabashedly, in the more accurate light of the analysis of Antonio

Gramsci, but keeping intact a basic tactical principle of that "radiant genius." Gorbachev has even taken the trouble to explain that basic tactical principle. In his book, *Perestroika*, he has explained:

> It would be appropriate to recall how Lenin fought for the Brest Peace Treaty in the troubled year 1918. The Civil War was raging, and at that moment came a most serious threat from Germany. So Lenin suggested signing a peace treaty with Germany.
>
> The terms of peace Germany peremptorily laid down for us were, in Lenin's words, "disgraceful, dirty." They meant Germany annexed a huge tract of territory with a population of fifty-six million. . . . Yet Lenin insisted on that peace treaty. Even some members of the Central Committee objected . . . workers, too . . . demanding that the German invaders be rebuffed. Lenin kept calling for peace because he was guided by *vital*, not *immediate*, interests of the working class as a whole, of the Revolution, and of the future of Socialism . . . he was looking far ahead . . . he did not put what was transitory above what was essential. . . . Later, it was easy to say confidently and unambiguously that Lenin was right. . . . The Revolution was saved.

Probably Gorbachev regards the insistence of the West on liberalization of human rights as undue intrusion, and the insistence of the former satellite nations to be free as "disgraceful" and "dirty" actions by "socialist brothers." But, to save the Revolution, to save the essentials of the Party-State, he does see it as necessary to liberalize the Soviet empire, even to disaggregate the present structure of the USSR. For only thus can he hope and expect to be admitted as a full-blooded member of the new globalist society of nations.

Leninist flexibility, colored by Gramscian subtleties and modified to supply whatever was lacking in Gramsci's blueprints for victory—this constitutes Gorbachev's program. For it is true that human affairs in the last decade of the twentieth century are not at all the same as in its first four decades, when Gramsci lived and thought and died. "Marx never saw an electric bulb," commented China's Hu Yaobang in November of 1986, "and Engels never saw an airplane." Just so, globalism was a non-thought for the politically battle-hardened Sardinian whose mind and outlook were polarized between the parochialism of Lenin's pseudorevolutionary Moscow and a Western European culture about to be drowned in all-out war.

Gramsci never saw the deadly mushroom cloud of a nuclear explosion, the fearful opening announcement of a new and unheard-of interdependence of nations. He never had even a glimmering of the idea of the computer chip, which has revolutionized industrial development in regions whose populations were, until what seems only moments ago, locked into their Asian rice paddies and their African savannas and their Brazilian rain forests. Nothing in Gramsci's pre–World War II surroundings so much as hinted at the possibility of a "global village."

In Gorbachev's hands, however, Gramsci has entered into the globalist competition. Of that Pope John Paul is convinced. As the Pontiff leads the tattered but still powerful and unique structure of his universal Roman Catholic Church through the unpredictable volatility of our times, he is certain that Mikhail Gorbachev will move confidently into the deep waters of the new globalism, with the ghost of Antonio Gramsci as companion and guide.

The Pope sees Gorbachev as supremely confident that he can maneuver the Leninist geopolitical structure and organization he now heads into a position of total domination in that new globalism. Nor has the Pontiff any of the illusions nourished by other West leaders about the General Secretary's vision of how that new globalism can be turned in the direction of Leninism and skillfully adapted to the Leninist geopolitical goal. Gorbachev's vision is still animated, as Chilean journalist Jaime Antunez has written, by "an immanentist sense, and [by] its purpose . . . to change social [and] economic relations with a view to producing a 'new man' fully liberated from 'old moral ties' [of] Western Christian civilization."

While, in the Pontiff's mind, the success or failure of the Gorbachev gamble with the new globalism remains an open question—the odds being heavily in Gorbachev's favor—John Paul's analysis of the new globalists and their plans makes him pessimistic about their chances of any acceptable degree of success.

Part Four

Champions of Globalism

14. . . . with Interdependence and Development for All

At some moment very soon after World War II, while the ghost of Antonio Gramsci was just getting up a good head of steam in the world, an extraordinary revolution he did not foresee began to take hold around the planet. The mood of the world arena began to change. Whether or not Gramsci's policies fed that mood, it seemed that almost suddenly there was a hankering for some truly workable system of interdependence among nations. A new kind of interdependence. An international unity that would not come riding like death on the back of conquest or subversion or crude takeovers. The time was past for yet another polished-up version of the ancient empire of Rome, in which all the world was forced to be Roman.

Rather, the new globalist mind envisioned an interdependence that would somehow accommodate the fact of the world as a shrinking place, but would also leave each nation its own identity.

As blurry as the concept of interdependence among nations might have been, a single aim did come to the fore fairly early on. And, though, since then, a great deal has changed among the many contenders for predominance in the global arena, that aim has remained constant at least for the most powerful of them: development. Some means was energetically sought by a few, was desired by many, and came to be expected by all, through which every national and cultural entity would actively share in and contribute to the material development of all. Everyone would have to be on board, for interdependence required an absence of strife. And an absence of strife required that there be no have-nots or "outsiders" among the nations.

Blurry or not, the new globalist vision was enough to ignite fires of longing among men and women the world over. Whole generations had

lived all their lives amid global, regional and local wars. Even peace—
what there was of it—could only be guaranteed by the threat of war.
Compared to such a world as that, interdependence and material development could only sound like heaven on earth.

By about the end of the seventies, it seemed that nearly everyone in
every nation and condition of life was following the barrage of practical
news and not-always-so-practical editorial opinions about what was commonly accepted as a global competition for power going on in earnest
among individuals, groups and nations. It became commonplace for
men and women in every walk of life to appraise their own interests—
their family situation, their job or profession, their company, their city,
their country, their cause—in the light of such global developments.
Increasingly, people came to see themselves and the circumstances of
their lives in what they understood to be new and unprecedented globalist terms.

Given such widespread globalist yearnings—or at least the widespread
yearning for international peace and material development—and given
the fact that no practical means for achieving such overall goals seemed
to emerge, the world was prepared in advance to be drawn into the orbits
of two powerful leaders. Karol Wojtyla as Pope John Paul II and Mikhail
Gorbachev as General Secretary of the Soviet Union loomed taller and
seemed able to stride farther than any of their contemporaries on the
shifting world stage.

As these two world leaders burst so unexpectedly upon the scene of
global affairs, one after the other within seven short years, there was a
common perception that, as different as they might be in every other
respect, one thing they shared set them apart from every other leader
and from every other globalist visionary: The Roman Catholic Pontiff
and the Soviet General Secretary each seemed to stand in sight of what
would perfect the incipient globalism on the horizon of our world.

That public perception of both men was and remains accurate. For
both came to their positions of power as died-in-the-wool globalists. Both
have a truly geopolitical bent of mind. Both have a clear geopolitical
mandate and purpose. And each of them is backed up by a geopolitical
organization.

John Paul and Gorbachev both understand already what practical
working structures are needed to create a geopolitical system among
nations. They have long since seen clearly that geopolitics must and will
transfer national politics to a global plane—will induce all the transformations and adaptations necessary in today's local political structures, so
that they may flourish in tomorrow's truly geopolitical system of inter-

dependence. They have long since understood that no nation of the world will remain in the next century as it has been or is in this century. They have long since seen that the very concept of nationhood will be deeply altered.

Much of the world may be uncomfortable with Gorbachev's Communism. Much of the world may be repelled by John Paul's Roman Catholicism. But it is clear to all the world—leaders and people alike—that over and above Communism and Catholicism, there is in each of these two men a secure point of view that can at long last take the idea of globalism beyond the stage of a blurry dream. Either of them can—and each of them intends to—infuse the present inchoate globalism with the values it lacks, give it flesh-and-blood reality, and transmute it into a veritable new world order.

Walking as they do in the unobstructed light of their separate globalist visions, these two men—the Pope and the General Secretary—act like magnets, drawing popular emotions and a vast enthusiasm to themselves around the world.

National leaders, meanwhile, are drawn in the wake of these two men. In such company, John Paul and Mikhail Gorbachev are perceived with less emotion and not always with enthusiasm. But they are seen as having a clear picture of what is needed to create a true geopolitical unity in a world groping for exactly that. They are known to have their differing blueprints of the global unity that would absorb all local unities. Blueprints, in other words, of the centralization needed in order to eliminate the thousand and one separate nationalist-minded governments pulling this way and that in the current international system. Blueprints, moreover, of the values that must act as the glue—the sticky tape of cohesion —indispensable to any geopolitical arrangement among nations but lacking to individual nations in the world of the 1990s.

The fact that John Paul and Mikhail Gorbachev are the towering figures in the world arena where globalism is perceived as the prize does not in the least discourage other contenders from crowding in.

On the contrary, champions of globalism are in ready supply. Some have entered the arena alone. Some have come with a bevy of camp followers. Some form short- or long-term alliances with fellow contenders. Some remain aloof from all the others. Most of them have an international forum they have never enjoyed before. And all of them are beset by problems they either deny, or have not yet figured out how to overcome, on their way to the future. But every one of them is bitten by the same bug—the will to lead the way to the new globalist pattern that will hold sway over all nations.

From John Paul's vantage point, the first big problem faced by most of his competitors in the globalist arena is that, as individuals and as groups, they still approach the world situation with a local mind-set.

Their second major problem is that with the sole exception of Mikhail Gorbachev, none of the other contenders has a system of values around which a new globalist structure for the nations of the world can form and maintain itself over time.

And yet a third difficulty is that none of them has managed to create or to gain control of the practical machinery they need for success—a functioning, up-and-running geopolitical organization such as Gorbachev's global Leninist machine, or John Paul's universal Roman Catholic structure.

Despite even such deep shortcomings, however, there are certain globalist-minded groups—some score or so in all, by the Pope's reckoning—that are powerful forces in their own right. These contending groups fall rather naturally, in the Pontiff's analysis, into three broad categories.

The first category is the most crowded. There are so many groups in contention here, in fact, that they form themselves into subcategories. But generally speaking, and allowing for differences and divisions aplenty, included here is every globalist-minded group of some importance that maintains a vision of the new world in its own image. Each of them is certain that the world is about to become what that group already is. Each sees the world as a whole in its own terms. These are the Provincial Globalists.

The second broad category comprises a smaller number of globalist-minded groups than the first—only three in all. And the number of people represented is not vast. Nevertheless, the characteristic of this category is that each group included within it sees the world as already in its own globalist basket. Without fear or favor, each will ride on the back of any current that will take it forward. But for them, it's not so much that the world will become what they are. It's that they are the world. These are the Piggyback Globalists.

The third category is made up of only two groups. But these are the true globalist contenders. Humanly speaking, very little seems to stand in the way of their ultimate success in the globalist arena. And though John Paul knows they have not yet crossed the Rubicon that separates globalism from a true and workable geopolitical system, he sees them nevertheless as the Genuine Globalists.

• • •

The Pontiff maintains an intimate knowledge of each of these many globalist groups. And he does analyze them in terms of such categories and subcategories as these. He has spoken about many of them publicly from time to time. In the Vatican, and around the world on his never-ending travels, he has met publicly and privately with representatives and leaders of them all.

No one is more aware than John Paul, therefore, that some of the groups in question may have a romantic idea of what global interdependence will look like, or of how it will be achieved. And no one knows better than he that some of these globalist contenders are downright unrealistic about the practical ways to get from one stage of development to the next.

Nevertheless, whatever their own chances of ultimate victory in the millennium endgame, John Paul takes them seriously for several reasons.

First, there is the practical reality that, with few exceptions, these groups stand in serious and very effective hostility to John Paul and his Church, far more than they do to Gorbachev and his Party-State. They constitute points of deep opposition to the Pope's own acceptance as a world leader. And they wreak harm on his Church through the influence they exert over its members.

John Paul feels impelled to take these globalist contenders seriously, moreover, because whether they are realists or not, and whether they are persons or nations or systems builders or religious or ideological groups, their contention revolves around the stern stuff of the world. Around finance, trade and industry, politics, territory and military matters, and—not least—around religion. Whatever may happen to them ultimately, at the present moment they influence the fortunes of the world as surely as Marx or Lenin or Stalin or Gramsci did. The undeniable influence of these groups and their globalist mind-set—their irresistible desire for interdependence among nations, and the total allegiance of the most important of them to material development—have already transformed the former rigidities of the nations into the soft, malleable material from which the world expects its new order will be formed.

And John Paul maintains that these groups are of major importance for yet another reason. It is among these incipient globalists that both he and Mikhail Gorbachev must now operate. It is within the climate these groups create as a passing condition of our world that John Paul must pursue his own vision and his own goal. And he knows that Mikhail Gorbachev must do the same.

. . .

From his vantage point at the hub of the Vatican—the world's greatest listening post—Pope John Paul is so acutely aware of the daily moves and the long-range plans of each major globalist group, that it is as though each of those groups maintained a "situation room." A sort of high-command headquarters in which tactics and strategies and ultimate aims are laid out across the maps and action models on display. It is as though the Pope himself could enter those imaginary "situation rooms," unseen in his white robes, to watch the leaders of each group survey those maps and action models. It is as though he could listen to all the discussions and debates about the shape of the coming world and about each group's hoped-for system of global order.

Such situation rooms may not actually exist in every case. But the concept presents an orderly and accurate way to track John Paul's intelligence, understanding and appraisal of the various individuals, systems and groups that have crowded into the arena of the millennium endgame. It is a way to see, as if through the Pontiff's eyes, the remarkable array of forces that confront him. Forces that are truly preparing the world for a geopolitical alignment, even while they themselves are caught and carried along in the deep and irresistible currents of human affairs. These are currents, John Paul maintains, upon which all of these globalist groups will exert some influence for a time, but which none of them appears to understand, or even to perceive.

15. The Provincial Globalists

Every major globalist group in today's international arena has a system of underlying ideas about the world, and a system of acting in relation to the world that is based on those ideas.

That being so, it has to be said that anyone walking with Pope John Paul through the imaginary situation rooms of the plethora of groups that form his first and broadest category of globalists would be hard pressed to see any trait common to them all.

Each group views the world in a different—and often in a sharply contradictory—light. Christian religions vie with each other. All of them contend with non-Christian religions, which in turn contend with one another. Religious systems compete with nonreligious ethical systems; and all of those compete with political ideologies. Groups that are relatively small and localized stand in brave and confident opposition to groups much larger in their membership and far more extensive in their geographical reach.

Despite all their differences, however, one prime characteristic is shared by all the groups in this first category, which impels the Pope to compare, contrast and assess them in similar terms. Because each of them is certain that its system of ideas, as it stands, is the basis upon which the new world order must be arranged, each is just as certain that the world will beat a path to its door. Each of these groups is certain that it can stay as it is; and that sooner or later the world at large will somehow take on the ideas and the mind-set of the group, forging itself on a grand scale into the group's image and likeness.

The likelihood that any of these groups will achieve the globalist victory it envisions is remote on the face of it. Each group's underlying system of ideas about the world cannot be adapted without essentially destroying the group itself. On the other hand, those underlying systems cannot be adopted as they stand by the rest of the world, without dislocating or displacing the primary globalist aims current among nations.

Nevertheless, to argue that these Provincial Globalists do not have a significant impact on the globalist tendencies of the rest of the world would be to go too far. Provincial though they may be, each of them has suddenly found itself on a world stage. To one degree or another, each has learned to play a role on that stage, using all the international instruments—globalized media, intergovernment and intercultural forums—to impress its outlook like a stamp on other minds.

Further, each of these Provincial groups enjoys a certain advantage in a world that is increasingly shorn of any commonly accepted system of values at the same time that it needs such a system as the glue for the new political arrangement among nations. In those circumstances, everyone feels impelled to give a hearing to any and every point of view.

It is precisely because each of these Provincial Globalist groups has a voice—and in some cases, even a certain appeal or vogue—beyond its own ken that John Paul has spent time with certain of his close associates analyzing each of them, reckoning the impact each is likely to have on the practical order of the world's new vision of itself, and assessing the future of each.

The first Provincial Globalist group stands alone. Its situation room is home ground exclusively to those the Pope describes as the Angelists.

That name is precise in its description. For the maps and action models in this imaginary operations post show the center of the world to be those lands that are the abode of Allah's Angels, lands illumined with the heavenly light of faith of the Prophet Mohammed, and of Allah's Sacred Law, the Sharia.

The leaders who frequent this situation room may differ in the degree of moderation or extremes with which they are prepared to pursue their globalist vision and intent. Nigeria's leader, for example—Ibraham Dasuki, Sultan of Sokoto and *Sarkin Muslimi*, Commander of the Faithful —is more moderate than either the irredentist Muslim Brotherhood of Egypt or its twin in the Sudan, the Islamic Front. Different from any of those was the late Ayatollah Ruhollah (Breath of Allah) Khomeini of Iran.

What unites them with all of Islam, however, is the same light of faith and the Law that shines over all Islamic populations of the world. A total of something over 700 million souls, including those who live in the nations that stretch from Morocco on the North African shores of the Atlantic Ocean to Indonesia in the Java Sea. The Muslim name for North Africa, in fact, is indicative of the Angelist mentality. From Marrakesh to Cairo, that whole geographical region is called the Island [of faith] in the [infidel] West.

Outside of the geographical limits where the light of Allah and his Prophet shines, all lands and peoples are figured on the Angelist map in the dreadful darkness of infidelity. All are held to be in hated alliance with the Great Satan—an identity presently shared in unequal proportions by the United States and the Soviet Union.

The impact of this mentality in the present globalist-minded world has been demonstrated with different effects in different nations. And not the least of it for other globalists concerned with the ebb and flow of alliances among nations is that the Angelist mentality—fired as it is by its vibrant faith, which is channeled by skillful leaders into military and political fields—makes it very difficult, if not temporarily impossible, to see Israel as an integral part of the economic and political structure of the Middle East comity of nations. This Arab-Israeli contention, as it is called, is a permanent disturbing factor among all the nations, for the present moment. From the Angelist side, clearly there is no geopolitical compromise possible between Israel as it is today and the Islamic forces arrayed against it. Experience since 1948 has shown that no power can afford to take up a neutral stance in this contention. Dissension, therefore, quite apart from the human losses in successive Arab-Israeli wars and through the ravages of terrorism, is the immediate fruit of Angelism.

In reckoning the future of Islam, Pope John Paul takes into account that as a genuinely religious faith, it preserves certain fundamental truths that the Holy Spirit reveals to all people of good will; and that, in God's providence, Islam can be a threshold from which its adherents can be prepared to accept the only historical revelation made by God in this world. There will come a day, John Paul believes, when the heart of Islam—already attuned to the figures of Christ and of Christ's Mother, Mary—will receive the illumination it needs. In the meantime, the Pontiff knows that Islam will stand against him and his Church and his geopolitical vision. Still, the Pope can foresee no possibility that the Angelist mentality, so graphically clear in this first globalist situation room, will serve as the practical stuff from which the world will be able to fashion its future.

In the second Provincial Globalist situation room, one set of maps and action models is shared by several groups of Christians (Adventists, Baptistic and Evangelical sects) and non-Christians (Christian Scientists, Jehovah's Witnesses, Mormons, Unitarians), who are as exclusive-minded as their Muslim counterparts, but without the expressly political ambitions and the revolutionary extremism.

Minimalists, some of John Paul's associates call these groups, because they expect to constitute a minimum of the world's population until some (as yet) unknown day—the "Last Day"—of mankind's earthly history.

Minimalist is an adequate term to describe these groups as far as their membership goes; except for the Baptistic and Evangelical sects, where the numbers are reliably placed around 50–70 million worldwide, none of the others exceed 7 million, the smallest number belonging to the Jehovah's Witnesses (mid six figures). And the term Minimalist aptly sums up the essence of whatever globalist outlook they have developed. Deliberately restrictive in their idea of how the vast majority of mankind will fare in the long and final run, they expect that their religious outlook, now shared by a minimum of human beings, will become the absolute norm for all those (a restricted number) who will fare well and achieve eternal happiness.

Because none of them are "churches of the poor," being largely located in the economically upper-middle and upper classes of society, their influence can be disproportionately larger than their numerical size would warrant. Most of the groups officially engage in very active and well-heeled missionary work, in which they compete with Roman Catholic missionizing attempts. Each one of them has a deeply rooted opposition amounting to a nourished enmity for all that John Paul represents as Churchman and as geopolitician.

In their quite evident globalism one cannot detect even the basic lines of geopolitical thought. Placing their central hopes for victory in the arrival of some particular "day of the Lord" and lacking any lived experience of geopolitical action, they are globalist in outlook but do not enter the georeligious contention. Their interest for John Paul lies in the element of opposition to him that they present. That opposition among the non-Christian Minimalists is obvious especially if, like the Mormons and Christian Scientists, they deny the central tenet of John Paul's Christianity: namely, the divinity of Jesus. Among the Christian Minimalists, the opposition is virulent and has a long history. Despite the mutual differences, for instance, between the Advent Christian Church, the Church of God of Abrahamic Faith, and the Seventh-Day Adventists, they are at one in the opposition to Rome as the "Red Whore of the Mediterranean."

Given their separate and separatist perspectives on the world, in one sense these groups are uneasy allies at best. But there is good reason for them to be placed by John Paul in one command center.

For one thing, their origins unite them in a particular point of view concerning Pope John Paul. They all arose within the context of rebellion against the authority and privileged teaching power of the Roman Church. At different times and places, each Minimalist group climbed off the battered but always advancing georeligious caravan of the papal Church. Each group remains at the place where it disembarked. And each retains its deep objections to the authority now embodied in the pontificate and the person of John Paul II.

Another important and practical trait shared by Minimalists is that all of the groups sprang up within Western democracies; and the vast majority of them are homegrown products of the United States. They have been formed in the very womb of Western democratic principles about the rights of man and the dignity of the individual. And with few exceptions, they accept the latter-day American interpretation of the "wall" that separates church and state.

The difficulty for John Paul—and indeed for the Minimalist groups themselves—is that the democratic principles to which they have bound themselves are about to swamp the systems of underlying ideas by which they identify themselves and on the basis of which they desire to interact with the rest of the world. In their eyes, their regard and respect for democratic principles impose upon them the obligation—the religious, as well as the civil and political obligation—to defend every person's right to be wrong. Every person must have the right not only to believe in Hell of the Damned and Heaven of the Saved. Every person must literally be assured the right to choose Hell over Heaven. That obligation carried to that extreme not only sets the Minimalists apart from John Paul; it sets them against him, as well.

It sets them apart from the Holy Father, because democratic principles cannot take precedence over divine revelation. No one can be forced to believe in Heaven or Hell, or to choose the one over the other. Nevertheless, it is axiomatic for John Paul that no one has the right—democratic or otherwise—to a moral wrong; and no religion based on divine revelation has a moral right to teach such a moral wrong or abide by it. In a world that has come to see itself in the "right to be wrong" perspective common to the Minimalists, the claim of each of these groups to be heard on an equal footing with everyone else cannot be shunted aside.

Like the Angelists, in John Paul's perspective all Minimalist groups contain some parts of the full revelation made by God to his Church, which he placed under Peter's care. On the Day of Reward and Retribution for which each of these groups waits, whatever elements of true religion each maintains will surely be integrated into a profession of the full faith of Christ.

In the interim, however, it is evident to Pope John Paul that as an array of groups who have crowded into the arena of the millennium endgame, the importance of the Minimalists is that they render the world a more congenial place for groups who profess to embrace the same democratic principles, but who are totally bereft and contemptuous of any truly religious elements embraced by the Minimalists, and who are far more ambitious than the Minimalists to establish a practical globalist agenda well before the "Last Day" arrives.

In the third situation room of the Provincial Globalists, John Paul gazes at maps and action models riven with the outlook of two groups whose pathos he cannot deny, but whose helplessness neither he nor any mortal man can relieve. For both groups are caught in historical crevasses from which there is no retreat, no advance, no escape.

The world map John Paul examines in this center has been fashioned to suit the Eastern Orthodox Christian mentality still preserved among Greek, Russian and other Christian minorities strewn throughout the Middle East. It is a map the Orthodox Christians willingly share with the tiny remnants of the once vibrant Anglican Catholic community.

For John Paul, the pathos of their position is accentuated by the fact that these groups are heirs to an ancient tradition that today avails them not. Within that tradition, they have an instinct for the georeligious and, therefore, for the geopolitical. But the passage of time and the development of circumstances exclude them from that georeligious and geopolitical stance they feel in their bones as part of their heritage, part of their mandate and part of their reason for existence as religious groups.

Because they climbed into their positions by breaking with the Roman papacy and so abandoned their only realistic hope of georeligious status, John Paul looks upon them with a special solicitude. But he knows that as they now stand, their future lies down one of two pathways. Either they will remain lodged in relative isolation in their historical crevasses, holding on to their traditions. Or, as some of them have already shown an inclination to do, they will decide to accept some form of merger with the various tides advancing on their positions. Beyond that, any final and satisfactory relief of their pathos must await near-future historical events of a worldwide magnitude.

In the meantime, because of their past they exercise a certain political influence of a localized nature, with which John Paul must reckon. The Russian Orthodox Church centered in the Patriarchate of Moscow not only wields considerable influence over some 100 million members; it also becomes the consenting, if unwilling, handmaiden of the Soviet Party-State. Its major officials accepted positions in the KGB. Its authorities acquiesced in the massacre of thousands of Roman Catholic clergy, and accepted—as spoils of war—many Roman Catholic churches and institutions. Indeed, today, at least one solid faction in the Patriarchal Church is virulently antipapal. Throughout the remaining branches of Eastern Orthodoxy there persists a deeply buried antipapal and anti-Roman prejudice; it is felt that any aggrandizement of the papacy can come only at the cost of Orthodox dignity and privilege.

For Greek Orthodoxy, centered historically in Constantinople, always claimed that this city (now Istanbul of the Turks) was the Second Rome replacing the First Rome (of the Popes); and Russian Orthodoxy, in its long-distant high days of preeminence, claimed that Moscow was the Third (and Final) Rome, replacing that Second Rome and that First Rome. History has not been kind to either of these delusions of religious grandeur. Yet, in both centers and patriarchates, those claims are still regnant and are the bases of the opposition and enmity John Paul has to deal with from them. Georeligiously, of course, they are not competitors of his. But globally, they oppose him.

The fourth Provincial Globalist situation room holds the special fascination of primitive things. For here is displayed a rendition of the world map that has been suited as well as can be managed to the mind and the outlook of four ancient but still subsistent non-Christian religions: animism, Shintoism, Hinduism and Buddhism. Each of these groups would claim that it possesses a religious outlook that *could be* georeligious and that it is therefore potentially geopolitical. In John Paul's view, they do have explanations of man's cosmos that would be georeligious, had the nations of the world ceased to develop about three thousand years ago. That did not happen, however. And in today's world, all four groups are at bay and threatened by the encroaching tides of modernism.

Yet they have to be counted by John Paul as a very important assemblage of globalists for the simple reason of their numbers. Between the subcontinent of India, a large proportion of Chinese, and a majority of Southeast Asians, there is a number somewhere in the region of 1.5 to 2 billion human beings involved here. Precisely among this vast population, the wheels of development have begun to churn faster and faster, producing the new "Asian Tigers" (Korea, Taiwan, Malaysia, Thailand) and promising to accelerate such technotronic development elsewhere throughout the landmass of Asia. Papa Wojtyla can be sure that with that development there will be a fresh development of globalism, always at least tinged if not deeply colored by the original religious and ethical outlook of those peoples. When the time comes that a geopolitical perspective enters their angle of vision, he can envisage an opposition from them to his own geopolitical undertaking.

Already, in the religiously jaded and ethically confused West, there has filtered from Buddhism, and to a lesser degree from Hinduism and animism, a new current of religiosity—belief and cult—which produces minds diametrically opposed to the Christianity John Paul professes and on which his geopolitics is founded.

All of the planning materials open to the Pontiff's view in the fifth situation room reflect real strife, deep contradictions between the globalist groups gathered here and between each of these groups and the wide world with which they are in constant and intense interaction.

For one or more of a variety of reasons, each of these groups maintains an "apartness" from the rest of the world, without standing aside from the world. Each wants to be part of that world, for each must have a globalist influence to achieve its own aims. The anomaly, of course, is that "apartness" is the tie that classifies these groups together in the Pontiff's global analysis of each of them.

The "apartness" involved here can take various forms, depending on the mind-set of each group. But it is most often based upon an established group tradition—usually religious or ethical or cultural but most times riven of necessity with economic and political dimensions.

While the extremism of such "apartness" has resulted in the apartheid system of the Republic of South Africa, fundamentally the same sense of "apartness" is shared by many white nations vis-à-vis the nonwhite nations, by many black nations of Africa, and many yellow nations vis-à-vis those differing ethnically from them. A similar apartness, but marked by a long-standing cultural tradition, is to be found in the people of the Indian subcontinent and of Japan. An identical type of "apartness" strengthened by powerful cultural factors gave rise to the distinction made by the ancient Greeks between themselves and all non-Greeks, whom they called "barbarians."

Just as the traditional name for China, the Middle Kingdom, indicated how its inhabitants held to the centrality of that country in the world and its "apartness" as the center of the world, so every group known to us as having this sense of special "apartness" from the rest of human society has its own way of looking at the map of countries and nations.

Whatever practical form "apartness" may take in any individual group, and whatever its basis, it is regarded by each group in this situation room as a basic given of its identity. It is lodged deeply in the lives, outlooks and folkways of its participants.

The "apartness" of these groups does not necessarily prompt all of them to seek a territorial integrity for themselves. But there is always a certain limit to the assimilation they will accept. And the ongoing affairs of human society are judged as favorable or inimical according as those affairs impact on the delicate balance each group maintains between the "apartness" it sees as essential to its identity and the interaction with the world essential to its vibrancy and its practical success.

The outstanding groups located in this fifth situation room, Japanese, Chinese and Jews, exhibit the fundamental mark of that genuine apartness which marks them Provincial Globalists. This is the absence of any formal element in them that would drive them to "convert" the world to their own way of life. In fact, as is generally known and acknowledged, a hallmark in all three indicates that they do not want to do so; indeed, that they consider it impossible. No non-Japanese or non-Chinese can really become Japanese or Chinese, even to the extent that men and women of different nations—including Chinese and Japanese—have become, say, thoroughgoing Americans or Frenchmen. It is axiomatic in Judaism that while anyone can and is allowed to convert to Judaism, Jewishness is restricted to those born of a Jewish mother.

In other words, whatever may happen to their members, singly taken, who may be absorbed into non-Japanese, non-Chinese or non-Jewish societies, for the bulk of the populations living in China, Japan and Israel, assimilation—loss of that apartness—is positively excluded. The special problems faced by these Provincial Globalists are best exemplified in the case of Jews.

Jews will assign a preeminence to the Land of Israel, even though they have no intention of living there, and to the Americas, where nearly half of the world Jewish population (fifteen million) live today. This self-consciousness and apartness of Jews has been set in ferroconcrete by the never-to-be-forgotten Hitlerian attempt at total genocide. For that Holocaust and the birth of Israel have, as Bruno Bettelheim pointed out, forever liquidated the old ghetto mentality of Jews. Jews will no longer seek out that type of segregation they once did when they petitioned Christian authorities to set aside a small portion (a *borghetto*) of the city (the *borgo*) for their exclusive use. But in no way is this exit from the ghetto mentality to be taken as a desire for assimilation. "Nonsegregation without assimilation, this is the new rule."

For John Paul, all three of these "apartness" groups are very important because all three have and will have important roles to play in building the geopolitical structure of the new world order. And each group presents different problems and will meet different difficulties. For, in a profound sense, their strengths derive in large part from their apartness. But once their globalism begins to face the transition to a geopolitical viewpoint, the first casualty will be that apartness.

The Provincial Globalists of our age are destined to undergo a series of severe shocks and mutations as, willy-nilly, they adapt themselves to the new globalism emanating from more powerful groups. There is no way that any one of them will be able to maintain itself in any vibrancy and progressive strength unless it allows—or suffers—its provincialism to be enlarged beyond the confines it traditionally observed. Individuals among them may for a while maintain themselves within those confines.

But, inevitably, as groups they will have to face dire alternatives. Either they will become thoroughly and realistically globalized and therefore capable of collaborating in the building of a geopolitical structure. Or, as groups, they will remain in place, diminish in numbers and influence, and finally lose their identity as operative parts in a new world order.

John Paul, in his papal travels, has constantly engaged in dialogue with representatives of these groups. In many cases, through the diplomatic arm of his Vatican, he maintains a relationship with them—at least a certain cordiality, sometimes even a mutual collaboration concerning some practical problem or need. He sees their individuality as a valuable asset in a world that tends to organize human beings into a faceless mass of undifferentiated peoples. And he knows that what is best in these Provincial Globalists—their sense of dignity and mission—can be sublimated by the grace of Christ and thus become a potent element in the building of a genuinely God-blessed structure for all nations.

16. The Piggyback Globalists

Within the second broad category of globalist-minded groups contending for supremacy in the millennium endgame, Pope John Paul counts just three entries—three groups of one-world-community builders: the Humanists, the Mega-Religionists and the New Agers.

Unlike the Provincial Globalists, none of the groups involved here has any thought of remaining aloof, or of waiting for the mountain of public opinion to move of its own accord, or of getting caught in some isolated crevass of history. All of these groups, in short, are global activists. Moreover, each has demonstrated from the outset that it appreciates the importance of transnational structures such as the Pope's worldwide Church and Gorbachev's global machine. Each has a structure of its own, in fact. But the true genius of each group, operationally speaking, lies in the fact that it has developed to a high art the ability to ride piggyback on the structural setups of everyone else's organization, whispering sweet universalisms into the ears of their leaders and adherents alike.

It is common knowledge that each of these groups has attracted its share of crackpot visionaries: so much so that the groups themselves are frequently lampooned. But the truth is that the membership in each case is weighty with the names of many highly valued men and women. And even a glance at the strides each group has made toward its own vision of a one-world community is enough to convince any observer that, as a whole, they cannot be dismissed as of no consequence.

The globalist groups within these three categories are strikingly compatible with one another. Indeed, compatibility is a basic watchword for all of them; and it rests primarily on two things.

First, though their ideas about the world differ somewhat, they are in agreement on certain bedrock issues—most especially those concerning the religions of the world, and those having to do with the desirability of a global community. Second, both in their ideas and in their strategies for acting in relation to the world, all of these groups are remarkably well suited to the already generally accepted aims of interdependence and material development among all the nations and cultures.

The similarities among these three groups are so striking, in fact, that John Paul sees them in the long run of historical evolution as neither more nor less than three interfacing programs formed within and locked onto the same ground plan. Reason and imagination lead one to conclude that the ground plan emanated from one intelligence.

Common to the ideas of each of these globalist groups is the conviction that man is even more than the most important figure in the cosmos. For them, man is the only important figure. Each group vindicates the exclusively human.

To one degree or another, albeit with different shadings, each group shares the view that mankind is not called to be holy; it is called to be happy, in the certainty that all the glory of life is right here, and right now. Happiness lies within the ambit of material development. Each of us is called to be a happy consumer of the earth's goods, living in a bountiful world. That is our supremest right and our only common destiny.

That exclusivity about the importance of material man in a world defined by its material bounty is directed against even the notion of God as worshiped by Christians, Jews and Muslims. It is directed against any notion of divinity that does not make God an integral part of this exclusively human cosmos. Beings loosely called spirits or devils or devas are not necessarily excluded. In fact, they are essential to New Agers. But because they, too, are conceived as constituent parts of man's universe, they are tolerated even by Humanists.

Concerning the strategy for action by which these globalist groups put their ideas of the world into serious play in the international arena, each of them has hit on a variation of the same action model. They do not seek to get rid of the colorful little diversities among the world's religions or cultures. That would only be counterproductive; for it would mean dismantling the structures upon whose backs they ride. And in any case, some individual traits turn out to be useful.

Nevertheless, it is not too much to ask in the sweet name of universal reason that all national, religious and cultural groups modify their traits so that everyone—every nation, every religion and every culture—can be accommodated as a division or subdivision of the future one-world community that is both the aim and the justification of each of these three groups.

For such globalist community builders as these, there is no earthly use in perpetuating any element that has historically divided human society into distinct, separate and sometimes warring parts, or that might do so in the future. Their chosen task is to hasten the day when all will be one in a materially comfortable world community, now abuilding, and to assist us all by teaching us how to become members of that global community of contentment.

The maps, action models and documents John Paul peruses in the first of these three situation rooms belong to the Humanists. Everything he sees here brings home to the Pontiff how very far their quiet, bloodless and altogether humanly pleasant revolution has come within a relatively short time. A glance at just one map shows him, for example, that there are sixty Humanist organizations flourishing today, in twenty-three countries.

The opening salvo of this group's ambitious assault on the world was heard in 1933, with the publication of the Humanist Manifesto I. Given great vogue and credibility by American educational philosopher John Dewey, and by other luminary cosigners of the document, HM-I put forward the basic Humanist proposal: Human perfection is to be attained by human efforts in this cosmos. By any measure, HM-I was a clarion call to work for no less a result than a real revolution. It was Humanist Manifesto II, however, that really made headlines. And with good reason. Written by University of Buffalo philosophy professor Paul Kurtz and published in 1973, HM-II was presented as a mere updating of HM-I. But it was so much more explicit that it deserves a special place among the action models in the Humanist command post.

HM-II clearly stated the goal of the Humanists with regard to all institutions, and with special emphasis on religion. It was not liquidation the Humanists should seek, said Kurtz, but "the transformation, control, and direction of all associations and institutions. . . . [This] is the purpose and the program of Humanism. Certainly, religious institutions, their ritualistic forms and ecclesiastical methods must be reconstituted as rapidly as experience allows."

In all their efforts toward such "transformation, control, and direction of all associations and institutions," Humanists were instructed by Kurtz to advocate "a socialized and cooperative economic order, autonomous and situational ethics, . . . many varieties of sexual exploration, . . . and the development of a system of world law and order based on a transnational federal government."

Piggyback tactics were not merely vindicated by HM-I and HM-II; they were positively mandated and on as global a basis as possible. Humanists everywhere promoted their revolution, as they still do, through the vital arteries of public education; federal, state and municipal administrations; publicity, advertising and entertainment; churches, cultural and political associations, colleges and universities. Nothing could be exempt.

In general, Humanists have always been adept at making their revolution as pleasant-sounding and as humanly appealing as possible for most of their targets. But when it comes to Christianity, the gloves are off. Pope John Paul read and reread the words of one enthusiastic author published in the January–February 1983 issue of *Humanist Magazine*: "The classroom must and will become the area of combat between . . . the rotting corpse of Christianity . . . and the new faith of Humanism."

John Paul does not brush such Humanist assaults aside lightly. He has real cause for concern that the Humanists represent a threat to his Church. In fact, he knows that Humanism has made converts even among his highest Church officials.

In 1986, for example, delegates from the Vatican traveled to Paris, without the Pope's blessing, to attend the World Congress of Humanists. There they joined the general omnium-gatherum of representatives from Soviet-dominated Eastern European countries and from Western Europe and the Americas. For they were all enmeshed in the anti-Catholic drumbeat of Humanism. At the very least, their example caused confusion among the faithful.

In September of 1988, again without papal blessing or by-your-leave, Roman Catholic Cardinals Poupard of Paris and Daneels of Belgium headed an eight-man delegation of Catholic theologians from France, Canada, Yugoslavia, India and Norway to participate with an international group of professional Humanists in a conference in Amsterdam. Among those professional Humanists were Dr. Paul Kurtz himself and the virulently antipapal Robert Tielman of Utrecht University.

There can be no doubt for John Paul that Their Eminences and the Catholic theologians accompanying them had all read and understood HM-II. And, informed as they are, it would seem virtually impossible that they were unaware of one recent and most public enterprise undertaken by Tielman. He had made a special trip to San Francisco during Pope John Paul's visit there just one year before, in September of 1987, in order to organize, coordinate and sharpen the homosexual demonstrations against the Holy Father's papal person.

Most Catholics will not lightly forgive those demonstrations, because of the open blasphemy committed against the Eucharist on the streets of San Francisco. Yet neither the Cardinals nor any of the theologians present at the Amsterdam gathering appeared unduly troubled by Tielman's attitude or his actions. In fact, the open joke repeated at their expense in stage whispers among the delegates was that Humanists sat on both sides of the conference table in Holland!

The year 1988 was a bumper year for the Humanist harvest, it would seem. For by that year as well, they succeeded in organizing the Church of the Good Humanist in the United States. And they succeeded in attracting representatives from the Catholic Church establishment in America and from several mainline Protestant churches as members. One major project in which they will all have a hand, surely, is the planned launching of the Vision Interfaith Satellite Network (VISN), which will beam the message of HM-II even more effectively over America's airwaves.

Not surprisingly, Pope John Paul's assessment of the effect of the Humanist assault on the world from its position in the globalist arena is a sober one. He sees the Humanists' revolution, which has succeeded beyond even their most sanguine expectations, as the cruelest and most radical kind of revolution imaginable. For it has not only denuded public education and university studies of any positive religious content. As Italian editor and commentator Alver Metalli wrote in 1989, it has affected "that point of human conscience, inviolate up to now, where desires, aspirations and one's life plans are formed."

John Paul has no need to look at any action models that might be open to view in the Humanist situation room in order to see into the future they prepare for us all. For that future is already upon many of us. Though their process advances at varying speeds in different quarters of the world, the Humanist ideal of the happy consumer enters the home and the personal life of every individual.

Cultures remain diverse, and the world's religions remain distinct. But that diversity is of secondary importance. According to the Humanist principle, in fact, the only true difference between the various cultures and religions is merely a chronological one. Each of them simply happened to develop and flower at different moments in history. Each represents no more than a different step along our common path toward material happiness and fulfillment. Whether you are talking about nations or religions—about America or Europe or Asia, or about Christianity, Judaism, Islam or Buddhism—it is a fact of the Humanist view of life that each simply needs to be synchronized with all the others. Once they are all brought up to speed, as the current saying has it, it will be clear to all that there is nothing to squabble about.

True to the Humanist formula for progress, little by little men and women of every culture and faith are now marked increasingly by the same characteristics in all areas of their lives. Whether in New York or Bangkok, Warsaw, Palermo or Buenos Aires, Addis Ababa or Nairobi, all have the same Humanistic aspirations. Everywhere, vital institutions and activities—sexuality, marriage, family planning, religious practice and preference, public rituals, public and private education—change and recolor themselves continually according to the Humanist principles of synchronization. And everywhere, culture and religion alike bow before the goddess of happy consumerism, kowtowing to her promise of the equitable distribution of luxury items and convenience goods for all.

As single-minded and effective as they are, the Humanists pale in many respects by comparison to their upscale counterparts, the Mega-Religionists. Take the sheer number of groups involved, for example. Where the Humanists have a respectable sixty or so groups around the world, the Mega-Religionists have some five hundred.

Or take their ability to ride piggyback on the structural setups of governments, religions and associations already in place around the world. Where the Humanists must seek the control and direction of such institutions in the best way they can, Mega-Religionists are very often expected to—and do—control and direct those institutions as a matter of course.

Or take the flavor of acceptability each group can foster on the basis of the names it can bandy about. The wish lists of the Humanists are the actual membership rolls of the Mega-Religionists, some of the most distinguished, widely known and wealthy men and women of the past sixty years, people whose names are frequently household words around the world.

In one Mega-Religionist group alone—the Temple of Understanding, centered in the United States and most often referred to by its initials, TU—there are more than six thousand such names: Nobel laureates, prominent individuals who hail from sixty-two countries on all five continents, people who, in one way or another, live their lives as though all political borders were already extinguished, who are as easily recognized east of Suez as west of it, who are as likely to turn up north of the equator as south of it and may do so for vacation or for business—or to attend a Mega-Religionist gathering, like as not. People who call themselves— and were for a while called by the world—the "beautiful people" are Mega-Religionists, people of the caliber of Yehudi Menuhin, Carlos P. Romulo, Dwight D. Eisenhower, John Foster Dulles, Henry R. Luce, George Meany, Queen Elizabeth II, the Duke of Edinburgh, Earl Mountbatten, Spyros Skouras, Teilhard de Chardin, Thomas Merton, Pierre Trudeau, Robert McNamara, John D. Rockefeller IV, Pearl Buck, Leo Cardinal Suenens.

Given the noticeable difference in the membership of Mega-Religionist groups as against those of the Humanists, something of a difference in purpose inevitably shows up as well.

Humanists are still preoccupied with what they call the "bane of religion." The Mega-Religionist mind, by contrast, is devoted to the proposition that comfort is not always as exclusively physical as Humanists like to insist. Religion, too, is essential to the comfort of human civilization, and to the comfort of its differing cultures. It's just that separate religions are neither necessary nor desirable. In fact, for the sake of peace, all religions must fuse into one great religion—one mega-religion—as quickly and painlessly as possible.

According to the University of Buffalo's Paul Hutchinson, once that fusion takes place, "the whole of Humanity shall remain a united people, where Muslim and Christian, Buddhist and Hindu shall stand together, bound by a common devotion, not to something behind, but to something ahead, not to a racial past or a geographical unit, but to a dream of a world society with a universal religion of which the historical faiths are but branches."

It is to just such fusion between all religions that the Mega-Religionists are principally dedicated. A fusion that is to be accomplished in a world of plenty; there is no quarrel with the Humanists about that. But the Mega-Religionists will entertain no question of liquidating the more harmless elements of each religion; for these have a folkloric and colorful function, and perhaps a certain function in terms of appeasement and camouflage. Still, all such details must be "absorbed," as the vocabulary of such groups puts it, into a "higher dimension" according as mankind matures in its own godliness.

The aim of this process of fusion was set out by a man of many interests. Writing in 1948, the Marxist, millionaire, publisher and Mega-Religionist Victor Gollancz said, "The ultimate aim should be that Judaism, Christianity and all other religions should vanish and give place to one great ethical world religion, the brotherhood of man." Further, said Gollancz, that aim should be achieved by "believers with different opinions and convictions . . . [who] are necessary for each other . . . [and who] work out the larger synthesis."

That process itself was given a name: "syncresis," or "syncretism." As part of the Mega-Religionists' special jargon for quite a while, those two words were shorthand for the Mega-Religionists' action plan. Meaning, basically, "to pour together," they were a letter-perfect description of what was to be accomplished.

All religions of mankind were, and still are, likened to wines—some mellow, some bland, some with a heady bouquet, some of young vintage, some with the cachet of greater age. Believers from each religion— "believers with different opinions and convictions," as Gollancz wrote— must gather small, select tastings; and then each of these choice tastings must be poured with all the others into one great new wine jar. The resultant blending will nourish the whole human community in a new harmony of thought and feeling. Finally, all political systems will follow the religions into the jar; they will be fused into a one-world political community under a one-world government.

The expected Mega-Religion that will accomplish all that has also been given a name. According to D. H. Bishop, writing in *World Faith* magazine in 1970, "since it would contain elements of every religion and would be universally acceptable," it would be called "monodeism."

The function of monodeism is to create and maintain among men a universal brotherhood. In fact, "brotherhood" is one of the most important, if not always one of the clearest, terms of the Mega-Religionists. For it describes the geopolitical condition of the world they envision once Mega-Religion has been established for us all. And it also describes the somewhat mysterious group—the Brotherhood, or the Elders—that

Mega-Religionists often speak of as the behind-the-scenes guiding force of their movement. No one has ever identified the members of such a Brotherhood in public. The Elders remain unknown. And at least for the uninitiated, they appear largely as figments of the Mega-Religionist desire: a little the way the Wizard seemed to Dorothy, perhaps, in her dream state, longing to get home to Kansas by way of Oz.

Leaving aside the Brotherhood, and to give credit where credit is due, the names of two men—both from the Orient and both long dead—must forever be listed as the prime forces that made possible the widespread and influential movement of the Mega-Religionists today. The first, a Persian named Baha 'U'llah, contributed the basic ideas and principles. The second, India's Swami Vivekenanda, developed the technique for spreading those ideas and principles. These two men could not have complemented each other more perfectly had they set out to do so.

Baha 'U'llah, having reached the age of fifty, proclaimed himself a divine figure with a new revelation for all the world. Baha'i, as his revelation is called, has three million followers and runs establishments in some 350 states and dependencies. As a religion or an ethical grouping in its own right, Baha'i has not set the world on fire in terms of its numerical membership. The principles of Baha 'U'llah's new revelation are quite another story, however; for to say those principles have gained widespread acceptance would be to understate their impact.

Baha 'U'llah taught that revealed religions—indeed, all religions—can be fulfilled only by being transformed into his own larger revelation. Though he never supplied the practical details of the unity he called for, he was clear about its practical consequences. As all religions were fused into one Mega-Religion—a term he never used—there would be a World Government, complete with a World Executive, a World Parliament, a World Police Force, a Universal House of Justice, a World Language, and a World Currency.

When all that was accomplished, there would reign among men what Baha'is like to call the Most Great Peace. For peace among men, which is to be maintained by the Council of Elders, was and remains the ultimate aim.

Any form of patriotism will disappear—a needless thing in the face of peace as a planetary condition. Similarly, all the particular traits of all the various religions having to do with truth and transcendence and salvation and all the rest of it will sink to a secondary level for a while, and will finally vanish—as needless things in the face of brotherhood and unity as planetary conditions.

Baha 'U'llah died in a Turkish prison in 1892. He left no instructions regarding how to effect his transformation. His son, and then his grandson, continued his work. But they gave no such instructions, either. In that regard, it can be said that Swami Vivekenanda was Baha 'U'llah's truest heir; for he did supply precisely the required formula.

It is difficult to resist the conclusion that Vivekenanda enjoyed some special gift of communication—some charisma, as television stars like to say about one another. The most heady reading of him by his devotees is that he was entrusted with a special mission by the Elders.

For, amazingly, in one summer visit to Chicago in the year following Baha 'U'llah's death, Vivekenanda, a Hindu by heritage, successfully inaugurated the technique by which Mega-Religion—already defined in its essence by Baha 'U'llah—has made such steady progress in the twentieth century.

Invited by the World Congress of Religions as the star attraction of the Parliaments of Religions held in conjunction with the 1893 Chicago World's Fair, Vivekenanda "dialogued" with all comers—Christians, Jews and Muslims, Shintoists, Jains and Taoists, Zorastrians, Confucians and Buddhists, atheists and Communists.

In tone and in substance, that was the start of a practice we all take for granted today: the interfaith meeting. Vivekenanda's example was infectious; his language, inoffensive; his thought, stimulating. And the overarching message of all three—example, language and thought—was the unity of all mankind, and the harmony that lay in store for us all on the day when, by just such a process as he demonstrated, all true religions would be melded into a higher belief.

Though he died young—in 1902 at the age of thirty-nine—Vivekenanda, by his extraordinary personality and example, provided the how-to action model for the achievement of Baha 'U'llah's vision. That, it was said, had been his mission. And sure enough, within scant years after his life in this "dimension" was over, important organizations began to form, follow his lead and thrive. In region after region of the world, group after star-studded group held congress after international congress, fellowship meeting after interfaith fellowship meeting.

In all of them, the signs and symbols associated with ancient and not so ancient religions were borrowed and displayed in unaccustomed places. Unity was visibly on the march. Yes, it was true that sometimes those symbols were bowdlerized, as was the case with Bertrand Russell's peace symbol—a broken cross turned upside down. But such violence to individual religions was not inconsistent with the aim of sampling for the sake of unity.

Most often, though, such symbols were borrowed with due respect. It became more and more common to find the Vedanta sign of the Hindus —a serpent coiling among leaves arranged in the shape of a six-pointed star—displayed at Mega-Religionist meetings in Prague, Czechoslovakia, or in Detroit, Michigan. It seems almost natural today to find the Buddhist wheel, with its six spokes representing as many religions— Buddhism, Hinduism, Islam, Judaism, Confucianism and Christianity— displayed in such places as Mother Teresa's principal house in Calcutta, and in New York's Cathedral of St. John the Divine.

Such expressions of universalism were not accepted all at once, of course. Nourishing a vision of world unity and peace takes time. Sinking all religious differences into the unifying ground of material plenty can be hard work. Plenty of humanly guaranteed reason and honesty and liberty doesn't just happen. Nor does plenty of food and shelter. Nor does plenty of all-seeing, all-wise godliness descend upon man overnight; he must be coaxed and nurtured with plenty of patience toward the Mega-Religionist ideal of a global, borderless and plentiful homeland.

On the other hand, things didn't go all that badly. To list even a tiny fraction of the many hundreds of Mega-Religionist groups that confront Pope John Paul as active and humanly powerful organizations is to display a clear and worldwide trend with which he must deal.

Within the decade in which Vivekenanda accomplished his mission of example and departed this "dimension," the rush to follow his lead was on. The now venerable International New Life Fellowship (INLF) made its first mark in the world in 1906. In 1908, the Universal Religious Alliance (URA) established its claim and its acronym, first in New York. The year 1910 saw similar important contributions to the Mega-Religionist advance by the Union of International Associations (UIA) in Belgium and the Union of East and West (UEW) in London. The World Alliance for International Friendship and Religion (WAIFR—the acronym that might have been designed to have some appeal of its own) and the Church Peace Union (CPU—not much appeal there) each count 1914 as their first hallmark year, in Switzerland and the United States, respectively.

The decade of the twenties saw the entry of more and more Mega-Religionist groups. The League of Neighbors (LN)—1920, United States —had a friendly ring to it. Then there was the International Fellowship (IF—a modest, even tentative ring to that one), 1922, India. International Brotherhood (IB) followed in 1923 in Paris. World Fellowship of Faiths (WFF), 1924, United States again. World Alliance (WA), the same year, Oxford, England. Peace and Brotherhood (PB), 1926, Louvain, Belgium. The Threefold Movement (TTM), also in 1926, New York. World Peace (WP), World Conference for International Peace Through

Religion (WOCIPR) and Order of Great Companions (OGC) all count their importance as groups from the year 1928, Geneva and London.

Even a small sample of the plethora of groups that emerged from about the mid-thirties to the opening of the seventies forces one to take account of almost ten more major Mega-Religionist entries. World Congress of Faith (WCF), 1936, London. The Self-Realization Fellowship (TSRF), 1937, Indiana. World Spiritual Council (WSC), 1946, United States. International Committee for Unity and Universality of Cultures (ICUUC), 1955, Rome. World Fellowship of Religions (WFR), 1957, New Delhi. The very impressive Temple of Understanding (TU), 1959, United States. Organization of United Religions (OUR), 1967, Paris, and Spiritual Unity of Nations (SUN), 1970, England, picked up again on the idea of acronyms that might have some appeal. One of the best-known in the dizzying welter of names, the World Conference of Religion for Peace (WCRP), scored its earliest contributions in Kyoto, Japan, 1970.

Because the patrons of the Mega-Religionist groups are the establishment figures of the world, and because such luminaries of world society attract one another as surely as they capture the attention of the general public, it is not surprising to Pope John Paul that such individuals turn up regularly at one another's interfaith celebrations around the globe.

It was accepted as a matter of course, even as early as 1955, that John Foster Dulles would appear at San Francisco's Cow Palace for just such a celebration, all but wreathed about with Hindu and Buddhist symbols as a member of the World Brotherhood. Similarly, no one could have been surprised to see Sir James McCauley, a Buddhist, turn up on the Mediterranean island of Patmos in 1988 as an official delegate of the World Conference of Religion for Peace (WCRP), to help the Greek Orthodox Patriarch of Constantinople celebrate two thousand years of Christianity.

What John Paul does find disturbing is the degree to which the higher-ranking clergy—cardinals and bishops—throughout his Church organization set an example of Mega-Religionist cooperation for priests and laity alike by joining celebrations that are intentionally neither Roman Catholic nor Christian.

The late John Cardinal Wright, for example, a Vatican figure of some importance, was one of the Founding Fathers of WCRP. Perhaps the Cardinal did not realize what he was getting into when he lent himself to the founding of that organization. Others, however, cannot claim ignorance as a fig leaf.

Surely Terence Cardinal Cooke, the late Archbishop of New York, understood the implications of his hosting a widely publicized meeting of TU in St. Patrick's Cathedral. To the accompaniment of silver bells and ceremonial horns, and before a gathering of some 5,000 TU devotees —including Roman Catholic, Armenian, Protestant and Jewish clergy— the Cardinal welcomed the Dalai Lama to his side as the fourteenth reincarnation of *Bodhisvatta Avalokitesvara*, Manifestation of Buddha's Compassion.

"We believers seek common ground," the Cardinal told the TU glitterati as he took the Dalai Lama's hand. "We make each other welcome in our houses of worship."

"All the major world religions are the same," the maroon-robed Dalai Lama corrected His Eminence, and received a standing ovation.

John Paul's concern goes still further. It is one thing—a dangerous thing, perhaps—to lend your Roman Catholic house of worship for the atheist ceremonies of Tibetan Buddhism. But systematic and worldwide cooperation with Mega-Religion carries the matter to an entirely different level. And that is exactly the situation in the case of the Pontifical Commission for Justice and Peace (PCJP).

Already known for its long cooperation with the policies of Antonio Gramsci, the PCJP, in each of its local branches throughout the four thousand dioceses of John Paul's Roman Catholic Church, consistently endorses the main themes of Soviet Marxist policy—the evils of capitalism in Western democracies, the call for unilateral disarmament by the Western powers, the absolute need to establish a one-world economic system based on the distribution of the riches, goods and services of the capitalist world.

That close collaboration of the Pontifical Commission for Justice and Peace with the foreign policy aims of the Soviet Union was institutionalized on the day the Commission cooperated with the World Council of Churches (WCC)—itself an instrument of Soviet policy since 1966— to establish a joint Committee on Society, Development and Peace (SODEPAX) in 1968.

SODEPAX fell into lockstep with the WCC on two capital points.

First, SODEPAX joined with the WCC in the condemnation of Pope John Paul's claim to head the one, true Church of Christ. Rather, making liberal use of the local offices of the Pontifical Commission for Justice and Peace, SODEPAX promotes the WCC's Mega-Religionist brief for the equivalence of all religions.

The second point on which SODEPAX fell into step with the WCC concerned the redefinition of "church," to give it the broadest possible interpretation. True to Mega-Religionist principles, the WCC decided in 1970 that the word should no longer be confined to "church of the

Christian faith," or even to believers. Rather, it should encompass people of any faith, and of no faith at all. This, it was maintained, was the new and genuine ecumenism, the true culmination of the ecumenical movement. Accordingly, it became a matter of principle for the WCC and its lackey, SODEPAX, to enlarge their "interfaith" meetings and "ecumenical" activities to include such ideas as would promote their adopted anticapitalist and anti-Western themes of Soviet foreign policy.

It is here that one point of capital importance lies for John Paul concerning the new interfaith Mega-Religionist wave. Where Mikhail Gorbachev rejoices from his Marxist position in the geopolitical arena, Pope John Paul is aghast. For a long time now, the Pontiff and his advisers have known that the Pontifical Commission for Peace and Justice, though still nominally Roman Catholic, has been taken over by converts to Marxism. Necessarily, too, the Pope and his advisers have concluded that four of the main Mega-Religionist organizations—WCRP, WCF, UB and TU—are under the control of a master puppeteer whose home base is surely that red-gabled building in Moscow's Red Square.

In 1944, in his book *Marxism and the National Colonial Question*, Joseph Stalin wrote, "It is essential that the advanced countries should render aid—real and prolonged aid—to the backward countries in their cultural and economic development. Otherwise it will be impossible to bring about a peaceful coexistence of the various nations and peoples . . . within a single economic system, which is so essential for the final triumph of socialism."

For John Paul, then, the threat of the Mega-Religionist movement is hardly in its quasi-theological self-justifications. It lies in the ease with which some of the most influential Mega-Religionist groups afford aid to Mikhail Gorbachev, persuading us all to dance to the classic tune written by Stalin "for the final triumph of socialism," a tune, John Paul is convinced, that is still piped, in a new arrangement, by the Pope's adversaries in Moscow.

There are now literally millions all over the world—millions of Roman Catholics and millions more Christians and non-Christians—who are persuaded that true human religion requires a commonly shared Mega-Religionist belief and practice that eliminates all the specific notes of their original faith and mitigates the rules of morality that once characterized their religious outlook. Moreover, there are as many millions who would never choose Marxism but who have been persuaded by the unlikely voices and examples of Mega-Religionist establishment figures that the prime cause—the very author and instigator—of all the world's ills is capitalist democracy, especially as exemplified by its chief proponent, the United States.

At first, one might not think New Agers are brothers under the skin to Humanists and Mega-Religionists. The world map on display in the New Age situation room is not dotted with scores of separate groups, hundreds of acronyms. Instead, it is gloriously illuminated by the vision New Agers see advancing day by day among the nations. A vision of our near-future world that is guaranteed by the forces of human evolution. A vision expressed with a certain ethereal and even mystical tone, and in a vocabulary borrowed from every religion and culture, every political and ethical system.

Though they appear to be in the thrall of the utter marvel of their own vision of what is to come, Pope John Paul sees in the New Agers something more practical for our near-future world. He sees in them the ideological ground troops of the Piggyback Globalists. Unlike the Humanists or the Mega-Religionists, they have no geopolitical power groups and not much glitter to speak of. But their success is practical proof that they have an appeal for the common man in all of us that is undeniable. And if it ever came to a contest between the three categories of Piggyback Globalists—between the Humanists, the Mega-Religionists and the New Agers—New Age would win the prize for riding atop everyone else's organizational systems, and co-opting the members of those organizations into the quest for the mystically material glory of the New Age.

Like the Mega-Religionists, the New Agers hearken to the teachings of a founding father. In 1931, Japan's Meishu Sama claimed to have received a special revelation. Unlike Baha 'U'llah's revelation, however, Sama's came complete with detailed instructions, plans for the New Age of mankind.

A New Age of light was coming soon, said Sama. It would be introduced by catastrophes on land and sea—"negative vibrations," he called them—that would purify our present age, the Old Age of darkness.

Both the purification of the Old Age, claimed Sama, and the establishment of the New Age would be supervised by a "Maitreya," or Messiah. Endowed with superhuman wisdom and fantastic psychic abilities, the Maitreya would bring to heel all powers of the universe and would establish the global village.

Lest Humanists or Mega-Religionists be alarmed that a nonmaterialist, transcendent heresy is afoot in New Age, let them be of good heart. According to Sama, the great Maitreya to come will be as much a part of the material human universe as, say, Moses or Buddha or Shiva or Baha 'U'llah or any of those great religious leaders of past ages. In fact, all those people—Moses and Shiva and all of that crowd—were Maitreyas too. And so was Christ, according to New Age doctrine. All were Maitreyas who came to teach us.

The whole point, in fact, is that the final and all-powerful Maitreya to come will correct the distortions mankind has wreaked upon the originally pure message of all those former Maitreyas.

When it comes to materialism, therefore, New Age will give Humanism a run for its money. And it will beat Mega-Religionists hands down. For, where Mega-Religionist groups are willing to accommodate certain malleable aspects of this or that transcendental religion for the sake of peace, comfort and consolation, New Age doctrine is rock-hard on two core principles that permit no such compromise.

The first point is that there is no reality beyond this world. No cheating, and no pretending. Everything—presumably including Sama's revelation—is exclusively human. Even the coming Maitreya and his attendant spirits, of which he has many, belong to this human universe. The words of poet Edwin Markham enshrine this basic New Age principle succinctly:

> We men of Earth have here the stuff
> of Paradise—we have enough!
> We need no other stones to build
> The Temple of the Unfulfilled—
> No other Ivory for the Doors—
> No other Marble for the Floors—
> No other Cedar for the Beam
> And dome of man's Immortal dream.

The second principle is harder to put into poetry; but it is even more important than the first for the New Age outlook. Man, according to that principle, is an animal evolving on an upward curve of increasing, all-inclusive perfectings that will result, very soon now, in millennial conditions for all mankind.

The nature of those conditions was set out by one prominent Roman Catholic New Ager, Father Matthew Fox, who was quoting witch Starhawk—a faculty member of Fox's Oakland Institute—much as athletes endorse cereals. The New Age, Fox quoted witch Starhawk approvingly, will be one in which "no one is ruled or ruler, where no promise of Heaven offers us false compensation for our present pain, but where we tend together the earth's living, fruitful flesh."

One area in which New Agers do not seem to stand as tall as Humanists or Mega-Religionists is highlighted by the fact that the map in the New Age situation room pinpoints only a handful of places New Agers can call their own. They do mark a single site as the New Age center of the world: Findhorn Bay in the north Scotch county of Moray, where the Findhorn River empties into the Moray Firth. Their community at Findhorn was to New Agers what the Vatican is to Roman Catholics. In its heyday, Findhorn already exhibited extraordinary fruits, plants and trees; its frequenters had extraordinary experiences. Findhorn was a "footprint" of the Maitreya to come.

But beyond that, the places of the world claimed by New Agers are so few that they can be quickly listed: the cliffs of Big Sur in California; the Victoria Falls, between Zambia and Zimbabwe; the gardens of Kyoto, Japan; the shrines of fabled Mandalay in Burma; the Hellfire Club in the Dublin mountains of Ireland; the standing slabs of Stonehenge, England.

That's a far cry from the sixty or so Humanist groups around the world; and it doesn't measure as much at all beside those hundreds of acronyms such as TU and SUN and WCRP and the rest that cover the Mega-Religionists' map. But if one were tempted on that account to dismiss the New Age ability to catch on in the world because of a lack of organization, or because they are too unsophisticated in outlook and setup to convert anyone but nonurban peoples—country bumpkins who have never heard of HM-II or seen the likes of John Foster Dulles—there are plenty of people to tell you that nothing could be more inaccurate.

David Fetcher, for example, a recognized expert on modern cults, points out that New Age indoctrination is taking place at all levels of religion, spirituality and culture. And John Randolph Price, one of the acknowledged world leaders of the New Age movement, claims that "there are more than half a billion New Age advocates on the planet at this time, working among various religious groups."

Given the subindustry of New Age publications thriving around the world, it is not surprising that even the most conservative estimates place the number of New Agers in the hundreds of millions, and find them sprouting like mushrooms not only in Western populations, but among the Chinese, the Japanese, the Indians and the Africans.

Further, where the Humanists and Mega-Religionists tend to appeal to the middle and upper-middle classes, New Agers seem to have something for everyone. Millions of individuals engage in self-training techniques at dawn and dusk each day. Individuals who run the gamut from laborers to laboratory geniuses, and from youths to senior citizens, all perform the same meditations. A housewife in Lincoln, Nebraska, a truckdriver in Scotland, a government official in Bonn, West Germany, a teenage freshman at Beijing University, a sheep farmer in Queensland, Australia, a chamberlain at the Royal Court of Bangkok, Thailand, a banker in Zurich, Switzerland—all nourish the same wild hopes for "the new world of man that is just around the corner, for the global village of the New Age."

No religion is immune from the zeal of the enthusiasts, converts and disciples of the New Age movement. New Age simply borrows all the words, melts them down like so many gold chalices and crosses, and pours them into the mold of their New Age globalism.

Networked throughout the Roman Catholic Church and all the main-line Protestant churches in the United States, for example, are teams of former Christian believers—bishops, priests and laity—who are subtly and gradually transforming the meaning of Baptism, Confirmation, the Eucharist, Marriage, Confession of sins, Priesthood and Anointing. Sacraments all, they become instead celebrations of "Earth festivals," cultivating man's relationship not with a loving God but with his own earthbound destiny in the global village to come.

In this particular misery, religion has company in all the main sectors of modern life, at least in terms of vulnerability to New Age zeal. No serious doubt can be maintained about the large and growing numbers of New Age adherents among those who want to succeed—to find the good life and promote it for others—in medicine, psychiatry, finance, politics, science, academia, the media and national and international business. More than a few large corporations, national and multinational, have even joined the crowd in an official and organized way. Intent on improving management skills and boosting motivation for success, they provide quasi-obligatory seminars based on the various techniques developed and perfected by New Age theorists for "self-realization" and "creative growth toward integration."

Generally speaking, New Age also rides especially well on the shambles left in the wake of the anti-God accomplishments of the Humanists and the religion-leveling accomplishments of the Mega-Religionists. Perhaps the firm if tatterdemalion teachings of New Age concerning "spirits" and "devas" give some measure of comfort to the former believers of the major Christian denominations.

The function of these "spirits" and "devas" is to aid men and women to enter the New Age. Chief among them all is Lucifer, the one whom all Christian denominations unjustly pillory and excoriate. "Lucifer," writes David Spangler, a former codirector of the Findhorn New Age

Center, ". . . is the angel of man's inner light. . . . Lucifer, like Christ, stands at the door of man's consciousness and knocks. . . . If man say, 'Come in,' Lucifer becomes . . . the being who carries . . . the light of wisdom. . . . Lucifer is literally the angel of experience. . . . He is an agent of God's love . . . and we move into a *new age* . . . each of us in some way is brought to that point which I term the Luciferic initiation. . . . We must say, 'Thank you, Beloved, for all these experiences. . . . They have brought me to you.' . . . At some point each of us faces the presence of Lucifer. . . . Lucifer comes to give us the final gift of wholeness. If we accept it, then he is free and we are free. That is the Luciferic initiation. It is one that many people now, and in the days ahead, will be facing, for *it is an initiation into the New Age.*"

Whether because or in spite of its belief in Lucifer and the lesser "devas" and "spirits," such New Age spirituality has demonstrated its attraction not only for former Christians, bur for men and women of all religious groups, and of no religion. It appears to be a perfect fit even for those atheists who are so really and truly godless that they see the need to deny the existence of God as equivalent to the need to deny the existence of the Three-Headed Cat of the Himalayas, or the Hairy Man of Norwood.

For such individuals, the appeal of the New Age effort lies in the fact that it is directed, above all, at enabling each person to manipulate his own experience for maximum personal benefit. Its aim is to allow the individual to project into reality the fulfillment of his desires. As cult expert David Fetcher concludes, in plainer, un-co-opted language, the aim for everyone is "to act like God, because you *are* God."

New Agers may be lampooned with greater ease than their Humanist and Mega-Religionist brothers. But the fact is that, where Humanists and Mega-Religionists tend to influence religious and other organizations on their own ground, New Age tends to suck them out like a vacuum. It has made the greatest strides in drawing believers and nonbelievers onto entirely new ground, convincing them that in its doctrine and revelation, New Age is the highest manifestation yet achieved on the evolutionary road to perfect enlightenment, an enlightenment, as they confidently expect, that will shortly engulf men and women the world over, persuading us all to enter the global village of the New Age.

That global village will be a more interesting place for some than for others, one would think. It will not be pie in the sky. It will be here. And if not now, it will be soon. Special "leaders" or "inspirers" or "instructors" will be all-powerful in that global village, making all the decisions about every human issue—economic and cultural as well as spiritual and religious. Above all, it will not be Christian or Jewish or Muslim.

For Pope John Paul, and for all who still remain genuine believers in the doctrine and revelation of Jesus, the rapid spread of New Age is less an illumination than a warning signal. John Paul denounces New Age doctrine, together with its materialist utopian principles and the mystical language in which they are presented.

Addressing the New Age concept of evolution of mankind and its institutions, the Pontiff insists that human development "is not a straightforward line, as it were, automatic and in itself limitless; as though, given certain conditions, the human race will be able to progress rapidly toward an undefined and limitless perfection of some kind or other."

As to the "liberties" claimed in the name of New Age—abortion on demand, contraception, divorce, homosexual marriages and life-styles, test tube babies, totally statist education—John Paul condemns them as sinful and absolutely forbidden practices that cannot lead to the human happiness figured by New Agers in their global village.

New Age appeals notwithstanding, John Paul maintains that man is not perfected by his own material experience, and certainly not by welcoming Lucifer as a beloved figure. Man is a being redeemed by Christ's blood and perfected only after physical death. There is no unity possible for men and women other than by an "exercise of the human and Christian solidarity to which the Church calls us all in the light of faith and of the Church's tradition."

No words could be more categorically Roman Catholic. Still, even as John Paul calls New Agers especially to the recognition of the age-old Catholic maxim that "outside the Church there is no salvation," he recognizes in the steady growth of their numbers yet another circumstance that must be welcomed by Mikhail Gorbachev. New Agers may not forge formal alliances with Marxist-minded groups such as the WCC and SODEPAX. Nonetheless, New Age prepares the way for exactly the conditions Marxism itself has been unable to create.

The Marxist ideal has always met its stubbornest rejection at the hands of several large blocs of people—in many cases numbered in the millions —who remained stoutly attached to a religious ideal to be realized only in the afterlife. New Age, on the contrary, not only envisages the ideal of the global village in the here and now. It serves the classic Marxist ideal by corroding and dissipating those blocs of traditional resistance to the notion of total control of human life and activity by all-powerful "leaders" and "instructors." Like many other "one world" groups, New Agers look forward to the elimination of existing political systems and national boundaries. They are prepared to welcome the subsequent blending of all nations and peoples into one planetary culture, with a

single court of justice, a single police force, a single economic and educational system—all under a single government dominated by a super-
bureau of "enlightened ones."

Allowing for the necessary change of language, that is very nearly the
formula set out by Vladimir Lenin. Indeed, the primary difference between the Utopia of New Agers and that of Leninist Marxism lies in the
stark fact that it was Lenin, not Meishu Sama, who devised and set in
place the practical geopolitical structures needed for success. That global
structural system rests now in the hands of a canny Soviet leader who
believes he knows how to use any element, expected or not, that will
work to the advantage of his own globalist ideal. On that score, the
utopian sages of Findhorn Bay are no match for Moscow. Of that Pope
John Paul is certain.

That all three—Humanists, Mega-Religionists, New Agers—are globalist
in mind and geopolitical in intent seems absolutely clear. That all three
are in fundamental opposition to John Paul, his claims as Vicar of Christ
and his papal teaching about mankind's destiny is equally sure and clear.
Much more ominous for John Paul is the obvious coincidence of aims
and organizational methods between Gorbachevism and these three Piggyback Globalist groups. They cannot of themselves move the economic,
financial and political mountains blocking mankind's path to their visionary global village. John Paul's apprehension only increases according as
he registers the disappearance of Roman Catholic faith among his clergy
and people and their quite obvious assimilation to New Age ideals and
goals.

For Gorbachevism, on the contrary, the Piggyback Globalists are a
godsend. The aim is to promote homogeneity and unity between what
was once the hermetically sealed Marxist society of the Soviet empire
and the cultures of Western countries. Standing in the way of such an
aim was organized Christian religion—notably, the institutional organization John Paul II heads.

Much like the "cheerful idiots" Dean Swift lampooned some centuries
ago as manfully digging their own grave site, the Piggyback Globalists
are excellent "front men" and "point men" for the advancing forces of
Gorbachevism now claiming to desire unity and cooperation with all
mankind. For on one capital point Gorbachevism and these Piggyback
Globalists agree: The exclusively materialist and this-worldly nature of
mankind is its essence and its destiny. John Paul and Gorbachev may be
alone stalking on the geopolitical plane. But waiting for Gorbachev in
John Paul's backyard is a host of supporters of Gorbachevism.

17. The Genuine Globalists: From Alabama to Zambia, Let's Hear It for Cornflakes

The two groups that constitute the final category of self-styled globalists are perceived already by the world at large as having such managerial power over the sinews of our daily lives that they are watched by everybody. Television, radio and print reporters do their best to ferret out every morsel of information about their activities, and commentators do their best to tell us what it all means. They are perceived as Genuine Globalists, as serious about setting up international systems and structures as Lenin ever was.

Like the Provincial and Piggyback Globalists, these groups see themselves as the future. The difference is that much of the rest of the world sees them as the future, as well. And increasingly, as members of both groups begin to talk about their globalist aims as "geopolitical"—that is, in the same league of capability as Pope John Paul II and Mikhail Gorbachev—very little laughter is heard; and none of it comes from the Vatican.

Though the members of both of these groups are managers by profession, the differences between the two groups are significant enough that they are commonly given two different names.

One of them, referred to most frequently as the Internationalists, is made up primarily of political bureaucrats: individuals whose activities center around the tough business of forging legal agreements and pacts between nations and, increasingly, between blocs of nations.

The second group, the Transnationalists, are money men and company men who operate at a certain rarefied level. Their action plan in the globalist arena was set out most clearly by one of their most convinced practitioners, Montagu Norman, who served as Governor of the

Bank of England from 1920 to 1924. "The hegemony of world finance," declared Norman, "should reign supreme over everyone, everywhere, as one whole supernational mechanism." As far back as 1756, Meyer Amschel Rothschild had expressed this principle in a more frank and direct way: "Give me the power to control a nation's money, and I care not who writes its laws."

In Pope John Paul's scheme of globalist situation rooms, the operational centers of Internationalists and Transnationalists are set side by side, with a wide and much-used swinging door connecting them. For, while he agrees that there are important differences between the two groups, they do share the same working model of the world. They both see each nation living in a global harmony that will result for us all from their tireless managerial efforts to fashion a truly interdependent one-world community. And it is common for members of both groups to serve in one another's bailiwicks from time to time.

Because there is so much traffic back and forth between the groups, and because both groups operate globally as a matter of course, it is not surprising to John Paul that matters we normally think of in terms of global politics often move in a lockstep pattern with what we usually think of as financial and corporate interests.

It could not be otherwise, given the fact that a man such as George Shultz, for instance, is comfortable in the role of a Transnationalist, as onetime eminent executive of the Bechtel Group, Inc.; and just as comfortable in his Internationalist role as secretary of state during President Ronald Reagan's two administrations. Or, to take another obvious example, a corporate Transnationalist of the stature of Armand Hammer regularly enters the Internationalist arena to undertake missions on behalf of the governments of the United States and the Soviet Union.

The crossover traffic between these groups works in both directions and at many levels. Richard Helms, an Internationalist in his role as the onetime valued head of the CIA, functions equally well as a facilitator and go-between for Transnationalist business ventures. J. Patrick Barrett, former CEO of Avis, became the New York State Republican chairman in 1989.

From Pope John Paul's vantage point, the thing that seems to bind these two groups most closely in practical terms is that at heart, and philosophically speaking, both are sociopolitical Darwinists. Of course, the Pope doesn't for a moment imagine that such activists as these are likely to take time out from their total immersion in world affairs to formulate their basic group philosophy in the same way that the Humanists have. There is no Internationalist or Transnationalist equivalent of Professor Paul Kurtz's Humanist Manifesto II.

Still, in John Paul's assessment, both of these globalist groups operate on the same fundamental assumptions about the meaning of human society today. Both agree on the face of it that the most important single trait that pervades the life of all nations is interdependence. And both agree that interdependence is a progressive function of evolutionary progress. Evolutionary, as in Darwin.

In practical terms, both of these groups operate on the same working assumption Charles Darwin arbitrarily adopted to rationalize his feelings about mankind's physical origins and history. If it worked so well for Darwin, they almost seem to say, why not expand the idea of orderly progress through natural evolution to include such sociopolitical arrangements as corporations and nations? In this view, the most useful of Darwin's concepts is that of human existence as essentially a struggle in which the weakest perish, the fittest survive and the strongest flourish.

When applied to sociopolitical arrangements, this Darwinist process seems almost to dictate the Internationalist and Transnationalist one-world view of things. The continuing clash and contention in the world as it has been until now has resulted in a slow evolution of those who have survived from one stage of interdependent order to another. From time to time, natural "catastrophes" have intervened, forcing "nature" to take another path. But at each new stage, interdependence has become more important and more complex.

The greater the interdependence between groups, the higher the evolutionary stage, the more the balance achieved between interdependent groups results in the common good.

The view of the Internationalists and Transnationalists is that they are the ones who are equipped to bring mankind to the highest level of sociopolitical evolution. Their effort is to bring together into one harmonious whole all those separate parts of our world that have not yet "evolved" into a natural cohesion for the common good.

In this effort, it is the task of the Internationalists to use their juridical skills to forge a high order of unity and harmony. The pacts and agreements among groups and nations that this group works out—and they have worked out quite a number—are practical instruments. They are real building blocks of institutions with global capabilities and wide-ranging interests. And these building blocks are backed up by the strength of each group or nation that signs on the dotted line.

The Transnationalists, meanwhile, see their task as the forging of unity and harmony not through juridical resources—such means can be useful, but are subject to restrictions and dangerous delays. The favored tool of Transnationalists is the greatest human strength of all, in their view. Hard cash.

• • •

Admittedly, the sociopolitical interdependence sought by these two closely related and practical-minded groups does not rest on anything like Darwin's Galápagos turtle. It rests on a three-legged creature of their own making: a real and living and evolving tripod that will carry us on its three legs into the globalist community of the near future.

The first leg of that tripod is international trade; and it is essential for the survival of interdependence itself.

The second leg of the tripod—an international system of payment—is essential to keep the first leg, trade, from collapsing.

Finally, physical security is essential as the third leg of the tripod, so that both trade and payment can be accomplished safely, and without any of those "catastrophes" that have diverted sociopolitical evolution from its true course in the past.

Avoiding catastrophes is more important now than ever before. For the Internationalists and Transnationalists have come far enough in their plans that the slow-boiling cauldron of our world rests on top of their evolving tripod. If a rough and unmerciful fate were to kick one of those legs out from under, the consequences would be so dire and universal that no Internationalist or Transnationalist would wish to contemplate the consequences for us all.

Not to worry, however. There may be a few bumps and rough spots ahead. But on the whole, so far so good.

The first leg of the tripod—the latter-day globalist version of international trade—got its start very soon after World War II. And until recently, it appeared to be doing splendidly, as it has so far been fashioned through the sensible cooperation of these two managerial groups.

For a full century before World War II, nations engaged in trade by means of networks of bilateral trade agreements and treaties of friendship, navigation and commerce.

Importantly, there had always been one power to serve as the solid underpinning of international trade, functioning as the marketplace of last resort, one power with enough military and naval strength, enough political clout and a strong enough sense of mission to provide the stability and economic stimulus necessary for world trade.

For a short while in the nineteenth and twentieth centuries, that one power was Great Britain, with its far-flung colonialist and commercial empire. But in the immediate aftermath of World War II, hegemony passed to the United States. And at the same time, a noticeable change —in effect, a liberalization and expansion—began to alter the direction of world trade. The widely felt need of so many nations at once to rebuild their shattered economies, and the new closeness of nations that had only recently been united in a common war effort, made multilateral trade the desirable and suitable option over the earlier bilateral network system.

Within two years of the end of World War II, two general arrangements were made under the hegemony of the United States. The first facilitated the building of the initial leg of the new tripod of interdependence—the new push to multilateral trade. And the second fostered the growth of the next leg—arrangements for multilateral payment for expanded trade.

The first of those two arrangements, and the more important, was the General Agreement on Tariffs and Trade—or GATT. Negotiated in Switzerland in 1947 after a series of five international conferences, GATT consisted of an integrated set of bilateral trade agreements aimed at the abolition of quantitative trade restrictions and the reduction of tariff duties.

Successful even at the outset, GATT was amplified in 1949, 1951, 1956, 1961 and 1965. After less than twenty years, sixty-four contracting parties, accounting for four fifths of all world trade, had signed on the dotted line. At the end of 1990, the "Uruguay" round of GATT talks will involve 105 nations. Meanwhile, GATT negotiations have already covered scores of thousands of tradable commodities, including such "intellectual properties" as patents and trademarks.

Up to this point, GATT has been the organized method both of creating and of strengthening—of "evolving"—the first leg of the globalist tripod. But it has also served another function. It has been a powerful force in convincing the world at large that interdependence among nations is as natural as—well, as evolution; and as essential to our well-being as the winds that circle our common home.

Largely on the basis of GATT successes, in fact, it is now generally understood and accepted that any nation's fitness to survive—and certainly its strength to flourish—requires that it engage vigorously in trade with other nations. Swiss Confederation President Jean-Pascal Delamuraz put the case for this globalist view of international trade as a basic ingredient for the survival of the fittest. "Isolationism," said Delamuraz, "(whether by retreats into nationalism, or by uncontrolled 'North-South' confrontations) has been a calamity. In the future, it will be an infirmity."

The nature of that infirmity is easily seen already, to take one of several possible examples, in Communist North Korea. Behind the severely ailing economy of that nation, as compared with the flourishing condition of South Korea, lies the refusal of dictator Kim Il Sung to allow his doctrinaire centralized economic system to join in international trade with "capitalist jackals."

In true evolutionary fashion, the second leg of the globalist tripod creation is essential to the first. If trade is to be increasingly international, then there must be an increasingly effective and acceptable system of mutual payment. Hence the scramble on the part of Internationalists and Transnationalists to find some universally acceptable monetary system.

As the first leg of the tripod, international trade, got its modern footing with the help of GATT, so the second leg was set on the right path by means of an international agency established in the same year, 1947.

Because the basic agreements making this new monetary agency possible were signed in Bretton Woods, New Hampshire, they are often referred to collectively as the Bretton Woods Agreement(s). The agency itself, however, was named for its function: the International Monetary Fund, or IMF. Because the IMF from the beginning was affiliated with the United Nations, it depends to a certain extent on the "umbrella" influence of the U.N.

By 1967, thirty-one members had accepted IMF obligations—to maintain full convertibility of their currencies (freedom of exchange transfer for current transactions). By 1968, there were 107 members (many former colonies joined). The IMF board is composed of finance ministers of member countries. Five board members are appointed by countries with the largest quotas; fifteen are elected the IMF governors of groups of countries with quotas ranging from 3 percent to 1 percent.

In today's climate of the fast-paced development of international trade, it is difficult to mount a practical argument against the need for an improved international monetary system to keep that first leg from running into serious trouble. Indeed, just how essential to our common good is the strengthening of this second leg of the globalist tripod was made clear by the specter of worldwide financial chaos that lurked behind the so-called Black Monday market crash in New York on October 19, 1987.

Still, looking on the bright side, that crash did have at least one salutary effect in the eyes of true Internationalist and Transnationalist managers of our global welfare. It demonstrated to nonglobalist politicians and money managers that, like it or not, the individual private money markets of the United States, Europe and Japan have already been globalized. They have already evolved to a higher state of interdependence.

It is argued, therefore, that a more efficient pooling of methods than can be provided by such arrangements as GATT and IMF is urgently needed. A greater homogenization of procedures and a tighter coordination of aims are required for a world economy in which the equivalent of the annual GNP of the United States changes hands every day on the international capital markets.

Some members of these globalist groups speculate about a single acceptable monetary unit—the shadowy "Phoenix" and "Bank of Ultimate Resort" surface in this regard from time to time in futuristic Internationalist and Transnationalist discussions.

Also discussed is some more clever convertibility plan that can overcome the hurdles IMF struggles with in our present and separate national monetary systems. Perhaps an overall and truly global agreement can be fashioned by Internationalists with the savvy input of their Transnationalist brothers.

In the view of some of Pope John Paul's expert advisers in the field, there is a more likely starting point for improved monetary interdependence. In such a scenario, they see the emerging stock exchanges in Asia joining forces over time, and eventually producing an integrated securities market. In the view of these Vatican analysts, this would shatter the already deficient nationalist monetary mold once and for all. It would provide at least the example of a healthy regionalism. And it would represent a new stage on the road to the worldwide securities system the nations will ultimately have to establish if they are to reach the heights of socioeconomic interdependence envisioned for the common good in the evolutionary scheme of the Internationalist and Transnationalist groups.

Whatever improved global monetary system is finally fashioned, certainly it will rest on some overall agreement devised by the cooperative efforts of Internationalists and Transnationalists. And certainly it will ensure that tariffs and trade arrangements will benefit the poor nations as well as the rich. Otherwise the final leg of the tripod—global physical security —will be jeopardized to the point of toppling the tripod creation before it reaches its full evolutionary potential.

There is little need for Internationalists or Transnationalists to argue the case for the need to establish and maintain the improved physical security of nations. They do have their own specialized view of the role of physical security, however, as the third leg of their global tripod. For international trade and payment systems to work, we must all be secure from such things as robbery and blackmail, harassment, depredation, destructive taxation and fines, and unfair competition. And such free-dom depends in large part, and in plain words, on military security.

Our recent history supports this globalist view of military security. Hitherto, the only purpose of NATO—on which the United States alone spends $150 billion annually for the maintenance of American forces in Europe—has been to discourage any attempt by the Soviets to interfere by military invasion with the free-market economies of Western Europe.

Similarly, the booming economies of Japan, Germany and the United States—economies that anchor the present uneven evolutionary development of interdependence in the rest of the world—depend on that all-important international commodity, oil. Thus, when the possibility arose in the 1980s that the bloody Iran-Iraq war would seriously interrupt international trade in oil, the presence of American military and naval power in the Persian Gulf was required for the duration.

Pope John Paul is not the only international leader to understand that among the several difficulties admittedly faced by the Internationalist and Transnationalist groups regarding their tripod creation, including its attendant systems and structures, is its dependence on the now insecure and fast fading hegemonic position of the United States in trade, finance and military-political power.

Take the areas of trade and finance, represented by the first and second legs of the tripod. For the first four decades following World War II, global foreign direct investment (FDI) was dominated by the United States.

By 1987, however, that picture of U.S. dominance in both areas had totally changed. Of the $250 billion FDI, fully 75 percent came from a whole spectrum of nations outside the United States: $70 billion from the United Kingdom; $51 billion from the Netherlands; $30 billion from Japan; $20 billion from Canada; and $17.5 billion from West Germany.

Single trade items tell the same tale. In the decade of the nineties, 20 percent of the cars in the United States will be produced by Japanese-owned firms, with similar trends in a host of other areas, such as office equipment, consumer electronics and many luxury items.

Given the loss of hegemonic leadership to provide drive and stability, the multilateral system of trade favored until recently by both Internationalists and Transnationalists is now gravely affected by the recent emergence of bilateral and regional arrangements. Rightly or wrongly, many Internationalist voices in particular are raised now, stating that GATT is dead. And no less a figure than George Shultz—a leading light for both the Internationalists and the Transnationalists—has said that "regional initiatives are playing an ever more important role in promoting free trade, closer economic cooperation and stronger growth."

Even the preparations for the much-heralded 1992 single-market program for Europe, together with the successful conclusion of the free trade agreement (FTA) to be implemented over ten years between the United States and Canada, have both increased the trend favoring world trade resting on bilateral and regional agreements fashioned through government auspices.

Harvard professor Lester Thurow, for example, claimed in 1989 that what we need now is "a system to manage business between the three blocs [North America, Europe and the Asian Pacific], rather than global liberalization measures" (modeled on GATT). A prominent Internationalist himself, Thurow was speaking as the point man for a thoroughgoing Internationalist structure of world trade, and finance as well, as the best way to avoid calamity, given the urgent need to fill the current vacuum in global leadership.

The second leg of the globalist tripod, representing global economic cooperation, has suffered many of the same difficulties as trade on account of the lack of hegemonic leadership. For international trade to be strong and viable, the all-important issue is not so much stable exchange rates per se as it is a stable anchor for exchange rates. And here again, hegemony is the indispensable anchor. One chief function of postwar American hegemony was its ability to provide that anchor, among all the others. But here again, the United States is by no means in a position to continue that role nowadays.

U.S. hegemony in financing has passed to others: notably to Japan, which is now the strongest financial power in our world—but not necessarily the most Internationalist or Transnationalist in spirit. And as we enter the nineties, United States military and political supremacy—the rule of the day for some thirty years after World War II—is over. America does still possess military clout, but not an exclusive military supremacy. It still has political assertiveness internationally, but without any moral surety that its political solutions are the best—or that they are even viable in today's world.

The classical and effective political assertiveness required for world hegemony—embodied formerly in the once flourishing British empire and later in the United States of the immediate postwar period—was pegged to its bedrock by two traits: an admitted and nourished patriotism, and a moral consensus springing from shared religious beliefs. The United States of the 1980s and '90s has lost its grip on both of those traits.

It no longer displays any nationwide acceptance of its old-time patriotism. And the only viable—but fragile—consensus is a legal one, based on legislation and case law.

The whole Internationalist-Transnationalist tripod system, therefore, appears to have developed a case of three wobbly legs. And yet, there is no denying that interdependence among nations has gone so far that the Internationalist and Transnationalist masters of our new global systems are more than justified in their concern for the consequences for all of us, should their programs collapse even before they are totally up and running.

The differences between the Internationalist and the Transnationalist approach to globalist interdependence are magnified in the ways they favor to solve the problems that face them at this most crucial juncture.

The Internationalist group appears willing to meet the world halfway. Internationalists do not see the nations of the world as a single community in quite the same fashion as the more doctrinaire among the Transnationalists do; they do not seem married to the idea that the nations of the world are already unevenly integrated members of a "global community."

Rather, Internationalists are essentially men of politics. They do realize that their own national political parties can no longer solve the economic and financial difficulties besetting their particular political systems and national economies. They believe that the answer lies in treaties and agreements that will team nations with congenial nation partners.

Internationalists, therefore, have come to view the world as made up of possible groups of nations. "Islands" of nations is a perfect image, in fact. Islands of nations afloat in a vast archipelago. The task to be accomplished, as the Internationalists see it now, is to build bridges between those islands, drawing them together into several communities according to regional interests, geographical location and certain economic-political conditions that favor successful bloc policies between them.

As professional bureaucrats, Internationalists choose for the creation of such blocs—and eventually, if time allows, perhaps the fusing of all blocs—governmental means. For the fashioning and maintenance of administrative structures through bilateral agreements is what bureaucrats do most efficiently and naturally.

It is in that context that Lester Thurow called for "a system to manage business between . . . blocs." It is in that context, too, that George Shultz touted the importance of regional initiatives; and that in 1989 he pinpointed again, and categorically, "regional economic cooperation and prosperity" as the primary challenge of the post-Reagan era.

The Internationalist chorus is an impressive one indeed. Major voices are heard almost daily, all calling for the same solution to the fairly swift disappearance of the stabilizing hegemony of the United States, in order to avoid the possibly disastrous results of the current vacuum in global leadership.

"There is only one way to make up for this grave deficiency (in world hegemony)," said C. Fred Beregsten, director of the Institute for International Economics, "and that is by agreeing upon a pluralistic management." Respected Japanese columnist Misahiko Ishizuka clearly sees the same need. Japan's function in such a pluralistic system of management, said Ishizuka, "will require a grand design involving not only economic but political and military matters."

So far, however, that grand Internationalist design has made only spotty and halting progress. The most advanced form of Internationalist regionalism as a solution to the crisis in global leadership is represented by the European Economic Community (EEC) and by the Free Trade Agreement (FTA) between the United States and Canada.

As a single-market program, EEC is—by prior standards, at least—the most ambitious enterprise on the horizon. Much has been made of the EEC aim to remove the tariffs within the region by 1998. But the plan concerns wider measures. The goal is to eliminate border controls on the movement of people and goods; to free up capital movement and trade in services; and to grant the right of establishment. Ultimately, there is to be a truly single-market community comprising the whole of Western Europe's 350 million people. Some Internationalists raise their sights for the future even higher. Norwegian Prime Minister Gro Harlem Brundtland, for one, has speculated that "in the light of the extended contacts between East and West, we have a vision of a future market, not merely of 350 million people, but of 700 million people in Europe alone."

Visions are all very well. But as impressive as the EEC program is, and for all the hope that Internationalists attach to it, Transnationalists will point out that virtually every other regional arrangement, except the FTA between Canada and the United States, remains bogged down in discussions, in exchanges of experience and in research and analysis. And to give the Transnationalists their due, the story does appear to be one of foot dragging and reluctance in region after region.

On one side of the Atlantic, there is the Caribbean Common Market (CARICOM), the Caribbean Basin Initiative (CBI) and the Central American Common Market (CACM). On the other side of the Atlantic, there is the Assembly of Regions of Europe (ARE), while across the Pacific there is the Pacific Basin Forum (PBF), proposed by George Shultz, and the Asian-Pacific Organization (APO), proposed by Australian Prime Minister Robert Hawke. There is even the Soviet bloc's Council for Mutual Economic Assistance (COMECON). The United Nations has its regional commissions as well—its Economic Commission for Europe (ECE), for Africa (ECA), and for the Far East and Asia (ECFEA).

The United States and Mexico actually drew up the framework for an agreement in 1987 that listed several specific areas for bilateral consideration, much in the manner that led to the U.S.-Canadian FTA. But no concrete concessions were granted by either side. Similar proposals have been entertained, so far with the same meager results, between the United States and Japan, and for the members of the Association of South-East Asian Nations (ASEAN).

As nearly as Pope John Paul can see, therefore, clearly the weakest link in the Transnationalist solution for the urgent need to provide stability in the tripod globalist system is that there is no sign of the broad formation of blocs required for their plan to work.

Even the three "Asian tigers" show no sign of unitary regional action. Indeed, Korea's and Taiwan's markets are even more tightly closed than Japan's. Moreover, while all the signs are that the European Community (EC) will achieve a certain intracommunity easement of border duties and labor movement, no one—least of all the Europeans themselves—thinks that the EC is going to trade as one bloc with the rest of the world.

As a group, dyed-in-the-wool Transnationalists are neither surprised nor entirely dismayed at the failure of the Internationalist initiative. In fact, blood brothers though they are, Transnationalists assail the regional approach of the Internationalists on several accounts. Their most important objection, perhaps, is that they are certain the legal machinery required to link one region or bloc of nations with another will involve protectionist restrictions—in such things as trade quotas, as just one example—as inducements to get certain nations to sign on.

To make their point, in fact, Transnationalists have only to point to GATT itself, the very underpinning of the Internationalist model. Transnationalists applaud the phasing out of the Multi-Fiber Arrangement by GATT members, because it will end the practice of developed countries to set limits on the quantity of clothing and textiles the developing countries can sell them. That phaseout is right down the Transnationalists' alley, because their effort is to avoid any head-to-head confrontation by which one economy attempts to protect its interests through legal restrictions that prevent others from full competition in the global market.

Happily for the Transnationalists, similar thorny issues concerning agricultural subsidies and protectionism are at least on the way to a solution. Unless such protectionist confrontations and arrangements can be phased out, say the Transnationalists, we will be faced with a regional system as mordant as any nationalist protectionism ever was.

Moreover, in the Transnationalist mind, solutions for problems and realizations of opportunities can no longer be achieved solely within a system of single nations, or even within a system of sectors or blocs of nations. No regional or bloc system, however interrelated it might be, will supply an adequate solution, because it is already too late to forge or control interdependence by means of blocs of trading partners. And it is too late because the nations are already interdependent.

If that argument sounds a little like the old saw about the chicken and the egg, Transnationalists make no apologies. Instead, they use that old saw again and again, to their increasing advantage. The complex issues presented by the interdependence that is already upon us, say the Transnationalists, require new dimensions of cooperation and collaboration at the global level. But collaboration not only of the old kind between governments and society: they see that effort as, at best, an evolutionary stage on the way to their own solution. What the world needs now, argue the Transnationalists, is a new sort of interdependence pegged to a regulated system of fresh and innovative interrelationships that cross all former boundaries, include all sectors and take in all disciplines.

In other words, effective and practical interdependence calls for a new systemic approach.

The Transnationalist mind draws back from the Internationalist solution of treaties and pacts, largely because that path implies a political consequence the Transnationalist mind is not ready to accept.

The Transnationalists, therefore, have in mind a different path to the same general goal, a different program for the nations. Quintessentially, they are managers—money men and company men. And their systemic approach is expressed in the creation of the global company.

The global company of the Transnationalists is sometimes confused with the multinational company, which has been around for quite a while. But the difference between those two creations is critical in this context. For, as Sir Edwin Sharp, chairman and CEO of the UK's Cable and Wireless Corporation, told an economic summit meeting in 1989, no matter how wide the network of a multinational company may be, the company itself remains essentially "a one-way street back to the parent company."

By contrast, the global company must have a genuinely international management: a management composed of several nationalities. And its decisions must have a worldwide character, so that plants and factories, for instance, will be located without regard for nationality.

The Transnationalist leaders themselves already transcend political and ideological boundaries. Television commentator Bill Moyers found out during a fifteen-day, globe-spanning trip in the company of David Rockefeller that "just about a dozen or fifteen individuals made day-by-day decisions that regulated the flow of capital and goods throughout the entire world."

In truth, Transnationalists form a social class—aptly dubbed the managerial class—that came into being only after World War II. And within that social class are to be found the very select few who regularly participate in weighty decisions about the regulated flow of capital, of capital goods and of capital services among the nations.

Their backgrounds usually include training in major business schools and sometimes graduation from prestigious colleges. They locate in companies of substantial monetary capital and "status" capital. They have strong ties with other corporate financial leaders and enjoy membership in elite groups around the world. They wield direct and indirect but always potent political power, belong to select clubs, and hold down multiple directorships and board memberships.

Together, these corporate leaders constitute a managerial system; this is the latest form that Western capitalism has taken—in a kind of chicken-and-egg process again—in response to the multilateral trading system as it has so far developed over the past forty years.

As multinational trade has developed, the flow of production and finance has become increasingly internationalized. Logically, that internationalization has resulted, in turn, in still further globalization of the policies by which trade and investment are carried out. Just as logically, therefore, the interests of Transnationalists are increasingly global, because their investments and their very lives have become global, encompassing all manufactured goods and all services, including money management.

In this Transnationalist managerial system, decisions are not dictated by the laws of individual nations or according to any system of morality based on religious beliefs and principles. Moreover, while Transnationalist decisions involve all-important elements in the economic and social lives of nations, they are not made primarily according to the political will, ethical consensus, traditional morality or social trends of those nations.

David Rockefeller once summed up the Transnationalist point of view in a nutshell: "We don't really mind what sort of government a country has, provided they can pay their bills."

The basic laws governing Transnationalist decisions refer to the balance needed between the supply and demand of goods and services— trade, in other words. And they refer to the movements of liquid assets —the global financial underpinning for trade. And they refer to the need to avoid any sociopolitical tensions or clashes between differing national interests that might upset the trade and finance applecart. And finally the basic laws refer to the need for homogenization of goods and services as produced and consumed all over the world.

Increasingly, decisions made on such a fluctuating basis follow the pragmatic judgment of nonpolitical men—Transnationalists—who occupy managerial positions within diverse but interlocking organizational groups. The professional occupation of these managers is primarily economics, industry or finance. And increasingly, as the chicken-and-egg syndrome spirals, those spheres transcend the boundaries of all political units—the units of city, state and nation.

As complex as this Transnationalist managerial system may be, its purpose is simplicity itself: the formation of the "good life." And at least in this respect, these globalists are exactly like the Piggyback Globalists. The goal is plentiful food, modern hygiene and medicine, an abundance of convenience and luxury goods, an abundance as well of the labor-saving devices of modern technology, from cars and computers to microwave ovens and toasters. And, not least, ever more plentiful and varied and audacious modes of entertainment—film and video, audio and print —for the general public everywhere.

Just how far the Transnationalists have come toward achieving their own hegemony to replace the leadership formerly exercised by nations such as Great Britain and the United States is clear to Pope John Paul in the reality that the most outstanding feature of international life today is, in fact, the interdependence of nations.

And it becomes clearer still to the Pontiff in the reality that such interdependence is based on the Transnationalist model; that it is furthered by the Transnationalist formation of global companies and related activities; and that it thoroughly reflects the materialist philosophy of the Transnationalist mind.

In a word, Transnationalists have already entered successfully on a new path in order to cope with the change in the fundamentals of the world economy. And the cause-and-effect element of the Transnationalist system itself—complex in nature and global in scale—continues to shape the future of the nations.

Some random samples of the impact the Transnationalist approach has on our lives, both as producers and consumers of goods and services, illustrate Pope John Paul's observations and reasoning here.

Every weekday afternoon, employees of New York Life Insurance gather all the claims that have come in that day and dispatch them by jet plane to Ireland, 3,000 miles away, to be processed.

Georgia Institute of Technology has established a privately held venture, China/Tech, with offices in Atlanta and Beijing.

British Petroleum is a British company; Siemens is a West German company; Honda is a Japanese company. Yet all of them have more employees and executive offices outside their home countries than inside. Honda, in fact, will soon produce and sell more cars in the United States than in Japan.

Fiber optics span all continents today. Millions of dollars move literally in seconds from Tokyo to New York to Milan to Frankfurt. Goods move around the world in a single day. One product emerging from an assembly line in Detroit, Michigan, can contain parts manufactured in five other countries. In point of fact, the major automobile companies can no longer accurately be called automobile "manufacturers." They are "assemblers" of auto parts manufactured elsewhere in the world.

The case is similar for electronics. As the chairman and CEO of the Sony Corporation, Akio Morita, observed in 1989, "Already our companies are partially American, partially European and partially Latin American companies, using local management, local raw materials and local production around the world. . . . Our slogan is local globalization." Michael P. Schulhof and Jakob Schmuckli, both Americans, were nominated to the board of Sony Corporation in 1989.

Major banks today have an effective physical presence in all the chief financial centers of the world. And the first truly global investment bank —CS First Boston, Inc.—has now been created by Rainer E. Gut, chairman of Switzerland's Credit Suisse. With operations in North America, Asia and Europe, 44.5 percent of CS First Boston is owned by Credit Suisse, 25 percent by its employees and 30.5 percent by the Olayan Group of Saudi Arabia.

The Philadelphia-based pharmaceutical company SmithKline Beckman Corporation has merged with the London-based Beecham Group P.K.C., to form the world's second-largest pharmaceutical company after Merck & Company. Their plans for management include a mixing of different nationalities, with special attention paid to the differing histories and cultures of those who will make up a Transnationalist management group. And they have a new business plan from the bottom up, reflecting how the newly united businesses could operate in combination, situated as they are on both sides of the Atlantic and in Japan. The target is a new corporate entity. A globalist entity.

Even film entertainment is going global in a way never before contemplated—a way that is becoming one of the most visible models of the Transnationalist success track. Hollywood is the repository for the seven major existing film libraries and studios in the world—Walt Disney Co., Paramount, MGM/UA, Warner Brothers, 20th Century–Fox, Universal Studios and Columbia Pictures. All of them possess powerful marketing and distribution systems to get films into theaters and on the air all over the globe.

Hand in glove with this global capability in distribution of existing product, an inexorable demand is created for what is now called new "software"—new entertainment programming.

Just as inexorably, therefore, companies and investors in other nations —notably Britain, Australia, Italy and Japan—are starting to snap up studios and production companies in the United States and elsewhere, while foreign concerns and U.S. producers are joining in financial deals, joint ventures and coproductions almost as a matter of course. Studios themselves, meanwhile, are starting to cast stars with an important eye on their international draw—Sean Connery as Harrison Ford's father in *Indiana Jones and the Last Crusade*, for example, because Connery's profile is high in Europe, Asia and sub-Saharan Africa.

Altogether, the global character of entertainment becomes more pronounced with each passing year. "What you end up with," concluded Charles B. Slocum of the Writers Guild of America/West, "is companies in all countries looking outside their borders." And that is as deft a description as you will find of one essential stage on the road to the Transnationalist goal.

In the chicken-and-egg, cause-and-effect syndrome that is such a hallmark of Transnationalist success, the consumer side of our lives is every bit as globalized as the production side.

Food tastes around the world are beginning to converge. Marketing experts point out that this convergence arises because of companies marketing their products on an increasingly international basis; because of increased travel; and because of vastly improved telecommunications. In short, and almost literally, the chicken-and-egg principle applies.

Coca-Cola, Kellogg's Corn Flakes and Nescafé sell in areas literally from A to Z—from Alabama to Zambia. Companies such as Kraft, Inc., Quaker Oats and Pillsbury are intent on creating global supermarkets.

McDonald's, which has already exported throughout much of the world what one supporter has called "McCulture," trained its first cadre of Soviets in that company's standardized food preparation techniques, and opened its first branch in Moscow in February 1990. Because the ruble is not presently convertible, McDonald's knows it will not benefit financially in the immediate future from the expansion of its franchise into the Soviet Union. But the benefits for its globalist aims are undeniable.

To speak of "McCulture" as a Transnationalist aim is neither lighthearted nor too farfetched. For while the agenda of this group is concentrated in the successful growth and operation of the global company, its full agenda is far more inclusive than that. For example, another important trait of the Transnationalists' agenda that receives close attention from Pope John Paul in his assessment of their new globalism is the Transnationalist formula for education.

That formula was summed up by Ernest L. Boyer, president of the Carnegie Foundation for the Advancement of Teaching. Schools must possess "an understanding of the new global agenda," said Boyer, and must reform their curricula so as to communicate that agenda to their students. Or, as President Claire Guadiani of Connecticut College said a bit more colorfully, schools must begin to satisfy the educational needs of people "who will operate in an increasingly internationalized environment, even if they never leave Duluth."

Transnationalist thinking is extremely thorough in this promotion of globalist education. It is not a matter of stuffing a few extra courses into the curriculum, along with some area studies and perhaps a foreign language. At most, such an approach would reduce global education to the status of just another subject. The Transnationalist idea is that globalism should permeate every subject taught; it should be a pervasive orientation. The globalist outlook and approach must predominate at least from junior high school through college and postgraduate studies. The cultural outlook must be such that no subject is regional in its focus.

Furthermore, issues of particular importance to Transnationalists must be studied at every level. Such issues as the environment, world hunger, the twin epidemics of AIDS and drug addiction, physical fitness, population control. At the moral level, equivalence must be the watchword. The cultural and legal values of, say, Sri Lanka's Tamils and Nigeria's Ibos must be studied for their own excellence, and not be added on by way of contrast or be seen as clashing with or inferior to our Western values.

Transnationalist educators have no serious fears concerning standardization of education in the so-called hard sciences. They are confident enough that what high-schoolers in Kuala Lumpur, Malaysia, will learn about mathematics, computer programming, engineering, chemistry, and the like will be exactly the same as what their counterparts learn in England, the United States, Canada, Germany, Spain, South America and Japan.

In the so-called soft subjects, on the other hand—in culturally loaded subjects such as history, literature, art, music, religion and ethics—the Transnationalist educator meets with greater difficulties. For example, in all the areas of the world molded by Western civilization, schools have taught those soft subjects with what Transnationalists regard as a pervasive "bias." That is, from a Western point of view.

A candidate for college has been expected to know about Shakespeare's *Hamlet* and Goethe's *Faust*, about the Magna Carta and the Napoleonic Wars. But he has not been expected to quote from the Indian *Upanishads,* or to describe the outlook of Gautama Buddha.

In short, education in schools of the Western world suffers from what Transnationalists have begun to call Eurocentrism—a provincial outlook that focuses overwhelmingly on European and Western culture, while giving short shrift to Africa, Asia, Oceania and Latin America. Only a Eurocentric mind would say, for example, that Columbus "discovered" America, as if there had been nobody on that continent before he arrived. Or again, history is Eurocentric when Westerners learn about Japan, India and China in terms of colonialist wars and other encounters Europeans and Americans have had with those peoples. By the same principle, African art is "primitive" to the Eurocentric eye. Schoolchildren learn about Marco Polo's travels to the Orient but never about Ibn Batutah, the fourteenth-century Muslim who traveled more extensively and in places Marco Polo did not even know existed.

All of that, according to the Transnationalist mind, must change. And Transnationalist educators are seeing to it.

In all of California's elementary and high schools, for instance, there is a new world history curriculum, explaining events through Hispanic, Asian and African eyes; and the civilizations of China, India, Africa and Islam are studied extensively. At Stanford University, Western civilization courses have been expanded to take in Oriental and African civilization. New York's Juilliard School of Music now has courses on the music of Japan, Africa, India and the Pacific islands.

The goal of such extensive changes and adaptations in educational curricula is to rear a new generation of men and women who will be able to view non-Western cultures not through a Western lens, but with the eyes of the peoples who make up those cultures—or at least, with the eyes Transnationalist educators attribute to the peoples of those cultures.

Education, then, is seen as the first step in fashioning a truly global outlook from the cradle onward. It is to be an outlook able to adapt with ease and according to circumstances to a point of view that may be Eurocentric or Afrocentric, Latinocentric or Asiacentric. An outlook that will be open to all cultural forms on an equal basis.

To make this utopian educational step a universal reality, ideally the same textbooks should be used all over the world in both the hard sciences and the soft curricula. And sure enough, a concrete initiative in this direction has been under way for some years now, undertaken by Informatik, a Moscow-based educational organization, and the Carnegie Endowment Fund.

In any case, whatever the specific steps and means employed to achieve the Transnationalist global education policy, that policy itself envisages a world permeated by cooperation and peace for the sake of constant and evenly distributed material development, a world permeated with freedom that is no longer exploitive, a world that allows for the diversity of the various cultures—provided cultural values never outweigh economic requirements. It will be a world that rejoices in the diversity of religions—provided theological differences never interfere with efforts to achieve the Transnationalist version of peace.

The Transnationalist outlook and line of reasoning here are crystal clear to Pope John Paul. If the Transnationalists are fully successful in their programs and policies, everyone will live and work in institutions that will be global in their organization and in their very essence. People will be doing "good" banking, or "good" engineering, or "good" manufacturing, if they are performing their tasks in institutions where all distinctions have collapsed between what is international and what is particular to any individual nation or culture or religion.

"Good" will no longer be burdened with a moral or religious coloring. "Good" will simply be synonymous with "global." Else, what's an education for?

.   .   .

As John Paul sees the future of this globalist agenda, educational changes will not be the half of it. The Transnationalist education formula is in essence one step in a drive to build a worldwide human infrastructure upon which an effectively working global economy can base itself with some security.

The emphasis is on homogeneity of minds, on the creation and nourishing of a truly global mentality. If the world's economy is going to be global in the Transnationalist sense, then those engaged in it cannot afford any provincialism in culture and outlook.

We must all become little Transnationalists. For the sake of the financial and trading interests upon which our world relies even now, a new mentality must be forged in legal systems, monetary systems, fiscal systems, defense systems, sociocultural values and demographic rules and regulations. Political ideologies and systems will all have to be modified by the natural, evolutionary processes that are already under way.

Further, while Pope John Paul is as aware as any man of the differences in preferred methods that are debated endlessly by these two globalist groups, the fact remains that at the most influential levels, cooperation between Internationalists and Transnationalists far outweighs any differences between them.

Whether they prefer to move along the path of greater and greater government bureaucracy, or greater and greater control by global management systems, both groups move in lockstep when it comes to the re-creation of our practical world. And should there be any doubts concerning either their will or their power to change that world through their sweeping policies, recent events put those doubts to rest.

Just one case history, in fact, is enough to illustrate just how closely the outlook and the effects of these two globalist groups dovetail with each other. And it is more than enough to demonstrate, as well, the power of these groups to shape our world and to dictate the fabric of our lives as profoundly as any revolution.

The name of John J. McCloy is not a household word. Nine out of ten of us would probably shake our heads if we were asked what this man had done in life. But as Bill Moyers discovered on his journey with David Rockefeller, anonymity is the welcome companion of men who operate at the heights of power where John McCloy spent most of his life.

In any case, it's not McCloy's fame or the lack of it, but his accomplishments that illustrate John Paul's point about the global reach and the near-geopolitical abilities of these globalists in their ambitions, their goals and their policies. For no one was a greater champion than McCloy of the fervent faith that the nations can be unerringly guided to a new world order—provided that talented and visionary globalists themselves design, install and maintain a controlled balance among the nations that deal in raw power.

The career of John J. McCloy spanned a period of sixty-four years, from 1925 until his recent death, on March 11, 1989. After serving in World War I as a staff officer to General Guy Preston, John McCloy graduated from Harvard Law School, and in 1925 joined the firm then known as Cravath, Henderson and Gernsdorf (CHG).

CHG handled much of the legal work that made it possible for American banks to become involved in foreign initiatives to rebuild Europe after the Great War. That was interesting, no doubt. But McCloy probably chose his entry point with a still keener eye. Paul Cravath was one of the founders of the Council on Foreign Relations (CFR). And CFR was the natural meeting place for such men as Cravath, Robert Lovett, Averell Harriman, Charles "Chip" Bohlen, George F. Kennan and Dean Acheson.

With good reason, those six men in particular were celebrated as recently as 1986 by authors Walter Isaacson and Evan Thomas in their book, *The Wise Men: Six Friends and the World They Made*. But what Isaacson and Thomas saw after the fact, John McCloy foresaw, at least in terms of general possibilities, in 1925. In McCloy's words, Cravath, Henderson and Gernsdorf "was where I would have a chance to run with the swift."

Run he did. Together with Lovett and Harriman, McCloy helped to paper together $77 million worth of bond issues for the Union Pacific Railroad. Also involved in that effort was Frenchman Jean Monnet, then an international financier with Blair & Company of New York and Paris, and later one of the architects and prime movers of what we now know as the European Economic Community.

McCloy become Monnet's lawyer. Together they worked at issues of securities for European municipalities; and they merged Blair & Company into Transamerica Corporation.

By 1935, within ten years of joining CHG, McCloy was already a megacorporate Transnationalist. In that year, he became fused as well with the Internationalists. In fact, he moved to heaven on earth from the Internationalist point of view—Washington, D.C. In the words of Isaacson and Thomas, he entered the tradition of "a group of hard-nosed Internationalists . . . [who] came from Wall Street and State Street, and thus understood well the importance of a prosperous and open global economy, and America's role in such a world."

One high-ranking member of that hard-nosed group was Henry Lewis
Stimson. Like Cravath, Stimson was one of the founders of CFR. And
like McCloy, he was a graduate of Harvard Law School who found his
own path to rarefied power in a law firm—the firm of the legendary Elihu
Root, where Stimson became a partner in 1897.

In 1941, with World War II already well under way, Henry Stimson
became Franklin D. Roosevelt's secretary of war. In the same year, John
McCloy became Stimson's assistant secretary of war; with Robert Lovett
as his counterpart in the same department.

It was clear that there was more to John McCloy than hard-nosed
politics and finance. There was as well the abiding mystique of the true
globalist, a certain fire that is the globalist's equivalent of religious fervor.
That McCloy burned with this fervor seems undeniable. On the day he
received the Distinguished Service Medal from his boss, Secretary Stimson, McCloy wrote in his diary that he looked up at "the steady gaze of
Elihu Root" in the portrait hanging on the wall behind Stimson. "I felt a
direct current running from Root through Stimson to me . . . they were
the giants." McCloy's World War II service provided him with the arena
he needed to become a giant in the same tradition, to become one of the
"Wise Men" who would be revered in his turn by other aspiring globalists.

John McCloy was an essential figure in such major wartime decisions
as the Lend-Lease program, which funneled $15 billion into Joseph Sta-
lin's Soviet Union, the internment of Japanese Americans in detention
camps, the dropping of A-bombs on Hiroshima and Nagasaki, a decision
symptomatic of the Wise Men's policy of balance. His energy was boundless. And as Stimson himself acknowledged, McCloy's authority was the
same as his own. Anybody who wanted to make progress in Washington
had to "have a word" with McCloy.

Conversely, he was prominent in the firing of General George S. Pat-
ton, who threatened to upset the balance of power McCloy's Washington
had determined should reign over postwar Europe. And in the later
Korean "police action," he was a major influence in President Harry
Truman's firing of General Douglas MacArthur, who threatened a similar upset in the Pacific.

After a busy and powerful stint as a partner in the firm of Milbank,
Tweed, Hope, Hadley and Miller—the legal arm of the Rockefeller family and its Chase Manhattan Bank—and as a board member of the Union
Pacific Railroad, the Empire Trust Company and the Rockefeller Foundation, McCloy was the natural choice to succeed Eugene Meyer as
president of the World Bank in 1946.

He was already a figure of enormous experience and power in global affairs, and a master of the ways of government Internationalist and corporate Transnationalist alike, yet McCloy's greatest and most far-reaching contributions still lay ahead of him.

In 1948, President Truman named McCloy to the postwar position of high commissioner for West Germany. As McCloy himself saw it, he now had "the power of a dictator as High Commissioner of the Allied Forces in West Germany." To trace the influence of John McCloy from this point on is to trace some of the most significant events in world history after World War II.

Within the balance-of-power tradition to which he was totally committed, the reconstruction of postwar Germany carried out by John McCloy became arguably the single most important policy for the Western world. Today, in fact, McCloy's West Germany is the key element in the fate of the European Community to be welded together in 1992. It is the key element in the near-future fate of NATO. And it is the key element as well in the fate of Gorbachevism.

As an Internationalist of the first order, McCloy was a key architect of the Marshall Plan. He drafted the Ausable Club proposals outlining the terms for Soviet-American arms control. He was one of the main movers behind the creation of OPEC. He negotiated the first agreements that resolved the Cuban missile crisis—yet another example of his embodiment of the Wise Men's policy concerning balance of power.

As a Transnationalist with few peers, meanwhile, McCloy was general counsel to the fabled "Seven Sister" oil companies—a Transnationalist role that dovetailed perfectly with his Internationalist role in the creation of OPEC. He originated many of the "New World Order" projects as chairman of the Ford Foundation. He was an active participant in Jean Monnet's first organization of the European Economic Community (EEC)—he called it "the United States of Europe." He presided over the merger of Chase National Bank with another Rockefeller bank, to form the third-largest bank in the world of that day.

All in all, among the Internationalist statesmen and Transnationalist businessmen of the post–World War II era, it would be hard to find one other individual who wielded such single-handed power and influence as McCloy. Those he promoted went far—Robert McNamara, for example, and Henry Kissinger, Dean Rusk, Eugene Black and George D. Woods, to name but a few. He was active and influential on the Warren Commission, which inquired into the assassination of President John Kennedy. He had a personal function in the selection of President Richard Nixon's cabinet.

So impressive—indeed, in the eyes of many of his colleagues, so superhuman—were McCloy's achievements, that he inspired in others that same quasi-religious fervor he himself experienced in Henry Stimson's Washington office as he looked up at "the steady gaze of Elihu Root."

At the black-tie tribute to McCloy on the occasion of his ninetieth birthday, Henry Kissinger called him "the First Citizen of the Council of Foreign Relations," and much more besides. Delving into that near-religious mystique that fires the globalist vision and fervor, Kissinger continued, "I believe John McCloy heard the footsteps of God as he went through history, and those of us who were not humble enough or who were not sharp enough had the privilege of knowing that, if we followed his footsteps, we were in the path of doing God's work."

With the stentorian achievements of this one Wise Man and his associates as an example of the globalist vision and power, it is difficult to argue against Pope John Paul's position that, for all their differences, Internationalists and Transnationalists pursue the same essential goals. And it is difficult to argue that the Pope need not assess these globalists as serious contenders with himself and Mikhail Gorbachev in the arena of the millennium endgame.

Indeed, most influential observers and commentators presently regard these globalist groups as having the predominant influence in shaping our near-future world. And with good reason. For already they have established development as the motor principle of our lives as individuals and as citizens of nations upon a shrinking globe.

Moreover, they have successfully pegged development itself to their tripod creation of international trade, finance and physical security; and they have enshrined the same idea of balance promoted by McCloy as the single key to our global well-being. Anything that will upset the tripod balance of trade, finance and physical security is understood as a threat to the world as a whole, and to each nation as a part of that whole. Everyone must cooperate, or everyone will suffer.

Just how pervasive this globalist outlook has become can be seen in the fact that virtually all nations are defined, and define themselves, in terms of how they rank on the world scale of material development. All agree that nations such as Ethiopia and Madagascar, for example, are "underdeveloped." That nations such as India, Pakistan and the Philippines are "developing." That such nations as Saudi Arabia, Chile and Norway are "developed." No one doubts that the most important feature of the United States, Japan, the United Kingdom and West Germany is that they are "advanced" nations. And no one doubts, either, that in each case, such labels have to do exclusively with the accumulation of wealth and with the greater or lesser availability of goods and services. For that is the basic and accepted globalist definition of development itself.

According as nations are successfully plugged into the tripod system, they progress upward on the evolutionary development tree. And in this globalist outlook, it goes without saying that, if the promotion and evening out of such evolution requires a progressive homogenization of values and behavior that some find painful, it is a small price to pay in the end for the material benefits we will all enjoy in the uniformly developed global village.

Pope John Paul does not categorically condemn the aims sought by such globalists. He readily admits that some of those aims can aid in the alleviation of conditions that make life today "solitary, poor, nasty, brutish and short," in the words of Thomas Hobbes, for some two billion human beings. John Paul means conditions such as poverty, disease, malnutrition, environmental pollution, inadequate wages and living conditions. In those areas and others like them, John Paul seems to see the globalist aims of these groups as beneficial to mankind as a whole.

At the same time, however, he also knows that the Transnationalist outlook, which seeks to admit developing countries rapidly as full partners in the task of managing the global economy, is not motivated primarily by humanitarian or moral impulses. Rather, it is a matter of strategic necessity, if tripod balance is to be achieved and maintained. For if almost four out of every five human beings continue to be excluded from the "good life," the global tripod economy itself will not escape the mortal blows of regional conflict and organized state terrorism.

Moreover, because the "good life" is the alpha and omega of the global thrust, Pope John Paul weighs in heavily and frequently with the criticism that "the mere accumulation of goods and services, even for the benefit of the majority, is not enough for the realization of human happiness."

Indeed, the Pope summarizes one main error of the Transnationalists in particular as "superdevelopment," which "consists of every kind of material goods for the benefit of certain social groups" and which "easily makes people slaves of 'possessions' and of immediate gratification, with no other horizon than the continual multiplication and continual replacement of things already owned with others still better."

John Paul gives the Internationalists their due, as well, in their efforts to forge closer internation and interbloc alliances. "We are one family," the Pontiff often remarks. And it would be all to the good if a closer and more intimate union of all nations in economic and financial collaboration were effective in eliminating the barriers of selfish, introverted nationalism.

However, if such collaboration necessarily implies artificial birth control and family planning techniques, together with ever-new genetic and eugenic "experiments," then the Pope's approval of the globalist ethos stops in its tracks. And he does know in dollars what Transnationalists are ready to pour into such efforts.

Papal criticisms notwithstanding, more and more the Transnationalist conviction takes hold among us that any point of view must be considered a disruptive "bias" if it upsets the material balance upon which world economic stability rests. And that conviction extends not only into general education and what we now call "corporate culture" but at least as deeply into the political, religious and moral areas of our lives where, admittedly, "bias" is very likely to crop up.

Increasingly, as this materialist view becomes more pervasive, the most vital elements in the personal, economic and social life of every individual in every nation are being affected, for good or for ill, by decisions flowing from the mentality and aims of global managers.

The evidence is clear that, as religious and moral "bias" is erased from our lives, the individual cannot but be affected by a massive onflow of modernity. What each of us values in life—what is "good" and "bad"; the very focus of meaning in life—must shift away from its traditional locus. It must shift away from everything that transcends the human scene, away from everything that was once identified with the God of religion, away from the laws of God and the demands of such religion. It must shift away from the individual's regard for family, and from the entire ethical consensus of whole peoples that was colored until now by religion.

John Paul sees some of the early effects to be expected from this profound dislocation, in what are now referred to—in bland and unbiased fashion—as the new "life-styles" that have already penetrated so deeply into the personal and social lives of many nations.

Moral considerations have largely been ignored or arbitrarily redefined in the global clamor surrounding such deep and frequently controverted issues as sexual equality of men and women, single parenthood, a woman's right to her own body, the growing acceptability throughout the West of RU-486 (the new do-it-yourself abortifacient pill), wombs for hire, fetal vivisection, fetal commodification and experimentation, homosexual rights, death with dignity, euthanasia, legalized suicide, the unacceptable character of the death penalty.

With the expert help of globalist organizations, forced abortions and sterilization are promoted in China and India, as matters having nothing to do with morality aside from the globalist "moral imperative" of population control for the good of global development. In those countries and elsewhere, the United States government alone spent up to half a billion dollars every year from the public treasury on stiffly promoted birth control methods.

If the wide-ranging programs of these two globalist groups develop unchecked, Pope John Paul sees the inevitable outcome for all of us in terms that are less benign by far than the picture painted for us by Internationalists and Transnationalists.

As the example of John McCloy and the Wise Men shows, the activities of these groups run hand in glove on the level of the creation of practical systems for the achievement of their vision of a balanced globalist world. Inevitably, therefore, a specific and expanding managerial program emerges from their efforts.

If followed to their logical conclusion, the methods and programs of either group point for Pope John Paul toward a human condition that will be irreconcilable with Christian principles and irreconcilable, too, with the generally admitted principles of human dignity and rights.

As the moral underpinnings of personal, social and political attitudes and behavior are displaced in a wholesale manner, both Internationalist and Transnationalist groups seem easily and naturally to take on the hue of an ideology as ironclad as any of the classical ideologies known to us from history. It is an ideology one hesitates to classify but one that has demands and conditions concerning ultimate governing authority in the world and that, at least by implication, entails prejudgments and conclusions about those elemental issues that have always divided mankind.

Life and afterlife is such an issue. The whole meaning of life—its purpose and significance, the meaning of personal worth and human honor, human rights, the purpose and the means of political governance. All of these are issues involved in the globalist ideology that drives the Internationalist and the Transnationalist.

In Pope John Paul's most candid assessments, the inherent tendency of both groups to build supranational systems for the establishment and maintenance of what they see as our global well-being is bound to lead to a completely new horizon for all men and women: an earth dominated by a new international bureaucracy to direct and control every citizen and every nation "for the good of all."

According as Internationalist and Transnationalist systems spread ever wider, forming a growing mesh for human life and activity, we all become subject to an increasing number of international bodies created to administer this framework.

By its very nature, the Internationalist program alone implies the creation of administrative bureaus placed in compartmented orbits around an ever-tightening network of nations. Even Harvard's Lester Thurow admits that if the world moved toward the Internationalist creation of three regional areas—North America, Europe and Japan—their three currencies would dominate the scene. But even without such an overarching dome of arrangements, there is no thinking observer of world events who does not expect trading blocs of nations to expand for the benefit of the competitive economic, financial and industrial positions of all concerned.

For all their weaknesses, their squabbling and their halting progress, even such regional associations as already exist—the European Parliament and the Organization of American States, for example—are growing more complex, as regional problems and developments place increasing demands on them. Incipient administrative sections of the United Nations already deal on a quasi-global basis with economic, sociological, educational and military sectors of life; and they, too, are expected to be endowed with wider powers.

For Pope John Paul, therefore, the importance of these globalists in the millennium endgame has very little to do with the differences in their preferred avenues of activity. For the Pontiff, these globalist groups are like two eyes looking out of the same face.

To be sure, the object of the globalists who confidently pursue their system-building agendas is benign. For along with John Paul and others, they recognize that as their globalist programs succeed, the "average citizen" and the "average nation" will no longer be able to cope on the basis of their own resources alone with the worldwide character of economic, financial and political forces.

Thus, Internationalists see their ever-widening grid of pacts and alliances as essential to tend the "best interests" of the average nation and to "protect" the average citizen from damage and destruction by those worldwide forces.

The systems-building program of the Transnationalists, meanwhile, tends strongly in the very same direction. Though as a group Transnationalists may draw back from the collectivist political implications of the Internationalist agenda, the supranational corporate and entrepreneurial globalists are well along in the early stages of their own program for the direction of human affairs. And because they aim at the same kind of homogenization and share the same fundamental ideology, the Transnationalists are happy enough to benefit by a treaty here, an alliance there, a regional or bloc association among nations now and again.

Transnationalists certainly don't intend to end up with governmental bureaucracies to answer to, however. They prefer the end product to be more in the nature of private, nongovernmental systems of global regulation of trade, finance and industry, systems already well enough along, as Bill Moyers discovered to his innocent surprise, that they can dictate the day-by-day flow of capital and goods throughout the world. These are systems already well enough along to affect education and cultural habits on a wide if not yet universal scale, systems that are not subject— in such important ways as treaties and other government arrangements are—to the ebb and flow of political, moral or ethical consensus.

For John Paul, therefore, there is very little to choose between these two groups. Were one to prevail over the other—or were they simply to continue their present de facto cooperation—the consequences would be very similar.

In both cases, the goal is global interdependence among all nations. To make interdependence a true and working reality, the homogenization already under way in our lives must progress and deepen. And to achieve further homogenization, further severe—in some cases, total— modifications will have to be introduced into the way every nation presently governs itself, and interacts with the world.

In either the Internationalist scenario or that of the Transnationalists, we will all by definition be subject to an increasing number of international bodies created to administer our global welfare. The future of the nations will be managed on a gridded and predictable global format.

In either scenario, the first and last order of the day, even in the conduct of national and local affairs, will be the globalist requirements of international balance. The good of each nation will depend on it.

Because political differences within and between nations tend to dislocate progress toward global balance, such differences will inexorably be diminished, and finally eliminated. The good of each nation will depend on it. That being the case, in the tradition exemplified by John McCloy and the Wise Men, global experts will come increasingly to the fore locally and nationally as well as internationally. The good of each nation will depend on their expertise.

Even in nations with a parliamentary system of government, the function of what we now see as the "loyal opposition" will become largely token. For such nations will be as reliant as all the others on the global grid of balance and protection. The good of every nation will depend on that balance and that protection.

The ultimate outlines of a globally interdependent world forged by means of global homogenization and regulation are not difficult for Pope John Paul to imagine. He foresees the outcome of such a process as one he would find repugnant, and as one that would be entirely at odds with the religious, moral and human values he is obligated as Pope to defend. Not altogether surprisingly, John Paul is not alone in his thinking. Indeed, perhaps the best summary of the outcome the Pope foresees was given by the late Paul M. Mazur, a man with professional credentials to rival those of any Internationalist.

A partner in the Wall Street firm of Lehman Brothers, and an economist-banker who was as familiar with the halls of Internationalist and Transnationalist power as John McCloy himself, Mazur saw the globalist dreams of his most powerful associates taking on an ever-darkening aspect. Over a decade ago, in 1979, in his book, *Unfinished Business*, Mazur foresaw that, as the system of interdependence among nations escalated in complexity, so the international bureaucracy required to control that system would escalate in scope and authority.

In Mazur's scenario, "finally the large number of governmental bureaus that will have their orbits in the atmosphere of our planet cannot be allowed the freedom to compete and collide with one another. So, in order to control the diverse bureaucracies required, a politburo will develop, and over this group organization there is likely to arise the final and single arbiter—the master of the order, the total dictator."

We who have never lived within such a tightly centralized and vast collectivist system as Mazur was describing—that he was all but predicting, in fact—cannot even imagine its details as they would affect our daily lives. But John Paul does not need to imagine those effects.

He does not need to use his imagination because he lived much of his life in the very heart of just such an ideologically based system. Further, he does not need to use his imagination because, as the man who now sits at the governing center of the universal, age-old and deeply experienced Roman Catholic Church—and at the center of the world's oldest chancery—John Paul is privy to the closest thing there is in practical terms to racial memory and wisdom. Besides, he has sources of knowledge and enlightenment denied to ordinary mortals. He is deeply aware of historical realities. And he is far more deeply aware of plans-in-the-making and of things to come than many a government or managerial body—newly born babes when compared to the Vatican in memory and experience—that is attempting to direct human affairs along the paths of evolutionary globalism.

And finally, Pope John Paul does not have to use his imagination, because the current thrust of international life itself persuades him that the scenario sketched by Paul Mazur is not beyond the capability and the cooperative efforts of the Internationalist and Transnationalist groups—however benign their intentions may be for the good of us all.

Certainly everybody would like to dismiss such a scenario as no more than hyperbole and speculation. John Paul himself would like nothing better. But by the admission of just about everybody concerned, the good of the nations already depends on what looks very much like a global economy; and Mazur's projection of one form that global economy could take must be considered in cold realism.

Ultimately, it becomes clear from the Pope's observations, analyses and projections that unless the sky falls, he expects not only that we will have a unified global economy, but that it will rest on something more than a true world trade zone. It will rest on carefully calibrated principles of homogenization, harmonization and balance among the nations. These principles are to be housed in a vast network of globally spread financial, industrial, commercial and cultural organizations, distinguished from one another but organized into a hierarchy of power according only to the magnitude of their operations.

All of the indicators point for John Paul to a system that finally could not tolerate any organization that would stand unremittingly against the most valued principles of that system itself. How much less, then, could such a system tolerate an organization that claims to be not merely independent of its control but endowed with the final word on the human worth of that globalist system itself. Indeed, by definition, such an organization would be regarded as the ultimate enemy of the system. And by definition, the Roman Catholic institution headed by Pope John Paul is precisely that organization.

Already and on many occasions, the Pope has made it clear that neither he nor his Church is going to be homogenized in those sectors of human life where he claims to have a unique and absolute mandate from Heaven. In all phases of education, in all aspects of moral behavior, and in all questions about the ultimate truths undergirding the life and death of every human being, this man claims for his papal persona the right, the privilege, the duty and the due authority to stand as judge. None of the present factors or future implications of the Internationalist-Transnationalist ideal are outside that claim or exempt from that judgment.

Any attempts to manage the world supply of food by curtailing human births through new techniques are within his purview to judge. All plans to rid education of any genuine religious and moral content, or to substitute a rational ethic for what he considers to be the ethical laws revealed by God, he will reject and oppose.

Moreover, he will do all of this following norms he insists are revealed by God to him as God's vicar on earth, norms confided to his principal care—and, if necessary, to his sole and supreme diktat.

There is no doubt in John Paul's mind that the Internationalist-Transnationalist groups are Genuine Globalists, who must be considered on a different level from their Provincial and Piggyback counterparts. For if the general Internationalist-Transnationalist program were to be followed at least by the United States, a once-more-united Germany, and Japan, as the principal economic and financial powers among the nations today—and were those three to make no concessions to regionalism or to exclusivist nationalism or to rabid protectionism—then John Paul would envision more than merely another contender in the globalist arena.

He would envision a third genuinely geopolitical competitor in the world by the end of the second millennium. A competitor aiming at the creation of a mentality common to millions of human beings all over the globe, and at a managerial system able to assert itself as the prime factor that will condition and direct the form of the new society of nations—the global village. No doubt exists in John Paul's mind that by such a time there will be a fourth and redoubtable competitor, mainland China in the grip of the CP of China.

John Paul's rockbound certitude—deriving from his Catholic faith and from his personal endowment as the sole vicar of God among men—is that any human effort that is not ultimately based on the moral and religious teachings of Christ must ultimately fail.

The question, therefore, is whether the rare sound of the genuinely geopolitical footstep is to be heard in the globalist situation rooms of the Internationalist and Transnationalist groups. The question to be addressed is whether those two groups can create for themselves a position that will place them in direct contention—contention of the ultimate kind—with the revitalized form of Leninist Marxism introduced by Mikhail Gorbachev, and with Pope John Paul's own beleaguered Roman Catholicism. There will be no genuine geopolitical contention between Gorbachevism and the Chinese Leninists—only a jockeying for pride of place in the ultimate victory parade of Marxism.

Finally, the question at the back of all the others is whether other geopolitical events not remotely contemplated by Internationalists and Transnationalists, Soviet or Chinese Marxists, will come upon the society of nations before even such powerful globalists as these have time to create the brave new world of technocrat and economist and financial manager.

Part Five

Shifting Ground

18. Forces of the "New Order": Secularism

In the arena of the millennium endgame, John Paul II and Mikhail Gorbachev may be crowded around with ambitious globalists. But in the Pontiff's geopolitical reckoning, there are chiefly four regions in which the near-future society of nations will be fashioned: the United States, the Soviet Union, mainland China and Western Europe.

Within the populations of each of those regions, specific major forces are at work. And from the accelerating interplay of those forces, from region to region and back again, will come all of the main developments affecting the papacy embodied by John Paul, all of the developments affecting therefore the spiritual salvation he claims to represent for all mankind.

If Pope John Paul's consideration of the future involves such sweeping terms as "regions" and "forces," it is not because of any papal indifference to single individuals—to their conditions of life, their needs, their rights, their hopes. The opposite is true, in fact. John Paul thinks and talks about regions, and about forces at work therein, on the same principle that stands behind his insistence that there are "sinful structures" underlying the rich man/poor man and the beggarman/thief relationships between the nations.

In other words, such terms signify realities for John Paul. They signify the very men, women and children he has seen all around the world, who are acting observably in a common manner. When he speaks of forces at work in regions, those terms embody the lives of individuals who behave in a concerted way, develop along common lines, move in the same general direction; and who do so now almost exclusively for economic, financial, political or demographic reasons, or for a combination of those reasons.

Like it or not, Pope John Paul has found that on the geopolitical level, there is no other way to encompass the huge flow of concrete circumstances that now affect our practical world and his Church within that world. There is no other way he can come to overall and practical policy judgments on the truly geopolitical plane.

And therefore there is no way to set out John Paul's point of view, to glimpse what he faces in the millennium endgame, or to explain his policy judgments, other than to understand the way he sees those four principal regions of the world and the forces that now operate throughout each of them.

John Paul's summary assessment of the regions involved has, in one sense, the smoothness of a mathematical equation. Because he has no ax to grind politically, economically or financially, the high emotions that generally surround those issues for other leaders are absent for him. But there is one constant in the Pope's equation, one all-important coefficient he prefixes to his assessment of these regional forces; and he does this with a certainty that is in itself beyond the reach of common emotions and the most lucid reasoning any man or group of men can perform.

In John Paul's perspective, those forces emanating from among the nations appear as the molding influences, the impersonal architects building a new structure to house the society of nations. John Paul knows: Whatever is being wrought by those forces has been already—and even before they set to work—assumed within a framework of salvation in the all-encompassing mind and the irresistible intention of God.

That factor, according to John Paul, stands prior to all human activity; and it will be the final determinant of how effective the human activity of men will be. It is not a surprising factor in a Roman Catholic pope. But it must be clearly understood.

It is not a vague and general belief that, no matter what men do, no matter what type of structure is put together by those human forces, God will go ahead and do what God wants. Believers often think and speak— and nonbelievers just as often understand believers like John Paul to be carrying on—as if God were the Ultimate Handyman called in by the Despairing Householder who, in his stupidity and cockiness, thought he could mend that leak in the roof but has ended up floating around his own house, now invaded by the destructive waters of a deluge. This is God as the Fixer of Bad Deals, the Lone Ranger reversing what looked like death and disaster, the Last-Resort Hero. But such is not the God of John Paul.

Nor must John Paul's persuasion be framed within the Tower of Babel scenario. Men decide to build the tower of their geopolitical dreams. Of course, it is all wrong, inspired by arrogance, reared by pride, a real challenge to God, an affront God cannot and will not suffer. So God, at the crucial moment, just as it seems men will succeed in their godless undertaking, will step in and by a unilateral action frustrate all they do, confound their plans, destroy their miserable efforts and scatter them as pygmies under the iron heels of infinitely superior strength. This is not how John Paul conceives the plan and intentions of the God he worships and serves. For he worships and trusts in a God of salvation who so loved the world and all men in it that God's own son died so that all men might live forever.

Whether anyone shares or repudiates John Paul's prime conviction, they must understand that conviction and the knowledge on which it is based. It is simply this: All that men under the impulse of these regional forces achieve—in the gross and in the smallest detail—has been foreseen and incorporated as working parts in God's plan of salvation. Not in spite of men's actions and achievements, but through them, God's ultimate will prevails.

Right enough, in John Paul's outlook about the present workings of men, there is one largely unnoticed element: his conviction that in our actual geopolitical situation, there will be—in John Paul's lifetime—a direct intervention by God in those four regions of the world, with Russia as its focal point and all other regions of man's earth profoundly affected by that focused intervention. But it will not be a Tower of Babel intervention, nor anything like a parting of the Red Sea waters to allow merely the Elect to escape terrible destruction. For John Paul's is a God of love, indeed, is Love itself at work. Intervention there will be. Apocalypse— clear revelation of how ultimate good and consummate evil are irreconcilable—there will be. But now and throughout all regional developments, that Love is working assiduously in order to bring the ongoing drama of human things to God's foregone conclusion.

For those who do not understand John Paul's vision and do not know his conviction, logically the general observations he makes about all four regions and the forces at work within them may be disconcerting—especially for those who are partisans of one or another of those forces. For in every case, the change John Paul emphasizes is fundamental. In some cases, there are changes he regards as catastrophic in their present effects on the lives of ordinary men, women and children.

In general terms, within the nations of all four regions, let it be said of

John Paul's observation that all the old truths that reigned supreme are being changed. In some cases, they are being liquidated. And all the old symbols—that common shorthand by which whole populations express and share those truths—are being changed and liquidated, too.

If ever there was a nation that lived by such shorthand symbols, it was the United States.

In America, military strength was a fact; but it was more. It was a symbol of power once unique to that country. But that power has now been distributed among others. In America, man-made democracy was a fact, but it was more. It was the ideal for freedomless people elsewhere. But democracy in the United States is undergoing huge strains. In city halls and statehouses, in the Capitol and the White House, and in all three branches of government—executive, legislative and judicial—re-alignments are being forced that are too profound to pass off as just another little shift in the system of checks and balances.

In America, the once self-perpetuating, independent economy was a fact, but it was more. It was the symbol of ultimate protection for those who were lucky enough to live there. But now the American economy depends seriously, even avidly, on the economy of the world around it; and the lives and fortunes of the people who live there depend on what happens in the lives and fortunes of over two dozen other nations. The American Bald Eagle is still the national symbol for high-soaring strength and pride and independent daring. But it is no longer the symbol of uniquely preeminent superpower strength. Pride and daring are not even cultivated as national virtues. One has been besmirched as "imperialistic," the other has been lampooned as inept. The propaganda of "blame America" has played its part in this. But chiefly this change is due to the new fact that the undertakings of America are no longer those of a "nation under God." The public consensus is that a wall forbids Americans to think and act as a "nation under God." But it was that original persuasion that instilled the pride and encouraged the daring.

In the Soviet Union, three symbols reigned supreme. Instead of the Eagle, they had the Russian Bear of incalculable menace. Instead of man-made democracy, they had the man-made Party-State, housed in the Kremlin and dominating all the Russias (and much more besides) from Red Square, Moscow. And with no parallel anywhere, they had the vast stretches of winter snows that were the ultimate guarantee that

Mother Russia could never successfully be invaded—not by Napoleon Bonaparte, who skulked back to France with barely 10,000 ragged survivors out of an invading force of 400,000; and not by Adolf Hitler, who lost three entire armies to those Russian snows. Not by anyone, went the Russian saying. Mother Russia was impregnable.

Now, by contrast, the West has to deal with what appears to be a very friendly, unthreatening teddy bear, who wants to eat our food and be like us. It appears that the professionally subversive Party-State has renounced all wishes to subvert democracy; it actually wants to democratize itself as far as possible. And were the Russian snows to drift even higher and even into summer, they would not affect the invisible invaders that penetrate everywhere and are welcomed everywhere as the new global information and communications networks fall across this region.

In China, too, there was a time not long ago when three symbols spoke everywhere of that nation that is a vast region in itself. These were symbols of its leaders and its people, of its inner strength and of its outward threat.

The Dragon was China's fierce and vengeful exterminating angel; it was the incalculable protector of China as the center of the world, the "Middle Kingdom"; and it symbolized the role of the ultimate dictator of China's fate. The man-made Great Wall told the world that China was separate, self-contained, a place that could not and would not be assimilated into the rest of the world. The long, winding Yellow River mirrored it its ever-flowing waters the perpetuity of the Chinese identity itself. Foreign devils come and go, that river had always said, but China goes on forever.

These days, the Dragon has been transformed into another reality: the diminutive figure of Deng Xiaoping heading the CP of China from behind the guarded walls of Zhongnanhai Compound, where China's emperors once lived and from where he and the dyed-in-the-wool members of the CP intend to maintain control through the classical means of Leninist terror.

Like the Russian snows, the Great Wall is no longer a barrier to information and ideas, or to jet planes and missiles. So weak is that barrier as a symbol now that, just as in an old Chinese legend the tears of Meng Jiangnui washed away that part of the Wall where she found her dead lover, so the tears of hope and suffering shed by China's people can threaten to sweep aside all that Wall has stood for.

As to the Yellow River, it does still flow as surely as it always has. But

for the Chinese mind today, its symbolism has been shunted rudely aside
by its practical function. Now it is the key to the flow of goods and
services required to satisfy the new capitalist desire among the people.
And those who talk about its color breathe not a word about the perpetuity mirrored in its yellow waters. Instead, they see riverine industrialization, on which China's near future will depend; and they see pollution.

As profound as the changes are in those first three of John Paul's crucial
regions, it is in Western Europe that he sees the deepest change and the
source of the greatest pathos in terms of human destiny. Long before the
symbols of identity lost their meaning for the United States, the Soviet
Union and China, Europe freely cast away the institutions that housed
the symbols of the only identity that region ever achieved as a unit.

Europe never relied on the natural protection of snows, or on the
man-made defense of a 1,500-mile wall, or on a river as the symbol of its
continuity.

During the centuries when European unity was at its height and vibrant, Europeans housed their hopes and found their believing trust
beneath the domes and Gothic spires of the churches they built. They
called that whole territory by a kind of family name: Christendom; and
in the span of just a hundred years—between 1170 and 1270 alone—they
built eighty cathedrals and major churches, the living symbols of the
reality in their lives: the Catholic faith.

Europe's protection was centered on its faith. Its identity was provided
in the papacy. The unifying principle of its civilization lay in its common
acknowledgment of the primacy of the Pope.

That Christendom has ceased to exist. The faith that was once Europe's protection is now dead in those nations. And the papacy is no
more a symbol of their identity than the primacy of the Pope is their
preoccupation or concern.

While it is true that Christianity is no longer understood as a force to
be reckoned with in Europe of the 1990s, it is just as true that Pope John
Paul displays no pointless insistence that it should be. This is one of the
mystifying traits of his papal policy. In a 1988 address startling to some
for its frankness, John Paul told a visiting group of European delegates
and students that they did not have to build their new Europe of 1992
and beyond on Roman Catholic principles. He did raise the caution that
they should not forget Europe's traditions of civilization and culture.
And while the Pontiff knows that was a far cry from standing in their
midst as the living symbol of that civilization and that culture, such was
not for a moment his intent.

· · ·

One fact of geopolitical life John Paul must deal with is that the disappearance of the forces that, until recently, dominated in these four major
regions has not resulted in a neutral situation for any of them. And
certainly not for the Pope.

In the United States and Europe—in all the market economies of the
West nations, in fact—Pope John Paul sees one mentality, a single persuasion. In its broadest lines, he sees the same mentality reflected in the
words and actions of Poles and Hungarians, Romanians, East Germans,
Czechoslovaks and Bulgarians—and, not surprisingly, of the Soviets
themselves—as they grapple with the newfound liberties Gorbachevism
has so far proffered to them. He detected the same persuasion in the
student protests of 1989 in Beijing's Tiananmen Square; and it obviously
stood behind the policies of Beijing's central government. It is, finally, a
persuasion that has always been shared by several of the aspiring globalist
groups that have the Pope's attention—by New Agers, Mega-Religionists
and Humanists, to be sure; and in most concrete terms by Internationalists and Transnationalists.

So common is this persuasion, in other words, that John Paul identifies
it as one principal force molding the society of nations today. There are
a lot of arguments about this force, but no single name for it has been
agreed upon. Those who exalt this mentality and defend its qualities
against all comers give it such general names as "secularism," or "realism," or "hard-headed practicality." Critics refer to it by another set of
names. "Materialism," "secularism" and "this-worldliness" are used frequently. Those who condemn this persuasion outright see it as "neo-
paganism," "godlessness," "apostasy," and even as "Satanism."

By whatever name it may be defended or attacked, there is very little
difficulty in recognizing this force—the power of this persuasion—as an
operating influence in individuals and in corporate groups. And there is
no difficulty, either, in identifying the obvious preferences and phobias
that are the constant companions of those who are guided by this mentality.

If there were a motto for this point of view, it would be something like
"Let experience be your guide." Your only guide.

Those who live by this motto—or, in any case, by its meaning—display
a constant and fundamental preference in every area for the experience
of living. In the practical business of daily life, in the grind or excitement
of daily work and in the daily dream and quest for prosperity, concrete
experience is acknowledged to be superior to any principle or rule that
might come by any other means—no matter what the source. That is

about as far as preferences extend. Experience is about *it*. Phobias, on
the other hand, are around every corner.

The primary phobia is for all principles and rules that come from any
source outside one's own experience. It is a rule of experience itself, in
fact, that one must refuse to be guided by any rule or any principle one
hasn't seen demonstrated with one's own eyes, and preferably in one's
own life. "What goes around comes around" is all right as a principle, for
example. Every person and every group over the age of three has seen
that one work in terms of experience, and it has practical applications.

But a rule or principle such as "Seek first the Kingdom of God" or
"What does it profit a man to gain the whole world and lose his own
soul?" is not hardheaded and practical. In fact, anyone of this persuasion
will tell you that such rules and principles are "abstract" and "impractical." The few who still speak in philosophical terms condemn such rules
and principles as "aprioristic."

For people—individuals, groups and nations—who share this persuasion, the judgment of what is true depends, as everything does, on their
own experience. How they must act in order to be "morally good" in
their own eyes, and in order to be successful in the business of living,
cannot be deduced from "abstract" principles. And it cannot be announced by pope or prophet, priest or philosopher. It can only be concluded by individual or common—but always concrete—experience.

At its highest reach, this supreme deference to experience means that,
in and of itself, only mankind has the ability to avoid defeat and despair.
In and of itself, only mankind has the ability to create salvation, right
here. And, if that brand of salvation isn't the Paradise of the Bible, or the
Heaven of Christians, it does hold the promise of greater or lesser relief
from pain and want. In fact, it holds the promise of material circumstances as favorable as can be fashioned.

Given such a reigning phobia for absolute rule and principles, and
given the companion phobia for any authority proclaiming absolute rules
and principles, it must be clear that secularists do not defer to the Bible
of Christians or Jews, or to the Koran of Islam. But they don't rely on
personal whim either. Unpredictable happenstance does not govern secularist behavior. Accumulated experience does that.

The accumulated experience of a nation is to be found in its national
documents, in its national story, in its folklore and in its traditions. All
of that, working in combination with presently lived experience, provides
a set of lessons and practical values for the members of each nation and
for each nation as a whole.

Within that setting, organized religion may well have a valuable function, provided that none of the moral precepts or doctrines of organized religion be insisted upon as the absolute rules and principles that must govern human behavior. Indeed, in order to be a useful element in preserving what secularists call the "soul" of a nation, religion must join art and literature in adjusting to the concrete level of experience.

Thus, Humanist Schuyler G. Chapin can safely speak of the arts as "vital to sustaining our national existence," despite our "present greed-oriented, anti-intellectual society" in America. But no good secularist would say the same of organized religion as long as it insists upon its absolute rules and principles, and upon its recourse to absolute authority —even if that authority is God's.

Historian Arthur Schlesinger put organized religion neatly in its place within the secularist scheme of things. Americans must save themselves, Schlesinger wrote, "at whatever risk of heresy or blasphemy . . . sustained by our history and traditions"; for "the American mind is by nature and tradition skeptical, irreverent, pluralistic and rationalistic . . . relativism is the American way."

It is typical of our age of global communications that the most accurate, and the most poignant, description and praise of the secularist phobia for religion and religious authority has come out of China. Astrophysicist Fang Lizhi, born and bred in the long day of Mao Zedong's rule, came to international notice during President Bush's 1988 visit to mainland China, when it was widely broadcast that the President had included Fang on his list of honored dinner invitees and the Chinese authorities had excluded him from that honor. A known dissident in Communist China, Fang saw the handwriting on the wall and soon took refuge in the American Embassy in Beijing, where he remained until the summer of 1990. He now resides in England.

The year before, in 1987, Fang wrote a canticle to the highest ideals of secularism. Man, he said in that work, is not made to be under the control of "overbearing power." Man has within him his own power, "the moral law within." Governed by that power alone, man must take to science as the only path worthy of his dignity. As one would expect, Communism and its absolutes fare no better than religion under the pen of Fang Lizhi. "Science has only disdain and disgust for the curses by totems, for the barbarities, the addiction to lies, and the worship of the nonexistent—all such constitute the bulwarks of political dictatorship." In Fang's mind, the "nonexistent" lumps the ideology of Marxists and the faith of believers in one heap of contemptible things.

In words that recall the earliest paeans of secularist praise uttered over two hundred years ago by France's Denis Diderot—he and his fellow *encyclopédistes* were the theorists and founders of modern secularism—Fang observed that "what brings man happiness and freedom is first of all wisdom, a wisdom that manifests reason and sobriety. . . . It is not cries of ignorance and benightedness, nor, even less, threats of bloodshed against freedom." With such wisdom, man can overcome all suffering and hardship. Man has it within himself and his natural powers to re-create his universe.

Pope John Paul has made it clear how important he regards secularism to be as a major regional force. It cannot be treated lightly, nor be expected to go away, nor written off as a philosophic debate of interest only to academicians, professional clerics and religious fanatics. For John Paul, secularism is a spreading disease of the modern world. And, as surely as medical sleuths trace an epidemic to its source, so secularism finds its birth to have taken place in that period of European history called the Enlightenment—a name chosen by the budding secularists of the age.

The sudden and exciting burst of scientific inquiry during the 1700s—the fundamental breakthroughs in knowledge of the physical universe, and the birth of new scientific methods—produced a mentality that rejected all the absolutes formerly presented by religion and religious revelation. Instead, the new thinkers latched onto experience as the source of knowledge and betterment for mankind. That, they said, was the only viable way for mankind.

From that Enlightenment were born the "certainties" on which all modern political and social systems in the West have been based—not excepting political Marxism. Westerners have brandished and still brandish human freedom and human rationality as the sole and sufficient creators of all the good man seeks in his historical endeavors: economic prosperity, peace and order among nations, scientific progress, technological breakthroughs, artistic flowering, literary excellence. On the sole basis of self-confidence, man—according to the secularism of the Enlightenment—can achieve all of that good. Mankind can be good morally.

A very strange and disturbing voice broke in on this roseate projection in the nineteenth century. It belonged to that twisted and perverse German, Friedrich Nietzsche (1844–1900), and announced damningly: "Men cannot be good without God." Then, lest men be tempted to agree and to seek out God again, Nietzsche added with his madman's laugh: "But of course, God is dead!"

Nietzsche's warning that men cannot be good without God fell on deaf ears; and his mocking assurance that God was dead was taken to mean that the notion of God preached by traditional Christianity had proved to be a fabrication of superstitious and ignorant minds. Instead, following the secularist line, the existence of God was affirmed. But it was either of God pushed so far distant from man as to be inaccessible, unfathomable, unattainable; of God stripped of his fatherhood of all men, of his loving salvation of all men and his infinite desire to be with men and have his glory glimpsed in perceptible beauty and thinkable truth; or it was God—as Mega-Religionists and New Agers configure him to be—completely identified with mankind and this human cosmos, God not only in this cosmos but God as this cosmos, God as each one of us, God as all of us cemented together in humanness.

So complete is the secularist distortion of God's image, and so completely does it leave man to his own devices, that it constitutes a subtle and cunning blasphemy and sacrilege. Within the seemingly noble and heroic secularist act of going it alone, Pope John Paul hears an echo of the perennially evil cry of that first and most ancient blasphemer: "I will not serve."

In concentrating on secularism as a major regional force in the world, John Paul focuses particular attention on the West. And he finds a radical but constantly narrowing difference between Europe and the United States.

In most European countries, secularism has already triumphed completely. In that region, organized religions—Catholic, Protestant and Jewish—are regarded as alike in their insistence on absolutes. They are considered to have little or nothing to contribute, therefore, to the current political, economic and cultural life of Western European countries.

John Paul is explicit about the condition of this "post-Christian" Europe. "There is a vacuum in Europe," he remarked to one journalist in the early summer of 1989, "but it is not a completely neutral vacuum, because certain forces move in this vacuum; above all, Western forces, which are linked to each other. One of those forces is the economy of the free market, the capitalist economy. The other force is modern science, dominated despite everything by the natural sciences, colored with positivism." And, the Pope concluded, "If one considers all these elements, it is easy to understand why this vacuum is not very adapted, very open and available, to be filled with Christian contents."

In John Paul's outlook, there is no possibility that Christendom as it once was will ever return to existence again—its faith expressed in the soaring spires of its cathedrals, its people kneeling beneath hooded domes to worship at the tabernacles of the divine Word made flesh. Certainly, religion and religious authority are no longer in serious contention within the national lives, economic considerations, educational structures or social engineering of the twelve countries gearing up for the much desired Europe of 1992+. Now that Mikhail Gorbachev has bid fair to have his ex-satellite nations as well as his own USSR associated with the twelve in Europe from the Atlantic to the Urals, the secularism of Western Europe is going to be reinforced.

The principles upon which Europeans are organizing themselves in all sectors of life are drawn exclusively from the icons of secularism, from the positive sciences and the lessons of experience.

Outside the American Embassy in Beijing, where Fang Lizhi has taken refuge, the selfsame secularism as he has proclaimed reigns supreme among the millions who belong to the Communist Party of China and the millions more who do not. For secularism is indeed a by-product of decadent Confucianism, and Confucianism has supplied the Chinese with a would-be ethical framework for well over a thousand years. There can be little doubt that the rioting students in Tiananmen Square in 1989 professed not only a rank secularism overgrown with the now noxious weeds of Marxism. They were insisting on *their* brand of Maoism and of secularism. The Chinese Party-State preferred its own brand. The students had to be liquidated—an old inflexible law of classical Leninism. An eerie parallel to the professed secularism of those students is provided us by some of the most influential of Eastern Europe's ex-Communists, now collaborating in the reconstruction of their Soviet-ravaged polities and economies. As the December 23, 1989, *Economist* noted, these "have been saying that Marx was just a well-intentioned stumble on the road that began in 30 A.D." (the purported year of Christ's crucifixion and, therefore, the beginning of human "liberation" from the sinful structures of capitalism).

Among what are commonly regarded as the major West nations, therefore, the United States is unique in this matter of secularism, insofar as a long-standing and bitter contention still burns between American secularists and certain groups within organized religion. The die has not been cast definitively one way or the other.

True to their ideals, the champions of secularism in the United States appeal to national history, and to a deeply felt patriotism of sorts, as witnesses to the rightness of their cause. They argue for secularism as the underpinning of democratic liberties, of basic human rights and of the personal integrity of each American. In the slippery slang of Arthur Schlesinger, Jr., secularism "is what America is all about." It is at the heart of what America means, he means.

Nevertheless, even such passionate and sweeping language does not paper over the crack that widens every year between two clearly distinct and opposing segments of the American population.

On one side stand the two thirds of America's current population of 250 million people who not only believe in religious absolutes and in some form of absolute authority based in religion, but who endeavor to organize their personal and corporate lives accordingly.

On the opposing side stands a singularly influential minority of Americans who hold as a dogma of life that secularism is as American as mom and apple pie. Solidly entrenched in the establishment—in faculties of universities and colleges, for example; in the print, radio and television networks; in associations such as the National Education Association (NEA); in state and federal government offices—this minority appears able to tip the official momentum of the nation in its favor. The preferred battleground of the secularist minority lies in important areas of religious interest: Issues such as abortion, contraception, homosexuality, pornography, euthanasia and school prayer have been carved out as key areas of contention.

Members of the majority complain that the constant movement of the United States toward secularism on these and other issues rests upon the positions of public influence of the secularist minority, and upon judicial decisions reached without consulting the views and wishes of the majority population. They point out that in the present "establishment" climate—secularist through and through—of the U.S.A., it is impossible to develop moral clarity, persuade Americans to undertake hard work and to save rather than spend their earnings, and persuade the body politic of America to nourish a genuine confidence in the United States and in the West.

What now shall be the foundations of political integrity and social justice? they ask. For economic stewardship based on today's sacrifice of wishes for tomorrow's promise? For social responsibility? Are all these to be defined in terms of U.S. nationalism? Of our consumerist ambitions? Of our science and our technology? Merely of "life, liberty and the pursuit of happiness"?

For a while among an influential class of American thinkers and politicians, the answers to those questions were sought in the political doctrine of John Calvin (1509–64). God was, according to Calvin, an utterly transcendent sovereign of the cosmos. All human life was corrupted by sin. Man's obligation was to undertake a faithful stewardship—economic, political, artistic—of this cosmos, thus transforming it. Americans of this inclination made a "transforming worldliness" their aim. It did not work, because, as Glenn Tinder wrote in 1989, "Politics is a realm of moral darkness, and the darkness cannot be dissipated by human virtue and wisdom."

For a while, yet another attempt was made to bolster the failing Enlightenment heritage. In a current of political theory started mainly by Karl Barth and furthered by such "Radical Reformers" as Jacques Ellul, it was proposed that, forever and a day, the true Christian will be at odds with the social and political structures of this world, while he awaits the arrival of the Kingdom of God in its fullness. He will function as witness or prophet, never allowing the others to forget that this is a world of sinfulness.

Both these currents, each one still alive to one degree or another, have proved themselves inept and helpless in the overwhelming tides of secularism that have been sweeping over U.S. society since the end of World War II. Both suffered from the bane of academic theorizing: They had no concrete religious expression readily accessible and attractive for the masses of Americans. Besides, the prophetic stance lacked politico-social clout; and political Calvinism underwent the corruption of politics in its effort to enter politics.

Neither these, nor the more well-known mainline American churches, nor the substantial Roman Catholic Church have been able to do much to impede the gradual but steady secularization of the American system. Yet it is impossible for John Paul to discount the possibility of a violent reaction in the rank and file of American believers. But, year after year, as secularization extends itself throughout America, the likelihood of such a reaction grows dimmer and dimmer.

It was instructive, but not surprising, in this regard for Pope John Paul to watch the performance of Mikhail Gorbachev on American soil in 1987. Supreme tactician that he is, Gorbachev obviously sees in the United States what John Paul sees. He managed to present himself, therefore, as a benign and affable secularist.

Speaking at the U.N. General Assembly in New York, in effect the Soviet leader stretched out his hand to say, "Look! I am not Lenin or Stalin or Khrushchev or Brezhnev. I am Mikhail Sergeyevich Gorbachev. I am a secularist, just like you hardheaded Americans. Let's shake hands and do some honest and profitable deals. May the best man win!" That appeal went right to the heart of the most powerful secularist-globalist contenders in the Western regions. And it was hardly lost on Pope John Paul—but for different reasons.

John Paul knew that a much different regional force lay behind the supple secularist mask of Mikhail Gorbachev. And he knew already, too, that the stunning surprises this canniest of Soviet leaders had in store for the world in the months to come made it imperative for him to command the stage in the West as a hero in the secularist tradition.

There are still many questions to answer about Mikhail Gorbachev; and it may be that Gorbachev himself cannot yet answer even some of the most important ones. But about his secularist stance there is no doubt in Pope John Paul's mind. The man behind the outstretched hand is a master of Antonio Gramsci's technique of cultural penetration. Following the edicts of Gramsci, he has clearly recognized the seductive value of secularism among democratic capitalists. As the direct heir to Lenin, and the first of his successors to abandon the Stalinist distortions of Leninism, Gorbachev has at last successfully presented Leninism to the West. And he has done so in respectable—not to say dazzling—secularist terms.

John Paul's moral appraisal of Gorbachev's style of secularism—what the Soviet leader calls his "new thinking"—rests on what the General Secretary himself outlined as the three dominant traits of that thinking: "the lessons of the past, the realities of the present, and the objective logic of world development."

Excluded totally from these traits is any tradition of reliance on the Creator of this world and the Savior of all men and women. The world as Mikhail Gorbachev thinks about it, at least for public consumption, is a world on its own. It is the world of the professional atheist and of the confirmed materialist. It is a world of bronze skies and dead earth, where man's gaze can find no infinite expanse to roam, and only the realm of endless matter to fascinate him. Let him look for no light from on high for the eyes of his soul, but only for the light that issues from gross matter.

The genius of Gorbachev is that, to a degree it is hard to exaggerate, he makes this view glitter for the secularized minds of Americans and Europeans. For such minds, Gorbachev has become the attendant angel of secularism, who beckons for them to reach as high as they themselves are willing to reach, with him as their guide.

He is their assurance that we are not condemned to suffer in the future from all those things that have plagued us in the past—from inequality, indignity, dire want of the necessities of life, gross and institutionalized injustice, early and ignominious death. He is their living guarantee that, together, we can reach to the very core of this earth, into every hidden place of this human cosmos. Together we can humanize it all.

We are not necessarily separate pygmy entities, dwarfed by the skies and stumbling on a darkened plain. For Gorbachev will show us how humankind's collective intellect can and will be accumulated within a new—a geopoliticized—form of the present United Nations. On that day of human history, man—the man each one of us is—will be made into a giant, standing as the center and focus of all our human activity as nations and as people. That is the beckoning height of Gorbachev's neo-Leninist reach.

Nor are we alone in this Atlas-like effort to carry the universe on our shoulders. Gorbachev may be the chief attendant angel in this globalist effort. But he points to other angels we must all obey. He points to the objective processes that, unbidden by us, form global channels for history's progress. And he points to the iron logic of history itself. These processes of which Gorbachev speaks are made evident to us in various ways; and they do seem always to point to that iron logic of history he talks about.

As a simple example, the environment of our world is threatened. If that means we must stop using plastic and chlorofluorocarbons, then the iron logic of history demands that we must find better ways to pack our fast foods and dump our trash, and better ways of refrigeration, and better ways to dispense our deodorants. Similarly, our planet cannot support too great a population. If that means we must have fewer people, then the iron logic of history demands that we practice contraception, abortion and even euthanasia.

John Paul agrees with Mikhail Gorbachev's view that such global processes as these are every day gaining a new momentum, and that, in their very acceleration, they are affecting world politics. What better proof, says Gorbachev in substance, that we have only to follow the mute but clear indications of these objective processes? History's logic will then take over. By such means will we arrive at happiness and fullness of life.

What better proof, responds John Paul, that Gorbachev's "new thinking" is not simply the secularism of the West? It is not mysterious or angelic or seductive, either. And, above all, it is not new. It is dialectical materialism, the same dialectical materialism that has been a major force in the world since it was elaborated and adapted by Karl Marx as the rationale and justification for his godless ideology of Communism, and finally incorporated into the sociopolitical machinery of Leninist Internationalism.

Ours is not a philosophically enlightened age. Our forefathers would have recognized Gorbachev's dialectical materialism as readily as John Paul does. But presented as Gorbachev offers it today—as a seeming gift placed at the feet of the secularist West—Leninism can be accommodated as easily as any other humanistic ideal. For it passes the only acid test required: It makes no religious and no moral demands that secularists have not already consented to follow.

To use an expression common and congenial to secularists of the United States and Europe, the "human values" of Gorbachevism are no more and certainly no less than the "human values" vindicated by Humanists, Internationalists and Transnationalists in the capitalist West.

For John Paul, there is a basic human fallacy crippling the regnant secularism of the West and of Gorbachevism. The prevalent idea (erected into a principle nowadays) is that a wall is to be maintained at all costs—at the cost of liberty itself—between church and state, between religion and public life. The Wall—capitalized frequently in order to personify it as a legal entity much like America—is more sacred than motherhood and apple pie. But, the Pontiff argues, the idea that we can be related to the world and not related to God is as false as the idea that we can be related to God without being related to the world.

In other words, given every substantial and constitutionally guaranteed freedom and human justice, there is no concomitant guarantee that human life will not be morally vacuous, spiritually degraded and culturally vulgar. The values of freedom and liberty have to be guaranteed by higher values. You cannot practice a system of politics without the spirituality of religion any more than you can exercise a spirituality that is not political—even in a thoroughly humane and civilized society. "Once bread has been assured," Russia's religious philosopher Nicholas Berdyayev commented, "then God becomes a hard and inescapable reality, instead of an escape from harsh reality." For, as John Paul points out, it is not enough for the individuals of a public institution to practice godliness in private (prayer, adoration, good works, etc.); their institution as an institution must acknowledge God and institutionally explicate that godliness. Holiness is the aim, not only of individuals, but of human institutions. All this, of course, is rejected by the current secularism.

To give the United States and its imitator capitalist nations their due, John Paul readily points out that capitalism itself has generated a third power force, which is gaining momentum and favor among the nations. It is a force at least as seductive as Gorbachev's neo-Leninism, a force we know as the open-market economic system of the West nations.

"The creative drive of the people," President Bush told the Hungarian government in July of 1989, "once unleashed, will . . . bring you a greater treasure than simply the riches you create. It will give each one of you control over your own destiny—a Hungarian destiny!"

Just as Pope John Paul's words to his beloved Poles in 1979 echoed in all the nations of the Soviet empire, so the words of this Chief Executive of capitalist democracy echoed around the desolate capitals of the satellites in local variations. "A Polish destiny!" "A Czechoslovak destiny!" "A German destiny!" "A Bulgarian destiny!" "A Romanian destiny!"

Between 1979 and 1989, in fact, times and leadership had changed in the Soviet Union; and in the West, as well. And Mikhail Gorbachev had gone to the United Nations looking for a handshake and a deal. Now he had what he wanted. Following his own precepts of objective processes and the iron logic of history, Gorbachev had rejected classical Marxist economies. He had done so for one simple and nonideological reason. The closed-market economy of the Soviet Union and its satellites had long since failed. That economy had merely insulated the Party-State from the vibrant market forces in the rest of the world and forced the economies of the East nations into grinding inefficiency and regional impoverishment.

The objective process at work for Gorbachev, therefore, was and remains the urgent need to find solutions to his economic crisis. The iron logic of history impels him to develop a market system compatible with his own aims. A market system that is open—but, as he says, "socialist." A system that will be more "humane and more productive" than the failed Marxist-Leninist system. But it must be a system that will not— cannot, he insists—mean adoption of capitalist democracy. It will be "socialist."

It is obvious to John Paul that, as a geopolitical grand master, Gorbachev understood from the outset he would have to pay a price in order to sever his neo-Leninism as an ideology from the debunked economics of Leninist Marxism. It is also clear to the Pope that Gorbachev had calculated well in advance the top price he would be willing to pay.

The first installment of that price was the small change of bureaucratic reform essential to sweep away ineptitude, corruption and institutionalized inertia. The next installment was a little steeper. State planning would have to allow important inroads to private initiative—to personal ownership and private exploitation for profit.

The third installment was tougher still; for it had to be paid in that most guarded currency of the Party-State: political sovereignty within and outside the Soviet Union. Without local control in all of the caged but never-dead sovereignties of captive nations—Poland, Hungary, and all the rest—there would be no economic innovation, no industrial competition, no fruitful production. Without some "liberalization" of internal USSR politics, there would be no way out of old-line Stalinism.

In fact, as John Paul knows, Russian sovereignty itself is not excluded from Gorbachev's calculations. "Our Party," Gorbachev told the Nineteenth All-Union Conference of the CPSU on July 1, 1988, "should in every respect be a Leninist party not only in content but also in its methods." Those methods already included Lenin's original idea of a government rooted in "the people's approval," and in state authority accumulated on the basis of soviets—some variation, in other words, of Lenin's concept of people's councils.

Thus, when over 300,000 Soviet miners in the Ukrainian coalfields went on strike in July of 1989, Gorbachev declared himself "greatly inspired" because they were "taking things into their hands thoroughly." And indeed the miners received unspecified promises of profit sharing, industrial management and shipments of food, clothing and other scarce consumer goods. The miners even went so far as to ask that Gorbachev scrap Article Six of the Soviet Constitution, which establishes the CPSU as the "leading and guiding force" in Soviet society. Still, said Gorbachev, the negotiations were "demanding . . . but good and constructive." Sure enough, by February 1990, that sacred cow, Article Six of the Soviet Constitution, was apparently sacrificed at a contentious meeting of the Communist leadership in the Kremlin. The CPSU will not, it was decided, have the monopoly in Soviet political power.

But the moment did come when Gorbachev made clear to the world the price he would not be willing to pay. Neither the Soviet Union nor the Warsaw Pact nations would be transformed into capitalist democracies. He has gone out of his way, in fact, to warn that under no circumstances would that be included in his deals with the West or with anyone else. "This would be very dangerous," he has said, rattling the sabers of conflict again, "and would merely revive the enmities of a former time."

The reference was obviously to the Cold War, to the bitter forty-five years of contention between East and West. And it was aimed squarely at the political and entrepreneurial leaders of the West, who are intent on their tripod balancing act—and therefore on stability, peace and expansion of trade. Gorbachev may not be a born capitalist; but he clearly knows where the capitalist heart lies, and he seeks to establish a de facto convergence between his East and the West, made possible by as wide an application as possible of the West's techniques in economics and industry.

When John Paul thinks of that convergence, he is thinking of much more than a mere fit or working convenience, a mere matching of needs and abilities. For in all frankness, both capitalism and Leninism have serious problems for which one or the other has developed some solutions.

Capitalism in its current libertarian form makes individual freedom its driving force. Leninism makes government control the driving force, but such control has proved to be inept for economic and industrial development.

Capitalist countries have not been able to correct the inevitable maldistribution of goods and services, or the dislocations that freewheeling markets cause. Hence, they move toward government control through such "safety nets" as welfare and related social remedy measures, environmental regulation, education subsidies, housing subsidies and other easements.

Soviet Leninism has not been able to limit the damage done by total government control. Hence, Gorbachev must lead the USSR and its former satellites into a system that will harmonize the economic needs of the system and the professional Leninist aim of the system.

There are more than a few such headings under which a deficiency on one side has been met by a solution—acceptable or not—on the other side. But when John Paul thinks and talks about convergence, such are not in his mind. He is thinking of the logical convergence that does arise between the two because both reject any religious or "faith" basis for human aspirations and activity.

The weakness and vulnerability of the West is thus laid bare for John Paul. Basing their stand on no absolute rule of morality, acknowledging the dominion and will of no divine person as the reason for or against this decision or that condition, not asking for divine protection from errors, Western negotiators are now locking minds and wills with a man who wears a supple mask that makes him look like them and talk the language they use. Any mention by them of what in the West are called human values—the dignity of the individual, human rights, democratic freedoms—can be and has already been matched on Gorbachev's lips by soaring expressions matching all of theirs.

The suppleness of that mask affords him almost endless opportunities to overcome Western suspiciousness. Permitting the apparent "democratization" of the USSR's former satellites, allowing (almost) a thousand flowers of criticism and self-opinion to bloom in public in the Soviet Union, apparently withdrawing from Afghanistan, opening up Moscow to the golden arches of McDonald's—the list is endless—Gorbachev seems to be giving endless pledges of his good faith and his attachment to those "human values" the West touts as its very own norms of acceptable human morality. In the meanwhile, the Soviet president offers his Western counterparts the heady wine of fresh markets, banking and brokerage and joint venture possibilities, and an end to the yearly waste of dollars on the defensive and offensive shield of the West.

The secularist approach to human problems that is shared by both sides has placed them both in this precarious position. For what secularism kills off is the force of moral obligation to an authority believed and held to be outside the human conscience and to all human consciences, superior to the human conscience as such, and provided with sanctions to enforce the moral law or penalize its violation. Secularism allows of no such absolute. "One cannot but regret," John Paul stated quite trenchantly during his January 1990 annual state-of-the-world address to the Vatican diplomatic corps of 120 ambassadors to the Holy See, "the deliberate absence of every transcendental moral reference in governing the so-called developed societies." That one word "deliberate" evoked a momentary buzz of comments among the otherwise decorous body of diplomats. God and his moral law, John Paul was telling them bluntly, have been deliberately omitted from your councils of state.

There is, therefore, a spiritual blindness, a myopia in things of the spirit and of God—this is John Paul's conclusion. It gets worse, according to the Pontiff. For that profundity of blindness to the moral dimension of human life brings on, as a consequence, a darkening of the mind's clarity, so that the practical and highly important judgments Americans have to make when tangling with a Master Juggler of Gorbachev's skill will be off the mark, awry, and unbalanced by unimportant elements. The February 1990 marriage of Susan Eisenhower, granddaughter of Dwight D. Eisenhower, to Roald Sagdeyev, adviser to Mikhail Gorbachev, evoked in millions the conviction that "the Cold War is really over." Maureen Dowd, reporting the day's events in Moscow on February 7, 1990, when the Kremlin Politburo decided to relax its monopoly on Soviet political power, wrote in *The New York Times* that in Washington that day, "some people were thunderstruck. Others were numb, unable to absorb one more remarkable blow to Communism. . . . So today the reaction was mostly muted wonder at the events in Moscow."

Unknowingly, Peggy Noonan, speechwriter for Ronald Reagan and President Bush, put her finger on the effect of that darkened perception of the American mind. "We may have exhausted our capacity for surprise and delight when we watched children in Tiananmen Square quoting Jefferson and children in East Berlin taking pick-axes to the Berlin Wall as East German guards smiled for the camera."

Neither surprise nor delight is required by those who have to do with Gorbachev and Gorbachevism. On the other hand, those emotions are the logical reactions of people who have become eyeless in the Gaza of Mikhail Gorbachev. And the danger is that once the passing delight and surprise are over, when cold reality sets in, the spiritual blindness and the chains of this moral prison holding down the human spirit will finally become too much. Men may well be tempted to shake and topple the very pillars of their material and earthly confinement and thus perish, unless a loving Father of all creatures still loves man so much that he will not abandon man in his self-made secularist prison and the darkness of his own unaided mind.

"All has been foreseen by God," John Paul comments. "The Father of all of us has arranged human affairs so that they end with man being saved from himself." For today men do need such a saving. "The growing secularism tends to obscure more and more and ultimately to negate man's natural creaturely values . . . which God's redemptive plan recognizes and empowers." Without those values, human society would disintegrate.

19. Forces of the "New Order": The Two Models of a Geopolitical House

In the shifting ground of human affairs today, the most surprising new contours are provided by two leaders, John Paul II and Mikhail Gorbachev. Gorbachev appears as the active agent of changes to which the West is reacting, while John Paul II gives all the impression of one who, not in mere reaction, is riding herd over these active and reactive partic-ipants. Why these two leaders should be able to exercise these key func-tions is a source of puzzlement to those who are not aware of the two men's importance; and to those who sometimes fail to appraise correctly and appreciate the reason for their prominence.

These two men are the only two among world leaders who not only head geopolitical institutions but have geopolitical aims. Geopolitics is their business. Now, the precise nature of the shift in world affairs is geopolitical. Alone among leaders, these two men have firsthand ac-quaintance with the geopolitical. But for the vast majority of onlookers and for many in government, geopolitics is merely a way of speaking about the mutual relationship of different systems of politics. Thus, the gargantuan change being effected in the shifting ground escapes them.

The term "geopolitics" is a relatively recent invention. It is composed of two Greek words, meaning "earth" and "political system," which the ancient Greeks never combined.

Those Greeks were very aware of the relations between different states and nations, each with its own political system, each being what the Greeks called a *politeia*. They saw all of these as constituting a loosely connected arrangement of differing political entities. Whether the rela-tionships between them were based on peaceful trading or on signed alliances and associations, or on subjugation and imperial domination, the Greeks' fundamental notion of internationalism was that it involved different politically structured systems. One state, one *politeia*, might dominate several others. Several states might group together in offensive and defensive alliances or in straight commercial and industrial partner-ship. But there never was a moment when the same political structure was accepted and established in what originally were politically different states. Nobody ever proposed that the same *politeia* be shared freely by the different states and nations.

This was the limited extent of their internationalism. Late in their history, some few individuals lauded and tried to practice the ideal of the *cosmopolitis*, the citizen of the world, the individual who felt "at home" in any and every one of the political systems of the day. But this was seen as an individual whimsy, a romantic and somewhat exotic experi-ence, not as a desirable condition of mankind in general, and certainly not as embodying a political ideal to be striven for. They never even conceived of a *cosmopoliteia*. They never conjoined a word for "earth" or "world" with the word for "political system."

Until the end of the nineteenth century and the beginning of the twentieth, this internationalism provided the only framework within which relationships between different nations and states were considered.

Sometime in the nineteenth century, the term "geopolitics" was coined by non-Greeks. By then, the constituent elements—states and nations—of internationalism had changed. For one thing, men could now speak of the whole of earth, the whole world, and all nations in it. Exploration had covered the face of the globe. For another, enormous commercial empires—British, French, Ottoman, Austrian, German, Dutch, Russian, Chinese—and some minor ones—Spanish, Portuguese, Italian, Japanese—dominated the world scene, cornering the raw power of earth's resources and the financial hegemony derived therefrom. The United States, neither a minor power nor a commercial empire in that society of nations, was still in the last stages of its own formation. Not until Woodrow Wilson boarded the *George Washington* for post–World War I Europe did the United States begin to flex genuinely internationalist muscles.

In this world situation, there had been born a certain homogeneity and overall standardization among nations and states. Internation relationships were more complex than ever before. Writers, thinkers and politicians, as well as bankers and economists, did think of that world as a loosely coagulated system of states regulated in their mutual relationships by some very generalized and generally observed rules of conduct. For a minute number of the very privileged classes, there was indeed a more developed form of the old Greek cosmopolitanism, but it remained an exoticism.

When the term "geopolitics" was used in reference to that world system, it implied the complex of relationships between all those world-spanning national interests and the "games" nations played, *Kriegspiel* and *Staatspiel*, the maintenance of peace and the conduct of statecraft in peacetime. Their peacetime was always defined in terms of an enemy. War was merely the conduct of statecraft and diplomacy in a more forthright way with that enemy. As the French cynically put it: *Plus ça change, plus c'est la même chose.*

Because the monopolies in trade and finance as well as military might rested in the hands of the Great Powers, "geopolitics" was also used to include the relationships between all minor and major powers. That network of relationships—reproducing the internationalism of the ancient Greeks in a more sophisticated and definitely worldwide ambit—was built and maintained with one end in view: the balance of power between the Greats, and between their allies among the Minors. The clashes, economic, cultural, military, between the members of that international society concerned the pride of placement, and hegemony either in one part of the globe—Great Britain in Europe, Turkey in the Middle East—or internationally, say, in overall financial clout or naval supremacy on the seven seas.

Fundamentally, nothing had really changed since the Greeks. Internationalism had as its basic unit the individual *politeia* rooted in a particular state or nation, whether that was imperial Britain, republican France, democratic America or tiny protectorates like Sierra Leone or Sarawak. In a genuine, if limited, sense, the whole could be described as geopolitical; the word included all the political systems all over the earth.

Along that road of twenty-five centuries from the Greeks to modern times, there had been only two instances when the thought and concrete goals of some men went beyond this notion and practice of internationalism and approached the point where the reality of "earth" and "one political system" could be conjoined in one word.

The first in time was clearly enunciated and targeted as goal and ideal by a group of men and women who started off in the twilight of Greek civilization as the ragtag association of fishermen, servants, slaves, small merchants, dirt farmers, artisans and laborers—Jews and non-Jews—whom their enemies derisively called "Christians." That name stuck. In the first days of their existence in and around Jerusalem, their self-description was of "one community with one heart and one soul, and holding all possessions in common."

One of their earliest leaders in the first century of this first millennium, Paul of Tarsus, scrutinized the microcosm of nationalities and kingdoms, religions and cultures around him, and formulated the Christian refinement of the then regnant internationalism. He used his usual brilliant eloquence in doing this, but necessarily in terms of what he knew in his day as the society of nations. And, although the farthest west he personally ever reached was Spain, the farthest east and north was Greece and Turkey, the farthest south was Arabia, he spoke for all nations and peoples of the human race.

"You must now realize," he wrote to the inhabitants of Colossae, a town located in what is now the Denizli province of western Turkey, "that you have become new men on account of the enlightenment you now have about your Creator and his preferred world, in which there is to be no distinction between Jew and non-Jew, Jewish Christian and

Gentile Christian, fellow citizen and foreigner, known and unknown people, slave and freeman. For, now, Christ is all of us, and Christ is in all of us." Paul's inventory of differences and divisions that separated the people of his day into different and warring systems and groups finds exact parallels in our modern society of nations, states and peoples. According to Paul, all differences and divisions have been transcended by a new unity.

Nor was Paul speaking of a purely spiritual unity. He was laying down a blueprint for a new society of peoples and nations undivided by nationalism, racial origin, cultural diversity, wealth or poverty, political systems or religious hatred. Nor did he envisage the goal of that society of peoples to be a balance of power maintaining the equilibrium of greater and lesser. In his pregnant phrase, it is full-scale unity in Christ. A georeligion centered and dependent on Christ: This is what Paul presented as the underlying framework for the ideal internationalism. In his context, Paul could have justifiably used that hybrid word "geopolitics," for he was speaking of a *geopoliteia*, one truly geopolitical structure for all mankind as one race.

Paul, as often happened, was the intelligent and perceptive formulator of a doctrine that would be taught and propagated to all peoples and nations by another man, Peter the Great Fisherman, and by his successors over in Rome. Despite his obscurity and cruel death, Peter had been given the Keys of authority to teach all men and women, and to establish thus the *geopoliteia* Paul had announced as God's plan for all men. That authority was guaranteed by the blood Christ shed. Within the span of some three hundred years and the pontificates of thirty-two successors to Peter as Bishop of Rome and official holder of the Keys of this blood, the initial obscurity of the Holder's office had been shed; Peter's papacy now assumed an increasingly dominant role in the development of nations. The Pauline goal, the Christian *geopoliteia*, was the goal of that papacy.

It took that papacy and its institutional organization, the Roman Catholic Church, almost the whole of two thousand years to attain, in the concrete order, its status and condition of a georeligion. It took all that time and the ups and downs of 264 pontificates for the political philosophy and goals of that georeligion to be purified and purged of the cultural and civilizational accretions that along the road impeded the development of papal and Roman Catholic geopolitics.

At the close of two thousand years since Paul expressed the worldview of a genuine georeligion, the 263rd successor to the obscure Great Fisherman reigns and governs in Rome as the titular head of that georeligion housed in a genuinely geopolitical structure. For John Paul II is not only the spiritual head of a worldwide corpus of believers but also the chief executive of a sovereign state that is a recognized member of our late-twentieth-century society of states. With a political goal and structure? Yes, with a geopolitical goal and structure. For, in the final analysis, John Paul II as the claimant Vicar of Christ does claim to be the ultimate court of judgment on the society of states as a society.

One of the eye-opening factors enhancing John Paul II as a prime world leader has been precisely the striking appearance of a genuinely political capability on the part of his Holy See, hitherto—and for some hundreds of years—regarded as an institution that should exercise whatever influence it exercises exclusively in the strictly "religious" and "spiritual" spheres. A wall stood—or should stand—between "Church" and "State."

The Noriega interlude of late 1989 was the most recent eye-opener. U.S. Army authorities, the Bush administration, and the ten or fifteen Latin American governments involved in that Caribbean standoff emerged from its successful conclusion with a totally revamped concept of John Paul's Vatican. His Vatican men, clerics all of them, displayed not merely a detailed grasp of the issues clustered around the refugee Panamanian strongman, but a sophisticated approach to the diplomatic, military, governmental, and political problems that bristled around the Holy See's Panama City embassy. Whether in regard to Papal Nuncio Laboa, his two principal aides there, or the relevant officers in the Vatican's "Second Section" (for Relations with States)—Archbishop Angelo Sodano, the "foreign minister," Archbishop Edward Cassidy, Vice-Secretary of State, Monsignor Giacinto Berlocco, special emissary, or the other in-house experts—the evolution in everybody's concept of the Holy See was quite manifest. One of the chief military spokesmen, General Maxwell Thurman, on his first appearance before newsmen referred to Archbishop Laboa as "some sort of ambassador." But, in the heel of the hunt, when announcing Noriega's capitulation, the General referred deferentially and correctly to "Papal Nuncio Archbishop José Sebastian Laboa," whose "professionalism" the General praised.

"These men didn't go around sprinkling Holy Water and shaking Rosaries," one military aide commented. "Actually, they led us to a solution." In the end, all concerned—Panamanians in their fears and desire for vengeance, Latin American diplomats accustomed to the slippery slopes of compromise, the Americans bent on "Operation Just Cause"—uniformly agreed that John Paul's men never allowed the moral issue to be lost in the scuffle between Noriega's supporters, his Panamanian enemies, and the righteous wrath of the U.S. expeditionary force.

Nobody from all three groups even thought for a moment that John

Paul's Holy See "should have nothing to do with such purely secular and state matters," as one Paul Blanshard–style East Coast commentator remarked.

The second thrust at a concrete goal beyond and transcending mere internationalism came from the brain of the most outstanding fanatic and zealot and the greatest organizing genius in ten centuries: V. I. Lenin. Conceived in that twisted mind, born in the carnage and cruelty of the Marxist takeover of Czarist Russia, that second attempt became embodied in the greatest hybrid political creation of all world history: the Party-State of the USSR.

Never a nation in any accepted sense of the word, nor an empire as we have known empires to be, the USSR was put together in the form of a state but uniquely designed and built to vehicle the Leninist-Marxist political takeover of all other states on the waves of an expectedly world-wide proletarian revolution. That is a thoroughly geopolitical goal, housed in a designedly geopolitical structure. Lenin and his successors built that geopolitical structure. Housing no religion, it houses an ideology that undeniably is a geo-ideology.

What many in the West find difficult to separate is the facade of national identity—the USSR as a member nation in the society of nations—and the Party-State of Lenin's building and design that exists and operates behind it. It is a troika of the CPSU, the Red Army and the KGB. Its raison d'être and sole goal is not the well-being of the inhabitants of the USSR but the ideological aim of all loyal and genuine Leninist-Marxists: a Marxist geopolitical structure spanning all the nations and peoples of the globe.

The possession, the nurturing and the advancement of that geopolitical structure, in addition to the rather rare mentality it has engendered in the Soviets, constitute a first and important parallel between John Paul II and Mikhail Gorbachev. But the parallel goes further.

Not only are both of these men Slavs and both of them heads of the only models of geopolitical organization available for us when we examine the society of nations and states today in its trend to a new world order that must be something more than a merely Internationalist or even Transnationalist structure. Both of these powerful world leaders have chosen to gamble.

Papa Wojtyla decided very early on in his pontificate that the geopolitical should receive the burden of his attention and be the focus of his papal activity. He would hew out for himself a special place in world affairs, while tending to the shambles of his own institution in only a marginal fashion. He was and is gambling, not only on the durability of his Church—that it could survive the continually growing shambles—but on the objective he had chosen for his papacy—that he could play an integral part in the geopolitical formation of the society of nations.

Mikhail Gorbachev, for his part, has severely modified and adapted the Leninist Marxism of the USSR, no longer pursuing the strategy hallowed, as it were, by the two greatest figures in the seventy-three-year-old history of that Party-State, Lenin and Stalin; he has set out to mold the structure and goals of that Party-State to the form passionately recommended by Communism's greatest but unsung hero, the Sardinian Antonio Gramsci.

No Marxist theoretician ever analyzed the proper geopolitical stance and strategy of the Leninist-Marxist Party-State more intelligently than he had done. Gramsci unerringly laid his finger on the only strategy that could possibly ensure a total victory of the Party-State through a world-wide proletarian revolution.

He purified the (to Marxists) sacred term "proletariat" of the nineteenth-century, outmoded meaning every leader from Karl Marx to Yuri Andropov stupidly accepted. Primarily, what is needed is not political penetration of capitalist countries, nor military superiority, Gramsci said, but corruption of their Christian cultural basis.

Gramsci proposed a new form of Marxization: Reduce all men's expectations of any salvation from on high—in art, in literature, in science, in medicine, in social works, in politics, in finance, in commerce, in industry. Promise all men liberation from what ails them by means of heightened human—and only human—effort by intellectual, emotional, scientific, ethical, means. Instruct them that all hope of progress lies within themselves.

Unerringly, too, Gramsci brought into sharp relief the fundamental postulate of Marxism: its total and thorough materialism. But this, Gramsci pointed out, will provide the common ground Marxists can share with capitalists in the West. Join them, Gramsci exhorted his fellow Communists. Participate in their profit-seeking, in their social "do-gooding," in their international peace-making and peace-keeping structures, in their art movements, in their literary efforts, in their efforts to raise health standards and living standards, and yes, even in their profession of ethical and religious goals. Become members of the global home they are building, genuine members of their human family, collaborating in liberating all men from slavery and the meaninglessness of daily life.

All this, but under one major proviso. Let the entire effort be solely by man for man's sake. Collaborate to fill his belly with fresh food and to fill his mind with a fresh knowledge. But make sure he believes both food and knowledge are his creation, the results only of his own noble efforts. Make sure man never repeats the famous cry of German philosopher Martin Heidegger: "I know that only God can save us." In 1989, the new leader of Czechoslovakia, Vaclav Havel, would tell his countrymen: "In organizational decrees, it is truly difficult to find that God is the only one who can save us." Mikhail Gorbachev, as Gramsci's disciple, would say: "Make sure no one listens to Havel."

Gorbachev's gamble is with the durability of the Party-State: that it can last through a period of territorial retrenchment and exposure to all the allurements of capitalism and Western democracy. The gamble is worth taking, he thinks, because of the geopolitical prize at stake.

Any worthwhile assessment and accurate estimation of these two men, Karol Wojtyla and Mikhail Gorbachev, must start from this geopolitical premise. Both men think and plan geopolitically. They do not see the world's nations as diverse and divergent groups of men and women who are learning with difficulty to get along together, or merely as an assemblage of powers who must modify and adapt their resources in order to survive. Each man, in his own way, presumes—assumes would be a better word—that the diversity and divergence are accidents of human history, that in reality all are finally being driven by a force greater than the force any one or several of them can muster. In his authentic Leninist Marxism, with its crass materialism, Gorbachev recognizes this force as blind historical destiny. In his genuine Roman Catholicism, Papa Wojtyla believes this is the power of Jesus Christ as head of the whole human race.

They differ profoundly on this fundamental point. But they are one in the vantage point from which they start: the totality of nations, their different tendencies and weaknesses as part of that totality. Without an appreciation of that unique geopolitical vantage point, it is not possible to understand the moves they make, the turns and twists in their strategies; and, because of their undoubted influence on international affairs, it would be difficult to plot the trajectory the society of nations will follow in the present decade as they progress toward what all envision as a new world order.

The two main vehicles of that progress are, obviously, the interdependence of single nations and the generalized decision and wish to undergo development. Distances, not merely geographical but economic and cultural, have narrowed between nations. For, every year, that economic interdependence intensifies as a means of development. To facilitate that interdependence, political differences and contentions are being diluted and weakened by enlightened self-interest. The current outstanding example of this necessary narrowing of political distances is provided by the 1988–89 changes in the political structures of the Soviet satellite nations and, to some small extent, in the political structure of the USSR itself. Even national prerogatives—say, a country's currency—are being curtailed, modified, abolished, as presently planned for the European Economic Community of 1992 +. Already, it is safe to say that the outlook in the society of nations as a whole is more intensely oriented to the international side of life than ever before. Under the impetus of the desire for development, this international attitude is being transformed into a transnational and globalist outlook according as interdependence gives birth to joint efforts and multilateral participation in mutually beneficial projects.

But that progress toward a new world order is stimulated not only by the desire for development and the demands of interdependence. Today, for the first time in history, the whole human race is facing geo-issues: the choice between peace and nuclear destruction of this planet's civilization; the deteriorating environment of the globe itself as a human habitat; and single-theme issues like the scourge of AIDS, the proliferation of drugs and widespread famine. None of these can be solved by any one nation without the cooperation of all others. For all, in their territories and their peoples, are deeply threatened in these issues. From these causes alone, a globalism would have to be born.

This new globalism is often discussed with a liberal use of the terms "geopolitics" and "geopolitical." But, to be very accurate, what is being discussed is the internationalism of the ancient Greeks with a small admixture of their cosmopolitanism—this last item rather as a matter of whimsy or poetic license on the part of some globalists.

Those who indulge in no whimsy, but are bent on themselves creating the new world order, speak as if that new order went far beyond internation collaboration, association and commingling transnationally on the basis of democratic egalitarianism as it has evolved in the individual Western democracies. But the Fukuyama interdict bans them from any explicit and detailed description of that new order. For Francis Fukuyama was correct: Out of the present internationalism there cannot come any level of thought and structure beyond what democratic egalitarianism supplies. What lies far beyond that level of perception and structure cannot be supplied by the most thorough internationalism and the most ardent transnationalism.

The fact of international life today is that we are in the middle of an intensely globalist period, and none of our political structures, national or international, are geopolitical. We do not possess the structure suitable or necessary for housing a geopolitical society of nations and states. Until such is created, all we can have, and do increasingly have, is a society of ever more interdependent nations linked by ever more numerous agreements between single units in that society.

That key term "geopolitical," in fact, refers primarily to structure, and only secondarily to the ideology, the spirit or ethos (democratic capitalism, Leninist Marxism, or other), infusing that structure. At the present stage of our human experience, we can arrive at a somewhat satisfactory idea of the geopolitical by starting with the structure we have known for a long time: the political.

To be geopolitical, a structure would have to be equipped with legislative, executive and judicial powers over all its inhabitants—and, in this case, that means all the nations. The creation and successful exercise of those powers depends on the unity within which all the inhabitants live. We do not yet know—we cannot even imagine with our fantasy or reason with our minds—what the principle of that unity could be, for all our political unities have been based on common territory, common racial origin, common language, even common religion or—its pale image— common ideology. And all those political unities—nations, states, "countries," or "powers," we sometimes call them—rest on apparently inviolable principles of human rights arising from a multiplicity of differences (linguistic, territorial, cultural, racial).

While, as Fukuyama pointed out, "democratic egalitarianism" is leavening all these different unities that make up the society of nations, nothing deriving from that same "democratic egalitarianism" in itself gives any opening for a consideration of a geopolitical structure within which all the different member states could be politically assimilated to one model. For that furthest reach of our political thought presupposes *national* unities. What could be the principle of the geopolitical unity necessary for a truly viable geopolitical structure? The Fukuyama interdict is a two-edged sword cleaving our present from our past but also clearly cutting us from any future based on "democratic egalitarianism" and its political base.

In all our recorded human experience and within the bounds of our reason, we cannot find any satisfactory answer about the principle of geopolitical unity. Our pathway to such an answer is blocked by the way we think, perceive and form judgments about that very familiar category of human grouping we call a nation or a state. The way we think about it is ingrained from centuries of experience.

When the upheavals in Romania freed the population from the iron grip of the Nicolae Ceauşescu government, the desire for change and for a new political structure washed over Romania's eastern border into Soviet Moldavia (part of Romania before Soviet-forced annexation in 1944). One of the Moldavian dissidents, Oazug Nantoy, expressed the terrible difficulty that now arose for Romanians and Moldavians: how to invent national Moldavian politics on the grass-roots level after so many years of Stalinism. "The worst we still have from the Stalin era," said Nantoy, "is the *way we think*. We cannot obtain new thinking on credit."

On the much broader and worldwide plane occupied by the society of nations, there is the same difficulty. Leaders and statesmen, as well as Transnationalist entrepreneurs and Internationalist activists, have inherited a way of thinking about internation relations that of itself precludes them from thinking geopolitically. It would be a mighty feat of reason and imagination for them to unthink—to free themselves from—the framework of those relations within which they have lived and thought and planned heretofore, and which is the spontaneously accepted way in which they understand all that is transpiring around them in our world. Unfortunately, as Nantoy remarked apropos of his fellow Moldavians, they cannot obtain "new thinking on credit."

It is relatively simple to state in so many words what geopolitics implies theoretically. It is very difficult to think in a practical fashion about the society of nations geopolitically and to understand the hard-fact implications of a geopolitical structure housing those same nations. Hence, it is very difficult for most moderns to understand what John Paul II and Mikhail Gorbachev are about.

Both these leaders are geopolitically minded, and they are both dealing with their individual situations from a geopolitical standpoint and with a geopolitical goal in view. Their statements and actions, their weaving in and out through current events, the welter of facts about them, and the wealth of international commentary on them, all this has a geopolitical thread running through it that is hard to unravel. Geopolitics is, at one and the same time, so grandiose in its assumptions, so broad in its worldwide implications, and yet so dependent on such a complicated machinery, that it lies outside the scope of our normal thinking modes.

Yet, if there is any one overall identifiable trend of internation relationships today, it surely is geopolitical. Even before Western leaders officially joined this trend, they already were conniving at it. Now that the geopolitical trend has become an active element in our world, there is a "new thinking" abroad—again, on credit from that prime agent of change Mikhail Gorbachev.

20. Diplomatic Connivance

At the earliest stages of any deep change in international affairs, there is a time-honored practice that governs the behavior of the great powers of the world. One of the most successful practitioners of that approach— the eighteenth-century French adventurer-statesman, Charles-Maurice de Talleyrand—artfully called that secretive process *la connivance diplomatique*. Diplomatic connivance.

Intelligent and farseeing statesmen who contemplate a brusque departure from an established policy, Talleyrand maintained, will keep the public mind and reaction of their nations in view. Consequently, long before they reveal their new policy, they will carry on a private dialogue among themselves, exploring the most sensitive and delicate aspects of their plans.

In the privacy of diplomatic chanceries, in highly classified correspondence, in privileged person-to-person communications, agreements of substance and principle are reached. Agreements about how far each participant is willing to commit itself; about what the overall timing will be; about who other than the main parties should be informed; and about the main steps by which the general public is to be acquainted with the planned change.

Precisely that process had been in operation for more than three years before Mikhail Gorbachev began his tenure as General Secretary of the CPSU in March of 1985, bringing with him changes of a truly shocking nature and extent.

By the time Gorbachev came to the top of the Soviet heap, in fact, knowledge of what was about to come had already begun to filter from government channels, ministries and diplomatic missions outward to think tanks and paragovernmental agencies, as well as to the most influential financial, industrial, cultural and media centers. All along the way, minds were disposed and acclimatized by a process of discussions and reactions, agreements and preparations.

The surprise for some was that Gorbachev—an untried leader, after all, with no experience on the world stage—seemed to move so rapidly after his advent as General Secretary; that he seemed to master so much so quickly as to take the world by storm, and never mind learning the ropes of the normal process of diplomatic connivance.

Pope John Paul was not surprised, however. For one thing, Gorbachev was better fitted for his new international role than most Soviet bureaucrats. Even in his Stavropol days, he had shown his geopolitical bent, as well as his avid interest in and talent for international networking, on official visits he made to Belgium, Italy, West Germany, France and Canada. But that was far from the whole of it.

By the opening of the 1980s, Gorbachev was entrenched as the special protégé of KGB head Yuri Andropov. In 1982, when Andropov succeeded Leonid Brezhnev as General Secretary, Gorbachev remained at his side. As the aging Andropov's health declined, it was the young and trusted Gorbachev who functioned as de facto General Secretary, shuttling back and forth between Andropov's sickroom and Moscow's General Secretariat. It was Gorbachev who conveyed the wishes and decisions of the master on matters of deepest confidentiality and high state security to Andropov's bureaucratic underlings. On a need-to-know basis, finally Gorbachev became privy to all there was to know. He knew all the executive decisions taken by Andropov. He saw to the transmission of those decisions into the hands of the relevant executive branches of the Soviet government and the Communist Party.

After the General Secretary's death, in February of 1984, Gorbachev performed the same function for Andropov's successor, Konstantin Ustinovich Chernenko. Already seventy-three years old and ailing, Chernenko was a dying man at the time of his election to the highest post in the Soviet Union.

When the time came that Chernenko was no longer able to sit with his Politburo colleagues, press photographs showed Mikhail Gorbachev—now highly experienced, uniquely informed and deeply connected to the sinews of Soviet power—sitting symbolically but discreetly behind Chernenko's empty chair. And during the 175 days immediately prior to Chernenko's death, when he was completely hidden from public view, Gorbachev was at his bedside.

As an accredited member of international leadership, Pope John Paul was another of those privy to the changes being planned. But, thanks to his own independent sources of information, John Paul was also able to correct most of the partisan distortions that inevitably pervade the diplomatic connivance process, as each side seeks its own advantage—including some distortions introduced by members of the anti-Church within his own chancery who never miss a chance in their efforts to transform both Church and papacy.

From his vantage point of the Vatican as a window on the entire world around him, and as a man born and bred to genuine geopolitics himself, John Paul saw at the opening of the 1980s unmistakable signs that a geopolitical strategy far superior to any understanding prevailing in the inner councils of the West had masterfully seized the prime initiative in world affairs. The society of nations was becoming locked into a scenario that appeared to be dominated by Moscow and that would be played out by the turn of the second millennium.

Quickly swept up in that millennium endgame were all of the various factions of the West; all of the diverse religious and antireligious globalist movements of the day; the People's Republic of China; that helpless giant we call the Third World; and the Roman Catholic institutional organization of John Paul, together with other forms of Christianity.

For Pope John Paul II, the most obvious sign that a major process of diplomatic connivance was under way—and that therefore a major departure from the world order that had prevailed for nearly half a century was coming—surfaced in a certain change of attitude that became noticeable in the conversation and behavior of high officials and power brokers in the capitalist nations. The consensus among the Internationalist and Transnationalist leaders of the West began to revolve around the notion that the Soviet leadership had finally realized the simple truth: The whole Soviet economic system was about to implode.

It seemed logical enough to anyone with an ounce of real capitalist sense that after seventy years of unrelenting Marxism—with its GNP being swallowed up in armaments, and with its privileged *nomenklatura* resting atop a hopelessly inefficient bureaucracy—the Soviet Union was at least sending signals that economically, financially, socially and psychologically, the USSR was on its last legs. It seemed inevitable that it would signal for help. And it seemed the Internationalist-Transnationalist moment of triumph was at hand.

Accordingly, signals began to flow back to the Soviet Union from the

West. And the process of diplomatic connivance being what it is, some of the signals were discreet—almost private, you would say. The Soviet submarines' behavior around Sweden's coastline was one such signal. For a number of years, Soviet submarines have been penetrating Swedish territorial waters, probing the accuracy of the rings of submarine sensors that protect Sweden's naval bases, thus testing Sweden's defenses. Under Gorbachev, Soviet violations rose to a record level in 1988. Even after one Soviet submarine, a Whiskey-class vessel armed with nuclear torpedoes, grounded itself on the rocks outside Karlskrona in 1981, the penetrations continued unabated. Why hasn't Sweden protested violently? Why has the United States, with its stake in Swedish defenses—even though Sweden is a neutral—not made it an issue with Gorbachev? Why, finally, does he persist in it? The final answer lies in the quest for signals, signals of permissiveness and nonbellicosity on Sweden's part, signals of the U.S. understanding of Soviet touchiness about its coasts in the Baltic. In a word, it is a diplomatic connivance.

Other signals are more overt. The economic condition of the Soviet Union, known accurately in the West, began to receive a great deal of play in European and American media reports. It became fashionable, for want of a better word, to discuss the opportunities for peace that might be implied by the fact that the Soviet Union could not keep up its foreign subsidies. That it could not rebuild its decrepit infrastructure. That it could not compete in the world economy. That it could not supply needed consumer goods to its own people. That it needed at least two decades—and a huge infusion of Western credits and other help— to correct its dangerous posture.

Rather soon, the companion idea began to surface that, while the failed Soviet economy presented an opportunity for a new approach by the West, there would be a downright danger to everybody should the West be too fainthearted or too doctrinaire to cross the bridge of economic cooperation. If the West were to force Moscow to the brink of its own destruction, the argument ran, what would there be any longer to hold the Soviet hand back from the ultimate strike against the West? Veiled though it generally was, the idea seemed to be that Moscow would not go alone into oblivion.

Somewhat less publicly at first, and during the same time period, the process of diplomatic connivance began to fuel some basic financial and trade initiatives. Two mechanisms were set in motion to supply a certain easing of economic pressures in the Soviet Union.

The first mechanism was a rescheduling of Soviet debts to the West. In practice, this mechanism meant that the Soviets were not required to pay down the principal they already owed. And it meant that interest payments could be finessed by postponement; or financed by new loans rolled from one banking consortium to another, and not listed in the information conveyed to stockholders. Involved here were such major United States banks as First Chicago, Chase Manhattan, Citibank, Manufacturers Hanover Trust, Chemical Bank, Bankers Trust, Marine Midland and the Bank of America.

Surely it was understood that this mechanism would place a heavy economic burden on the West itself. In the United States, for example, the losses sustained by the banks in this operation were deducted as far as law allowed from tax payments. The American taxpayer was thus loaded with about half of the losses.

Nonetheless, for policymakers the gamble of increased public debt was apparently worth taking. No doubt it seemed literally to be a once-in-a-lifetime opportunity to extend at least the first two legs of the capitalist tripod—trade and finance—into the Soviet Union itself. If that much could be accomplished, who could doubt that the third leg of the tripod —the physical security of all nations—would be greatly strengthened?

The second mechanism for easing the economic burdens crushing the Soviet system was convertibility. The Russian ruble was and still is not convertible on world currency markets, nor is it directly convertible even between the Warsaw Pact nations of the East. A new convertibility mechanism was, therefore, devised to facilitate the ruble. An agreement was reached between West German and Japanese banks to support a limited amount of rubles on the market at a pre-agreed level. By this means, the Soviets became eligible for membership in all the international money organizations that function as conduits for American capital.

That this major financial process in favor of the Soviets enjoyed acceptance in important spheres of influence was made clear by William Verity, among other high-level spokesmen. Verity was one of the founders in 1973 of the U.S.-USSR Trade and Economic Commission (USTEC), and he chaired that Commission from 1978 to 1984. "The U.S.," Verity declared in 1987, "is going to have to get used to the idea that the Soviets are good trading partners."

Whatever about their worth as a trading partner, the Soviets did prove themselves to be masters at the game of diplomatic connivance. Even before what came to be called Gorbachevism was felt by the general public, the Soviets had been provided with $16 billion in credits and unsecured loans by Western European and Japanese trade and financial deals.

By 1988, with Gorbachev at the helm, total Soviet debt to the West came to $179 billion in low-interest, unsecured loans and was rising at the rate of $2 billion a month. Moreover, financial experts in East and West alike were in agreement that the Soviet regime would need $100 billion more in Western capital over the next five years.

How much Gorbachev may have contributed to the early stages of the Soviet end of diplomatic connivance for the economic salvation of the Soviet Union, and how much it was the brainstorm of KGB head and later General Secretary Andropov and others, may never be known. What is certain for Pope John Paul, however, is that whether Mikhail Gorbachev was the master planner or not, once he reached the pinnacle of power, Gorbachev showed himself to be the aptest genius of all at the process of diplomatic connivance.

With Gorbachev on the scene, a new energy began to heighten the action in the sphere of international affairs claimed by the capitalist nations as their own. During the years between 1985 and 1988, the General Secretary's openness and candor, so stunning to most in the West, was exactly what the financial doctors ordered. Apparently flying in the face of traditional Soviet secrecy in such matters, Gorbachev readily talked about his budget deficits. He publicly deplored the condition of the Soviet infrastructure. He complained about the folly of Soviet efforts to restrain inflation with price controls, which only aggravated the already disastrous shortage of food and consumer goods of every kind.

His experts in the financial field soon joined their ebullient General Secretary in a kind of Greek chorus of Soviet helplessness. The USSR was portrayed to the West in the starkest terms by Soviet economist Victor Belken as "a cannibalistic economy feeding on itself." Not only that, chimed in Belken's fellow economist Vladimir Tekhonov; the Government's ability to print money in the circumstances was "like putting an alcoholic in charge of a liquor shop." Yet a third leading Soviet economist sounded the note that no Internationalist or Transnationalist wanted to hear. There was a real danger of a "rightward swing" in the Soviet Union, warned Leonid Abalkin, unless some rapid economic progress is registered "within two years."

On still another front, arms control and disarmament matters were the subject matter of more connivance, even before the Soviet president reached Washington in December of 1987. Soviet pre-event planning and the seeding of minds among U.S. authorities was admirable. It was done so well that today, in the light of recent occurrences at the opening of 1990, it is impossible to resist the conclusion that the demilitarization of Europe—East and West—was already planned by Gorbachev in conjunction with the unification of the two Germanys, three years before Gorbachev would call those shots, numbing U.S. authorities with relief.

Already, in April 1987, ten retired U.S. flag and general officers sat down with eight of their Soviet counterparts, under the sponsorship of the Center for Defense Information. Up for discussion: Arms reduction on both sides. The Soviet proposal: The U.S. and the USSR should remove all troops from foreign countries. The Americans' question: Wouldn't that mean the Communist governments of Eastern European satellite countries would fall? The Soviet reaction: So what? The next question: Doesn't this revive the whole question of the two Germanys— and the Berlin Wall and . . . and . . . and . . . ? The Soviet reaction: Yes.

The meetings were continued in Washington, Moscow and Warsaw. The net effect was a dissipation of the basic reason for the enormous expense and trouble the U.S. had shouldered for forty-five years—a defensive European shield against those Soviet troops garrisoned all over Eastern Europe. That basic reason was fear. Hence, NATO. Hence, a minimum annual U.S. expense of $150 billion.

By the time Gorbachev reached Washington in December 1987, Washington was ready to receive him, ready to go forward with diplomatic connivance. "Everyone feels just cozy," remarked one prime television news commentator. The best example of just how cozy everyone had become with everyone else, and of just how quickly everything was moving along a very straight track, was provided when Mikhail Gorbachev set foot at last on the pavements of Washington, D.C., that December. His greatest achievement during that visit was not at the White House, or among the excited crowds of Americans who pressed in to shake his hand when he jumped from his motorcade. His chief triumph was at the Soviet Embassy, where he participated in a meeting, organized by USTEC, with the most prominent advocates of easy-credit trade between the USSR and the United States. Among those present at the meeting were Armand Hammer, grain mogul Dwayne Andrews and USTEC President James H. Giffen.

In the best traditions of diplomatic connivance, Giffen was explicit in an interview with NBC about USTEC intentions. "The level of [non-agricultural] trade," he said, "could go from a billion dollars . . . up to four or five billion per year, and maybe even higher, into the ten-to-fifteen-billion range." In response to the implications of such a scenario, Giffen was asked, "Do you really want to make the USSR an economic superpower?"

The reply was to the point. "I think we do."

Subsequent developments confirmed what John Paul already understood to be the case. Giffen was speaking for a broad range of important interests in America and elsewhere in the West.

As early as the following spring, in April 1988, USTEC held its twelfth annual meeting in Moscow. Led by William Verity—not in his role as USTEC founder now but as United States secretary of commerce—five hundred American businessmen set about an unprecedented deal-making process with a corresponding number of Soviet businessmen. In late 1988, another flurry of business deals involved West Germany, the United Kingdom, France and Italy in the extension of a fresh credit line of $11 billion to the Soviet Union.

On March 30, 1989, the American Trade Consortium, consisting of six major United States corporations—RJR Nabisco, Mercator, Eastman Kodak, Chevron, Archer-Daniels-Midland and Johnson & Johnson— signed a major trade agreement that is expected eventually to inject $10 billion into the Soviet economy. By the second quarter of 1989, close to two hundred companies from Western Europe and the United States had formed joint ventures with Soviet counterparts; and in May of that year, five European banks and three Soviet banks announced the first joint banking venture in Soviet history: the International Bank of Moscow.

On top of all that, through bond sales, security firms, insurance companies and corporations, the Soviets were granted access to Western financial markets, free of all oversight. That is, they were not required to divulge basic economic data.

From Pope John Paul's point of view, it made little difference at the practical level how much of all this was prearranged theater—diplomatic connivance, in other words—and how much each side was maneuvering in a dead-earnest competition for advantage in its own globalist agenda. Most striking for the Pope were three things. First, the level and the extent of the aid extended to Gorbachev by the West were being consistently heightened. Second, East and West seemed to be most compatible as newlyweds—or anyway, as bedfellows. And third, the truly uncommon geopolitical mind-set, vision and ability of the Soviet General Secretary were evident in every move he made.

There was Mikhail Gorbachev, being courted by the Western suitors until he caught them, finally consenting in blushing innocence to accept Western money, Western credit and Western trade.

And there was the West, consenting to Gorbachev's conditions. Consenting, for one thing, to the disturbing role of the KGB in all business deals. True, the West did require a little prenuptial counseling in that matter. Paul Konney, vice-president of Tambrands—one of the participants in the March 30, 1989, deal—asserted that "there is a very aggressive, hostile intelligent presence in all our deals." However, Gorbachev's

early nurturing at the breast of the KGB during his Andropov years
seemed to present no serious problem. "People need to get used to it"
was Konney's opinion. "There will be a KGB representative in the organization of everyone's joint venture."

Listening to such advice, and glancing perhaps, if one got that chance,
at the bronze medal of the Kremlin that rested on the desk of Mercator
Corporation's James Giffen, one could not help but see something more
than the old predominant desire to turn a profit. There was a new element that did not exist in the international mix before Gorbachev's arrival on the world scene. There was a blithe and trusting spirit filtering
down from high places to comfort many who might otherwise have been
nervous. And that is the central idea and purpose of the whole process
of diplomatic connivance.

By the time the way was clear for Italy's Prime Minister Ciriaco De
Mita to call, as he did in 1989, for a "Marshall Plan for the Soviet Union,"
it was beyond any doubting that the most serious process of diplomatic
connivance in fifty years was already well along the way.

Within scant months of Mikhail Gorbachev's election in March of 1985
to the post of General Secretary of the Central Committee of the CPSU,
he and President Reagan met at their first summit, in Geneva, Switzerland, on November 19–20, 1985. With that meeting, the first signal was
raised for the general public that a profound change in the arrangements
among nations was under way.

When President Reagan returned from that summit, he gave a low-
key report to the Congress and the American nation. "It was," the President said summarily, "a constructive meeting."

Constructive was hardly an ample description. The depth of agreement reached in that meeting was better gauged by scanning just one of
its products.

The General Agreement on Contacts, Exchanges and Scientific Technical Education and Other Fields—the General Agreement, some Vatican analysts called it for convenience—was drawn up by Secretary of
State George Shultz and Soviet Foreign Minister Eduard Shevardnadze,
and was signed by Reagan and Gorbachev at the summit. The canvas
covered in its provisions ranged over the entire cultural life of the United
States and the Soviet Union. All phases of education and all branches of
the arts were dealt with. It authorized mutual exchange programs, the
homogenization of curricula, the sharing of facilities and the mutual
indoctrination of the two peoples involved.

One portion of the *General Agreement*—Article II, Section 3—provided that both nations were to encourage "cooperation in the fields of science and technology, of humanities and social studies."

The basic idea of "cooperation," according to Article IV, Section 1.d., seemed to be "to conduct joint studies on textbooks between appropriate organizations of America and the Union of Soviet Socialist Republics." Cooperation would cover all computer-based instruction, instructional hardware and curriculum design for all grades of primary and secondary education, as well as college and university studies.

The obvious goal was a total homogenization not only of the methods of teaching and learning, but of what was to be taught and learned. Ideally, the content of all curricula would become identical. One day soon, one assumes, schoolchildren in Gorbachev's birthplace of Privolnoye and schoolchildren in Reagan's birthplace of Tampico, Illinois, will all learn the same materials.

This may have seemed to the Transnationalists a giant preparatory step toward their long-held dream of unbiased, uniform global education. To Pope John Paul, it was a giant step taken into the near future with closed eyes and obliterated memory.

Cooperation, for instance, in the "social sciences" turned a blind eye to the official prostitution of psychiatry and psychology by the Soviet Union as clinical tools for inflicting mental and physical torture as political punishment and for disposing of dissidents. The USSR had been effectively banned from the World Psychiatric Association in 1983 for just such practices. It had not been readmitted at the time of the signing of the *General Agreement*; and in fact, a delegation of American experts reported after their 1989 visit to the Soviet Union that nothing substantial had changed in the field. Diplomatic connivance seemed not to be strained by this factor, however.

Or take cooperation in the humanities. As taught in the Soviet Union, all humanities are marinated in Leninist Marxism as a matter of course. And as a matter of course, history is distorted by a thoroughgoing Marxization of ideas, by the systematic suppression of facts, and by downright lies. One might wonder, therefore, what common curricula might be drawn up between the USSR and the United States, or any other country of the West. Presumably, the same blithe and trusting spirit that reigned in trade and finance assumed that such problems would take care of themselves.

Cooperation in science and technology presented interesting problems of its own, meanwhile. John Paul was hardly alone in seeing all the advantage flowing to the Soviets in these areas. He saw nothing but a greater hemorrhaging than had already taken place of vital American technology in favor of the USSR.

Without the 1985 *General Agreement*, the Soviets went to great lengths to obtain such technology, chiefly by the subterfuge of espionage, and by the adulterous actions of third-party governments and entrepreneurs. Just how far the *General Agreement* would go in making such irregular activities unnecessary for the Soviets became a fascinating subject of discussion among some in the Vatican.

According to Dr. Stephen D. Bryen, who headed the Pentagon's security program for the Reagan administration, in 1988 over half the technology that makes the weapons systems of the Soviet Union possible already came from the West. And the United States Department of Defense has stated on the basis of actual figures that trade and technology transfers to the Soviet Union have already saved the USSR billions of dollars, have reduced weapons-development time, and have amounted to a gain of $6.6–$13.3 billion in military technology.

Apparently, however, there is no such thing as too much technology; and, apparently, the Soviets would rely only so far on the *General Agreement* to acquire it. In 1989, four years after the Geneva summit, the Soviets paid, to the Toshiba Company of Japan, a good chunk of that hard cash the West was providing. In return, and acting in violation of solemn agreements, Toshiba supplied the Soviets with the American machine-tool technology that enabled them to build nearly undetectable submarines. The case made headlines and met with public outrage. But it was hardly an isolated incident; and Japan was not the lone transgressor.

In something of the same vein, the Soviets continued their aid to foreign surrogates, to the tune of some $127 billion in 1988—$1 billion to Nicaragua; $2 billion to Vietnam; $5 billion to Cuba; more billions to Central Europe, Afghanistan, Ethiopia, Angola and Latin American surrogates such as the powerful Shining Path Marxist group so troublesome to Peru.

Without a shadow of a doubt, the aim of the *General Agreement*—at least from the point of view of the Wise Men of the West—was "to transform the shape of the world," to quote Internationalist George Ball, because "sooner or later we are going to have to face restructuring our institutions so that they are not confined merely to the nation-states. Start first on a regional [U.S.A.-USSR] basis, and ultimately you could move to a world basis." In that quintessentially Internationalist view, the

General Agreement is a blueprint for what is called a "comfortable merger" of the populations of the United States and the Soviet Union.

Taking into consideration not only the sweeping scope of the *General Agreement*, but his own intimate knowledge of the Soviet Union and his equally intimate knowledge of the process of diplomatic connivance, Pope John Paul came to an inescapable conclusion. That *Agreement* was not drawn up specifically for approval at the November 1985 summit. It was not put together in a day, or even in the few months between March, when Gorbachev was elected to the top Soviet post, and November, when he met with Reagan.

Rather, that *Agreement* came from already established drawing boards. It took time, effort and organization to produce that *Agreement*, just as it took time, effort and organization to effect the helter-skelter eastward rush of banking and trading interests.

Without question, the policies visible in both areas reflected the sweeping ambit of Gorbachevism, as well as the equally sweeping intentions of the Wise Men. For both parties intend to create nothing less than a new arrangement in all human affairs—a "new world order," to use a consecrated phrase both Gorbachev and the Wise Men employ.

In John Paul's assessment, however, the early advantage rested with Gorbachev. For those early policies also reflected that blithe and trusting acceptance by the Wise Men of basic Leninist thinking. An acceptance —a continuing connivance—that was becoming the hallmark, if not the battle cry, of the Wise Men, as they took the field with the leader who had been judged—and not by Yuri Andropov alone—as most likely to succeed in fulfilling Vladimir Lenin's ultimate dream of Soviet messianism.

21. "Cold-Eyed, I Contemplate the World"

Following Mikhail Gorbachev's seminal speech at the United Nations in December 1988, spokesmen in Pope John Paul's Holy See felt constrained to underline the positive promise the Soviet leader held out for world peace and development.

John Paul himself, however, withheld any papal comments. On his ultimate analysis of what makes Mikhail Gorbachev tick, and of what gives Gorbachevism its momentum, depends a whole gamut of important papal decisions that bear directly on the welfare of his universal Church and the success of his papacy. Because the specific terrain for both men is the society of nations, the Pope must make that judgment of the Soviet leader in a geopolitical context that necessarily involves the vast world forces with which Gorbachev is either in collusion or in contention.

And while it is true that ultimately John Paul must make his judgment in the light not merely of facts derived from his intelligence sources, but of facts coming to him by papal privilege, it is also true that, on this occasion, as Gorbachev took his bow in the U.N., the Pontiff was in possession of his own sources of information about Kremlin councils, about Mikhail Gorbachev's outlook, and about what had passed between President Reagan and the General Secretary at their Geneva and Moscow summits. He was aware of the possibilities, acquainted with the assurances and apprised of the realities behind the public relations and propaganda efforts on both sides.

As 1989 progressed, therefore, all during the startling actions that were to propel Gorbachev into the middle of the organized policies and plans of the United States and the West nations and the Wise Men, Pope John

Paul's attention remained on the fundamental mind-set of the parties involved. And there, he found little to surprise him.

Before reviewing those startling events of 1989, and in order to understand how Papa Wojtyla views the astounding success achieved by Mikhail Gorbachev before the spring of 1990, one should become acquainted with the Pontiff's summation of Gorbachev and his Gorbachevism, which goes a long way toward explaining where John Paul stands today, and how he views the present geopolitical structure that is abuilding among the nations and peoples of Europe (including the USSR in an altered condition) and of the North American continent.

The familiar process of the Wise Men was over forty years old. It had congealed all international activity in well-worn ruts. It progressed by fits and starts. It sometimes took two steps backward for each step forward. It relied on an "either-or" atmosphere, warning of an ultimate lethal collision or, at the very least, of a series of shocks to the entire world system of nations. In terms of ultimate international harmony and cooperation, it appeared more and more to be barren of real hope and meaningful change.

Yet so taken did the West remain with its position on the world stage and with its own in-club program for the development of nations, that its reaction had become predictable to every new *ballet d'invitation* orchestrated by Leninist intelligence. Each time, the West was first surprised; then fascinated; then mesmerized; then taken in; and finally disappointed—but always ready to enter the cycle again.

By the time President Reagan was prepared to break that pattern with his own principle of "Trust, but verify," the difficulty was that no Western government was capable of the verification required.

Obviously, no Western intelligence agency—and therefore no Western government—had any inkling that the Soviet system could actually produce such a character as Mikhail Gorbachev from its enigmatic innards. Or, once they took note of him, that he could be promoted to the position of supreme Soviet power. Or that, once promoted, he would—or even could—steal such a long march on his Western colleagues in statecraft and in the molding of international opinion. "It breaks protocol!" sputtered one French official, as if to make John Paul's very point, when Gorbachev dropped his July 14 letter like a Bastille Day cannonball into the "Group of Seven" meeting. "Protocol be damned," answered a Britisher. "What do we do with it?"

But the principle followed by the Pope in assessing Western reactions

to the Gorbachev phenomenon is much more fundamental than observations about oversmug policies or debilitated intelligence capabilities.
Rather, it has to do with the fact that the Western mind has found no
way to fathom the attitude of the genuine Leninist mind; and that it is
unlikely to do so. For not even the basic notion of arid humanitarianism
has a place in the rulebook of Marx, Engels, Lenin, Stalin and Mao. In
moral terms familiar to the Western mind, there is no way to understand
the Communist mentality—what Dostoyevski called "the fire of the
mind"—that animates the champions and guardians of the Leninist
Party-State.

The information sources at the disposal of John Paul's Holy See indicated to him that, true to form, throughout the varied reactions of the
West nations to the early phases of the Gorbachev phenomenon, there
were grains of truth mixed with generous dollops of fond and wishful
thinking, long-standing distrust, latent and patent fears, and the inertia
of Western bureaucrats in their analytic thinking.

On the other side of the coin, the fundamental principle used by Pope
John Paul in making his own overall judgment of the Gorbachev phenomenon stands in stark contrast to the one he applies to the West. And
the principle in this case, while confirmed by John Paul's Kremlin-watchers throughout Soviet territory, is drawn from his long firsthand experience of the Leninist mentality as he learned its real features at close
quarters in his Polish motherland.

In essence, that principle recognizes the keynote of the Leninist Party-
State as a counterintelligence organization from start to finish. And in
practice, that principle takes President Reagan's cautionary slogan,
"Trust, but verify," to its deepest significance.

Trust Gorbachev, Reagan was saying; but verify his words by his deeds.
John Paul's experience has taught him that promises made and deeds
accomplished both come from the heart of an institutionalized counterintelligence operation. One way or another, both words and actions aid
the overall purpose of the Party-State to strengthen itself in all circumstances and to achieve its ultimate aims for its own exclusive success
throughout the capitalist West and the world at large.

As unpleasant and cynical as that principle may sound, every information source and reliable indication at the disposal of John Paul tells
him that the bones and structure of the Leninist Party-State—the secretariat, the KGB and the Red Army—remain intact and operative.

That being so, it defies credibility to think that Gorbachev is an entirely original mind secretly bent on turning the Party-State system upside down and restoring the Soviet Union to the comity of free nations. The Leninist system does not allow for such a character—even if he is Mikhail Gorbachev—to live any longer than it takes to snuff out a human life. Thus, as long as the Leninist Party-State remains intact and operative, so long does John Paul's fundamental principle of understanding Gorbachev remain intact and operative.

None of all that is to say, however, that little or nothing has changed in the Kremlin with the advent of Gorbachev. Leninist principles do remain valid. But there has been a switch in operations. And that switch has been based mainly on two things: on the special personal and geopolitical talents of Mikhail Gorbachev himself, and on the principles urged upon his Communist brothers over fifty years ago by the unsung Italian genius, Antonio Gramsci.

Of those two elements in the new mix of Leninism, in certain respects Gorbachev has been the greater surprise for Pope John Paul. For he is the first Soviet leader who has risen to the top free of the ham-handed crudity, personal unculture and counterproductive provincialism of his predecessors in high office. It is no wonder to John Paul that even Margaret Thatcher, never a friend of Leninist Marxism, said on meeting Gorbachev for the first time that she felt the impact "in every molecule of my being."

Nor was Mrs. Thatcher alone in her enthusiasm as the vibrant General Secretary displayed to the world an undoubted superiority in statecraft and leadership by comparison to the already known and uninspiring performances of his European and American counterparts. His success on the world stage became so palpable, in fact, that as throaty chants of "Gorbi! Gorbi! Gorbi!" followed him all through his triumphal state visit to West Germany, the tabloid *Bild* cooed that "what meant fear and threat to us has become a cuddly animal without bloody paws."

In reaction, Soviet spokesman Georgi A. Abatov could afford a little modesty: "We did not expect such a welcome."

The second element of Gorbachev's neo-Leninism—the full implementation at long last of the principles of Antonio Gramsci—is surprising for John Paul only in Gorbachev's singular mastery of the techniques required, and the icy nerves he displays as he carries them out.

Central to this element of Gorbachev's neo-Leninism is one point of Gramsci's with which Pope John Paul is in total agreement: Between raw Leninism and raw capitalism, there never was and still is not any essential difference. In each case the driving force is materialism. At heart, each system is exclusively materialistic. Neither looks beyond the material here and now. Neither values or defines man and the life of each individual beyond the material goods he produces and consumes.

It seems clear to John Paul that Mikhail Gorbachev's reading of Gramsci is the same as his own. It's just that, from their vantage points on opposite sides of the materialist fence, these two leaders must and do see the whole process of Gramscian policy from an exactly contrary point of view.

Gramsci warned that Leninism could not compete with the West in the economic and military fields. More, he warned that, even if such a competition were possible, it would not mean the ultimate victory of Leninism. Instead, said Gramsci, such competition would likely lead to a long and wearing struggle, would erode the willpower and the resources of the Leninist Party-State and, worst of all, would leave intact and unconquered the high cultural ground of the West—the popular mind, complete with its transcendent ideals so alien to Leninism.

At the very best, predicted Gramsci, any such economic and military struggle between Leninism and capitalism as he knew it would come down to a boring stalemate.

Competition there must be, of course. But, exhorted Gramsci, as if speaking directly to the genius of Gorbachev, let it be for the popular mind. Let that competition be led by the Party-State; but let it be waged day by day in the bailiwick of the capitalists themselves. And let the means be not military might but sweet acculturation of ideas and ideals. Promote all areas of cultural convergence. And above all, strip the West of any last clinging vestiges of Christianity's transcendent God. Then will the West be gravely vulnerable to penetration by the fundamental "dialectic" of Marxist materialism.

By what appeared to many—but not to Pope John Paul—as the luck of the draw in this round of history, Mikhail Gorbachev came to power at a moment so perfect that Gramsci himself could not have wished for a better one.

By 1985, the influence of traditional Christian philosophy in the West was weak and negligible. The influence of Christian believers was restricted. The truly vibrant areas of Christian life were reduced. The secularization of church hierarchies, bureaucracies and clergy—including the Roman Catholic Church and its once vaunted religious orders—was extensive. And the ever more pervasive moral license of Western countries was well entrenched.

Looking coldly at the genius of Mikhail Gorbachev, and attending always to his own principle of judgment regarding the Soviet Party-State as an intact counterintelligence organization par excellence, John Paul knew that Gramsci's master strategy was now feasible. Humanly speaking, it was no longer too tall an order to strip large majorities of men and women in the West of those last vestiges that remained to them of Christianity's transcendent God.

In Pope John Paul's analysis, in fact, the bigger challenge for Gorbachev would be for him to mesmerize the capitalist West in its single-minded preoccupation with its tripod model for international development and stability.

For that reason, the Pope was not surprised at the General Secretary's "new thinking" in his United Nations speech. It was in that speech, in fact, that the Soviet leader himself confirmed John Paul's analysis that there had been a switch in Kremlin operations, and that Gramsci's blueprint was on the table in Moscow.

In a nutshell, Gorbachev's speech was Gramsci brought up to date. It put the mind of the West at ease about military preoccupation and danger. It sought to fascinate that mind even further with money and goods and profits and technological advances. And underpinning it all was a fascinating change in emphasis. Gorbachev was asking for help, all right. But he was doing so by proposing what appeared to be a genuine partnership with the West in the areas of its deepest preoccupation. Surely, Gramsci would have been proud.

Given the papal analysis of Gorbachev and the neo-Leninism of the USSR, John Paul did not find the deepest significance of the General Secretary's U.N. speech in its contents. It was not even all that significant in the Pontiff's view that Gorbachev had effectively claimed for himself the center spot of international action; that much, at least, was not new, for the West had always reacted to Soviet initiative. The real importance of the hour he took to deliver his address lay in that fact that Gorbachev was able to disassociate himself so successfully from seventy years of history. And it lay in the fact that he had taken over the center spot of international acclaim. That was new.

From John Paul's point of view, therefore, the fact that Gorbachev had been able to fly in the face of history and stand before the world as its new hero was the only new element that had to be factored into the formula by which the Holy See must judge the changed and changing condition of human society.

To understand the Pope's reading of what made Gorbachev's U.N.

triumph possible in those terms is to understand the deep difficulty John Paul faces in Gorbachevism.

For one thing, even on the face of it, when Gorbachev rose to address the U.N. delegates that December day, in actual fact no one there had done less than he had to ease the problems of which he spoke with such passion. No one had done less than he and his Party-State for world peace; or for the cleansing of our polluted environment; or to relieve the misery of millions. Of East Germany's forests, 41 percent are dead or dying; 10 percent of its people drink substandard water. Air pollution is so bad in northern Czechoslovakia that life expectancy is shortened by three to four years. In Hungary, one in seventeen deaths is due to air pollution. Almost all the water in Poland's rivers is unfit for human consumption, and 50 percent is so toxic it is unfit for industrial use. The river Vistula, flowing through Warsaw, is a lifeless sewer. At least 25 percent of Polish soil is too contaminated for safe farming. Vegetable farming in the Silesia region will have to be forbidden because of the abnormal quantities of lead and cadmium in the soil. In the Soviet Union, 102 cities (50 million people) are exposed to industrial pollution ten times greater than safety norms. The Aral Sea and Central Asia have been polluted by indiscriminate use of water, pesticides and fertilizers. Large tracts of Poland and the USSR now are witnessing the birth of deformed babies and the mysterious outbreak of skin diseases not described in medical books—apparently the results of the Chernobyl disaster.

In addition, many of the delegates listening to Gorbachev's speech represented governments that had labored and had spent their time and resources to help cure the ills of nations that had suffered grievously from the wrongdoing of the system now headed by Mikhail Gorbachev. Many more of those delegates came from nations whose fields and gardens and unborn babies had been sown with seeds of death from Soviet inefficiency and fecklessness in dealing with the environment. Still others represented peoples who had been ground down by the heels of Soviet militarism.

Moreover, in and of themselves, Gorbachev's words that day were not different or fresher or more heartening than the clarion calls to our consciences that President Reagan had made on at least half a dozen occasions—in his Normandy address commemorating the Allied invasion of 1944, for instance, or in his Moscow University address of May 1988.

Yet, no such appeal by the American president—or by any other leader of the West nations—was ever received with anything like the enthusiasm meted out to Gorbachev's U.N. address.

Where did the difference lie? Pope John Paul's answer to that question was disheartening—but, once again, not surprising.

The difference, it would seem, lay in the religious, political and moral climate that now attends the nations in their efforts to find new leadership for the world at the end of the second millennium. For that climate is such that an international body as widely representative of the nations as the U.N. wishes no reliance on God and has no intention of presenting gifts on any altar.

In that climate, the American president as titular head of the West is not in a position to galvanize the nations, because Americans typically announce their plans and ideas with a righteousness originally born of a religious womb. And their European counterparts are even worse off, because they speak of their ideas in the jaded terms of leaders who once tended the Altars of God, but have now turned their backs on their own past.

In the present climate, only someone resident at the heart of the only self-proclaimed and officially antireligious, anti-God empire our world has ever known could carry the day. Only someone above the slightest suspicion of being morally good for an otherworldly reason. Only someone dedicated to success and triumph in this world exclusively. Only someone at the center of hard-core, hard-nosed Marxism. Only that someone had a chance of being heard on his own terms—and of moving the West from its ingrained and long-held policy of containment.

Given all the givens, therefore, Mikhail Gorbachev was the perfect leader to herald the new era. And he was the perfect servant of the natural forces the society of nations has now agreed we must all obey.

Given the difficulties of the Soviet Union, it was only logical that he would ask for help and cooperation. Given the desire of the West nations to find new and profitable markets for their goods and services, it was only reasonable that they would respond with a heady combination of relief and enthusiasm. Given the fact that, as a generation, we are notorious even among ourselves for knowing little or nothing of what preceded the forty-five years that have molded the actions and initiatives of nations, it was only natural that Gorbachev's carefully honed appeal would meet with resounding success.

Even granting the four or five half-truths uttered by Gorbachev in his U.N. address, and the one or two major lies he repeated, and the duplicitous and merciless behavior of the Soviet Union past and present, it was obvious to John Paul and his advisers that this Soviet's globalist sense was far superior to that of any Internationalist or Transnationalist leader. They had simply been outclassed.

Moreover, as official point man of the Leninist process, Gorbachev had even managed a more accurate reading than the Wise Men of the deep emotions running like a current beneath the surface among the peoples throughout all the nations. The bravura effect of Gorbachev's U.N. performance traced to that very fact. For he put into words straight out the widely felt, if not always frankly expressed, sentiments among peoples and nations.

As someone who might have been expected to brandish intransigence and threat, Gorbachev spoke instead of solving the problems that beset us all. Assuming an unsurpassed globalist posture, he declared for the world that we have all had enough of those problems. Assuming an almost unique geopolitical posture, he proposed that we face into the erection of international structures and begin to deal with economic repression, to deal with pollution of air and land and water, to deal with starvation and disease and broken lives.

Reading the popular mind of the West as if born to it himself, he proposed an end to mortal fear for our survival as a race. And in that, Gorbachev tapped the deep urge of men and women everywhere to leave behind all the threats of extinction. He held out the hope that the human family can revise—if all goes well, perhaps even shatter—the sense of drifting helplessness that has come to lie like a secret sorrow within our lives.

Finally, that was the glittering attraction of Gorbachevism. Help for all our pain and all our fear lay in perfectly achievable human institutions that would unify society economically; and, ultimately, politically as well.

The bloody history and the present problems of the Soviet Union notwithstanding, within a mere four years as General Secretary of the Central Committee of the CPSU, Mikhail Gorbachev had forced a redefinition of the terms on which international development will be pursued from now on. And he had left his political peers on the world stage to eat his dust.

During the spring of 1989—that is, in the months between Gorbachev's U.N. statement of intent and his forays into West Germany and France to begin its implementation—Pope John Paul had an unneeded and unwelcome confirmation that, no matter what the country or the context, the basic principles remain all too accurate by which he judges the Leninist mind as against the mind of the leaders of the capitalist West.

The context this time was China, where another *ballet d'invitation*—not the first since Mao Zedong's revolution won the day—was played out in Beijing's Tiananmen Square. While it is true that China's Leninist regime is not so far along in history's march as Gorbachev's Soviet Union and that Chairman Deng Xiaoping is no rival to Gorbachev when it comes to urbanity, the tragic events that began in Beijing on April 21, 1989, took the West through each step of reaction so familiar by now to the Holy See.

Still taken with its own international agenda, the West was first surprised, then fascinated, then mesmerized, then taken in, and finally, it was disappointed—but ready to enter the cycle all over again. And again, the mind of the West could not fathom the attitude of the genuinely Leninist mind. As Western intelligence had failed to predict, analyze correctly or even keep pace with the phenomenon of Gorbachevism, so that intelligence made gross miscalculations about the students who led the Beijing uprising, as well as about the nature of the Chinese government.

With regard to the Chinese students, Western ignorance and illusion passed for reliable information and understanding. There seemed no inkling in the West of student discontent in China until the magnitude of that discontent was clearly manifested by events. And, once their discontent had boiled to the surface, the West had already lost sight of the fact that the students themselves were rockbound in Leninism. They were China's version of one young French factory worker quoted in *The New York Times:* "I couldn't think of not being a Communist," said that young man. "It's my life. I don't make an effort to be a Communist. I live it."

When the demonstrations began in a smallish way in Tiananmen Square following the funeral of the liberal Party leader Hu Yaobang, the students were asking for an end of "corrupt practices" in the government, and for "significant and meaningful dialogue" between Party leaders and the ordinary people. But they were not calling for an overthrow of the Maoist socialist system.

When some mischief-maker splattered paint on the giant billboard depicting Mao Zedong's rotund face overlooking the square, the students hastened to clean it, shouting Mao's sayings, and exclaiming, "Long live Comrade Mao who set us free!"

Nevertheless, Western self-deception persisted, and nourished itself on media reports that displayed what Western reporters described as a homemade statue modeled on Lady Liberty holding freedom's torch high over New York Harbor. As little as possible was made of the fact that the students did not have the Statue of Liberty in mind, but the "Goddess of Reason." No doubt the upraised arm and the torch were modeled on

Lady Liberty's. But her name and her Phrygian cap were taken from the French Revolution. And she was greeted by the students with the singing of the "Internationale," the socialist anthem for all nations.

One commentator, a Belgian, remarked, "Those kids don't know how many human beings were killed to this tune, and how many democratic rights have been trampled underfoot by singers of that dreadful song." Perhaps. But it would not be long before hundreds of "those kids" would themselves join many a martyr who had marched into oblivion singing the tune they sang.

With regard to the Chinese Communist government, meanwhile, the ignorance of Western intelligence and analysis passed all bounds of wishful thinking and deficiency, and entered the realm of nescience.

The rapid spread of the students' demonstrations and of their very vocal discontent into other major cities and even to the Chinese countryside was enough to lead many Western governments and businessmen to make gross miscalculations.

Mesmerized by the way the Chinese had taken to Kentucky Fried Chicken, Coca-Cola, computers and capitalist profits, they failed to take into account either Deng Xiaoping's obsessive Leninism, or the functional nature of his classically organized Leninist Party-State. What analysis there was appeared to be based on skewed information provided by liberal intellectuals in the Chinese Communist Party (CPC) and the vast Chinese bureaucracy.

About Deng Xiaoping himself, ignorance in the West was profound. People remembered Deng's visit to the United States, and the news pictures that showed the diminutive Chinese leader wearing a ten-gallon hat at a Texas barbecue. They knew he had been touted as a personal friend of President Bush since Bush's earlier days as ambassador to Deng's China. With such pitiful information as their guide—and from the opening shouts to the last rifle shots in what was dubbed by state-controlled Beijing television as the "Beijing happening"—Western analysts echoed a persuasion that bore no resemblance to Pope John Paul's intelligence.

Commentators present in Beijing, as well as U.S. government statements and even some off-the-cuff remarks by President Bush himself, all seemed to point to the conviction that, in the face of such widespread and peaceful protest by perhaps as many as a million Chinese, the CPC headed by the good old boy Deng Xiaoping would have to make concessions. Democratic concessions.

When the days drew on and no concessions were forthcoming, the illusions about Deng were ringed around with fantasies. Deng was in favor of the students. There was a bitter fight behind the scenes in the CPC Politburo between the soft-liners led by Deng, and the hard-liners led by Li Peng. Deng was ill. Deng was dying. Deng was dead.

In all this, Pope John Paul saw again the deep and universal accuracy of his perception that the West has no means of penetrating the Leninist mind. On the contrary, Deng was seen as a completely Westernized man subject to the influence of compassion, in sympathy with the underdog, horrified by bloodshed, informed by the same vestiges of the Christian civilization that still stir the Western mind and heart. Those Christian remnants may now be called "humanitarian motives." But, by any name, the West expected Deng to behave according to such norms.

Deng did not. More, Deng could not. Deng Xiaoping was formed by Mao Zedong. And not only was Mao Zedong formed by Lenin; he was formed within a society that had never been deeply penetrated, as Russia had, by Christian ideals.

The deception and illusion about Deng and about Communist China trace directly back to the time of Mao. When that revolutionary shot his way to the post of Chairman of the CPC, in control of all China, in 1949, the reaction in the West was an almost exact copy of the rosy-eyed adulation that had hallowed the first thirty years of Stalinism in the Soviet Union.

Mao's China ate well. Mao's China was orderly. Mao's China was quiet. Mao's new China Man and Woman sprang whole and healthy from the Chairman's wise brow like Athena from Zeus in the ancient Greek myth.

Before any other major Communist leader, Mao Zedong understood the importance of Antonio Gramsci's basic teaching: You have to transform the culture of the people.

In Mao's translation, that came out: Cleanse the people's memory of the past. Teach the people: "Do not think. We will think for you. You will be happy."

Thus, Mao's New China Man and Woman rose each morning to the tune of "The East Is Red." Everyone flung himself into aerobic movements to greet each fine new day in Mao's land. Everyone worked with no concern for money. Everyone was ecstatic at being a faceless, humble unit in the huge anthill of Mao's classless society. Everyone wore a copy of the Mao suit in preference to decadent Western dress. And, in preference to decadent Western pornography, everyone read the Party paper and Mao's *Little Red Book* of wise and profound sayings. They read little else, however, because—as the *Little Red Book* itself admonished—"If you read too many books, they petrify your mind."

In 1966, after fifteen years of "The East Is Red" and the *Little Red Book*, the ancient Chinese culture Mao sought to eradicate and replace was still very much alive.

Mao pondered his problem. Resting at the exquisite Lu mountain resort of Kuling in the Lushan Highlands of central Kiangsi Province, perhaps he remembered the maxim he had included in his *Little Red Book* that goes like this: "Revolution is not a dinner party, or writing an essay, or painting a picture, or doing embroidery. It cannot be so refined, so leisurely and gentle, so temperate, kind, courteous, restrained and magnanimous."

Gazing out over the vista of gardens, lakes, temples and beetling cliffs, Mao penned one of his more famous poems: "Cold-Eyed, I Contemplate the World."

When the Chairman came down from the mountain, he launched the devastating "Cultural Revolution" of 1966–76. He sent millions of young men and women out to uproot all traces of China's ancient culture. Mao's holocaust of human lives and torture certainly exceeded the European holocaust under Adolf Hitler, and the Ukrainian holocaust under Joseph Stalin.

Included in that holocaust were some of Mao's oldest and most faithful comrades. Deng Xiaoping—one of the early followers of the Supreme Leader Mao Zedong—was rewarded for his lifelong Leninism and Maoist fidelity by becoming the No. 2 target of Mao's Cultural Revolution. "No. 2 Capitalist Roader": that was the scornful title given him. "No. 1 Capitalist Roader," President Liu Shaogi, was murdered by Mao's order. Deng, who was to be next, was spared only because, as an exception to the rule, Deng's son, Pufong, would not bear false witness against his father.

A brilliant physics major at Beijing University, Pufong was tortured, sodomized, beaten to a pulp and thrown out a window by his interrogators. He survived with broken fingers, damaged hearing, internal organs ruptured, and a broken back that left him permanently confined to a wheelchair.

Thanks to his son's constancy, Deng Xiaoping also survived. Humiliated in public, denounced and spat upon, Deng was imprisoned in Jiangxi military compound to be "reeducated" by a Leninist committee of prison instructors.

Despite the torture and humiliation both he and his son had under-gone, Communism remained "a fire of the mind" for Deng. And, in that regard, he was following in a tradition that had long since been hallowed in blood. He was following in the footsteps of the Old Bolshevik Nikolai Bukharin, for example. Before he was shot to death by Stalin's firing squad on March 14, 1938, Bukharin pleaded in his last will and testament that the comrades who were about to execute him should remember "that, on the banner which you will be carrying in the victorious march of Communism, there is also a drop of my blood." He died confessing his "guilt" to charges he knew had been fabricated, and urging on to victory the Party that had decreed his death to please Joseph Stalin. Similarly, Hungarian Communist Imre Nagy went to his hang-ing on June 16, 1958, protesting, "If my life is needed to prove that not all Communists are enemies of the people, I gladly make the sacrifice."

The willingness to die in order to show one's loyalty to the system that is about to end one's life is the "cold eye" of Leninism at its coldest. Still, there can be no doubt that Deng was formed and bred in that same tradition. Had he been put in front of a firing squad, or quietly garroted in a secret prison, one can be sure he would have died asserting his loyalty to the ideology of his assassins. Like the students in Tiananmen Square, he would have cried out not for his life, but his loyalty to "Chair-man Mao who set us free!"

As it was, when the horrors of the Cultural Revolution were ended and order was restored, Deng was still in one piece; and the same proces-sion into China from the West took place as had wended its way to Stalin's Soviet Union years before. China was hallowed all over again by a procession of university dons, amiable clergymen, international do-gooders, self-appointed world philosophers, drawing room socialists and millionaire Marxists in their private planes.

By the time the United States decided to play the "China card" against the Soviet Union during the Nixon administration, it was easy—it was almost a Western tradition, in fact—to ignore the brutality. To ignore the one million Tibetans killed and the million and a half more driven into exile by the brutal Tibetan genocide by Mao's China, for example. And to ignore Pakistan's genocide in Bangladesh, because it was Pakistan that had opened Mao's front door for the West. Any dislike of the Chinese was confined with some care to Chiang Kai-shek's "corrupt" Kuomintang in Taiwan.

• • •

As things turned out, Deng Xiaoping's unremitting Leninist loyalty led
him to a fate far different than Nikolai Bukharin's or Imre Nagy's. The
year 1982 found him not in a martyr's grave or even in a military compound, but in Mao Zedong's place as Chairman of the Central Committee of the CPC.

Once again, the ignorance gap between the Leninist and Western
mind led many to believe that, because Deng had suffered so terribly
during the Cultural Revolution, his rise to the top power spot would
surely mean the dawn of a different day. His would be a more humane
outlook and a more open regime. The fact was, however, that Deng was
what he had always been and what he remains today—a bone-bred Leninist in the pattern of Mao Zedong.

Under Deng's chairmanship, his son, Pufong, was made director of
the China Welfare Fund for the Handicapped (CWFH), and he founded
the Kanghua Company (KC). The plan was for the KC to see to financial
backing for the CWFH. In practice, however, the scheme seems to have
aroused Pufong's entrepreneurial instincts; the funds he collected
through the KC's activities never reached the CWFH, but were transmitted instead to the KC branch in Shensen, near Hong Kong. So blatant was Pufong's activity that it contributed to the public sense of
corruption in high places, and Deng had to reprove his son in public for
"allowing himself to be exploited by others."

What went largely unremarked, and was probably little understood in
the West, was the fact that the entire CPC is a close network of interwoven family relationships. Entrepreneurial corruption there surely was,
for that is as endemic to the Party-State as to the capitalist system. But
curiously, that does not dilute a highly orthodox sense of Marxist ideology. And, above all, even the lure of profit does not dilute the drive to
protect the Party-State from activities that might endanger its Leninist
control over the people. In that, as in all essential things, Deng could
not be expected to bend.

When the Chinese student demonstrations began in April of 1989, Western analysts may have known of Deng Xiaoping's secret speech to top
party officials in which the Chairman warned, "We can afford to spill a
little blood" if necessary to arrest the student movement. But, if they did,
they seemed taken nonetheless with the public charade of permissiveness
played out by the eighty-two-year-old Chinese president, Yang Shang-
kun, aided by the security apparatus chief, sixty-five-year-old Qiao Shi.

Western media personnel was beefed up at just about this time in preparation for a visit from the ubiquitous Mikhail Gorbachev, who was to arrive for a kind of Soviet-Chinese summit of rapprochement that had been arranged some time before. It is fair to say, therefore, that at a critical moment, most reporters and commentators on the scene were not part of the tiny corps of more experienced China-watchers.

Thus, at a crucial moment, it was probably a little easier to create the illusion not only that the control of the CPC was in shambles, but that the aging regime led by Chairman Deng Xiaoping was disintegrating. As Edgar Marin, director of the National Council of Scientific Research, put the case, "The disintegration of the hope for earthly salvation by Communist revolution among its believers brings regeneration of the rights of man and the idea of democracy."

Most Western analysts seemed unaware that President Yang had himself been secretary general of the CPC's Military Commission; or that Yang's youngest brother was then chief commissar for the army; or that Yang's son-in-law was chief of staff; or that another Yang relative was commander of the 27th Army Unit.

In any case, the government's convincing performance lasted for as long as necessary to uncover the organized centers of revolt against obedience to the regime. The students seemed caught in a big-time media dilemma. They welcomed the cameras as a means of popularizing their demands; and they feared the obvious fact that if the world was watching, so was the CPC.

As to the Western press, it seemed to mirror the gamut of the usual responses of the West to unexpected Leninist activity. First they were surprised at the events that were unfolding. Then they were mesmerized. Then they were taken in. And finally they were disappointed.

So complete and so effective was the CPC deception that after the tanks and armored personnel carriers had rolled into Tiananmen Square on June 3, one horrified American TV anchor asked, How could the Deng *we* thought *we* knew do this?

Still, the illusion persisted that, somehow, it would all turn out according to the Western script. Reports surfaced that the 27th Army Unit was on its way; that it would defend the students against the hard-line contingents who threatened the brave movement with extinction; that a miniature civil war was about to take place in Tiananmen Square.

Inevitably, disappointment turned to horror when the 27th Army Unit —closely controlled by, and deeply loyal to, the CPC—shot Tiananmen Square clear of demonstrators, crushing many of them beneath the tracks of lumbering tanks, mowing down some thousands with their guns and quickly instituting what can only be called a public reign of terror.

"A very small number of people created turmoil," Deng Xiaoping said at last in a public statement, "and this eventually developed into a counterrevolutionary rebellion. They are trying to overthrow the Communist Party, topple the socialist regime, and subvert the People's Republic of China so as to establish a capitalist republic."

Such a statement was only to be expected as the final act in the terrible charade. On all counts, Deng was lying through his teeth. The number of people involved, and the number in obvious sympathy and ready to be swept up in the protest against corruption, was anything but small. And the students themselves were anything but counterrevolutionaries. Deng knew the students had no intention of overthrowing the CP or of abandoning Marxist socialism. He had heard their fervent shouts in support of "Comrade Mao who set us free." But he had also heard their demands for dialogue and for an end to corrupt practices in high places; and he would have none of it. As in the time of Mao, so in the time of Deng: The Party-State was all-wise. And it was all-powerful. And so it would remain.

The horror and confusion of the West at the action orchestrated by Deng Xiaoping's CPC was an exact portrait of the inability of the Western mind to fathom the fundamentally inhuman attitude of the truly Leninist mind. Deng knows what torture is. He knows what cruelty and brainwashing are. He knows the pride of a father, and he knows what it is to see a son suffer. He knows the pain at the loss of one's personal freedom. Yet, all of that can obviously be burned away by "the fire of the mind" that is Leninism.

In the cannonades that blasted the students in Tiananmen Square; in the young bodies crushed beneath tanks; in the hasty midnight pyres fed by gasoline thrown upon mounds of tangled bicycles and mangled corpses; in the shotgun trials and the death sentences that followed—in all of that was displayed the inhuman fire that animates all the policies and all the *ballets d'invitations* of the Leninist Party-State, whether in China or the Soviet Union or anywhere else.

Yet even as the "Beijing happening" reached its pitch of horror, Pope John Paul had no doubt that the West would somehow find a way to see in all of it the scenario it wished to see.

It was of intense interest to John Paul in that regard that, in the midst of Mikhail Gorbachev's first full-fledged campaign to win over Western minds, and almost as a curtain-raiser to the "Beijing happening," a similar "happening" was played out in the Soviet Union.

On April 4, 1989, 158 Georgians went on hunger strikes in order to force some degree of autonomy from the Soviet Union. By April 8, over 8,000 citizens were on the streets of Georgia's capital city of Tbilisi.

Though the fiery, independent-minded Georgians were unaware of it, Moscow knew exactly what the Georgian National Democratic Party and its leaders, Chairman Georgi Chanturya and second-in-command Vano Khukhunaishvili, had planned. On the very day of the Tbilisi demonstrations, April 8, a Supreme Soviet decree drafted by Gorbachev, signed by him and issued in his name sealed the fate of the Georgian secessionist movement.

By that decree, anything and everything animating the Georgian uprising was made a felony. It was aimed directly against all those who called for the alteration of the Soviet system "in ways contradicting the USSR Constitution." It was aimed at those who manufactured "materials" arguing for the alteration of the Soviet system, and at those guilty of "incitement of ethnic or racial hostility or strife." It was aimed at those challenging the role of the Communist Party of the Soviet Union "as the leading and guiding force of Soviet society."

One day later, on April 9, and on orders from Mikhail Gorbachev's Politburo, security troops—not local militia, as later claimed by Moscow —were sent in with tanks and armored personnel carriers. The crowds were sprayed with a tear gas called chloroacetophenone and then with a poison gas known as CN. Those who still remained were finally dispersed by soldiers wielding guns and shovels with specially sharpened edges—a tool strapped, twenty each, to the outside of each tank. At least twenty Georgians were killed in the offensive, and more than 180 were hospitalized. Gorbachev's foreign minister, Eduard Shevardnadze, himself a native son of Georgia, quickly flew to Tbilisi with instructions for the local Party leadership. Martial law was declared on April 10; and, by that same evening, over 120 tanks and armored cars occupied key intersections, bridges and squares.

In subsequent days, some five hundred people were arrested and imprisoned for interrogation and punishment. Military helicopters monitored the streets and rooftops from above. Nearly all shops, restaurants and public buildings were closed. The only signs of protest left finally were pitiful enough. Most women and many men, when they ventured out of doors at all, were dressed in mourning and sobbed openly. At Lenin Square, thousands of flowers were strewn where citizens of Tbilisi had been killed by bullets or gas or shovels.

Meanwhile, the authorities confiscated sixty thousand legally registered firearms, arrested two hundred people for curfew violations,

banned all foreign journalists from Tbilisi, and broadcast coverage of
Mikhail Gorbachev fulminating against "extremism" and "adventurist
elements," and reasserting the Soviet government's resolve to fight "destructive" nationalist actions.

Nevertheless, according to a Kremlin announcement, the decision to
use riot troops and toxic gas and sharpened shovels in Soviet Georgia on
April 9 "was made locally by Georgian authorities." Gorbachev was
"completely shocked."

Shocked or not, on April 12, Gorbachev drew the same Leninist line
in the sand that would soon be drawn by Deng Xiaoping. "We are absolutely against" the demands of the Georgians for autonomy, he said,
because it would be tantamount to "breaking up the national-state structure of our country."

Just how absolutely the Western mind is set in the cement of its illusions
was demonstrated in this situation for John Paul when—unperturbed by
the events of Tbilisi, and fully apprised of the student demonstrations
that had begun in Tiananmen Square—Mikhail Gorbachev arrived amid
great speculation and excitement for the summit with Deng that had
been scheduled some time before.

It was fascinating for many who serve the Holy See to observe the
enthusiasm that was displayed for Gorbachev, both on the part of the
Chinese students who clamored to see him and by many seasoned members of the Western press, who had come primarily to cover the Deng-
Gorbachev summit.

Once he had left China, Gorbachev's published reactions to the "Beijing happening" were of a piece with his comments about Tbilisi, and
with what John Paul would have expected, based on his reading of the
Leninist mind. Once Deng had displayed the same tactics that Gorbachev had used in Tbilisi, the General Secretary expressed "regret"
about the Chinese government's cruel suppression of the student demonstrations, but confided to reporters that Soviet information about the
situation was "still vague." On June 15, during his triumphal visit to West
Germany to promote the end of "artificial barriers" between East and
West—and though, at the very least, Gorbachev had read hourly tran-
script reports emanating from Beijing to the Kremlin—he cautioned that
"We must display great responsibility and balance in our assessment" of
the situation in Tiananmen Square; "we don't know everything yet about
the situation."

Meanwhile, Gorbachev's rubber-stamp Soviet Congress of People's

Deputies condemned all pressures from the West on Beijing to respond democratically to the student demands. The massacre of students, said the deputies, was "an internal affair" of China. "Any break in the process of reforms in this enormous state [China] . . . ," added Gorbachev, "would cause major damage to the whole process of recovery in the world." In the wake of Tbilisi and Tiananmen, the world might well have asked, "What process of recovery?" But, like any true Leninist, Gorbachev knew the drill to follow when any serious obstacle to the Leninist process presented itself. He reached beneath the conference table to pound the floor with the iron club of military threat.

By now, however, threats seemed unnecessary. The West appeared so caught up in Gorbachev's idea of recovery that there was more worry about dangers to Gorbachev's survival at home than about the events in Tbilisi or Soviet reactions to the events in China.

The chief worry seemed to be for Gorbachev's durability against the Soviet hard-liners in the Kremlin. During an interview given in his Moscow home and published in January 1989 in France's respected *Le Figaro*, the late and celebrated Soviet physicist and human rights activist Andrei D. Sakharov had already predicted that "the conservatives [the Stalinists] will overthrow Gorbachev, or at least impose their views on him." At that same interview, Sakharov's equally famous and equally activist wife, Yelena Bonner, had gone even farther: "I would not bet ten rubles on Gorbachev [surviving]."

Nothing seemed to throw the General Secretary off balance, however. In the very teeth of the doubts about his ability to face down the oft-quoted hard-liners, 74 members of the 301-member Central Committee "voluntarily" resigned. To be sure, this was not Mao's Cultural Revolution, nor a Stalinist bloodletting. But it was a classic Soviet power purge. Managed with surgical precision by Gorbachev, it effectively swept away the veteran "Icy Survivor" himself, Andrei Gromyko, plus a former defense minister, nine generals, many regional leaders and onetime Politburo figures, and a certain number of "dead souls," as the Russian novelist Gogol once branded corrupt bureaucrats.

If the cold eye of Leninism looked out upon the world from the center of such events of 1989 as Tbilisi and Tiananmen, and from the bloody purge of Beijing and the bloodless purge of the Central Committee of the CPSU, there were and still remain certain exceptional aspects of the behavior of Mikhail Gorbachev that have raised a question for the world that had not been raised in over seventy years of Leninist-Marxist leadership of the Soviet Union. That question concerns faith. Christian faith. Gorbachev's faith.

"Surely," Gorbachev said not long after his emergence as General Secretary in 1985, and to the astonishment of many, "surely God on high has not refused to give us wisdom enough to find ways to bring us an improvement in our relations."

That was not the language of a cold-eyed Leninist. And it turned out not to be an isolated incident. "Jesus Christ alone knew answers to all questions," Gorbachev said in the course of that same year, "and he knew how to feed twenty thousand Jews with five loaves of bread. . . . If God and the Politburo are well disposed to me, I will find the answers."

One cannot imagine Vladimir Lenin saying things like that. At one stage, Joseph Stalin did speak of Mother Russia. But one cannot easily picture him saying to Franklin Roosevelt or to any American official the words Secretary of State George Shultz heard from Gorbachev as the Soviet leader began his first visit to the United States in 1987: "The visit has begun. So let us hope! May God help us!"

As Gorbachev's tenure lengthened, so did striking events continue to raise this unheard-of question. In fact, during the 1988 Jubilee Mass in Kiev that marked the millennium of Russia's conversion to Christianity, a remarkable cry was heard from the pulpit: "At last God has sent us Gorbachev, but Satan wants to kill him." Even granting the close connection between the Soviet clergy and the KGB, the fact remains that thousands of believers—young men and women as well as old, many of them sobbing—crowded the streets of Kiev on that occasion to venerate the sacred icons openly, and apparently with none of the accustomed fear of Party-State repression or reprisal.

Still more compelling for many were Gorbachev's pointed, off-the-cuff remarks after the earthquake that devastated Armenia later that year. Gorbachev cut short a visit to the United States to tour the stricken region. While there, he took the opportunity to blast his domestic opponents again in much the usual terms. "They're striving for power," he grumbled. "They should be stopped by using all the power at our command—political and administrative." But then he added a striking and unexpected dimension to his warnings: "Let God judge them. It's not for them to decide the destiny of this land. . . . This is the edge of the abyss. One more step and it's the abyss."

In December of the same year, when Mother Teresa of Calcutta visited the Soviet Union to aid in the Armenian recovery efforts, she was received in the Kremlin with all honor by Soviet Prime Minister Nikolai Ryzhkov in the company of Foreign Minister Eduard Shevardnadze and the General Secretary of the Armenian Communist Party. Mother Teresa was assured in the warmest terms that the Soviet Union expected great things from the work of her Roman Catholic missionaries in the USSR's devastated areas.

Pope John Paul, his entourage and his Kremlin-watchers do not ignore such words and behavior on the part of Mikhail Gorbachev. On the contrary, this question of Gorbachev's relationship with God—with the God of his youth, with the God of history, with the God of divine grace and of man's salvation—is among the most important questions for John Paul to consider.

In fact—and notwithstanding the Pope's personal experience with the cold eye of Leninism, and his present intelligence information—a crucial dimension of the papal assessment of Mikhail Gorbachev in present-day geopolitical terms lies in the Pontiff's view of this particular Soviet leader as a special instrument of God. The question of Gorbachev and God, therefore—the question of a possible ambivalence in Gorbachev between the cold eye of Leninism and the eye of faith—is a crucial factor for John Paul in the millennium endgame. And for the believer John Paul is, these are not mere words. They are norms of thought and action.

That the West, as well, has become interested in, if not fascinated with, this question was underlined during a press conference Gorbachev held at the Élysée Palace in Paris on July 5, 1989. Asked if he had been baptized, Gorbachev answered almost breezily that he had, and that such a thing was "quite normal" in the Soviet Union.

Despite the General Secretary's easy reply, the fact is that neither baptism nor virtually any other facet of a Christian way of life is a "normal" element in a successful public career in the Soviet Union. Rather, such things are sure and certain obstacles even to obtaining entry to university studies. And they are absolutely insurmountable obstacles to entry—never mind advancement—in the Soviet Communist Party system. The documentation of that fact is far too extensive to allow for any dissembling.

An accurate judgment on Gorbachev in this matter must take into account the Leninist womb from which he, as a hard-core Leninist, has come. In 1905, Lenin echoed Karl Marx and said that "Religion is a kind of spiritual gin in which the slaves of capitalism drown their human shape and their claim to any decent human life." In 1915, his tone was more brutal. "All oppressing classes of every description need two social functions to safeguard their domination: the function of a hangman and the function of a priest. The hangman is to quell the protest . . . the priest reconciles them to class domination, weans them away from revolutionary actions." In 1917, his pronouncement was horribly antihuman: "We must be engineers of souls," and he went on to describe how his Bolsheviks were bound to destroy the traditional identities of all those human beings now in their power, and to reconstruct them as specimens of the "new socialist humanity."

Given this ideological heredity coming to him through Joseph Stalin ("Kill the eunuch priests and you kill this Christ") and Nikita Khrushchev ("Belief in God contradicts our Communist outlook"), John Paul has to consider closely the apparent contradiction between Gorbachev's position as General Secretary of the Soviet Union and his words and his permissiveness concerning religion. Just three alternatives suggest themselves; and, while the consequences of each alternative are fairly clear, the papal jury is still out on a final decision concerning which scenario the Pope is facing.

One possible God-and-Gorbachev scenario is that, in speaking of "God" and "wisdom" and the "abyss," and the like, Gorbachev is using vocabulary and ideas emptied of all mystical or transcendental meaning, much in the way Hitler's elite SS troops adopted the motto *Gott mit Uns* —God with us. To be sure, that was monumental and self-righteous hypocrisy on the part of men bent on staining all God's creation with brutality and overkill; but it was credited by no one as an expression of believers.

If this is the case with Gorbachev, then his behavior in this regard is probably no more important than that of any man who uses certain ways of talking learned early in his family life to emphasize a point. As John Paul well knows, Russian is as rich in such expressions and images as Polish.

The second possibility is that Mikhail Gorbachev is the classic crypto-Christian: that he is a fully believing Christian of the Russian Orthodox variety, truly attached to Orthodoxy's fundamental beliefs, secretly worshiping in his heart, fully dependent in his prayers and hopes and career on the help and inspiration of God.

If this is the case, then Gorbachev would truly be God's "mole" placed at the pinnacle of the Soviet atheist system at a crucial moment of history. If this is the case, then Mikhail Gorbachev would be the twentieth-century man chosen by God for a most singular role and fate. And if this is the case, then the world has been assisting all unknowingly at the highest drama of our time, a drama that has only just begun.

The third possibility is that Gorbachev's story may be much more typically Soviet and "cold-eyed" than some would like to believe. It may be that within himself, and in his closely guarded relations with the Council of Elders, the General Secretary is a rabid Soviet atheist, a full believer with Lenin that "all religion is utter vileness," a thoroughgoing Leninist of the classical vintage—but an extremely cunning one, who realizes that a certain level of convincing Christian lip service can still help to secure the deep and extensive integration with the West that is needed by the Soviet Union, of whose fate he is now the chief guardian and propagator.

If this third scenario is the true one, then it would have deadly significance for Pope John Paul and for the West. If true, it would mean that in the Soviet inventory of enemies to be penetrated, deceived, leavened and taken over, Gorbachev has put religion and formal religious organizations at the top of his list—just as Antonio Gramsci advised. If this is the true scenario, it would mean that Pope John Paul's Roman Catholic organization is the prime target. If true, it would mean that Gorbachev is the most dangerous Soviet leader the Church has faced, the author of the ultimate seduction, practitioner par excellence of KGB intelligence deception, and the coldest "cold eye" Leninism has yet produced.

There is only so much empirical evidence one can expect to uncover in assessing the real meaning of such unexpected behavior on the part of a supposedly atheist leader of a professionally and militantly atheist Party-State. And what evidence exists is so equivocal that it can be, and in some Vatican conversations often is, used to bolster opposing positions on the question.

All four of Gorbachev's grandparents and both of his parents were genuine believers in the Russian Orthodox faith. The familiar Russian icons of Christ and his Mother, Mary, were concealed behind the required portraits of Lenin and Stalin that hung in his paternal grandparents' house.

Born on February 2, 1931, Gorbachev grew up in the worst of Stalin's terror. We know that he was baptized; that his patron saint was solemnly declared to be the fierce defender of Heaven itself, St. Michael the Archangel; that he went to church regularly; that he participated with his parents in the liturgy—he sang the old Slavonic hymns, confessed his sins and received Holy Communion.

More, we know that all of this went on at the height of the Stalinist purges, the mock trials, the torture, the midnight interrogations and the sudden deportations and executions that decimated the Church of its

clergy and its pious laity. Even in the provincial town of Privolnoye, to
practice one's faith as the Gorbachevs did in the thirties was an act of
Christian heroism.

Did Gorbachev remain a hero, at least in his heart, as he grew to
maturity? Or was the pressure too much for him? Or was faith not
enough for him? Whatever the answer might be, at the age of fifteen
Gorbachev was accepted into Komsomol—in effect, the "Little League"
of the Communist Party. No one known to be an active believer could
have managed that. Komsomol indoctrination requires not only formal
denial of religion, but formal profession of the atheism officially propagated by the Party-State. Gorbachev must have passed the basic requirements.

From that time on, in fact, he must have paid his Leninist dues all
along the line. For he was not merely accepted; he flourished. He went
to university. In 1952, he joined the Communist Party. And he set out
on a career so distinguished among his fellows that he came to the
particular notice of the head of the KGB, Yuri Andropov, who became
nothing less than his mentor. And, having passed every test and challenge, he came finally to the peak of Soviet success as General Secretary
of the Communist Party of the Soviet Union.

Given three such contradictory scenarios, how is Pope John Paul to
read such a history?

If Gorbachev has been a crypto-Christian all along, then his motivation must have been extraordinarily pure to remain intact for so long,
and in such alien and personally dangerous circumstances. More, his
faith must have been nothing less than heroic in its profundity and
reach, because the only aim of such an exercise could have been to go
as far in his career as God would make it possible for him to do, with the
intention of liquidating the official atheism of the Party-State.

When seen in those terms, the first or third alternative—either a benign or a deadly turning away from faith—seems more likely. In both of
these scenarios, despite the early exposure of the young Gorbachev to
all the "furniture" of Christian thought within the intimacy of his family
life, by the time he joined Komsomol—and certainly by the time he
graduated from university and entered the Communist Party—he had
renounced the Christianity of his family.

Perhaps the objective reasons were fairly ordinary. The all-enveloping
materialist and atheistic outlook that surrounded him away from home
and hearth; peer pressure; Party pressure; the pressure of personal ambition; the doctrine and motivation as he moved along in Stavropol University, in Moscow University, in the Communist Party. All of this would
have led Gorbachev away from Christian belief and worship.

That road is not such an extraordinary one these days. In fact, it is more or less the same road followed by so many like-minded people in the West that they have been given a special name. "Anonymous" Christians, they are often called. What then, fundamentally, would be the difference between Gorbachev and Nikita Khrushchev, who avowed in 1958, "I think there is no God. I freed myself long ago from such a concept." Or between Gorbachev and Deng Xiaoping's son Pufong, who told Mother Teresa some years ago that "we start from a different standpoint, but we are doing the same work. . . . I myself am an atheist." Or between Gorbachev and U.S. historian William Shirer, who admitted to a reporter in 1989 that "my father was an orthodox Presbyterian and I'm sure he believed in heaven and hell and that sort of thing. For me, all that is gone."

If, like Khrushchev and Shirer, Gorbachev is an "anonymous" Christian, he has ceased to believe in the spiritual importance of organized and formal religious practice, and in the truth of Church teaching about the supernatural. But neither, in that case, would he be an enemy dedicated to the final death of all such practice and belief. Indeed, he might well retain some vague idea of a redefined and benign God. And whatever anybody else believes would be fine by him, and fine by the benign God he vaguely acknowledges.

After all, when speaking to the Central Committee on February 5, 1990, he called for a wide range of measures "to enrich the spiritual world of people," especially on the educational and cultural levels. "Industrial growth figures," he asserted, had obscured "human values." In this age of information, he went on, "we are nearly the last to realize that the most expensive asset is knowledge, the breadth of mental outlook and creative imagination." While this is not religious language properly so called, it is language of the spirit—such words would never pass the lips of a Stalin or a Lenin.

If Gorbachev is that low-grade specimen of anonymous Christian, there is always the chance that, now or later, Gorbachev may "revert to type." Faced with the ultimate in dilemmas, he may reach for that source of salvation and solution of all problems he sang about in those old Slavonic hymns and learned at his mother's knee to acknowledge as the real governor of man's fate. Perhaps there was even a glimpse of such an attitude when Gorbachev spoke so unexpectedly in earthquake-ravaged Armenia of "the edge of the abyss."

On the other hand, perhaps—after the model of Stalin—the third possibility is the real case for Gorbachev. If he has renounced his faith, how likely is it that the reasons were not ordinary or benign at all? How likely is it that, carried by his own gifts and by the invisible hand of destiny to the highest position in the Soviet Union—the nation and the system—he has simply understood in his penetrating and no-nonsense way that he could not go on behaving as his six predecessors did, and approaches the Pufong model?

Surely Gorbachev is more sophisticated than Nikita Khrushchev and Leonid Brezhnev, with their ready stock of lavatory jokes about religious believers. It was not unusual for them to wine and dine their honored guests in the magnificent Granovitaya Palata of the Kremlin. Completed in 1491 by Czar Ivan III to memorialize his bloodiest victory over Russia's greatest enemies, the Tatars, the Palata is decorated from its ceilings to its floors with Master Andrei Rublev's priceless icons of Christ, his Mother, the angels and the saints, all dominated by a giant fresco of the Last Supper, meant to remind everyone who ate there that we are intended to partake finally of the Bread of Angels and the Blood of the Lamb.

For Gorbachev's more recent predecessors, all of that, and the Palata's warm, red-orange hue so suggestive of Christ's Resurrection, were probably about as significant as the agonies of the Tatars were for the Czar when he had stakes driven through their living bodies from chin to chine on the morrow of his victory.

Still, to say that Gorbachev is more knowledgeable and less crude than Khrushchev or Brezhnev is not to say that he cannot have done more than turn good-naturedly away from the faith of his childhood. It is not to conclude that though he does not foul-mouth all religions as Lenin did, he cannot now share the mordant atheism of Lenin. Nor is it to deny the possibility that behind a more agreeable facade by far, Gorbachev might prove to be as lethal in his way as Stalin was. Once his seminary days were over, Stalin was probably responsible for more acts of sacrilege and blasphemy than any man in history.

There are temptations for John Paul in his analysis about God and Gorbachev. Because the matter is so important in terms of what the Pope can expect from the Soviet leader during critical events to come, the greatest temptation is to go to one extreme or the other.

It would be easy enough to make fond and wishful judgments. The Pope knows, after all, that Mother Teresa could only have received the welcome she did in Moscow with the General Secretary's fullest concurrence. But he also knows that as a recipient of the Nobel Peace Prize, and as someone already accepted in Cuba and Communist China, Mother Teresa has become an internationally acceptable symbol of man's "humanitarian" feelings for man.

The Pope knows that Gorbachev's mother, Maria Panteleyevna, goes to church as faithfully as ever; and to this day she has a birthday cake prepared each year for her son and sees that it is decorated with the two letters that stand for the animating cry of Russian believers: "XB!" *Xristos Boskres!* "Christ Has Risen!" But he knows as well that Khrushchev's daughter, Mrs. Aleksei Adzhubei, asked Pope John XXIII to bless her religious medals; and he remembers the Christian piety of Leonid Brezhnev's grieving widow at her husband's open casket in Moscow.

On the theory that it is better to make a wrong decision for the sake of caution than to make no decision at all, shall the Pope be tempted to the other extreme, then? Will he apply to Gorbachev, for example, the pen portrait Haing Ngor left us of Cambodia's Leninist leader, Pol Pot, who rid his country of nearly two million of its citizens by the most brutal and callous methods known? Those who met Pol Pot, wrote Haing Ngor, "saw a neatly groomed, soft-spoken man who smiled often; he had tiny, soft, almost feminine hands. Most of all, they remembered something special about his character: they said he was easy to trust."

The truth of the matter is that John Paul is too hardheaded and cool-eyed himself to be overborne by evidence from surrogates. And so, too, are the other realists he relies on in the Vatican and elsewhere. He requires of himself judgment that is calm and independent. And, above all, he is mindful of the bedrock principle of the classic "cold-eyed" KGB operation: If you are willing to be deceived, you will be. A key moment in John Paul's assessment of Mikhail Gorbachev's Christianity and religious belief will have come during the Vatican summit of December 1, 1989. He will have been very discreet and noncommittal about his perception of Gorbachev's religiousness. He will have commented that the Soviet president, apart from being an obvious instrument of divine providence and a specific sign of the times, remains "open to the grace of Christ."

As such, Gorbachev may be a onetime believer stumbling his way back to his ancient faith, while acting in the meanwhile like Shakespeare's character and like Pol Pot of Cambodia—somebody who "smiles and smiles and is a villain." Whatever words Gorbachev uses that are humanly well-intentioned, even if partisan and only residually Christian, will go from his mouth to God's ear; and they will evoke divine grace for the ends God has in mind, whatever about Gorbachev.

On the other hand, whatever destructive intentions Gorbachev the Leninist entertains in relation to Christianity and its tatterdemalion civilization in the West will be frustrated by the Guardian Angel whose name he still bears and who always sees the face of God.

Meanwhile, however, John Paul cannot afford simply to wait; to turn aside into the grandeur of papal isolation in a vain effort to sit out the onslaught of Gorbachevism. His whole policy has involved him, his papacy, his churchly institution and his Roman Catholic people in the millennium endgame. His policies regarding Gorbachev, therefore, must be wise as a serpent's, but simple as a dove's. Until the evidence tells him clearly otherwise, he will take the General Secretary to be the Leninist he professes to be; and, as has always been his practice, John Paul will not expect from the Leninist mind what he knows the Leninist mind cannot contribute.

22. "New Thinking"

Though there are many who will not easily acknowledge it, a barely concealed fact of international life is that for the past forty-five years, the Soviet Union has been the major catalytic factor in the communal life of nations.

The actor par excellence on the world stage has not been the United States. It has not been any globalist group, religious or otherwise. It has not been even the most militant or the most strategic among the developing or underdeveloped nations. And it has not been Pope John Paul's Roman Catholic Church.

When John Paul talks about his own Church in these terms, he is not referring merely to the success of Soviet agencies in developing and popularizing the deceitful Gramscian penetration of Christian doctrine with Marxist Liberation Theology—though that is his greatest headache among the people of Latin America. Nor is he talking about the failing doctrinal orthodoxy of seminaries and religious orders throughout his Church; or about the thousands of bishops, priests, nuns and laity—

including entire monasteries, convents and churches—systematically destroyed by the USSR.

What John Paul is talking about—what John Paul always talks about —is foreign policy. He is talking about the general foreign policy the Holy See has followed over the past thirty years and more.

Beginning with Pope John XXIII's reign, from 1958 to 1963, and continuing through the fifteen-year reign of Pope Paul VI, the Soviet factor has been paramount in crucial policy decisions. It even induced John Paul's predecessors to delay obedience to the mandates of Heaven in matters of supreme importance. And while John Paul would never gainsay his predecessors, those decisions have rendered his own governance of the Church all the more complicated and thorny.

Any other current head of state, political leader or power broker, if he is frank, will make the same acknowledgment in regard to his own foreign policy decisions. The Soviet Union has been the prime actor. Everyone else has reacted.

When Mikhail Gorbachev came to full power in the Soviet Union in the spring of 1985, therefore, all the world was his stage. In no way was he prepared to turn a blind eye to that fact of recent history—not in the matter of the *General Agreement* he signed with President Reagan in 1985 and not in anything else. And so, by the end of 1988, having dominated the process of diplomatic connivance to his enormous advantage —not only in terms of aid and comfort garnered from the West but above all in terms of ideological acceptance—Gorbachev was ready to make that stage his own.

In May of 1988, in the final year of his presidency, Ronald Reagan was granted permission by General Secretary Gorbachev to address the students and faculty of Moscow State University. Accordingly, the "Great Communicator" stepped forward in Moscow to deliver "a message of peace and good will and hope for a growing friendship and closeness between our two peoples." The President's manner was smiling and confident. Absent from the content of his speech was any reproach. He made no veiled hints about the "evil empire" he once saw and surely knew still to be alive in the Soviet Union.

Instead, President Reagan dwelt on America's freedom and its fruits, and on the possibility of "a new world of reconciliation, friendship and peace." Over and over again, he referred to the "many hours together" he and General Secretary Gorbachev had spent. "I feel that we're getting to know each other quite well."

Just what those two men said to one another during those "many hours together" has been the subject of much speculation around the world. But what seems certain is that Gorbachev so successfully impressed Reagan as to elicit from him what amounted to a public endorsement of the General Secretary's program for future relations between the United States and the Soviet Union. That endorsement was a major triumph for Gorbachev in his steadily mounting drive to change fundamentally the official policy of the United States toward the Soviet Union. Characteristically, however, the Soviet leader did not wait for anyone to catch up with him. He used his own triumph to leapfrog to a still greater one. And quickly.

On December 7, 1988—Pearl Harbor Day on the calendar of American history—as President Reagan was preparing to turn the White House over to President-elect George Bush, Mikhail Gorbachev strode forward to address a plenary session of the General Assembly of the United Nations in New York.

In an hour-long speech delivered with vehemence, and with his passion written clearly on his features, the Soviet leader presented the first full, clear formulation of Gorbachevism—of his "new thinking," to use the concept of his book, *Perestroika*, which had been published internationally not long before. As his living words filled that forum of nations, there was no other leader in a position to challenge his formulation, and, judging from the reaction, no one wished to do so in any case.

Gorbachev set the stage for his program in what seemed the most classic Internationalist-Transnationalist terms. "The world economy," he observed, "is becoming a single entity outside of which no state can develop." For him, as for his contemporaries, this world was now built on a tripod system; and so: "It is virtually impossible for any society to be 'closed.'" At the same time, however, "knots have appeared in our world's main economic lines: North-South, East-West, South-South, East-East." North-North, he might have added, and West-West. But he did not.

As a master geopolitician, Gorbachev called for a solution that lay in the formation of seminal geopolitical structures.

Our situation, he said, calls for "creating an altogether new mechanism for the furtherance of the world economy . . . a new structure of the international division of labor . . . a new type of industrial progress in accordance with the interests of all peoples and states. . . . Further progress is now possible only through a quest for universal consensus in the movement toward a new world order." With such a bold geopolitical sweep as his basic platform, Gorbachev launched into the principles of the geopolitical world he sees as desirable.

Beginning with the bedrock Leninist idea, untroubling by now to many Western ears, of "humankind's collective intellect and will," the General Secretary proposed "the supremacy of the idea central to all mankind over the multitude of centrifugal trends" as we find them today between East, West, North and South. Only by letting "this central idea dominate will the society of nations develop into the ideal: a world community of states with political systems and foreign policies based on law." Gorbachev left no doubt that he was talking about international laws binding all nations.

Of course, in order to let "this central idea dominate," the nations must change their philosophical approach to the task of achieving world unity amid the diversity of nations. For in this way, they will also change their political relations. To accomplish this task, continued the passionate Gorbachev, the nations must rely on "objective world processes."

One such process, he offered, would be reliance on the Helsinki agreement of 1975, so that Soviet territorial integrity would be accepted as final and definitive. Another "objective process," said Gorbachev, would be reliance on the natural unity of the two Germanys, thus allowing West Germany to take up a more neutral position vis-à-vis the rest of Europe.

In a third example, Gorbachev addressed the twin realities of an interdependent world and the need for the integrity of world peace. Like it or not, he said, we are all now interdependent. None of us can have peace if the others have no peace. Peace has become indivisible. Therefore, exhorted Gorbachev, let us start a world political dialogue among all nations; for within that dialogue, the arduous negotiating process between East and West can go forward.

Moving onto the broadest geopolitical terrain, Gorbachev advanced the need for a central agenting authority to organize and galvanize all of these objective processes. And he declared that alone among all the world's institutions, the United Nations itself is "an organization capable of accumulating humankind's collective intellect and will."

If the nations consent to cooperate in such a manner, then "cocreativity" or "codevelopment" would benefit all. If the nations consent, cooperation can include space exploration and environmental protection. It can lead to the conversion of arms production into a disarmament economy. It can wipe out the crippling debts of South nations. Through such cooperation, a homeland can be created for the Palestinians. Through such means, indeed, can all the pressing global problems that tear at our unity as a human community be addressed and solved at last.

Gorbachev was clearly not talking about internation politics; for that is no more than our present condition. He was talking about genuine geopolitics. And he had a warning: "Without the U.N., world politics is inconceivable." Alone of all the institutions so far created, "the U.N. embodies, as it were, the interests of different states. It is the only organization that can channel their efforts—bilateral, regional and comprehensive—in one and the same direction."

The geopolitician in Mikhail Gorbachev may be striking; but it never overwhelms his immediate political instinct. Did the General Secretary's global program mean that capitalists must renounce their way of life, and Marxists renounce their Marxism? Not at all! None of us "need give up our convictions, philosophy and traditions, or shut ourselves away" from the new order.

Did the General Secretary claim, as his predecessors had all done, that the Soviets were the only ones who are right? Not at all! "We don't aspire to be the bearer of ultimate truth."

What, then, did the General Secretary propose happen between capitalist and Marxist? "Let us transform our rivalry," he offered with a smile, "into sensible competition . . . an honest competition between ideologues! Otherwise, our rivalry will be suicidal."

And finally, the ultimate appeal. Why did the General Secretary propose this panorama of "new thinking" for the nations? Because, he explained at length, "the world is at a turning point in its development. . . . A new world is emerging." Today, "international relations must be humanized . . . the world must be made a safer place, more conducive to normal life." International relations can be humanized only if "man, his concerns, rights and freedoms, are placed at the center of things. . . . The idea of democratizing the entire world has grown into a powerful surge and political force . . . and I have a feeling of responsibility to my own people and to the international community."

When Gorbachev had said all he had come to say and had taken his chair, the delegates who had jammed into the tiers of seats in the U.N. chamber to hear him burst into loud and unaccustomed applause. This was not the ritual ovation due any head of state who takes it into his mind to address the United Nations. It was much more than that. It was a personal tribute to Mikhail Gorbachev. It was an enthusiastic acceptance of his words. It was an international endorsement of his person as the vehicle of their own fond and universally shared hopes.

In a single hour, Gorbachev had shriven himself and his Party-State of all the specters of Soviet leaders past—Stalin, Vyshinsky, Molotov, Gromyko, Brezhnev, Khrushchev—whose memories had for so long haunted the halls of the U.N. with the pall of distrust. In a single hour, he had dismissed all those baleful memories as so many outworn superstitions. In a single hour, he had become the embodiment of a hope and a warning—a hope that sorrow could at last be replaced with human joy; a warning that the only alternative to the hope he held out to them all was the merciless fratricide of Cain.

Finally, in a single hour at that podium, Gorbachev had shouldered aside all his peers in the nations and the power centers of the West, to claim the center spot of international attention and approbation. So prolonged was the tribute to himself, to his achievement and to his call to action, that Gorbachev stood up and took a bow!

If the troubles that already beset Gorbachev at home fostered worry—or, in some quarters, a momentary hope—that the Soviet leader might not be up to the role of the prime actor in international affairs, he himself seemed to have no such thoughts as he masterfully mounted pressure on the new American president, George Bush, to react to his proposals. By a combination of carrot and stick treatment, and through a complicated series of carefully contrived international moves, Gorbachev raised the level of tension and expectations in the United States, Europe and Japan.

While behind-the-scenes plans were being discussed by West leaders in the early months of 1989, Gorbachev made advance announcements of his own plans to carry his campaign forward in visits to West Germany and France in June and July. The reactions in those two countries and elsewhere, riven as they were with expectation, heightened the pressure still further on President Bush. "We look like a bunch of bean counters," said Wisconsin Representative Les Aspin, head of the House Armed Services Committee, "and Gorbachev looks like a guy who wants a different relationship in Europe."

Before Bush had caught his breath as President, the Soviet General Secretary had created for him the classic put-up-or-shut-up situation, from which there was no escape. There was no question in anyone's mind now who was the actor on the world stage, and who was the reactor. "What we have now," said Gary Orren, professor of public policy at Harvard, "is not a perceived crisis, but a perceived opportunity without any apparent deadline. Instead of a bad guy, we have Gorbachev."

Given that opportunity, so long hoped for, what did the Bush administration plan to do? What was the administration's thinking? Had the new administration any answer? Any leadership to offer? One U.S. editorial specifically chided the President himself, whose "excuses for going ever so slowly are now likely to . . . sharpen the contrast between a dynamic, lively leadership and an American administration stalled in its own caution." Within certain quarters of the Vatican, it was clear that the American administration was stalled less by its caution than by complicated discussions with allies, and by deep consultations within the sustaining traditions of the "Wise Men" of the West.

Then, in a series of four speeches—in Hamtramck, Michigan, on April 7; in College Station, Texas, on May 12; at Boston University, on May 21; and at New London, Connecticut, on May 26—President Bush carved out the clear position of the United States and the West. No doubt it was music to Gorbachev's ears.

"It is time to move beyond containment," declared the American president. And in that sentence, the Kennan policy—the basic doctrine that had guided the West nations' reaction to the Soviet Union for sixty years, the fundamental policy Gorbachev needed to remove and replace for *perestroika* to work—was consigned to the inactive file.

There is now a "new policy," Bush went on, "one that recognizes the full scope of the change taking place around the world and in the Soviet Union itself. . . . We seek the integration of the Soviet Union into the community of nations. . . . Ultimately, our objective is to welcome the Soviet Union back into the world order." There was no mistaking the thinking of the Wise Men in such an objective. They had always envisaged a "new world order."

The President did lay down conditions for welcoming the Soviet Union into that world order. It amounted to a line-item veto of certain Soviet actions. Soviet devilment in Cuba and Nicaragua had to stop. Soviet stealing of Western technology had to stop. Soviet use of the international drug trade to debilitate the populations of the West had to stop. Soviet restrictions on the free exchange of books and ideas, and on the movement of peoples, between East and West had to stop. Soviet suppression of human rights had to stop. Soviet maintenance of armed forces obviously poised for attack and not needed for defense had to end.

"A new breeze is blowing over the steppes and cities of the Soviet Union," said Bush, reacting to the popular hope Gorbachev had raised by his very presence on the stage of titans.

"Why not, then, let this spirit of openness grow, let more barriers come down? . . . Perhaps the world order of the future will truly be a family of nations."

The picture of that "family of nations" painted by President Bush, and the portrait he drew of the "new world order," was the model of the Internationalist-Transnationalist vision of the future. We now see before us, the President declared, "a growing community of democracies anchoring international peace and stability and a dynamic free-market system generating prosperity and progress on a global scale."

He then embraced the highest moral aim possible for human reason unaided by the grace of a transcendent God. The era of a new world order, he declared, has "an economic foundation: the proven success of the free market; and, nurturing that foundation, are the values rooted in freedom and democracy."

The hallowed voice of John McCloy echoed in those words. And so did the voices of Elihu Root and Henry Stimson and the other giants who had so inspired him; the voices of all the Wise Men whose still-dominant aim was the landmark goal of a new world order regulated by economic progress beneath human skies. A new world order achieved without the intervention of a Heaven beyond the visible heavens. A new world order achieved within the lordship of man, and without the Lordship of the Son of Man. President Bush had gone as far as he could and still remain within the mental and moral guidelines of the Wise Men.

Once again—in Vatican analysis, at least—the only fundamental change had been in Gorbachev's favor. The original processes of the West, based on the Kennan policy, had been designed as a reaction. Bush had announced to the world a change in direction, a change of gears for which the West was thankful. Still the West would meet and offset—but not liquidate—the fundamental aim of the Leninist process. Absent the central Kennan doctrine of containment, however, the questions in some minds were: What new centerpiece policy would replace it, and whose policy would it be?

And so the first and most difficult phase in Mikhail Gorbachev's geopolitical plan had been accomplished. Containment was out as basic American and Western policy in his regard. And the way was open for a key element in the new geopolitical endgame to be put in place by the leader who had already secured the greatest advantage. The adversaries of the Leninist process had fallen into perfect position.

What better moment, then, for Gorbachev to follow up his now towering advantage? What better moment than this to begin the first clinical demonstrations of the "objective world processes" that had brought the nations to their feet in admiration at the United Nations? What better moment to do more than leap from one triumph to a greater one? What better moment to take a full and open run at a major geopolitical goal?

Summer was nigh. And if a "new breeze" was "blowing over the

steppes and cities of the Soviet Union," as Bush had said, so too were
the winds of Gorbachevism blowing across the West.

West Germany's reception of Gorbachev during his June visit, which he
had announced with a politician's timing after his U.N. speech, was
dazzling. The crowds were dazzling. The brisk sales of Gorbachev coins
and stamps were dazzling. The Red Star earrings and bright-red clothes
the people wore in his honor were dazzling. Gorbachev's obvious relish
at plunging into the crowds to sign autographs, to shake hands, to be
touched by well-wishers—all of it was dazzling. "He could be an American," one student remarked, "or at least advised by Americans, the way
he does public relations."

Gorbachev needed no advice from the Americans, however. And he
was after something far more than dazzle.

In his visits to Bonn, Stuttgart, Dortmund and other cities, it became
clear that he was after a new union. And it wasn't just talk. At the U.N.,
he had spoken of West Germany taking up a more neutral position vis-à-
vis the rest of Europe. Now, on German soil, he put flesh on the bones
of that proposal.

A new stage in Soviet–West German economic might, he suggested,
bolstered by the Soviet Union's vast resources, would create a colossus
that, given time, could dominate Europe. In short, Gorbachev—never
for a moment blind to history, and ever a geopolitician to the marrow of
his bones—was after the Europe of Lenin's dreams. Of course, he didn't
put that dream in Lenin's terms. "Our common European home," was
how he put it. But in that appealing phrase, he was not talking about the
Europe of the "Europeanizers" who aim at a new unity in 1992.

Rather, he was holding out to the West Germans the possibility that
they—now an economic giant, but still a political dwarf—could achieve
a new status in partnership with his Soviet Union. "This calls for new
political thinking," Gorbachev sloganeered with the best of them, as he
and West German Chancellor Helmut Kohl signed a Joint Declaration
and eleven other agreements. "Courted by both world powers," responded the liberal newspaper *Süddeutsche Zeitung* in an editorial, "the
political dwarf, West Germany, is waking up and growing into its normal
size as the central power in Europe."

Asked about the Berlin Wall, Gorbachev took even that emotionally
loaded question farther than anyone had expected. At the U.N., he had
spoken of a reliance on the natural unity of the Germanys. Now, on
German soil, Gorbachev drew aside the barest corner of the curtain still

shrouding the astounding "objective processes" he had in store for East and West alike. "Nothing is eternal . . . ," he said. "I don't think the Berlin Wall is the sole barrier between East and West. . . . Conditions on the continent may someday make all border obstructions obsolete." Nobody among his listeners, indeed no one in the West, could have dared to think at that moment: Within eighteen months, the Wall would be gone, and the two Germanys would be discussing unification.

Gorbachev had timed his July visit to France to precede by a matter of days the 1989 meeting, scheduled to take place in Paris that year, of the "Group of Seven" whose decisions and actions are fundamental to the federation of the European Community. During that visit, a few more details emerged about the General Secretary's vision of the "common European home" he envisioned. It was not the vision of the Group of Seven.

That common home, said Gorbachev, extends from the Ural Mountains in Russia to the Atlantic. Still more striking was his addition to those contours: "The USSR and the United States constitute a natural part of the European international political structure. And their participation in its evolution is not only justified, but is also historically determined." In fact, Gorbachev railed against those "who would like to place the USSR outside Europe."

With equal force, he condemned all who would like to create a Europe from the Atlantic to the Urals by abolishing socialist governments in the Soviet satellites. In Germany, he had already said that the USSR was aiming at the creation of a "socialist market system." Now, in France, he warned the world not to expect the East to "return to the capitalist fold . . . this is unreal thinking and even dangerous." With that much understood, however, he also signaled that he did not mind the idea of a multiparty system.

When Gorbachev returned home to Moscow, by no means did he leave the field to the Group of Seven. In fact, it was in the midst of their Paris summit that he made his most direct and audacious move. He interfered with the deliberations of the Group of Seven—to say he dominated those deliberations would not be a great exaggeration—by the unheard-of tactic of sending them a letter.

Dated July 14—Bastille Day on the calendar of French history—Gorbachev's letter was addressed to French President Mitterrand as the head of the nation hosting the Group of Seven meeting. But it was read to all the visiting heads of state, President Bush among them. And in terms of its far-reaching implications, as well as in terms of headline-stealing media coverage, it was as big a bombshell as his December speech in New York had been.

Gorbachev's proposals in that letter were skillfully calculated and were hinged upon his geopolitical outlook. The Soviet Union, he said in essence, intends to join the West's efforts at mutual economic cooperation. "The formation of a cohesive world economy implies that their multilateral economic partnership be placed on a qualitatively new level."

What new level? Nothing less than a direct association of the Soviet Union in the Group of Seven and in the Europe they planned for 1992 and beyond.

"Multilateral East-West cooperation on global economic problems is far behind the development of bilateral ties," Gorbachev declared. "This state of things does not appear justified, taking account of the weight our countries have in the world economy." It was one thing to make a European union out of twelve nations. But wouldn't a union between the USSR and its client states in Eastern Europe, on the one hand, and the twelve Western European nations, on the other hand, make more sense? More economic sense? More financial profit sense?

Having opened with his bold and sweeping geopolitical platform, as he had done at the United Nations, Gorbachev proceeded in his letter to make proposals that, if implemented, would radically alter the planned course of European union. He proposed beginning with "meetings of government experts" to develop "a common economic language" and to exchange information on areas including economic development and lines of credit and aid to the Third World.

Gorbachev's aim was clear: "The world can only gain from the opening up of a market as big as the Soviet Union." And he drove his intention home in what can be described as a diplomatic oath: "Our *perestroika* is inseparable from a policy aiming at our full participation in the world economy . . . within our common European home."

The shock of the Group of Seven at receiving Gorbachev's stunning challenge was so palpable it was felt in public. President Mitterrand tried to laugh it off with a Gallic twist. We can sit and talk in the living room of "our common European home," he joked; perhaps we can even troop out to the kitchen and "have a snack together." But let's wait "before we retire to the master bedroom." President Bush was somewhat more conservative in his use of a similar image. They could, of course, "wander from room to room" and that sort of thing. But "anything else" would be premature just now.

They might have saved their breath. Gorbachev wasn't after a bawdy interlude or a tour of the house. Not even a shotgun marriage would do. He wanted everything. And, for some, his timing only highlighted yet again his lightning-quick perception of how best to follow up his own advantage.

Pope John Paul, for one, read Gorbachev's reasoning and his action as a textbook exercise in geopolitics. Gorbachev had made a deep thrust at the heart of the Internationalist-Transnationalist program. He had made that thrust in their own terms and pretty much in their own tripod language of trade, finance and military security. And finally, he had used a double-edged sword to do it.

On the one hand, Gorbachev's *perestroika* was the only solution for his own internal Soviet problems. On the other hand, the Group of Seven could not afford a return to the pre-Gorbachev status quo between East and West. But if *perestroika* should fail, that would be the only alternative.

"The old artificial barriers between different economic systems are being liquidated," Gorbachev had said. Therefore, the economic system of the East could not be left out in the cold. It was no longer possible to fall back on the Kennan doctrine. And so another fundamental policy of the West—the long-planned European Economic Community—had become vulnerable to fundamental change at Gorbachev's say-so and at his timing. Gorbachev had become the active agent in international life. Other nations assumed the role of reactors. But the initiative was in his hands.

In Gorbachev's geopolitical perspective, the time was right for his boldest step of all. "It is virtually impossible," he had said at the United Nations, "for any society to be 'closed.' " He had disposed of the doctrine of containment. He had hinted in Germany at the creation of new conditions that would make current "border obstructions obsolete." He had issued a put-up-or-shut-up challenge to the Group of Seven.

Secure in his own position within the Party-State structure—still comprising General Secretary, KGB and Red Army—and having secured at least to some degree the partnership of the West, as well, Gorbachev headed full swing into the rearrangement of the Eastern satellite nations needed to fit the reordering of human affairs for which he was preparing.

All during his challenges to the West nations, in fact, he had been taking parallel actions that made it stunningly clear that he was already following the path of his own challenges. At home in the Soviet Union

and all throughout the Eastern satellites, events that made observers very
jittery indeed confirmed that this was a Soviet leader who meant what he
said, even if he took his own sweet time to follow through with actions
matching his words.

Geopolitically, John Paul realized in 1988, it made no sense—and he
knew his fellow geopolitician Mikhail Gorbachev would have the same
realization—for the Soviet president to have lunged so decisively at including the USSR in "a Europe from the Atlantic to the Urals," and
presumed at the same time to leave the Soviet empire as it was: a Gulag
Archipelago with many Gulags tied to it. That proposal would merely
evoke all the "old thinking" of East versus West. There would be no "new
thinking." The two adversarial structures would still stand. No common
structure housing East and West would be possible; and, in the end,
Gorbachev's *perestroika* (reconstruction) would devolve into *perestrelka*
(a shooting war).

The script to be followed in Gorbachev's upcoming diplomatic maneuver for 1989 had to be crafted by him in such a way that it evoked the
"new thinking" in the West but did not imperil his own position of power
in the USSR. In this doubleheaded play, John Paul could see that his
own Poland and the other satellites could very well become helpless
pawns but with a capital role to fulfill in the diplomatic maneuvering to
come.

Already, at the opening of 1989, when it became clear that Gorbachev
would be coming to Italy on a state visit in December, the question arose
naturally: Why shouldn't Pope and Soviet president meet? "That," answered one Vatican aide softly to a reporter's query, "makes for interesting speculation." But if the Pope was going to admit the Soviet
representative into his Vatican and sit down with him, it must not be
seen or turn out to be merely one more of those "nice-to-have-seen-you-
because-you-didn't-bite-my-hand-off" encounters, as Harry Hopkins
once described his first meeting with Joseph Stalin.

The Vatican had already had numerous encounters of that type with
Soviets. Beginning with Nikita Khrushchev's birthday greetings to Pope
John XXIII on November 25, 1961, there was a series of Vatican-Kremlin
"contacts": the visit of Khrushchev's son-in-law, Aleksei Adzhubei, editor
of Moscow's *Izvestia*, in 1962; Pope Paul VI's brief encounters with So-
viets at the United Nations in 1965, his reception of Soviet President
Nikolai V. Podgorny in 1967 and his by-the-bye short contacts with other
Soviets and Communist bully boys from the Eastern European satellites

in the Vatican on four further occasions. John Paul met with Soviet Foreign Minister Andrei Gromyko twice (January 24, 1979, and February 27, 1985) for substantial conversations. But in 1984, when the Pope wished to visit Lithuania, he was refused permission. So much for such encounters! John Paul needed them no more. He would not again be on the "asking-for-permission" end of the stick.

Consequently, in 1988, when the already bouncy Mikhail Gorbachev invited Papa Wojtyla to come "with all the other religious leaders" to the "Moscow Celebration" of 1988, John Paul refused, sending instead seven cardinals (led by Secretary of State Agostino Cardinal Casaroli, bearing a letter expressing the Pope's complaints). Casaroli had a ninety-minute interview with Gorbachev and another talk with Foreign Minister Shevardnadze, during which he let both men feel the steel beneath the smooth glove of *romanità*. The maneuvering had begun.

Gorbachev desired a much-publicized summit with the Holy Father. He now realized who this man was and what he represented. He was no mere prelate like the subservient Patriarch of Moscow or his fellow Orthodox prelates, who had gone along with the atrocious treatment meted out to religion by Gorbachev's predecessors. He was an international figure, a potentate with overwhelming moral influence. And he was a Pole of the Poles. If anyone could help smooth Gorbachev's path with the Catholics in Lithuania and the Ukraine—both potential trouble spots for Gorbachev—it was Papa Wojtyla. Besides, this Pontiff was a card-carrying member of the Western "establishment." A summit with him was a must for Gorbachev's credentials as the newest—if unexpected—candidate at that club's door.

So the maneuvering into desirable and mutually acceptable positions began, accompanied by the usual signals. John Paul started "talking at" Gorbachev while actually talking with third parties—Poles, Czechs, Lithuanians, Ukrainians. In February 1989, the Soviets restored the Cathedral of Vilnius, Lithuania's capital, to the Catholics, and the hierarchy was expanded. The same month, John Paul gave the go-ahead signal for Polish bishops to sit in a joint committee with Communist government delegates in order to outline a new relationship between Church and State in Poland. By June, the Vatican and Warsaw had agreed to establish diplomatic relations; the fifty-nine-year-old CPP Central Committee member Jerzy Kuberski became Poland's ambassador to John Paul; the fifty-one-year-old Archbishop Jozef Kowalczyk became John Paul's representative in Warsaw. "I have done it [helped the reforms in Poland]," John Paul said with an eastward glance, "as part of my universal mission, and it should be seen as this. . . . It is integrated in

my mission as it is integrated in the historical evolution of the world."
This was a message in diplomatic language destined for the listening
Gorbachev, and it told him: "What I do in my papal backyard of Poland
today has significance only in your whole context."

Third-party intermediaries then sounded out the probability/possibility
of a Wojtyla-Gorbachev summit in December. The Vatican reaction was
a "Yes-of-course-but" answer. In July, Gorbachev (mindful of the Pope's
complaints) sent another signal: He allowed John Paul to nominate a
Catholic bishop in Byelorussia—the first such appointment in sixty-three
years. John Paul forthwith instructed his "foreign minister," Archbishop
Angelo Sodano, to start negotiating about a possible meeting with the
Soviet president during his already planned state visit to Italy.

Meanwhile, within weeks of his December 1988 speech at the United
Nations, and all through that spring and early summer of 1989, headlines
around the world began to take on a stunned and breathless tone in their
effort to keep up with the pace of Gorbachevism at home. A mere sampling of the headline news, when reread today, still evokes wonder at the
skilled guidance and staging of events—all the more remarkable because
Gorbachev was dealing with volatile forces of popular passion and nationalist sentiments. Gorbachev's repertoire of reassuring happenings for
jittery observers was bottomless.

[March] Leningrad's Communist Party Left in Tatters [after the elections of March] . . . Gorbachev Hails People's Power . . . Soviets Agree
to Discuss Terrorism, Drugs and Environmental Issues . . . KGB Head
Vladimir A. Kryuchov Meets with Jack F. Matlock, U.S. Ambassador to
Moscow . . . Gorbachev Condemns Stalin's Farm Collectivization, Proposes to Return Farms to Families . . . Gorbachev Sanctions New Proposed Laws About Religion, Religious Education, Religious Services,
Free Publication of Religious Books, and Church Activity in Charitable
Works . . . Free Soviet Elections . . . Soviet Insurgents Bask in Victory's Glow . . .

[April] Kremlin Proposes a Sweeping Purge of Corrupt Members from
Its Top Leadership . . . Soviet Communist Party Need Not Dominate
in the Satellite Nations of Eastern Europe . . . Change Is Urgent, Gorbachev Insists . . . U.S. and Moscow to Exchange Diplomatic Experts
. . . Soviets, After 33 Years, Publish Khrushchev's Anti-Stalin Speech
. . . Bells Are Ringing as Soviets Return Churches to Faithful . . . Hungarian Communist Official Says Top Priority Is to Institutionalize Political Pluralism . . . Moscow Imports Consumer Goods to Appease Public
. . . Soviet Political Upstarts Form a Coalition . . . Gorbachev Plans to
Stop Producing Uranium for Weapons . . . Soviet Newspapers Announce the Finding of the Remains of the Slain Czar and His Family . . .

[May] Twenty Washington Experts Say "Gorbachev Is for Real" . . . U.S. and Russians Working Together Quietly in Exploring Space . . . KGB Is Seeking a Friendly, More Upbeat Image . . . Polls Find Gorbachev's Rule Eases American Minds on Soviets . . . Soviets Print Report Saying Stalin Agreed to Split Poland with Hitler . . . Lithuanian Legislature Declared That the Republic Wanted Independence . . .

[June] KGB Head Says New Soviet Legislature Should Ride Herd on the KGB . . . Ex-KGB Head Vladimir Semichastny Says Former General Secretary Yuri Andropov Carried Out Stalin's Purges [killings] and Turned a Blind Eye to Corruption . . . "The bloody history of the main building [KGB headquarters] on Dzherzhinsky Street [Moscow] is too unforgivable. This is the place from which orders went out for the destruction and persecution of millions. This service [KGB] sowed grief, cries of agony, torture and misery all over its native land" [Yuri Vlasov speaking in the New Soviet Congress] . . . Pointed Questions for Chief of KGB before Soviet Legislature; He Hears Denunciations . . . Siberian Miners' Strike Spreads as Authorities Make Concessions . . . Hungary Dismantles the Entire 150-Mile Barbed-Wire Curtain Between It and Austria . . .

The headlines about Poland were "quite unbelievable," commented the *Frankfurter Zeitung*. For those with memories, they were:

[April] Solidarity Gets Full Legal Status . . . Polish Parliament Agrees to Talks with Solidarity . . . "Poland Has Joined Europe," Says Lech Walesa . . .

[May] Communist Poland Acknowledges Soviet-Nazi Pact on Its Fate . . . "Poland now has a new possibility allowing for transformation in the social, political, economic and moral life of the entire society" [John Paul II] . . .

[June] *Gazeta*, First Independently Published Newspaper in the Soviet Bloc . . . Solidarity's Overwhelming Victory [in national elections] . . . Communists Call for Coalition with Solidarity . . . Warsaw Accepts Solidarity's Sweep [in elections] and Humiliating Losses by the Party . . . Polish Communist Official Admits the Massacres of Polish Officers by Stalin's Direct Orders [4,254 at Katyn; 3,841 at Degachi; 6,376 at Bolugaye] in June 1940 . . . Solidarity Seeking $10 Billion in Relief for Poland . . . Solidarity Has Accepted Responsibility for the Country . . . France to Give a New Bank Loan to Poland [$1.15 billion for reconstruction, $110 million in further loans] . . . "Solidarity doesn't need to rule, only to exercise control and to broaden democracy" [Lech Walesa] . . . Walesa to Back Any Communist President . . .

All of these quick-fire happenings, besides evoking wonderment, satisfied a certain hunger in the West, where governments, commentators and the ordinary public desired to see changes in the Soviet empire, changes that would reassure them the East-West tension was truly gone. But all of what had happened so far in 1989 turned out to be a mere prelude to the heady wine the Soviet president was about to proffer his hoped-for cohabitants in the House of the New Order in "a Europe from the Atlantic to the Urals." John Paul could already write the geopolitical script of the forthcoming Gorbachev menu for the remaining months of 1989 and into the decade of the 1990s.

Beginning in August and ending in December, all six satellite nations are convulsed in change. On August 19, strongman Wojciech Jaruzelski designates senior Solidarity official Tadeusz Mazowiecki as the first non-Communist prime minister of Poland since 1948. On September 10, Hungary opens its borders with Austria to allow hordes of East Germans access to West Germany (almost 200,000 crossed over by early November). On October 17, the Hungarian Communist Party disbands and drops the name Communist from its self-description. János Kádár, old-time Stalinist, had departed from the leadership on May 22. On October 17, the new Hungarian parliament rewrites the Constitution, allowing a multiparty system and free elections.

That August, too, Wojtyla-Gorbachev contacts and signals multiplied. On August 24, Yuri E. Karlov, personal representative of Soviet Foreign Minister Eduard Shevardnadze, hand-carried a message from Gorbachev, declaring his "readiness for further development" of Vatican-Kremlin relations. He also mentioned "drastic issues"—the environment, nuclear war, world hunger—that needed airing between the two leaders. John Paul responded that he was going to send Archbishop Sodano to Moscow for discussions.

The next day, three Russian Orthodox metropolitans arrived at Castel Gandolfo, the Pope's summer home fifteen miles south of Rome, to discuss the problems existing between Russian Orthodox prelates and the Catholics of the Ukraine. In 1946, the Russian Orthodox Church had acquiesced in the massacre or deportation of all Catholic prelates, had also taken over Catholic churches and institutions. What was going to happen now? Already the Orthodox could see from afar that a reckoning day was drawing near. But the price: to hand back their ill-gotten gains? Negotiation, replied John Paul, and, of course, some restitution.

Conversation and contacts and good-will gestures—with an occasional rough passage—ensued. That same August, John Paul received in private audience Tadeusz Mazowiecki, the new non-Communist prime minister of Poland—an old friend and ally in his Krakow days—together with Communist Commerce Minister Marcin Swiecicki and Foreign

Minister Krzysztof Skubiszewski and Solidarity's parliamentary leader, Bronislaw Geremek. Clearly, if you wanted to know what was going to happen next Monday in Central Europe and the USSR you could learn that the previous Saturday, if you had an entrée to John Paul's Vatican.

During his October 6–7 overflight in USSR airspace on his way to the Far East, John Paul relayed a radio message to Gorbachev, asking God to bless him and the Soviet people, and sending his blessing to them all. In the same month, Sodano returned to Moscow with a request concerning peace in Lebanon, meeting both Gorbachev and Shevardnadze. With Gorbachev's permission, too, a Russian Orthodox Mass was celebrated in the Cathedral of Michael the Archangel in the Kremlin on October 13. This was a direct appeal to John Paul's religious heart, for October 13 was the seventy-second anniversary of the appearance of the Virgin Mary at Fatima, Portugal. John Paul's whole foreign policy is built on the meaning of that heavenly appearance, and he also ascribes to the Virgin of Fatima the fact that, on May 13, 1981, the bullets fired at his head by assassin Mehmet Ali Agca missed him. In addition, another Russian Orthodox Mass was celebrated on October 22 in the Cathedral of the Assumption, also in the Kremlin, in honor of the Virgin of Tenderness—Mary as portrayed in a very old icon preserved in the Cathedral. Without the knowledge of the Soviet authorities, an expatriate Czech bishop walked into the same cathedral at about the same time and quietly celebrated a Roman Catholic Mass, concealing what he was doing behind the ample folds of the Pope's own newspaper, the *Osservatore Romano.*

With the blessing of John Paul and the permission of Gorbachev, ten Christians and eight Soviets sat down at a U-shaped table in a seventeenth-century château at Klingenthal, outside Strasbourg, France, and for two days (October 19–21)—beneath a portrait of Charlemagne, the ninth-century emperor who has been called the original father of Europe —discussed the possibility of Christians and Marxists being able to build a new Europe together.

"We want to create a new Europe," declared Nikolai Kowalski, Gorbachev's top expert on religious matters, "for the good of man, for his political and spiritual freedom." With Cardinal Poupard, president of the Pontifical Institute for Culture, listening, Viktor Garadja, director of the Soviet Institute for Scientific Atheism, asserted: "Marxism's opposition to religion is a thing of the past." But, warned Mikhail Narinsky, Soviet historian, "Christians must help . . . or our present *perestroika* could turn into *perestrelka.*"

To them, to jurist Aleksandr Berkov and the other Soviet delegates, the Christians present emphasized that "freedom of conscience is now regarded in the West as a basic human right that requires legal guarantees." Yes, the Soviets responded, a new law, now in its second revision, was being debated in the Soviet parliament. "We need time," said Aleksandr Berkov, "time and your patient understanding."

Meanwhile, on October 18, Erich Honecker, Communist leader of East Germany, is replaced by Egon Krenz and imprisoned to await trial. Krenz will last only a few weeks. Down in Bulgaria, Todor Zhivkov, Stalinist leader since 1954, is forced to resign on November 10. The previous day, the East German government announced the opening of the Berlin Wall at all points. Within a month, the Wall will effectively be no more. By mid-December, slabs and portions of it will be on sale in Bonn, Paris, London, New York and Los Angeles.

By mid-November, amid the echoes of what was happening around the Berlin Wall, in Czechoslovakia, in Bulgaria and Romania, all arrangements had been made for the Vatican meeting. Gorbachev had removed the contentious and chauvinist Metropolitan Filaret from his post as chief-in-charge of the Russian Orthodox Church's "External Office" (it handles all meetings and dealings with the Vatican), replacing him with the very pro-Roman Archbishop Kirill of Smolensk. It was a move obviously desired by John Paul, a delicately intimated wish of his, which the Soviet strongman had no scruples about satisfying. That was what these Orthodox prelates were for—to assist the Soviet government.

On November 27, Metropolitan Juvenali of Kolomna came, with a mixture of pleading and complaining, to tell John Paul that "we cannot conduct Christian brotherly negotiations under the muzzle of a gun." Juvenali, who wanted John Paul to halt the now triumphant Catholics taking back the Transfiguration Cathedral of Lwów, was reminded that back in the 1940s, his Church had done nothing when Soviet muzzles spat bullets at the Lwów and Ukrainian Catholics. But all can be negotiated, he was told—in the shadow of President Gorbachev's policy of *glasnost!*

On November 29, Czechoslovak Communist leader Milos Jakes will step down. Alexander Dubcek—hero of the ill-fated 1968 "Prague Spring," since disgraced and demoted—and Vaclav Havel, once imprisoned for his anti-Marxist views, will become the national leaders. It will be December's end before the last holdout of the old Stalinists, the "Pig of Romania," Nicolae Ceauşescu, will be tried, summarily found guilty and—still not believing that it is all over—will be executed with his wife, Elena, already nicknamed bitterly, "Lady Macbeth."

By November's end, all was in place for the Vatican summit. Raisa

Gorbachev, dubbed the "Queen of Kremlin chic" by Italian newspapers, performed her solo engagement in Messina on November 30, evoking cries of "Viva Raisa!" from crowds of Sicilians and groups of Catholic nuns waving red flags. She was there to lay a wreath at the memorial honoring the Russian sailors of four of the Imperial Russian Navy's warships who came ashore and saved the lives of a thousand Sicilians who had been buried by the three-day earthquake of December 1908.

If ever the Western onlookers needed a sign that Mr. Gorbachev intended vast and peaceful changes in view of democratic egalitarianism, surely they had that sign in the gloom that swallowed up all those faithful stalwarts of the Party-State—János Kádár of Hungary, Milos Jakes of Czechoslovakia, Erich Honecker of East Germany, Todor Zhivkov of Bulgaria, Wojciech Jaruzelski of Poland. All of them departed because the Party-State decided they should, because the Soviet troops garrisoned on their territories would, they were assured, no longer cow the masses. In a sense, those onetime Party bosses were victims of the "new thinking"—only if they consented to their own demise could they now, by self-immolation, serve the Party-State. In any case, they had no choice. In the face of Ceauşescu's refusal to so serve the cause and depart, together with his hated Securitate bully boys, there were threats both from Warsaw Pact authorities and from NATO people that they would, if necessary, back up those rebelling crowds with arms and ammunition. The connivance was at work even there. George Bush's administration had consulted its NATO allies and the Warsaw Pact nations about a "coordinated response" to Ceauşescu within the framework of the Conference on Security and Cooperation in Europe (the CSCE of the 1975 Helsinki accords), should Ceauşescu prove to be an intractable problem. In the event, he did not.

"New thinking" is hardly an adequate term to describe the overall reactions among the Western onlookers of these events. It was a veritable wonderment, punctuated with that hopeful sigh of relief: "The Cold War is really over!" For many governments, those changes chased away any lingering doubts about Gorbachev's being an honest broker. Ludicrously but tellingly, the beleaguered dictator of Cuba, faced with a severe reduction in his annual alms from the Soviet Union, and fearful that his number was up next, used a mild understatement to complain in early December that "it is getting very difficult to build a Communist state" while "the reformers are slandering socialism, destroying its value, discrediting the Party, and liquidating its leading role . . . sowing chaos and anarchy everywhere." But John Paul delivered a scathing postmortem on the Marxist ideology of these erstwhile Communist regimes, describing that ideology as a "myth" and a "tragic Utopia."

Now, for the West, the Soviet president—like the maître d' praised by the bridegroom at the marriage feast of Cana—had reserved the good wine until the end of a banner year that was to usher in the new decade. In retrospect now, Gorbachev's timing—and luck—was perfectly adapted to his personal situation within the USSR and out front, in the eyes of contemporary leaders. He would have his "new thinking."

"The Soviet leader's difficult task," John Paul had stated, "is that he must introduce changes without destroying the Party-State." It was a pithy summary of the major danger Papa Wojtyla saw threatening Gorbachev's internal situation in the USSR. The danger was a total loss of support for his geopolitical aims among those who alone made him viable as General Secretary and now must make him viable as the Soviet president with czarlike powers. Only in that guise had he a realistic chance of holding together the ungainly USSR, already straining under the impulse of centrifugal forces, and to salvage from it a reduced core of territory.

For within the very structure of the USSR, huge and vicious strains were beginning to appear. Wildfires of ethnic conflict and economic woes were suddenly blazing throughout the six Muslim republics—Azerbaijan, Turkmenistan, Tadzhikistan, Uzbekistan, Kazakhstan, Nakhichevan—challenging Moscow's central control in an area covering the Soviet Union's southern flank, a strategically sensitive area. In Kirghizia, Moldavia, Armenia, Georgia, Byelorussia and the Ukraine, the winds of opposition and local autonomy were setting off high-decibel alarms in the USSR's very top-secret Defense Council.

The three Baltic States, Lithuania, Estonia and Latvia, gazing hungrily at the successive "liberations" of the Eastern European satellites, said quite bluntly that they wanted out of the USSR. Already in 1988, the Lithuanian parliament declared it was sovereign and not subordinate to the USSR. The Lithuanian national movement, Sajudis, had the backing of a majority of Lithuanians, including—in a very Catholic population—the support of the non-Catholic minority represented by, for example, the Jewish writer Grigorijus Jakovas Kandvivius, who was elected to parliament. Estonia's elected representatives have made the same assertion of independence. The Latvians celebrated Independence Day on November 18, 1988, with public demonstrations lit up by thousands of maroon-and-white national Latvian flags.

Meanwhile, *perestroika* had as yet produced no tangible results. Food queues at depleted shops were just as long; necessities were scarce; fuel was expensive; demoralizing stories were spreading about dissatisfaction in the Armed Forces, about continuing Soviet atrocities in Afghanistan; about the special supplies of rich food and beautiful luxury items available to the sacred *nomenklatura;* about revolts against Gorbachev within the Party—even within the all-powerful Central Committee. Besides, the Soviet economy was and still is suffocating from a worsening but hidden inflation, enormous budget deficits compelling billions of current rubles to lose their buying value, while price controls distort resource use and force goods onto the flourishing black markets, which only nourish an underground economy that does nothing for state revenue enhancement.

By the time the Soviet president would meet President Bush at Malta on December 2, 1989, the question most often heard abroad would be: "Is Gorbachev on the way out?" Several officials in the Bush administration openly stated that Gorbachev "cannot hold on." Many spoke about "saving Mr. Gorbachev."

In order to rebuff and beat down the "conservative" elements in the USSR who could prevail over him—so the message was conveyed to the West in a thousand and one ways—the endangered Soviet president needed a new type of cooperation from the West. Western pressures and demands must be tailored to suit his convenience in repelling the basic charges looming up against him on the home front. *Perestroika* was not working, his adversaries complained; and in all this *glasnost*, he was giving away the whole Soviet shop—selling out to the capitalists is what his opponent Ligachev meant—and at the same time demoralizing the Soviet Marxist spirit. Retired Colonel Igor Lopatin, as leader of the Council for Interfront, the Moscow lobby of Russian nationals in Latvia and the other Soviet republics, railed against Gorbachevism as threatening the units of loyal Communists throughout the Soviet Union.

Faced with such virulent opposition, Gorbachev let all concerned in the West know that he must not be perceived as conceding "humiliating" and debilitating conditions to the Western democracies. This was the much-desired "new thinking." With Western cooperation, he could elude his enemies and pursue his main internal goals. There was much admiration in John Paul's Vatican for the terrier-like tenacity of will with which Gorbachev relentlessly pursued the dismantling of the Soviet satellite nations abroad while countering the "hard-liners'" reactions at home to that very policy, seeking even greater powers for himself at home and a more complete endorsement of his ideas. For that foreign policy vis-à-vis the satellites was intended to elicit—as one of its chief effects—the "new thinking" of the West, and that "new thinking" would enable him to overcome his enemies at home.

As long as he could retain his general secretaryship of the Central Committee, his alliance with the KGB, and therefore his control over the officer corps of the Red Army, those czarlike powers he needed would be his because guaranteed by 230,000 KGB troops (with tanks, helicopters, artillery and planes of their own); by 340,000 Internal troops; by elite units like the 30,000 Spetsnatz; by some 70,000 paratroopers; and by some particularly trustworthy Guard divisions. All in all, his ultimate strength resided in this military arm of over three quarters of a million highly trained and carefully indoctrinated "effectives," who could count on the blind ideological support and allegiance of perhaps 15–20 million citizens throughout the USSR. Gorbachev's personal fate and fortunes came down to that.

John Paul's observation to French journalist and writer André Frossard, although it anticipated by two years the surprising events of autumn and winter 1989, indicated how penetratingly he had understood the Soviet chairman's position vis-à-vis the West and to what lengths Gorbachev would have to go in order finally to elicit from his Western contemporaries the type of cooperation and collaboration that was needed if his reformed and renewed Leninist Marxism was to get the Party-State over the top of the biggest hurdle in its path since November 1917. "The Soviet leader must change the way the [Soviet] system works, without changing that system," the Pontiff remarked to Frossard.

In spite of all Gorbachev brought about in the Eastern satellites and the USSR by the end of November 1989, there remained that fundamental difficulty for the mind of the West: the Soviet system. The fright and apprehension it had engendered and generously fed for over seventy years was a fire that burned in the Western mind. The most impressive expression of that fright and apprehension was composed and published by an anonymous "Z" in autumn of 1989. "Z" was quite frank and forthright: No matter that the Soviet leader *is* making his socialist system more humane, and no matter even that by some political sleight of hand he apparently replaces it with a market economy—and even with the trappings of a Western democracy. No matter, asserted "Z"; the brute fact is that the Party-State remains intact. It is the monster. That is the only fact that merits attention. As long as that Party-State remains, "Z" recommended, it should be a hands-off policy for the West. Let Gorbachev and his Party-State stew in their own juice and perish—for surely they will perish.

The "Z" attitude, in other words, gave a negative opinion about John

Paul's questioning summation of Gorbachev's difficulty. No, "Z" answered; in order to survive and succeed, Gorbachev cannot do what the Pontiff suggested he had to do. But "Z" was speaking—as the Pontiff was —about facts. The wily Soviet president knew and knows that, fortunately for him, it is not facts that move international opinion and individual men's minds today; it is their perception of facts. Their perception becomes for them the reality, no matter what the facts.

The gambit in which the Soviet leader indulged between December 1, 1989, and mid-February 1990 would all but assure him that the overall Western perception became as follows: The Party-State, if not as dead as a doornail, is certainly on the way out of all effective existence. The "new thinking" would be pushed to its logical conclusion. "Z" was derided, in the words of Vladimir Simonov, political analyst for the government-controlled Soviet press agency Novosti, as "a hybrid of far-right extremism and naïveté . . . the position of *perestroika*'s gravediggers . . . that still regard the Soviet Union as something diabolic."

If anything was needed to show convincingly that the "Z" thesis had had no appreciable impact on the progress of the "new thinking" in the official mind of the West, it was the arrival of President Bush, on December 1, at the United States warship *Belknapp* in Maltese coastal waters, where he was scheduled to "summit" with Mr. Gorbachev on December 2. On the eve of the Vatican summit, the wryly humorous Soviet spokesman, Gennadi Gerasimov, commented: "They have been talking for years about a dialogue between Christians and Marxists. This time it will be real. This time it will be a conceptual talk." On Gerasimov's Marxist lips, "conceptual" meant "down-to-earth" and "practical"—the opposite of religious emotion and ideological passion.

23. Vatican Summit

In the range of summits and "summitry" the world has witnessed since 1945, the Wojtyla-Gorbachev summit of December 1, 1989, struck a peculiar chord of its own. It displayed the usual characteristics of summits: two supreme leaders sitting down together to discuss their mutual relationship; panoply and power in evidence from both sides; worldwide interest in the meeting and its consequences; and a vital function of their meeting in the ongoing concrete affairs of their contemporaries.

But, unlike the other summits, when this one was over and done with, there was no satisfactory precision available about what was transacted between these two men, the Pope of All the Catholics and the Leninist Leader of All the Russias. For transaction there surely was, a transaction much desired by the Soviet leader in his race to achieve a wholly new international status for his USSR, and a much prized transaction for this Slavic Pope, whose papal policy and personal devotion are irrevocably oriented to the lands of the Slavs. And, let it be said, it was a transaction that was assiduously monitored by leaders in the West, who had been stimulated by the meteoric Soviet president to link the future of their countries and nations intimately with this man's future.

Yet neither in the weeks preparatory to that summit nor in its aftermath was any precision to be had. There were fourteen hundred journalists and reporters assigned to cover the state visit of Mikhail Gorbachev to Italy. He was to hold important meetings with government officials. But that side of his visit was put on a "newsworthiness" par with Raisa Gorbachev's visit to Messina on November 30. "Good copy," certainly, but not front-page, large-headline news. The Wojtyla-Gorbachev meeting was the main focus of interest.

It was announced, analyzed and critiqued extensively and intensively by the media for weeks before it took place. Comments by world leaders and predictions by pundits filled the newspaper columns and editorials. But no estimation of the forthcoming get-together between the reigning Pope and the current strongman of the largest, the most powerful, and still the officially anti-God state sounded satisfactory, even approximately accurate. Everyone knew some details. No one seemed able to spell it out in the round.

For patently it was not a religious event, as we normally understand such a happening. Yet who could doubt that religion would be a conditioning factor on that day's exchange between papal host and Soviet visitor? This was no ordinary meeting of the "greats": a gelid encounter of wary warriors around the green-topped table of raw power. But still, if any genuine power existed on that day, it surely rode on the shoulders of Papa Wojtyla and Mikhail Gorbachev.

The Soviet man was not in Rome on a social visit "to trace the footsteps of the Caesars" and, just by the way, "to see the Pope." Nor was it a bargaining session, a "hard-tack" negotiation between international "horse dealers." Lesser men, the "gremlins" and "back room" boys in Vatican and Kremlin, would do all the haggling and point-by-point bargaining.

Nor, finally, was it foreseen as one of those "celebrations," a diplomatic get-together wreathed in smiles and handshakes, punctuated with photo opportunities, highlighted by a public "signing" ceremony and giveaway memento pens, evoking good "feelings" about "the other side" and culminating in the clinking of champagne goblets at a state banquet for the glitterati. There would, indeed, be handshakes, and smiles, and photo opportunities, and—for the working "gremlins" backstage—refreshment *alla italiana*; but all that usual panoply was rendered in the chiaroscuro peculiar to the age-old *romanità* of the Holy See.

During the last weeks and days of November, there were diligent attempts to downplay the meeting, to describe it as a quiet triumph of the Vatican's long-suffering, almost fifty-year-old *Ostpolitik* originating in the Vatican of Pope Pius XII, maintained by Popes John XXIII and Paul VI, and crowned by Secretary of State Agostino Cardinal Casaroli. But this was not so. The twists and turns of that *Ostpolitik* had provided temporary easements in isolated cases. But the forthcoming meeting, if the child of that *Ostpolitik*, would be as surprising as a brilliant flamingo born from two bewildered barnyard fowl. Casaroli's *Ostpolitik* was a long, winding, dark tunnel with never a speck of light, with no end in sight ever.

If there never had been an *Ostpolitik*, that meeting would have taken place anyway. If there had been only that *Ostpolitik*, it would still be mired down in the morass of deliberately awkward protocol, and tortured on the brambles of intentional ill will. Only because of what Wojtyla had accomplished in his first ten years, and only because Gorbachev in his desperation looked beyond the here and now of mummified Leninist Marxism, was the forthcoming meeting possible.

Other analysts saw it as a chance for those men—each one needing something from the other—to display their bargaining chips and claim their IOUs. But this was not the case. The IOUs had been paid. The chips had eliminated each other. That had been the essence of *Ostpolitik*.

Still others contemplated the coming meeting with misplaced piety and historical myopia, seeing it as a fatal compromise bordering on blasphemy—the Church entertaining, beside the Tomb of the Apostles, the one man closely resembling the unclean Beast of Apocalypse foretold as polluting the Holy of Holies! But Papa Wojtyla had no intention of allowing that Tomb to be besmirched—he relied on the protection of the Archangel Michael for that proviso. President Gorbachev had no intention of trying to desecrate, to desacralize, or even to trivialize the Vatican ground he trod on and the sacred presence of the Most High housed immemorially within those walls. Anything of that nature was as distant from Pope and President in their intentions as a banal act of common lewdness.

Between any such motivations and what actually animated the two leaders in the December meeting, the distance and the difference can be aptly compared to the distance and difference between a pigsty on a dirt farm and Mount Everest in the Himalayas. Not cluttered with busy details of personality and career, not hobbled with little vanities (complaints, preferences), and not designed even partially with a view to "the voters back home" or homeside parliamentary politics, the meeting concerned the structure of our human society, its substance, its promise, its perils and its ultimate foreseeable fate.

In spite of the pervasive imprecision coloring the forthcoming summit, when all the conceivable forecasts and pre-analyses had been endlessly set forth, there remained one solid and widely shared persuasion, never expressed fully in words, but nevertheless washing around the minds of people.

If anything really newsworthy, really important for the man in the street, was going to transpire on that December 1 in the Vatican, it would be in the nature of a drama; and all the rest belonged to "the grease and the paint" of the supporting cast, the carefully planned decor and the barely audible accompaniment of a very ancient and very modern voice reminding all and sundry of our deepest, wildest human hope—to see the Father of us all face-to-face and, finally, to taste the peace of true home on earth.

This sense of drama, this universally experienced feeling that not merely were two important personages about to talk but something affecting all was about to happen, pervaded the minds of observers and commentators. The fate of all in the coming years was going to be not merely discussed but molded powerfully.

For the generality of people today, there was no new thinking available "on credit," and, therefore, no way they could think the thoughts Wojtyla and Gorbachev would verbalize carefully. Yet, it was realized that now, on the eve of the most important decade in two thousand years, someone with vaster stature than a mere "religious leader" was in close colloquy with someone endowed temporarily with more transcendent intuition than any of his Leninist predecessors.

In effect, as that first Friday in December dawned, a sea of the same awareness about the drama unfolding in the Vatican was lapping around the minds of all—the proximate witnesses, those interested from afar, the inimical, the suspicious, the cynical, the hopeful. That sea of awareness seems to have been as universal as the waters of the oceans that ebbed and flowed around the edges of all five continents, providing a symbolism and an imagery peculiarly apt for the occasion. Whether it was around Soviet Archangel in the Arctic Circle, around the meandering coastlines of Old Europe, washed by its three main seas—the Atlantic, the Mediterranean, the North Sea—around the continental bulks of Africa, India, Australia, or around the newly named Pacific Rim, these same ocean waters mirrored the widespread consciousness of the Vatican event. No one was not touched. Just as no human shore could escape the washing ocean waters, so no one could be unaware, even the most adversarial—the Hermit Crab of the Adriatic's Albania, the Clown of the Caribbean in Cuba, the Beggarman Dictator of Nicaragua, or the frightened band of Touch-Me-Not Purists in Beijing.

Symbolically, too, those same waters heaved and rolled around the island of Malta, where President Bush, guarded by U.S. naval might, with a Soviet flotilla standing by, already awaited the Soviet president, straight after his visit with John Paul. There was a symbolic message and a daunting imagery carried by the wild waves of those waters, whipped slowly into fury by a winter storm around Malta. The Soviet president would have to wait and wait before getting together with the American president. The American leader would have to hazard a motor-launch trip through those troubled waters in order to reach the Soviet leader.

By contrast, the coming together of Papa Wojtyla and President Gorbachev proceeded in great tranquillity and with customary Vatican punctilio. St. Peter's Square, sunlit beneath a clear blue sky, was closed from early morning to all traffic. Behind barricades, a policeman stood every fifty feet. At 10:50 A.M., the Soviet motorcade of five Russian-made ZIL limousines, carrying Gorbachev, wife Raisa, and twenty-four officials and aides and led by an ever-watchful army helicopter, swept in quietly through the Renaissance archway into the Courtyard of St. Damasus. A group of black-suited gentlemen, the receiving line, stood by.

Not waiting for the chauffeur to open the door, Gorbachev was out that door, hand extended, a broad smile on his lips as he walked over the Oriental rug spread on the ancient cobblestones, in order to greet Bishop Dino Monduzzi, prefect of the Pope's own household. Raisa followed him, dressed in a red dress, Gorbachev in a dark-blue suit but without the usual panoply of medals Soviet leaders used to display, even when dressed in "civvies." There were smiles and handshakes all around. Twenty-four Swiss Guards, dressed in the blue-and-gold-striped uniforms designed by Michelangelo, performed, as guard of honor, their four-point *picchetto* drill with halberds.

Then the President, followed by his retinue, entered the Apostolic Palace and advanced along a red carpet up the corridor, studded with blinking pieces of audiovisual equipment. Fr. Giovanni D'Ercole, assistant press spokesman and "traffic director" for the moment, kept whispering into the microphone tucked behind his Roman collar as the Soviet party advanced, Gorbachev's every step being watched on the ubiquitous digital monitors as the cortege approached the elevator.

Arriving on the third floor of the Apostolic Palace, the Gorbachevs found a smiling John Paul II standing and waiting for them. He wore his papal white robe, with a gold cross pendant on his chest. He addressed the Soviet president in Russian as "Mr. President." Gorbachev alternated between "Holy Father" and "Your Holiness," as did Raisa Gorbachev.

If these two men, Wojtyla as Pope and Gorbachev as Soviet strongman, had met ten years earlier—the moment when John Paul was fresh from Poland in his office as Pope and Gorbachev just up from the province of Stavropol and installed in Moscow as Secretary of Agriculture and Central Committee Secretary of the Communist Party—surely some exuberant commentators would have waxed poetic in their imaginations.

They would have been fed by the lithe, almost panther-like loping stride of a still fresh-faced Karol Wojtyla—the Polish yeoman straight from the *polanie* (fields) of his motherland and in search of Poland's traditional enemy to the East. They would have seen an invisible aura of mute confrontation between him and the bustling, husky figure of the Soviet man as the self-assertive, overriding and fast-talking Russian *boyar* ready at a moment's notice to hack and hew his way stolidly with a broadsword to the goal of empire and foreign possessions.

But the intervening decade has taken its toll on both men. On one as the Holder of the Petrine Keys to Heaven, which shine with the human blood of his God. On the other as the quintessential Leninist commissar, Champion of the Hammer and Sickle, which he claims today he has wiped clean of the human blood of millions mowed down in the ugly harvest of death on the way to the never-never land of the Marxist Utopia. Both men have paid their dues for their personal access to the cold, bleak plane of geopolitics they now occupy and on which they will converse alone this December day.

Perhaps, indeed, neither of them is any longer aware of the vast change of mind he has undergone because of what he has had to suffer in order to achieve a tolerable balance and equilibrium on those little-frequented heights. That was not suffering of body but of spirit, leaving invisible wounds that never heal, never scar.

Wojtyla and Gorbachev are far, far older than ten ordinary years will ensure of themselves; and the twelve-year difference between Pope (seventy) and President (fifty-eight) makes no difference. They have learned, as leaders, when to pause in wait on events and when to leap ahead of them; as inspirers, what hopes not to evoke; as commanders in chief, what commands not to give. They are wiser, not sadder, but certainly more sober and relaxed because surer than ever before that the construction they have put on events will be verified by what is going to happen for the remainder of their days on earth.

A first look at each other as they advance to shake hands, the first eyes-to-eyes stare crisscrossing between them in quick appraisal of mood and temper, the press of palm on palm and fingers on fingers, the very sound of their first syllables—all that is quite enough for quick recognition, for establishing between them the authenticity of the forthcoming conversation.

With conventional preliminaries over, Vatican aides softly and deftly guide everyone: Foreign Minister Shevardnadze with his aides and advisers off in one direction for a sit-down discussion with Cardinal Casaroli, with the Vice-Secretary of State, Archbishop Cassidy, and with their teammates from the Vatican's "Second Section"; Raisa Gorbachev on

her way to see the Raphael Rooms and "Loggias" (she has already seen
their replicas in the Leningrad Hermitage) and to be frustrated in this,
her second attempt to see the Sistine Chapel. When she and her husband were here as little-remarked visitors in 1971, the Chapel was
closed for repairs; likewise today, December 1, 1989, she cannot get to
see it.

At 11:03 A.M., Pope John Paul ushers Mikhail Gorbachev into his
private library, motions him to a chair, sits down opposite him, opens his
notes and starts talking. A reproduction of Poland's national treasure,
the icon of Our Lady of Czestochowa, bearing the slash mark of a Tartar
saber on the cheek, has been placed on an easel to the right of the two
leaders and some few feet from the table at which they sit. It is John
Paul's "touch" to the scene.

Outside the closed doors of the papal library, four Swiss Guards stand
on watch. All approaches to those doors, within the Apostolic Palace,
are littered with elements of the Vatican Secret Service, the Italian police, some of President Gorbachev's personal bodyguards. Television
monitors and radio communications sweep every inch of corridors,
rooms, elevators and lobbies. Outside electronic and "body" surveillance
on the grounds around the Palace and in the air above it seal off the two
men from any interference.

As planned, the two men will have about five minutes alone, conversing
in Russian. Then they will be joined by interpreters and some others.
The switch ensures accuracy and correctness of understanding, as well
as a witnessed record of what transpires between the two leaders. Enemies and friends of both men in the Vatican and the Kremlin must have
some crumbs to chew on and digest.

The initial minutes together and alone permit these men some things
they both need. The meat of today's transaction between Papa Wojtyla
and President Gorbachev is reviewed here. Before any third party from
either side participates, they must be able to agree on what will not be
aired verbally during the full session. For both men have dissidents and
adversaries in their political households, and those must not be privy to
certain ultimate goals and certain decisions Papa Wojtyla and President
Gorbachev nourish in the only confidentiality that is absolute—their
own hearts and wills.

In addition, one or two subjects are to be touched on that are best not
mentioned in public communiqués. Perhaps some particular individual
on one side or the other? A forgotten prisoner in the Gulag? An intelli-

gence matter between Vatican and Kremlin? A fleeting exchange about John Paul's would-be assassin, Mehmet Ali Agca?

And then there are assurances to be given mutually, about which the wide world will never hear: John Paul's deepest intention in visiting the Soviet Union, Mikhail Gorbachev's ultimate disposition regarding God and religion and Russia. These themes are ultimately connected, since both men are convinced that the papal visit will be much more than a mere papal visit. On that event will hang the ultimate judgment of history about the significance of Gorbachev and Wojtyla. Perhaps, indeed, that is why the Soviet president interspersed his actual words of invitation to John Paul with an "if God keeps us all alive and well in the meantime" phrase.

Lastly, between the two there is an agreed-upon assessment of where world affairs stand and the most desirable directions in which they should go. It is not the first time this subject has arisen between them. They already share common words, concepts and principles, so there is no need for long-winded explanations or detailed exposition. Already, through trusted personal intermediaries, they have had substantial communication on the ticklish issues. So now they act more or less after the manner of two master mariners preparing to set sail who finger the key rigging, test the rudder, ensure the working order of the ship's radio, glance at their provisions and scrutinize momentarily their already planned voyage on the map. There is very little need of talk or extended discussion; just telling phrases and indicative gestures. Then they are ready to give orders to the working crew.

The session with interpreters using a mélange of Polish, Russian and Italian will get down to the details on which the two leaders wish to establish a protocol of agreement. Prior consultations between Vatican and Kremlin people have located the general areas in which the two leaders can form a public agreement: the establishment of a permanent channel of official communication between Kremlin and Vatican; full diplomatic relations; the passage of an effective freedom-of-conscience and religious-liberty measure through the Soviet Parliament; the demands of the Holy See on behalf of its faithful in the Baltic States, the Ukraine, Byelorussia, and elsewhere in the Soviet Union; Soviet policy in Latin America and the Middle East; an official visit by Pope John Paul II to the Soviet Union in response to Gorbachev's official invitation; and, lastly, the present and future relationship between the Holy See and the Russian Orthodox Patriarchate of Moscow.

Who, even from among all our current world leaders, could have usefully joined in that transaction—for transaction it was—at this geopolitical summit? That question is greeted by the same silence of unknowing that cloaks the Vatican meeting.

Essentially, that transaction between the two consisted in identifying the similarities, parallels and coincidences between their individual geopolitical minds and intentions. The agreement between the two was reached by matching up and measuring mind to mind, intention to intention. The disagreement between them was evident where mind did not meet mind, where intention flew in the face of intention.

But always, as should be the rule between the two sole participants in a genuine and tense endgame in which both are gambling all in order to win all, there was no clash and no infringement upon the individual differentials between them. Knowledge of those, and mutual acknowledgment of them, this was all that the success of the meeting required. This was no battlefield, no competition—all that belonged outside, on the open terrain of living millions, competing ideologies, governments, armies, and the stuff and matter of economics and industry.

Between these two players, it is to be "all cards face up." John Paul knows that the Soviet leader is a hard-core Leninist. "I am a Communist, a convinced Communist," he proclaimed publicly some days previous to the meeting. "For some that may be a fantasy. But for me it is my main goal." As for the Pope he is about to meet: "We [Marxists] do not conceal our attitude toward the religious mind. We look down on it as deficient because it is nonmaterialistic and unscientific."

Mikhail Gorbachev knows, and John Paul knows Gorbachev knows, that this Polish Pope does not see any chance even of survival—let alone success—for Gorbachevism unless Russians convert to religion, renounce, denounce and execrate Leninist Marxism. "No political system and no ideology built on a materialistic concept of man and human life can do anything more than plunge man into deepest misery and send him into darkest exile from his true destiny." This was one of John Paul's earliest excoriations of Leninist Marxism, while he was still a Polish cardinal. He still thinks so.

Between these two men, therefore, no camouflage, no deception, no playacting, in this mutual estimation as well as in the reading of the other's "face up" cards.

Obviously, some cards on both sides of the table are identical—those, for instance, that picture the elements both men agree are major in the endgame now being played for the formation of the new world order: Western Europe, Central Europe, the USSR, the U.S.A. and the People's Republic of China (PRC). All the other elements—Japan, Latin

America, Africa, the subcontinent of India and Pakistan, Southeast Asia, Korea and the remaining members of the society of nations—will be drawn willy-nilly into that play of major elements.

Of those major elements, there is mutual agreement that the PRC is the one that dominates the arrangement of all the others. It is the basic reason that dictates Mikhail Gorbachev's moves within the USSR and Central Europe, and those moves in turn have decided the direction in which Western Europe and the U.S.A. will move.

On each side of the table, there is one card always lying beneath the right hand of the players: it identifies the overall and ultimate geopolitical goal of its owner. The hand gesture is merely that, a gesture, to indicate inviolability, not to conceal its message. For each one has already read the other's hole card; that is why they have come together as endgame players.

As Gorbachev knows, John Paul's goal is a geopolitical structure for the society of nations designed and maintained according to the ethical plans and doctrinal outlines of Christianity as taught and propagated by the Roman Pontiff as the earthly Vicar of Christ. He is neither for Gorbachev's "East" nor for capitalism's "West," for neither can create the needed structure of the nations. There can, finally, be no compromise with the dialectical materialism of that "East" or with the capitalist materialism of that "West."

Nor will any compromise be necessary even in the short range. John Paul is convinced neither "East" nor "West" can succeed of itself in creating a geopolitical structure; and this is so mainly because, before any definitive moves in such an effort are made, the condition of all the major players will be severely modified by an act of God. That act will have as its epicenter precisely that Central European area between the Oder River in the west and the Caucasus Mountains in the east.

As John Paul knows, Gorbachev's goal is a geopolitical structure corresponding to the Leninist ideal: the Marxization of the entire Eurasian landmass from the Atlantic to the China Sea as the first step, then the Marxization of the Western Hemisphere. It is presumed as axiomatic by John Paul that the much touted Sino-Soviet falling out is a long-range tactical move designed to facilitate Soviet rapprochement with the West, while keeping intact pure Leninism in the raw among China's billion-plus population. Now more than ever, since Gorbachev's thrust at some form of integration with the nascent Europe 1992+, this double-headed policy has become of capital importance.

John Paul has followed all the moves that his Soviet opposite number has made in the last two years. Indeed, the first of those moves—the liberalization of Poland, key territory and nation of Central Europe, which set all the satellite dominoes toppling—was largely made possible by the policies of Archbishop Karol Wojtyla and Polish Primate Stefan Cardinal Wyszynski. He can predict, without being told by their chief author, what the subsequent moves will be. He has read Gorbachev's words at the Student Forum on November 5, 1989: "We are carrying forth a Marxism-Leninism freed from layers of dogmatism, staleness and shortsighted considerations. . . . We are returning to its roots and creatively developing it in order to move ahead."

But those two hole cards remain outside all discussion. There is a certain element of "See you in Central Europe" between the two men, not so much in the challenge of "See you tomorrow in the O.K. Corral" of Wyatt Earp fame, but certainly in the spirit of Thomas More addressing the executioner who is about to chop off his head: "Pray for me, as I for you, that right merrily we meet in Heaven."

All the other cards are available for examination and for the play, even the trump card, the ace each man is counting on. There is John Paul's reliance on a heavenly intervention, the evocation of an utterly new state of consciousness in all of mankind. There is Gorbachev's almost servile belief in the coming of "Leninist socialism" as "the inevitable result of civilization's development and the historical effort of the working class and all working people," as he told the Moscow students on November 5.

John Paul knows it does not matter in Gorbachev's long-range view that he has had to loosen the control reins over the Central European satellites. The Soviet president knows that schools of Marxist and para-Marxist thought and persuasion have been born throughout the claimant intellectual elites of the West—at Stanford University, among Critical Legal Studies Groups (the "Crits") of Harvard Law School, in Frankfurt's School Critical Studies Group, among France's "Structuralists" and "Deconstructionists," in the leftist Black Studies movements, the World Council of Churches, the Third World Studies groups, among the radical feminists, and throughout the art departments of a majority of major universities. On the top of that Marxist-colored wave, there are scores of clergymen and nuns, seminary professors, intellectuals, writers, all from John Paul's Roman Catholic Church and all translating Marxism into hallowed Christian terms so that basic Marxist thought can become palatable for the hundreds of millions of Catholics in Third World countries, particularly Latin America.

No, Gorbachev need not fear. Marxist theory and enthusiasm will never die as long as such elites carry them forward. Wasn't that the basic twist Antonio Gramsci gave to classical Leninism? And isn't he, Gorbachev, the prize pupil of the dead Sardinian theorist? Nor need John

Paul fear. He knows that the fate of Marxism—theory, theoreticians and practitioners—and of Gorbachev's structural plans for Europe and Asia will be decided not on the earth but in the Heaven.

Agreeing to disagree on ultimates, agreeing to agree about several interim measures and conditions affecting the Catholic Ukraine, Lithuania and Latin America, both these men cover the U.S. concept as developed by President Bush and Secretary of State Baker: the three concentric spheres of international unity—the European Economic Community, the North Atlantic Treaty Organization (now assigned a political role) and Greater Europe (the Western European states, the former satellites, the Soviet Union and the United States). In sum, a first geopolitical structure housing some 800 million souls from the Urals in the USSR to the coast of California, washed by Pacific waters. Theoretically rounded and finished as a working concept, there is no way it can be reduced to a practical working system, unless the ominous promise of the PRC to be the spoiler is not offset and diverted.

Some cards, finally, are discarded: the anomaly of Albania, sour and inimical and bitter, in the middle of the European euphoria; the devilment of Castro's Cuba, which has ceased to be of use to Moscow; the PR gyrations of Nicaragua's Daniel Ortega; the prostitution of the Russian Orthodox Patriarchate of Moscow to the policies of the Leninist Party-State.

Ranging over all these issues, securing agreement where possible, underlining irremovable differences, emphasizing further steps in a gradual rapprochement between Holy See and Kremlin, each man has sized up the other and determined as of now how far he can be trusted and where the points of utter divergence may provoke open hostility, even warlike reactions. This mutual review, essentially completed before they met, is now reflected in how they, together with their aides, conduct the actual discussions at the meeting: point by point and, at times, word by word.

Methodically and deliberately, sometimes with difficulty, the two men ratified in mutually agreeable terms their understanding and commitments on those subjects.

When you have gone over all the details of that meeting, there is one conclusion that allows you a mere glimpse of its geopolitical function. No agreement reached by the two men during the sixty-eight minutes they were together with aides and interpreters (11:10 A.M. to 12:18 P.M.), and no agreement hammered out by the parallel meeting running concurrently for some fifty-seven minutes between Soviet Foreign Minister Eduard Shevardnadze and Secretary Agostino Cardinal Casaroli, supplemented by their aides, could have been achieved without the person-to-person meeting of the Pope and the Soviet president.

Why, then, that meeting? What was the element only these two men in a personal get-together could and had to contribute, if the Vatican-Kremlin rapprochement was to succeed?

Quite simply expressed, the Vatican meeting concerned a welter of procedural and permanent arrangements—the stuff and matter of the agreement. Only John Paul and only Mikhail Gorbachev could take the general trends and principles (all to be practiced) of the proposed agreement and together place those details within the framework of their geopolitical intentions and ambitions. This was a special process, which the two leaders were capable of carrying out satisfactorily only in each other's presence.

Something proposed from the Kremlin side during the pre-December meeting preparatory talks may have been incorporated into the proposed text of agreement as worthy of consideration and as a possibly acceptable point by the Vatican. Likewise, from the Vatican side, there may have been something advanced by John Paul's agents and it, too, incorporated as a possibly acceptable point by Gorbachev's agents.

But, during the actual meeting, when one leader proposes such a point for mutual agreement, and goes on to explain that point from his geopolitical point of view, only then will it be clear to the other leader that the point is acceptable or unacceptable from his geopolitical point of view. For the two of them are discussing each point against the backdrop of geopolitics, and only within that framework are all points incorporated into the general agreement.

Hence, the need for interpreters on both sides, to ensure verbal understanding of each key term used—it may be as simple as "and" in place of "or"—and hence, also, the need for specialized aides for on-the-spot information. Hence, above all else, the need for the direct, face-to-face, voice-to-ear meeting of the two leaders. For there is more to language than the dictionary meaning of words. There is the connotation of a word for its user. And there is his intention in using it. Both connotation and intention are best perceived in a *viva voce* exchange. So much depends on the geopolitical mentality that the two leaders can use language understood by all present but what those two understand and mean can escape all others. They are literally talking over the heads of all present.

The term "peace" is a case in point. Politically, for those listening to the two leaders, the term meant an absence of conflict and an agreement between possible or actual enemies to forgo conflict. Geopolitically, the term meant and means something else for John Paul and Gorbachev: not the conflictless arrangement of their duo, but the unitary condition of a new order between them. Will promoting the Ukrainian Catholics fit in with that unitary condition? It may well meet all current political requirements by John Paul, the Ukrainians, or Gorbachev. But it may damage the process of unitary development. What, therefore, does John Paul mean when he speaks of "peace" as his goal? And Mikhail Gorbachev? Each one of them is aware of what the other means geopolitically when he speaks of "peace."

There could, in other words, be no really solid agreement between John Paul's Holy See and Mikhail Gorbachev's Kremlin unless both met in person and, laboriously communicating through interpreters and aides, arrived at a mutually acceptable understanding consigned to written language they would both accept.

At 12:18 P.M., the two leaders emerged from the papal library. Raisa Gorbachev, seated in a chair in the hallway outside the library, had been waiting for some time. A microphone flanked by two chairs had been arranged beneath a painting of Christ's Resurrection by Renaissance artist Pietro Vannucci ("Perugino"), known in his day for his profession of atheism and simultaneously for his religious devotion. Like the icon of the Virgin on that easel in the library, the choice of location for Mikhail Gorbachev's post-meeting remarks was John Paul's.

Gorbachev characterized his meeting with John Paul as "a truly extraordinary event. . . . We had much to discuss. I felt that my thoughts and concerns have been duly appreciated, as well as my explanations of the problems that now exist . . . including problems between the state and various churches, which we are addressing in a spirit of democracy and humanism."

The Pope and he had reached an agreement in principle to establish diplomatic relations; and "we announce that we have invited the Holy Father to visit the Soviet Union." Gorbachev reiterated the changes taking place—"within the framework of *perestroika*"—in the status of believers in the Soviet Union, and he thanked "the Holy Father" for making his visit possible.

Then it is the Pontiff's turn to conclude this meeting, with some remarks in Italian. Gorbachev sinks into a plush white high-back chair, glancing at a Russian translation of Wojtyla's speech, half understanding the Italian, nodding in silent assent now and again, throwing an odd glance at the small ring of dignitaries and aides around them. The deep basso tones of this Priest, the smell of the Sanctuary hanging in the air, the icons of saints and mysteries on the walls, even his half understanding of the spoken words, all are powerfully evocative. "This meeting will be interpreted as a sign," John Paul is saying, "as singularly meaningful, as a sign of the times that have slowly matured, a sign rich in promise. . . ."

There is no way this Soviet man, with his mercury-fast intelligence streaking back and forth over all the details, can escape the voice of deepest remembrance in him. Signs have abounded in his life. Once upon a time, when all was fresh in him—his early teenage years—indelible and unspoken convictions were imprinted on his soul and imaged by the lively sensations experienced only in raw youth. He lived those early impressionable years amid an abundance of such signs.

The Easter Days and Holy Days at Russian Mass in his native Privolnoye. Standing between his father and mother, facing the iconostasis that hid the priest from view as he consummated the Mystery, listening and trying to join in the rising and falling cadence of the old Slavonic hymns, half understanding the words but fully understanding the meaning of it all. Surrounded by signs that cozened the Mystery and its meaning—the flickering candles of adoration; the sweet smell of the incense of prayer; the privileged taste of Holy Communion bread tinctured in the consecrated wine; the blue and gold and silver and red of the sacred icons on the walls from which his patron saint, the Archangel Michael, together with saints and angels, with Christ and his Mother, gazed down on him; the oneness of himself with parents, with the other worshipers, with the priest, with the Mystery—their *sobornost*. That child of Privolnoye was "father of the man" now listening to another priest in another Sanctuary embodying the same Mystery.

Nothing in the fugitive years since that springtime of life had erased those profound imprints of his soul. No, not the youthful, dutiful avowals of atheism in the Komsomol, not the solemn professions of Scientific Atheism in the Party, not all the oaths of office up along the ladder of hierarchy, not even the craven submission to the diktat of the Council of Elders required for admission to the leadership of the Party-State. Nothing had changed, really, in him. Merely the choice of his will, and his outward behavior. Both could be changed in an instant. "There are no atheists in foxholes," was a comment of one soldier returning from the trench warfare of World War I in Flanders. This day, in the Vatican, no atheist is listening to Pope John Paul II.

"The Soviet president is a long-awaited guest," Wojtyla continued, "a man whose words truly demolish the idols and remove the boulders along the path of the human caravan. . . ." An elegant tribute, certainly, to Mikhail Gorbachev's geopolitical savvy and superior skill. But, also, a momentary stab of light into his heart and the inmost councils of his mind. Once you demolish the idols, Wojtyla was intimating, there remains only the divinity those idols aped. Once you clear the boulders of fratricide from our road, there remains only love. "In the heart of man, there remains always a certain space which only God can fill, always a desire only God can satisfy." It was both an analysis and a warning. Wojtyla the geopolitician bespoke the analysis. Wojtyla the priest issued the warning.

In franker terms, he could have said, "Your Lenin, in 1905, called religion 'a kind of spiritual gin in which the slaves of capital drown their human shape, and their claims to any decent human life.' And a little later, Lenin spoke of 'the only idol we permit and maintain is godlessness.' Even if your demolition of that idol is a temporary and temporizing proviso, Mr. President, beware of the one that idol was meant to supplant. You knew him once. You worshiped him once. It is terrible to fall into the hands of a living God. For he conquers all by love, because he is love itself. Even if your abandonment of fratricide is merely today's ploy to buy tomorrow's time and next week's dollar credits, beware because you have given love a breathing space. And that love conquers all, including the death you might be reserving in your heart as the ultimate fate for your adversaries."

These intimate resonances of Papa Wojtyla's words do not echo from the printed text of newspaper reports. They were palpably present in his living voice as he spoke.

For the rest of his speech, Papa Wojtyla was sensible and moderate. He supported *perestroika*, "if it helps to protect and integrate the rights and duties of individuals and peoples so that peace may ensue in Europe and the world." Of course, he remarked, "many believers in the Soviet Union had suffered painful lives since 1917. . . . On their behalf, whether they be Latin, Byzantine or Armenian, I nourish the firm hope that they will be able to practice freely their religious life." John Paul was thinking of such situations as that of Leningrad's venerable Cathedral of Kazan, now a Museum of Soviet Atheism, as well as of its congregation of believers. With some more remarks about the hopes he had for the full normalization of conditions in the Soviet Union, and a last word of thanks to the Soviet president, John Paul concluded.

There remained the exchange of gifts. Papa Wojtyla gave the Soviet man a three-foot-high reproduction of a mosaic from St. Peter's tomb depicting Christ. "This," he said, "is a memento of this historic event." Gorbachev had a two-volume reproduction of a fourteenth-century Kievan Psalter for John Paul. "I believe," he said to the Pope, "you will find this interesting." For Raisa, John Paul had a Rosary with a gold cross and mother-of-pearl beads. His murmured words to Mrs. Gorbachev were not recorded. In Roman diplomatic parlance, the gifts were neither "neutral" nor "slaps in the face." They were "tentative" and "positive" but "safe" expressions of genuine satisfaction and cordiality.

There finally was that last moment between the two men, the final final moment of leaving each other's presence, a last meeting of the eyes, a parting gesture of the hands, when instinctively John Paul would say a "God speed you on your journey, Mr. President," then turn away, breaking the delicate filament of person-to-person contact between them, and return to his papal study on the third floor, his head crammed with details, his heart pressured by wild hopes and deep apprehensions. From up there, he could only hear the powerful strokes of the escort helicopter leading the five limousines out of the Courtyard of St. Damasus. But, in his mind's eye, he could see it all clearly.

More than any help John Paul had promised or could deliver to Gorbachev, there was the protection of the Archangel Michael, after whom Mikhail Gorbachev had been named, as his personal patron; and there was the protection of the Virgin of Tenderness, whose shrine stands within shouting distance of Gorbachev's working desk in the Kremlin and without whose approval and favor this Soviet president could never succeed, could not survive the ravening wolves of dissension, hate and violence out there in Moscow's streets, in Azerbaijan, in Georgia, in the Ukraine, on the Baltic Sea and over in China.

Was it Goodbye, until Heaven? Or *Do Zwidanya*, until once more on this earth? Was Gorbachev a temporary instrument of God's providence, this day his finest hour, and soon to be cast aside? Or was he the one destined to preside over the coming unveiling of human fate back there throughout the ancient homeland of all the Slavs and all the "Europeans" between the Elbe River and the Caucasus Mountains? There remained for John Paul the crying words of the dying Pius VI, a man who had acquaintance with those ravening wolves: "May the sweet mystery of God's love consume us all in his peace."

The Soviet president left the Vatican at 12:57 P.M. He was off to lunch and an afternoon visit to the Colosseum, where he would, American style, "press the flesh" in the crowds of gusty Romans, as he had done in Washington, New York, Bonn, Paris and Beijing.

He had participated in what the Pope's own *Osservatore Romano* had described as "a moment of singular intensity" and one Italian paper called "the summit of the century." Vatican Vice-Secretary of State Archbishop Cassidy was more sober: "Our impression is that Mr. Gorbachev has a vision of a world not just in which conflict is missing, but a world in which there is a real decent cooperation . . . but Catholic communities will have to be normalized . . . bishops recognized and established in their sees . . . churches opened . . . a community able to worship in normal situations" before Gorbachev achieved full credibility. John Paul, through his Vatican aide Cassidy was stating his requirement that Gorbachev perform what columnist Cal Thomas aptly called "a conscious and public departure from the convictions of the German and Russian founders of Marxist Communism."

In the weeks following the meeting, there were many reflections on it, many analyses of its meaning and many practical decisions taken as a consequence. Gorbachev, in his New Year's message, declared that "the world is now forging ahead in pursuit of happiness, freedom and democracy." We now have, he asserted, "the goal of a humane, democratic socialism, and a society of freedom and justice. . . . Everyone in the Soviet Union must now shoulder part of what the entire country is experiencing in the complexities and passions of the Soviet Union. . . ." Give me, he appealed over television, "a practice of reason, kindness, patience and tolerance." You almost expected him to end with a "God bless you all, my fellow Soviet citizens!" sniped journalist Yves de la Coste.

In his New Year's message, Czechoslovakia's writer, saint and president, Vaclav Havel, urged John Paul to visit his country (John Paul went in April). In his annual address to the vast diplomatic corps of Rome, on January 13, he announced the coming birth of a "Europe of the Spirit," the "common home" of all Europeans; and he congratulated the U.S.A. and the USSR for their new approach to "peace and unity."

Each one of these men returns to his own habitat fully persuaded that, under the circumstances, he has taken the wisest step toward his ultimate goal and won the best possible conditions from his counterpart. Each hopes the other will fulfill his part of the agreement. Each one in his own way hopes the other will have the strength and time to do so. For each one, in his own way, is tied to a rather inevitable schedule, already running out along the passage of the minutes, hours, days and weeks that slip by. That schedule is the monkey on each man's back, continually screeching about the unavoidable deadline he has undertaken to meet by entering the colossal gamble of geopolitics.

Mikhail Gorbachev must preside daringly but prudently over the process of disaggregating the huge and ailing Soviet giant, already palsied in its extremities, anemic in its internal arteries and deeply disturbed in what has passed for its soul, all these years. What has already happened

to it can be accurately viewed as disintegration, even if it is an allowed
disintegration governed by a principle of Lenin that Gorbachev has
learned well: "Do not put what is transitory above what is essential." The
former pacific unity of all parts of the hybrid USSR was and is transitory
compared to the essential of preserving the "Revolution." That union
represented merely immediate and here-and-now interests. In the continuing "Revolution" lie the external interests of "the world's working
class as a whole."

But the monkey will scream its alarm more and more loudly, as the
fitful palsy shakes more and more parts of Gorbachev's USSR; and the
fateful deadline will draw nearer, according as the troika of Central Committee, KGB and Red Army finds its strength more and more diluted
while, over in the East, along a border of 4,000 miles, the other partner
in preserving the "Revolution" waxes stronger and more palpably Leninist than the stricken USSR. How far should the new permissiveness
go? Surely not so far that Gorbachev or his successor presides over something resembling the tiny Duchy of Moscow five centuries ago. That
would be the point of no return. But how far? In principle: as far as is
required for the integration of the Party-State in the "common European
home." But what about the in-between time?

In that "in-between" lies Gorbachev's gamble: that, before the point of
no return, he effectively occupies the living room and bedroom of that
"common European home." A full marriage. Then he will have actual
or potential power over a union greater than the former USSR's. He can
confidently face eastward and purify the Chinese "socialist fraternity"
from its terrible deviation in substituting a modern version of its very
ancient "warlordism" for the pure Leninist internationalism, and in mis-
translating Lenin's universal victory of the worldwide proletarian revolution as the paltry "territorialism" always claimed by the ancient and
hateful Middle Kingdom. Capitalist corruption can be tolerated—even
used. But the "Chinese deviation" destroys the soul of Leninism.

John Paul, too, must go on presiding daringly but prudently over the
disintegration of his Roman Catholic institutional organization. He, in
his way, just as the Soviet president in his way, is committed to that
course of action—and inaction. But how far is too far?

He must go on with his mission as he has understood it to be ever
since he became official Holder of the Keys. He does believe those Keys
are guaranteed by the human blood of the man he worships as God. He
does also believe that this geopolitical mission he has chosen to fulfill as
Pope will be crowned with a success never registered in the life of any
preceding pope. That, in effect, in the sight of all nations, his authority

by right of those Keys will be declared in the skies above every nation so that across the face of Earth all men and women will see clearly where they stand in relation to the one who shed his blood to make those Keys perdurable until the end of all human time.

But the more his institutional organization descends into the shameful shambles of disintegration; and the fewer become the number of those who are Catholic in belief and practice; and the greater the number and power of those within his Church who are no longer genuine Roman Catholics, the more that monkey on his back screams in alarm at the approaching deadline, the point of no return, beyond which it will not be truthful or accurate to speak of a visible Roman Catholic Church.

24. *"New Architecture"*

Whether it was a tacit perception that the Wojtyla-Gorbachev summit at the Vatican outclassed the Bush-Gorbachev summit in Maltese waters, or whether the guesses and estimates about that Maltese summit had already and accurately forecast the results of Gorbachev's short meeting with President Bush, the fact is that no noticeable excitement surrounded the American and Soviet flotillas for those few days at the beginning of December 1989. The ugly winter waters, the annoyance of the Soviet president at being kept waiting, the critiques of Gennadi Gerasimov, these and suchlike details were what created news. It was taken for granted by all observers that the two presidents were going to put their final stamp on the "new thinking."

So it came as no great surprise when Mr. Bush, in the immediate aftermath of the Malta summit, summed up the results by saying: "We stand at the threshold of a brand-new era in U.S.-Soviet relations." The President was thus announcing the official American entry into the millennium endgame. Its basis? The "new thinking" was carried to its logical conclusion: "I, the President of the United States, will kick our bureau-cracy and push it as fast as I can," on trade and credits, on two arms control agreements—both treaties to be finished and ready for signing at the next summit meeting, in June 1990. Mr. Bush did not explicate in so many words, but it was part and parcel of the "Malta understanding" that the United States would exert great circumspection in its words and actions so as not to make Mr. Gorbachev vulnerable at home to the attacks of the new Russian "Patriots" and of those who were already screaming out loud about Gorbachev's "caving in" to the Yankees.

Doubtless, the Soviet president acquainted Mr. Bush with his Decem-ber–February program as well as with his planned schedule for the re-mainder of 1990, thus getting himself confirmed as "our man in Moscow." The "we must help Mr. Gorbachev" rule went into full vigor. It would be some weeks yet before Vaclav Havel, new president of Czechoslovakia, would gently but pointedly criticize this Western atti-tude. "In the West, there is a tendency to personalize history," Havel told journalist Lally Weymouth. "It seems to me that no matter how big Gorbachev's share in this [the changes in the USSR], this is something that doesn't exist and fall with his person." But Western leadership pro-ceeded on that principle. "You have a love affair going with Gorbachev," one Lithuanian activist told an American visitor, "but we do not love him as you do."

Loved or unloved, Gorbachev went ahead with the propaganda value of a promised papal visit to the Soviet Union and John Paul's help in calming Catholics in the Baltics and in the Ukraine as the palpable results of the Vatican-Moscow meeting on December 1; and, following Mr. Bush's post-Malta resolutions, the "new thinking" was definitely "in." The Soviet leader had been assured of Western cooperation in his domestic struggle for those czarlike powers he needed for complete con-trol of his situation. Gorbachev had now become the key element in the millennium endgame as Western leaders planned it.

But the contrast in aims between Western leaders and John Paul was clear to the Pontiff. The West's cooperation was granted in view of the "Wise Men's" ultimate aim of the "new world order." John Paul was carrying on Christianity's perennial tradition of accepting forced cohabi-tation with evil, knowing that, in general, no new world order could successfully emerge that was not based on the rule and kingship of Christ; and that in this particular historical situation, the final solution of the world's difficulties would be effected through the intervention of the Queen of Heaven.

In the meantime, he could once more have written the veritable scenario of Gorbachev's achievements between December 1989 and February 1990. The achievements were phenomenal, the "new thinking" they generated so exhilarating for the West that an almost Alice-in-Wonderland atmosphere pervaded the international atmosphere for a while.

"Moscow feels immeasurably more comfortable in the international arena than ever before," Soviet Foreign Minister Eduard Shevardnadze crowed on December 5. Well he and all his colleagues might crow. President Bush had undertaken: to have the two treaties—strategic nuclear arms, conventional forces—ready for the June summit meeting; to facilitate the economic reforms in the Soviet Union; and—most important—not to embarrass the Soviet Union's adventurism in Afghanistan, Syria, Cuba, Nicaragua, Ethiopia and El Salvador.

The events following up these beginnings took on the air of the inevitable.

By the end of December's second week, U.S. Secretary of State Baker had sketched out a "new architecture" built on the "old foundations" of NATO, the European Security Conference (CSCE) of 1975–76, and the European Community (EC). The U.S., the EC and the USSR would meet in June at a CSCE thirty-five-nation assembly to map out the place and function of a unified Germany in that "new architecture." For a Germany reunited will be the capstone of the inmost circle in that "architecture"—the Western community of nations. The second circle will include the Soviet Union and its former satellites. The third and outermost circle will embrace all in a wide sweep from Helsinki to Vladivostok on the Pacific Ocean. Mr. Baker was planning as an Internationalist, of course. True to that mentality, he had now presented his so-called two-plus-four framework: Within this arrangement, the two Germanys would agree on a path to be followed, leading them to unification; then the four powers—the U.S., Britain, France and the USSR—would sit down with the all-Germany delegates and negotiate the delicate issues of new and old borders and of international security.

Rightly, Mr. Gorbachev spoke rambunctiously about it all. "No one has the right to ignore the negative potential formed in Germany's past." He added that "the Soviet Union has an inalienable right to expect, and the capability to exert efforts to ensure, that our country should not sustain either moral or political or economic damage from German unification." The fine combination of saber rattling and righteousness showed that Gorbachev saw in this "new architecture" the fresh outlines of his geopolitical plan. "Our Leninism," he told Moscow cadres, "is now purified and capable of reaching its destined goals."

John Paul noted, in this same period, that "the time is ripe to reassemble the stones of the battered walls" and "construct together our common house," based upon the "spiritual roots which have made Europe"—but that all efforts would fail if nations did not end "the presence and spread of countervalues such as selfishness, hedonism, racism and practical secularism." His geopolitical agenda remained the same because his reading of all these events had not changed: On an exclusively materialistic basis, not even all the nations involved in the CSCE (NATO and Warsaw Pact nations, plus twelve European neutrals) could achieve even a limited success. But they were going to try anyway.

For there was no gainsaying the effect now evoked in the Internationalist minds of the West. Even the schedule of free elections now promised for 1990 was startling for minds that, over forty-five years, had never associated such a democratic process as a free election with the Soviet Gulag Archipelago: February 24, Lithuania; February 25, Moldavia; March 4, the Ukraine; March 18, East Germany, Latvia and Estonia; March 25, Georgia and Hungary; May 20, Romania and Bulgaria; June 8, Czechoslovakia; and, to round all this off, the December elections in Germany to pick a *Reichskanzler* for all of Germany.

The changes promised by Gorbachev started to appear slowly but surely. At Brussels, Eduard Shevardnadze joined the United States in condemning Nicolae Ceauşescu's repression of dissidents in Romania. "I can only express my very profound regret," he said. "We are categorically against the use of force." An extraordinary public relations effort was launched by the hated KGB to recast its image as "just an intelligence service like the ones possessed by all the other Western powers." But it was in Lithuania that Gorbachev began to reveal his biggest surprise.

As far back as February 1986, he had told the landmark Congress of the Soviet Communist Party that "no party has a monopoly over what is right. We need," he went on significantly, "to restructure the Party's internal apparatus, greater democracy within the Party, and national election reform." In June 1988, he told his Soviets: "The Party's leading role will depend entirely on its actual prestige, which, at every point, will have to be reaffirmed by concrete deeds." Now, in late December, Lithuania's Communist Party broke its ties with the Communist Party of Moscow and declared itself the Independent Communist Party of Lithuania. It was a direct rejection of Article Six of the Soviet Constitution, which guaranteed the CP of the Soviet Union the "leading role" in world Communism.

In mid-January 1990, Gorbachev flew to Lithuania for three days of cajoling, threatening and argumentation. He was well briefed on the situation. The local Communist Party had already declared its independence from Moscow's control. "We have passed the threshold," said Algirdas Brazanskas, Communist Party first secretary and Politburo boss, "and there is no turning back." Anyway, as another member of the Lithuanian Politburo remarked, "Gorbachev will be overthrown within a year."

Nothing daunted, Gorbachev took on all comers in Party meetings and on the streets of Vilnius, Lithuania's capital. His efforts were backed up by very efficient KGB teams, who worked assiduously to undermine the anti-Soviet sentiment that animated Lithuanian workers, management and intellectuals. On his last day there, at the end of a marathon four-hour public debate with Lithuanians, one Lithuanian stood up and asked the Soviet president bluntly: "Are you in favor of a multiparty system?" Gorbachev's answer was totally unexpected. "I do not see anything tragic about a multiparty system," Gorbachev said, shrugging his shoulders, "if it emerges and meets the realistic needs of society. One should not dread a multiparty system." That was on January 13.

Less than a month later, on Sunday, February 4, the day before the opening of the Plenary Session of the Central Committee of the Soviet Union's Communist Party, there was a very strange gathering in Moscow's Red Square. It was strange for Moscow because it was the first assemblage of so many people—over 250,000—in that square in seventy years. It was strange for the Party-State because, as an absolute rule, Soviet law and practice prohibits any gathering of even 100 people in the street without official permission, and because it came together precisely to urge the Communist Party to resign its political monopoly in that vast territory. "Resign! Resign!" were the cries shouted under the walls of the Kremlin. "Long live the peaceful revolution of February 1990 that is now under way!" shouted Yuri N. Afanasyev, member of the Congress of Deputies.

Finally, it was strange because neither when the jam-packed thousands crowded into Marx Prospekt after a four-mile march nor when speaker after speaker denounced the Communist status of the USSR, and clamored for a multiparty political system, did the police take any action. Radio Moscow, in fact, broadcast the rally in advance. Unofficially, this rally had official sanction! "Keep your hands off our President!" warned one hand-lettered sign.

Up at the windows giving on to Marx Prospekt, Gorbachev could point down at those thousands; they were going to be his best allies when he faced the 250-member Central Committee on the morrow. Nobody had to stress the obvious: Only one man could have sent out the word that

summoned the crowds, that muted the police, that instructed the media.
"These are democratic forces," the television reporter commented at the
news hour, as the screen showed the placard held high by the marchers:
"Gorbachev! We're with you!" Lest anyone miss the change-or-die message, evening television followed the news with reports from the former
satellites.

Western observers had a choice. They could regard Gorbachev's very
recent railing against a multiparty system and his visit to Lithuania as
last-ditch attempts to stave off a dreaded result. Or, they could regard all
that as skillful use of psychological pressure in order to place him in the
position of the French revolutionary who excused his sudden change of
allegiance, saying: "I did my best. But the people are leading. I must
follow them!"

On Monday, February 5, Gorbachev opened the Plenary Session of
the Central Committee of the Soviet Union's Communist Party. He
dropped his bombshell right at the beginning: The Communist Party
must renounce the absolute power guaranteed it by Article Six of the
Soviet Constitution. "The crux of the Party's renewal is the need to rid
it of everything that tied it to the authoritarian-bureaucratic system. . . .
The Soviet Communist Party intends to struggle for the status of the
ruling party. But it will do so strictly within the framework of the democratic process, by giving up any legal and political advantages."

There could be no doubt now: The CP's monopoly was over. Pluralism
was in. The multiparty system would be legal and constitutional. As if to
prove further how far along the de-Marxizing of the USSR could go, the
Central Committee's platform published on February 7 contained an
endorsement of private property. This was a surrender not only of the
Party's economic dictatorship; it was a repudiation of one of Karl Marx's
basic principles and an apparent adoption of the principle on which all
true capitalism is built. The CC did not proclaim the principle, however.
It just permitted private property. The CC also faced the conundrum
posed by private ownership of property in a closed and planned Marxist
economy: "how to find an organic combination of plan and market methods to regulate economic activity." And the drafters of the platform spoke
of "a need for a procedure in which planned, centralized economic
management will be exercised through prices, taxes, interest rates,
credits, payments, etc."

All of this sounded like capitalism in the making. Gorbachev airily
dismissed the wonderment-filled questions of reporters on Friday, February 9: "These changes have been under way in this country since
1985." All of this was a normal evolution, he was saying, in the Soviet
democratic process. Why the surprise?

It was score 1 for the "new thinking." There was still more to come as added reassurance.

On February 12, leaders of the Soviet parliament voted in favor of holding "an extraordinary session . . . in the nearest future" in order to vote on new powers for the Soviet presidency—Gorbachev's post. "A democratic presidential power would be his: to maintain the country's stable development, to speed up *perestroika*, to guarantee its irreversibility, to ensure the normal and effective functioning of all state and public institutions in the process of democratization, to ensure law and citizens' security, to protect the Soviet Union's interests, and to represent our state in the international arena."

These were the absolute czarlike powers he needed. What Lenin and Stalin had accumulated by bloodletting, torture, the massacre of millions, lies and propaganda, this Master Craftsman of Statism had obtained unbloodily and by overwhelming vote. It was score 2 for the "new thinking" of the West.

Finally, as score 3, there was the big surprise of February 13. At Ottawa, the Soviet Union agreed with the leaders of the West that talks should start immediately, on a rapid schedule, with a view to reunification of the two Germanys into one. The significance of this mutual decision was mighty. It meant that the USSR was directly involved in shaping the future of all Europe; for, in that Europe made whole, the economic hegemony and the dynamic leadership would reside in a reunified Germany under conditions guaranteed by the USSR. It meant, even in the short run, the diminishment of U.S. hegemony—and that, also, in a military sense, for no one was fool enough not to realize that Germany would rearm, perhaps within a European force, perhaps not. It also laid the groundwork for the emergence of an ancient dream: the Northern Alliance Tier, or Russo-German Alliance. On all those developments, Gorbachev as czarlike leader would have immense influence.

In the "new thinking" now foremost in Western capitals, all major government policies and activities would be geared to the thirty-five-nation meeting in June and the U.S.-USSR summit at about the same time. The United States and its allies were determined to "help" the Soviet president and to avoid giving his enemies any handle with which to beat him down.

Gorbachev was given carte blanche to fix the date of the next U.S.-USSR summit when it best suited him politically. Nor did Secretary of State Baker emphasize in any way the U.S. objection to the USSR's sending a supply of new Mig-29s to Cuba and India. He would not publicly reiterate U.S. insistence on the independence of the three Baltic states. Nor would a word be breathed about the thirty million land mines the Soviets had sowed in Afghanistan. For the "new thinking" bids the West to make Mr. Gorbachev's avowed aim—to terminate the Communist Party's totalitarian rule—as easy as possible. This is why many would rather speak of conspiracy between the U.S. and Gorbachev than "new thinking" by the U.S. about the USSR. Many more go further and insist that basic Leninism is Gorbachev's motivation, and that behind all the smiles and concessions to "democratization" there abides a cold, calculating eye.

"The Western image that Gorbachev is democratic," admonished Lithuania's Bronius Genzelis, a member of the Congress of People's Deputies (the new superparliament Gorbachev has created in Moscow), "is not correct. . . . Gorbachev is playing with the West the way a cat plays with a mouse. . . . He is a realist who saw the precipice of decay and destruction, and hurried to the West to avoid an explosion in his own country."

Nevertheless, it remained that at the end of this skillful bout of geopolitical statecraft by Mikhail Gorbachev, the excited mentalities of the nations had predictably accepted the reactive posture on which he had counted. "The West does not fully realize that the Soviets have not won the Third World War, the unarmed war [for economic victory]," said Vytautus Lansbergis, leader of the Lithuanian Sajudis independence movement. "They, on the contrary, have collapsed. But they are talking terms of peace as if they had won. The West talks to Gorbachev as to an equal."

That summed up pithily Gorbachev's achievement. Instead of being relegated to stew in his own Soviet-made, homegrown juice, he and his USSR were now welcomed into the millennium endgame.

Soviet satisfaction was almost oleaginous. Foreign Minister Shevardnadze cast an eye back over the Cold War days when Stalin predicted an "inevitable victory" for Marxism and Nikita Khrushchev told the West, "We will bury you." To be frank, Shevardnadze told his Western colleagues at the Ottawa meeting in mid-February, "our country took too much time grappling with the dilemma of truth versus happiness." The Soviets, he said, had thought they should "prefer the anxiety of someone who knows the truth"—that the proletarian revolution would succeed—"and not choose the tranquillity of those [the West] who ignore it." But, he went on magnanimously, "Today our country is sick. . . . We shall become not only a big and strong country but a genuinely comfortable and civilized home for men and women. Such a state has to survive." As a mea culpa, this dripped with delusory self-righteousness, which, under normal circumstances, would have been greeted in the West with hoots of laughter and catcalls of "Hypocrite!" But in the "new thinking," this was music in Western ears.

More was to come from the Soviet parliament, that February. The parliamentary working group, on February 21, came up with a draft law giving President Gorbachev new and extensive powers over the legislative and executive branches of government: power to bypass parliament, power to bypass the Politburo, power over the Ministry of the Interior, the KGB and the Red Army. Absolute power, in other words.

One final and effective blow in favor of "helping Mr. Gorbachev" and, therefore, in favor of total U.S. dedication to the millennium endgame was provided by the new president of Czechoslovakia, Vaclav Havel. In his childlike, almost holy-man manner, the former playwright addressed the U.S. Congress on February 21. It is doubtful if, when he had finished, he left any dissenters in the tiers.

"We enter an era in which all of us, large and small, former slaves and former masters, will be able to create what your great President Lincoln called the family of man. . . . After World War II, the Soviet Union . . . was a country that rightly gave people nightmares because no one knew what would occur to its rulers next and what country they would decide to conquer. . . . Europe turned into a single enormous arsenal divided into two parts." But now "the totalitarian system in the Soviet Union, as well as in most of its satellites, is breaking down. And our nations are looking for a way to democracy and independence. . . . These revolutionary changes will enable us all to enter into an era of multipolarity . . . and to create the family of man.

"How can the United States help us today? My reply is as paradoxical as my whole life has been: You can help us most of all if you help the Soviet Union on its irreversible but immensely complicated road to democracy."

By that time, Havel had said all his audience wished to hear: a clear, unambiguous endorsement of the "new thinking" and of U.S. engagement in the millennium endgame. But there was, in his estimation, one other fact they needed to recall. No one could have better expressed Pope John Paul's deep reservation about the situation—and in secular language as effective as the Pontiff's. "Without a global revolution in the sphere of human consciousness, nothing will change for the better in the sphere of our being," Havel said quietly. Then he put his finger on the central lack. "We still don't know how to put morality ahead of politics, science and economics." Then this retiring and shy man underlined the remedy. "We are still incapable of understanding that the only genuine backbone of all our actions, if they are to be moral, is responsibility, responsibility to something higher than my family, my country, my company, my success."

It only remained, for complete frankness, for Havel to invite all the members of Congress listening to him to kneel down, to worship God and to ask God's blessing and help and divine light. Under the circumstances, Havel knew this was not the thing to do. But he must have regretted—at least momentarily—that the dominant secularism of the age and of the United States precluded such an ending to his remarks.

No doubt, his speech clinched the "new thinking" in many a mind and helped orient it to the millennium endgame. He himself would be skeptical as to the number of those who would in reality place all this within the framework of godliness. For them, the family of man was the result of genetics, evolution and politics. For Havel, for Abraham Lincoln, for Papa Wojtyla, the family of man was a supernatural bonding of all the creatures of God, Creator and Redeemer.

There remained, at the end of this exercise of brilliant geopolitical statecraft by Mikhail Gorbachev, the excited mentalities of the nations now involved in the consequences of his skill, in contrast to the almost detached tranquillity of John Paul. For, once again, the leaders of the West (and with them their peoples) had dutifully and predictably accepted the reactive posture on which Mikhail Gorbachev had successfully counted. And the source of that difference between the Holder of the Keys and his contemporary competitors in the fateful millennium endgame was to be sought in the radical difference between the visions drawing each side on unresistingly.

Thus, as of winter's last days, in February 1990, the geopolitical vision of the "Wise Men of the West" had been squared and tailored and trimmed to Gorbachev's "common home" of some 800 million "Europeans" occupying the landmasses and plying the ocean waters between the Urals in Russia and the Pacific coast of California. More peace, more prosperity, more manufactured goods, more trade, more stable currency of exchange, more freedom from threat of sudden destruction, more healthy and happy populations—all within a geopolitical structure beneath whose roof the chauvinist bickering of ideologies and the jingoism of nationalisms would no longer have any voice. None of this was being planned in obedience to the divine precept "Love each other, as I have loved you." Nor did the moral law as Christ has revealed it stand as the measure of what was good and what was evil. The visionaries, in this case, will not acknowledge success as dependent on God's providence.

He will not be adored and praised officially beneath the roof of the house abuilding.

Mikhail Gorbachev, within a relatively short time, will find how far the "new thinking" will permit him to venture—again as chief agent of action —in conducting the already reactive posture of the West. The Gramscian penetration of Western culture will be, he hopes, thorough and deep and pervasive. In the light that guides him, he will at any given moment see the opportunity that all genuine Marxists believe will surely arise under the irresistible dialectic of material forces. The geopolitical house now abuilding will need very little adaptation—perhaps a thorough housecleaning, followed by some interior decoration and design— in order to fit the frame of universal dictatorship of the Party as the host of the soon-to-come and stateless "Paradise of the Workers." Mikhail Gorbachev has tranquillity, yes, but with ebullient outbreaks of legitimate rejoicing. He has had his way with the society of nations so far.

While the first weeks of 1990 are full of novelty and excitement for all others and lit up by the near-future prospect of further harmony and homogenization of goals within the USSR and Europe, John Paul stands apart. He is tranquil in his unshakable trust and hope, yet he forever repeats his fundamental message: Not principally fratricide of the body is the capital sin of man against man, but fratricide of the spirit. The only way to avoid that is by a total conversion to God.

He undertook an eight-day trip, January 25–February 1, through five impoverished West African countries: Cape Verde, Guinea-Bissau, Mali, Burkina Faso and Chad. It was a mirror image of his Scandinavian trip during the days of Mikhail Gorbachev's first diplomatic onslaught of Europe. There, speaking among people dedicated to the "good life," he was paternally warning both Gorbachev and all Europeans that their presently uppermost intent—primarily in their negotiations—should be to revivify the spirit of and belief in God as the viable foundation for the "new Europe" and the "new world order" Mr. Gorbachev preached and they envisioned.

Here in Africa's belt of poverty and hopelessness, his eyes were glancing northward to the capitals of Europe and North America and to the diplomats, agents, ministers of state and emissaries who shuttled back and forth in torrid negotiations. This poverty of Africa, he said, "is an open wound. . . . How will history judge a generation that, having every means to feed the world's population, refused to do so, with fratricidal indifference? What kind of peace can be expected by peoples who do not put the duty of solidarity into practice?"

There was special significance in his assertion to the Marxist-oriented rulers—Aristide Pereira in Cape Verde, João Bernardo Vieira of Guinea-Bissau, Blaise Compaoré of Burkina Faso—that "neocolonialism presented under the guise of cooperation is an evil the Church cannot accept." His indirect reference was to African Marxism, which is nothing more than a loose weave of slogans and social goals. His direct reference was to the straitjacket of ideology animating Gorbachev and now eliciting a close cooperation from the West. "There is the colonialism of territory," he had said during his 1980 visit to Burkina Faso, "but the most pernicious colonialism is of the spirit."

Pavel Negoitsa, a reporter for the Soviet trade-union newspaper *Trud*, and the first Soviet journalist to go on a papal trip, wrote that this Pope "is a great moral force" and his method was not unlike "continual drops of water on a stone"—this time "the hard stone of world opinion." Eventually that stone would "wear down" and "give in." But Negoitsa could not explain that constancy in the Pontiff's behavior.

For John Paul, the wheel of international developments has turned men's gaze definitively on that portion of the globe—Central Europe and the western Soviet hinterland—where, John Paul is persuaded, the foundational events of the veritable new world order will take place, surprising men and women infinitely more than the events of 1989–90. Immensely secure in his faith as the "complete slave of Mary," he could look on February 13, 1990, as a day of confirmation of his faith and trust. The thirteenth of each month was and is the preferred day for his patron of Fatima.

Whether celebrating Mass in Oslo, or kissing little children in the leprosy clinic of N'Djamena, Chad, or consoling an old couple in a miserable hut in Burkina Faso's Ouagadougou, or parleying with the Master of All the Russias in his Vatican library, John Paul remained firm in his intent and his confidence. Neither the secularism of the West, nor the Leninism of the Soviets, nor the neo-Maoism of the Chinese, would or could alter that. For the patterns had been set for the millennium endgame. The society of nations was locked into a set course leading to that final clash of two geopolitical views—that of Heaven and that of men resorting to their own devices.

25. The Millennium Endgame

Thus, before the onset of a new spring in 1990, all the patterns were formed and set for the conduct of the affairs of nations in the foreseeable future. Now, in these trailing times of the second millennium, the long-standing game of winner-take-all between the two superpowers and their partisans had to all intents and purposes ceased; their great and decisive endgame had begun in earnest.

Everywhere, as John Paul had analyzed the situation, one whole generation passed away, another was born and grew past maturity, and a third had just been born, during the global winner-take-all game. It was a seesaw contest or, if you will, a tug-of-war initiated by the utopian dreams of a Lenin and a Stalin, fomented by their henchmen in many lands, and animated by the principle of fratricide. "We will bury you," Nikita Khrushchev had screamed, pounding his desk at the United Nations with his shoe.

For close on seventy years, the well-being and progress as well as the suffering and difficulties of all nations have been gridded on the seesawing patterns traced by the varying fortunes of the two superpowers. The West stood for certain basic values: free enterprise, free markets, free trade, all housed in free political institutions; the primacy of the individual socially, economically, politically; the creation of wealth, not its mere distribution or redistribution, as the goal of the economic order. Still one other value ruled the American mind in particular: a sense of its responsibility as the only power capable of engaging in that tug-of-war, the only power capable of outweighing the Soviet adversary.

Ensuring peace overall was defined strictly in terms of a fratricidal enemy. Peace was the capacity to discourage the enemy's lethal wishes. Each side aimed at outweighing the other on the seesaw. But neither actually succeeded, because neither successfully straddled the center and controlled the two ends. One way or another, all the strains and stresses undergone by the nations, as well as their successes and sureties, resulted from the back-and-forth veering victories in the relentless tug-of-war between those two giant contestants, who were bent, each one of them, on eventually hauling the other, kicking and contentious but captive, over into its own terrain.

That is all those generations had known. Theirs had been a world of dangerous seesaw, of the lethal tug-of-war. The value and the safety of their lives as nations came to be measured along that great divide between the two contestants.

Among the successive waves of Cold War, thaw and détente, there ran the flummery of never-ending disarmament talks; the mutual recriminations; the occasional bloodletting; the regularly occurring "tit-for-tat" expulsions of diplomats for "undiplomatic behavior" because the other side had done just that; the horrid "sideshows" in Vietnam, Afghanistan, Nicaragua, Namibia, Ethiopia; and, hanging over all this, the fear of sudden nuclear holocaust.

As a cap on this wearing-down process, there was the constant pressure on all nations to make a choice, to take a side between sides, or to remain neutral—which each side labeled as a covert taking of the other side. Hence those horrid coordinates "East-West" and "North-South," which John Paul excoriated. It was the worst of times—so much so that the best consolation offered was that at least World War III was being avoided. "We haven't had a major world war for over forty years," was the comment. As if that was the best man could hope for.

Quite recently and quite suddenly, this wasting global game ended. Unbelievably, but actually, it ended. There was no longer any counterweight on the seesaw, any tension in the tug-of-war. Nobody could explain precisely why to everybody's satisfaction. Reasoning and fancy vied to explain the sudden change.

Whatever the driving power behind the sudden change, one main fact is clear:

The two main contenders have decided to converge; to seek out, identify and enlarge every possible area of cooperation, collaboration and sharing; to excise all the hardened warts of hate and distrust that have marred the faces they displayed between them; to create trust by opening up to each other their parliamentary processes, their defense and strategic measures; to establish a unity of purpose and of action in various scientific and humanitarian sectors; to introduce among their peoples ways of living, of learning, of understanding and of judging that cannot be tagged as either typically American or typically Soviet or Russian but will merit being described as human and common to both. For only thus can you understand what is being said by the leadership on both sides of the fence today.

The decision to seek that convergence and the concrete steps already taken in that direction do outline the basic character of this new game of nations: There are to be moves by one nation, then follow-up moves by the other nation. Then the creation of new mutual relationships and forces, enabling and evoking further moves on every player's part; and all this purposefully aimed at achieving convergence. Every time a forward step is taken, the foot must land on a square of already confirmed trust. President Ronald Reagan's publicly announced principle of his trust in Mikhail Gorbachev has been elevated to a universal principle: "Trust, but verify." On both sides.

Clearly, this also is an endgame. Not so much because its beginning marks the end of the winner-take-all game that racked the society of nations for two generations. Principally because, in this new game, the nations are writing a definitive coda to what they have been as a society for most of this now-ending second millennium.

Its end, barely ten years away, will signal a farewell to a nation system of human society that, in its worst paroxysms, had almost decided to commit suicide—by wholesale industrial slaughter of millions of human beings or in a nuclear oven—and, at its very best, enabled the nations to put up with the soul-deadening boredom of perpetual contention because some tasted sweet victory and the rest lived on the hope of victory —as if that were the best man could do for man.

But there are, in high places, no illusions about the nature of this endgame. The heart of it lies in competition. It is still a winner-take-all arrangement. The West has renounced none of the basic values it has defended and propagated for the last seventy years. The Soviet East has not renounced its utopian goal; but, under the pressure of unchangeable circumstances, the leadership has decided to adopt a different way to that goal. They both have agreed to conditions that mean, in effect, that either one or the other will predominate finally and will finally bury the other without the horrors of a shooting war. The Gramscian conversion of Leninism preserves the burning core of Leninism.

There is not one normally aware and normally well-informed member in the various power centers and interest lobbies of "East" and "West" who has not recognized the terminal effect of this endgame, although few can readily imagine that planned society of nations in which the present accepted differences that mark all nations are eliminated. And some find it frightening, even appalling. Nobody expects a world order to evolve that will, as an optimist might say, combine the best of Leninism and capitalism. Neither a "Leninized" capitalism nor a capitalistic version of Leninism is possible. Neither does anyone know for sure the factors that hastened the end of the old game and, in a certain true sense, imposed the endgame with such ease and with such rapidity, dictating the new rules, even fixing the timetable. The endgame follows a new calendar.

Everyone recognizes one salient fact: This sudden, apparently benign changeover started almost simultaneously with the accession of Mikhail Sergeyevich Gorbachev to the leading position of power in the USSR and with his meteoric ascendance as the dominant personality and the primary catalyst of international life.

From the beginning of his pontificate, John Paul has been talking incessantly about the convergence of the nations. He had the endgame in view some ten years before other men faced into it; and, for his pains, he has been seen by many in the West as a man of the East, and by many in the East as a man of the West. Deterred in no way by such misunderstanding, John Paul hinged the success of his pontificate on what was and still remains a gamble concerning the present endgame. He would endow his papacy with an international profile and, as Pope, move around among world leaders and nations, vindicating a position for himself as a special leader among leaders, because in that competition he plans to emerge as the victor.

He did accomplish his immediate aim. The papal profile of high international definition was achieved. It was the first step in his gamble. The second step has been more hazardous but is intimately linked with the first. The gargantuan effort he has put forth on the international plane has not been even half matched on his part by an effort at halting the year-by-year deterioration of his Church structure. There has been no genuine policy of reversing the shame of his Church today; namely, the slow but sure transmogrification of that Catholic structure into a most un-Catholic thing, a misshapen, limping, scar-ridden and diseased version of what it was twenty-five years ago.

His energies, his interests, his time and his talents have been almost exclusively preoccupied with the endgame. And, now that it has started in earnest, more than ever his concentration is focused on the emerging patterns and on the master magician Mikhail Gorbachev. For John Paul's gamble is riding on the back of Gorbachevism.

That endgame, into which Gorbachevism has forced everybody to enter, came as a relief for the generality of people everywhere.

In the "West," where men and women have grown weary of soul in the ceaseless rounds of tensions, thaws, rearmament, armed clashes and endless fears. In the East, where every promise of Leninist Marxism has been fulfilled by its direct opposite—imprisonment of mind and body instead of freedom, hunger instead of plenty, dismal backwardness instead of progress, inefficiency instead of high efficiency, privilege-ridden society instead of equality, hopelessness instead of hope.

In the now not so Far East, whose food, languages, religions, wars, refugees have become daily news fare for Mrs. Calabash, wherever she is. In the Western Hemisphere, where, up north, men and women are finally getting tired on their treadmill as it aims ceaselessly to produce a better mouse trap; and where, down south, men and women are beginning to suspect that there is no humanly acceptable exit from the swamps of economic helplessness and inept nationalisms. The miserable of the world now know how the "other half" lives; and the "other half" has not only lost its energy, it is caught in its own rhetoric of challenge.

This mass of spiraling strains had to end; and while the start of the endgame was a surprise, men and women everywhere are taking it in their stride. It is as if they know there had to be some way out of the one-way street into which they had been hemmed by the Leninist process and by that process of the Wise Men of the West, the amoral tomfoolery of raw capitalism as it played with the human environment and with the lives of helpless millions in the Third World, who cut themselves off from the sustenance of their old traditions because they had been led by hollow hopes and false promises to commit themselves to the new gods of economic expediency.

For quite a while now, and for quite an appreciable time before Gorbachevism became the catalyst within international affairs, John Paul has resolutely faced into the inevitable happenings and accompaniments of the endgame.

Certainly, the formerly segregated society of nations dubbed the "East" is being penetrated by the technology, the business know-how, the managerial skills of the "West," together with the garish panoply of symbols announcing the goodness of the Big Mac, Kentucky Fried Chicken, Nestlé chocolate, French champagne, Italian clothes and wine, and German do-it-yourself over-the-counter drugs.

But the penetration of the West by the East, while it will include some choice consumer goods, and some panoply of the East's symbols of the good life (no doubt adapted to American and European tastes), will be of a more profound kind. It will take place on the level where culture and the human spirit intermingle, and where human sensibilities are molded through the silent operation of basic ideas and judgments about the human condition. For this penetration is to be accomplished by the planned convergence of minds and wills.

The West, already profoundly secularized, is going to converge on that all-important level with minds and cultures already impregnated with the officially nourished secularism of the Leninist homeland, and—this much all can be sure of—under the watchful surveillance, the skillful manipulation and the expert monitoring of the Party-State. It would be foolish on the part of any statesman or politician in Europe of the 1990s, with Gorbachevism in full swing, not to realize and act according to the fact that political penetration and control of Europe in its continental institutions as well as in its state-by-state legislatures is the key aim of Gorbachevism. John Paul must now assist at that Soviet penetration and control, and be helpless to prevent it. The ghost of Gramsci will flit triumphantly over the Marxization of European political culture and its first continental institutions.

For John Paul could predict, as early as 1988, that the Eurocommunist parties of Europe (Italy's, France's, Spain's, Germany's, Belgium's) will be accepted and granted equal status in the EEC as well as in the other European institutions. With the birth of political alliances between Communists and Socialists on national levels, the European Parliament would be a reality. Under the Gorbachevist "liberalization" plans for the Soviet Eastern European satellites, and because of his 1989 proposition (he did not request; he proposed) that at least those Eastern nations, if not the Soviet Union itself, be admitted to the "common European home," Europe from the Atlantic—or at least from Calais on the English Channel—to the Russian Urals would in a short time be a socialist Europe, whose legislators owed ultimate allegiance to the Soviet Union and whose executive, legislative and judicial functions would be occupied by men and women of the same ideological brand. When Greek Prime Minister Andreas Papandreou announced on July 28, 1989, that "our Socialist party and the Left [the Communists] must have the opportunity to govern the country democratically, progressively and patriotically," he was wisely reading the writing on the wall that told how Greek politics and Europolitics would go.

This planned penetration of Europolitics will go hand in hand with the Moscow-controlled "liberalization" and "democratization" within the Soviet satellites. Both "liberalization" and "democratization" will be introduced through the Communist parties, through the cooperation of particular individuals who are already "deep" Soviet plants in supposedly anti-Soviet bodies, and through the clandestine plans of the KGB. Any apparent "liberalization" and "democratization" within the Soviet Union itself will be vehicled by the same means—all the state institutions coordinated by the KGB.

John Paul, as well as some others, has learned that Western statesmen, politicians, analysts and thinkers find it almost impossible to imagine that dissident movements such as the 1968 Alexander Dubcek movement in Czechoslovakia, the Solidarity and KOR movements in Poland of the eighties, the Sakharov and other Russian dissident movements within the Soviet Union, have always been and still are shaped, guided and controlled by the CP apparatus. Very few moderns in the West are acquainted with the thoroughness that has always characterized the Leninist process.

John Paul, as of 1988, therefore, has had to live with the knowledge that both the United States and Western Europe are now caught in the beginnings of a political embrace whose only purpose is to control them both, and thus make inevitable the harnessing of their economic power to consolidate a veritable Leninist empire.

The third step in the papal gamble involves, of course, Gorbachev and his USSR, but not as the key element.

That is the mystery of divine providence, in which John Paul firmly believes and on which the brilliant success or the miserable failure of his papal gamble totally depends. Practically considered, the success of his papal participation in the endgame depends on an event whose timing and occasion he is powerless to determine, and the nature of which he cannot in any way influence or fashion. Without that event, he will be impotent just at the height of the endgame. Backed up by that event, he cannot but emerge as the most powerful man alive in his time.

But the price he has to pay is full of bitterness for him.

From the point of view of strict Roman Catholicism, it is a bleak outlook in the short run. The bulk of Churchmen (bishops, priests, cardinals) and vast masses of the laity in Europe and on the North American continent are already alienated from that strict Catholicism, calling themselves "Catholics without the Roman" and members of the "Church without the Pope." The anti-Church, John Paul's direct enemies within or without the Catholic fold, have developed a specifically Roman Catholic secularism, which will now enjoy a fresh fillip in the direction of an ever-greater panreligious feeling and mode of behavior. The "supermarket" (pick 'n' choose) Catholicism fostered or permitted by so many Churchmen, the "ecumenical" (all religions come to the same thing) egalitarianism of so many more, the blunted edge of Catholic education, the antipapalism of bishops and theologians—all of this provides an open and ready seedbed for the planting of a new and more thorough abandonment of Catholic essentials. And this situation, for the moment irremediable in John Paul's estimation, will provide him with more frustration and annoyance than he could ever have bargained for.

For the moment, and until the new secularism registers some signal victories, the neo-Catholicism of the anti-Church will mingle with and not be clearly—and deliberately—separated and distinguished from the pockets of genuine traditional Catholicism. For authenticity is still sought by the anti-Church, Catholic authenticity. They want to appropriate the entire legacy of Rome. But inevitably the two will separate when the penetration is consummated.

John Paul's Catholics, in that consummation, face the real possibility that for the first time since A.D. 315—1,675 years ago—their genuine Catholicism will lose all its precious footholds in the Western civilization it created and in all the cultures it brought forth in the nourishing and protective shade of that once mighty tree of apostolic and Catholic Christianity. It is now possible that the Roman Catholic Church in its Catholicism will become a socially negligible and a politically invisible entity; that it will become a cultural pariah as indeed it was for the first three hundred years of its existence.

The endgame par excellence.

The anomaly of the millennium will be provided by the sole figure of John Paul. His high international profile still invulnerable to the anti-Church, he will still hold the Keys of that Blood as the enviable source of unique authority, and on his back will rest the hope and guarantee Christ once and for all time made to Peter in a deserted spot near the Roman town of Caesarea Philippi in ancient Judea.

Not only are calm nerves of steel needed to play such a role, and not only must he have an unbreakable grasp on the intangibles of faith preserved in profound tranquillity. He must be clear in his own mind, must have thought it all through to the end, not in a series of abstract concepts but within a programmatic vision inwoven with the Tree of Good and Evil man once ate of, the death cry of the Man God on Calvary, the terrible raid on humanity by the Four Horsemen of the Apocalypse, and the ecstatic song of the thousands destined from all eternity to eat at the Banquet of the Lamb in the final Kingdom.

If his contemporary generation of men and women realized how fitted and equipped this one man, this Polish Pope, has been in order to have that vision and fulfill this role, they would already be blessing their destiny to live these Catholic times with him. A later and wiser generation surely will venerate him as his contemporaries have never dreamed of doing. For his is the vision. For his is that role, as Servant of the Grand Design.

II

The Geopolitics of Faith

Part Six

The Vision of the Servant

26. Polishness and Papacy

Since the start of his pontificate in October 1978, Pope John Paul II has conducted papal affairs and behaved himself in such a way that there really are only two plausible readings of him by his contemporaries. Either he is a prime example of the classic "straw man," with a very good "act," to boot. Or he heralds a new and as yet unrecognized force in the geopolitics of the nations, a force that, as he actually claims, will be the ultimate and decisive factor determining the new world order. In the final analysis, there are no other feasible ways of rationalizing this Pope's performance on the world stage.

The straw man at English country fairs was decked out as king or queen or noble lord or governor or rich man. The clothes, jewels, diadem, money and features were painted straw, animated by a circus performer wearing the straw and following the script of an act that inevitably ended in the total discomfiture of the straw man amid the hoots and catcalls of an audience delighted at the unmasking of a pretender. All the panoply was shredded. All the gestures of the act turned out to be ludicrous. The end was always the same: a pile of discarded straw, and the total indifference of the crowd, which moved on to other attractions.

The most outstanding "straw man" in modern times was surely dictator Benito Mussolini, who in the thirties claimed to have founded the Third Roman Empire, to have an unbeatable army, air force and navy, and to be the arbiter of Europe's fate. Army, air force and navy were completely, rapidly and devastatingly destroyed by the Allies. His "Third Roman Empire" fell to pieces—like straw—overnight. He was betrayed and killed ignominiously by his own people. It all ended in discarded ruins and derision. The empire, the invincible armed forces, the new Rome—it was all a sham: a straw man's act.

His Holiness, since 1978, has assiduously carved out for himself an international profile. Precisely, he himself has done it—not press agents, not an international team of zealous partisans, not a clever propaganda machine, but he himself in person. And he has done it as if it was his right as well as his duty. No pope ever did this on a like scale. Nor has any human being in known history even attempted it. This papal gambit is unique.

By February 1990, he had spent 8 percent of his pontificate—a total of 326 days—on 45 papal trips to 91 countries, giving a total of 1,559 speeches in 32 languages, being seen and heard in the flesh or on audio-video circuits by over 3.5 billion people, and logging enough international miles to have flown 17 times around the circumference of Earth. Within Italy, he has made 85 trips up and down the boot-shaped peninsula (in mileage, the equivalent of 34 times up and down the whole country), thereby consuming 23 percent of his pontificate's time.

A straw man's clever act? Hardly. The governments involved have not treated him as a passing show, nor have the watching media or ordinary people. The hundreds of thousands who thronged to meet and hear him, and the extensive media coverage (which other visitor to the United States has had 16,000 journalists assigned to cover his visit?), were the stuff of many a politician's fond but vain dreams.

Nor has John Paul ever gone anywhere as a mere tourist or even as a distinguished visitor or famous character. With few exceptions, every visit to those 91 countries was formally a state visit or was treated as such by the host government, even if in an anticlerical Mexico, a Protestant England, a Stalinist Poland, efforts were made to avoid any appearance of acknowledging him in his claim to moral and religious leadership of the whole human race. All realize, seemingly, that he is in a category superior to the Dalai Lama, the Patriarch of Constantinople, the Archbishop of Canterbury, Billy Graham, any renowned itinerant Indian swami, or any other religious leader who travels.

Above and apart from all religious leaders and all current heads of state of major or minor powers, John Paul has established personal relationships with the governmental leaders in all 91 countries. They have discussed the serious business of government and world affairs with him as with an equal who talks to all of them about religion and morality.

At home, around his Vatican, are 120 diplomatic missions, sent there by their governments. When he comments on their affairs, he passes sober judgment, and the nuances are noticed. They noted that he did not, in 1989, join the general euphoria at the meltdown of the Berlin Wall and say "the Cold War is over"; he said only that "the year 1989 could well signal the decline of what has been called the 'Cold War.' "

He speaks as somebody to whom major powers appear responsible. "U.S. and Soviet leaders have assured me of their desire to place international relations on a more secure foundation, and to regard each other even more as partners instead of competitors." The tone is paternal, not paternalistic. And it is authoritative. This man speaks as if he had the right to do so—in the eyes of those who are the subjects of his commentary. No government has bridled at him.

There is no way, in all realism, that John Paul II and his international behavior can be put down as a "straw man" engaged in an amusing "act." When Mikhail Gorbachev addressed John Paul as "the world's highest moral authority" on December 1, 1989, in the Vatican, surely he was merely acknowledging the reality of how he and other government leaders, East and West, see and treat this Pope.

If the world is not dealing with a straw man in this Pope, there remains only that other alternative. But the mere idea that John Paul embodies or represents a force to be reckoned with in the current geopolitical trend of global affairs is very distressing and unpalatable to many; for many more it is unintelligible, and by still more, totally unrecognized. There are solid reasons for these reactions.

The newest game in the City of Man is the building of a geopolitical structure. Everyone who is anyone in terms of sociopolitical and economic power is engaging in it, some deliberately, some willy-nilly; and ultimately, it is conceded, all nations, great and small, will be involved. It is the millennium endgame.

The science of geopolitics is being formulated now for the first time. The first faltering steps on the geopolitical plane are being essayed by the infant Internationalism and Transnationalism of the last few decades. For the vast majority of actual and would-be participants, geopolitics appears as a new way, the "millennium" way, of rearranging the distribution of wealth, political power and human freedom across the face of the globe. The subject of geopolitics is the whole material universe. The molding and fashioning force of our geopolitics is the combined will of millions of men and women co-opted into the creation of a new world order. The instrument for building a geopolitical structure is organization on a new and unprecedented scale because it is intended and planned to be more international, more than supranational. It will be, in the minds of its planners, geopolitical. And no one but a fool would suggest that the major "movers and shakers" of this organization are acting primarily or even secondarily out of purely religious motives.

Here comes John Paul, striding among the "great ones," speaking to all the "little ones," and the point of what he keeps saying incessantly about this geopolitics is strictly religious. His comments do not turn on a purely ethical or moral basis. It is religious and specifically Christian from a Roman Catholic perspective.

No one really suspects him of seeking territorial aggrandizement, gold, political power or personal pleasure. At his vaguest—and this is already specific enough to be disturbing to our secularist world leaders—he insists that just as no system of politics is viable unless it is based on the spirituality of genuine religious belief in God and in Christ, so no religious belief is viable unless it is deeply involved in political systems.

At his most specific, however, he insists that men have no reliable hope of creating a viable geopolitical system unless it is on the basis of Roman Catholic Christianity. "One can only regret the deliberate absence of all transcendent moral references," he told all and sundry in his January 13, 1990, speech to the international diplomatic corps of Vatican Rome. "Christ is the sole strength of Europe and the king of all nations," he asserted.

No one, individual or corporate body, has formally conceded him the right to act and speak as religious authority and moral monitor of the society of nations. He has assumed this mantle, and no one of consequence really disputes his assumption of it. No one except the present "touch-me-not" Leninist Marxists of Beijing resist him—and even they are now making what can pass for remotely conciliatory sounds. Why is it that a man from a backwater Polish town called Wadowice and now the head of a religious institution has come to be a respected commentator and successful participant in our geopolitics? The question becomes more acute when you consider what every informed world leader knows about John Paul.

It is widely known that the main personal emphasis in Karol Wojtyla's life has always been and still is on his relationship with Mary, the mother of Jesus. His personal motto—*Totus Tuus* (Entirely Yours)—concerns her and memorializes special acts of self-consecration to her, which he personally undertook years ago.

For the general mind and, particularly, for the minds of other world leaders, it is an arresting—if not somewhat disconcerting—thought that this intensely active man in all he does is consciously and expressly seeking to implement a mandate given him as Pope by a person he venerates as the mother of the God he adores. If he confined himself to the sacristy and the altar and the pulpit; if he looked and sounded like what literature and the worldly imagination depicts as "the holy man in his cell," as the guru type, even as the otherwise harmless religious fanatic, they could understand him.

But they watch this man stalking the minds and hearts of millions across the world stage. They are closeted with him as movers and shakers of our present history. He discusses complicated and far-reaching issues of politics, economics, finance, war and peace, technology and ethics. They find themselves dealing with a genuine intellectual, mature, informed, aware, a person of stark realism and moving compassion for the bread-and-butter needs of ordinary men and women. On the diplomatic circuit, in the power plays between nations, he has shown an agility and a sensitivity second to none. He is a professional respected by professionals.

Yet, with all that, they have to take into account that John Paul is following a timetable he asserts has been established in Heaven; and he fully presumes that what he does and they do will succeed only if it conforms to the foretold sequence of historical events he confidently ascribes to a woman he, along with other millions, venerates under the symbol of her heart—they call it the Immaculately Sinless Heart of Mary.

The apparent anomaly, therefore, that Papa Wojtyla presents to the normally secular mind of his peers and contemporaries is this combination of hardheaded geopolitical perception and analysis with a religious devotion and world outlook based apparently on a deep religious and devotional persuasion. The choke point for the secular mind is that the geopolitical dovetails with the religious: One does not suppress, inhibit or disqualify the other. In fact, he is geopolitical in bent of mind because he is of this religious caliber. He is of this particular Marian religious mentality because of his geopolitics.

The ultimate question, then, about Karol Wojtyla reduces itself to this: Why is he so sure—as well as skillful—geopolitically, in view of his totally unworldly attachment to the unseen, intangible world of Mary and Christ and God? He commands and receives attentive hearing on the geopolitical plane; how come? What formed this geopolitical ability in him? What has all that to do with his ever-insistent Marian devotion? How do you explain this Pope in terms of background and heredity as well as papal office? That he should have a perfervid devotion to the Virgin Mary is not surprising in a very Catholic Pope. But a thoroughly geopolitical mind coming out of Poland—that would strike many as very unexpected, and for one capital reason: the history of Poland in approximately the last 195 years.

Poland as a separate country, an independent people and a sovereign nation literally ceased to exist in 1795.

With a brief twenty-one-year interlude (1918–39) of relative freedom for Poles, that period of nearly two hundred years constitutes an appalling litany of natural entombment, demographic enslavement, linguistic persecution, bloodshed, economic impoverishment, religious oppression, a general connivance among powerful nations to obliterate Poland as a nation-state from human memory, two world wars, a true genocide attempted by the Nazis with the scientific thoroughness of the German mind, a further attempt by the Soviets to eradicate Polishness with the ruthlessness achieved only by Stalinism. Poles as a race should have been demoralized beyond recovery, and their Polishness should have been mongrelized beyond repair by that sustained brutalization.

If any ethnic group in the society of nations today has an absolutely unassailable bill of indictment to urge at the bar of human justice, it is the Poles. But more important than the quest for a justice that is not available is the double question about Poland's survival. How, out of that crippling maelstrom, have the Poles emerged as the one Eastern-bloc country capable of forcing the iron hand of imperial Leninism? And how is it that the grandiose figure of the "Polish Pope" comes striding tranquilly and carefully out of the same destructive obscurity, with rancor for none, not hobbled with parochialism, and with a spirit ranging over a geopolitical plane so all-inclusive and so universalist that he finds few genuine peers there?

Given those antecedents, this "Polish Pope" should not have so emerged, and Poland should have no real identity, unless, as has always been implied by "Polonia Sacra," the Poles are assigned a special role in our history by the sacralizing hand of the Lord of history. For sacra in that phrase means precisely "set apart," "consecrated," "specially appointed," by the All-Holy.

Deepening this conclusion is the most glaring fact about the "Polish Pope." Polishness made him.

The men and women who as role models, mentors, instructors, advisers and exemplars formed the character of Karol Wojtyla as the "Polish Pope" are all known to us. His parents, foster mother, brother; his priests, teachers, professors, personal friends; the bishops and cardinals who from early on had a say in his formation, the popes and politicians who overshadowed his days; the thinkers, philosophers, writers who took his mind by storm. We know their names and their occupations, where and how they lived, and how they died. And he is genuinely their child, the product of their highest ambitions and their deepest desires. We are not talking of predecessor Poles as distant as Archbishop Nicholas Traba of Gniezno or Stanislaw Cardinal Hosius of Warmia, each of whom was nearly named pope in the fifteenth and sixteenth centuries.

John Paul's fashioners in Polishness were in their majority Poles who were themselves without exception formed in that period of history that was admittedly the worst for Polishness—a matter of about six quite recent generations. Karol Wojtyla belongs to them; he is no Melchizedek, without pedigree, without ancestors; nor is he some "troubled" integrist, breaking away from the tradition that made him and seeking a new identity, wider than that into which he was born and fitted by his fashioners. His spiritual heritage came into his hands from them. His politics and his Polishness, his geopolitics and his faith, are their gifts to him. What transformations he has wrought in the meantime are merely a function of his larger-than-life destiny as presiding Pope of the millennium endgame.

If any of those now dead men and women were to walk the earth today, they would readily recognize this "Polish Pope" as theirs. His challenge to Poland's Stalinist government in 1979 would be the same as the challenge they flung at equally godless destroyers in their own day. The prime victims of "sinful structures" imposed on them by the malicious consensus of Austrians, Germans and Russians, they would identify immediately with John Paul's excoriation of the "sinful structures" evolved from the consensus of East and West and imposed on East European nations during the 1945–85 period. The materialism of Leninist Marxism and raw capitalism was no worse than the materialism of Poland's captors during her long night of entombment, the evil of materialism they knew firsthand; and more than two generations of them felt the Soviet whip across their backs.

More important than any other gift to Karol Wojtyla, those predecessors and ancestors were forced by historical circumstances to adopt a geopolitical attitude of mind and outlook when all around them and among them there reigned an arrogant set of nationalistic, parochial-minded emperors and kings and governments. Peculiar to the Poles was the deep-set conviction that geopolitics implied georeligion, and that their georeligion—Roman Catholicism—implied geopolitics. On top of all that, each of those ancestors of Wojtyla could have chosen—many did—Karol Wojtyla's personal motto, *Totus Tuus*. For the Virgin Mary was their chosen icon of hope during a long, dark night.

For all of that is the patrimony, the spiritual heritage of Karol Wojtyla specifically as a son of Poland; and it came into his hands from his Polish ancestors and mentors. In their majority, they were themselves formed in the period that was at once the worst and the most miraculous time for a nation of people whose singular history is based on improbabilities and miracles. They were the bearers and the embodiment of the Poland that has always been and still remains the geopolitical *plaque tournante* of "Europe from the Atlantic to the Urals." This is the Poland that has long been called *Polonia Sacra*, a people certain that its nationhood is guaranteed not by any government or state but by a sacred undertaking of God, with whom they have, as a nation, made a series of three solemn pacts. Poland might be crucified as a nation-state; but Poland would not die. God would not fail the Poles.

Still, there are deep questions about the policies and actions of Pope John Paul II to which even some of those who understand him best cannot find the answers. What precisely does he envisage for his present world by way of geopolitical structure? Why has he not undertaken a thorough reform of his crumbling Roman Catholic institutional organization? He justly abhors Marxism, and he holds socialism to be merely the anteroom of spiritual decadence that prepares the way for Marxism. He sees and has said in unexceptionable terms that capitalism of itself has no human solutions, only human skills and techniques for material advantage and economic aggrandizement. What, then, does he think should be the economic-political character of a viable new world order? At times, both in Church and in state questions, he seems to be waiting, to be preparing, to be temporizing. What is he waiting for? Why does he hesitate or temporize?

The roots of his geopolitical and georeligious outlook are already discernible in the history of his beloved Poland; half the enigma John Paul presents to the world outside him can thus be solved. But the other half is all the more enigmatic and the more important for ordinary men and women. At a time when many are convinced that the dawn of ultimate world peace has already started by 1990, John Paul II manifestly disagrees. Clearly, he is convinced that the world as a family and the nations as a society face the same danger of extinction that Poland once faced. Yet he is no pessimist. What is the basis of his negative reading of our human chances? And, then again, why the apparent optimism? For the answer to that half of the enigma, we have to do more than understand his Polish heritage. For the solution, we have to look outside Poland to *the* georeligious and geopolitical event par excellence.

27. The Pacts of Polishness

The geopolitical idea so often expressed by Pope John Paul and Mikhail Gorbachev that the world, or at least a good part of it, comprises "one family" is not farfetched. There is a broad consensus among anthropologists, linguists, agrospecialists and cultural experts that some relatively short time after the last glaciers receded from the Eurasian landmass—about twelve thousand years ago—there flourished the remote ancestors of almost all the peoples now occupying "Europe from the Atlantic to the Urals," and North America, as well.

"Caucasians," as this ancient race is called, are identified by scholars as possessing the "Kurgan culture" and as speaking the mother tongue that is considered the root of all Western languages of today. They hunted and fished and foraged for food in the steppe lands between the Caspian and Black seas on the northern side of the Caucasus mountain range, that three-hundred-mile-long bastion that blocks passage south into the fertile plains of what we know as central Turkey and the Middle East.

In the west of that mountain range, Europe's highest peak, the 18,841-foot dormant volcano of Mount Elbrus, brooded down upon them, capped with its clouds, cloaked in its winds, its mists, its gods and its imagined mysteries. To the north, green expanses rolled into the heartland of Russia, all the way to the Ural Mountains and the Siberian lowlands.

Sometime before 7000 B.C., a vast revolution changed the Caucasians' way of life and ushered them on to their destiny. From being simple food gatherers, they became food producers. The earliest farming communities known to us existed in that area. They discovered and learned the early techniques of crop rotation and stock breeding. Human procreation became a source and a cause of blessings in the new society. More hands were the key to tilling more soil. Some of the oldest and most frequently found relics from this period are figurines of a goddess whose most distinctive traits—distended belly, large breasts—emphasized female fertility.

The sequel is easy to understand. More soil—more land—meant outward expansion. According as the population increased with every generation—each thirty years or so—more land was tamed and more was needed. Anthropologists speculate that the population would have expanded outward by thirty or forty miles with each new generation. It may have been much faster, however; for by 6500 B.C., Caucasian farming methods had reached Greece. And by 3500 B.C., they were practiced as far west as the Orkney Islands, off Scotland.

Mount Elbrus and the Caucasus range, which blocked the east and south, determined that part of Caucasian expansion and conquest would be northward into the Russian heartland; and then westward as far as Galway Bay and the Atlantic and—give or take a millennium or two— on as far as the eastern rim of the Pacific Ocean.

Constantly on the go, the Caucasian people superimposed themselves and their language where they went. The basic linguistic unity of "Europe from the Atlantic to the Urals" is scarcely violated by the Asianic origin of Finnish, Estonian and Hungarian. Even languages such as Basque and Albanian, which seem so alien to modern Western languages, are offsprings of the original Caucasian mother tongue.

In the millennium of their first great expansion, their constant migration and the tyranny of distance meant inevitably that whole groups of Caucasian peoples became separate and lived apart. Dialects of the original language developed—Slavonic, Teutonic, Celtic and Italic, for example. By sometime around 3000 B.C., whole areas were distinguished one from another by different languages—the dialects of the original Caucasian.

One newly developed language in particular—Old Slavonic, spoken by people who were called Slavs—held sway some hundreds of miles eastward from the Elbe River into the Russian heartland, southward as far as the Peloponnesus in Greece, and southeastward into what is today the Ukraine; and of course, it remained in the original steppe lands between the Black Sea and the Caspian. To describe themselves, as historiographer Iwo C. Pogonowski points out, Slavs said that they were people "who communicated by word of mouth" (*slovo* = the spoken word), as distinct from people of unintelligible language or those who were dumb and speechless.

Long before Athens reached for the glory that was Greece, the Caucasian populations of eastern Europe had subdivided into Balts and Germans to the north, with Slavs covering the remaining portion of central and eastern Europe. Once the Caucasians had taken possession of the vast landmass, only small pockets of racially different peoples established themselves within the Caucasian domain—the Asianic Estonians on the Baltic, and the Asianic Finns in Finland by the first century A.D., for example, and the Magyars in Hungary about the ninth century A.D. The South Semitic peoples, inflamed by Islam, tried for a thousand years, from about 600 A.D., to subdue the Caucasians and occupy their lands; but, in the end, even that bloody enterprise was ended.

The Slavs formed closely knit communities. They lived by their agriculture and traded with surrounding communities. They had a communal system of self-government that depended for its stability on the consensus reached among themselves. And they laid great store by the agreements they hammered out in frank discussions as among equals. The practice of the *sobor*—the communal gathering where all decisions affecting the community were reached by consensus—was typically Slav. The principle was not of the majoritarian one-man, one-vote variety. Rather, the principle was *sobornost*, the feeling and thinking consensus of the *sobor's* participants.

By about 700 A.D., two powerful Slav kingdoms emerged. One was centered in the area between modern Poland's two rivers, the Oder and the Vistula. The other, calling itself Rus, was centered in Kiev. Both were considered integral parts of that "Europe from the Atlantic to the Urals" of which John Paul II and Mikhail Gorbachev speak so passionately and persistently today; and both were part of that "one family" about which both of these leaders speak. From Poland's Oder River to Russia's Dnieper River, the entire area was considered the traditional homeland of the Slavs. There, the different and definitive traits of Polishness and Russianness were molded out of the lineage and the language of their common Caucasian heritage.

A tradition of Polish folklore tells us that a man named Lech—one of three brothers of the Piast family, which belonged to the tribe of Polanians, or Polanie—was fatefully led one day by a white eagle to a place near its aerie. There, at a site called Gniezno—a name that means "nest" or "cradle"—Lech founded his new kingdom of Polania, which would be ruled by the Piast dynasty for four hundred years.

What seems undoubted in this tradition is that the founder of the Piast dynasty was what we call today an ordinary man of the people, living on the land of the Poles. The white eagle he is said to have followed is still the official emblem of Poland; and the dynasty he is said to have founded came to symbolize the tradition of Poles in their unity as a people in unbroken continuity on the land of their ancestors.

It was of that ancient and enduring tradition that Pope John Paul reminded the world when he spoke at Gniezno in 1979. "Here," he said, ". . . I greet with veneration the *nest* of Piast, the origin of the history of our motherland and the cradle of the Church. . . . We are a people he [God] claims for his own. All together, we form also the royal race of the Piasts."

The historical record tells us that sometime around the year 840 A.D., the leader of the Polanian Slavs—a man of the Piast family whose name was in fact Chrosciszko—founded the Piast dynasty and that he formed its kingdom mainly by the union of his Polanians with five other tribes: Vistulans, Polabians, Silesians, Mazovians and Cassubians, or East Pomeranians. The members of that kingdom called themselves *Polacy*.

For the first hundred years of its existence, Poland was a ragged patch of territory, a hazardous enterprise from the beginning. Lacking any effective natural land barriers for its borders, separated only by vast forests from the normal trade and migration routes, the territory and nation of Poland, with its capital city at Gniezno, was in a precarious position. Situated in the middle of the Slav peoples, the inhabitants of the "Polish fields"—*pola* means exactly that: fields—were an obvious target for greedy neighbors. And from the beginning such neighbors were plentiful—mainly German, Slav and Asianic tribes on the search for fresh territory.

To Poland's immediate south lay the Slav kingdom of Great Moravia. To its east, the duchy of Kiev bristled with warlike intent. To its north and west were the Balts and the Germans. Within that first century, one part of Great Moravia disappeared into the German empire, and the rest was overrun by invading Magyars. To Poland's east, the Ruthenian Slavs constituted a new threat.

By the time Poland made it into the second century of its uncertain existence as a nation, two different but authentic Christian traditions had taken hold in most of Europe. Except for a large portion of Scandinavia and the territory until recently called Prussia, Europe from the Atlantic to the Urals was known as Christendom. "Europe," as Hilaire Belloc wrote, "was the Faith, and the Faith was Europe."

Although one as far as religion went, Christendom nonetheless was divided into two distinct portions following two distinct traditions. The line of division fell roughly along the meridian that separates the European landmass into east and west, running from Finland in the far north, stretching southward along the Elbe River in today's Germany to the Adriatic Sea around the heel of Italy.

Europe east of that line was the territory mainly of the Slav peoples. Their formative religious and cultural tradition stemmed from the most glorious and most long-lived empire ever fashioned by man—the Byzantine empire of the Greeks—whose capital, Constantinople, was perched strategically on the connecting water lane between the Mediterranean and the Black Sea, that is to say, between the European and Asian landmasses.

Europe west of that line was populated in the main by Nordic, Germanic and Romance peoples. Their formative religious and cultural tradition sprang from the Roman and Latinate mind. During the first thousand years of Christian papal Rome as a visible power among men —from 400 to 1400 A.D.—the Roman papacy and its ecclesiastical structure, the Church, were the fashioners of that Western culture and tradition.

Poland found itself in a peculiar position. Geographically, it was already the *plaque tournante* of inner-European political stability and power balance. While most of its territory lay in the western region, it straddled the east-west division. It stood as an open gateway into the heart of Russia in one direction, and into the lands of the west in the other. Moreover, it was the vital middle ground between northern and southern Europe. Given the fact that both Rome and Constantinople were vibrant and expansionist in every sense—religiously, culturally, politically and territorially—neutrality was not an option. Poland had to chose between east and west, or be overrun.

It was Poland's fifth Piast king, Mieszko I (921–992), who made the choice. He was a Slav leader of a Slav people, and the most natural thing would have been for him to turn eastward, to ally himself with what certainly seemed the superior power of Constantinople, and to opt for that Christian tradition as an inevitable part of the bargain. But Mieszko did not.

In the year 965, Mieszko married Roman Catholic Princess Dubrovka from Roman Catholic Bohemia. Clearly, however, his decision went much farther than a simple political alliance. In fact, it went farther even than his own baptism, in the year 966. For not only did he set about the conversion of Poland to Christianity. By a solemn pact—the Piast Pact of 990 A.D.—he made the entire nation and state of Poland over to the ownership of the Holy See of Peter, in the person of Pope John XV.

Mieszko's act was one of those fateful decisions made by key people of history under the pressure of concrete events, and according to their understanding of the issues at stake. Their problem is usually an immediate one. Their choice is practical. But the effect of what they do decides the fate and fortunes of unborn generations. Mieszko's decision was of this kind.

We have every reason to believe that Mieszko foresaw at least in outline what consequences would follow his choice. Any examination of the circumstances in which he made the donation consecrated in the Piast Pact convinces one that it was done primarily for religious and spiritual reasons. By an act of such enormous improbability as the Piast Pact, Mieszko was saying in effect that only Christ could assure the Poles of safety; that not only was the Roman See the center of the world, but its titular head was as well the titular overlord of the world; and that the Petrine authority of the Pope was God's authority. The Rome of the Popes was where the Poles would look for inspiration, leadership and authority.

Predictably, not everyone agreed with Mieszko. As always in known cases of mass conversion, there remained a solid core of the original religion—the paganism Poland's Slavs had brought with them in their long trek from beneath the shadows of Mount Elbrus in the steppe lands between the Black and Caspian seas. The supreme god of the Caucasians, represented for them by towering Mount Elbrus, had traveled outward with them over all of Europe, metamorphosing into Wodan of the Germanic peoples, Odin of the Norsemen, Zeus of the Greeks, Jupiter of the Latins, Perun of the Russians.

We do not know what name the pre-Christian Poles gave him; but by 1038, less than fifty years after Mieszko's Piast Pact, the tribal cult of that pagan god erupted against conversion to Christianity. So virulent was the revolt that historians have called it a return to paganism. That it was not. But it was a costly cleansing of the Poles as a people; and, for a time, most of what had been achieved in the first few decades of Polish Christianity was destroyed in a last flick of the old serpent's tail as it protested eviction from its long-held position among the Poles.

When it was over—and it was over quickly—by Polish choice and by Polish armed force, Poland was securely lodged in the West as Europe's eastern anchor. It shared that western commonwealth of the peoples in territories now called France, Spain, Portugal, Belgium, Holland, Italy, Austria, Germany, the five Scandinavian countries, England and Ireland. All were directly and exclusively formed by the missionizing emissaries of the Roman Church and its head, the Bishop of Rome. For, attributed to him and claimed by him were not only the spiritual and

religious regulation of those peoples, but also supervision of all sociocultural and political structures. As spiritual leader and political overlord,
the Pope was the preeminent—often disputed, but persevering—keystone in that portion of ancient Europe.

The peoples living there—even the xenophobic natives of England—
could and did circulate throughout their lands with relative ease. The
peoples of that western territory shared the same holy days, cultural
symbols, educational sources (mainly Greco-Roman), food, living habits
and social and political structures. Intermarriage was common. Trade,
commerce, banking, the arts, moral standards and laws, the sciences,
such as they were—all these strategies of living were homogeneous at
least in their broad lines.

It was in that context that the foundational traits of Poland were
formed. There would never be another eruption of paganism among the
Polish people. Since that time, in all its seesawing fortunes, neither the
nation nor any freely chosen government of Poland would ever repudiate
the overlordship of the man who occupies the throne of Peter. The
orientation of Poles to Rome became a national trait that has never been
eliminated. And that fact alone came, in time, to mark a special destiny
for these people and their land, and a specific geopolitical outlook for
generations of its leaders.

The choice made by Mieszko I and declared with such depth in the Piast
Pact determined the two main directions in which the spirit and the
attitudes of his nation would develop. Their orientation toward Rome—
their *romanitas*, as the Poles called it—became the force that molded
the vertical pillar and the horizontal plane of their national identity.

Vertically, *romanitas* was the means of the ascent of the Polish mind
and soul to God. For Poles, Rome was truly the Eternal City on the Hill;
it showed them the source of their safety and their salvation in life and
in afterlife. In spirit and in attitude, Poles transcended all time and space
within their Christian ambition to regard God's Heaven as the ultimate
reason and goal of all earthly life.

On the horizontal plane, meanwhile, the *romanitas* of the Poles joined
the practical life and fortunes of Poland with those of the See of Peter as
a visible power spread throughout the world. The place where those
vertical and horizontal planes of life met and formed a cross was the
motherland of Poland. This was to be the geographical place on earth
where the heavenly and the territorial joined to fashion the Roman
Christian ideal.

In the shadow of that cross, the Poles would build a sociopolitical

model that must rank as the eighth wonder of the world. Upon that
cross, the Poles themselves would again and again be crucified. With
that cross as their guarantee as a nation, the Poles would never die.

During the next five hundred years, the foundational traits of Poland
were developed. Its territory expanded. At one stage, the Piast king took
the throne of Prague, and conquered his way eastward as far as Kiev.
Poland fought its first major battles as the bastion of Western Christianity
against the Mongols; and it saw the creation of its mortal enemy—the
German Monastic State in Prussia—by the German brethren known as
the Teutonic Knights. The European powers recognized Poland's political equality with France, Italy and Germany. The Poles acquired their
first national patron, St. Stanislaw, together with eleven other canonized
and seventy-one beatified saints. The general law of the realm was codi-
fied. In 1264, Piast King Boleslaw Pobozny—Boleslaw the Pious—
granted to the Jews the General Charter of Jewish Liberties, essentially
creating an autonomous and self-governing Jewish nation within Poland
that was exempt from the defense of the land and that had its own courts
and tribunals, based on Talmudic Law. In 1364, Krakow University was
created.

So obvious was the Latinate and Roman mind in all of Poland's foundational traits and development, that an Arab geographer writing in the
middle of the twelfth century described Poland as "a country full of
wisdom and of Roman wise men." But the best—and certainly the most
improbable—was yet to come.

With the death of Elzbieta Bonifacja, infant daughter of King Wladyslaw,
in 1399, the Piast dynasty was at its end. Any betting man of the time
with an ounce of sense and a modest amount of experience would have
put his money on the side of bloody strife and contention to settle the
matter of power and the crown in Poland. That was pretty much the way
things were done. But any betting man who did that in Poland in 1399
would have lost his shirt.

What the Poles did do had no sociopolitical parallels in history or in
their contemporary world—and precious few in our own time. They
created out of the whole cloth of their view of the world a period of
elected monarchs. Following that period, from 1493 to 1569, they went
still farther and created a constitutional monarchy. Finally, from 1569 to
1795, the entire process blossomed into a full-blown system of republican

government—the First Polish Republic—so astounding that not for several hundreds of years would a democratic system as impressive as the Polish *Rzeczpospolita* be developed anywhere.

The first stage of that improbable historical transition got its start when Poland, represented by the remarkable Piast queen Jadwiga, accepted Grand Duke Wladyslaw Jagiello of Lithuania as its leader. However, the Poles had two conditions: Poland and Lithuania would unite; and the Duke would convert to Christianity. The Duke did convert, and in 1386 he married Jadwiga. The more remarkable event, however, was the union of the two states.

Formalized in the Act of Union of 1413, the united territories stretched eastward to Moscow and to the Volga River. And it was this Act of Union that was the extraordinary and improbable thing. For not only was it the constitution by which the two states agreed to govern themselves as a single unit; it laid the basis for an island of civilization in the sea of warring peoples that surrounded it. Like the preamble to the American Constitution, the central statement of that Act of Union reflected and remained forever the ideal of the nation that would live by it. It was an ideal emerging from the thought and teachings of such men of the Roman Church as Thomas Aquinas, Antonois of Florence, Nicholas d'Oresme and William of Ockham, among others.

"It is known to all," the Jagiellonian agreement declared, "that a man will not attain salvation if he is not sustained by divine love, which does no wrong, radiates goodness, reconciles those in discord, unites those who quarrel, dissipates hatred, puts an end to anger, furnishes for all the food of peace. . . .

"Through that love, laws are established, kingdoms are maintained, cities are set in order, and the well-being of the State is brought to the highest level. . . . May this love make us equal, whom religion and identity of laws and privileges have already joined."

Suddenly, a new geopolitical principle was defined. Two independent states agreed upon union through love rather than conquest. And, with that new principle, came three cast-iron consequences: No use of armed forces to conquer others, recourse to armed force only in self-defense, and enlargement of the state only through voluntary union between peoples.

The blessings on Jagiellonian Poland were as extraordinary and improbable as the Act of Union itself. It would take the other important powers of Europe three hundred years before they were capable of establishing the social organization, the legal bases and the political institutions sufficient to guarantee—at least in principle—the fundamental rights of human dignity and freedom that came to be constitutionally and civilly granted in the full flowering of the Republic of Poland.

The structural principle of the new republic—for so it was—was a political system of local legislatures (*sejmik*) and a national legislature (the *Sejm*) based on a pluralistic society and aimed at a perfect equilibrium between power and freedom. In 1494, the *Sejm* became bicameral, with a chamber of deputies and a senate. From that time on, organs of democracy clearly recognizable to us as our models fairly sprouted from the constitutional monarchy of Poland.

General elections were instituted—the first in the world as we know it in history. Watchdog senatorial committees were set up to attend to such worries as the rights and limitations of the Polish constitutional monarchy—only the *Sejm*, for example, could commit the country to war and ratify treaties—and to guard against corruption in government. A state treasury and a tax court of the treasury were established. Lower courts with elected judges led upward to a Supreme Court of Appeals, and dealt with intricate legislative, civil and religious systems based on the principle of *habeas corpus*, which had already been adopted by the Act of Krakow in 1433.

The list of Poland's sociopolitical accomplishments during the course of the fifteenth century went far beyond the merely improbable. The development and concrete application of such principles as government with the consent of the governed, freedom of religion, the definition and protection of personal rights and freedoms, general elections, and constitutional checks and balances to curb any autocratic tendencies on the part of the state, all remain enviable today.

Improbable developments in Poland were hardly over, however.

From 1520 to 1650, religious wars tore the entrails of all European countries. Virulent anti-Semitism decimated European Jewry, and in the first half of the sixteenth century, the term "Catholic" became distinct from "Christian."

In the midst of all that, in 1569, Ruthenia—a large swath of territory in what later became the western portion of the USSR—joined Poland and Lithuania in what was called the "Unitary Republic," or the First Polish Republic. The three territories were determined to form a single state coagulated as one family by the Christian mystery of God's love for all his creatures.

A careful reading of the constitution promulgated by Poland's King Zygmunt August, and of the other historical documents relevant to this

Unitary Republic, demonstrates the surprising internationalism of Poland, well before anything resembling it was born in the rest of the world. These Polish creations were already grounded in a geopolitical framework that had even then progressed beyond mere transnationalist thinking.

There were no religious wars and no anti-Semitic pogroms in the Unitary Republic. Rather, there was a consciously adopted principle of religious freedom. Filled with a vast majority of Roman Catholics, the Republic practiced a form of religious pluralism and toleration still lacking in Europe and the Americas. Nor was this principle of religious freedom based on some vague theory of the rights of man. It was rooted in the specific and basic law proposed at the Council of Constance (1414–18) by a Polish delegate, Pawel Wlodkowicz: "License to convert [by preaching and example] is not a license to kill or expropriate."

Thus, as the religion-based hate generated by the Protestant Reformation reached its height in the 1600s, the First Polish Republic was an extraordinary spectacle—a multi-ethnic and multiconfessional commonwealth based on a cosmopolitan idea of human membership in the family of nations and peoples. Poland had developed a working model of participative democracy.

So determined were the Poles to live by such principles that in 1645 at Torun, King Wladyslaw IV held the *Colloquium Caritativum*—the Loving Dialogue—which was exactly what it was billed to be. At a most improbable time, when religious hatred fueled wars and drove political policies in Europe, Polish Roman Catholics, Orthodox Eastern Christians and at least two Protestant sects—Lutherans and Calvinists—agreed to live and let live, to disagree unbloodily, and to foment their mutual love.

This was the classical expression of the Polish ideal, of Polishness lived on the practical—the horizontal—plane of worldly existence. This republican form of national government, aligned with the fixed orientation of Catholic Poles to Christ's salvation through Rome, summarized for a warring world what Poles conceived themselves to be as a nation.

It was not lost on the Poles, increasingly surrounded by Protestant powers, that a certain vulnerability was present in a system of government where kings were not hereditary but elective, and where time was needed to elect a suitable and acceptable successor after the death of a reigning monarch. The vulnerability lay in the transition period between one king and the next one; in the interregnum. Given their demonstrated love of

"Golden Freedom," the Poles wanted no strongman coming in to take charge by force of arms.

To solve the potential difficulty before it became a problem in fact, in 1573 the *Sejm* of the Unitary Republic conferred on the Primate Bishop of Poland the right and duty to act as head of state and chief executive during the period between the death of one king and the election of his successor.

Henceforth, the Primate Bishop of Poland would fill the gap of power and authority when no legally elected head of government was seated. By parliamentary title, the Primate Bishop was *Interrex*. His special function as *Interrex* was to protect the sovereignty and the religion of the Poles from affront and danger. He represented the Poles as a people, and oversaw their political and constitutional sovereignty. In times when they were deprived of their due and lawful political head, he embodied their rights and aspirations. In practical terms, he would form a regency-style government in order to further their interests.

Cut from the same cloth as the Piast Pact of King Mieszko I, which preceded it by some six hundred years, the *Interrex* Pact held in vigor down the centuries and still holds today. Like the Piast Pact, it would never be forgotten or broken. It was activated by the fifteenth-century Primate Bishop of Gniezno, Zbiegniew Olesnicki, by the sixteenth-century Primate Bishop, Jan Laski, and, perhaps most fatefully, in the twentieth century by Primate Bishop August Hlond, and by his successor, Stefan Wyszynski, who, besides discharging the function of *Interrex* in a twentieth-century and Stalinist context, was the closest mentor of Papa Wojtyla.

For those who habitually think in terms of a wall between Church and State, the concept of *Interrex* is unintelligible. Worse, it is even repugnant for those who think in terms of all religions as the same and who thus hold in essence that no religion is authentic or true.

Poles, however, based their reasoning on the alignment of their daily life with the vertical pillar of their faith, the alignment of the worldly with the divine that had been the hallmark of Polishness for five hundred years by this time. They rejected as an unacceptable outlook for Polishness any idea that there was no unique transcendent of a Saving God who requires worship and belief. Such a view was and would still be death for the greatness of Poland's Catholicism, which has recently achieved a degree of civil justice and religious freedom and toleration with no contemporary models or peers on the face of the earth to imitate.

The *Interrex* Pact has been so crucial to Poland's survival as a people —a survival that was to prove nothing short of miraculous—that it must be ranked beside the Piast Pact as the Second Pact of Polishness.

· · ·

The Third Pact of Polishness came about in circumstances far different from those that led to the Piast Pact and the *Interrex* Pact, circumstances of mortal danger for Poland. Even more than the first two, the Third Pact reflects the intimacy with the divine that lies at the heart of Polish Catholicism and of the Polish nation as a people.

By the 1600s, Poland was a power to be reckoned with in Central Europe. It was commercially and industrially prosperous. It possessed a well-trained army that included forty thousand Cossacks and was backed by multiple reserves. It had defeated the Russians and brought back their Czar Szujski in chains to Warsaw. It had defeated the Teutonic Knights at the terrible battle of Tannenberg in 1410. Internally, it was the mecca of Humanism—one of its brightest stars in that regard was the astronomer Copernicus, who stands as one key to modern astronomy. And it remained robustly Roman Catholic in the face of a rampant Lutheranism and Calvinism, and of a bellicose, expansionist Ottoman Turkey.

In 1648, the Unitary Republic of Poland was invaded and attacked by both Swedish and Turkish forces. At a certain stage of the war, only the Paulite Monastery on Jasna Góra—the Bright Mountain—overlooking the town of Częstochowa held out against the Swedish invaders.

Preserved in that monastery was the most famous Polish icon of Mary and the Infant Jesus. A special object of veneration since ancient Polish Christian times, the icon had been lodged at Jasna Góra since 1382. It is said to have been painted by St. Luke the Evangelist on a plank that originally served as a table for Jesus, his mother, Mary, and his foster father, Joseph, in their home in Nazareth. The right cheek of Mary's face on the icon bears a scar inflicted by a Tartar saber in 1430. Miraculously, as it seemed, Jasna Góra was never taken. After forty days of siege, the Swedish army retired.

In 1655, after peace came, King Jan Kazimierz proclaimed Mary to be Queen of the Kingdom of Poland. Like the Piast Pact and the *Interrex* Pact, that proclamation—together with its implicit promise of special fealty to Mary and reliance on her protection—has never been rescinded or denied or abandoned by the Polish nation or by any Polish government, Catholic or Communist, since 1655. Poland was often described as, and was in fact, the Garden of Eden of the New Eve: of Mary, the Virgin Mother of that Jesus whom Poles worshiped as God, Creator and Redeemer.

For the de-Catholicized and de-Christianized nations of the West today, the problem presented by the Polish Pact with Mary is even worse than the problem of the *Interrex* Pact. It appears simplistic, downright superstitious and objectionable, in fact. Yet, from the start of Roman Christianity in Poland, Mary was accorded a special position, corresponding to the dignity that had always been accorded her in the Church as the mother of God's Son: as the heavenly mother, therefore, of all who belong to Christ.

At the basis of this veneration of Mary is the Roman Catholic certainty that the whole purpose of knowing about Jesus is to love him. The whole purpose, for example, of confessing sins and of assisting at the Sacrifice of the Mass is to be closely linked, personally and intimately, with Jesus. Nor is that intimacy a group event. Catholicism was never a religion of mass feeling or group sentiment. To be sure, each Catholic belongs to the community of believers; but the bond of each Catholic with Jesus is personal.

According to Catholicism, there is no possibility of knowing and loving Jesus unless he is accepted as he presents himself to us. As he presented himself, in other words, in his life, in his physical sufferings, in his resurrection, and as he presents himself today in his Church, under the veils of the Eucharist as the central sacrament of Roman Catholicism. For, in that sacrament, Catholics hold that they really participate in all that Jesus did, both before he died and subsequently—that they are united with Jesus in the actuality of his earthly and his celestial life.

"Behold! I stand at the door and knock," Jesus is believed to say in the biblical words. "If any man will admit me, I will come into him, and eat with him, and he with me." God's guarantee of personal intimacy.

That certainty is the basis for what Catholics of vibrant faith have always spoken of as their spiritual—their "inner" or "interior"—life. That is their vocabulary of personal identification with Jesus, and of their conviction that Jesus desires a personal intimacy with each one.

Traditionally in Catholic life, such intimacy is brought about by God's grace in the individual, and by cooperation with that grace on the part of each person. Intimate association is fostered, in other words, by entering into all the details of Christ's life on earth and in Heaven through prayer and ascetical practices and mental effort: by entering into his words, his thoughts, his actions, into his earthly and his eternal relationship with his mother, with his foster father, with his saints and his companions, with his heavenly Father and his Holy Spirit, with his sacraments and his laws, with his governance of human history. All of that is part of each individual's intimacy with Jesus.

In all of that, Mary has held a special place since the earliest days of the Church. Catholics have understood by the knowledge of faith that as the woman selected from eternity to be the mother of Christ without any collaboration of a man, Mary was privileged from conception in her mother's womb. For many centuries before it was declared as dogma, the faithful have held that when Mary's mortal life was done, she was transferred body and soul to the Heaven of her Son's glory, where she occupies a special position.

It is that certainty, and that inexpressible joy of intimacy touched with the glory of God, that King Jan Kazimierz proclaimed as the Third Pact of Polishness in 1655. But even before that—fairly early in Poland's history as Unitary Republic—the relationship with Mary as the mother of Jesus and, therefore, as an essential aspect of Catholic intimacy with her Son was given lively and concrete expression.

In 1617—within an area of several square miles that lies between Wadowice, where Karol Wojtyla was born, and Krakow, where he lived, studied, was ordained as priest and served as Cardinal Archbishop—a remarkable project was begun by the Palatine Count Mikolaj Zebrzydowski in fulfillment of a penitential vow. Within two generations, that area, marked by four hills and known as Kalwaria Zebrzydowska, was covered with constructions—monuments, houses, churches, chapels, shrines, walks and trails and roads—that reproduced the main events in the life of Jesus and his associates. Represented at Kalwaria are Jesus' birthplace in Bethlehem, his home in Nazareth, the ancient Jerusalem that witnessed his preaching, passion, death and resurrection, and the founding of his Church.

And there, dwarfing the reproductions of Mount Zion, Mount Moriah and the Mount of Olives, stands the basilica dedicated to Mary as the Angelic Mother. There today, every year at the celebration of Christ's resurrection at Easter, and at the celebration of the Assumption—the taking of Mary in her whole person, body and soul, into her Son's eternal Heaven—anything up to sixty thousand Poles share in the intimacy between the divine and the human. They express a special love for Mary, because Jesus chose her as his mother. They place themselves in her charge and protection, because as babe and boy, Jesus freely chose to do exactly that. So said the Third Pact of Polishness in 1655. And so it says today.

Those Three Pacts of Polishness—the Piast Pact with the Holy See, the Pact with the Roman Catholic Primate of Poland as the *Interrex*, the Pact with Mary as the Queen of Poland—define the heritage, the meaning and the strength of Polishness. Nowadays, the one Pole whose Polishness is of vital interest to the world at large is Papa Wojtyla, and in one specific regard: What has that Polishness to do actually with the papal character and policy of the "Polish Pope"?

It is a curious detail about the twelve-year pontificate of John Paul that, in the beginning, he was almost constantly referred to as the "Polish Pope," but that with the passage of the years, the Polish tag has been most frequently omitted, almost as if people had stopped wondering and saying "a *Polish* Pope?" This change can be put down to the international stature Pope John Paul has achieved during the intervening years; today he is seen primarily as a cosmopolitan citizen, as belonging to the whole world. It is the surest sign of his successful drive to achieve geopolitical status and stature in the eyes of his contemporaries.

But a neglect of his Polishness as a major factor in his papal character and policy entails a misunderstanding of the role he has intended and does today intend to play as Pope, and of the geopolitical vision that animates him.

The first time that phrase, the "Polish Pope," rose in people's minds and passed their lips to describe Karol Wojtyla was the first time the world laid eyes on him as Pope John Paul II; and it was, in all probability, because of one simple spontaneous gesture of his on that occasion.

At 8:17 P.M., the evening of the day he was elected Pope, October 16, 1978, he stepped out onto the front balcony of St. Peter's Basilica, Rome, flanked by some cardinals and officials. The golden light of the illuminations caught the blood-red and white colors of his vestments, the blue of his eyes, but it revealed one other detail—a particular gesture of his —that took all Vatican-watchers by surprise. In living memory, no Pope had ever used that gesture; it was not "Roman," in that sense, nor was it "Roman Catholic" in the experience of the millions of Roman Catholics in the Western world who gazed on that scene live and by television satellite. And yet it seemed totally fitting and, because unwonted and new, a sign that this Pope represented a new era.

It was the position of his hands. Photographs and video records of the five previous popes (John Paul I, Paul VI, John XXIII, Pius XII, Pius XI), going back to 1922—the only popes in history who were caught on film at that solemn moment of their first appearance in front of the wide world—show a uniform tradition. As a newly elected pope, each one held both hands together at the level of the breastbone, palm on palm, fingers on fingers, thumbs crossed. It was and still is the normal Roman Catholic gesture of prayer and divine worship.

Karol Wojtyla's hands were closed in fists, and his right forearm was laid over the left, thus forming a cross on his chest, a fist almost touching the right and left shoulder. Many of the viewers that night had never seen this gesture; it meant little to them. Some realized they had seen it depicted in icons of saints from Eastern European countries, particularly of martyrs going to their death or lying in the repose of death. Most of those who remarked on it took it as a "Polish" or "Slavic" gesture of prayerfulness. This was reinforced by the tones of his first three words: "*Sia lodato Gesucristo*" (May Jesus Christ be praised). The language was Italian certainly, and the expression was Roman Catholic. But the basso voice with its unmistakably Slavic pronunciation—particularly the *l* and the *o* and the other long vowels—resonated with that lilt so many had heard only in Slavonic hymns.

This Pope was quite new. This was the "Polish Pope."

Most people in the West knew little about Poland and still less about Russia when Karol Wojtyla became Pope. But with his election to the See of Peter, at least some accurate information about modern conditions in Poland has reached the general public in the West. But what filters through the news media and the current spate of novels and travel books about both countries is not sufficient to give any substance to the term "Polish" when applied to the present Pope. His Polishness remains a vague, ill-defined adjective indicating only where he was born but little else that is clear. Such a poverty of detail and lack of clarity about John Paul's Polishness becomes a crippling liability in view of the geopolitical turn Karol Wojtyla has given to his papacy. Has that geopolitical bent of his eliminated his Polishness as a factor, or—conversely—how genuine can the geopolitical mind of someone be who is genuinely Polish?

Are we dealing here with two opposites (Polishness and geopolitics) in one and the same character?

The facts of history may be mind-boggling for many. Whoever says "Poland," meaning the Polish nation, and with full knowledge of what he is talking about, is saying three things about that "Poland," which boggle the modern mind as irreconcilables: Poland the bastion of papal Rome as the center of a georeligion; Poland the veritable shrine of that religious intimacy with divinity that is specifically Roman Catholic; and Poland the commonwealth of nations. That "Poland" is the direct result of the Three Pacts of Polishness; and the salient traits of John Paul as Pope have a clear lineage back to those Pacts.

The Piast Pact itself is the very womb of Polishness; and it is also the crucible in which the dimensions and the unremitting certainty of John Paul's driving political vision were formed and purified. This foundational Pact ensured that his association with Rome was as natural as his association with Christ and his mother, Mary. It made second nature for him the idea and goal of human membership in the family of nations—

more than a mere Internationalist, more than a simple Transnationalist, both of whom conceive the nations as an association of distinct parts related by human-fashioned pacts. Giving him form as a geopolitician because of his georeligion, it enabled him to start from the real unity of all men and women according to the Jagiellonian principle.

Beginning with the Piast Pact of 990, the Poles as a nation of people had identified themselves increasingly and uniquely as a people who not only communicated intelligibly with God but formed their practical and daily associations with one another and with the nations around them on the principle of that "divine love," cited in the Jagiellonian Act of Union, through which "laws are established, kingdoms are maintained, cities are set in order, and the well-being of the State is brought to the highest level."

The wondrous effect of that Pact and its georeligious consequences could be seen in Poland of the sixteenth century, which housed a population of ethnic Poles, Lithuanians, Russians, Germans, Armenians, Tartars, Ruthenians, Estonians, Latvians, Danes, Norwegians, Jews and the largest expatriate community of Scots in the world. All of these represented a dozen religions—including Roman Catholicism; and all of them considered themselves to be Polish citizens within a framework that catered to their ethnic and religious rights. Poland of 1939 housed nearly 40 percent of all Jews in the world then—10 percent of Poland's total population; Poland was the preferred homeland of Jews away from their homeland in Israel.

Polishness, in fact, and in the sense of those diverse groups, had no distinctive ethnic, religious or nationalistic note. It had geopolitical over-tones—and this on the territory of a nation that, without the shadow of a doubt, was thoroughly and confessionally Roman Catholic. How or why did the Polish nation arrive at that concrete estimation of human liberty and human commonality which did not begin to dawn on the reputedly more enlightened peoples of Western Europe and America before the middle of the twentieth century?

This trait of Polishness gave Papa Wojtyla his deep love for and under-standing of freedom—and his hatred for the prostitution of freedom by those who mouth its name in the cause of something-or-other. It gave him his deep understanding of the potential of Western democracy and republicanism—and his repulsion at Western unfaith. It gave him his model for free associations among the nations on the basis of love—but not on the basis of conquest or greed for power or profit.

There is even more implied in the name Poland that is relevant to John Paul II's papal career. If a search and examination were to be made, say, among the countries of Europe—and even extended to the Americas—for a country whose national history could be regarded as a "natural" preparation for geopolitics in general and papal geopolitics in particular, about the only country to answer this description would be Poland. This does not mean that every miner in Silesia and every shipyard worker in Gdansk and every farmer and housewife and intellectual in Poland is or could be a practicing geopolitician. But it does mean that, peculiarly to Poland, its national ethos and aspirations, the concrete historical events lived by Poles, together with their art and folklore, would be the most favorable conditions in which a geopolitically inclined mind would be nourished and developed, given the required will and opportunity. Wojtyla had the education, the sensitivity and the interest that facilitated his adopting a geopolitical attitude and policy.

Much more deeply and intricately than meets the eye at first sight, the Polish Pact with Mary, the mother of Jesus, has been and will always be an operative key element in this Pope's geopolitical mentality and—it must be stressed—his career as Pope. Long before he became Pope, he had concretized the general Polish Pact with Mary in a personalized form by consecrating himself as priest, as bishop, and as cardinal to Mary. His motto, *Totus Tuus*, reflects that decision.

But all that has been preparation for the signal role he firmly believes Mary will one day play in bringing into visible existence the geopolitical structure he has made his goal. Again, in keeping with his mind, he bases this expectation on a georeligious event in which Mary figures as the instrument of divine providence. God, through Mary, he believes, has already forewarned the nations and predicted that geopolitical outcome.

The school in which was developed Wojtyla's keen sense of the geopolitical as distinct from the national, the nationalistic, the regional and the ideological was his during all his days as a cleric in Poland. From 1948 onward, he was overshadowed by Stefan Cardinal Wyszynski, Primate of Poland and—in the Stalinist circumstances of post–World War II Poland—the effective *Interrex* who, over a period of some thirty-three years, successfully protected the Polish people from the Leninist demoralization planned by the Moscow masters. He not only did that; he reduced the Polish Stalinists to impotence—they who, in theory, had absolute power—and directly made the Gorbachevist "liberation" of Poland and the other satellites of Eastern Europe an inevitability. Ruefully or gratefully, Gorbachev owes Wyszynski a debt.

As Archbishop and later as Cardinal, Wojtyla worked hand in glove with Wyszynski, learning from him firsthand not only the function of

Interrex but, more important, the geopolitical way to reason about the then all-embracing Leninism of the USSR and about the fateful weaknesses of the capitalist West.

Centuries before Karol Wojtyla walked the fields and forests and climbed the mountain slopes of Poland, the Pacts of Polishness earned for Poles the same enmity of worldly powers that Christ bequeathed to his followers. The Pacts provided Poles with the only means imaginable by which they were able to survive as a people for centuries, although deprived of their own sovereign government, their own nationhood and a territory they could call their own. Completely partitioned among Austrians, Russians and Germans from 1795 to 1918, then thoroughly sovietized structurally for forty years, Poles en masse were impermeable, and proved that resident in them was a self-propelling and unstoppable dynamism that maintained cultural, social and spiritual protective mechanisms and ensured the perseverance of the Polish *racja stanu*, the unforgettable and unbreakable will to survive. "As long as we live," Poles always sang in their national anthem, "Poland lives. . . ."

28. The Pacts of Extinction

The death and entombment of the First Polish Republic as a sovereign nation-state was an accomplished fact by 1795. It was the direct result of pacts for its extinction concluded between the Great Powers of Europe. It lasted a full 125 years, until 1919, when the Second Polish Republic was established, to live a precarious twenty-year existence until 1939, when, once more, its extinction was accomplished by Hitlerian Germany and Stalinist Russia, whose avowed aim was to liquidate forever not merely the nation-state of Poland but the Poles as a distinct ethnic and national group. No other great power in Europe really objected to that result. As David Lloyd George wrote in a well-publicized letter of September 28, 1939, "the people of Britain are not prepared to make colossal sacrifices to restore to power a Polish regime represented by the present government. . . ." Lloyd George goes on to say that the USSR had every right to swallow up the Polish republic.

When the Western allies, Great Britain and France, did finally wage real war on Germany, ostensibly to free Poland, manifestly it was because they themselves were faced with a lethal threat. The "phony war" of September 1939 to March 1940 was a time of intensely studied options. It need not have ended with the waging of the real World War II at the beginning of spring 1940.

The "real proof of the pudding" came with the tragically erroneous Yalta and Potsdam agreements between Joseph Stalin and the Western allies: Poland was once more condemned to extinction, its people once more to be merged indistinguishably into the "peoples" and the "republics" of the Stalinist Gulag Archipelago—and that for another forty-three years. Another pact of Polish extinction.

Apart from the mortal blow to the rights of Poles as individuals and citizens, however, Poland's planned extinction for a terrible total of 168 years was a geopolitical and historical mistake of universal proportions. Because the net result was a lopsided and unbalanced view of history, of history's models and of history's lessons for later generations, it was a mistake that was doomed to be repeated; and not only in Poland. And despite all its twists and turns and complications, Poland's story from Renaissance times right into our own day makes it clear that the Soviets were by no means the first ideologically driven group to practice the professional elimination of whole blocs of history; nor were they the first to think up the dreadful stratagem of the "nonperson"—the person other people agree to pretend never existed.

But this extinction of Poland had one more result of far-reaching consequences: It bred among Poles and particularly in the men and women who were Karol Wojtyla's intellectual, religious and moral mentors and political forebears a vivid realization of geopolitics. For their fate as a nation, their daily lives as a people, and the very reason for being Poles depended on vastly intricate affairs involving the Great Powers of world politics. The *racja stanu* about which the Poles were and are justifiably preoccupied—the raison d'être of Poland as a nation-state—has been so long entwined with international affairs and world-wide events that Poland has taken on a permanently geopolitical connotation.

The upper reaches of that connotation and its global dimension was guaranteed by the inherent Romanism of Poland and what it stands for. In a true but not derogatory sense, Poland became and is a regularly played pawn in the geopolitical game. Small wonder then that John Paul would come equipped geopolitically. The Pacts of Extinction ensured that much.

The three major forces that led directly to the demise of the First Polish Republic in 1795 sprang from such varied motives and backgrounds that, without the advantage of hindsight, one would have expected war to break out between them, rather than the fusion of interests that grew instead.

Two of those three major forces had their earliest beginnings in the deep and violent strains placed on European order and unity by the relocation of the papacy to Avignon in France for sixty-eight years, from 1309 to 1377; and by the Great Schism that followed for another thirty-nine years, from 1378 to 1417. If ever a door of change opened in the affairs of men and nations, those 108 years constituted such a door.

Until then, the papacy had been the only highly developed and stable institution for hundreds of years, giving to the medieval world a sense of order, unity and purpose. In that world of early Europe, everything—politics, commerce, civil law, legitimate government, art, learning—all depended on the ecclesiastical structure that stretched from pope to cardinals and bishops, priests and monks, and outward through all the ramifications of life.

With the Great Schism came a sudden shock of universal doubt as to which of three rival claimants was the valid successor of Peter the Apostle. And along with doubt, the first seeds of challenge to the established order blossomed among the intellectual, artistic and aristocratic circles of European society. Again, only historical hindsight allows us to see now that, with the Great Schism and the Avignon papacy, something vital had departed from papal Rome, something precious and valuable for the papacy's name and standing. Men, for the first time, started to question papal claims. It was in this context that Catherine of Siena (1347–1380) announced the words she had heard in a vision of Heaven: "The Keys of this Blood will always belong to Peter and all his successors."

The doctrinal revolt of John Wycliffe (1330–1384) in England, imitated and followed by Jan Hus (1370–1415) and his Hussites in Bohemia, was early warning of the trouble that was brewing. For on doctrinal bases, such men began to challenge the civil and political order established on the basis of papal authority.

In this unaccustomed climate of uncertainty and challenge that came to mark early-Renaissance Italy, there arose a network of Humanist associations with aspirations to escape the overall control of that established order. Given aspirations like that, these associations had to exist in the protection of secrecy, as least at their beginnings. But aside from secrecy, these humanist groups were marked by two other main characteristics.

The first was that they were in revolt against the traditional interpretation of the Bible as maintained by the ecclesiastical and civil authorities, and against the philosophical and theological underpinnings provided by the Church for civil and political life.

Given the first characteristic, the second was inevitable: a virulent, professional and confessional opposition to the Roman Catholic Church and, in particular, to the Roman papacy, both as a temporal power and as a religious authority.

Not surprisingly given such an animus, these associations had their own conception of the original message of the Bible and of God's revelation. They latched onto what they considered to be an ultrasecret body of knowledge, a *gnosis*, which they based in part on cultic and occultist strains deriving from North Africa—notably, Egypt—and, in part, on the classical Jewish *Kabbala*.

The *Kabbala*, the highest reach of mysticism in Judaism's long history, was a direct descendant of the ancient pre-exilic Jewish mystic tradition rooted in the Carmel figures of Elias and Elisha. It left definite traces in the canonical Jewish Bible—the Assumption of Elias, the Millenarianism of Amos, the Servant Songs of Deutero-Isaiah, the Chariot Visions of Ezekiel, the New Covenant prophecies of Jeremiah, the haunting beauty of Malachi's prophecies.

The Jewish *Kabbala* itself was an attempt to outline how mere mortal man, within the strict Mosaic tradition of God's total separateness from man, could attain knowledge—and ultimately, possession—of the divinity. For that knowledge, or *Kabbala*, would itself be possession. Toratic purity was the only preparation for the reception of *Kabbala*; and it would bring with it profound effects and changes in the material cosmos of man.

The *Kabbala* was, in other words, a spiritual doctrine about the intervention of the wholly alien and supernatural life of the one God, the Creator of all things, into the material cosmos.

Whether out of historical ignorance or willfulness or both, the Italian humanists bowdlerized the idea of *Kabbala* almost beyond recognition. They reconstructed the concept of *gnosis*, and transferred it to a thoroughly this-worldly plane. The special *gnosis* they sought was a secret knowledge of how to master the blind forces of nature for a sociopolitical purpose.

In the prescientific, pre-Enlightenment world, before Francis Bacon "rang the bell that called the wits together," around 1600, that mastery involved, among other things, what is popularly but erroneously called "cabalistic" methods of alchemy—the effort to change the elemental nature of substances, mainly metals. In fact, the dedicated humanist cabalists were always seeking what was called the Philosopher's Stone— a mineral that, by its merest touch, could transmute base metals such as lead into gold.

However, behind all that—behind the cabalists' search for a secret knowledge of the forces of nature, and behind the myth of the Philosopher's Stone—lay the yearning to regenerate the world, to eliminate the base or evil forces, and to transmute them into the gold of a peace-filled and prosperous human society.

Initiates of those early humanist associations were devotees of the Great Force—the Great Architect of the Cosmos—which they represented under the form of the Sacred Tetragrammaton, YHWH, the Jewish symbol for the name of the divinity that was not to be pronounced by mortal lips. They borrowed other symbols—the Pyramid and the All-Seeing Eye—mainly from Egyptian sources.

On such bases as these, the new associations claimed to be the authentic bearers of an ancient tradition that bypassed normative rabbinic Judaism and Christianity alike; a tradition from which both of those religions had sprung but which the cabalists insisted was purer and truer than either of them.

How far these occultist associations might have progressed and what their influence might have been in different historical circumstances must remain an open question. For, as it was, the humanist movement that produced such occult societies found fertile soil among dissidents beyond the Alps. As far as historical researches have gone, it would seem that through the entire swath of Central Europe—from the Alps right up through Switzerland, Austria, Poland, Germany and Scandinavia— there ran the same discontent with the established order, and the same tendency to throw over the dogmas of the Roman papacy in favor of a "more primitive" and, therefore, more faithful interpretation of the Bible events.

Without a doubt, the new secret associations were ready vehicles of that discontent. Over time, in fact, and through an unpredictable series of mergers and mutations, the offspring of these early-Renaissance humanist associations developed into a potent international religious and sociopolitical force that would determine a whole new set of European alliances, and the fate of nations—including the dismal fate that awaited Poland.

For one thing, as they spread northward beyond the Alps, they found adherents among already existing dissident groups such as the Moravian Brethren of Hussite origin, the Unitarians and the neo-Arians. There was no doubt that revolt was building. As that climate intensified, the northward spread and acceptance of the occultist humanists meshed chronologically and most importantly with the beginnings of the Protestant Reformation in the early 1500s.

As we now know, some of the chief architects of the Reformation—Martin Luther, Philip Melanchthon, Johannes Reuchlin, Jan Amos Komensky—belonged to occult societies. And both Fausto and Lelio Sozzini, the Italian anti-Trinitarian theologians, found patronage, funds and a supporting network outside their native Italy. Socinianism, which takes its name from the two Sozzinis, was in fact well received among the brothers of the occult up north in Switzerland, Poland and Germany.

In other northern climes, meanwhile, a far more important union took place, with the humanists. A union that no one could have expected.

In the 1300s, during the time that the cabalist-humanist associations were beginning to find their bearings, there already existed—particularly in England, Scotland and France—medieval guilds of men who worked with ax, chisel and mallet in freestone. Freemasons by trade, and God-fearing in their religion, these were men who fitted perfectly into the hierarchic order of things on which their world rested. In the words of one ancient English *Book of Charges*, medieval freemasons were required "princypally to loue god and holy chyrche & alle halowis [all saints]."

Freemasons were quite separate from other stoneworkers—from hard hewers, marblers, alabasterers, cowans, raw masons and bricklayers. Freemasons were wage earners who lived a life of mobility and of a certain privilege. They were traveling artisans who moved to the site where they would ply their skills, setting up temporary quarters for their lodging, rest and recreation, and for communal discussions of their trade.

As specialists employed by rich and influential patrons, these artisans of freestone had professional secrets, which they ringed around with guild rules—the "Old Charges" of English and Scottish freemason guilds. That being the case, their lodging, or lodge, was off limits to all but accredited freemasons.

To foil intruders, they developed a sign among themselves—what English freemasons called the "'Word" but which might also be a phrase or a sign of the hand—by which to recognize a member who enjoyed the privileges of entry and participation in their lodge.

No one alive in the 1300s could have predicted a merger of minds between freemason guilds and the Italian humanists. The traditional faith of the one, and the ideological hostility to both tradition and faith of the other, should have made the two groups about as likely to mix as oil and water.

In the latter half of the 1500s, however, there was a change in the type of man recruited for the freemason guilds. As the number of working, or "operative," freemasons diminished progressively, they were replaced by what were called Accepted Masons—gentlemen of leisure, aristocrats, even members of royal families—who lifted ax, chisel and mallet only in the ultrasecret symbolic ceremonies of the lodge, still guarded by the "Charges" and the "Mason Word." The "speculative" mason was born.

The new Masonry shifted away from all allegiance to Roman ecclesiastical Christianity. And again, as for the Italian occultist humanists, the secrecy guaranteed by the tradition of the Lodge was essential in the circumstances.

The two groups had more in common than secrecy, however. From the writings and records of speculative Masonry, it is clear that the central religious tenet became a belief in the Great Architect of the Universe —a figure familiar by now from the influence of Italian humanists, a figure that cannot be identified with the transcendent God who chose the Jewish race as a special people or with the transcendent God of Christian revelation incarnated in Jesus of Nazareth. Rather, the Great Architect was immanent to and essentially a part of the material cosmos, a product of the "enlightened" mind.

There was no conceptual basis by which such a belief could be reconciled with Christianity. For precluded were all such ideas as sin, Hell for punishment and Heaven for reward, an eternally perpetual Sacrifice of the Mass, saints and angels, priest and pope. Indeed, the whole concept of an ecclesiastical organization charged with propagating that Christianity, like the concept of an infallible religious leadership personalized in a pope wielding the irresistible Keys of Petrine authority, was considered to be false and antihuman.

In the inevitable rivalry that would develop between the Catholic and Protestant powers of Europe, the Roman papacy—still a temporal power well into the 1600s—would logically if unwisely take sides, even as the Lodge would associate itself with the Protestant elements involved in burgeoning struggle.

In the midst of all this gathering ferment stood Poland, still foursquare and vibrant in the strategic heart of Central Europe, and still foursquare in its fealty to the Holy See of Rome as declared in the Piast Pact. For well over five centuries, as hereditary monarchy, then as constitutional monarchy and as Unitary Republic, Poland had been the bulwark of Roman Christianity, and the one military force that halted the onrush of the Ottoman Turks.

However, even before her third and final victory under Jan Sobieski, over the Turks at Vienna in 1683, Poland's geopolitical position in Europe had been radically altered by the Protestant Reformation launched over 150 years earlier, in 1517, by Martin Luther. In fact, whatever else it was intended or proved to be, in geopolitical terms the Protestant Reformation was a mega-earthquake. By the time of Sobieski's 1683 triumph over the Turks, Poland was practically surrounded and certainly menaced by a newly Protestant world: Prussia, Sweden, Saxony, Denmark, Transylvania (Protestant Hungary). The enmity of those countries for Poland was shared by other emergent powers in Europe—notably England and Holland, both Protestant nations by then.

In calm retrospect, it seems beyond the shadow of any doubt that one major contributing factor in the demise of the First Polish Republic was the influence—mainly among the Protestant enemies of Poland, but eventually, and to an important degree, within Poland as well—of the now humanist Freemasons.

In the era of Accepted Masonry, membership in the Lodge spread throughout the governing and academic classes in Protestant countries. The great universities of Europe in Germany, Austria, France, Holland and England, as well as the scientific establishments, all provided recruits to the Lodge. European Masonry became, in fact, primarily an organization of aristocrats, large landowners and realtors, bankers and brokers. Princes of the royal blood joined the Lodge in important numbers— George IV of England, Oscar II and Gustav V of Sweden, Frederick the Great of Germany, Christian X of Denmark, to name but a few.

The aim of the cabalist humanists had always been sociopolitical change. But with such a membership as it attracted, European Masonry wanted no social revolution. The main aim of European Freemasons was political: to ensure the balance of power in Europe for England, Prussia, Holland and Scandinavia.

The nub of the matter was, however, that any strategic reckoning of these countries, which had been newly reborn as Protestant powers, had to envisage the removal of the First Polish Republic, if their dream of the great northern Protestant alliance was ever to take flesh.

In the 1500s, Poland's eyes for culture, learning, art, thought and philosophy were on Paris. Its sabers were directed to the nascent duchy of Moscow in the east, and to the European Ottoman power to the south. Its heart remained fixed on Rome. Within its own borders, it was a federation of five or six ethnic groups within a republic based on constitutional freedom of religion and worship, which fostered Catholicism, lived at peace with the Protestants in its midst, and provided Jews with legal, religious and civil autonomy in a homeland away from their homeland. The country had become militarily strong, economically prosperous, politically mature, culturally advanced.

Most important for the dream of the northern Protestant alliance, however, was that in two respects Poland remained what it had always been.

Geopolitically, it was still the strategic *plaque tournante* of Central Europe. Out of Europe's total population of 97 million, only France, with a population of 15.5 million, exceeded Poland's 11.5 million. Poland's borders ran from the river Oder, in the west, to 200 kilometers beyond the riverine land of the Dnieper, in the east; and from the Baltic Sea in the north to the river Dniester in the south.

Religiously, meanwhile, Poland was still thoroughly Romanist and papal in its heart, its mind and its allegiance.

As a people, as a unitary nation and as a strategic linchpin, Poland therefore was the one major power standing in the way of a Northern European hegemony for the Protestant powers.

The basic plan for the final liquidation of the Polish Republic began as early as the latter half of the 1500s, as a strictly military undertaking. First, it seems to have taken the form of a classic and unremitting pincers movement: the Ottoman Turks attacking from the south, the Swedes from the north and the war flotilla of Protestant Holland acting in coordination with the Turkish and Swedish attacks by harassing Polish beachheads in the Baltic.

Sweden's Gustavus II Adolphus had an added impetus for his involvement in this effort against Poland. As a brilliant strategist, he surely appreciated the importance of liquidating Poland for the sake of establishing the desired Protestant hegemony. But in a world where royal bloodlines crossed every border and were part of every international initiative, whether friendly or hostile, he had his own dynastic quarrel— an ill-fated one for him, as it turned out—with Poland's King Zygmunt II, who was in fact King of Sweden from 1597 to 1604.

Bloody as they were, these early efforts against Poland came to ruin with the Turkish defeat of 1571 at the naval battle of Lepanto, the second Turkish defeat, at the hands of the Poles, in 1621, and the sudden death of Gustavus II Adolphus in battle, in 1632.

When war alone failed to achieve the aim of the Protestant powers to deliver Poland's territory into the hands of the Protestant allies and eliminate her from the scene as a power, the effort shifted toward a carving up of the territory of the First Republic on the apparently legitimate score of dynastic succession.

While there is no doubt at all that constant wars weakened Poland seriously, it was this "diplomatic" effort—long and complex and with many players involved—that was to prove Poland's undoing. And into the bargain, finally it would set a new pattern for international dealings that would reach well into the twentieth century.

Among the many and complex factors in this new assault on Poland were the wide-ranging plans of Oliver Cromwell as Lord Protector of the English Republic from 1653 to 1658. Cromwell's foreign policy aimed at a weakening of imperial Spain and at the creation of a grand Protestant alliance between England, Germany, Denmark, Sweden and a Holland freed from Spanish domination.

A second, closely related factor was perhaps the oldest of the secret associations that arose in Germany in the 1600s: the Order of the Palm. The order recruited its members in Germany, Scandinavia and Ottoman Turkey; all three had long since understood that the presence of Poland constituted the gravest obstacle to their mercantile and trading plans. The historical researches of the Polish scholar Jan Konapczynski have rightly pointed to the importance of Cromwell's attempted cooperation with the Order of the Palm. But with or without Cromwell, by the closing years of the 1600s, the order concerned itself seriously with the choice of who would become Poland's elected king.

Given those complex royal bloodlines of Europe, such an idea was far from frivolous or unattainable. For the Order of the Palm included such active and powerful leaders as Swedish Chancellor Axel Gustafsson Oxenstierna, Swedish King Gustavus II Adolphus, and Friedrich Wilhelm, Grand Elector of Brandenburg. Moravian bishop Jan Amos Komensky acted as agent for the order between the Swedes and the Germans. And German philosopher Gottfried Leibniz, as secretary of the Alchemist Society of Nuremberg—an affiliate of the Order of the Palm—employed his undoubted talents in favor of getting Palatine Philip Wilhelm elected as King of Poland in 1668–69, when the Polish crown did in fact fall vacant. The Leibniz effort failed; but it was a portentous stab at the legalistic dismemberment of Poland.

As the 1600s drew to a close, another effort to take Poland from within, as it were, came much closer to success. Friedrich Augustus I of Saxony was elected King of Poland in 1697. Like the first Piast King, Mieszko I, in 966, and like Jagiello in 1386, Friedrich converted to Roman Catholicism. But in his case, it was no more than a drill to pass muster; for he was and remained a devotee of the "reconstructed" *Kabbala*, and indulged in so-called cabalistic experiments.

Friedrich's German prime minister, Baron Manteufel, was clearly of the same stripe. A few years later, in fact, in 1728, he created the Masonic Court Lodge in Dresden, with an affiliate Lodge in Berlin. The seal of this Court Lodge was the Rosy Cross—the cross surmounted by a rose; and it counted among its members Friedrich Augustus I himself, and two Prussian kings, Friedrich Wilhelm I and Friedrich Wilhelm II.

Unlike Mieszko and Jagiello, Friedrich Augustus I did not last long as King of Poland. But during his seven-year reign, his foreign policy was directed toward the eventual partitioning of Poland's lands among her neighbors—an effort he continued even after he was deposed, in 1704.

It did not help Poland's position in this new political onslaught from within that she had been continuously at war since 1648. At one stage, she had sustained what contemporary Polish historians called the "Deluge"—a combined invasion of her territory by Swedes, Brandenburger Germans, Transylvanian Hungarians and Muscovites, all of whom were banking on the support of Cromwell's England and on an internal revolt of Protestants and pro-Protestant Catholics within Poland.

Poland survived the "Deluge," just as she had survived so many wars. But by the opening of the 1700s, she had sustained over a century of nearly continuous armed conflict. Now an abuse of constitutional privileges by Poles themselves, and a succession of weak and unacceptable rulers—Friedrich Augustus I was but one—brought the country to the condition of the "Sick Man of Europe."

The first half of the 1700s was, as well, a time that witnessed the great efflorescence of European Masonic Lodges—the true dawning of Accepted Masonry; and Poland by no means escaped its impact. Undoubtedly, in fact, Masonry had been introduced as an important dimension among Poland's ruling classes by Friedrich Augustus I; and the influence of Prime Minister Manteufel doubtless accounts for the Prussophile character of Polish Masonry underlined by some historians.

This was also the Enlightenment era. Inevitably, therefore, philosophy and science entered the fray; for many brilliant exponents of the new disciplines were also adherents of the principles of Masonry. Human intelligence, as a reflection of and participation in the wisdom of the Great Architect of the occultist humanists, was now seen as the infallible element in man's progress.

While the notion of the Great Architect was maintained, the alchemist element of the old humanist associations fell into disrepute and disuse with the onrush of scientific discoveries. The energies of the new initiates were channeled into more practical ways of attaining their sociopolitical goals.

Much of the symbolism and ceremonial that had been evolved in that earlier prescientific cabalism survived. But Masonic humanism as a living force now relied on uninhibited human inquiry, free from any adjudication—especially on the part of the Church and of religion; for that bedrock anti-Church ideology inherited from the thirteenth-century Italian dissidents remained intact—as the only foundation of human civilization. Catholic beliefs were seen as retrograde, as the great inhibitors of human happiness.

Predictably, such political and philosophical elements involved in Masonry as ideological foundation blocks exacerbated the already virulent hatred of the Roman papacy. And this was true especially in the Catholic heartland countries of France, Belgium, Italy and Spain.

The most powerful and all-directive Masonic Lodge in Europe, for example, was the Grand Orient of France. The anti-Roman and anti-Christian hostility in the Grand Orient became almost legendary. With true Gallic logic, in fact, its participants abolished even the old Masonic obligation to believe in the Great Architect of the Universe. In this step —bold even for Accepted Masons of the Enlightenment era—the French Masons were being very French: ahead of everybody else, and discomfiting in their frankness. Still, it was the Grand Orient type of Masonry that took hold in Catholic countries such as Portugal, Spain and Austria, and in Italy itself.

As early as 1738, Pope Clement XII could see the full georeligious and geopolitical implications of Accepted Masonry, whose Lodges included not only the new and deeply influential intellectual leaders, but the most powerful political personages of the day. Clement condemned Masonry as incompatible with Catholic belief—as indeed it was. And he condemned its secrecy as an unlawful practice that would make possible the subversion of nations and governments.

By then, however, it would appear that the die was all but cast. And Poland was to become the classic fulfillment of Pope Clement's warning concerning the subversion of nations and governments.

• • •

During the first half of the 1700s, Masonic Lodges—many modeled on the Grand Orient and on English-Teutonic Masonry—proliferated in Poland like eggs in a henhouse. According to historians of the stature of Stanislaw Zaleski, Jedrzej Giertych and Stanislaw Malachowski-Lipicki, some 316 Lodges dotted Poland in the seventy-seven years between 1738, when Pope Clement issued his condemnation, and 1815, when the Great Powers of the world agreed at the Congress of Vienna to ratify, under international law, the then accomplished fact of the obliteration of Poland from the face of the geopolitical world.

As in every other country, it was not the number of Lodges in Poland, or the size of their membership—reported by historians as 5,748—that was the determining factor in their influence over Poland's fate. Rather, it was as always the fact that Masonry successfully recruited leading and influential intellectuals and the politically powerful members of royalty and the aristocracy—the "superstructure" of society that Karl Marx and Friedrich Engels would point to, within a mere thirty-three years after the Congress of Vienna, as the oppressors of the "working masses."

The historical track of the founding of important humanist Masonic Lodges in Poland, and that of the three successive land grabs—partitions, they were called—of Polish territory, are compelling in the way that they seem to intertwine.

One of the more important Lodges, Wisniowiec, was founded in 1742 at Volhynia. In Warsaw, four major Lodges—Three Brothers, Dukla, Good Shepherd and Virtuous Sarmatian—were founded in 1744, 1755, 1758 and 1769, respectively. The Grand Polish Lodge dated from 1769, as well; its doctrinal authority was the Scottish Chapter of St. Andrew, and the Rosicrucian chapter founded in Germany by Poland's former prime minister Manteufel.

Within this stunningly fertile period for Masonry, Poland saw the election of three monarchs—her last as a republic—who ranked among the most ardent promoters of Polish Masonry. Augustus III died in 1763. He was succeeded by Stanislaw Leszczynski, who died in 1766. He in turn was succeeded by Stanislaw Poniatowski, who outlived the Republic by about three years.

Within that period, as well, Poland was subjected to unremitting invasion, to commercial harassment, to an increasing international isolation, and to what was probably the most crippling influence of all—internal subversion on a wide scale.

Recent studies by scholars demonstrate that during the first two thirds of the eighteenth century, large numbers of the Polish political and intellectual elite were won over to the humanist ideals of Masonry. As a consequence, they willingly collaborated in producing a numbing constitutional paralysis in the First Polish Republic. For clearly, in all their breadth and implications, the Three Pacts of Polishness—the Piast Pact with the Holy See of Rome, the Pact with the Primate Bishop as *Interrex*, and the Pact with Mary as the Queen of the Kingdom of Poland—were irreconcilable with the secularizing intent of Masonry. As it happened, sweetly enough for Masonry, the political fortunes of the Holy See were in visible decline all over Europe by this time.

It is more than merely ironic that the first great model of modern democratic government was also the first to fall victim to all the pitfalls that have lately become familiar all over again.

Poland's legislature began to use its oversight powers to encroach on the powers of the elected head of state. The supreme court followed suit, encroaching onto the domain of the legislature. Representatives began to resort to political ruses to ensure their constant reelection. Democratic liberty was cited as the basis to undermine the moral foundations on which that liberty had been based, and to paralyze government along doctrinaire lines of ideological humanism.

All of these embittering and inhibiting conditions had contributed their generous share to Poland's political decadence and to its internal weakness by the time Stanislaw Poniatowski took power in 1766 as the third in the line of Polish Masonic kings.

By 1772, Poland was so weakened by wars and international intrigues and corrupt government, that the first partial dismemberment of her territory—the First Partition of Poland—became possible. Russia and Prussia, in alliance with Austria, were the beneficiaries, carving up the first spoils three ways.

At about this time also, there started in Russia and Prussia that process that was to become so familiar: the slandering of everything Polish and the poisoning of the European mind with a dislike that amounted to contempt for Poles, and what remained of Poland.

On the Masonic front in Poland, an intra-Masonic rivalry broke out for predominance in Polish Masonry. After much contention between the English, French and German Masonic authorities, the Royal York Lodge of Berlin won the day. In 1780, it organized a new Polish Lodge, Catherine of the Polish Star, and obtained for it from English authorities a patent as a Grand Provincial Lodge. In 1784, it became the Polish Grand Orient.

By 1790, on the political front, the First Polish Republic had deteriorated into such a helpless condition that it was successfully forced into an unnatural and ultimately deadly alliance with its mortal enemy, Prussia. The Polish-Prussian Pact of 1790 was signed. Its chief architect, Ignacy Potocki, was Grand Master of Polish Masonry. And the conditions of the Pact were such that the succeeding and final two partitionings of Poland were inevitable, in the circumstances.

The final blows fell quickly upon Poland. In 1793, the Second Partition reduced Poland from its original population of 11.5 million to about 3.5 million. In effect, however, it was merely a prelude to the Third Partition. By the end of 1795, the long struggle to take Poland from the Poles was over. The last freely elected chief executive of the First Polish Republic, King Stanislaw, was forced to abdicate by Russia, Prussia and Austria. Triumphant at last, the Three Powers proceeded to divide the cadaver of Poland between them.

In a great foreshadowing of things to come in the twentieth century, Russia grabbed all of Lithuania and the Ukraine, with a combined population of some 1.5 million people. Prussia seized Mazovia, with Warsaw as its center—a million people more. And Austria made off with the Krakow region and its one million people.

With Poland's extinction complete, all that remained to accomplish was the eradication of the name of Poland from the map of Europe; and the obliteration of the memory of the Polish presence in Europe. It was precisely to that declared and openly pursued policy that the Three Powers made a joint commitment.

Among the ordinary Polish people, now forcibly parceled out among other populations, hope lingered that the tripartite decision to liquidate their country would be reversed. That hope was given an enormous boost by the sudden and stunning military successes of France's Napoleon Bonaparte. Beginning in 1796—only a year after the Third Partition of Poland—his resounding victories against all comers threw all the powers of Europe into violent flux; and, in geopolitical terms, it made sense for Poles to take hope.

In spite of his extraordinary genius as a military strategist, however, and in spite of his grandiose imperial ambitions, Napoleon was and remained a man of the French Revolution. When he looked at a map of Europe, he saw only lands to conquer, and the contours of military campaigns by which to do it. He never once grasped the geopolitical forces at work in Europe.

As a consequence, he attacked where he should have defended and befriended—his natural allies were in Poland, Russia, Spain and Italy; and with them, he could have beaten the northern alliance ranged against him. Further, he preserved what he should have destroyed—Prussia, for example, after soundly defeating it at the battle of Jena. And finally, he neglected to build strength where he needed it. A divided Poland was the most pathetic example of that neglect; for while he did create the duchy of Warsaw, it was no more than a sorry caricature of Poland, and neither restored the Polish nation-state nor constituted anything that could be of help to Bonaparte.

At the end, the whole world wanted to be done with the "little corporal," for, as long as he held strong, there would be no peace in Europe. After rampaging around the continent for almost twenty years, Napoleon was definitively eliminated. Banished to the remote island of St. Helena in June 1815, he died there on May 5, 1821.

Even then, however, Bonapartism was to produce perhaps the most important of its enduring consequences: Raw power, and the preponderance of such power, was thenceforward accepted as the international yardstick for the arrangement of human affairs.

The victorious powers of Europe assembled at Vienna in September of 1814 to rearrange the map of their continent. Europe would never again be as it was before Napoleon. At the Congress of Vienna, there was neither a religious principle nor any kind of moral suasion for the decisions made. Certainly, Europe was not even remotely ready for anything resembling the geopolitical principle expressed fully four hundred years before in Poland's Act of Union, by which powers agreed to unite and to govern themselves on the basis of that divine love through which "laws are established, kingdoms are maintained, cities are set in order, and the well-being of the State is brought to the highest level."

Quite the contrary, the Congress of Vienna was the first international meeting of European powers where the rule of thumb was to divide the spoils of war. Aside from the aim of preventing a recurrence of the danger all had been subjected to by Bonaparte, the purpose of the victorious parties was to balance raw power among themselves. And in that, it provided the model that would be followed by the Versailles Conference of 1918, and by the Yalta and Potsdam conferences at the end of World War II.

The historical track of the geopolitical involvements of Masonry and the demise of Poland appears to have continued; for historians have pointed out the Masonic identity of the main movers at the Congress of Vienna—Metternich for Austria, Castlereagh for Britain, Czartoryski, a Pole, and the Russian Czar.

Ercole Cardinal Consalvi as papal secretary represented the interests of the Pope. But his involvement was little more than what might be called an act of presence, required only by the fact that participants saw the Papal States as part of the world order they wanted to restore after the tumult caused by Bonaparte. In fact, "Holy See" as an internationally recognized papal title originated in the agreements of the Vienna Congress. Beyond that, however, the Cardinal's presence had little more effect than the nonpresence of any papal representative at the Versailles Conference a century later, when it was explicitly agreed in advance by the victors of World War I that the Holy See would have no say in the terms that dictated the end of that war with Germany.

In the circumstances that prevailed at Vienna in 1814–15, then, whatever hope there might have been for reversing the Third Partition of Poland evaporated. In its balance-of-power arrangements, the Congress ratified the tripartite mutilation of Poland, and the continued crucifixion of the Polish people as a nation, by what was asserted and maintained to be international law.

The First Polish Republic, with its constitutional monarchy and its splendid democratic institutions, was to die. Poles as a nation of people in Europe officially ceased to exist. Poland as a geopolitical entity was effectively to disappear from all the maps of Europe. For Poland—people and country—death and entombment was the decision of the Congress.

In the flush of their victory, the participants at the Congress of Vienna suffered from a lack of prescience at least as severe and costly as Napoleon's lack of geopolitical acumen. As members of the ancien régime of crowned heads and of autocratic and privileged landed aristocracy, they failed to appreciate yet another legacy Napoleon had left them.

As a child of the Revolution, Bonaparte had sown the seeds of dissolution all over Europe. He had smashed the hard surface imposed on European peoples by the ancien régime. He had shown its flaws, demonstrated its weaknesses, proved it was not perpetual. It was now a matter of time before the people—as distinct from the traditional superstructure of society—would clamber out and demand their place in the sun. It was, in fact, a mere matter of thirty-three years before Karl Marx and Friedrich Engels would publish *The Communist Manifesto*.

By then, however, Europe had fully deprived itself not only of the Polish democratic models for freedom of political and religious rights in a European context. It had deprived itself as well of the land that had stood strategically for a thousand years as Central Europe's strong and vibrant northern bulwark.

Given that the internationally agreed aim, as recorded in the sentiments at the Congress of Vienna, was to inculcate the persuasion that "nothing good can come out of Poland," and "nothing good and acceptable must be ascribed to Poland and its Poles," the question of what to do about Polish Masonry became an interesting logistical problem.

In essence, the difficulty was neatly finessed. The Polish Grand Orient, which dated from the period between the First and Second Partitions of Poland, was dissolved on September 24, 1824, by order of Czar Alexander I. All other Lodges in the territories formerly known as Poland—the Congress Kingdom, the Grand Duchy of Lithuania, parts of the Russian Empire and the Free City of Krakow—were likewise dissolved. German Masonic organizations took over the Lodges that remained in Poznania. And the liquidation of Polish Masonry was completed when the Polish Lodge known as "Piast Beneath the Three Sarmatian Columns," together with the German Lodge *Zur Standhaftigkeit*, or Endurance, was merged into a new German Lodge—*Tempel der Eintracht*, or Temple of Unity—to which the Prussian government gave full support, as it did to all other German Lodges in its territory.

It was only after the Polish insurrection of 1831 that purely Polish Lodges raised their heads tentatively but identifiably once again—in Besançon and Avignon, France, in 1832; in London (the Polish National Lodge) in 1846; and in a new Lodge in the famous Polish Armed Forces School in Cuneo, Italy, in 1862. Otherwise, even Polish Masonry would have to wait until the beginning of the twentieth century for its revival.

If it is to be said that the ultimate aim of Poland's enemies was the obliteration of the Roman papacy as a georeligious and geopolitical force in Europe, then it must be said as well that the flourishing Freemasonry of the Enlightenment accomplished at least two major victories over the Roman Catholic Church on both counts.

In 1773, the year following the First Partition of Poland, and a time when Rome found itself weakened in the traditional political sense, the suppression of the Society of Jesus was achieved under the architectural direction, as one might say, of dedicated Masons—the Marquis de Pombal, royal adviser in imperial Portugal; Count de Aranda, royal adviser in imperial Spain; the Duc de Choiseul and Minister de Tillot in imperial France; Prince von Kaunitz and Gerard von Swieten at the imperial court of Maria Theresa in Habsburg Austria. With that coup, the Roman papacy was deprived of an internationally distributed, highly trained, deeply respected and maddeningly resourceful battalion of papal loyalists. Their suppression at a critical moment removed the most dedicated offensive and defensive instrument ever placed in the hands of the Roman pontiffs. It was a loss whose consequences were to be felt by the papacy into the present day.

The second achievement—liquidation of Poland in the same general period—was a blow in the very same direction as far as its specific impact on the papacy was concerned. For the destruction of Poland as a nation-state stripped Roman Catholicism as a geopolitical force of a northern bulwark and of a powerful Catholic influence in the international affairs of Central Europe. And it stripped Roman Catholicism as a georeligious force of a powerfully radiant center for Catholic doctrine.

Some idea of the confessional enmity entertained by Masonry for the Roman papacy can be gleaned from the *Permanent Instruction* drawn up a few years after the Congress of Vienna, in 1819–20, by the French, Austrian, German and Italian Grand Masters of the Lodges:

> . . . we must turn our attention to an ideal that has always been of concern to men aspiring to the regeneration of all mankind . . . the liberation of the entire world and the establishment of the republic of brotherhood and world peace. . . . Among the many remedies, there is one which we must never forget: . . . the total annihilation of Catholicism and even of Christianity. . . . What we must wait for is a pope suitable for our purposes . . . because, with such a pope, we could effectively crush the Rock on which God built his Church. . . . Seek a pope fitting our description . . . induce the clergy to march under your banner in the belief that they are marching under the papal banner . . . make the younger, secular clergy, and even the religious, receptive to our doctrines. Within a few years, this same younger clergy will, of necessity, occupy responsible positions. . . . Some will be called upon to elect a future pope. This pope, like most of his contemporaries, will be influenced by those . . . humanitarian principles which we are now circulating. . . . The medieval alchemists lost both time and money to realize the dream of the "Philosopher's Stone." . . . The dream of the secret societies [to have a pope as their ally] will be made real for the very simple reason that it is founded on human passions. . . .

The Masons, it would seem, had stolen a march on Antonio Gramsci and the brilliant plan he proposed to his Marxist brothers for the extinction of Roman Catholicism as the central force impeding the de-Christianization of the Western mind. For both Marxists and Masons, however different and opposed they may be politically, are at one in locating all of man's hopes and happiness in a this-worldly setting, without any intervention of a divine action coming from outside this cosmos and without appointing an otherworldly life as the goal of all human life and endeavor. Marxism and Masonry transcend, both of them, individuals and nations and human years and centuries. But it is rather an all-inclusive embrace, holding all close to the stuff and matter of the cosmos, not in any way lifting the heart and soul to a transhuman love and beauty beyond the furthest limit of dumb and dead matter.

There are similar and disturbing echoes of these extreme policies in the activities of the superforce and the anti-Church faced by Pope John Paul II today, as well as in the statements of some who call themselves "progressive Catholics." For all of these elements of influence in today's Roman Church wish to carry on with a new ecclesiology that would in effect eliminate the Catholic exercise of the Petrine Office. But in 1820, the actual possibility that such an agenda might be accomplished was still over a century away. Today, it is the ongoing policy of John Paul's intra-Church enemies.

Meanwhile, the commitment to obliterate Poland and its Three Pacts of Polishness, and to see that "nothing good and acceptable must be ascribed to Poland and its Poles," was carried to outlandish lengths in particularly important instances.

One curious and instructive case in point touched the papacy itself, a little more than eighty years after the writing of the *Permanent Instruction* was completed, and a little less than eighty years before the 1978 election of Pope John Paul II. It concerned the village mailman in the Italian town of Riese in Upper Venetia, one Giovanni Battista Sarto by name, and his wife, Margherita, a seamstress.

Sarto had been born Jan Krawiec in Wielkopolska, Poland. When his part of the country fell into Prussia's hands, Sarto found political asylum in Italy, first in Godero, near Treviso, and finally in Riese, where he earned a ducat a day delivering the mail to the townfolk.

On June 2, 1835, a son was born to the Sartos, and they baptized him Giuseppe Melchiorre Sarto. The boy, "Pepi" to his family, was schooled in Castelfranco and Asolo. As a young man in 1858 he was ordained a priest. As a middle-aged man in 1884 he became Bishop of Mantua. And as he was getting on a bit in age in 1893, he was nominated cardinal and promoted to the See of Venice.

Following the death of Pope Leo XIII on July 20, 1903, the papal Conclave narrowly avoided fulfilling the dream of the *Permanent Instruction* and electing Mariano Cardinal Rampolla del Tindaro—the Vatican Secretary of State and an inducted member of the Masonic Lodge—as Pope and Vicar of Christ. In fact, Rampolla did actually receive the required number of votes. But Jan Cardinal Puzyna of Krakow—which was then part of the Austro-Hungarian Empire—exercised the veto power enjoyed at that moment by His Imperial Master, Franz Josef of Austria. Franz Josef knew of Rampolla's Masonic identity, but he probably had as many politico-financial as religious reasons for excluding Rampolla from the Roman See.

It took seven more voting sessions before the Cardinal Electors chose the sixty-eight-year-old Giuseppe Melchiorre Cardinal Sarto of Venice, who chose the papal name of Pius X.

On Sarto's election as Pope, the scramble of high officials in the Austrian monarchy was almost as comic as it was tragic, as they scurried to destroy all certificates and records that might reveal the Polish origins of Pius X. In accordance with the expressed sentiments, aims and intentions of the Congress of Vienna, nothing as good as a pope could come out of Poland.

At least one trace of Sarto's Polish heritage did survive, however, in spite of all the efforts to the contrary. The elder Sarto's original surname, Krawiec, is also the Polish word for "tailor." That, in fact, was the reason he chose Sarto as his Italian surname; for *sarto* is the Italian word for "tailor."

Still, so vigorously was the death and entombment of Poland and Polishness pursued that grown men of presumed probity swarmed like carpenter ants to devour all the official records in Krakow and in Italy, as well, that might reveal the Polish origins of the Krawiec-Sarto family.

29. Papal Training Ground: *"Deus Vicit!"*

"Poles," Czar Nicholas I remarked loftily to a visiting delegation of Polish nobles in 1833, "must remember that the lands they occupy traditionally are of supreme value to the interests not only of our Imperial Majesty but to those of other major European powers. Nature itself and Divine

Providence have written this destiny of the Polish people clearly for all to see in geography and history." If the concept (as well as the actual words) of "geopolitics" and "geopolitical" structure had been in current usage during the 1830s, His Majesty would surely have told his Polish visitors that not national Polish politics but geopolitics should frame their thinking and determine their actions.

Similarly, without a geopolitical framework in mind, no accurate understanding of John Paul II is possible. He will remain an enigma for non-Catholics and a stumbling block for his own adherents.

As a politician, he has not interfered in any massive way in the internal politics of Poland either to save Solidarity from its present fragmentation, or to foment a forceful Catholic or Christian democratic movement. Everyone knows where his heart goes as a Pole, as a Catholic and as Pope. Yet he manifestly remains immersed and actively involved in the geopolitical relationships between Poland and other Europeans as well as in the slow dismemberment of the USSR. Obviously, he is looking far beyond the confines of Poland and the local political interests of Polish Catholicism. He is thinking and planning as a geopolitician.

But the difficulty his contemporaries are experiencing in assimilating this role in a modern pope surely stems from what Czar Nicholas called euphemistically the Polish combination of "geography and history." Over one hundred years later, a Stalin and a Khrushchev did, each in his own inimitable way, employ more blunt and brutally frank language than the Czar when referring to Poland's importance for the security of the USSR within the European continental system.

By that fact of Poland's importance for the USSR, Poland automatically becomes important for the other European nations who share the continent with the USSR as well as with the U.S.A. For, as of the summer of 1990, the U.S.A. had declared itself to be "a European power," and Europeans were already so describing the U.S.A. Thus, the Europeans of 35 nations, the former Soviet satellites (minus Romania, for the moment), the new "Russia" of Mikhail Gorbachev, and the U.S.A. are now engaged in creating an integrated economy and a geopolitical structure in which to house that economy. John Paul's instinct for geopolitics and his in-house training, so to speak, in matters geopolitical have been his as a Pole. For his Poland has been a geopolitical pawn for nearly two hundred years.

That is not to say, however, that Poles failed to exhibit the behavior that has become so familiar to us in the many brutalities, repressions and "little" wars that are used in our day to gain or maintain some share in the world's balance of raw power. All along the line, in fact, the first long night of Polish enslavement was punctuated by the flaring explosions of successive Polish rebellions. There was the 1830 Warsaw uprising against the Russians, and the uprisings of 1846, 1848 and 1863 against their other occupiers and oppressors.

Aside from their internal rebellions, thousands of Poles emigrated to take up arms under the flags of other nations—of Turkey, for one, a power that had its far different reasons for opposing the Three Powers of Austria, Prussia and Russia. More thousands of Poles, such as the great composer-pianist Frédéric Chopin, formed a kind of army of expatriates who flooded out through Europe and dedicated their lives and careers to keeping Poland's cause before the eyes of the world as best they could.

But the unique element in the situation of Poland, and the one that made its long-sought death impossible to achieve, was the radical distinction between the Poles as a nation and Poland as a sovereign state.

From the time of the Piast Pact of 990 with the Holy See, the Polish identity—*polonicitas*, or Polishness—was something more than "Frenchness" or "Italianness" or "Americanness" or "Germanness." For Polishness was anchored not so much in the ever-shifting borders and fortunes of its territory but in that vertical configuration of the faith of the people, entwined with and expressed on the horizontal plane of their daily lives as Poles.

The orientation of Poles was to Rome. It was the same *romanitas* that had for so long been the means of the ascent of the Polish mind and soul to God: the joining of their practical lives and fortunes as a people to that Roman Christian ideal. That remained the central reality for the Polish nation. And that reality remained rooted in the Three Pacts—their Pact with the Vicar of Christ as overlord of Poland, their Pact with Mary as Queen of Poland, and their Pact with the Primate Bishop as *Interrex* of Poland.

Truth to tell, in the persons of Pius VII and Gregory XVI—which is to say from 1829 to 1846—the papacy lived up poorly at best to its responsibilities in the Piast Pact with the Holy See. Gregory in particular —who was elected through Austrian influence and was protected by Austrian arms—had such a clumsy hand and so little knowledge or understanding of what was going on that in June of 1832 he actually issued a formal encyclical roundly condemning the Polish uprising in Russian-held Warsaw.

Such papal collaboration in the partition of Poland cost the Poles dearly. But even that factor made no deep or lasting difference in their survival. For one thing, of course, Gregory XVI did not have the last word in the matter of Poland's Pact with Christ's Vicar in Rome. From the time that Pius IX succeeded Gregory, in 1846, each Roman Pope has become more aware than the last of the profound issues at stake in Poland.

Aside from policy changes in Rome, however—in fact, well before 1846—there had already begun what Polish historians have described as the "organic labor" of self-preservation, the silent constructive work of preserving Polishness. Poland and Polish culture lived on, because Poles as Poles lived on.

A whole new and cohesive literature came into being that celebrated Polishness and Polish *romanitas*. Writers who remain as unknown in other Western nations as do the Polish roots of their own democracies were among the men and women who fueled the fires of perseverance among their compatriots. Henryk Sienkiewicz was to Poles in that terrible time what playwright-cum-president Vaclav Havel came to be for Czechoslovakia in 1990. There is a long honor roll of such Polish writers —Maria Konopnicka, J. I. Kraszewski, Boleslaw Prus, Eliza Orzeszkowa, among many more—who became part of the passionate refusal of Poles to give their consent to their enslavement or to see their enslavement as the extinction of Poland.

Nor was Poland's Pact with Mary ever in doubt or in danger among the people. Never in their "organic labor" to preserve their Polishness did they neglect on special Holy Days to gather in their tens of thousands, as they have done for over two hundred years, at the Kalwaria Zebrzydowska, near Krakow, with its basilica dedicated to Mary. Never did they fail in their mass pilgrimages to Częstochowa monastery on their "Bright Mountain" of Jasna Góra, where the scarred icon of Mary and her infant Son remained housed. Always the queenship of Mary that such icons represented shed beams of light through the darkness of this first Polish night.

Still, without leadership and organization, it is doubtful that either fealty to Rome or the most intimate piety toward God and his holy family would alone have preserved the identity or cohesion of Poland in any practical sense as a nation. And that was where the *Interrex* Pact—by which the Primate Bishop of Poland was obliged to head the nation when constitutional government was suspended and political leadership failed —proved itelf as the essential element for survival.

Around the Bishop of Gniezno and Warsaw, and around what he stood for, Poles successfully erected the paradigm of Polish culture, Pacts and all. From the time of Pius IX in the mid-nineteenth century—and particularly since the turn of the twentieth century—the Polish Catholic hierarchy has been filled with Churchmen who were all Rome-oriented in their deepest core, all utterly devoted to Mary as the Queen of Poland, all furnished with a faith untouched by the wildfire storm of Protestant- ism or the deluge of Masonic humanism. Over the decades, tens upon tens of thousands of bishops, priests, nuns and faithful laity suffered torture, deportation, execution, enslavement and constant serfdom on their own soil. But none of that, nor all of it together, could eliminate or diminish the function of the *Interrex* as a primary force uniting the people in a way that seemed beyond the power of their adversaries to comprehend.

There was just one point in time when the Catholicity of Poland was almost led onto a fatal path. That moment reached its paroxysm around 1848—the year of revolution in Europe, the Springtime of the Nations —when the deep Polish night was subjected to the torture of the false and meretricious light of an illusory dawn.

Among the expatriate Polish leaders and intellegentsia, mainly in France, there arose a deep and moving conviction that Poland, in imi- tation of Christ himself, would be resurrected from the tomb of territorial dismemberment. It was nothing less than a national Messianism; and it developed into a fierce belief among the Polish émigrés in Paris.

The comparison they made between Poland and Christ was full-blown. Poland, they said, had died a violent death at the hands of enemies, as Christ had. Poland's sufferings and death were redemptive, as Christ's were. As Christ was resurrected from the dead, so would Poland be. As the Risen Christ set all men free from sin, so the Risen Poland would set all nations free from oppression. So far did the Messianists go in their febrile enthusiasm that they believed the dead Polish heroes of the past would be reincarnated, and would even develop angelic powers of moral persuasion.

The range for this Risen Poland envisioned by the Messianists would not be geopolitical in the sense that had become normal by now in Polish thinking; it would be supergeopolitical. They felt Poland would provide in microcosm a model for the new world order. And in the dreams of these enthusiasts, that world order would forever exclude the old divisive internationalism still so deeply embedded in the contemporary empire- builders of the nineteenth century—the French, the Dutch, the English, the Germans, the Russians and the Chinese.

This new Polish identity was prophesied principally by three Polish poets, each of whom was born and died within the time of Poland's official nonexistence: Adam Mickiewicz (1798–1855); Zygmunt Krasinski

(1812–1859); and Julius Slowacki (1809–1849), whose verses were used to express the deep bond between Pope John Paul II and the Polish people in 1979, as they cheered him and sang with him and wept to see him when he went to Poland to issue his first direct, geopolitical challenge as Pope to Moscow. For he was theirs in a most special sense, their *Interrex* in Rome itself. "We need strength / To lift this world of God's," Slowacki's words rang out in the sudden hush of the crowds on the eve of John Paul's departure. "Thus here comes a Slavic Pope, / A brother of the people!"

Each of these poets insisted on the Christ figure of Poland; and each took Poland—the center of the cross formed by *romanitas* and *polonicitas*—as the point of salvation for Poles and for all human beings.

In the awful circumstances in which the Messianists found themselves, their dream is understandable as an errant offshoot of the "organic labor" of self-preservation. But at base, their Catholicism was erroneous—a fact that was pointed out to them by their countryman and archcritic the great poet, philosopher and patriot, Cyprian Norwid. There was one and only one Christ in human history; there cannot be another. There was only one cross on which a redeeming crucifixion could take place. There was only one human death and divine resurrection—Christ's—that could have universal redemptive value. No other individual—and no nation at all—could be described accurately in these same terms.

In time, most of these Polish Messianists came to recognize the error of confusing Poland with Christ. Further, in reaction to their own mistake—and in a move that would have deep and long-lasting repercussions for Poland, for Polishness, for the nearly unbelievable strength *Interrex* would provide for Poland's survival, and for the direct formation of Karol Wojtyla as priest and Pope—some of the Messianists formed a new religious order, the Resurrectionist Fathers.

Founded with papal approval, the vocation of the Resurrectionists was to reinterpret Polish history in an orthodox way; to preach accurately the one and only divine resurrection—Christ's; and to prepare for that eventual day when *Polonia Sacra* would be called upon to play a special role in the society of free nations.

In 1866, the Resurrectionist Fathers founded the Polish College in Rome, where Polish priests could be trained. "This college," Pope Pius IX declared, "will be mine, and I will be the ruler for these poor Poles here in Rome, since they have no ruler of their own."

With their Catholicism screwed on straight again, and with their geopolitics firmly rooted in that bent of mind, the Resurrectionists established their Polish College fairly quickly as an indispensable place for the orthodox ecclesiastical formation of the Polish Catholic hierarchy. At a time when all of life in Central Europe was based on *imperium*—on the power and the dazzle of imperial majesty and glory—and at a time when not only Poland but Rome itself was stripped of its former status as a temporal power and seemed at the mercy of the *imperium*, the Polish College purified itself, and the many priests who served or studied or stayed there, of all the retrograde instincts that had led the Messianists so far astray.

All in all, it may well be true that without the Polish College in Rome, there would have been no *Interrex*. And it is true almost beyond question that without *Interrex*, there would have been no Second Polish Republic; and there would have been no survival possible against the cruel and bloody tides of Nazi genocide and Stalinist enslavement. There would have been no Poland.

What happened instead was that the Polish College in Rome influenced and helped to form the generations of Polish bishops and priests who themselves could be broken neither in spirit nor in will by the vilest brutality of their oppressors. Nor would they allow the will of Poles or their spirit of Polishness to be broken.

The twentieth century that dawned upon Poland would prove to be a new crucible of suffering and hope for her people. By then, the Church in Poland was peopled with priests and bishops who were to become the fashioners, the teachers and the exemplars of twentieth-century *polonicitas*, of an untainted Polish *romanitas*, and of a georeligious and geopolitical mentality that was as unparalleled in their world as the First Polish Republic had been in the world of the sixteenth century.

These were the men who were the direct ecclesiastical and religious ancestors of Karol Wojtyla.

At the outbreak of World War I in 1914, Poland's Bishop Primate and *Interrex*, Edmund Cardinal Dalbor, saw fully two million of his people forcibly conscripted to fight the war of their Russian, Austrian and Prussian oppressors. By war's end, 220,000 Poles serving in the armies of Austria had been killed, as well as 110,000 in the German Army, and 55,000 in the Russian Army. In the territories that had been Poland before the partitions, two million buildings and two thirds of all railroad yards and stations were destroyed. In all, $10 billion in Polish property was sacrificed in somebody else's war.

Finally, in the teeth of all that destruction, the Austrian forces were in retreat from Polish lands by the beginning of 1918, and a German-Austrian defeat was at last on the horizon. Even before the November 11 armistice, Cardinal Dalbor set in motion a whole series of political events, and a cascade of new hope for Poland.

Early in 1918, in his mandated role as *Interrex,* Dalbor assembled a Regency Council composed of Archbishop Alexander Kakowski, Prince Zdzislaw Lubomirsk, and Dr. Jozef Ostrowski. The Polish delegates to the Austrian parliament took advantage of the fast-developing situation to declare their independence from Austria as citizens of a freed Poland.

Though Poles had not been permitted to govern themselves for over a century, they had by no means forgotten how. On November 7, 1918, a provisional Polish government was formed in Lublin. On Armistice Day itself, November 11, the Regency Council dissolved itself and transferred power to the commander of the Polish Legions, Jozef Pilsudski. Pilsudski in turn issued a decree declaring Poland a republic—the Second Polish Republic—with himself as provisional head of state. Within barely two months more, a general election for a constitutional Polish parliament was conducted.

Hardly had this cascade of hope poured out, however, when a shadow of what lay in store cast itself over Poland. In February of 1919, with the new Polish *Sejm* barely elected, Lenin's Bolshevik government in Russia made a bid to annihilate the Second Polish Republic before it could consolidate itself. Lenin flung an army of 800,000 men into the effort. With a three-to-one superiority in artillery over the defending Poles, Bolshevik Marshal Mikhail Tukhachevsky was soon advancing to the very gates of Warsaw.

Even in the face of certain disaster, Cardinal Primate Dalbor would not allow Poland to be denied again. He did the one thing the Pacts of Polishness dictated. Before the decisive battle was engaged, in August 1920, he led his bishops in a formal rededication of the Polish nation to Mary as its Queen. He made for the Second Polish Republic the very same pact of trust that had been made by King Jan Kazimierz for the First Republic just before the Swedes were unexpectedly driven out of Poland in the seventeenth century.

Sure enough, it had the same results. Despite all the odds, the Poles routed Lenin's superior army and pursued its remnants well beyond the Vistula River and the eastern borders of Poland. The date of Tukhachevsky's unexpected rout and defeat was August 15—the Feast of Mary's Assumption into Heaven. And, as any Pole will declare to this day, that victory was a miracle—the "Miracle of the Vistula." That miracle was the effect of Mary's protective intercession with God, who finally decrees the outcome of all human battles. Military strategists certainly had no better explanation. And, in the eyes of the faith that has always been Poland's privilege, there was no doubt about it.

Lenin's army or no, the Poles never had paused in their efforts to put their Second Republic into working order. On February 20, 1920, with the Russians still pounding at them, the newly elected *Sejm* adopted a constitution and proceeded to erect an orderly system of government for Poland.

On the international front, meanwhile, Poles hadn't lost any of their ideals or their ability to see the consequences and benefits of international alliances freely formed. Jozef Pilsudski proposed a federation of nations led by Poland and to include Finland, Georgia, Azerbaijan and Armenia. It was a brilliant proposal, designed to block all advances of Lenin's Bolshevik state, and to stabilize Central Europe. Had Pilsudski's plan been carried out, in fact, there would have been no World War II.

That was not to be, however. The ideological animus against Poland as an integral Catholic power in Central Europe was still vibrant and would prove to be as costly to the world as ever. The devilment of English and French Masonry raised its head again—personified now in David Lloyd George, Prime Minister of wartime Britain and ardent Freemason, and in France's Georges Clemenceau. Lloyd George went so far as to falsify the line of demarcation between Poland and the new Russian state —the so-called Curzon line—agreed upon in December of 1919 by the Allied ministers. Lloyd George illegally and dishonestly shifted that line to include the Lwów region of Poland in Soviet territory.

In the early months of all this anticipation and activity, as World War I was clearly in its last phase and Cardinal Primate Dalbor was working toward the establishment of the Second Polish Republic, Polish quartermaster Karol Wojtyla retired from the Austrian Army Headquarters in Krakow. With his wife, Emilia, and their young son, he took up residence in the industrial town of Wadowice, some fifty kilometers southwest of Krakow. There on May 18, 1920, just three months before Poland's reconsecration to Mary and the "Miracle of the Vistula," a second son, Karol, was born to the Wojtylas. He would grow into young manhood in the brief twenty-one-year springtime of Polish independence, and under the influence of some of the most extraordinary Churchmen ever to be assembled at the same moment in a single nation.

The men who set the tone for Poland and Polishness during Karol Wojtyla's boyhood and youth following Cardinal Dalbor's death were led by Cardinal Primate August Hlond, whose policies were clear, concise and of a piece with Poland's geopolitical ideal rooted in the Three Pacts. It doesn't take much to see that those policies are of a piece, as well, with the exhortations of Karol Wojtyla as Pope John Paul II in the eighties and nineties.

Poles as a nation, said Hlond, were not merely to believe in some passive fashion what the Church teaches, but were "to go into action with the Church . . . with a mighty Catholic offensive on all fronts. . . . We want parochialism to die, and what is the truth of the spirit and the substance of the supernatural life to live."

Like the influential Resurrectionist Fathers at the Polish College in Rome, Hlond consistently and energetically voiced the modern ideal of Polishness, and of Polish *romanitas*, purified of any retrogressive tendencies or longing for imperial glories, and certainly purged of any messianic errors. But he was firm, as well, in the conviction that temporal life and spiritual life cannot be walled off from one another without grave consequences.

With an eye cocked toward the Masonic humanism that had been so costly for Poland, and toward the seemingly everlasting effort to malign and isolate both Poland and Rome, Hlond insisted that the Church is not "a hothouse plant," or "a museum filled with people retarded because they practice holiness" or "a great fortress surrounded by barbed wire . . . occupied solely with staving off attacks."

Rather, he maintained with all his energy that the Church is "the builder of the world" and "the guardian of the nations . . . structuring the relationship between temporal progress and the supernatural cultivation of the human soul."

Clearly, then, Hlond rejected any thought that the Church Universal should contemplate turning back to earlier temporal glories. "Erroneous is the attitude," he argued vigorously, "that somehow the task of the Church is to turn back the present to the past forms—to the baroque, to a medievalism in the clouds. It is not the task of the Church to impede mankind's movement into the future."

Nevertheless, in Hlond's view, the Church in the twentieth century had the same georeligious and therefore geopolitical mandate it had had since the first century, when Christ as its founder had charged it with its worldwide mandate. In one ringing sentence, Hlond summed up that geopolitical function of Rome. Its task, he said, was not "to be concerned that the epochs of world history be all alike in terms of the structure of social and political conditions, but rather that every epoch might live by the spirit of Christ."

Long before Karol Wojtyla became a priest, he and all of Poland heard this local Polish bishop give clear definition to that universalist Catholic attitude, which bishops and priests in other lands have forgotten or never knew. It is an attitude that many bureaucrats in the Vatican now headed by Karol Wojtyla have a difficult time understanding in this consummately Polish Pope.

It is an attitude countered, in fact, by many bishops, who take it upon themselves to move in exactly the opposite direction as they retire into the regional parochialism of the "American Church" of the United States, or the "Hinduized Church" in India, or the "Liberation Theology Church" of Latin America.

The *romanitas* that Hlond fostered in his Poles—clergy and people alike—allowed for no trace of any such provincialism and for no ethnic bias or peculiarity, Polish or otherwise.

On the contrary. The Cardinal Primate admonished Poland in powerful terms that "when the smallest portion of the Church's hierarchical form loses vital contact with the rest of the Church . . . it ceases to be an organism and a portion of the Church." Moreover, he insisted that the balance is complex but important between the hierarchical element —the bishops—and the laity, which "is aware that *it* is the Church . . . having a part to play with the hierarchy in the mission of the Church."

August Hlond lived what he preached. He was plainly no hothouse Cardinal Bishop, but a vibrant and effective leader who concerned himself and his nation with developing the classical Polish persuasion of a commonwealth of nations resting upon the ideals of the First Polish Republic. There was a difference, however. Times had changed, and Hlond enlarged even those advanced ideals, purging them of the Eurocentric traits that had undeniably been part of classical Poland.

The mind of August Hlond and the mind of Poland's hierarchy were essentially one in all respects. Clustered around him, and creating a cohesive atmosphere in Poland, were all the ecclesiastical ancestors of Karol Wojtyla, prelates known for their piety and zeal, some of whom have since been proposed for canonization in the Church they served. Alexander Cardinal Kakowski of Warsaw, Latin Archbishop Eugeniusz Baziak of Lwów, Bishop Zygmunt Lozinski of Minsk and Pinsk, Bishop Jozef Sebastjan Pelczar of Przemyśl, Bishop Konstanty Dominik of Chelmno; Bishop Michal Kozal of Wloclawek, who would die in Dachau. The balance in that outstanding team of Polish ecclesiastics was rounded out by Churchmen of the caliber of Armenian Archbishop Jozef Teodorowicz of Lwów, Bishop Josef Felix Gawlina, head military chaplain, and Ukrainian Archbishop Andrzej Szeptycki of Lwów, in whose seminary a young Ukrainian, Josyf Slipyj, was rector and would later be the famous Cardinal Slipyj.

These and thousands more who worked with them were the men whose ideas and ideals always remained in complete cohesion with Catholic Poland's distinctive history, but who nonetheless developed the ideas of *polonicitas* and *romanitas* beyond any scope that could have been entertained in Eurocentric Poland of the nineteenth century.

The first member of that Polish hierarchy who directly and personally affected the life and career of young Karol Wojtyla was Adam Sapieha, a man so extraordinary that his character seemed to embody the strength and the weakness—the hardiness and the pridefulness—of *Polonia Sacra* in its heyday as the third-largest power in Europe and as Roman Catholicism's bastion against both military incursion and doctrinal attacks against its millennial faith.

Born in 1867, Sapieha inherited all the characteristics of a family of princes that had won its prominence in the First Polish Republic by sheer determination and grit. In war, they were fearless fighters, troublesome enemies, ungovernable prisoners and magnanimous victors. Faith, honor and freedom were the rules by which they lived and, not infrequently, died. Accustomed to command, skilled in battle, they became equally skilled at the niceties of leadership in a democratic monarchy. And in the multiracial Polish commonwealth, they acquired, as well, a style of diplomatic language and negotiation that seemed to die in the rest of the world, as it succumbed instead to the crude language and the industrialized slaughter of war that has blemished diplomacy and international relations since World War I.

By the time Adam Sapieha became Archbishop of Krakow, in 1912, his Polishness and his *romanitas* had been leavened and enriched by his studies at the Canisianum, the international college at Innsbruck, Austria, and by a stint at Rome, where he not only received diplomatic training, but became private secretary to Pope Pius X, whose lineage as the son of a Polish mail carrier in Riese so many had done so much to obliterate.

In intimate association with Cardinal Dalbor as *Interrex*, Sapieha saw the people of his region through the awful suffering and ruin of World War I. Moreover, because of his lineage, his papal and diplomatic associations acquired in Rome, and not least because of his indomitable personal bearing and prestige, he was often more influential than Dalbor himself in the complexities involved in forming the Second Polish Republic.

In 1938, as a youth of eighteen, Karol Wojtyla came under the direct influence of this proud, influential, highly experienced and articulate proponent of Polish *romanitas*. Wojtyla's mother, Emilia, and his elder brother, Eduard, had died. He and his father moved into an apartment in the Debnicki sector of Krakow. As Sapieha was always on the lookout for vocations, and because it was his habit to visit widely and frequently among his people, it is sure that Sapieha and the young Wojtyla met soon after the move to Krakow.

By then, war was already on the horizon again. Pope Pius XII urged Cardinal Primate Hlond to leave Poland; and, in anticipation of that move, Archbishop Sapieha was given wider ecclesiastical jurisdiction. In effect, during Hlond's World War II absence from Poland, Sapieha would function as Primate; and, in practical if not strictly legal terms, he would assume the function of *Interrex* as well.

On September 1, 1939, Adolf Hitler poured seventy armored divisions —a total of nearly a million men—across the Polish border in a blitzkrieg assault by land, sea and air. Once again, Poland became the prime Killing Field of Europe. And Poles themselves became the object of planned genocide.

On January 25, 1940, on the instruction of Nazi Field Marshal Hermann Göring, the provisions of the so-called *Secret Circular* went into effect in Poland. In the words of the German Governor General of Poland, Hans Frank—the "Pig of Poland," as he was justly dubbed—the *Secret Circular* was the handbook for the German policy of "making certain that not one Polish man, woman or child was left alive to soil the territories now and forever a part of the Third Reich." Under Frank, those policies reached an advanced degree of thorough ruthlessness and unmerciful cruelty.

Poles were divided into two classes. Those engaged in industries essential to the German war effort were to be kept alive on the barest possible rations. The rest—women, children, clergy, scientists, teachers, doctors, architects, merchants, unessential craftsmen—all were to be got rid of by execution, starvation and deportation.

The records are almost incredible. Six million Polish citizens were killed by the Germans, including 644,000 killed in combat and a million more deported to die in Siberia. The Nazis developed their efficiently brutal network of 8,500 concentration camps in Poland and organized them, as the industry they were, into thirteen administrative districts. Of the 18 million Europeans imprisoned in these camps, 11 million were killed—3.5 million Poles and 7.5 million from other nations.

The Roman Catholic Church and its hierarchy became a concentrated target for General Frank. All bishops were at least harassed. Some were only placed under house arrest. Others, however, were tortured; and many were deported or killed. One of the most notable cases was Father Anton Baraniak, who had been secretary to Cardinal Primate Hlond before Hlond had left Poland for France and Italy. During his imprisonment, Baraniak was made Bishop and so became the only Polish bishop imprisoned by the Nazis.

It was obviously Baraniak's close association with Cardinal Primate Hlond that interested Hans Frank. There were sensitive Vatican secrets to be had; and beyond that, if Baraniak as a cleric closely associated with the redoubtable August Hlond could be forced into a public endorsement of the Nazi presence, Frank's life would be easier in Poland. Despite the torture to which he was subjected, however, Baraniak became a disappointment for the "Pig of Poland," and a symbol of resistance for the Poles.

By 1942, well over 7,500 Polish priests had been deported to the especially infamous concentration camps of Sachsenhausen-Oranienburg, Buchenwald, Radogoszcz and Opausa. All diocesan offices were closed. All Polish seminaries and all secondary and higher educational establishments were shut down. All Polish libraries that were not destroyed were transported to Germany, and no new books or periodicals could be published. The historic primatial palace in Gniezno was destroyed, and the Gniezno Cathedral became a German concert hall.

As Governor General, the "Pig of Poland" decided to make his residence and headquarters in Archbishop Adam Sapieha's Krakow and to make that city a special example of his thorough Nazi brutishness.

Frank took Wawel Castle, a gorgeous and priceless antiquity, for his private residence. The Mining Academy of Krakow became his official headquarters. The "Institute for German Labor in the East"—the hateful euphemism for those who masterminded and directed this concerted genocide of Poles—was housed in the buildings of the Jagiellonian Library, whose collections and contents were shipped to Germany. The venerable Jagiellonian University was closed, and its professors were deported to two of the most feared concentration camps, Fort VII and Lawica, where all prisoners were degraded, vilified and tortured, and where many of them joined the toll of the dead.

Krakow's street names were all changed to German ones. The German officer corps took up residence in the comfortable houses on what had been the proud avenues of Krasinski, Mickiewicz and Slowacki. But worst of all was the prison on Montelupi Street, where night and day anyone passing by could hear the noises of the charnel house that place became—the screams of the tortured, the moaning cries of the starved and the dying, the maniacal laughter of prisoners driven insane and, not infrequently, the staccato sounds of firing squads.

From the outset, the German occupation, in general, and the presence in Krakow of the "Pig of Poland," in particular, were to Adam Sapieha as red flags are to a bull. In the frigid interviews that took place between the two men, it is doubtful if Hans Frank's brutishness and Nazi arrogance were a match for Archbishop Sapieha's haughty, calm and superior dignity, which had always served Cardinal Dalbor so well.

In his daily life as functioning *Interrex* of Poland, however, Sapieha was anything but calm. Rather, he was the living, breathing example of Cardinal Hlond's dictum that the Church cannot deal with its lethal enemies by "running into the shadows," nor can it be "occupied solely by staving off attacks." The call instead was one of "carrying off and establishing the victory that overcomes the world."

In one sermon at his residence, Sapieha spoke of the need to purify *Polonia Sacra* of "the filth of these swine"—but "intelligently done," he said, "for we are Poles."

In his cold, hard way, the Archbishop meant every word; and he found many and varied ways of doing exactly what he said. As early as 1939, seeing the handwriting on the wall, he had already established underground seminaries and universities. Now, in an unremitting labor of fine judgments and practical decisions upon which depended his own life and the lives of thousands of others, Sapieha entered into what was nothing less than a Polish national conspiracy against the Nazis. He kept the Vatican informed about the actual state of affairs in Poland; and, through the Vatican and the Polish government in its London exile, he collaborated with the Polish partisans. He issued false baptismal certificates to Jews, and organized networks to feed and conceal those who could not be got out to freedom.

Undoubtedly, Adam Sapieha was the most prominent, influential and capable Churchman left free in Poland. And, for the Polish Roman Catholic mind, his active presence as functioning *Interrex* during those bloody and waning years of the Second Polish Republic was yet another clear indication of God's providence over *Polonia Sacra*.

Two years into this planned desolation of his homeland, young Karol Wojtyla made his decision to enter clerical life. He applied to Archbishop Sapieha for permission to study for the priesthood. He had already spent a year studying linguistics at the Jagiellonian University; and when the university had been shut down by the Germans, he had spent another year as a boiler-room helper at the Solvay Chemical Works.

After Sapieha accepted him into the underground seminary, there was no outward sign to the Germans that Wojtyla's life had changed. That would have been fatal, in all likelihood. He continued to live at home with his father, and he put in his hours at the chemical plant. But in his off hours, along with the other underground seminarians, he followed philosophy and theology courses at the Archbishop's residence. And he came under the close personal direction of Adam Sapieha, the first of two extraordinary archbishops who would be most responsible for his own formation as the Churchman he was to become.

In his two years under Sapieha's direction, Wojtyla was the recipient of many of the older man's reflections and of much of his experience. At the Archbishop's hand, he received his first schooling in how a true Churchman deals with a mortal enemy of the Church's faith. As another of Sapieha's underground seminarians later recalled, when the Archbishop of Krakow set forth from his official residence in his carriage, he created an immediate atmosphere of respect. "Not a mere man but a whole, grand institution—the Church—was passing by you."

Suddenly, on September 7, 1944—Black Sunday—German squads fanned out through Krakow. They were preparing to leave in the face of the Soviet armies advancing under Marshal Ivan Koniev. All adult Poles were to be rounded up and deported to Germany. Karol Wojtyla's name was on their list.

Whether in their haste the squads failed to comb the Debnicki section of town, where he lived, or whether Wojtyla eluded them is not clear. At any event, they did not take him. A later message from Sapieha told him and other underground seminarians to make their way to the Archbishop's residence and hide there.

By January of 1945, the Germans were gone. But the Allied agreements of 1945 and 1946 at Yalta, Teheran and Potsdam "assigned" Poland and its people to the Soviet zone of influence, and to their second dark night of entombment as a nation. Now the Stalinists were in charge.

There can have been no doubt in Sapieha's mind what was to come; he was too much of a realist to play mind games with himself or anyone else. With that same foresight and acumen that marked so much of what he accomplished as a Churchman, he singled out Karol Wojtyla from among his seminarians and arranged for him to leave Poland in 1946 to pursue doctoral studies in Rome.

Already ordained a priest by then, for the next two years Father Karol Wojtyla lived in Rome at the Belgian College, which was not run by the

Resurrectionist Fathers, but was still imbued with the same spirit of Polish *romanitas* that had furnished the Church in Poland with its indomitable clergy for nearly a century now.

Wojtyla pursued his studies, meanwhile, at the Angelicum—in that day still hands down the best school anywhere in the Church, and still run by such Dominicans as Garrigou-Lagrange, who were hands down among the best minds anywhere.

By the time Wojtyla returned to Poland in 1948 to take up his own post as parish priest, Poland was a one-party Communist state under Stalin's quisling Boleslaw Bierut. Adam Sapieha, now a cardinal, had three years to live. August Hlond had died, and Poland's Primate and *Interrex* was the "Fox of Europe," Stefan Wyszynski.

There can be no doubt that the brutalization of the Polish nation by the Germans, followed by the Allied betrayal of the Second Polish Republic and the ruthless Stalinization of all things that ensued, dispelled any aery-faery romanticism that may have lingered in the Poles.

Like many of his generation born between the world wars, Karol Wojtyla had been influenced by the Messianist poets of the nineteenth century. Mickiewicz, for one, had acquired world status; and images he and the others had used, their genuine lyricism, the language they fashioned, the concepts they evolved, had easily entered the people's consciousness as part of their Polish heritage during their emergence into the brief daylight of the Second Polish Republic after more than 120 years of enslavement.

Now, however, the great world had once more offered Poland as a non-nation into the total control of a merciless power. And once more, it was a power that aimed precisely at eviscerating and cremating classical Polishness.

In this second night that fell over *Polonia Sacra*, Poles of Wojtyla's generation saw a clear signal from God that neither the messianic role imagined for their country by its past and dead dreamers, nor its republican status attempted between the two world wars, was to be Poland's destiny. All that was null and void. It did not fit with God's overall plan for Europe. Nor did it fit with God's particular providence for this people. Their true greatness, it seemed, tied always to the Three Pacts of Polishness, was to be linked to the larger Europe that had always extended, in their geopolitical reckoning, from the Atlantic to the Urals.

What was needed at this fresh moment of oppression, however, was a new attitude. A fresh initiative. A plan for coping with the here and now of the in-house Soviet Stalinists. In the vulgar but vivid image used by

Jozef Swiatlo after he defected from Soviet Marxism to the West in 1953, Poland at this moment of its latest betrayal was like a virgin whose bedroom was filled with rapists. "Unless she has a plan," said Swiatlo, "probably the sun will rise on the morrow, but surely she will no longer be a virgin on that morrow."

Poland's plan was to be devised by Stefan Wyszynski. And as that plan unfolded, it was to be implemented in all of its wiliness and tenacity by his whole hierarchy.

Under Archbishop Adam Sapieha, Karol Wojtyla had learned to survive in the face of an enemy who dealt almost exclusively in gore and death. Hitler had decided to liquidate the Poles because he knew he could not change what they were as a people. Hitler's problem was that he was dedicated to evil. But he was not stupid.

During his years under Archbishop Stefan Wyszynski, the younger man would now begin to learn the hard, down-to-earth, nuts-and-bolts lessons of how to live and cope day by day with forces irremovable by ethnic unity and intent upon snuffing out all allegiance to Polish *romanitas* and all religious faith itself.

At the outset, in 1948, Wojtyla was a parish priest in Krakow, still "wet behind the ears" and with much to learn. Quickly enough, however, he would come to be one of Wyszynski's most valued associates, once he was nominated Bishop. It took very little time for the two men to find the collaboration between them easy and fruitful. Wyszynski found that already, as a young Churchman, Wojtyla was thinking along universal lines—like himself—and that there was no hint of parochialism in Wojtyla. Added to this was Wojtyla's sense of timing and his wide knowledge of men and human affairs. The two men thought alike. In time, it would be Wojtyla who would be at the Archbishop's side through the thick of Stalinism and the thin of the world's pointed neglect of Poland.

For the fate of Poland, for the formation of Karol Wojtyla, and for what can only be called the geopolitics of sheer survival, there could not have been a more apt *Interrex* as Poland's leader than Wyszynski; nor a more important time for Providence to bring him onto the world stage.

A professional and widely traveled sociologist with over a hundred publications to his name by the early thirties, Wyszynski had never made a secret of the fact that he regarded the National Socialism of Hitler's neighboring Germany as "a return to the barbarism of the jungle." One result was that he spent all the years of World War II on the move, with a price on his head. The fact that he was never caught may have been the first of the thousand and one reasons that, by and by, people began to call him the "Fox of Europe."

Soon after war's end, in 1946, Wyszynski was made Bishop of Lublin.

After the death of Cardinal Hlond, two years later, and despite the fact that he was the most junior of Poland's bishops, he was named Archbishop of Gniezno and Warsaw. At the age of forty-eight, he was Primate and *Interrex* of Poland. The task of keeping Poland and Polishness alive was his.

What Wyszynski wanted was a third road between revolutionary Marxism and liberal—or "rigid," as some people thought—capitalism. As everyone knew by then, however, that was not what Stalin had in mind for Poland.

Even before the end of World War II, in fact, Stalin had decided that this time he would ensure the Soviet Union's possession of Poland. He would tolerate no repetition of Marshal Mikhail Tukhachevsky's ignominious defeat of August 15, 1920. There would be no new "Miracle of the Vistula," because this time Stalin would see to it that no Polish legions remained on Polish soil to resist the invading Soviet forces, led now by Marshal Ivan Koniev.

Stalin's decimation of the Polish officer corps began with a string of massacres. The first batch to be slaughtered numbered 4,143; all were buried hastily and surreptitiously in Katyn Forest, near Smolensk, in Russia. Other massacres of Polish officers followed. These atrocities were followed by the formation of a Polish army as part of the Soviet armed forces, and by the deportation of some hundreds of thousands of Poles into the Gulag.

On the political front, meanwhile, Stalin had no intention of allowing the Polish government, still in exile in London, to take over again in wartime Poland. For that government was led by the great Peasants Party of Stanislaw Mikolajczyk, a staunch anti-Communist who was anathema to the Soviets.

As early as July of 1944, therefore, the Soviet dictator had created a postwar Polish government-in-waiting, which he located in an obscure provincial center on the Polish-Soviet border. Selected to lead this Third Polish Republic of Soviet design was Boleslaw Bierut. Born a Pole, Bierut was Stalin's head Soviet security agent, former chief of the Polish Desk at the NKVD for seven years. By December of 1944, within five months of its formation, Bierut's government had been installed in Warsaw by the armor of Stalin's Soviet divisions advancing steadily against the Nazis.

Just about two months later, in February 1945, the Yalta Conference was held. Stalin came away with the agreement of American President Roosevelt and British Prime Minister Churchill to his imprisonment of Poland.

Another two months and, in a charade that again signaled the international acceptance of such a fate for Poland, Wincenty Rzymowski signed the Charter of the United Nations as the new "Foreign Minister" of the new "Democratic Republic of Poland." Three months later, in July, the Potsdam agreements confirmed Stalin's possession of virtually all of Central Europe. The Iron Curtain was in place.

Though one of over half a dozen free nations locked up in the dungeon of Soviet totalitarian control, Poland was a special sort of captive and was to be treated differently from the others. The East Germans, the Bulgarians, the Hungarians, were all to be treated as serf nations supplementing the USSR. Finland was already an autonomous state and nation within the "Soviet orbit."

Poland was to be like none of those. The Stalinist aim, like the aim of the Three Powers in 1815 and the aim of Germany in 1939, was to liquidate all social structures that were spiritually, culturally and nationally Polish. Imprisonment was a prelude to planned death. Poland was to be a non-nation.

The old senate was abolished and replaced with a new *Sejm*, put together in Soviet-rigged elections. To no one's astonishment, Boleslaw Bierut became the first President of the Third Polish Republic, with Marxist Jozef Cyrankiewicz as his Prime Minister and Russia's Marshal K. Rokossovsky as his Defense Minister.

Throughout all of Poland, and under Boleslaw Bierut's direct and personal control, politicians and "social technicians" imported from the Soviet Union instituted a thorough program of Stalinist totalitarianism. Political commissars carefully weeded the Polish Army corps and police of all dissidents. Soviet NKVD trainers developed a new secret police and militia. A vast registration was undertaken of every Pole, and of every Polish activity. Over every phase of Polish life there loomed the shadow of the trained missionaries of Sovietization, the political commissars.

Between 1946 and 1949, Poland was Sovietized in a three-year "reconstruction" plan; another five-year plan would be in store after that. Culture in all its organized forms—the media, scholarship, educational institutions on the primary, secondary and university levels—was subjected to the most rigid political and ideological control according to strict Leninist orthodoxy. Private property and private trading in goods and services were eliminated. Agriculture was collectivized, and a new form of serfdom, state farms, was established. Everything was to be governed by the economic and political dictates of Stalin's Soviet Union. The aim was to eliminate the independent, individualist Western and Latinate mind of Poland, and to replace it with the Eurasian system of thought and morals that Leninism had so successfully imposed on Russia.

Cardinal Primate August Hlond never abandoned his toughness and independence of spirit. He had not been a young man when he left Poland in 1939, however, and when he returned after World War II, he no longer commanded the sheer physical vigor to meet the incredible new onslaught of Stalinism with the wit and energy it required.

By the time Stefan Wyszynski was elevated in 1948 to the impossible position of Archbishop Primate and *Interrex* of Poland, Stalinist "reconstruction" had already gone very far. Nothing and no one moved outside the steel net of totalitarian control thrown by President Bierut over the whole country and the daily lives of its millions.

In those circumstances, only the most sanguine could have foreseen even a fraction of the success Wyszynski achieved. Poland was not a nation where waves of national feeling could be expressed in open confrontation, as they could in India or America. It was not a place, therefore, where great men could walk in the spotlight of world opinion to shape such passions and exhort the powers in charge toward decolonization or civil rights. Unlike a Martin Luther King, Jr., or a Mahatma Gandhi, a Stefan Wyszynski was not inevitable in the Poland of 1948. Given the forces against him within Poland and beyond its borders to east and west, neither Wyszynski nor the power he developed was even probable, much less inevitable.

Nonetheless, the reach of the power he finally came to command was geopolitical to such a compelling degree that, within his lifetime, it would mold all of the vital realities of the millennium endgame that would come to a head in the 1990s; the endgame in which Wyszynski's protégé of thirty years, Pope John Paul II, would become so deeply and perilously engaged. Wojtyla would learn the ropes from a master tactician, and understand how one can start from the extreme position of underdog but end up leading the pack.

The nub of Wyszynski's attitude toward Stalinism and the Stalinization program in Poland was summed up in one blistering cannon shot he included in an early sermon. "It is almost madness," he charged, "to demand that a whole nation renounce Christianity only because a small group of people believe the reconstruction of society is impossible without a materialist ideology."

For anyone else, that might have been an interesting thought. For the Soviet-controlled Communist government of Poland, however, and for Marxist President Boleslaw Bierut, it was one more confirmation that the total victory of Leninist Marxism would not be assured in Poland until

Polish Catholicism had been extirpated lock, stock and barrel. There were no two ways about how to resolve the issues at stake. No useful compromises were contemplated. No half-victories were possible. From their point of view, each party was in it for all or nothing.

Given their experience to date with Churchmen in other countries, it is doubtful that the Soviet government in Moscow or in Warsaw contemplated any serious problems with Poland's hierarchy. Already Cardinal Mindszenty in Hungary and his counterparts in Romania, Czechoslovakia and Lithuania were behaving much as the Russian Orthodox clergy had in the 1920s. That is, they had battened down the hatches; they put up a "moral resistance" from behind their moats of separation, and they hurled missiles as unimportant to Stalin and his Eastern bloc surrogates as Church anathemas and dogmatic definitions. If experience was any guide, then, the Church in Poland would end up somewhere between martyrdom and corruption—and totally ineffective in its supposed battle with Stalinism.

The irony was that the one thing about Stefan Wyszynski that neither the Soviets nor their puppets in Warsaw understood was the element that would finally defeat them. The irony was that in Archbishop Wyszynski, the Polish Communist government had no enemy. For he regarded Boleslaw Bierut and his regime as misguided and delinquent children of the motherland of Poland; as men who, in the words of the Christ he served, did not know what they were doing.

That wasn't the whole of it, of course. For Wyszynski would do his level best to provide his errant countrymen as the Poles they were with some of the lessons that had escaped them until now.

One lesson he intended to teach the government in Warsaw was that, in the Primate of Poland, they were not up against the "clerical" mind they despised so much and held in such contempt. Instead, they were up against the power of the Eternal God who had repeatedly sacralized their common homeland.

A second lesson that would no doubt follow from the first was that the whole face-off that was to come between the Communist regime and the Church was to be an unequal fight. And while the government members could not know it, in Wyszynski's eyes they would be the inferior contestants. For they had been convinced that the only two forces in the world that mattered were the brute reality of Stalin's USSR and the decadent capitalism of the West. Further, they had been convinced that the only importance of the Church—whether in Poland or elsewhere—was as the chief bastion of capitalism. Scuttle the Church, therefore—especially in Poland—and they would be in the vanguard of the proletarian revolution that had been appointed by blind forces of history to transform the world.

Poles they might be; but in such persuasions, Wyszynski knew they were victims and dupes of a simplistic, abstract and primitive myth. Their minds had been removed from reality, impoverished in knowledge and blindsided by lies. For all that, however, he made no mistake about the ardor of their convictions.

In the circumstances, perhaps the third lesson the Primate had in store for them was in fact the first and most practical one the government members would have to deal with. For it concerned the fact that Wyszynski was not the weak-bodied sort of cleric the Soviets had found elsewhere. He would not scurry for cover in his scarlet robes. He would stand in the open, flush them out on their own ground; and, in ways that confused everyone, he would, in the words of Cardinal Hlond, "go into action with the Church" and conduct "a mighty Catholic offensive on all fronts."

Almost immediately upon his consecration as Archbishop Primate in 1948, Wyszynski took the initiative in his clash with Stalinism, which would continue for thirty-three years. Faced with a thoroughly installed Stalinist system, Wyszynski took the government entirely off guard with an outrageous proposal. In a meeting with the minister of public administration, Wladyslaw Wolski, the Archbishop suggested, of all things, that there be an agreement between the Church and the government.

"Let us formulate an understanding," he suggested. "The government and the Church will establish a mixed commission of government officials and three Catholic bishops." The object, he explained, would be to establish and maintain an "understanding" between the Episcopate and the government.

The idea was literally stunning. And not only to the Communists. Nobody had ever thought of or proposed such a thing. To his own surprised bishops, Wyszynski admitted that it was a "hazardous" undertaking but the only path open to them. To gauge the matter by his personal negotiations with the government, however, one would never have thought for a moment that hazard was involved for anyone.

His immediate problem, in fact, was that his adversaries were likely to see his call for an understanding as a call for compromise. Considering that they had total political, civil and military control of Poland—including Soviet divisions stationed on Polish soil, the secret police organized by the NKVD, and the sinister Ministry of the Interior, with its intermi-

nable files on every Pole and its blatant surveillance of their daily lives—
the men he had to deal with would not be prone to compromise.

Wyszynski came at the problem from a point of view that was as outrageous as his proposal itself. His argument was that his program was the
only realistic one the government could follow.

To drive his pugnacious argument home, the Archbishop took full
advantage of the fact that, Communists or no, he was dealing with men
who were Poles. In effect, he told them that they were as hidebound as
he was in their common *racja stanu*—in that particular Polish nationalism that is interwoven with the interest and the good of the state.

Perhaps it was the smallest possible premise of concrete Polish reality;
but for such professionally faithless men as these, it was also the most
basic thing they had in common with Wyszynski. For *racja stanu*, like
Polonia Sacra, was an ancient phrase embodying an ancient principle.
Poles had always used it to express their nation's right to exist; to express the right of Poland to have neither its territorial integrity nor its
national identity threatened by anyone outside its borders, or inside them
either.

Intentionally, Wyszynski was invoking the common heritage of all
Poles, who had, as a people, been the object of annihilation since the
1700s. But he was not about to rely on a purely emotional appeal. Shifting his argument to include a good chunk of new ground, in successive
meetings he challenged Bierut's regime to explain how the government
could hope to maintain even national order, much less their precious
racja stanu, unless they had the cooperation of the Archbishop's hierarchy. Poland was, after all, 98 percent Catholic. Clearly, therefore, the
Church was the most permeating force among Poles; and the hierarchy
was arguably the most strategic element the government had to deal with
in Poland.

The argument could only have come from Wyszynski. Never mind all
those Soviet divisions on Polish soil and all the security forces and all the
surveillance. Wyszynski knew his Poles. His velvet-glove appeal to motherland and people had a powerful pull, even for Polish Marxists. And his
iron-fist threat of civil disorder had its effect, too.

Encouraged by the fact that the government did not reject his proposal
outright, and never a man to stand on one foot when he could stand on
two, Wyszynski, before his adversaries had time to digest his opening
arguments fully, recommended to the government's attention a series of
political and quasi-geopolitical considerations.

One of the more complex issues he raised involved the so-called Western Lands—territories lying west of the line drawn between the Oder

and Neisse rivers, plus a small portion of East Prussia. Originally part of the First Polish Republic, the Western Lands had been inhaled by the German Empire, and had been returned to Poland in 1945. But it still remained to arrange an international treaty with Germany to secure those lands to the present Polish government. Such a complication was perfect grist for Wyszynski's mill.

How, he wondered, could the Polish Communists hope to secure that treaty for the Western Lands if the influential German hierarchy, repelled by the anti-Catholic attitude of the Polish regime, should decide to pressure for endless delays? Or perhaps the German hierarchy would manage to kill the treaty altogether.

And then, of course, there would be the complication that international acceptance of Poland's claims to the Western Lands would be impossible unless the Vatican appointed Polish bishops to the dioceses in that territory. Wyszynski granted that the government might hate the Vatican. But let's be realistic, he said in effect. How could the Polish Communists hope to secure the treaty if the Holy See, also repelled by Warsaw's anti-Catholic attitude, refused to replace the present German hierarchy with a Polish cadre instead?

And there was still more, as Wyszynski pointed out. For both of those matters dovetailed with the desire—the downright need, in fact—of the Polish government to sign a purely commercial treaty with West Germany. Already by 1948 the Americans had got the West Germans on fairly solid footing compared to the East bloc nations. It seemed only likely that if the German bishops and the Holy See chose to stall or kill one treaty, the other would probably go aglimmering as well.

All in all, in a series of meetings to wrangle over Wyszynski's proposal for the establishment of the Mixed Commission, the Archbishop not only taught his misguided and delinquent children a lesson or two; he conducted a clinic in brash negotiations.

For the four preceding years, since the Bierut government had been installed by Stalin's army in Warsaw, that government had pursued its ham-handed policies in Poland on the assumption that it was tackling a purely parochial problem. But for all its history and in all its bones, Poles had never been a parochial nation.

Now, having opened the door to Wyszynski—something it could not have avoided—suddenly the government began to see chasms opening up on every side. For openers, chasm number one: a cleric-fomented, never-ending revolt of the Catholic Polish population. Chasm number two: loss of the Western Lands. Chasm number three: more trouble with the Vatican. Chasm number four: failure of the desired good relations with West Germany for commercial purposes.

As far as the agenda went, that was an impressive survey. But off the record, there was another chasm. The chasm between what Soviet and Polish government officials expected to find in the Primate of Poland and what he turned out to be.

Explicitly in words and implicitly in his actions, Stefan Wyszynski was refusing any notion of passive martyrdom or of active corruption. He would not compromise like the Orthodox clergy of Russia; or be a martyr like the Primate of Hungary; or be like any of the rest of them. How were the Communists to deal with him, then?

In that regard, in fact, Wyszynski minced no words and left nothing to the imagination. "If God demands our martyrdom yet again," he said, "we will not hold back our blood. . . . But today's ideal must be the ability of the Church and of Poland to live rather than the ability to die —we have already shown our ability to die in Dachau and in the Warsaw uprising. . . .

"I want my priests at the altar, in the pulpit and in the confessional. Not in a prison. . . . I want martyrdom only as a last resort—always a grace and an honor."

As to himself, Wyszynski would add later: "It is all the same to me whether I have to sow words or my own blood—as long as Poland remains Christ's kingdom."

In the end, apparently the government felt that the best way to deal with this fox was to do just that. Deal with him. Despite the enormous odds against him, within five months of his consecration as Primate of Poland, Wyszynski sat as a member of the Mixed Commission of government representatives and Polish bishops, to begin hammering out an "understanding," just as he had proposed.

It is a measure of the enormity of the miracle Wyszynski had achieved that in occupied Germany of the early Cold War years, run as it was by the Allied commissioners, the powerful American, British and French contingents found it hard even to get the Soviet *Kommandantur* to meet with them to discuss the sewage-disposal problem in Berlin.

In truth, the Mixed Commission in Poland was as nervous-making a proposition for many who took an interest from afar as it was for the Polish Communists on the scene. Acrid and sometimes lethally intended criticisms were hurled against Wyszynski from progressive-minded circles in Western Europe and America. Animus against any Catholic-

Polish success cropped up again in various predictable quarters. And not least, there were rumblings in Rome among those Vatican authorities who shunned diplomatic pleasantries with even the humblest Soviet official.

One element in Wyszynski that was particularly baffling for his adversaries, whether at home in Poland or abroad, concerned the question of his attitude toward Marxism, and where he stood on the political spectrum in general. For, after all that had gone on in Central Europe and in Poland in particular over the past two centuries, there weren't many left in the world who were naive enough to swallow some tomfoolery about separation of church and state.

Marxist philosopher Leszek Kolakowski tried to pin the Archbishop down by asking him whether he was against the Polish Communist system because it was atheist, or because it permitted only the Communist Party and was not politically pluralistic.

Wyszynski never answered Kolakowski directly. But in point of fact, he rejected Communism, and he fought tooth and nail against bureaucratic Marxism built on a materialist ideal. As far as he was concerned, moreover, that Marxist ideology was totally impractical and unworkable for Poland. In fact, he would see to it that it was.

What of capitalism, then? Was Wyszynski going to try to inject that hated element into the "agreement" he wanted between the Church and the government?

Again, the Primate's position was unsettling for many who monitored these discussions and events from abroad. For the practical and unswerving materialism of raw capitalism repelled him, just as Marxist materialism did.

The fact was that Wyszynski never veered from his idea that there surely should be a middle road—a third road, as he called it, between Marxist Communism and materialist capitalism: the third road that would permit genuine democracy while not fomenting materialism. For in whatever form it came, and whatever its sociopolitical trappings, materialism had always led to practical atheism.

Despite all the theoretical questions in the world, however, Wyszynski's immediate problem was a pragmatic one. He had to fashion a course of action in the face of a statal power with which the Poles had to live, like it or not. There had to be an agreement that would serve as a working base between him, as Primate and *Interrex*, and the Communist state government.

In the two years of interminable discussions and haggling of the Mixed Commission between 1948 and 1950, the government showed how much it detested the whole idea of having to contend with this upstart bishop.

The negotiations were always inimical, contentious horse trading, and sometimes bordered on something very close to warfare.

The government members of the Mixed Commission hurled insults at Wyszynski, threatened him, vilified him in propaganda published in local newspapers, and not infrequently they stomped out of meetings vowing not to return.

For his part, Wyszynski gave as good as he got. He cared nothing for the insults and never returned them. But he made it plain that he was prepared to respond to threats with information that, if made public, would disgrace government members in the eyes of Poland and the world. And when the members of the government delegation stormed out of meetings, he knew they would have to come back. For it was true that they needed Wyszynski, and he didn't lack for ways to show them how much.

They needed him chiefly as a stabilizing factor in a very restive, inimical population. Wyszynski, ably backed by Wojtyla, was always in contact with the population through sermons, addresses, newspaper articles, continual visits to various parts of the country. The cultural and social machine he was always abuilding kept his visibility high among the people and his accessibility wide open. No member of government was as well known as he at the grass roots. He was trusted—uniquely trusted— always to tell the truth, always to protect the people.

Having progressed a miraculous inch in getting the Mixed Commission negotiations going at all, and despite all the difficulties over the next two years, Wyszynski proceeded to mark off a mile. His propositions right through were as brash as his original proposal had been.

During one six-hour meeting at Wilanów Palace with Franciszek Mazur and the government contingent he headed, the Primate argued openly, albeit with some subtlety, against Marxism. He characterized it as something indigenous to the Anglo-Saxon background that had been applied to a people—the Russians—whose souls were Eastern Orthodox. This Russian variety of Marxism was rife, therefore, with three elements that made it impractical for Poland: It was Eurasian; it displayed an enmity for Roman Catholicism; and it was anti-individualistic.

Poland, on the other hand, was Western, Latinate and individualistic. If Marxism was to be applied to the Poles, Wyszynski argued, it could not be the Russian variety. And it could not be hostile to the Roman Church. He insisted now, as he had always done, that there was no theoretical connection necessary between atheism and Marxism. More important, he insisted that there was no practical connection necessary between atheism and Poland's new system.

Subtlety, however, was not always the order of the day for Wyszynski in the heat of these meetings. "There is nothing more vile than state religion—the worst form of slavery," Wyszynski fired at the government negotiators at one point. Why would they want to evacuate the Polish mind and soul of their vital energy—a vibrant Catholicism? Couldn't they see they would be cutting off their collectivist noses to spite their Marxist faces?

Mixing insult and implication in a rhetorical question, Wyszynski asked his adversaries on the commission if, when it came right down to it, the government would rather have the independent and practical morality of Roman Catholicism or the craven subjugation of Polish consciences to worship of the state, and the sheer venality that would go with it.

Would it not be better, he argued—would it not in fact be wiser and more practical—to use Polish energies in reconstructing the cultural life and the political vigor of Poland?

Worse, he accused the government of a kind of backwardness that was particularly odious to them as Poles, given the history of the Three Partitions. "Forget all that 'salad,' " he charged with open contempt, "of Freemasonry and individualist philosophy picked up by mentally impoverished Polish nineteenth-century politicians and intellectuals in France. It is unworthy of twentieth-century reality." Wyszynski abhorred the potpourri—the "salad"—of half-baked democracy, popular totalitarianism, rabid anticlericalism and utopian ideals that became a staple of French radical politics in the nineteenth century and filtered into Poland through its émigrés.

Finally, with the constant activist backing of his clergy all over Poland during two years of what amounted to sociopolitical guerrilla warfare, Wyszynski and his bishops on the Mixed Commission finally corralled their adversaries and dragged them, kicking and screaming and still viciously opposed to him, to the point of at last signing an agreement with the Polish Episcopate.

On April 14, 1950, it was officially agreed in a legal document that religious education in the schools would be guaranteed. Guaranteed in the status of Catholic institutions and associations like Lublin University and all charitable organs of the Church. The Catholic press and Catholic publishing houses were free to function. The building of new churches was to be unhindered; seminary education and Church nominations and appointments of clergy to ecclesiastical positions were to be unfettered by government interference.

In effect, Wyszynski had proposed, fought for and got a legal agreement that covered the main needs of the Church. Whatever happened from now on, the Church and the people in Poland had an unassailable position to hold up to the government and the world. They had a leg to stand on.

Now, as Wyszynski understood, the real war would begin.

Over the next twenty-five years and more, the tactic of the government was systematically to violate each provision of the April 1950 agreement by every means at its disposal. The government set about an orchestrated program of scraping away every vestige of freedom they had granted: the freedom to worship, to associate religiously, to learn about Catholicism, to exercise that Catholicism in its traditional forms, and to act as living members of the Roman Catholic Church.

New government regulations and prohibitions were aimed at every sector—education of children, training in seminaries, publishing of books and newspapers, pastoral activity of priests and bishops and religious orders. Passports that would have enabled Wyszynski and his bishops to pay their bounden visits to Rome were not forthcoming. Entire editions of Catholic books were seized and shredded—sixty thousand copies of three books written by Wyszynski met this fate in a single day. Trucks and vans equipped with blaring loudspeakers would circle around churches during Mass so sermons couldn't be heard.

To those in Poland and elsewhere who called this duplicitous policy of the Polish government a policy of bad faith, Wyszynski had a blunt and practical answer. In his mind, it made about as much sense to speak of "bad faith" or "good faith" in Leninist Marxists as it would to speak of "hygienic" or "unhygienic" policies among wild polecats.

For the Leninist-Marxist mentality, there is neither truth nor falsehood. There is only expediency. In Leninist-Marxist thinking, if it served the purpose at hand to make certain solemn promises on Monday, then they would make those promises. Come Tuesday, if it no longer served the purpose to keep those promises, they would not be kept. In Marxism, crass expediency is the rule for him who is not a fool.

On a certain level, Wyszynski's response to this government rule of crass expediency was simplicity itself. He would make it expedient for the government to come to heel and keep its word. In a protracted and difficult struggle, again and again the Primate would find ways to use the legal agreement he had won to hold the government's feet to the fire of its own burning failure.

. . .

Wyszynski and his entire body of clergy set about building that fire at the grass roots. For the strength of Poland has always been in its people and its pacts. The genius of Wyszynski as *Interrex* was never to break definitively with the government, but never to permit government infractions of the agreement to pass without hurling violent protests.

As has always been the case, however, the true tour de force of Poland's fight for survival as a nation was to unleash on the alien government all the forces of the supernatural, all the forces that are today inconceivable by many otherwise enlightened observers, commentators and analysts.

By sheer organization, and a febrile activity that defies the imagination, the Polish bishops and clergy worked in close phalanx fashion under Wyszynski's constant and canny leadership, in order to mold and forge that basic strength of Polish religious belief into a blazing torch that came, in time, not only to threaten the Communist government in Poland, but to shatter the very grip of the Soviet Union in Central Europe.

Intense pastoral activity kept them all in close contact with the people virtually twenty-four hours a day every day of every year. Archbishop Wyszynski alone delivered at least six hundred sermons a year, and gave uncounted public addresses, in addition. He made pastoral visits to every part of Poland. And from his chancery on Miodowa Street in Warsaw there poured out a flood of personal letters, memoranda, aides-mémoire, telegrams and instructions.

The Polish regime probably needed no such activity as an excuse for the brutal and treacherous tactics that became a standard part of their anti-Church arsenal; for President Boleslaw Bierut and his government displayed authentically deadly enmity in the physical sense. Priests and bishops were arrested and temporarily imprisoned. Nuns were harassed. Priests and prominent Catholic lay people were mugged. Organized bands of toughs looked for threatening confrontations. Sudden and rude government inspections were visited on Church installations. Seminaries were disrupted with sudden violations by inspectors.

Through all of it, however, Wyszynski stood his ground with the Bierut regime in Warsaw on the basis of the agreement they had signed with him. Whether they liked it or not, that "understanding" was an unassailable legal instrument that could be held up to the world.

When a new oppressive legal sanction was clamped on Church activity, he went on the offensive with a reminder of what was truly expedient for the government. "These restrictions," he warned, "will be harmful to Poland's image abroad." If they couldn't be counted on to respect so simple a matter as the official agreement of April 1950 at home, how could other nations have the confidence to deal with them?

When government officials claimed the right to carry out intimate surveillance of all Church associations and to permit or forbid them, he came back at them with a charge of violating the fundamental and internationally recognized right of free association. "Nobody can give anybody the right to free association—or deny it. By merely existing, each man has this right. The United Nations says so. The constitution of the USSR states this."

When the government denied Wyszynski and some of his bishops their passports, he reminded them that the expedient thing for them was to think of the matter in terms of Polish territorial integrity. "Does this government really expect the Vatican to give canonical recognition to the Polishness of the Western Lands? Well, then, why can't we, the Polish bishops, go legally to talk with Vatican officials about this crucial issue?"

When, always mindful of the wider role they saw for Poland, Wyszynski and his bishops wrote a letter to the German bishops suggesting a postwar reconciliation between Germans and Poles—"We forgive, and we ask forgiveness," the letter proposed—the Bierut government tried to use the Archbishop's tactics against him. The Primate was a stooge of "Wall Street bankers" and the CIA, they charged; in league with the Vatican, he was plotting against Polish nationalism—the *racja stanu* he professed to hold so dear.

Wyszynski was not about to be had up on any such charge, however; and, in return, he hauled his accusers into the cold and rarefied sea of geopolitics. "The sooner the government realizes that our letter [to the German bishops] has paved the way for a Polish–German Republic agreement, the better for their own political health. By that agreement, the USSR is helped. For it is bedeviled by the rise of an inimical China. The USSR needs to put its European back garden in order, achieve some unification there. Our letter has helped that policy."

Not all of Wyszynski's arguments and ploys won the day in terms of this or that particular issue. But what was going on was not entirely about those particular issues. For Wyszynski, it was about the relationship of Poland—Poles, their Polishness and their territory—with Heaven. And for Boleslaw Bierut and his regime, it was about brute power and the position of the "Democratic Republic of Poland" in the march to the "Paradise of the Workers."

Bierut had brute power; there could be no doubt about that. But Wyszynski seemed stubbornly to ignore that fact. He was tireless in the face of constant and often dangerous government harassment. And he understood that under the ragged surface of the government program, there was always the intention to trap him into some precipitous decision, some unwise move or some situation that would justify his removal from the primatial residence, and from the public scene altogether.

To the government's consternation, however, there was no trapping this Fox of Europe—for so he was widely known by now. Time and again, one or another outflanking maneuver by Wyszynski set this or that government plan on its ear. And, time and again, Prime Minister Jozef Cyrankiewicz would mutter in frustration, "Again, that Bishop! That Bishop again!".

The Polish government was not pleased to learn that in November of 1952 Archbishop Stefan Wyszynski would be elevated to the rank of Cardinal, with public ceremonies to be conducted by Pope Pius XII in Rome in January of 1953. As was more than once the case, Bierut's government knew of the secret decision taken in Rome before it was publicly announced, and even before Wyszynski knew; for the Vatican had long since been penetrated by Eastern bloc intelligence.

Of course, "that Bishop" would not be allowed to go to Rome to receive the red hat. But, as Wyszynski's presence in Rome was not required for his new dignity as Cardinal to be valid, the victory for the Communists was a poor one indeed. His nomination by the Pope made him a cardinal. The public ceremony was merely solemnization of the fact.

In the face of such a slap against their own policies, the Polish government ratcheted its policy of harassment up to a new level. By government decree, monasteries were dissolved and plundered, and whole classes of seminarians were drafted into the army for national service. Printing and publishing were crippled by drastic cuts in the supply of paper. Onerous taxes were assessed against Church institutions. Religious teaching was thrown out of a third of all schools.

Wyszynski and his Polish bishops later wrote one of their letters to the Polish people in which they set down the pith and nub of the havoc continually wrought by the Bierut government in Poland: "Whatever served the system or certain persons was called moral, and whatever bothered them was called immoral or evil. In this way, morality was made a slave to people and the system. . . . Words lost their value. Untruth reigned in the means of social communication, information was falsified, the truth passed over in silence, perverse commentaries given. Everyone said that the press lies, the radio lies, the television lies, the school lies. Until, in the end, the lies turned back on the liars."

Thus, on and on went the struggle, until one day the government tried the impossible. It moved to take direct and legal power in the appointment of bishops and other diocesan officials.

This time, Wyszynski would not budge an inch. There was no diversionary tactic, no refuge in the premise of *racja stanu*, no warnings about international consequences or geopolitical benefits. The only premise at stake now was the right of the Church to govern itself. The Cardinal and his bishops replied to the government move with a quick-fire response in unmistakable Roman terms.

On September 22, 1953, six of Poland's bishops were arrested on trumped-up charges. All were imprisoned, and one of them, Bishop Czeslaw Kaczmarek, was sentenced to twelve years.

Wyszynski knew his turn would come soon. Five days before Bishop Kaczmarek and his companions were taken, in fact, the Cardinal told his bishops, "Granted a choice of alternatives, I will choose imprisonment over privilege, because in prison I will be at the side of the most tormented ones. Privilege could be a sign of leaving the Church's proper road of truth and love."

On September 25, as the Cardinal was preparing for bed just after ten in the evening, seven cars with windows obscured by caked mud drew up at his residence on Miodowa Street. Within minutes, police officers were inside the house.

Wyszynski knew at once what was happening. He came down from his bedroom and was handed a government decree ordering his "removal" from the city of Warsaw. No reason was assigned; no law was invoked. His signature was required on the decree. Wyszynski refused to sign. "I cannot acknowledge a decision for which I see no legal basis. . . . I will not thus voluntarily leave my residence."

"At least read the decree, sir," came the response. "And sign it."

He had read the decree. Instead of his signature, he wrote: "I have read this."

The Cardinal fetched his Breviary and his Rosary. His coat and hat were brought to him. He was escorted to one of the waiting cars, and within minutes the convoy was swallowed up in the darkness of Warsaw's streets.

Some details of Wyszynski's arrest are now clear to us from government records and the diaries of government officials. It is clear that the decision to seize him was hatched in Warsaw and that it was approved in Moscow. It was to the Minister of the Interior himself that the Primate had said, "I would rather sit in a Polish prison than be comfortable in Biarritz." Now it is clear that, in the words of that same minister, Wyszynski's removal was to be "final and irreversible."

Except perhaps as a declared public enemy who had at last been unmasked by the vigilant guardians of socialism, the Cardinal was not to be allowed to surface again as a public figure in Poland.

With Wyszynski's voice stilled and his directive functions terminated, the government moved swiftly. President Boleslaw Bierut's terror machine went into action throughout Poland, demoralizing, harassing, interrupting, blocking all Church-related activities. Karol Wojtyla moved swiftly in counteraction. He communicated with all the bishops, gave special instructions to all his priests, communicated privately with the Vatican, and established a monitoring system to track the Cardinal's movements and location.

On September 28, just three days after Wyszynski's "removal," his interim replacement, Bishop Michal Klepacz, terrorized by hours of menaces and threats, was forced to issue a pro-Communist declaration. Menaced still further, on October 17, Klepacz vowed obedience to Communist rule. Wojtyla made sure that everyone knew what was afoot in this government charade.

Letters smuggled out of Poland to Rome and to Western capitals told the whole truth. On top of that, a former aide to the brutal Boleslaw Bierut—none other, in fact, than the Jozef Swiatlo who now compared Poland in its early years under Stalin to a virgin whose bedroom had been invaded by rapists—had become a well-known and exceedingly well-informed expatriate and anti-Communist commentator, who broadcast daily reports over Radio Free Europe about the internal state of Poland.

As to Wyszynski himself, meanwhile, several possible ways to dispose of him were considered. For a brief time, serious thought was given to direct assassination—an "accident" on the road could be arranged. But it was decided instead to milk his arrest to the fullest. His confinement would be such that if it did not kill him, it would enfeeble him physically and unbalance his personality. He would be putty in the hands of his captors.

While the brainwashing was going on, government propaganda would prepare the public mind in Poland and abroad for a huge show trial to convict "Mr. Wyszynski" of "sins against the people"—gross currency violations, for instance, plus collaboration with the CIA, plotting with the Vatican to overthrow the People's Republic of Poland, and moral turpitude among his entourage and in his own private life.

That, it was hoped, would write an end to the troublesome presence of Stefan Wyszynski as Primate and *Interrex*; thus the frustrating opposition among his clergy and laity would fall to pieces. Of course, none of this was going to happen. Wyszynski, far from being reduced to putty and brainwashed into admitting horrible crimes, only seemed to wax mentally stronger and more active than ever. Then there was the ecclesiastical mechanism he had created, and the intricate ramification of Catholic organizations he had created and prepared precisely for such a government tactic. There also was Father Wojtyla. Junior in years to all of the bishops, he rapidly came to the fore as the leader during Wyszynski's imprisonment. He was confident and tranquil, thus evoking confidence and tranquillity in those around him. The reports to Rome were clear-minded and balanced. He obviously understood all the factors, national and international, that were at play in this crisis.

Wyszynski's first place of imprisonment was in the cold northern reaches of Poland, at a Capuchin monastery in Rywald. Then, in October, he was taken to another dilapidated monastery, at Stoczek. Location in the north, with inadequate protection against the frigid temperatures and dampness of the Polish winter, was intended to ensure at least the Cardinal's physical breakdown; the more so since, as the government was aware, Wyszynski had suffered from a weak chest in his younger days. If the government was lucky, he might even die.

The government should have known better. But even after all their years of dealing with "Mr. Wyszynski," it is fair to say that, except for the faith they refused, there was probably nothing that could have prepared them for what was to come. For it would belong to a terrain made accessible to the human mind only by the special grace of the God Wyszynski adored, by the Christ he worshiped as Savior, and by the special privileges granted by God to the mother of Christ as the Queen of Heaven.

In the face of a hopelessness as bleak as the winter landscape of Stoczek, Wyszynski searched for strength and perseverance in his pain. Cut off from his Church, from Rome, from his people, from his country, he searched for the confidence to maintain optimism in the darkness that enveloped his life as a prisoner.

In the deepening misery of this "final and irrevocable" banishment from his work, this Pole of the Poles entered into the only dimension left to him; into the largest dimension of all: Poland as the sacred possession of God; Poland as the nation that had confided itself, in the intimacy of faith, to the protection of the woman who had been chosen by God to protect his Son; Poland as the Kingdom of Mary.

On December 8, 1953—the day on which the Church commemorates and celebrates the special sinlessness of Mary, which had been granted her by a "unique grace and privilege of Almighty God," as Pope Pius IX had written nearly a century before—the imprisoned Cardinal, as

Primate and *Interrex* of Poland, made an act of devotion and consecration to Mary.

In that act of "voluntary servitude," Wyszynski affirmed for himself, and for Poland in the mid-twentieth century, the same Pact of Polishness that had been declared by King Jan Kazimierz in 1655, after he defended the Bright Mountain of Jasna Góra against the Swedes. Wyszynski linked himself and Poland with Jan Sobieski's victories over the Turks at Chocim in 1673, and in Vienna in 1683. In the intimacy of faith, and in tangible history, he followed the same path that had led to the Polish rout of the vastly superior Soviet army at the "Miracle of the Vistula" in 1920.

In sum, as each of those predecessors had done, Wyszynski was asking Mary, within God's will, to use him still for the task of saving souls and saving Poland. He was drawing down upon himself and upon his nation the supernatural protection of Poland's great Queen.

And so it was that the avowedly atheist government in Poland—by violating the Cardinal's persona as Primate and by rendering him impotent to deal with them on the tangible plane of their contention—had led him to a renewal of Poland's immemorial Third Pact of its national identity. They had forced him onto the high ground of Heaven's terrain.

Over the next two years, the Council of Polish Bishops under the acting head, Bishop Michal Klepacz, and following Wyszynski's directions from his prison, reactivated the Mixed Commission, organized pilgrimages and prayer meetings—the theme of which was the unjust imprisonment of the Primate—and kept up a barrage of requests that he be released on legal and constitutional grounds. The ground swell of protest about the imprisonment, over the two years, was one contributing factor in Wyszynski's final release. But just as important was the hard lesson learned by the government: The religious machinery created by Wyszynski only doubled its energy and performance because of the harsh treatment the Primate had received. It was a no-win situation for the government.

In the fall of 1954, Wyszynski was transferred from Stoczek in the north of Poland to Prudnik Slaski in the extreme south. Then, in October of 1955, he was taken to his final place of imprisonment, at Komancza, in Sanok Province, near the Czechoslovak border.

With the onset of spring in 1956, the national and political landscape of Poland began to change. Communist mismanagement in general had now produced breadlines, hunger, a shabby and broken-down condition in cities and towns, inflation, unprofitable enterprises and a crumbling industrial infrastructure.

In March, the First Secretary of the Communist Party, President Boleslaw Bierut, went on a visit to Nikita Khrushchev in Moscow to account
for his dismal record. Aside from Bierut's failure, and Khrushchev's personal dislike of Bierut, the Soviet dictator did not take kindly to his
visitor's oily and ill-timed hints that he knew much that was damning
about everybody in Moscow's leadership, including Khrushchev himself.
Bierut was given a bullet in the back of the head.

At Komancza, Cardinal Wyszynski prayed for the eternal soul of Boleslaw Bierut, the man directly responsible for his imprisonment. The
top spot in Poland's government, meanwhile, was given to the lugubri-
ous, ruthless, skirt-chasing Soviet security agent Edward Ochab, who
had earned the sobriquet "Gloom-and-Doom-and-Boom" Ochab among
the Polish populace.

Ochab had his hands full. Poland's economic misery was finally beginning to erupt in the sort of discontent that would lead to the defeat of
political Communism in the 1980s. In June of 1956, "bread and freedom"
riots of workers broke out in Poznan. Communist Party offices were
destroyed, secret police files were burned; and, in the city's unrest, fifty-
three people were killed.

Sparked by the Polish example, Hungarian workers exploded in riots,
and finally rose up in full revolt against their Soviet masters. Red Army
tanks rumbled across Hungary and crushed the revolt. But the lesson
was not lost on Moscow.

In the midst of the Eighth Plenum of his Central Committee, Nikita
Khrushchev took some of his top men and flew to Warsaw. Simultaneously, Soviet tank corps moved westward toward that city. In talks
held in the Polish capital on October 19 to 21, the Soviet and Polish
comrades agreed to cool things down. More exactly, Khrushchev made
it clear that he would have no further riots. The country was to be
pacified. After the bloody quelling of the Hungarian uprising, they could
not take a second international black eye in Poland.

Wyszynski's isolation at Komancza was not so complete that he was
unable to follow the unfolding situation. And he clearly saw something
new in these events; something more than the troublesome sociopolitical
unrest in Poland was now motivating Moscow's policy and behavior.
Gradually, news filtered through the underground pipelines undergirding all political and social life in the Soviet empire. The Party-State in its
inner councils was going through a deep upheaval. The Kremlin geopol-
iticians were in a profound reassessment of their world situation.

On March 15, 1956, as he contemplated the changing panorama, the

Cardinal came to a simple-seeming but grave decision that was unique, and at the same time totally in keeping with the permanent worldview inherent to his Polishness. This decision was, as he told two visitors to his prison on that day, not simply the only remaining solution to Catholicism's peril in Poland, but the only proviso against the unsure future of the USSR. He would dedicate Poland as a nation, as a people and as a territory in voluntary servitude to Mary for the sake of Europe and the world—and he would do so together with all of Poland's bishops, and with all Polish Catholics. It would be a truly national act of voluntary servitude for the sake of the world.

There was thus something more to Wyszynski's decision than mere private devotion. His proposal contained a unique element that lifted the whole plan and vision from the outset onto the unmistakably georeligious and geopolitical plane that had always been implicit in Poland's outlook. His proposed dedication would not be for his personal freedom, or for Poland's national freedom. The intention now would be for the whole Roman Church, and for the world in which that Church now found itself. More, the intention would be that the slow torture of the Church and of the world by Leninist Marxism would cease; that the hate would be ended; that the cancer of Marxism would be removed from all of humanity.

In two thousand years of Church history, never had one nation offered itself, as Wyszynski now intended that Poland would, for the sake of the world. Nor is it likely in the purely natural course of things that any nation that had been treated by the world as Poland had would have had any such inclination.

Perhaps there was in Wyszynski's idea a trace of the nineteenth-century Polish Messianists; for it did presume a messianic role for Poland. But if so, it rested on none of the false Catholicism of those poet-dreamers. And it was eminently achievable.

Wyszynski's plan was laid out quickly and realistically. It would take time and concerted effort to arrange for the entire nation to come together as one in a solemn vow of dedication. Wyszynski looked, therefore, to the perfect timing of the millennium of Poland's conversion to Christianity as the date of full-blown national consecration. That one-thousand-year anniversary would fall in 1966. The Cardinal would have ten years in which to prepare for the celebration. Preparations would begin with a solemn vow of national dedication by the nation and its bishops on August 26, 1956. Each year, in August, Wyszynski's bishops would organize popular processions in which reproductions of the holy icon of Our Lady of Jasna Góra would be carried from city to town to village. Each year, the bishops would lead their people in the millennium vow as composed by the Cardinal Primate. And during each of those yearly celebrations, the bishops would deliver sermons emphasizing the overall themes of that vow. Finally, in 1966, the bishops would lead all the people in one final, national repetition of that vow.

How Wyszynski would manage to coordinate all this from his isolation at Komancza was not a matter that troubled him. Heaven—and his bishops and people—would supply what was needed; for now he was acting as Primate and *Interrex*. Besides, the overall animator of the spirit of this national dedication was Karol Wojtyla. He grasped, apparently, the geopolitical and georeligious issues involved in the whole proposal. On that future date in 1966, Wojtyla would preach the keynote sermon and display a wide-sweeping grasp of the hugely vital world issues involved in Poland's conduct under pressure from Leninist Marxism.

On the very day he made his decision, therefore—March 15, 1956—with no glitter or fanfare to mark the occasion, Wyszynski wrote out the words to be used in the dedication. Those words were simple, mentioning only Poland, its families, its country, its work, its religion, its hopes. But it was the religious offering of all these—"in the spirit of the vows of our ancestors," the Three Pacts of Polishness—that constituted the moral power of that national dedication.

Once he had composed that national vow, he started on practical plans. The supernatural intention of the Cardinal Primate seemed to develop among the Poles with a striking internal energy. On August 26 of that very year, just five months after Wyszynski's decision, the people assembled all over Poland for the first of the annual celebrations. At Jasna Góra alone, a million people assembled around the monastery where the quintessentially Polish icon of Mary is preserved. In every corner of the land, as each of the promises of the vow was announced by the bishops, Polish voices everywhere cried out in answer: "Queen of Poland, we promise!"

Alone in his prison at Komancza, Cardinal Primate Wyszynski stood before a reproduction of the Częstochowa icon and recited the vow he had composed. Later, it was determined that the first dedication had been carried out in all parts of the country within the same time span of about twenty minutes, and with remarkable spontaneity.

From that moment on, Stefan Wyszynski's release from his "final and irreversible" confinement and his restoration to his public duties as Primate would seem to have been no more than a matter of time, and of timing.

Pressures that had already been building on the new government of

Edward Ochab were becoming intolerable. The situation was becoming increasingly fraught with the danger of wide-scale riots and national revolt. Even Polish Communists were dissatisfied with Stalinist methods, and Ochab found he could not curb the national unrest. In mid-October, Ochab was replaced by Wladyslaw Gomulka as President and First Secretary of the Polish CP.

There were those who always suspected that Gomulka suffered from deep psychological disturbance. If so, the problem didn't get in the way of his understanding that for the vast majority of Polish workers—for the bulk of the population, therefore—Stefan Wyszynski represented the only credible vestige of acceptable authority. That being the case, Gomulka quickly dispatched two emissaries to Komancza to talk with the imprisoned Wyszynski.

There was no question that the Cardinal would simply step out into the sunlight of his personal freedom. As had always been the case, he understood himself to be dealing in the Communist regime with an adversary of inferior force. Gomulka would have to negotiate. And Wyszynski was a past master at the art.

What, the President's representatives asked, were the Primate's conditions for consenting to leave his confinement, for accepting restoration to his rightful place, and for helping Gomulka restore and maintain order in Poland?

The Cardinal's reply was a simple and straightforward litany of terrible wrongs to be righted. There must be a restoration of all ecclesiastical freedom in Poland, including Church appointments of clergy and bishops. The Mixed Commission was to be reinstated, to its full if cantankerous functioning. Through Wyszynski himself as Primate, negotiations were to take place with the Holy See in order to reach a formal and internationally valid agreement, a Concordat, between the Holy See and Poland. All bishops, priests and theologians who had been imprisoned were to be released. All restrictive laws were to be lifted so that newspaper press runs would not be restricted, passports and publishing licenses would not be denied, and banking facilities could operate on something approaching a reasonable basis. And, not least, the Party must repudiate the forced show-trial "confessions" of Bishop Kaczmarek; and Kaczmarek himself must be released and restored to the Church.

In making his demands, Wyszynski was not relying on anything as flimsy as the changing and deepening conditions of social and political unrest in Poland. For one thing, to do so would have been to ignore the known arrogance of the Leninist-Marxist ideologues in both Warsaw and Moscow of the 1950s. Very shortly, in fact, some of those ideologues would venture in their arrogance even as far as the brink of nuclear war with the United States. For another thing, Wyszynski understood that, now no less than before, the Polish Communists truly and deeply desired to be rid of him and the very existence of his Church.

But mainly, for the believer Wyszynski was, and for any believer examining the circumstances of his successful return as functioning Primate and *Interrex* of Poland, all those conditions of social and political unrest that had brought the regime to this interesting juncture were precisely the elements used by God's providence in Poland's behalf. The "bread and freedom" riots in Poznan; the Hungarian revolt; Boleslaw Bierut's failure; the gross mismanagement of Poland's economy; the failure of Edward "Gloom-and-Doom-and-Boom" Ochab—all of that Wyszynski understood on the plane of spirit, of God's grace, and of human destiny as a matter planned by God, the Lord of human history.

In his venturesome recourse to the intercessory power of Mary as the Mother of God, Wyszynski knew that on a national scale he had called on God's power. As far as he was concerned, therefore, he held all the cards. And he had not overplayed his hand.

By the evening of October 28, 1956, Wyszynski was home again in the Primate's residence on Miodowa Street, with all the conditions he had demanded in his pocket, and on his record a total and unexpected victory over an enemy that had appeared to be overwhelmingly powerful. Wyszynski's Poles were the first to understand the Cardinal's laconic comment on his successful defeat of the government: *"Deus vicit!"* God conquered!

Wyszynski was not adapting a phrase from Julius Caesar. He was echoing the victory statement of Poland's King Jan Sobieski III after his successful rout of an overwhelmingly powerful Turkish army at Mount Kahlenberg, Vienna, on September 12, 1683. The Ottoman Turk, at the zenith of his power, almost conquered all of western Europe. *"Veni, vidi, Deus vicit!"*—I came, I saw, God conquered!—was Sobieski's retort to the acclamations he received for his victory. Forever after, that patch of ground with its memorial chapel on Mount Kahlenberg has been ceded by the Austrians to Poles as a piece of Polish territory.

30. Papal Training Ground: Under the Sign of *Solidarność*

It is true that the Karol Wojtyla who has come to be known to the world as Pope John Paul II was formed in the womb of Poland's proud and terrible history, and that he was raised in the cradle of Polish *romanitas* and the Three Pacts of Polishness. But it is also true—and every bit as important—that he came to maturity as priest, as bishop and as geopolitician by the side of Stefan Cardinal Wyszynski, who was the Primate Churchman of Poland and its most redoubtable *Interrex* for over thirty years—precisely the years of Wojtyla's formation as a Churchman.

As Archbishop Adam Sapieha had done before him, Cardinal Wyszynski singled out Father Karol Wojtyla from among his fellow priests as someone with a cluster of personal talents that marked him out for a special Church career. Wojtyla had a comprehensive mind that always placed details within the larger context. He had a profound personal piety that was authentically Roman Catholic; at the same time, he had a voracious intellectual curiosity, an up-to-date acquaintance with currents of political and religious thought, and a sturdy independence of judgment. He also had "presence"—that indefinable but definite mark of a powerful personality. Of such stuff, Wyszynski knew, were leaders made.

Over twenty-two years, from Wyszynski's return to Warsaw in 1956 until Karol Wojtyla's election as Pope in October of 1978, there grew between these two temperamentally different Churchmen a symbiosis of religious devotion, of attachment to the Polish motherland, of agreement about Poland's destiny within the society of nations, and about the geopolitical function of the Roman papacy.

In the words of his perceptive biographer Andrzej Micewski, Stefan Wyszynski "created no new doctrines or ideologies. He simply paid attention to the worst possibilities," while pursuing the best that his people were capable of. And in doing that, he followed the dictum of his own immediate predecessor, August Cardinal Hlond. He went "into action with the Church . . . with a mighty offensive on all fronts." Until the end of his life, Wyszynski worked with his whole Church, with his bishops and priests and people, to see that parochialism—whether of the Marxist variety, or any other—would die; and to ensure that "what is the truth of the spirit and the substance of supernatural life" would live.

Because of the complex role the Cardinal was called upon to play in this crucial period of Poland's history (1948–80), it was perhaps predictable that not everyone in the world would see Wyszynski's actions in quite so favorable a light. From the moment he was called upon by Party Secretary Wladyslaw Gomulka to provide the help the Communist government needed so badly—which is to say, virtually from the moment of Wyszynski's return to Warsaw—the Polish Primate had his critics at home, abroad and in the Vatican chancery.

Gomulka's government was composed in its top leadership of frightened men and in its lower echelons of Party stalwarts, really old-time Stalinists. The Party leaders had come to the point of admitting, at least in private, that their weakness lay in the fact that the mass of Poles would not go along with any form of intense Sovietization of Poland. As First Secretary of the Party, therefore, Gomulka—together with Aleksander Zawadzki as head of state, Adam Rapacki as foreign minister, and Prime Minister Jozef Cyrankiewicz, who had just come a cropper in his intention never to see Wyszynski a free man again—came up with a plan to fashion a "Polish Road to Socialism."

For their plan to work, they needed Stefan Wyszynski and his calming authority over the people. And to the confusion and surprise of many inside Poland and abroad, Wyszynski acquiesced.

In doing so, the Cardinal drew the reproach of a good number of Poland-watchers, who might not themselves have had the grit and the wit to search for ways to come out on top, had they ever been forced to share their homeland with a Leninist-Marxist totalitarian government.

In their own poverty of alternatives, perhaps some of those critics nourished the idea that Wyszynski was no more than a political conservative who would, if he could, return to the state of things before Communism took over. Like the Polish Party leaders themselves, however, such fault-finders might have found greater profit in the thought that, given the prior ideologies that had so often cost Wyszynski's nation so dearly, there would be precious little gain for Poland in turning back the clock.

More than that, however, the truth was that the Cardinal was neither conservative nor liberal in any classical political sense of those terms. Rather, his outlook was thoroughly ecclesiastical and authentically Roman Catholic. Moreover, it remained true that the Polish Communist leaders had no enemy in Stefan Wyszynski. He would fight their ideology and their stiff-necked policies and their stubborn wrongheadedness with all his wiliness and courage and might. But even after his brutal treatment at their hands, he still regarded Gomulka and that whole crowd as his errant Polish children.

Finally, it was also true that the Cardinal had not been born yesterday. Gomulka might call his plan a Polish Road to Socialism; but Wyszynski called it a government ploy to gain time. He understood as well as Gomulka did that the urgent object of the government exercise was less to be found in Poland than in the Soviet Union. For, as Poles themselves, Wyszynski's "errant children" wanted at all costs to avoid a complete takeover of the country by the armed forces of the Soviet Union. To do that, they had to head off any further riots, demonstrations and industrial unrest. And for that, Wyszynski was indispensable.

In such circumstances, it is doubtful if the Cardinal cared two inflated zlotys whether he and his clergy were said by some to have gone "soft on Communism" or were perceived as "men of the Left." For the truth of the matter was that despite a common desire to keep the Soviet armies out of Poland, the war between the Polish Communist government and the Polish Episcopate was not over.

In fact, despite Gomulka's need for the Cardinal's help, there wasn't even a truce between the two sides. If it seemed otherwise to some distant observers for a time, it was just that no one else had ever fought such a war as Wyszynski and his clergy had taken on; nor had anyone even tried. So almost no one except some members of the Vatican chancery and some few others had the remotest appreciation of the new struggle that began in Poland in October of 1956 under Wyszynski's direction.

That there was a war between Wyszynski and Gomulka is beyond cavil. From the start, and despite the Cardinal's cooperation in calming his Poles and inducing the idea of patience with events, the government's "programmed laicization, atheization and demoralization," as Wyszynski called it, was incessantly promoted. Indeed, the inventory of harassment, subversion and personal attacks was only longer and more detailed than before.

New tax assessments on Church real estate were so heavy that to pay them, all Church properties would have had to be sold off. There were sudden raids on diocesan chanceries and heavy-handed inspections of seminaries. The Church's account at the National Bank of Poland was canceled and the funds transferred to the Polish Savings Bank—a move that meant the Church was no longer a public institution and therefore in another tax bracket. Passports were again refused to some prelates. Taxi-loads of theatrically drunk government lackeys dressed as priests careened around the main streets of Warsaw, noisily asking the way to the nearest brothels. Priests were systematically excluded from the state's health insurance coverage. Catechetical centers at schools were closed. There were continued attempts to interfere with the nomination of Churchmen to ecclesiastical positions. Attempts were even made to enlist members of Wyszynski's own family and his barber as informants.

All in all, if the government was lacking in fruitful imagination, its energy and ingenuity were stupendous in its war of unremitting harassment against the Polish Episcopate.

For his part, meanwhile, Wyszynski appeared on the surface to do no more than take up his end of the warfare where he had left off when he was "removed" from Warsaw in 1953. He was engaged again in continuous rounds of consultation with his bishops and such key members of his activist clergy as Karol Wojtyla, who became Bishop of Krakow in 1958 and immediately showed his mettle in the tortuous dealings with government officials. Wyszynski wrangled endlessly with the Mixed Commission and with his dedicated adversary Prime Minister Cyrankiewicz. He took up his unflagging pastoral visits throughout Poland, each year giving hundreds upon hundreds of sermons and public addresses. Always and continuously, he sustained an incredible level of private conversations and correspondence.

In reality, however, there was now a totally new dimension to Wyszynski's end of the struggle with ideological Communism and materialist Leninist Marxism. The Cardinal was intent upon harnessing the personal hopes and national prospects of the people with the universalism of their Roman Catholic Pope in Rome. His aim was that the minds of Poles generally should move with familiarity and facility, as his own mind did, on the plane of international life and geopolitical trends. He wanted it again to become a commonplace of Polish thinking to consider their position and their prospects within the framework of the greater Europe they had always understood to extend from the Atlantic to the Urals.

More, he aimed at a universalist perspective in Poland that would be coterminous with the universalist perspective of the Roman papacy. In all this, with his innate love of Poland, Wyszynski wanted to see his people and their country prosper.

Except for the part about prosperity, Wyszynski's vision for his people, as well as the agenda it entailed, was extremely rare, if not absent, in Western democracies in the late 1950s. Certainly, they were totally nonexistent in any other Soviet-bloc nation. Nevertheless, it was that vision and that agenda that would prove to be lethal for the Leninist-Marxist system in Poland. As had so often been the case, Poland would be the spearhead nation in Central Europe.

Cardinal Wyszynski had a number of advantages in his contention with Gomulka and the government regime. One of the most important was the wholehearted and unwavering support given him by his Polish bishops and clergy—by and large, a group of men with unusual talents and with great and untainted Catholic faith; and by and large, as well, a group of men in whose selection the Primate had a chief hand. In the face of endless harassment, constant personal sacrifice and not a little bodily danger, they understood rather well the breadth and intent of the Cardinal's policies; and they found resourceful ways to carry those policies out in practical terms.

Another summary advantage Wyszynski enjoyed—especially in view of the universalist geopolitical element in his thinking and his program —was the support he received from the heads of the Holy See. Four very different papal administrations—those under the aristocratic Pius XII, the gregarious John XXIII, the liberal-populist Paul VI, and the radical reformer John Paul I—all supported Wyszynski. Despite concerted government efforts to undermine Wyszynski's standing with the Vatican, all refused to deal over the Cardinal's head with Warsaw—something that would surely have been fatal for Wyszynski's entire position and for his Church.

In this regard, it was as important as the Cardinal's knowledge of how to deal with the Polish government that he also knew how to hold the loyalty of the Holy See to his policies. He understood as few others the careful distinction to be made between the Vatican bureaucracy and the Holy See. And this was not the least of the lessons Karol Wojtyla learned from the older man.

There was, by way of example, the case of one hardheaded Vatican emissary, Monsignor Luigi Poggi, who took just a little bit too long to understand the Polish game going on between Wyszynski and the Gomulka government. The Primate minced no words in the situation.

"Monsignor Poggi's status," he said to his bishops, "is that of an employee of the Vatican Secretariat of State and not a representative of the Holy See." That was the neatly cut phrase of one who knew what hands truly rested on the levers of power.

Within five months of release from his imprisonment, Wyszynski himself went down to Rome. On May 18, 1957, he at last received his scarlet-red cardinal's hat from the ailing Pope Pius XII and spent some time in private talks with the Pontiff. The following year he was in Rome again, this time as Cardinal Elector in the Conclave that chose Angelo Roncalli as John XXIII.

Stefan Wyszynski had a special value in Papa Roncalli's eyes. This was a cardinal primate from behind the Iron Curtain—the only cardinal in a Communist land—who had fought well and survived, along with his Church. Archbishop Josef Beran of Czechoslovakia, Jozef Cardinal Mindszenty of Hungary, Cardinal Stepinac of Yugoslavia, Cardinal T'ien of China, were either in prison or in exile, and their Church was orphaned of top-level leadership. Wyszynski's ideas about how to deal with the Soviet Union met with great welcome, therefore, in John XXIII. The two men did differ on one chief topic—the timing of a spiritual assault on the Soviet Union. The Pope wanted to temporize, while the Cardinal wanted action immediately.

Despite that difference, Wyszynski was clearly more helped than hindered at home in Poland by Papa Roncalli's Eastern policy. The Pope also protected Wyszynski from the "Marxizing" elements of the Vatican, who sought accommodation at any price with Moscow. In 1960, Pope John held a conversation in the Vatican with Nikita Khrushchev's son-in-law, Aleksei Adzhubei, editor of *Izvestia*. In addition, John accepted an agreement with Khrushchev himself, by which a trade-off was made concerning the upcoming Second Vatican Council: The Council would issue none of the usual statements condemning the Soviet Union's Leninist Marxism; and in return, two prelates of the Russian Orthodox Church, Metropolitans Borovoy and Kotlyrov, both with KGB status, would attend Vatican II as observers. Wyszynski privately saw no value for Rome in this exchange. But he respected the Pope's decision. Only Wyszynski and Wojtyla realized that the "deal" between Khrushchev and this Pope entailed a grave decision whose consequences would come to haunt Wojtyla as Pope in the 1980s.

Because Khrushchev let his admiration for Pope John be known, and because John's regard for Wyszynski was well understood, the circle was completed in a nervous Warsaw. The Cardinal's Polish enemies feared that Wyszynski, too, would find favor in Khrushchev's eyes. And then?

Cyrankiewicz in particular must have shuddered at the possible answer to that question.

While there can be no doubt about the advantage to Wyszynski of policies that derived from direct papal support and the cooperation of his own Polish hierarchy, it is also true that his supreme advantage lay in the Polish people. Like Karol Wojtyla, and like Stefan Wyszynski himself, the people had been formed in the womb of Poland's proud and terrible history. They, too, had been reared in the cradle of Polish *romanitas* and the Three Pacts of Polishness. As readily as birds take wing, they took to Wyszynski's efforts to bring them to the best they were capable of. For in truth, they wanted nothing less than the Cardinal did for themselves and for their beloved *Polonia Sacra*.

The process that had been initiated by the government was their so-called "Polish Road to Socialism." The counterprocess initiated by Wyszynski was calculated to guarantee that no ideology—not the Leninist Marxism he had to deal with at the moment, whatever it might be called, and not any other materialist ideology he knew to be waiting in the wings —could take over and infect the people confided by Providence to his care and guidance.

Further, even in these days of continuing struggle for their survival, Cardinal Wyszynski had one eye cocked for that future day he always seemed so certain would come, when Poles would again take over their own governance. He spoke about it, predicted it and aimed his policies at it.

With both of these motives undoubtedly balanced as part of his reckoning, Wyszynski set about welding a new unity among Poles, a unity based on three elements that were fundamental to his people, still vibrant as a nation in their faith.

The most basic of those elements was the traditional grass-roots Roman Catholicism of the Poles. That long-ingrained system of religious beliefs, moral principles and pious practices was anchored in their Three Pacts, with the Holy See as their true overlord, with Mary as their true Queen, and with the Primate *Interrex* as their true leader in the absence of a legally constituted government.

The second element, rooted in the first, was composed of the centuries-old sociopolitical characteristics of the Polish people: attachment and esteem for education and the arts, and an obstinate and unquenchable insistence on freedom—not least, as they so often demonstrated to the Communist authorities, freedom in the fields of labor relations and culture.

The third element was a consequence of their checkered history as a nation following on the brutal partitioning of their territory, and the repeated imposition upon them of alien and inimical rulers over an inhumanly long period of time. As a result of that experience, Poles had learned already to identify themselves as a people rooted and domiciled forever in one particular land—without their own government, yet distinct as a nation from any false "Poland" consisting of an odious political structure with an ideologically colored state and government.

The key factor in Wyszynski's successful evocation of a community spirit was undoubtedly the untiring efforts he put into organizing his own collaborators among the clergy and the people. His prewar years as a sociologist and lecturer, his travels around Poland, his natural gregariousness, gave him an instinct for what people needed and how people thought about and understood public events. In general, he was very fortunate in the type of bishop to be found under his governance of the Church in Poland. By and large, it would have been difficult to find another group of bishops who were so attuned to their Primate that they could second all his efforts so efficiently and loyally. In particular, the young Bishop Wojtyla gradually worked his way into the counsels of Wyszynski by the sheer power of his acumen, his fearless methods of dealing with the bullying legal power in the land. Wojtyla also appealed very effectively to the intelligentsia of Poland, for his scholarly qualifications and his literary accomplishments were undeniable and attractive. And yet he was a man of the people.

Sheltering all of this planned activity over the years like a great umbrella were the ongoing preparations for the 1966 formal declarations by Poles of their voluntary servitude as a nation to Mary. And Mary already seemed to be doing her part, for it turned out to be an effective cover.

To the thoroughly secularized minds of Wyszynski's rabid Communist opponents in Poland, his preparations for the millennium anniversary of his nation's baptism into Christianity seemed so removed from power politics and from the hard realities of life—and were in any case so useful in the pacification of the people—that they seemed never to guess at the ferroconcrete consensus the Cardinal was building in the Polish nation.

To be sure, the preparations were impressive in their extent and their organizational effort. But it all seemed so "churchy" and so removed from the brute sociopolitical strength that was Gomulka's primary concern, that he and his government were content to deal with it by their usual means of harassment and brutality.

Both in its intent to trash supernatural faith and religious devotion, however, and in its failure to discern even the slightest ray of intelligence behind it all, that government response was the clumsiest, most ill-begotten, fundamentally crass and thoroughly stupid mistake that the Communist regime could have chosen to make.

Fortunately for Wyszynski and for Poland, the Cardinal knew his people far better than did his "errant children" who were running the government. "There have been situations," Wyszynski wrote to his bishops, "where we have lost with the government. And we may lose again with this or that government. But we can never lose with the Nation! Our sensitivity to what is going on in the soul of the Nation must always be acute."

With that sensitivity as his watchword, and with their common faith always as a guide, Cardinal Wyszynski directed his bishops and clergy in the creation of one consolidated and strikingly efficient network of catechetical centers attached to local churches. It was this network that would prepare Poland for its vow to Mary. It was this network that would forge the unity without which Wyszynski knew that no later economic structuring of the nation could succeed and no political structuring would be possible. And it was this network that ultimately would see to the death of Leninist Marxism as the overlord of Wyszynski's Poland.

Government harassment or no, four million children and young people were involved in the effort. Fully 88 percent of students at the elementary level attended 20,000 centers administered by 10,000 instructors, including 1,785 nuns and 700 lay people.

Diocese by diocese, Wyszynski's organization supervised the pastoral activities of his priests, especially in the personal needs of their parishioners. Social assistance was provided at many levels: general advice and counsel, small loans, food and clothing, moral support—in the true sense of both words—in family difficulties, help in paying for medical costs and hospitalization. A special corps of chaplains occupied themselves with students, attending to their spiritual welfare, their academic performance, their social behavior and group spirit.

Aside from the practical aid provided, this nearness to the ordinary people in their homes and their workplaces, in their leisure time and their personal trials, bore the supernaturally handsome harvest of an increase in the already great loyalty of Poles to their Church and to their Primate. Wyszynski was seen as the national leader who stood foursquare for the good of the people and for the happiness of their families; and it was an accurate perception, which, of course, he aimed at evoking.

Over this churchly organization with which he clothed Poland parish by parish, street by street, home by home, always Wyszynski spread the extraprotective mantle of the preparations for the Marian devotional vow of national servitude set for August of 1966 and focused on Our Lady of Częstochowa. And, always, a part of those preparations was the explication of what this vow implied for Poland and Poles as a nation, for the Soviet Union with its nineteenth-century Leninist-Marxist mythologies, for Europe as a common home for all Europeans, for the society of nations as a whole, and for the Roman papacy as precisely what Cardinal Hlond had called it so many decades before: "the builder of the world" and "the guardian of nations . . . structuring the relationship between temporal progress and the supernatural cultivation of the human soul."

Had Wyszynski made a serious procedural mistake in dealing with the unceasing government policies directed against himself, his clergy and his Church, or had he miscalculated the temper of the people and unintentionally sparked the kind of uprising that had been Hungary's undoing in 1956, all his years of effort would have been derailed, and all his hopes for Poland's future would have been sent spiraling into oblivion.

Though either of those scenarios was always a possibility in a climate that was frequently as explosive as a tinderbox, it was the first problem—dealing with the government—that was consistently the most demanding. For while Gomulka and his government cadres never appeared to grasp the full political or geopolitical significance of Wyszynski's counterpolicies, they never let up on their pressure against him.

Though it cost him dearly in some ways, Wyszynski never did make such procedural mistakes. Indeed, he accepted willy-nilly such things as the nomination of certain priests he knew to be in the government's pocket, if not in its employ. He continually received government agent Boleslaw Piasecki as a visitor to his residence, despite the fact that he regarded Piasecki as an arch-apostate and a double-dealing agent for Gomulka. And when the Marxist head of state, Aleksander Zawadzki, died, the Primate sent his condolences in the proper diplomatic manner.

In other words, Wyszynski never violated the code of public conduct in dealing with these or thousands of other issues that had constantly to be fielded. For none of those issues, nor all of them together, were more than trivialities in comparison with the swelling volume of awareness among the people concerning the universal significance of their coming vow of national servitude to the Queen of Poland.

Nevertheless, Wyszynski was not about to become a passive, wimpish whipping boy, helpless against government onslaughts or their base calumnies. He protested every inimical government move. To one non-plussed government representative who had gone too far by half in his abusive threats, Wyszynski vowed, "We will talk about this issue from the pulpit, and we will talk about it with the Party. I will talk to everyone, with the first secretary and the prime minister, if need be."

Without a doubt in the world, he would have done just that. Public rules and decorum were one thing, but in closed-door meetings Wyszynski was always prepared to give as good as he got—and a little bit more if the situation called for it. In one such meeting—a marathon conference in June of 1958 that lasted from five in the afternoon to four o'clock the next morning—he made that point ringingly clear.

First Secretary Gomulka and the Cardinal's old enemy Prime Minister Cyrankiewicz had beseeched Wyszynski to come to the meeting. As always, they needed his help to keep popular discontent in check.

The unstable Gomulka threw all caution out the window at one point and began shouting at Wyszynski at the top of his voice. The Primate understood the situation and managed first to stop the shouting and then to calm the first secretary.

When Cyrankiewicz started to play his old games again, however, attempting to control Wyszynski by accusing him of unlawful procedures, it was an entirely different matter. The Cardinal turned the full blast of his personality and fearless authority on the prime minister. More, he hit him in the face with a brazen counterthreat. "I did not come here as an accused person . . . I came here to present the facts. I do have an unsettled account with you, sir. The fact that I haven't brought up personal grievances doesn't mean that I've forgotten them. If you want to take up accusations, I will first of all accuse you . . . and demand a public rehabilitation, which will disgrace you in the eyes of Poland and the world." Wyszynski had driven his point home; there can have been no doubt in the prime minister's mind that the Cardinal was talking not only about his own illegal arrest and imprisonment but about Cyrankiewicz's personal corruption and his participation in certain sordid actions of Joseph Stalin.

There were no more such threats from Cyrankiewicz. At least, not in that meeting. But years of contention still lay ahead. And more often than not, success or failure for the Poles depended on the ability of the Primate and his bishops to maintain balanced judgment and to keep the people calm in what sometimes seemed a madhouse run by the criminally insane.

· · ·

In October of 1962, the opening session of Pope John XXIII's much publicized Second Vatican Council drew virtually every Roman Catholic bishop—there were 2,500 in all—in the world to Rome, and any number of non-Catholic observers, as well.

With Bishop Karol Wojtyla at his side as his closest protégé, Cardinal Wyszynski led the Polish bishops as delegates to this extraordinary geo-religious and geopolitical event, which was to have deep and lasting effects not only on the Roman Catholic Church but on the configuration of world politics for the remainder of the twentieth century. Among the Polish bishops present at the Council, Wojtyla was to achieve a promi-nent place in the eyes of his fellow bishops and of those who would one day elect him Pope. The unison and the differences between the two men came out in clear relief—not that those differences made a whit of difference to Wojtyla's devotion to Wyszynski or to Wyszynski's belief in Wojtyla's star as one destined to ascend in the firmament of the Church and the broad expanse of human skies.

Wyszynski had been part of the Preparatory Commission appointed by Pope John XXIII to draft the official agenda of his Second Vatican Council. The Commission's work resulted in what were officially called *Schemata*; each of these dealt with some important topic the Commission judged should be discussed by the Council. When the Council went into session as of October 1962, it quickly became clear that a very well-organized faction among the bishops and the assistant theologians was bent on abrogating the Commission's *Schemata*. Although a minority, this faction succeeded by excellent parliamentary maneuvers to encom-pass their purpose.

The net result was that the idea of the Church in the world and of how the Church should function and of what it should achieve—all these vitally important ideas were changed. In the original *Schemata*, the traditional Roman Catholic point of view on all three questions was dominant. In the new *Schemata*, that traditional Roman Catholic view was replaced by a new standpoint, which had more to do with modern (particularly American) concepts of democracy and people's power than with Roman Catholic teaching. Successfully sold to the bishops of the Council, adapted by them and incorporated into the official documents of the Council, these new ideas gave birth to a new ecclesiology, a new view of Catholicism, of the Roman Church and of the papacy.

The new ecclesiology could have been reconciled with the traditional ecclesiology, if great care and deliberate efforts were forthcoming. They weren't. The net result was that an ambiguity floated through all the Council's official statements. Wyszynski and Wojtyla both saw the dan-

ger. Wyszynski did not want to live with that ambiguity. Wojtyla thought
the Church could live with it and that in time the reconciliation of the
two viewpoints could be and would be effected. Actually, as it happened
in the twenty years following the Council, that ambiguity wreaked havoc
with the institutional organization of the Church that Wojtyla as Pope
would inherit in 1978. But at the time of the Council, all that was hidden
in the future; in the Council's immediate aftermath, a false euphoria,
expressed as the "Spirit of Vatican II," successfully—because pleasantly,
as most people judged—put the majority of bishops and others off their
guard. Only when the high and rough winds of screeching dissidence
starting blowing, and only when the central authority of the papacy
under Pope Paul VI was ripped to pieces by the "democratization" of
religious belief and practice, only then were Wyszynski's warnings recalled. But by then it was too late to reconcile the old and the new
Vatican II viewpoints.

Back in the Council days, 1962–65, however, Stefan Wyszynski's Polish agenda was never absent from his thinking; and in that regard there
were a few matters of particular importance he deemed it necessary to
discuss personally with Pope John. In two private interviews, the longer
of which lasted for fully an hour and three quarters, the two men reviewed such matters as the issue of the Western Lands disputed between
Poland and Germany and the question of the nomination of bishops—
Polish or German!—for that territory.

Mainly, however, Wyszynski wanted to urge upon Pope John that he
dedicate the Council, the bishops of the Church, and the laity of the
world, whose servants they were, to the same bond of servitude to Mary
that the Cardinal was preparing in Poland.

It seemed to the Primate that there would never be a better moment
in terms of opportunity, or a more urgent one in terms of need. All of
the bishops were gathered in Rome at this moment, and they would be
back again for succeeding Council sessions. And across the whole world,
every continent was obviously suffering to one degree or another from
the power meddling and totalitarian oppression exerted by the Soviet
Union.

But more than that, just about the whole world was aware by now, as
Wyszynski was, that two years before, Pope John had opened and read
what was purported by credible investigators to be instructions taken
down from the lips of Mary during a supernatural visitation to three
peasant children in the remote district of Fatima in Portugal. Though
the contents of those instructions were secret—in fact, they were referred to as the "three secrets of Fatima" by the increasing number of

people who got wind of their existence—it was nonetheless widely known by now that Mary had called for a dedication of more or less the same kind Wyszynski was urging on Papa Roncalli; and that she had apparently done so for more or less the same georeligious and geopolitical reasons that had motivated Wyszynski.

Given such crucial events in Poland's history as the Jasna Góra victory of 1665 over the Swedes, and the "Miracle of the Vistula" against Lenin in 1920, the little he knew about Mary's purported request at Fatima seemed as reasonable to the Cardinal as it did to any Pole. In fact, taking into account the condition of the world in the early 1960s, and given the perfect occasion in the form of an assembly of the world's bishops in Rome, why not just get on with it? Why not get things started?

Of course, Vatican protocol being what it is, the Primate didn't put the matter in just those terms; but his meaning was clear enough.

Roncalli listened with interest and indulgence. He respected Wyszynski, and admitted that, if he had heard Wyszynski out before he had made and implemented his decision, he might have acted differently. But his attitude to Wyszynski's urgings was the same as it had been when he had first read the secret instructions of Fatima in 1960. The purpose of such an act of dedication, as the Poles themselves had emphasized, would be to end the Soviet Union's lethal mischief-making in the world. To ask for such an intention would be to incur a face-to-face confrontation between the Roman Church and the USSR at precisely the time when Pope John had decided to leaven the Soviets instead through the spirit of his Council, which would spread throughout the world as his bishops returned to their dioceses.

The Pope's answer to the Cardinal, therefore, and almost in so many words, was that this time, "our time as Pope," was not the time for such an act of dedication. Had the Cardinal been privy to the full contents of the "three Fatima secrets," he might have wondered if there would be another time. Still, while Poland's choice was a matter confided to his hands, the choice for the world lay in the hands of his Pope. Wyszynski would not cavil at the Holy Father.

Anyone who knew Wyszynski would not have expected him to let the matter rest there. He saw Papa Roncalli again in May of the following year, during the second session of the Council. By then, Pope John knew that the Council was out of his control; his agenda for a deep renewal of activist faith in the Church had been set on a course the Pontiff had not foreseen, and it would serve someone else's agenda instead. And he also knew that he would have no time to alter that fact. On June 3, Angelo Roncalli died in his faith and his regrets.

Wyszynski finally persuaded John's successor, Pope Paul VI, at least to proclaim Mary as Mother of the Church. Paul did so solemnly on November 21, 1964, in front of the whole Council of Bishops. The Cardinal would have to be content with that; for Papa Roncalli's decision to politicize the idea of any wholesale dedication of the Universal Church to Mary, and his companion decision to temporize with reference to the Soviet Union, were to remain principles of Vatican policy for many years to come in this century.

Nearly twenty years later, those twin decisions by Pope John would almost literally have a stunning effect on the policies of Wyszynski's protégé, Karol Wojtyla, in his role as Pope John Paul II.

Meanwhile, the decision to so honor Mary had deep implications. It meant that explicitly the officials of the Church transposed the already great importance of Mary (as an active participant in Christian life) from the merely devotional and purely religious to the georeligious plane on which the Roman Church operates. Mary was now, whether one liked it or not, recognized as a geopolitical element in Christian salvation. It was a capital point in the formation of a prepapal mind in Wojtyla.

Wyszynski and Wojtyla and the rest of the Polish hierarchy were not much slowed at home by the Council going on in Rome. If anything, it almost appeared that Wyszynski's failure to change the mind of the Holy See concerning the dedication of the Church and the world to Mary caused him to redouble his concentration on Poland as a paradigm of the world, and on the Church in Poland as a paradigm of the Church Universal in its worldwide struggle with the evil abroad among men since the creation of the world.

Such a view was not a fanciful thing, for Wyszynski was a practical man; a doer. And he had expressed just such a view as far back as 1952. In that year, before Prime Minister Cyrankiewicz had so rudely removed him to imprisonment, the Cardinal had written to his hard-pressed Catholics with advice and instruction he never failed to keep in mind himself and never failed to impress upon Wojtyla and his other bishops.

"As a background for your perseverance," the Primate had written them, "let me remind you of the fundamental position of the Church in the face of our Polish condition. In the course of 2,000 years . . . the Church has faced various situations; but she was never surprised by those situations. The wide world was [surprised] when it found itself Arian, Albigensian, humanistic, Protestant, rationalistic, capitalistic. . . . She [the Church] faces Communism with serenity . . . because she is compelled to exist with that reality . . . and, today, that relationship must be maintained even with her enemies—and they are not only the Communists but the Freemasons and pagan capitalism."

Even in cohabiting with their most lethally intentioned enemies, Wyszynski urged the Poles, they should be true to every aspect of their Polishness, harboring neither fruitless dreams of returning to past fortune nor baneful plans for future retribution: "The Church in Poland . . . must educate Poles not to nurture any idea of revenge or a complete restoration of their past. Polish Catholics in whatever circumstances—even in those that are adverse for the Communists—will not raise their hand against them. . . . Catholics will respect an accomplished social evolution. . . . The present reality shows bold signs of social changes. . . . God has placed us in the condition in which we must live."

Such was the attitude constantly displayed by Wyszynski and his clergy; and to a surprising degree as well by the populace at large, as the Primate continued to network Poland with his endless organizational efforts. By 1963, the effect of Wyszynski's minutely planned and faithfully executed arrangements for the millennium celebrations at last began to daunt the Gomulka government. In response, the first secretary trotted out every tactic he and his underlings could come up with.

Sharp personal attacks on the Cardinal Primate surfaced yet again. It was charged that Wyszynski had received gifts from that incorrigible Fascist, General Francisco Franco of Spain. He was accused once more of tampering with state affairs in seeking a reconciliation between Poles and Germans. In fact, as the Cardinal was leaving a church where his policy of forgiveness of the Germans for their war atrocities was proclaimed, he was confronted by a gang of government-hired toughs, who chanted, "We won't forgive!" True to his own lights, Wyszynski chose to pass directly through the rough bunch, answering one of them pointedly and sincerely, "Brother, that doesn't matter." Another, who was hassling a woman in the crowd, he chided, "Brother, be decent."

By 1965, the year before the ultimate national celebration and dedication, the preparations had taken on such a vigor of their own that they became one continual celebration, complete with constant processions everywhere, in anticipation of the millennium vow that would be led by the Cardinal at Mary's shrine at Częstochowa on the Bright Mountain of Jasna Góra.

Accordingly, so too did the government step up its activities of harassment. Its tactics ranged from the hyperbureaucratic to the sleazy and the physically dangerous. Permits were refused for religious processions carrying reproductions of the Częstochowa icon. Other processions were diverted from their routes or were prohibited from entering certain zones. In one incident, the police stopped a car displaying the Częstochowa icon, wrapped the picture up in a tarpaulin and tied it securely with rope, and only then allowed the automobile to continue on its way.

On another occasion, sham reports of an outbreak of smallpox forced would-be pilgrims to return home. Time and again, military vehicles would be driven dangerously along roads frequented by priests on their way to icon celebrations, forcing clerics off the road in "accidents" that disabled their cars, and that sometimes caused serious injury. Pilgrims who were not physically roughed up were continually under surveillance by the "sad people," as Gomulka's secret service agents were called. Regularly, gangs of toughs took to disturbing even normal liturgical celebrations. And, in a pointed and threatening move, a permanent militia guard was placed around Jasna Góra itself.

By then, however, it was already far too late to stop what Wyszynski had begun, not only with respect to the millennial celebration and vow of "national servitude" to Mary, but with respect to the sociopolitical element of his agenda. For in 1965, the first signs of that organized element of the Cardinal's agenda popped to the surface when thirty-four prominent intellectuals issued a declaration of freedom for artists and writers as a basic right. What Wyszynski was counting on was thus beginning to happen. Segments of the population, such as groups of intellectuals and people who were not Catholic or had long since abandoned any practical belief in their original Catholicism or had lapsed into complete nonobservance of Catholicism's laws, were now attracted at least to the point of supporting Wyszynski, because his general goals were for the betterment of Poland's dire economic and social conditions.

By the time that much prepared date August 26, 1968, rolled around, there was nobody in Poland who was unaware of what would be transacted at the monastery at Częstochowa on Jasna Góra—the Bright Mountain—with Mary as Queen of Poland. It is very difficult for those who have known life only in Western democracies to realize that the great majority of Poles thought about that forthcoming celebration as an event affecting not merely Poland but Poland's neighbors in Europe, Poland's Europe in its entirety, "from the Atlantic to the Urals," and, farther afield, the wide world in Asia, Africa, and the Americas. That familiarity and facility of identifying one's local cause with a universal cause is absent to a large extent in Western democracies.

On August 26, Wyszynski himself presided over the ceremonies at Częstochowa. Over a quarter of a million pilgrims gathered on the hillside around the monastery and again responded to the words of the national dedication. True, the militia was present. Extra government troops, police battalions and teams of Zomos—bully boys—stood by watchfully, but not daring to make any move. While the voices of that quarter million rang out again and again—"Yes! We swear it!"—in response to ritual requests for their assent to the dedication, the same ceremony was being performed at literally thousands of locations throughout Poland.

Wyszynski had successfully tied the goals of democratic liberty in Poland to the celebration of a Roman Catholic belief, and both of them were now held in the minds of Poles to be linked with supranational goals and with the well-being of the society of nations.

It was Archbishop Wojtyla's function to piece all of it together in words. He spoke of the "supernatural current" let loose by the millennial celebrations of Jasna Góra and irresistibly overcoming the "totalitarian threat to the nation" and "the atheistic programs supported by the Polish United Workers Party"—the Communist PZPR. He quickly transposed Poland's harassed and embattled position to the international plane: "Poland faces biological destruction . . . as does the entire world of man. . . . As Poland, so the rest of the world is in absolute danger." Then he hammered home the supreme lesson: "Our temporal theology demands that we dedicate ourselves into the hands of the Holy Mother. May we all live up to our tasks."

There was no doubt in his listeners' minds about the "tasks." "The Archbishop," one visiting expatriate Pole told newsmen, "was reminding us Poles that, if we fulfill our destiny, it will be a European destiny, a worldwide destiny."

The next twelve years were to be a concrete fulfillment of Wyszynski's undertaking as Cardinal Primate and as *Interrex*. "In accepting the duties assigned to me by the Church—the episcopal sees of Gniezno and Warsaw—I also accepted a moral and civil duty to undertake appropriate discussions on the requirements of Polish state interests." This was as bold a statement as Wyszynski could make to the faithful gathered in the Warsaw basilica. "This is a dictate of my conscience as a bishop and as a Pole."

In brief terms, Wyszynski now saw his role as *Interrex* coming to the fore in a very explicit fashion. He was to be the defender of the people's rights, of Poland's rights, and the supplier of their needs. He would do this under the sign of Solidarity—*Solidarność*—with them as Poles, as Catholics, as human beings.

But in taking up this stance, he was not in any sense saying that his own difficulties as Primate were over. In actual fact, until December 1970, the usual pressures exerted by the regime on him and his colleagues were more intense than ever before. His seminaries, his schools, his priests, his own status in Poland, the ordinary function of his churches—all were again the object of frenzied attacks. Wyszynski's immersion in national and labor problems was his way of carrying war into the enemy's camp. Constantly criticizing the government, constantly defending the workers, constantly underlining the mistakes of the regime, using public opinion at home and abroad, he was finally instrumental in the liquidation of the Gomulka regime in December 1970.

To the new Communist government, under Edward Gierek, Wyszynski said plainly: "We cannot forget that we have been sent to lead the Nation to the Gospel. . . . We must fulfill our obligation to the Church in such a way that we are able to assist the country in difficult circumstances." He was putting the government on notice that the fight would continue.

On May 28, 1967, Pope Paul conferred the Cardinal's hat on Karol Wojtyla. For the next eight years, Wojtyla's figure began to loom over the national scene with a newly authoritative voice. "The Primate of Poland," he wrote in an article of May 1971, "bases his position within the universal Church on his roots in that part of the Christian community to which Providence has linked him, the Church in Poland. The very existence and activity of the Church becomes a fundamental trial of strength." He too thus put the Gierek administration on notice that the fight would continue and that Gierek's fight was with the Church Universal.

Continue it did, and along the usual lines of harassment, false accusations, denial of passports, aggression by the "Patriotic Priests" of the Communist-sponsored Pax organization, denial of building permits for churches and schools, attempts to replace the Sacraments of Baptism and Marriage with state-sponsored lay ceremonies; and by all the other means devisable by the Communist bureaucrats of Warsaw.

The Wyszynski-Wojtyla tactics continued: sustained attack in the Catholic press and in sermons on every violation of human rights; constant pressure through Rome on the government; constant diplomatic connections with West Germany and the United States brought to bear on the Polish scene.

A change started to manifest itself in the government's attitude to the two cardinals. By 1976, Gierek went so far as to praise Wyszynski as "a great man and a great patriot," but—as he told his Politburo colleagues —Cardinal Wojtyla was "the worst of all." The truth was that Wyszynski had attained a position of moral superiority in the eyes of the people that was unassailable. But this young Cardinal Wojtyla, fiftyish and active, was the future danger. Obviously he was being groomed to succeed Wyszynski as Primate. Besides, in that year, 1976, Wyszynski was operated on for cancer. The Wojtyla danger was nearer than they had thought. During Wyszynski's illness, Wojtyla was his replacement as spokesman and Church standard-bearer for all public issues; the government thus had a foretaste of what lay in store for them, should he become Primate.

The two successive Communist governments were not far off the mark when they read, first, Wyszynski and then Wojtyla as potential destroyers of the Leninist-Marxist system in Poland. The first internal Polish revolts among lay Poles were accurately read as a consequence of the example set by the Cardinal Primate and his fellow bishops. They had successfully challenged the totalitarian regime, had survived and were flourishing.

In the seventies, there was, therefore, the revolt of the Polish intellectuals. There followed the Committee for the Defense of the Workers (KOR) and the Committee for Social Self-Defense (KSS): The working classes in Poland found it necessary to defend themselves against the Party that claimed to vindicate their claims as workers. Later, the strike power of workers in Gdansk, Szczecin and Jastrzeb would lead to the social contract between the workers and the government and, later still, to the official registration of Solidarity.

By now, Cardinal Wojtyla was down in Rome, fulfilling his duties on special Vatican committees, deeply immersed in the negotiations of a Poland-Vatican Concordat, and preaching a spiritual "retreat" for Pope Paul and his papal household. The aging Paul and the young Polish cardinal developed a very close relationship, and the Pope saw in Wojtyla a future Pope for the Church—but quite a distance in years from the seventies. "Your Eminence," he told Wojtyla, "will be shortly very much needed in Poland. God will provide after that." Both men were obviously thinking of Wyszynski's failing health; and both were aware of Paul's own decline.

That was not the only vague hint of what the future might hold for Wojtyla. There was the venerable and saintly Josyf Cardinal Slipyj, the Ukrainian Catholic leader, survivor of eighteen years in the Soviet Gulag, now exiled in Rome but always dreaming of his beloved St. George Cathedral in Lwów, the Ukraine. Wojtyla's reverence for Slipyj was as much for the physical tortures the Ukrainian had undergone as for what he represented—the Ukrainian Catholic Church. "Your Grace will bury me in St. George's," he told Wojtyla. "It is God's will." (Slipyj died in 1984 at the age of ninety-two, and his body waits in Papa Wojtyla's Rome for the day of his homecoming—an event that became highly probable in 1990 after Papa Wojtyla's meeting with Mikhail Gorbachev.)

It was one more straw in the winds of destiny ushering Cardinal Wojtyla to his near-future appointment, and it was of a piece with everything that had gone into the making of Wojtyla. In its heyday, the Polish commonwealth was closely bound to the Ukraine religiously and politically. Even when Poland's enemies tore them apart and Joseph Stalin with the connivance of the Russian Orthodox Churchmen raped the Church in the Ukraine, the bond between Poles and Ukrainians persisted underground. By the late seventies, Wojtyla's orientation was eastward to the Ukraine and to Russia.

At Pope Paul's suggestion, Cardinal Wojtyla established contact with other Church leaders in the world, and visited the United States on an extended tour throughout the land. It was a simple project to let the world outside the Gulag know of the young Polish cardinal's character and ability. It also allowed Wojtyla to experience firsthand the secularism of Harvard, the provincialism of American bishops, and the dynamism of New York and California. For, as Paul used to say, "nothing beats living."

Despite every attempt to put Cardinals Wyszynski and Wojtyla in opposition to each other—this was the explicit aim of the Gierek government in the late seventies—the two men were absolutely loyal to each other. No one could tamper with the stature of Wyszynski in Poland, in Rome and in Europe. No one could breach the confidentiality Wojtyla maintained toward Wyszynski or even touch on his personal relationship with the aging Primate.

In those last years of the seventies, Wyszynski sometimes spoke about matters that still escaped the watching observers of the West. Very few realized that already by early 1976, the inner-council discussions of the Moscow Politburo no longer turned on the well-worn opposition of capitalism-proletariat. This for the Kremlin was antique language and thinking. Instead, as Wyszynski expressed it in an earlier letter to one of his Polish bishops, in February 1976: "Today the question moves significantly away from the level of 'capitalism-proletariat' to another level, not foreseen by Karl Marx—establishment of 'neocapitalism' in a collective economy, exercised by a Communist state in the name of the primacy of export production over the working man." Only in hindsight do we today know that this is as neat a definition as any of what Mr. Gorbachev has in mind.

It was advance notice of a slowly evolving mentality among the Kremlin masters that oriented the minds of these two concerned Poles toward the USSR as a seedbed of change for Europe and the world. What was distinctive—and, for non-Catholic and secular minds, severely offputting—was the Marian coloring these Polish cardinals gave to what, after all, was a geopolitical viewpoint.

Wyszynski bridled at any suggestion that this so-called Marianism of the Church in Poland was a matter of subjective feelings. It was a West German historian and commentator, Brigitte Waterkott, who analyzed that Marianism accurately in its geopolitical significance.

"It would be," she commented, "a complete misunderstanding to treat Polish Marianism as exclusively a matter of feelings. . . . The Polish Church affirms the affirmation of its national history, which finds its peak in the idea of the Polish nation's special calling in relation to the universal Church, to Europe, and to the world, in devotion to the Blessed Virgin of Jasna Góra. . . . Częstochowa is the central point of a historical image of messianic lineaments. . . . When the nation, after the Three Partitions, came together before the Altar of the Virgin, the external unity of the state was succeeded by an internal, mystical one."

It is quite an extraordinary fact about the Catholic Church in the twentieth century that one of its cardinals—and a Polish cardinal, at that —was the first Churchman we know of who intuited where the gaze and interest of the Church would be directed at the end of the second millennium. Moreover, that this latest orientation to Europe and to the USSR in particular should be channeled through an all-pervading presence of Mary, the Mother of Jesus—this is the most surprising element. And Stefan Cardinal Wyszynski was the chief instrument in the redirection of that gaze and interest. He did and does belong among the great men of the age.

In the Catholic optic, and indeed in any optic that is unbiased, it appears sure that the effective conclusion of the act of "national servitude" of Poles to Mary in 1966 brought on inevitably the liquidation of the Polish Communist government in 1989; but, more immediately, it merited that out of Poland would come the Polish Pope. At a particularly dangerous moment in the history of the papacy, for Roman Catholics the outstanding fact is that God chose a Pope from the Slavic nations. Wyszynski had tutored Karol Wojtyla in churchcraft and statecraft and in Polishness. Wojtyla became a cardinal in June 1967, and was thus eligible for a papal election. Long before the wide world learned that international equilibrium depended on a Russian Slav, Mikhail Gorbachev, it had to get used to a Slavic Pope.

In churchcraft, Wyszynski was without a peer among his twentieth-century colleagues either in the College of Cardinals or throughout the Roman Catholic episcopacy worldwide. In another age and under less straitened circumstances for Poland, he would have been elected pope. He was of that rare timber epitomized by Winston Churchill in describing Pope Innocent XI: "In manner gentle, in temper tolerant, in mood humane, in outlook broad and comprehending, he nevertheless possessed and exercised an inflexible will and an imperturbable daring."

Being appointed to one small province of the universal Roman Catholic Church, and of sheer necessity engaged personally in an all-absorbing and dangerous combat with narrow and localized minds—"pygmies on stilts in high place," he called them—for life itself, Wyszynski knew how to transform it all with a greatness that as yet escapes many.

Wyszynski's life and actions testify to the chasmic difference between him and many Churchmen today. Under his guidance, the Church of Poland was transmuted into a paradigm of the Church Universal. The nasty little infighting with homegrown Marxists was translated into a phase of the Church's worldwide struggle with the evil abroad among men since the Creation. The beloved motherland of Poland was promoted as a front-line element in the beginning geopolitical gamble of the nations. The essentially simple religious intimacy of Catholic Poles with the divine was channeled for a cosmic purpose—indeed, was used with childlike daring to wrest from the Almighty a singular grace capable of softening the hearts turned to Marxist stone, and promising to put living flesh back on the arid bones of Western man's judgment desiccated by reason left to its own treadmill devices.

"Today," Wyszynski remarked to an American visitor at Częstochowa in 1966, "we have been granted the favor of a power beyond all the powers that be, around us." He made no secret of the cause of his success. Yet it must always remain a mystery.

31. The Politics of Faith

Pope Paul VI died on Sunday, August 6, 1978, at 9:40 P.M. Within that same hour, a telephone call from Rome to Cardinal Wyszynski's residence in Warsaw gave the news, thus effectively halting him and Cardinal Wojtyla in the middle of complex Church-State negotiations in Communist Poland and intergovernmental discussions with West German authorities. The Pope was dead. The Holy See was without a legitimate leader. The vast georeligious institution of the Roman Catholic Church lacked its geopolitical guide. Better than most other cardinals, the two Poles understood: The most important business now was to remedy that lack. A new pope had to be chosen.

Of course, for the Church Universal that was important; all authority and religious authenticity depended on the approval of the Pope. But in the perspective of those Polish cardinals, the selection of the next pope was weighted with a new gravity at that precise moment of history.

These two, living and working within the confines of the Soviet Gulag Archipelago, had between them waged a relentless struggle in Poland—Wyszynski for thirty years, Wojtyla for nearly twenty—with the Polish surrogates of the Leninist Moscow masters. They had waged it and won it. As had been Poland's lot for nearly four hundred years, so in mid-twentieth century her internal state was conditioned by geopolitical factors; and these two had always made their plans and executed them in that geopolitical perspective. They could consider the choice of a pope only in that same perspective. This was their Churchmen's mode. This, too, was their advantage.

More attuned than anyone in the West to the enigmatic heartbeat of the Soviet Party-State, better informed than most Western intelligence analysts about conditions in the Soviet satellites and captive republics, these Poles had become convinced, at the opening of 1978, that, deep within the Party-State, a profound change was under way. Not a change of heart in the sense of a conversion from malignity to benignity toward the capitalist West. Rather, a growing conviction that the Cold War could not be won by Moscow, and that a new approach to the West was called for. "This," Wyszynski reported to Paul VI in late 1977, "is the underlying feeling. Stalinist politics even when modified by Khrushchev and Brezhnev are leading the USSR nowhere . . . the same obsolescence in the captive nations . . . just hardening pockets of increasingly inept local Parties. . . ."

Paul's Vatican, of course, had seen in this a vindication of the *Ostpolitik* inaugurated by John XXIII, intensified by Paul VI and particularly championed by the Vatican Secretariat of State. Wyszynski, though, regarded that *Ostpolitik* as a dark tunnel without any lights at its end. "Quiescence in the status quo," he called it bluntly.

Now, change was coming in the Soviet Union. Paul VI was dead. Whoever succeeded him would have to—or, at least, should—steer the Church into that change. For, quite predictably, if the foreign policy of the USSR changed, if the Kremlin masters chose another pathway toward their cherished geopolitical goals, the whole of international life would be caught in a flurry of changes—changes planned by those masters but unexpected by the West and bypassing the dead-end tunnel of the Vatican's current *Ostpolitik*.

Yet, the only other institutional organization on the face of the globe that measured up to the geopolitical reach of the Soviet Party-State was the Roman Catholic Church. It would have to adapt itself to whatever changes were introduced—not merely react to the changes, but foresee them, prepare for them, and assimilate them to its own provisos. That, in brief, would be the task of Paul VI's successor. Rarely in the long history of papal elections had the choice of pope held such portentous consequences for the decision to be taken shortly by 111 Cardinal Electors in Rome at the next Conclave.

Within days of Paul VI's death, Wyszynski and Wojtyla each received from the papal Camerlengo, Jean Cardinal Villot—now chief executive in charge of the Vatican caretaker government and all Conclave matters —his personal summons to come and participate in the Conclave that would elect a successor pope. Opening hour for the Conclave was preset precisely for 5:00 P.M. on Friday, August 25. But it was advisable to arrive in time for pre-Conclave discussions with their brother cardinals—all 111 of them, each with the same personal summons in his pocket, hurrying to Rome from the four quarters of the globe—before being immured in the heavily guarded isolation of the Conclave.

When the two Polish cardinals eased themselves into their seats for the Warsaw-Rome journey on August 18, they were traveling light. Each man carried a small valise, really an overnight bag containing the usual personal necessities for a short stay away from home. In his pocket each had an open ticket. Wyszynski could reasonably expect this to be the last Conclave he would attend. In three years' time, at age eighty, he would be ineligible to vote in a papal election. He expected now to discharge his normal functions as a Cardinal Elector and then go on his way tranquilly toward oncoming eternity. His younger colleague, Cardinal Wojtyla, was configured differently. Poland needed him. Especially when Wyszynski passed on.

This journey southward would be just long enough to allow them both to adjust their minds to the issues of the forthcoming election; but, together with a quick Conclave, it should impose only a short stay away from home matters. In no time, they both would be back and take up where they had left off. Indeed, in that August of 1978, the fact was that neither of them nor, for that matter, the Camerlengo himself expected a long-drawn-out Conclave. All three were realists. They and most of the

Cardinal Electors knew the bottom line: At this particular juncture, a protracted Conclave was ruled out by the condition in which Pope Paul VI had left his Church and by the almost irreconcilable factionalism among the Cardinal Electors as an electoral body.

Sitting side by side on that journey to Rome, chatting together, napping occasionally, reading and discussing Conclave-related documents, Wyszynski and Wojtyla had the great advantage of their already very close association. Ever since Wojtyla's appointment as auxiliary Bishop of Krakow in 1958, and more intensely since he became a cardinal in 1967, the two men had worked together hand in glove, Wyszynski as the guiding hand, Wojtyla as the quick-learning and resourceful *secondo*. Ecclesiastically senior and junior cardinals, personally they were more like father and son.

Between the two of them, they had successfully driven the desperately confused Stalinist government of Warsaw into a diplomatic and political corner, making the first breach ever in the rigid control exercised locally by Moscow. They could, in 1978, look forward confidently to a possible break in Marxist control of Poland's work force. The Solidarity of the eighties was on the drawing boards. Poland, as the geopolitical pawn it had been for so long, might be in the vanguard of the huge change both men sensed was under way. Wyszynski and Wojtyla were a matchless combination.

But with that close association and personal bond between them, there remained the inevitable differences arising from age and seniority. Wyszynski himself, seventy-seven, had been formed in a world that had literally passed away by the time Wojtyla, now fifty-eight, was born. Already, Wyszynski was a veteran of two capital papal Conclaves (of 1958 and 1963, respectively), had lived under six popes, and was personally acquainted with four of them. What there was to be known about Rome's Vatican and the vital issues of the Church Universal, Wyszynski knew. All of that still lay in the future for Wojtyla. What Wyszynski could communicate to his younger colleague he had done, and particularly now on this journey was doing.

There were, however, matters he could not communicate to the younger man—if nothing else, the secrets of the two previous Conclaves; those were protected by a solemn oath. And then there were other things —the fruits only of experience, what one Polish poet called the "long thoughts of old age"—which Wyszynski camouflaged with his sense of humor. In time, he was confident, Wojtyla would come to share them. In time.

The crux of the forthcoming Conclave was something they had already discussed before the death of Paul VI. Wyszynski had been down in Rome the previous year for forty-one days, conducting very delicate state matters with Pope Paul. In August of 1977, Paul had been near death. He and Wyszynski had had several prolonged private conversations. The old and very weary Pontiff had confided in the Pole about his fears for the future of the Church because of his own failures, and the triumph of the anti-Church elements both in his own Vatican and throughout the structure of the Church. He also spoke of the fearful force installed—enthroned might be a more apt word—in the heart of the Vatican as of 1963, the year of Paul's election as Pope.

All in all, Pope Paul's summary regret was that when death came to him—and during that last eighteen months of his life he daily prayed for it—he would bequeath to his Church a baneful ambiguity concerning the sacrosanct and vital papal office and the Church, an ambiguity that he had not effectively dispelled in all his fifteen-year pontificate. On that journey down to Rome in August 1978, both Polish cardinals realized that ambiguity had by now ballooned into a constitutional crisis. Both the papal office and the integrity of the Church were threatened. The ambiguity was largely the creation of the anti-Church and was its chief weapon.

Wyszynski could track that ambiguity as far back as the thirties; Wojtyla had come across it much later, in the fifties and especially during the Second Vatican Council (1962–65). It consisted of two opposing and mutually exclusive beliefs rife among the official personnel of the Roman Catholic Church: cardinals, bishops, priests, nuns, professional theologians and philosophers, and—at that time—a very restricted number of the laity. Those opposing beliefs concerned the Roman Catholic institutional organization, including the papacy. Both Wyszynski and Wojtyla realized that the Cardinal Electors in the coming Conclave were split down the middle between these two opposing beliefs and that probably there was no way of reconciling them. As a theologian, Wojtyla would describe them as two irreconcilable ecclesiologies: i.e., fundamental and mutually exclusive concepts of what the Church was, what the papacy was.

In one ecclesiology, that churchly organization is aptly described as a "kingdom" or "monarchy," with all the classical connotations of those terms: a hierarchical structural pattern; a single authoritative head—the Pope—delegating authority throughout the structure; appointive, not elective, power centers—the bishops; the preservation and handing on of tradition; veneration for symbols; the sublimation of all social as well as personal ideals to the views of the "Kingdom"; inequality and subordination of all members of the "Kingdom" within the untouchable hierarchical patterns—the laity subject to the clergy, the clergy to the bishops, the bishops to the Pope; the exclusion of women from the priesthood; the uniqueness and exclusivity of all members of the "Kingdom"—only within the "Kingdom" and by the "Kingdom's" ministrations could divine salvation be achieved: "Outside the Church, there is no salvation."

This was the traditional belief and doctrine about the Roman Catholic organization: the Pope, as Vicar of Christ, endowed with personal infallibility (guaranteed only within stringent conditions); with a universal primacy of unity—he was the one unifying element of all Christians; with a universal primacy of teaching authority—his was the last word in matters of faith and morals; and with a universal primacy of jurisdiction —all power in the Church to teach and to govern, whether locally or universally, derived its legitimacy only from him, directly or through the channels of the appointed hierarchy.

The opposing ecclesiology described the Church as the "people of God," endowing the key word, "people," with a world of meaning. The people as source of all power and legitimacy—therefore of all clerical power, be it of priest, bishop or pope. The people as source and authorizer of all faith standards; of all religous order; of all laws—including the definition of what is sinful and what prayers are to be said; and of all pastoral ministry and all liturgical celebration. The people as constituting the majoritarian vote by which all of religious and moral life should be regulated. The people as composed of equals with equal rights, no distinction being made between male and female, between ministers of religion and those they minister to. The people as strictly pluralistic in its attitude to differences, without homophobia or heterophobia, without restrictions on sexual expression. The people as seeking greater and greater homogenization with and assimilation to the generality of mankind, without any idea that one religious way of life is superior to all others or unique in itself, without any trace of the old "missionizing" and "converting" syndrome or of the old propagandizing efforts, without any attachment to one liturgical language, like Latin.

The ecclesiology of the "people of God" proposed, in other words, a thorough democratization of all religion, and shunned like the pest any trace of the former and traditional "specialness" of Roman Catholicism.

The anti-Church element within the institutional organization of the Catholic Church was, by 1978, a long-standing thing. The names of prominent anti-Church partisans were well known to all, as were their alliances with non-Catholic forces. They existed throughout all the limbs and channels of the Roman Catholic organization—particularly at many of the key choke points in the functioning system of Roman Catholic Church governance. They were bishops, theologians, cardinals, even members of the Vatican bureaucracy.

What had always been disturbing for Wyszynski was the peculiarity that the anti-Church partisans insisted on remaining within the Roman Catholic governing system. They worked to alter that system profoundly. They never called themselves anything but Roman Catholic, and never left the Church in open apostasy, schism or heresy. They insisted they were Roman Catholic and that the new ecclesiology—the "people of God" idea—was the truly Roman Catholic idea. They constantly undermined the persuasion that the Bishop of Rome—the Pope—had any special overriding authority over the other bishops of the Church. Rather, the Bishop of Rome must behave like any other bishop of the Church, be subject to the votes of the other bishops and the laity. Any notion of a special Petrine Office, of the Petrine Keys of authority, must be relinquished as outmoded and contradictory and irreconcilable with the democratization of religion and the bill of human rights.

For that ancient papacy was the one obstacle blocking "the people of God" in the Catholic Church from joining all "the people of God" throughout all the other religions, thus to achieve the full human unity of "the people of God." Likewise, the old distinctions between priest and laity, between the "teaching Church" (the clergy, from Pope to priest) and the "learning Church" (the laity), had to go.

One triumph of the anti-Church was registered at the Second Vatican Council. The bishops present at the Council had deliberately chosen to describe the Roman Catholic Church as "the people of God." In the official texts they approved as their joint statements, they referred to the Church eighteen times as the "Kingdom of God," but eighty times they called the Church "the people of God." The bishops may not have understood the implications of what they were doing, but Protestant observers did. "This image . . . means that an ecclesial function is assigned to the laity," Peter Meinhold wrote. "Many of the old distinctions between clergy and layfolk . . . will now disappear."

Franz Cardinal Koenig of Vienna put it even more explicitly: "The old distinctions between the teaching Church [the official personnel] and the listening Church [the laity], between the Church that commands and the Church that obeys, have ceased to exist. . . . It is the layman who directly represents the Lord Christ vis-à-vis the world."

The big crisis for the anti-Church came with the Conclave that assembled in June 1963 to elect a successor to Papa Roncalli. Wyszynski, who had been present at the Conclave, could not reveal the details of what went on. But sufficient was known about the two main factions among the Cardinal Electors to indicate how close the anti-Church came to disaster. At stake was the election of one of two front-running Cardinal candidates: Giovanni Battista Montini of Milan and Giuseppe Siri of Genoa. They were poles apart in ecclesiology.

Montini, not an accepted member of the anti-Church but belonging to them in liberal sentiment, progressive sociological outlook, anti-Romanist persuasion and neomodern humanism, was the most favored candidate of the anti-Church. With impeccable credentials in Church government and ecclesiastical statecraft; politically acceptable in Italy, France, Holland, England and America; of irreproachable personal piety and life-style, Montini was made to order for the anti-Church. He was a great enthusiast of the "people of God" ecclesiology. He could possibly be induced to *not exercise* the Petrine Office and thus let it lapse into desuetude—hopefully, to become thus otiose and obsolete. At all events, being a man who loved peace in his own house above all other things, he would probably fight shy of challenging the anti-Church or of taking sides as regards that ambiguity.

For the traditionalist-minded among the cardinals, the undoubted champion and choice was Giuseppe Siri, Cardinal Archbishop of Genoa, a man whose traditional credits were as sure and as well known as those of the dead Pope Pius XII or of Pope Pius XI, earlier on in the century. Siri was also a no-nonsense Churchman. You might have to "tolerate" rheumatism or the ravages of cancer, but not corruption of doctrine or abandonment of moral principle. "Tolerance," he once said, "is not a virtue. It's a mere expedient, when you cannot do otherwise." Siri, as pope, would not tolerate the anti-Church tendency. He would exercise the Petrine Office to the full—and immediately and unmistakably. Siri was a man after Wyszynski's own heart. With Siri as pope, Wyszynski could have worked as with a companion spirit.

Whatever Wyszynski communicated to Wojtyla about the Conclave of June 1963, it is certain he did not violate his oath of secrecy during that journey southward to Rome or at any other time. But he could have had no compunction about telling his younger colleague that the crisis in that Conclave was the violent reaction by the anti-Church partisans against the Siri candidacy; they could read the handwriting on the wall. Siri would have meant the end of the anti-Church, the end of all ambiguity about what the Church was, and an end to all the hopes entertained by the extra-Church enemies of the papacy that the papacy would be effectively eliminated.

It is equally certain that within the 1963 Conclave voting, Siri had garnered the required number of votes to make him Pope-elect. But the law of Conclave is of iron; for any Conclave election to end with a validly elected pope, the Pope-elect must freely accept his election. "*Acceptasne fieri in Romanum Pontificem?*" (Do you accept to be made Pope?), the question ritually put to every Pope-elect, evokes a short but profound abyss of silence on earth and in Heaven, for now the will of one single individual has the deciding of much future history.

It is certain that Pope-elect Cardinal Siri responded: "*Non accepto*" (I do not accept). It is also certain that, as often happens, he added a few words indicating at least in general terms why he did not accept. It is also certain that, in those words, he suggested his refusal was given because of his persuasion that only thus could foreseen possibilities of grave harm be avoided—but whether harm to the Church, to his family, to him personally, is not clear. He did indicate that his decision was made freely and not out of any duress—otherwise any subsequent election in that Conclave would have been invalid. All this was current coin of Conclave information; and Wojtyla would have known it.

What he would not have known in the same way was what Wyszynski could not permissibly tell him: what forced the hand of Siri to refuse the papacy. This never became part of general information. Wojtyla would have heard the firmly asserted rumors—Wyszynski would not confirm or deny them if Wojtyla asked him. And Wojtyla would not ask him. He would not, out of respect for Wyszynski's oath of secrecy, have asked Wyszynski if the rumors of the "little brutality" were accurate. Without any means of establishing it by notarized statements and duly sworn-in eyewitnesses, the rest of the world is still left with the information that the Siri nomination and election were set aside by what has been called the "little brutality."

Once the Conclave area of the Vatican has been sealed off—double-locked doors, posted sentries, electronic surveillance—there are supposedly no communications with the outer world except in the gravest necessity and by authorized persons. Such grave necessity could be the physical needs of the electors (cardinals have died in Conclave or been taken out of Conclave to die) or grave reasons of state—such as the very existence of the Vatican City State or of its members or dependents. For "necessity knows no law."

What is firmly stated is that at least one Cardinal Elector did have a conversation—however short—with someone not participating in the Conclave; that the someone was an emissary of an internationally based organization; that no explicit rule of Conclave privacy was violated by the event; and that the conversation did concern the Siri candidacy.

Such an incident during the Conclave could, with a certain permissible stretching of the terms of Conclave law, be justified as concerning a "grave matter of state security."

What is certain is that the Siri candidacy was laid aside and most probably in connection with that conversation—this, in sum, is the "little brutality" firmly rumored in Roman circles at the time of the June 1963 Conclave and ever since. The only other viable candidacy available and acceptable to both sides was Montini's. After a three-day Conclave, he emerged as Paul VI.

The anti-Church forces had narrowly avoided having a pope who would end their hopes of success; they now had one whom they could manage. Those with a diametrically opposite ecclesiology still had grounds for hope. Montini, progressive in social and political matters, was known to be orthodox in theology and of deep personal piety.

So, the Cardinal Electors emerged with the crisis in full blast among them, and that fateful ambiguity hanging over a vital Church issue. In the event, Papa Montini would give the anti-Church its head. He would never resolve the ambiguity that now would reign: What is the Roman Catholic Church? An essentially hierarchic organization based on authoritarian rule? Or a loosely knit assemblage of churches in which all sacred functions and all temporal stewardship were democratized according to the choice of the "people"? That ambiguity cloaked the organization for all of Paul VI's pontificate.

As the two cardinals discussed and reflected upon that crisis of ambiguity, they saw clearly that there was no hope of resolving it within the coming Conclave. The two main factions proposing irreconcilable ecclesiologies were stronger, more deeply entrenched and more irreconcilable than ever. Another compromise candidate would be chosen—and quickly. The redoubtable Siri would be at this Conclave. He would garner many votes, if he were to announce his willingness to be considered. But, they both knew, he would not.

For them, living and struggling on the cutting edge of geopolitical power, this conclusion was gloomy. A compromise pope would not be free to exercise any geopolitical leadership. Nor could he be really effective georeligiously. The ambiguity would plague all his days as pope. Wyszynski must, at least once during that journey, have glanced at his junior colleague and wondered if his name would come up. Wojtyla was unwilling to enter the competition; that much was clear. Nor would Wyszynski advise him to do so if he was asked. Apart from being badly needed in Poland, Wojtyla would be saddled with that ambiguity and be a target for the anti-Church. No, this was not Wojtyla's day.

In the Conclave, matters proceeded as expected. In one day, August 26, after three rounds of voting—one to eliminate possible runners-up, one to test the strength of the main candidate, and one to confirm his election by unanimous vote—that main candidate accepted his election.

The candidate was Albino Luciani, the sixty-six-year-old Patriarch of Venice, born the son of a socialist migrant worker on the Street of the Half Moon in the village of Forno di Canale; a priest at twenty-three, a bishop at forty-six, a cardinal at sixty; an outspoken opponent of Communism (although always on good terms with local Communist bosses); a humanist of some distinction, a conservative theologian, conversant with but not overly enthusiastic about ecumenists and their dreams; and with forty years of solid, undistinguished service as a prelate behind him. He chose his own papal name, John Paul, in honor of John XXIII, who made him bishop, and Paul VI, who made him cardinal, and he promised to continue their policies, while keeping intact the "great discipline of the Church in the life of priests and laity." The "Smiling Pope," as he was called, offended nobody but was nobody's man, apparently. The perfect compromise. The anti-Church settled down to wait. Their opponents prayed in hope.

Many of the Cardinal Electors, after the Conclave was over, described John Paul I as "God's candidate"; and at least on the lips of certain electors, the phrase would seem to have had a significance for them beyond the obvious and apparently pious meaning. His election foreclosed the chances of neither contending party. It merely delayed the day of confrontation.

We probably will never know in great detail what passed between John Paul I and the two Polish cardinals during their separate interviews with the new Pope. When a man sits alone on that peak of papal responsibility, he has what Italians call a "second sight"—meaning an extra dimension of perception—for the dangers of high position. Wyszynski had been to that high place in his own day and his own way. He understood the heroism required of a man to remain calm and serene—even if he is the "Smiling Pope"—while the ground beneath his feet starts to tremble.

The two Poles left Rome and returned to Poland with a rather accurate picture of the internal crisis in the Church of Rome. The transition from one pontificate to another had been too smooth to be true. Meanwhile, Wyszynski had an important rendezvous in Germany.

•   •   •

Wyszynski had prepared the ground for the German visit. His letter of 1965 to the German bishops was blunt: "We forgive and we ask for forgiveness." Polish-German hatred had to end. Wyszynski could not conceive of a "Europe from the Atlantic to the Urals" without Germany and without Poland. In response, the chief bishops of Germany had come to Poland on what could be described as a visit of penitence and reconciliation. Suddenly, all the governing circles in Poland, Germany and the USSR saw the long-range effect of Wyszynski's letter. All this took place in the sixties.

In September of 1978, on his return from Rome, Wyszynski set out for a five-day visit to West Germany, accompanied by Karol Wojtyla and a delegation of Polish bishops. Now he had created a platform to broadcast his geopolitical views on that "Europe to come."

"Our two nations," he said in his first speech, "have been educated by the Roman Catholic Church. Providence has given us a basis for unity because we have not merely common borders but also a shared religious heritage." At Fulda, West Germany, on September 20, he was more specific: "Many times we hoped that the day would come when we— Poles and Germans—could do what has been done in the past and as we are doing today: namely, build a Europe of Christ, a Christian Europe." The next day, he warned that "our meeting . . . might even be an outrage in the eyes of politicians," and then he brandished the source of his confidence: "We have worked for centuries in Central Europe to establish here the Kingdom of Christ." Whether Marxists or Socialists or Christian Democrats liked it or not, "Europe must realize once again that she is a new Bethlehem—of the world, of peoples and nations." Wyszynski's implied reservation, which today is John Paul II's reservation, was clear to all listeners: "Europe from the Atlantic to the Urals" is possible only if based on Christian civilization and motivated by Christian values—both finally depend on the millennial tutelage of the papacy.

When Wyszynski returned to Warsaw that week of September beginning on Sunday, September 24, he was given a piece of news that greatly, but strangely, disturbed him. Pope John Paul I had received a certain Russian Orthodox cleric, Metropolitan Nikodim of Leningrad and Ladoga, the second-highest-ranking clergyman in the Soviet-run Russian Orthodox Church, who enjoyed the status of colonel in the KGB. Nikodim, eleven times the object of KGB interrogations on suspicion of treason, the unofficial negotiator of the arrangement between Pope John XXIII and Nikita Khrushchev in 1960, had died of an apparent heart attack in the papal study in Rome, receiving Absolution of Sins and Blessing for the Dying from John Paul I.

Wyszynski's sense of trouble was confirmed in the early hours of Thursday of that same week: a telephone call from Rome announced that John Paul I had been found dead in bed. The Primate knew the consequences: another Conclave, another pope, yes, but now, most probably, a confrontation. No other Albino Luciani was available for election. The College of Cardinals had already been polarized. A first-class hierarchical crisis hovered over the Polish cardinals' return journey to Rome, for which Wojtyla again packed a small overnight valise. Whatever happened would have to happen quickly, so few alternatives remained for the Cardinal Electors.

Down in Rome, during the days and hours immediately preceding the Conclave, there was no doubt among the future Cardinal Electors on two scores.

First, they were divided down the middle—almost evenly—with ostensibly no common plank to share between them in choosing a successor to the now dead "Smiling Pope," John Paul I. That dreadful ambiguity, Paul VI's legacy, underlay their irreconcilability. Second, the one dominant figure among them was cut by Stefan Cardinal Wyszynski.

The "people of God" partisans, ecclesiastical "heavies," all of them, wanted a candidate who would pursue the decentralization of Church administration, who would be a symbol of unity, not of jurisdiction. The papal Curia should become a local diocesan chancery. The bishops should act by general consensus. The laity should have full access to all posts in the Church. Unity of faith was to be forged with other religions as equals in possession of truth. Religion should become the handmaiden of men's efforts to create a one world order. The leaders of the bloc were formidable—Giovanni Benelli of Florence, Leo Suenens of Belgium, Jan Willebrands of Holland, Franz Koenig of Austria, Paulo Evaristo Arns of São Paulo, Brazil, Eduardo Pironio of Argentina, Basil Hume of England, François Marty of Paris. They had their preferred candidates: Hume, Marty, Benelli.

The opposing bloc grouped itself around Giuseppe Siri of Genoa, Josef Höffner of Cologne, Pericle Felici of the Vatican. The first was truly the ancient lion of Church politics, once a pope-elect in his own right, a formidable adversary in argument, and very influential in political circles. Höffner, aristocratic in outlook, intolerant of any idea about "democratization" of the Church, chief prelate of a very "well-heeled" province of the Catholic Church, respected creditor of Catholics in many Third World countries, was backed up by personal prestige and towering political stature not only in West Germany, but in the countries of Central Europe. Felici was a veteran of the Second Vatican Council as its Secretary, an excellent canon lawyer who did his best, but failed to prevent the "hijacking" of that Council by the anti-Church party.

From the start of the pre-Conclave discussions in Rome in preparation for the Conclave now set to begin at 5 P.M. on Saturday, October 14, 1978, one cardinal, Wyszynski of Poland, stood out because of one impressive trait in his behavior—his unique flexibility—and because he quite obviously did not speak in terms, partisan or other, of the divisive ecclesiology alienating the two blocs. Wyszynski's focus of interest was elsewhere. He was speaking of the near future, and in geopolitical terms. The superpowers—the United States and the USSR; the major powers —Germany, France, Japan, Europe from "the Atlantic to the Urals" as a unit; the grinding poverty of the Third World; the Westernization of African and Asian nations through trade and industry; these constituted the substance of his comments.

Furthermore, this Pole, his brother cardinals realized, had been to Hell and back, so to speak. And he came bearing his permanent scars of mind and will as trophies of a strength beyond the strength of all human cleverness. He came furnished with rare lessons and insights; rewarded for his genuine heroism with a deep sense of what the Church is; ready with unbeatable skills for close combat; enlightened in ultimate truth about the Petrine Office beyond the capacity of any other in Conclave to gainsay him. He was, for all, venerable.

Clothing this personality was a unique and attractive flexibility, a genuine ability to enter the other man's mind, understand it and find whatever common ground there might be between them. He had only one limit: no compromise on essentials. In one who always spoke with the "big picture" of human affairs in view, this flexibility made him unique. He had no match, and everybody knew it, curial cardinals and "home" cardinals alike, although all had to acknowledge their impasse before they turned seriously to him for a way out. And no other Cardinal Elector was able to tackle the crisis with an ability matching his. Bureaucrat cardinals, "pastoral" cardinals, academician cardinals, "limousine" cardinals, cardinals *de salon*, saintly cardinals, politician cardinals, de-Catholicized cardinals, aristocratic cardinals, "popular front" cardinals, reactionary cardinals, apostate cardinals—none of them walked into Conclave with the indwelling power of spirit that Wyszynski had earned in the killing fields of Poland, adjacent to the Leninist Gulag Archipelago. The volatility of a Benelli was stabilized into reverence in Wyszynski's presence. The tawdriness of a Hume, the raw ambition of a Pironio, the fecklessness of a Willebrands—all were muted when faced with the well-known Wyszynski stare and the knowledge of the Polish Primate's firsthand experience on the front lines.

By the time they entered Conclave on October 15, two elements went with them: the impossibility of a genuine compromise candidate of Albino Luciani's kind; and the dependence of the Conclave outcome on Wyszynski's stance in the actual voting. The first day was ritually devoted to putting each of the blocs on notice officially—by successive and issueless voting sessions—that neither bloc could muster the required majority of two thirds plus one to put a candidate over the top. Wyszynski's greatest hour came on the following day, Monday, October 16.

From the memories of those who were actively concerned with the choice of a candidate pope—for a certain number were more passive than anything else—it is clear that the Wyszynski mental mold became a fixture in the Cardinal Electors' minds. They came to see the world around them as he did, although they did not all share his assessment of that world.

There were Wyszynski's three Internationals: the Red International of Leninist Marxism, the Golden International of Great Money, and the Black International of the Clerical Church. Those elders who had made their compromises with Marxism or with the Lodge winced, of course, at his strictures. But they had to agree with his structuring of the society of nations.

Then there was the Wyszynski policy of "no more catacombs" and of actively dealing with Leninist Marxism—cohabiting with and defeating it on its own ground and aboveground in the sociopolitical fields. Finally, there was his very sober, very vibrant, authentic-sounding forecast about the fate of the Church organization in the remaining years of this millennium. The USSR, with its Gulag Archipelago of oppression and its gaggle of captive nations and "republics," was on the way to dissolution—a dissolution deliberately engineered by the wise architects of the Party-State. The key territory and focal area of the change would be Central Europe. The "mover and shaker" of the change would be Russia. The whole society of nations would inevitably be influenced by that gargantuan change.

Whether they were "people of God" partisans or "hierarchic Church" partisans, all of them supported and shared the Second Vatican Council's document that presented the Virgin Mary as the Mother of the Church—"people" or "hierarchic." Wyszynski played on this unity. "The whole constitution [of the Church]," he said, "is at once Christocentric and Marian. It is as if there are arms to embrace the Family of Man. . . . The [Vatican] Council brought Mariology together with ecclesiology."

Wyszynski was implicitly invoking a spiritual force—Mary's all-powerful intercession with God—as Poles like him had done in all their vicissitudes. His was the same voice as Jan Kazimierz's, Jan Sobieski's, Primate August Hlond's. Wyszynski went even further than they; he called down Mary's blessing on his brother cardinals, using the title Poles had always conferred on her: Our Lady of Jasna Góra, the Bright Mountain. His plan to break the deadlock was, in its essential terms, as simple as that.

But no one listening to this man in a private conversation or in a public address could mistake him for a simple pious, devotional character with no realization of the hard facts of life. They knew otherwise about Stefan Wyszynski. They had seen him in action. Some of them had taken him on in an argument, only to find themselves outclassed.

"Nothing beats living" is an old adage. Wyszynski had lived it all: brainwashed prelates, apostate priests, ecclesiastical double agents, screaming commissars, bribe offers, calumnies, isolation, imprisonment, financial ruin, vindictive laws, boneheaded diplomats. If anyone like Giovanni Benelli or Eduardo Pironio decried papal leadership, he could tell them how the papacy and its Secretariat of State had saved Poland. To the ecumenical fantasies of a Jan Willebrands he could oppose the reality in Poland between Eastern Orthodox (under Moscow's thumb) and Roman Catholic. Whoever from the United States or Belgium or Holland spoke airily about female liberation or the mitigation of clerical celibacy was inundated with the lurid facts of the Polish experience with the Mariavite sect in Poland. (Mariavites had married bishops and priests, ordained wives. Aberrations in doctrine and behavior have blotched and marred the Mariavite history.)

Any attempt by a Paulo Arns to plead for compromise with Leninist Marxism was met with an array of facts and the cruel truth about the nature of Leninist deception. Any Marxist-inspired attack on capitalism was rebuffed by a careful explanation of what Leninist Marxism really meant in terms of malnutrition, miserable living conditions, fettering of the mind, corruption of the family. The grandiose generalities of a Basil Hume about democratizing the hierarchical structure of the Church were exposed by Wyszynski as the most vicious fallacy of the Anglo-Saxon mind. When anyone from the United States or France even hinted that the perennial Catholic devotion to Mary was a hindrance to Christian unity with Protestant churches and sects, he was told summarily that without Mary there was no hope of Christian unity.

Wyszynski could back everything up from experience. He was not theorizing. He spoke from lived experience. No doubt about it: Many of those hardheaded Churchmen were overcome by Wyszynski's dialectical

skill, by his obvious kindness, and, yes, by the obvious superiority of a
Churchman who was not indentured to any sociopolitical elite, and
whose soaring vision of earth, of man's time and God's eternity, recalled
many of his fellow cardinals to their duty to choose a *Catholic* pope.

Still, the sudden change in the pattern of voting during October 16,
the quick leap of Karol Wojtyla's name to a small majority, then a comfortable majority, and quickly to that irresistible two-thirds-plus-one majority took most Cardinal Electors by surprise and left the diehards on
both sides—a Basil Hume of Westminster, a Giuseppe Siri of Genoa—
somewhat dazed. Wojtyla's election was miraculous.

Wyszynski, as was his wont, did not hesitate later to tell it as he saw it:
"If people doubt there are signs and miracles in the world today, I say to
them, 'If anything is a miracle, what happened in the Sistine Chapel on
October 16 is one.' . . . When I approached John Paul II to pay my first
homage, he and I almost simultaneously pronounced the name of Our
Lady of Jasna Góra; this was her work. So we believed, and so we decidedly still believe."

In the end, therefore, it was not the iron will of the power brokers, and
not the political savvy of crafty Churchmen, but the childlike simplicity
of a few great men relying on the truth of Catholicism's central mystery
—God's entering the womb of a human mother—that obtained the saving grace for an institution racked in its essentials by a malignant cancer.
His American brother cardinals, many Europeans and not a few media
commentators had gently—and sometimes not so gently—mocked and
lampooned the childlike simplicity and trust of seventy-four-year-old
John Cardinal Carberry of St. Louis. The ten chocolate bars he took into
Conclave as provisions, and his quite obvious and childlike reliance on
an actual revelation from the Holy Spirit to guide the final choice of this
October Conclave, were lumped in one category: irrealism and the "out-
of-touch" attitude of an old man with passé ideas.

But it was the power of such faith in a Carberry, as in the *Ave Marias*
of millions of obscure Catholic believers during those three days, and as
in the hearts of the two Polish cardinals with their personal dedication to
that human Mother of God, that moved the mountain of difficulty
threatening the Roman Catholic institutional organization that autumn
of 1978. Canny Cardinal Confalonieri's remark after the Conclave was
heard by many as merely an evasive truism. But he told the absolute
truth of that Conclave: "*Abbiamo un Papa cattolico!*" he said. We have a
Catholic Pope! He surely implied that the opposite had been possible.

There are many still alive today who know now that during the sixty-
four hours of this Conclave, the huddled but confused leaders of the

Roman Church peered more than once over the edge of the abyss between mortal flesh and divine spirit, realizing that in the final count of affairs, they and they alone would be held accountable by the tremendous, sacred God of Heaven and earth for what would happen yet to literally billions of human souls.

Some of these 111 men had not said a Rosary for years; some had identified the glory of God with all their own petty ambitions; and some had worked silently for the liquidation of the Petrine Office of Pope. But, in that hour, they all became willy-nilly the instruments of providence. In their fears, in their nescience of the future, and relying on the saving grace of Mary's divine Son, two thirds plus one of them gave the world a Slavic Pope anointed under the seal of the human Mother of God.

Doubtless, at a later moment and a more tranquil time for Poland, for this Slavic Pope, and for his Church, Stefan Wyszynski will be declared to have been a Servant of God—the first step in the long process of being declared a Saint of the Church. In the meantime, and in the immediate aftermath of the October Conclave, there were two scenes of this great man's life that are indelibly etched on human memories as memorials to his greatness and signposts of the Slavic Pope, Wyszynski's protégé and pride, his gift to the Church Universal.

On Sunday, October 22, there was the Obeisance. It took place at the solemn investiture of the new Pope with a single symbol—the pallium, an embroidered woolen stole placed around his shoulders. The ceremony was witnessed by a live audience of some 75,000 and an estimated television audience of a billion and a half people. One high point of the ceremony came when the cardinals walked forward one by one to perform in public their personal obeisance to this new Vicar of Christ.

John Paul II sat on a low thronelike chair, wearing his pontifical vestments and the pallium. Each cardinal came up to him, knelt at his feet, kissed the Ring of the Great Fisherman on the Pope's fourth finger, whispered a few words of blessing and congratulation, and retired. There were variations with this or that particular cardinal. The Pope might take the cardinal's hands between his, he might exchange a few quiet words with him; with a few he exchanged the Christian kiss of peace.

But with Wyszynski, there was a different exchange. Onlookers could see, between these two, an interchange that was at one and the same time breathtaking and heartrending. In ceremonial, and in ritual symbol, they were Pope and Cardinal. In the reality of spirit and in ultimate truth, they were son and father, friend and friend, comrade and comrade. They were all of that, and something else besides, something too deep even for the sudden, unbidden salt of tears we cannot explain, and too intangible for any image of the fantasy or thought of the mind. It could only be witnessed.

In that obeisance of Wyszynski, it was the gesture of their hands and the movements of figures—the Pope seated, the Cardinal kneeling—that spoke. Wyszynski did ritually kiss Papa Wojtyla's ring, and then the Pope took the Primate's hands between his and kissed them. For brief seconds as they embraced, Papa Wojtyla seemed to be kneeling also. Doubtless, neither of them could utter many words. It was what they did that said all. About Poland. About the pain of the years they had worked together. About the ineffable sweetness of having together served the beautiful Christ they both adored as God and Master. And about the shadow of the Great Fisherman that now cloaked one of them for all his days, and amply consoled the other for having upheld the authority of those Keys Simon Peter received from an exultant Christ on one distant day at Caesarea Philippi in ancient Judea.

On Monday, October 23, there was the Adieu. Again, it took place in public, before the eyes of the Polish pilgrims who had come with the Primate to greet the new Holy Father in the Nervi Hall of Audiences. In this scene, it was the two faces, the Pope's and the Primate's, that elec-trified the onlookers in the hall and the distant millions gazing on the scene through the eyes of a satellite hovering far out of sight above Roman skies.

Both were faces already made according to that saying: After the age of fifty, you deserve the face you have. Wyszynski's seventy-eight-year-old craggy, weatherbeaten face was drawn in that unmistakable calm of a man who, having been tried and tried a thousand times, then worn out by the harshest human adversity for another thousand times, still was able to survive and to come back intact, only because he would not let go or give up. The calm that meets no more surprises. The calm that permits a smile of humor but rarely the belly laughter of amusement.

The fifty-eight-year-old Pontiff's face had features that were still rounded and sleek, with that sheen of freshness and physical fitness remaining only in a man not yet devastated in his own flesh by the rack of physical assault and, as yet, not oldened by the inner anguish of knowing how deeply he was hated and wished to death.

"We Poles know what a high price Your Holiness has to pay"—this was the theme of Wyszynski's speech of greeting—"in leaving the moth-erland in order to obey the command of Our Lord: Go forth and teach all nations." Papa Wojtyla's answer was simple: "On the Throne of Peter today, there would not be a Polish Pope . . . if it had not been for your unceasing belief in the Mother of the Church, or if there had not been Jasna Góra and . . . your ministrations as bishop and primate." The words were true, but it was the expressions of their faces that told all.

Wyszynski fell to his knees in a last act of homage. Without hesitation, Papa Wojtyla fell to his knees, the two men holding each other in a long embrace, Wyszynski's face bowed over the Pope's encircling right arm, his eyes closed, his left hand lightly touching the Pope's wrist. Wyszynski was suffering the worst of pains—the irremediable stab of human loneliness, for he was returning home without his right-hand man, his alter ego, his support. Wojtyla's face in the reality and in photographs has an unwonted expression. He is looking at the inclined face of his mentor and friend, and every line of his features is speaking of compassion and understanding, of regret for Wyszynski's pain, and of strength offered the older man so that he may carry on. "I understand," Wojtyla was saying. "We both understand. It is you who are paying the highest price. But we both know for whose sake you do it."

That wordless embrace, the momentary brokenhearted look suffusing the old Primate's face, the strength and distress evident on Wojtyla's mouth, around his eyes and his arms holding the Primate—the scene left no dry eyes in that audience. For all were Poles, and some soundless instinct of their commonality made each and every one a momentary participant in the ache of that Adieu.

In any other age of the Church but the present one, those scenes— the Obeisance and the Adieu—would have set Christian imaginations on fire and entered into their art and folklore. Depicted by artists and icon masters, chanted in hymns as sacred events, dramatized in the theater, perpetuated in marble or bronze or stained glass, they would have typified the faith in things unseen and the substance of things to come by which Christians have always lived and died in order that they might live forever.

Unfortunately, we have no inclination to celebrate. We do not feel it is the time for celebration. Ours is the age of the Roman Catholic anti-Church, with its Hell-bent purpose of desacralizing Catholicism, no matter what the target—the once venerated Office of Peter the Apostle, the Sacred Presence of Christ in the Eucharist, or the towering identity of Catholic Poland as a wellspring of grace for the Church Universal. And many of our contemporaries are convinced they are living in the slowly passing, uneasy twilight hours before the Day of the Man dawns in a blood-red sky engraved with the bizarre Sign of the Upside-Down Cross, reminding us: "In this sign, you will die."

So the age has shrunk our possibilities of human greatness, deprived us of the freedom to be noble. Our deepest regrets are not for the extinction of goodness, of purity, of compassion, of trust, of personal honor, of love and, finally, of all reason itself—our most precious faculty. Our brooding expectation is of unnamed catastrophe. Our wild hope is in an eleventh-hour salvation from beyond the rim of our human horizon. But we have no margin of mental ease to dwell on obeisance as greatness, no leisure time of the heart to marvel at martyrdom offered and not refused, no humility to kneel and kiss the hem of holiness's robe as it passes us by. We have shed so many tears that we have few, if any, left for the adieu of saints or for the last words of heroes.

32. The Politics of Papacy

Karol Wojtyla was elected Pope on October 16, 1978, by what eventually became the virtually unanimous vote of his brother cardinals. His election was firmed up on three main planks. He would, like his two predecessors, continue on the work of the Second Vatican Council, started by John XXIII. He would not, by simple papal fiat, decide that divisive ambiguity. He would specifically attend to what had to be done in the light of the predicted change in the Soviet "East."

Undeniably, he was no traditionalist. Equally, he was no liberal-progressive. Quite clearly, he was stalking an international stature. Undoubtedly, he was immersed in the outcome of the struggle in Poland between the Stalinist Polish government and the budding strength of the Solidarity movement, urban and rural, which Cardinal Wyszynski and he had laboriously nourished.

It seems certain now, in retrospect, that both he and Wyszynski configured the rise of the Solidarity movement in one definite geopolitical light. If, as they judged to be possible in the last years of the seventies,

Solidarity achieved acceptance in one strategically important unit of the Soviet empire—Poland—it could provide a model for a peaceful change within the Soviet system that would be acceptable to the Soviet masters of the Kremlin. For the original Solidarity proposal left all political, military and security issues untouched and in the hands of the Soviets and their surrogates in the various units of the system. The Kremlin masters could be reassured of their domination. There was to be no challenging it.

The Church's gain would be a welcome freedom in the religious and cultural fields. The Soviets' gain would be, or at least should be, a genuine cooperation of the subject populations in solving the already horrendous problem of an utterly failed economy.

This was Wyszynski's—and Wojtyla's—geopolitical thrust at the heart of the Soviet system. And seemingly, at its inception, their proposal was received at least permissively by the Soviets and their supreme leader, Leonid Brezhnev. It was an adaptation of the policy developed by successive Polish bearers of the *Interrex* responsibility. Wyszynski had learned it from his predecessor, August Hlond; and he from his predecessor, Edmund Dalbor, and so on back through the unending line of tough-minded Polish Church primates through the long night of Poland's entombment since 1795. The policy principle was simple: Cohabit with the opposition, fight it with the weapons of faith and culture; vivify the Poles as a people even though they had no land of their own and no national sovereignty; eventually outlive the foreign occupiers. This was the meaning of the refrain in the Polish national anthem: "as long as we live, Poland lives."

There was one very constant characteristic of the Wyszynski-Wojtyla geopolitical outlook and program: the function of Mary, the Mother of Jesus. This was not merely because of the Polish Pact concluded centuries before with her as the Queen of Poland. The high point in the Wyszynski-Wojtyla assault on the then impervious Stalinist government of Poland had come in 1956, when Wyszynski, a prisoner at Komancza, organized his plan to have the whole Polish nation dedicate itself in submission to Mary as her nation of slaves. On August 26 of that year, the act of dedication was accomplished throughout Poland and at Mary's shrine at Częstochowa, with the open consent of literally a vast majority of the millions of Poles.

It is difficult for the secularized minds of the West to realize that this official act of dedication to an invisible person—Mary—was meant not merely as an act of public piety and devotion, but explicitly as a geopolitical strategy with which to encompass relief for Poland from the lethal throttling of its spirit by the geopolitical giant the USSR was. It is most accurate to state that both Polish devotion to Mary as Queen of Poland and Mary herself were, for Poles, geopolitical in meaning and in function.

Wyszynski and Wojtyla, together with their fellow countrymen, expected Mary's action in their favor not only to aid their souls and minds and wills with graces interior to each individual. They fully believed her action would effect their sociocultural—and, eventually, their political —liberation. Marian devotion was not merely a private affair of an individual. It was public, communal. All was geopolitical, since Poland's fate was tied to the geopolitical stance of the West and the geopolitical system of the Soviets. Liberation through Mary from that fate would be a geopolitical event. So the Polish Church leaders configured their future.

Thus the initial stage of John Paul's papal policy took form within a geopolitical mold. As head of a georeligious organization, as someone personally consecrated to Mary, and as the Pope from a Poland likewise dedicated to Mary, he would enter the arena of international life via the narrow corridor of Communist Poland, proving there that he was nimble-footed and mentally too agile to trip over the obvious traps. He would inspire and guide the first steps of Poland's Solidarity and with its success pursue its extension into other units of the Soviet empire. He would critique both the Soviet "East" and the capitalist "West" from the strict standpoint of Christian morality. He would seek an international profile of the highest definition possible, nourished by a fixed policy of papal travels, and a voracious appetite for and genuine concern about every main issue involving the society of nations. He would essay an end run around the Soviets by establishing personal relations between himself and the authorities of the Greek and Russian Orthodox churches.

This papal policy was pure Wyszynski-ism transposed from the confines of Poland to the boundless plane of the globe, taking in all nations and all religions. The same basic confidence behind Wyszynski's strategy animated Wojtyla: belief in the geopolitical action and power of Mary as Queen of the world.

In only one respect did he deviate from Wyszynski's strategy and tactics. No matter how caught up Wyszynski was in matters of state— Poland and the USSR, Poland and the Holy See, Poland and the West, the Polish people versus the Polish Communist government, Poland and West Germany—he constantly paid minute attention to the Church in Poland. His contemporaries marveled at the versatility and attention to detail he applied to priestly formation, an intricate network of catechetical centers, social help-and-aid organizations, religious orders of priests and nuns, universities and institutes, the Catholic media and trade book publication, pilgrimages, devotions, sermons, parochial visits, convents, monasteries, wayside shrines—the list was unending.

Wyszynski did this as a leader because he knew his only strength against the enemy was a people with a vibrant faith grounded in regulated practices and supervised by competent ecclesiastical authorities. If he looked over his shoulder, he could see phalanxes of Catholic Poles, well instructed, well informed, unified and inspired.

Papa Wojtyla, in his wider field of jurisdiction over the Church Universal, has acted in almost the opposite manner. By the time he became Pope, in 1978, the deterioration of his churchly institution was striking. Every statistic pointed downward—Mass-goers, priests, nuns, communicants, confessions, Catholic schools. There was no longer any unity of doctrine among theologians. Over half the bishops of the Church wanted no papal control. The traditional philosophy, piety and devotional practices were in disfavor. Abortion, contraception, homosexuality, extramarital sex were on the rise. Ever since he became Pope, all statistics still continue to pursue the downward plunge.

Apart from now and again repeating traditional doctrine, he did nothing and is doing nothing to halt that deterioration. Isolated words not followed by concrete application have done nothing effective to correct it. John Paul has, in sum, not even attempted to reform the very obvious deformations afflicting and finally liquidating his churchly institution. One cannot imagine a Wyszynski as Pope behaving in this way. John Paul has acted as if reform was a lost cause from the beginning of his papacy. This is one of the most enigmatic traits of his reign as Pope. It must finally be explained in a Pope who is Catholic in his bones and in his soul.

What has guided his papal undertakings and required all his attention has been the geopolitical calculation he and Wyszynski formulated so well.

The small but significant inaccuracy in that geopolitical calculation was perhaps inevitable. It concerned time. Poles were already schooled in waiting; and to outwait the impregnable strength of the Leninist-Marxist system would, Wyszynski and Wojtyla calculated—as indeed most others in the West were thinking then—surely take time.

It had already taken Wyszynski almost thirty years of incredible effort to arrive at 1978, with the promise of Solidarity's existence more or less assured from Moscow's point of view. The Polish Pope could watch over the further development that in their calculations at the time of his election could easily stretch over the twenty to twenty-five years that, the actuarial tables predicted, remained to him. This calculation was, perhaps unavoidably, inaccurate. The error lay in the acceptance of a carefully built myth of Soviet impregnability. Wyszynski and Wojtyla did believe that the Soviet system would eventually implode, but that this disintegration would be slow in coming to a head.

It was an inaccurate calculation because of a sudden change in circumstances in Poland and Moscow, a change no one could foresee.

During the last years of Leonid Brezhnev, in the inner councils of the all-powerful Central Committee, the new mind of the Party-State was evinced in a Yuri Andropov—KGB chief as of 1967, Politburo member as of 1973—and in a Mikhail Gorbachev, his protégé, whom Andropov appointed as Secretary of Agriculture, and to membership in the Central Committee of the Party, in 1978. This new mind was a persuasion that the Stalin-founded Cold War policy was coming to a dead end, and that the Soviet Union was being successfully matched militarily by the Western alliance, while economically the USSR was falling way behind the capitalist world.

This new mind had no confidence in the "Polish model" as proposed by the Poles and permitted by Brezhnev. The anti-Brezhnev thinking of these men in the Moscow Politburo recognized the Wyszynski-Wojtyla tactic for what it was: a slow erosion of the Marxist system among the subject peoples. We can be sure that the name of the Polish Pope found a significant place in the discussions of the Party-State. With this disciple of Wyszynski in charge of the Roman Catholic institutional organization, there loomed a real danger for the European holdings of the Party-State.

The second change was in Poland. In a new momentum, Solidarity altered its carefully planned course. Wyszynski had once warned its leaders: "Do not let yourselves be drawn into alliances with those who would use you for aims that are alien to our Polish dignity and heritage." To reinforce that warning, both John Paul and Cardinal Wyszynski were thanked by the Polish Prime Minister, General Wojciech Jaruzelski, in March 1981, for their help in bringing about a peaceful solution between the Communist government and the Solidarity workers who were on a crippling strike. The danger had been that the strike could have encroached upon the political and security preserves of the government.

Wyszynski and Jaruzelski had their eye on the developing affiliation between the Solidarity movement and two radical organizations: the Committee for the Defense of the Workers (KOR) and the Conference for Workers' Self-Government (KSR). Both carried within them the seeds of political and military revolt.

As long as both Churchmen, Primate and Pope, were actively in control, Solidarity may well have continued to function within the Communist system, restricting its ambitions and activity to the fields of culture and labor relations.

But by 1980 Wyszynski was mortally ill with stomach cancer. By March 1981, the illness had become acute. Actually, he had barely two months to live. Perhaps the radicalization of Solidarity was inevitable. Some have suggested it was a deliberate scenario guided by the hidden hand of the Party-State in order to liquidate the whole idea of Solidarity. In any case, the removal of Wyszynski and John Paul from active, day-to-day participation greatly facilitated the radicalization of Solidarity.

May 1981 was a month of double tragedy. By May 3, Wyszynski was confined to his bed at his Warsaw residence on Miodowa Street. He was dying. On May 13, contract killer Mehmet Ali Agca pumped bullets into John Paul II in St. Peter's Square, in full view of 75,000 people and a television audience of some three and a half million. Bullets entered his torso. The two bullets aimed at John Paul's head missed their target, because just in time the Pontiff, standing erect on the "popemobile" circulating among the crowd, bent down to greet a little girl who had a picture of Mary pinned to her blouse. He was rushed to the wrong hospital, the Policlinico Gemelli, where he was given transfusions of tainted blood, thus adding to his body wounds the complication of hepatitis.

Cardinal Wyszynski could follow all this only from his deathbed, far off in Poland. By May 24, he was obviously entering into his agony, and there was very little time left to him in this life. His dead body would be cold within seventy-two hours. Papa Wojtyla lay in Rome's Policlinico Gemelli, his body still in shock from the brutal attack on May 13. Wyszynski and John Paul had to speak before the Cardinal departed. They had words of farewell for each other.

Wyszynski's cup of pain was almost filled on May 24. The convalescent Pope placed a call from Gemelli; the phone rang in Wyszynski's Warsaw bedroom; his attendant answered it, told the dying man the Pope was on the line; Wyszynski turned his head weakly and raised his hand to take the receiver. No use. The telephone cord was too short, and the Primate could not get up. By the next day, the cord had been lengthened, so the two could speak together one last time.

Both were extremely weak. Both were in pain. Both knew it was the end for one of them and, perhaps, for the other. Both, in other words, felt the ultimate sting of being mortal, felt the whip of punishment bite across their backs. It was not so much the number of words used on such an occasion or what was said that mattered now. What counted was rather the overtones of the voice, the message of the deepest self communicating its existence and its feelings.

Besides, from long association, they had their own shorthand. No one can even imagine, nor should anyone try to imagine, the very last words of that quiet conversation—what they were, who spoke them, and finally who hung up first. Only those two knew. Only they could with equanimity say goodbye for all the time that remained to each one—hours for Wyszynski, years for Wojtyla.

Wyszynski went up to his Maker and to his Maker's Mother in the small hours of May 28—that day, forty days after Easter, which Christians call Ascension Day. The theme of the ancient Roman Church in celebrating that day of Christ's Ascension could not have been more apt: *captivam duxit captivitatem* (he took captivity captive). A very old and weary warrior had surmounted the last barrier to his freedom. He had defeated all earthly captivity.

While John Paul lay convalescing that summer in the Policlinico, in the aftermath of Wyszynski's disappearance from this world, the first period of his sorrow and bereavement, we are told, gave way to a feeling of gratitude that he was still in life and could look forward to further years at his work. The deterioration of relations between the ever-burgeoning Solidarity and the ever more confused and fearful Communist government in Poland only emphasized his gratitude. In that June, July and August of 1981, wildcat strikes, public denigration of the government in straw polls, food shortages, defacing of Soviet war memorials in Poland, public demonstrations acclaiming Nobel Laureate Czeslaw Milosz (an archcritic of Marxism) in Gdansk—the birthplace of Solidarity—bitter infighting between the "hard-liners" and the liberals in the Communist Party, repeated growls from the Kremlin: all indicated a growing crisis.

Not able personally to exercise any effective monitoring and direction of Polish affairs, John Paul turned more and more intently to prayer. Prayer, especially, to Mary as the geopolitical hope of Poland and of the world. Because, he was now sure, Mary had saved him from intended death in St. Peter's Square that May 13—the official feast day of Mary as Our Lady of Fatima—he fell into a mode of prayer to her as the Lady of Fatima. She would save Poland from destruction—autodestruction or destruction by the ever more restive Soviets. From across the Atlantic came the head-on condemnations by President Ronald Reagan of the "evil empire" and news that the United States was rearming and repositioning its military forces.

It was in this mode of prayer and this mood of total trust in Mary that John Paul had what has been, as far as is publicly known, his only supernatural vision of things to come. There is no gainsaying that he did have that vision. What he finally understood by it will be a matter of opinion and speculation until the day that he himself speaks openly, if ever, about it.

Apart from the incidental fact that he received that vision while convalescing in the Policlinico, the most noteworthy trait of the vision was that it came as an exact repetition of a miraculous happening recorded sixty-four years before at the hamlet of Fatima in Portugal. It was just as if he had been present at Fatima around midday, October 13, 1917.

We have no difficulty in knowing all the details of that 1917 happening in Portugal. All was seen and recorded by press photographers, media reporters from Portugal and other countries, writers, scholars, government officials, and a substantial crowd estimated by the press of the time to have topped 75,000. What those on-the-spot witnesses saw and recorded is what John Paul saw in the luminous skies of Lazio above the Seven Hills of Rome, in August 1981.

The happy circumstance that so many witnesses were present at Fatima that day was due to a simple fact: As of the previous July, the October 13 happening had been predicted.

Involved as chief actors in the whole Fatima event were three peasant children, a brother and sister—Francisco and Jacinta Marto, nine and seven years old, respectively—and their ten-year-old cousin, Lucia dos Santos. The brother and sister were illiterate. Lucia could barely read or write. They spent their days herding their families' sheep. These three children claimed that on the thirteenth day of each month, beginning with May 13, 1917, Mary had appeared to them at a particular spot called Cova da Iria in the neighborhood of their sheep pastures; that she told them she had an important message for all the nations and all men and women; and that, after coming to see them each thirteenth day of the coming months, on October 13 she would by the power of God perform a miracle in order to substantiate the authenticity and vital importance of her message.

By one means or another, news of the successive appearances spread throughout Portugal, Europe and the two Americas. Hence the throng of people gathered at Cova da Iria in Fatima at midday on October 13. Not only the month and day and place were predicted by the children; the exact hour—midday—was foretold. What happened at that precise hour was a cameraman's dream, something even Cecil B. DeMille could not have fantasized.

It had rained torrentially all that night of Friday, October 12. On the morning of the thirteenth, the hamlet of Fatima was blanketed in driving rain beneath a cloudbound sky. Everyone and everything was sodden; the dirt roads were quagmires of mud; there was a good three inches of water at Cova da Iria, where the three children were waiting with their families, surrounded by those thousands of visitors. Toward midday, the voice of Lucia, the eldest child, was heard: "Look up at the sun!" All looked up. The rain suddenly stopped. The heavy veil of clouds broke asunder. The sun appeared. At the sight of that sun, uncontrollable waves of surprise, awe, fear, panic, joy swept through the crowds. The sun they now clearly saw was the same sun John Paul II later saw in August 1981.

This was not the unbearably bright midday sun normal in the skies of Portugal and Rome, the sun you cannot stare at without damaging the eyes. This sun was a fast-spinning plate of brightly shining silver, a giant pinwheel turning on its own axis, casting off beams of colored lights—red, orange, yellow, green, blue, indigo and violet—that tinted faces, clothes, cars, carts, umbrellas, animals, ponds, grass, mountaintop and horizon in all the successive hues of the rainbow. Everyone was able to stare fixedly at this brilliant disk, but yet without pain and without being blinded. All were fascinated by the rim of color around the spinning disk of that sun. At first deep red, the rim's color changed successively to all the colors in the rainbow.

That was the first part of what the onlookers later described picturesquely as the "dance of the sun." It lasted two or three minutes.

The second part of the "dance" started with a cessation of the spinning motion. Now the sun roamed back and forth among the clouds, seeming to tremble and pulsate within itself, appearing and half disappearing behind puffs and strips of cloud, occasionally stopping and spinning again on its own axis and throwing off those brilliant shafts of multicolored light, then resuming its roaming among the clouds.

The third part of that exotic dance came when the roaming stopped. That brilliant disk was stationary for a while, trembling, pulsating, rotating on its own axis. Then, without warning, it plunged from its position above the clouds, hurtled in zigzag fashion toward earth and toward the upturned faces of those tens of thousands. One observer described later how the smiling look of wonder on the faces around him in that crowd changed first into looks of puzzlement, then immediately into white-faced fear according as that solar disk, ever rotating and pulsating, came closer and closer, appearing bigger and bigger in its reeling descent, the heat increasing as it came nearer and nearer.

As this molten mass of light and heat zigzagged downward, cries of anguish and horror, prayers and exclamations, rose up: "It's the end of the world!" "We will all die!" "God forgive me my sins!" and the like. But in the middle of the downward plunge of that blazing sun, the voices of the three children were heard above the cries of anguish: "Pray and pray hard! Everything is going to be all right!"

But for a time it did look as if that disk was going to smash into the crowds, crushing and burning all before it. At the peak of these fears and horror, the disk halted, reversed its path, ascended back to the sky. It stopped moving. The spinning ceased. There were no more colors thrown off. The people could no longer look at the midday sun. It had just its usual unbearable noonday glare. The winds started to blow with noticeably greater force. All noticed the rise in the force of the wind. They noticed, too, that there was no movement whatever in the branches of the trees. No sooner was it noted that the leaves and branches were motionless in the middle of strong winds than they noticed—again, all together—that there was no water on the ground, no mud. All was dry and dusty.

Then someone shouted: "I'm dry! Bone dry!" The cry suddenly became universal. Everybody's clothes, a few minutes before heavy and cold from rainwater, were now dry and light and crisp and warm. "They looked as though they had just come from the laundry," one still-surviving witness recalled in 1989.

There is one more set of facts about the Fatima happening that is relevant to John Paul's August 1981 vision.

From the beginning of their reported conversations with Mary, the three children insisted she had given them three messages. Before their early deaths, Francisco Marto on April 4, 1919, at age eleven; Jacinta Marto on February 20, 1920, at age ten—the two Martos and Lucia dos Santos were questioned extensively about the Fatima happening and their six extended conversations with Mary. They never wavered or changed in their testimony, but they would not reveal the contents of the three messages immediately. They maintained that Mary had also given them precise instructions on this point. Since the death of the Martos, Lucia, now eighty-two and living as a Carmelite nun in Coimbra, Portugal, has been the sole living source of information about those three messages of Mary.

The first two messages of Fatima became very well known in the years since 1917. The first put the Church and all men on notice that the world as a whole society was following a path of sin along which a multitude of men and women were being led to the eternal punishment of Hell. The second message was a prediction about the outbreak of World War II. In that message, Mary also spoke about Russia and asked that the Pope and all the bishops of the Church consecrate it in an especially solemn manner to her. If this was not done, the children reported Mary as saying, Russia would spread error and evil throughout the world; many human beings would suffer and die as a consequence.

The third Fatima message still remains officially a secret. Lucia was adamant about its being kept secret. In 1944, under orders from her bishop, she wrote down on one sheet of paper the bare details of that secret, sealed it in an envelope and gave it to him. She told the bishop it was to be opened in 1960, because "by 1960, things will be clearer." But rumors spread about the contents of that envelope, to the effect that it concerned the USSR and other nations. Geopolitical-minded Vatican authorities began to feel queasy about the "Third Secret," as the contents of that envelope were now called. Under Vatican order, the envelope was brought to Rome and deposited in a small humidor-type box on a mantelpiece in the Pope's private apartments in the Apostolic Palace, there to await the man who would be Pope in 1960.

That Pope was John XXIII. He opened and read the contents of the envelope in the course of 1959–60 and decided those contents had no relevance to his pontificate. The envelope was returned to the box. His successor, Paul VI, read the contents and decided to do nothing about the matter. John Paul I also read Lucia's document, but he lived only thirty-three days as Pope. One of the first things John Paul II did on becoming Pope was to take out that envelope, read the document and place it back in that box. He, too, like John XXIII and Paul VI, decided it was not directly relevant; there was nothing to be done about the message. That was in late 1978.

The actual contents of that "Third Secret" remained by and large a secret until the pontificate of John Paul II. By that time, the contents had been revealed to a sufficient number of people on a private basis, and both John Paul himself and Joseph Cardinal Ratzinger had spoken with sufficient frankness about the contents so that at least the essentials could be reliably outlined.

Lucia's single-page written formulation of the "Third Secret" covers three main topics. A physical chastisement of the nations, involving catastrophes, man-made or natural, on land, on water and in the atmosphere of the globe. A spiritual chastisement, far more frightening and distressing—especially for Roman Catholics—than physical hardship, since it would consist of the disappearance of religious belief, a period of widespread unfaith in many countries. A central function of Russia in the two preceding series of events. In fact, the physical and spiritual chastisements, according to Lucia's letter, are to be gridded on a fateful timetable in which Russia is the ratchet.

The chastisements were meant to punish the nations for their ungodliness and abandonment of God's laws. The whole dire process could be averted—need not happen, in fact—if two requests of Mary were granted. One: that whoever would be Pope in 1960 (actually it was John XXIII) should publish the text of the "Third Secret" for the whole world to read and know. Two: that then the Pope, with all his bishops acting collegially, should consecrate Russia to Mary. Russia, according to the text of the "Third Secret," was the regulator of the timetable.

If those two basic requests were satisfied, then the two chastisements —physical and spiritual—would not be inflicted on mankind. Russia would be converted to religious belief, and a period of great peace and prosperity would ensue. If the requests were denied, the chastisements would then follow as surely as night follows day. Russia would spread its errors throughout all nations. Many millions would die. The practice of religion and the profession of true faith would diminish to a shadow of what they were. Widespread corruption would infect the Church's clergy and laity. The Holy Father would have much to suffer. A little glimmer of hope existed: In the end, after all this dreadful devastation, there would be a restoration of faith and tolerable living conditions.

Unmistakably, the "Third Secret" was formulated as an ultimatum, an "either-or" proposition.

In 1978, shortly after becoming Pope, when John Paul read Lucia's text of the "Third Secret," he had drawn the obvious conclusion. The Pope of 1960, John XXIII, had not satisfied those two requests of Mary. "These [predictions]," John had noted for his successors, "do not concern our times." John had refused to publish the text of the "Third Secret." He had not organized the collegial consecration of Russia to Mary—although he had a made-to-order opportunity to do so when 2,500 Roman Catholic bishops assembled in the Vatican on October 11, 1962, for the opening of his Second Vatican Council. He did not accept the "either."

Therefore, the fateful timetable of spiritual and physical chastisements was locked into place and, in that August of 1981, was running full tilt. The Roman Catholic Church and the society of nations were now operating under the sign of that dire "or" proffered in the Fatima message. John Paul needed no one to tell him the initial results of Pope John

XXIII's refusal of those two requests of Mary. Already whole sections of the Church in France, Austria, Holland, Germany, Spain, England, Canada, the United States and Latin America had fallen precisely into unfaith. There subsisted only a faithful remnant of practicing Catholics. His own Vatican chancery and the various diocesan chanceries throughout the Church were in the hands of the anti-Church partisans. Heresy and grave error resided in the seminaries. An intricate and self-protective network of actively homosexual priests, nuns, bishops and some cardinals now throttled all attempts to reform morals. Contraception was advocated explicitly or implicitly by a plurality of bishops, and abortion, together with divorce, was connived at. A Swiss bishop went on television with a valise in hand and opened it, cascading thousands of condoms before the eyes of viewers. "This," he said, "is the answer to overpopulation and AIDS!"

Most frighteningly for John Paul, he had come up against the irremovable presence of a malign strength in his own Vatican and in certain bishops' chanceries. It was what knowledgeable Churchmen called the "superforce." Rumors, always difficult to verify, tied its installation to the beginning of Pope Paul VI's reign in 1963. Indeed, Paul had alluded somberly to "the smoke of Satan which has entered the Sanctuary"—an oblique reference to an enthronement ceremony by Satanists in the Vatican. Besides, the incidence of Satanic pedophilia—rites and practices—was already documented among certain bishops and priests as widely dispersed as Turin, in Italy, and South Carolina, in the United States. The cultic acts of Satanic pedophilia are considered by professionals to be the culmination of the Fallen Archangel's rites.

No. John Paul needed no one to tell him the Fatima timetable was running in vigor. Already in 1980, speaking to a group of German Catholics about the "Third Secret," he had been quite explicit. Yes, he responded to one question. Lucia's text does speak of such chastisements. No, he said in answer to another question, those chastisements cannot be averted now. The die is cast. But they can be mitigated by praying the Rosary, he asserted.

Why, one questioner asked, did John XXIII refuse to obey the requests of the "Third Secret"? John Paul's answer was pregnant with his own pre-1981 reading of the text. "Given the seriousness of its [the "Third Secret's"] contents," he explained, "my predecessors in the Petrine Office [John XXIII, Paul VI, John Paul I] diplomatically preferred to *postpone* publication [of the text] so as not to encourage the world power of Communism to make certain moves."

This attitude toward the "Third Secret" and its demands for papal action was quite consistent with the original Wyszynski-Wojtyla time calculation, according to which they reckoned that the huge geopolitical change in the offing would run a gradual course of many years. John Paul's answers to the questioners at the 1980 Fulda meeting also threw light on why he has not undertaken any serious, papal-directed and comprehensive effort to reverse the continual and rapid deterioration of his institutional organization. No, he said in response to one question, the Church cannot be reformed at the present moment.

Manifestly, John Paul had accepted the fait accompli that inevitably followed the decision of John XXIII not to follow the dictates of the "Third Secret." He accepted the fact that the Church was now in the period of the Fatima "or," since the "either" had been refused by John XXIII.

His words also point to a mortal danger facing the capitalist nations, about which Lucia is quite explicit in the text of the "Third Secret." Understood in its depth and extent, John Paul's reference can be shocking: "so as not to encourage the world power of Communism to make certain moves." The Pope and the grizzled men who run the Vatican are not quixotic idealists living in a dream world of superstition and irrational fantasies. In fact, their realism can be numbing. If they or he could come to such a conclusion and make such a statement, it must be accurate and based on objective facts.

In that "Third Secret," indeed, Lucia's words are so explicit and so *verifiable*—and therefore so authentic—that, were the leaders of the Leninist Party-State to know those words, they would in all probability decide to undertake certain territorial and militaristic moves against which the West could have few if any means of resisting, and the Church would be plunged into further and deeper subjugation to the Party-State. Lucia's words underline a terrible vulnerability in the capitalist nations. That is the "seriousness" of Lucia's words. The capitalist West could be entrapped by the USSR. In Vatican parlance, Lucia's words have a dire geopolitical meaning. They must not be treated as pious and devotional outpourings. Her words from the Fatima happening are primarily related to the fierce politics of nations. Ever since John XXIII opened and read those words, the Vatican has treated them gingerly. Fatima has been politicized. John Paul, from the start, has gone along with that politicization. In Vatican foreign policy since the opening of the envelope, the cardinal principle has been to foment devotion to Mary as Our Lady of Fatima but never to make political decisions very obviously in the light of the "Third Secret." The "Secret" has to be buried, as Cardinal Ottaviani said in 1957, "in the most hidden, the deepest, the most obscure and inaccessible place on earth."

It must also be added, however, that the anti-Church partisans in the

Vatican bureaucracy and throughout the Church abhor anything savor-
ing of devotion to Mary, to Fatima and to divine revelation. For they
have forsaken the divine faith of Catholicism, of which Mary, the
Mother of God, is an integral part. They also know the present Pope is
under the special protection of Mary.

As he convalesced in the Policlinico Gemelli that August, the concrete
facts of the situation worked a change of attitude in John Paul. Those
facts were: the growing crisis in Poland between Solidarity and the government; the new twist in Moscow's attitude to Solidarity, as something
dangerous and to be crushed; the gap left by Wyszynski's death, a gap
that the new Primate of Poland, Jozef Cardinal Glemp, could not fill; the
significance of his own attempted assassination on May 13, feast day of
Our Lady of Fatima, and—as he firmly believed—his own deliverance
from sudden death by Agca's bullets through the protection of Mary as
Our Lady of Fatima.

John Paul could not put all those details into a coherent order without
coming to the conclusion that the geopolitical timetable was much
shorter than he and Cardinal Wyszynski had thought. The (for him)
obvious intervention of Mary in preserving his life placed him—in his
own eyes—in a direct relationship with Fatima and its "Third Secret." If
there was one dominant element in that "Third Secret," it was Russia.
The provisos of the "Third Secret" made sense only in relation to Russia.

He had accepted as fact that John XXIII's decision not to do as the
"Third Secret" asked—to publish the actual text, and to undertake a
collegial consecration of Russia to Mary—had placed the Church and
therefore the world in the "or" situation. He had no difficulty in accepting the predictions of dire physical and spiritual chastisements, and that
Russia would spread its errors throughout every nation. But all of that,
he had assumed—up to that August of 1981—was gridded on a long-
drawn-out timetable. Now he saw that the geopolitical timetable had
been inaccurately calculated. The geopolitical change implied by the
"Third Secret" was not far off. It was imminent. It was about to take
place. Russia was its womb. Russia was its focal point. Russia was to be
the main agent of change. Russia was to be the source of a universal
blindness and error.

A certain febrile character entered John Paul's behavior now. From
his sickroom in the Policlinico, he sent over to the Apostolic Palace for
that envelope. He read and reread portions of Lucia's testimony before
diocesan commissions inquiring into the Fatima happening, and he stud-

ied some of her other writings. He called in for consultation a certain Sister Mary Ludovica, an expert on Fatima, and after some discussion, he dispatched her posthaste over to Portugal, to speak with the retired and saintly bishop of Leiria-Fatima and with Lucia in her convent at Coimbra.

Into September and the fall of that year, 1981, events in Poland took on a correspondingly febrile and ominous character. Relations became more and more strained between the Polish government and Solidarity. The KSR-KOR elements associated with Solidarity had pushed the organization's demands beyond the limits of stated Soviet tolerance. The Moscow masters now feared Solidarity harbored ambitions that went far beyond the field of labor relations and culture. By November, the crisis in Central Europe was at its height; rumors of a Soviet invasion were rife.

The Cardinal Primate, Jozef Glemp, acting as *Interrex*, met with Solidarity's Lech Walesa and the head of the Communist Party, General Wojciech Jaruzelski, on November 4. The proposal: to form a triumvirate that would calm the situation, cool tempers on both sides and halt the slide into an anarchy requiring Soviet intervention. Walesa refused. By December 10, the crisis was full blown. The Moscow Politburo sent a last warning note to the government, advising the Poles that the situation must be cooled down and Lech Walesa must be beaten back. Walesa, on behalf of Solidarity, stated categorically: "We cannot retreat anymore." The war of nerves extended to the two Germanys; Helmut Schmidt of West Germany and Erich Honecker of East Germany held a summit of their own—what happened in Poland would have great import for them. They wanted no part of Lech Walesa and his miserable Solidarity.

On December 12, the straw that broke the camel's back: Solidarity proposed a national referendum on four major issues—all of which boiled down to an open invitation to Poles to vote the Communists out of office. General Jaruzelski spoke successively to Walesa and to Glemp by telephone. John Paul was alerted in Rome. At 6:00 A.M. on December 13, Jaruzelski declared martial law. Marshal Viktor Kulikov, Soviet commander of Warsaw Pact forces, threw a ring of steel around all neural points in Poland. Solidarity was suspended, as were all civic rights, all educational institutions, all telephone and telex communications. Poland was once more a prisoner nation.

As if in imitation of the former Pacts of Polish extinction, Western bankers in Paris rescheduled Poland's national debt. West Germany together with other European leaders assured the Soviets and Jaruzelski that no sanctions would be imposed, no matter what happened to Poland

and Solidarity. Business would be as usual. After all, by now all Solidarity leaders had been imprisoned. Solidarity's activities were now confined to midnight Masses throughout Poland. Only President Reagan's U.S. administration applied sanctions against the Polish Communists.

John Paul could read the handwriting on the wall of his times. His beloved Poland was not destined to achieve independence in, as it were, a solo flight. Its fate was tied to a much vaster geopolitical development, involving all of the USSR and all its captive nations. And, to be logical, if all those were involved, then all of Europe and the Americas would be involved.

Thus, as 1981 ended, his own fate as Pope and Poland's fate as a nation were seen by him as mere functioning parts in a new geopolitical pattern already setting in. Russia, indicated as the key factor by the "Third Secret," constituted the dominant orientation of that new and vaster pattern. And, suddenly, it became of vital importance to John Paul that the text of that "Third Secret" had not been published, and that the Pope with his bishops had not consecrated Russia into the care of Mary.

For now, immediately looming on his papal horizon, he could see the shape of things to come. The decreasing vibrancy of faith in Catholic communities, the darkening of European minds, the betrayal by his Churchmen of their proper pastoral function, the spreading net of Leninist-Marxist deception looping in all the nations in a geopolitical trap, the onslaught of physical chastisements to come—disease, disorder, earthquakes, tidal waves, all kinds of natural catastrophes from the hand of nature's Creator.

But during his examination of the Fatima material the previous autumn, he had come across the papal records of what Pope Pius XII had done in 1954. Pius had been in close touch with Lucia through intermediaries. He had learned from her that, failing a publication of the text of the "Third Secret" and a collegial consecration of Russia by Pope and bishops, some mitigation of the coming tribulations—but only a mitigation—could be achieved by merely consecrating the world to Mary, "with a special mention of Russia."

John Paul's immediate step was to write to all his bishops, telling them he would do just that on May 13, 1982, in Fatima, and inviting them to join him. A small minority answered him positively. A still smaller minority joined him on that actual day, May 13, 1982—either by their physical presence or by parallel actions in their home dioceses. The bishops of his Church were not at one with their Pope, either in his devotion to Mary and Fatima or in his solicitude for the survival of the Roman Catholic institutional organization.

For them, he was Bishop of a very ancient and important diocese— Rome. But the Keys of his authority were historical relics, not symbols of actual authority guaranteed by the human blood of God's Son. The Keys of this Blood no longer meant anything realistic for a plurality of his bishops.

For himself, John Paul was now held within a different paradigm of historical development. He had come into the Petrine Office in 1978 hailed as the Polish Pope. Now, more accurately, he saw himself as the Slavic Pope, giving the term "Slavic" a connotation that was somewhat different from the meaning given it by the poet Slowacki, who had been the first to speak of the "Slavic Pope." This Pope would be called Slavic because, originating among the Slavs of Poland, he was destined to preside over a geopolitical upheaval and sea change affecting the whole society of nations and directly springing from a Slavic—Russian, in this case—source tainted and corrupted by the primordial sin of Lucifer: hatred of all that God is and of all that is good.

John Paul now saw himself as all that, and then as something more. For that key message of Fatima had spoken of more. "In the end," the text of the Fatima message stated, as it wound down, quoting Mary's words to the children, "Russia will be consecrated to me, the chastisements will cease and the world will enjoy peace for a while."

That "more"—in John Paul's outlook—would be another era, long or short, in mankind's history, when a grand design of God's would be inaugurated for the society of nations. It would be a geopolitical unity of all the nations. It would come after all the efforts of Transnationalists and Internationalists, of all the globalists, had come to utter shipwreck because of the malignant geopolitical plans of the Party-State, which were more efficient, more thoroughly elaborated and more zealously executed than theirs.

There would be general shipwreck because on both sides, not the will of the Creator and Redeemer of mankind was the absolute rule of the contenders' efforts, but primarily greed for power and indulgence in mutual fratricide. Following that shipwreck, the Grand Design of God would be executed. He, John Paul, would be the Servant of that Grand Design.

There was both irony and pathos attendant on that late recourse of John Paul to the example of Pope Pius XII, a papal figure who had been denigrated as a hater of Jews—when, in reality, he had personally saved over 1.5 million Jews from the Nazi ovens—and as a medieval-minded prelate outshone and outclassed and consigned to the compost heap by the "glories" of the Second Vatican Council.

To find some palliative for the dilemma of his Church and the world at the beginning of the eighties, John Paul had to reach over the heads of the vacillating and permissive Pope Paul VI and of the strangely irresponsible "Good Pope John XXIII," back to the last Roman Pope who firmly maintained his hold and exercise of the precious Keys Peter had received and passed on to all his successors.

That Pius XII should be the point of recourse was ironic. That, after all the vaunted and falsely triumphalistic blowing of trumpets about "Vatican II," the Pope of 1981 had to reach back to Pius—this was papal pathos. John Paul II, self-proclaimed champion of "Vatican II," had to bypass all that "Vatican II" connoted.

Among this Pope's intimates, the very discreet word is that this is not and has not been the only earthly connection between Pius XII and Papa Wojtyla. Meanwhile, the subsequent private conversation between his would-be assassin, Mehmet Ali Agca, and himself in the Turkish hit man's Roman cell confirmed all of John Paul's surmises about the place assigned to him in the geopolitical plans of his enemies. The contents of that Confession-like conversation will one day come to light. For there was a pattern of destiny weaving the new venture of the Soviet Party-State and the geopolitical plans of Rome's enemies into the whole cloth of the Grand Design. And Mehmet Ali Agca, with his malign paymasters, was but a bit player in a drama just beginning then and now developing rapidly at the opening of the nineties.

33. In the Final Analysis

In the final analysis, John Paul II is a geopolitician-pope who spent the first part of his pontificate establishing himself and his Holy See as authentic players in the millennium endgame, which, during the same period of time, has become the "only game in town" and in this last decade of the second millennium will absorb the energies, the efforts and the vital interests of the great powers in our world.

He is a Pope who is waiting. That is the essence of his action. And in the meantime, he is busy in all the highways and byways along which the men of his age are moving helter-skelter. They have figured their present onrush as the last stages on the road to a new world order already in view, a true City of Man, built by Man's ingenuity for Man—this, finally, is the avowed goal they forecast for themselves, shimmering on the mountains of the future. John Paul is waiting, but not for that city to be built in order, as it were, to find out if there will be a place in it for him. He knows it will not be built, at least not as men have configured it.

He is waiting, rather, for an event that will fission human history, splitting the immediate past from the oncoming future. It will be an event on public view in the skies, in the oceans, and on the continental landmasses of this planet. It will particularly involve our human sun, which every day lights up and shines upon the valleys, the mountains and the plains of this earth for our eyes. But on the day of this event, it will not appear merely as the master star of our so-called solar system. Rather, it will be seen as the circumambient glory of the Woman whom the apostle describes as "clothed with the sun" and giving birth to "a child who will rule the nations with a scepter of iron."

Fissioning it will be as an event, in John Paul's conviction of faith, for it will immediately nullify all the grand designs the nations are now forming and will introduce the Grand Design of man's Maker. John Paul's waiting and watching time will then be over. His ministry as the Servant of the Grand Design will then begin. His strength of will to hold on and continue, and then, when the fissioning event occurs, to assume that ministry, derives directly from the Petrine authority entrusted solely to him the day he became Pope, in October of 1978. That authority, that strength, is symbolized in the Keys of Peter, washed in the human blood of the God-Man, Jesus Christ. John Paul is and will be the sole possessor of the Keys of this Blood on that day.

For John Paul, there is no personal glory attached to this ministry. There has already been hard labor and much hardship for him; and the future holds the promise of deep suffering and of trials by the fire of contempt and enmity. He accepted all that freely, it is true, and knowingly. Yet, no life of any past pope was more unitary in its thrust than Papa Wojtyla's has already been. By race, in character, through training, and vehicled on the happenings of his life, he appears to have been custom-fitted, as the phrase goes, for this unique role. Like his Master, for this he was born and came into the world.

. . .

Just a little over ten years ago, Karol Wojtyla walked onto the world stage as His Holiness, Pope John Paul II, and eyed each of his contentious globalist contemporaries from a geopolitical standpoint. For it was as a geopolitician he had been elected Pope. And he entered the ranks of world leaders as the Servant of a Grand Design he claimed was God's will for the society of nations.

Rife among his contemporaries, he found, was the persuasion of an imminent sea change in human affairs, and a competition to establish what many called a new world order on the back of that change. The society of nations, in fact, was starting to formulate a Grand Design of its own; but there were many competitors, each with his own ideas. One by one, he examined their proposals. He measured their behavior with the gauge of his Roman Catholic morality. He appraised their individual prospects for success. He knew, as they knew: There could be only one victor in that competition.

He had already decided to join that competition. For he also had his ambitions in the vital matter of a new world order. Those papal ambitions had been formed and nourished in him by the Polishness of his ancestors, and in the hard school of Stalinist Poland under the tutorship of the greatest cardinal in modern Church history, Stefan Wyszynski. The historical pacts of that Polishness provided him with a geopolitical outlook on all things human, crystallizing that geopolitical instinct in Mary, the Mother of Jesus. In his school, Wyszynski taught him the perennial lesson Christians have always had to learn: to seek no exclusive territory in the City of Man, but to establish the City of God within the very walls of that City of Man. Hence, John Paul's decision to enter into contention.

From that Polishness and from Wyszynski he also came to realize that in the growing crisis between the Gospel and the anti-Gospel, the resolution of the crisis would begin in the historic home area of the Slavs. Logically, then, he launched his entry onto the geopolitical stage from that area. He began in the Poland of 1979. For, in his conviction, Poland was the keystone in the area out of which would come the forces of change that all globalists were counting on.

Over a period of ten years, and among ninety-two nations across the length and breadth of five continents, he established himself as a world leader, one who was free of all disfiguring partisanship; as someone endowed with an all-embracing mind, a rare political savvy, a nimble diplomatic agility; and as the possessor of an international profile of perhaps the highest personal definition achieved by any one individual in recorded history. He became, on those terms, an acknowledged and accepted contender in the competition.

Everywhere and to everyone he presented himself as the Bishop of Rome and the only lawful successor to Simon Peter the Apostle. Everywhere he claimed the authority and the duty to advise, admonish and exhort all men, regardless of creed, race or ideology, on their duties to God and their due place in God's Grand Design for the society of nations. His own Catholics understood better than anyone that the Keys of Petrine authority he held were guaranteed by the sacrificial blood of Christ.

As Pope, as embodiment of the Holy See, he presided over a steadily declining and decadent Church organization. The organizational institution of his Roman Catholic Church was honeycombed with the usual ecclesiastical defects and human deficiencies: heresy, schism, sexual immorality, greed, pride, wholesale lapse in religious belief and practice, breakdown of Catholic family life, corruption in the major religious orders of men and women. The Church has always known these, and has its remedies. But the lethal factor slowly killing off the soul of Catholicism was something other.

The unifying element in that worldwide institutional organization—his own apostolic authority as Holder of the Keys Christ confided only to Simon Peter—that element had been bypassed, diluted, explained away, neglected or denied outright by a solid half to two thirds of the Church's bishops by the time Karol Wojtyla became Pope in 1978. By that time, the big, dirty secret in the Roman Church was that it now consisted of regional and local communities, all giving more or less guarded lip service to their unity with and under the Pope, but really hard at work creating a series of Catholic churches molded and fashioned on the various cultures and politics of the differing regions. John Paul's day as Pope was the day of the great illusion. Catholic unity was gone, but the facade of unity was still maintained.

Complicating his position as Pope and head of the Holy See was another and more sinister element: the presence of a committed anti-Church faction among his ecclesiastical officials throughout his Church, and its embodiment in his own Vatican household. In a true sense, John Paul is a pope at bay in his own Vatican. The lethal-minded opposition to him as Pope had been likened by one of his immediate predecessors to "the smoke of Satan invading the Sanctuary and the Altar."

Nevertheless, John Paul's concentration and febrile activity were directed almost exclusively to the geopolitical issue in human affairs. He did not undertake a serious and professional attempt to restore the former unity or to extirpate from the Church the known sources of its inner decadence. At one early moment, he even asserted that his Church structure could not be reformed. Anyway, his all-absorbing interest lay in the emergent geopolitical outline of the nations.

On this capital point, he did not—perhaps could not—imitate his beloved mentor, Stefan Cardinal Wyszynski.

Now, after those ten years of unremitting travel and labor, he was provided with a golden opportunity to reexamine the globalist scene. It was at the opening of the decade of the nineties—the last decade of Christianity's second millennium of existence and, by anybody's count, a watershed decade in world history. Specifically, this opportunity came during the first week of February 1990. Representatives and spokesmen for the most potent globalist currents—some 1,350 captains of industry, finance, politics, government, the media and telecommunications— trekked up 4,400 feet above sea level to the Swiss winter resort of Davos, the "Magic Mountain" of Thomas Mann's masterpiece, there to participate in the annual congress of the World Economic Forum.

This was no paltry meeting of theoreticians or academicians, or even of second-level personnel from finance, government and industry. The assembly included seventy government ministers—giants such as Helmut Kohl of West Germany, along with Foreign Minister Hans-Dietrich Genscher; Hans Modrow, prime minister of East Germany; President François Mitterrand of France; Austrian Chancellor Franz Vranitzky; Italy's Foreign Minister Gianni de Michelis; Japan's Deputy Foreign Minister Koji Watanabe, with Eishiro Saito; Singapore's Prime Minister Lee Kuan Yew; France's Philippe Gerard d'Estaing and Edward Heath of England—both former prime ministers; Jean-Pascal Delamuraz, president of the Swiss Confederation; Indonesia's Finance Minister Johannes Sumarlin; Mexico's President Carlos Salinas de Gortari; and a list of high officials from the European Economic Community—the European Commissions vice-president, Sir Leon Brittan; the European Commissioner for External Affairs, Frans Andriessen. This list was topped off by the active presence of an impressive Soviet delegation: Deputy Prime Minister Nikolai Ryzhkov, Deputy Prime Minister Leonid Abalkin, Nikolai Shmelev of the Soviet Academy of Sciences, along with six Soviet vice-ministers. They were flanked by Vitali Korotich, editor of the powerful *Oganyok*, and Oleg Bogomolov of the Soviet Academy of Sciences. Clara Hills and Michael Farren, U.S. Secretary and Under Secretary of

Commerce, were the two most active and vocal officials of the Bush administration who were present.

World banking and finance had its greats at Davos: the Federal Reserve's Wayne Angell; World Bank head Barber Conable; Otto Poel, finance minister of West Germany's Bundesbank; West Germany's Finance Minister Max Waigel and Economic Minister Helmut Haussmann; East Germany's Central Bank president, Horst Kaminsky, and Economic Minister Christa Luft; Daimler-Benz chairman Edward Reuter; Robert Jaunich of the multinational Jacobs Suchard; Rand Araskog, chairman and CEO of ITT Corporation; Robert Hormats, vice-chairman of Goldman-Sachs International; Henry Kaufmann, former vice-chairman of Salomon Inc.; Renault's vice-president for international affairs, Jean-Marc Lepeu; officials of GATT; and a slew of bankers, industrialists, finance and science experts from Europe, Asia and the United States.

Even more interesting and significant than this roster of truly important personages was the theme around which they gathered: Where were the emergent lines of the expected sea change leading them all? The question uppermost in all minds: How best could they facilitiate and pursue those lines? The concluding question, which nobody at Davos dared to examine too closely, much less answer: When the sea change was over and past, in what shape or form would the society of nations be?

For John Paul, the first and most unsurprising lesson to be learned at this globalist meeting in Davos was the confirmation of his initial analysis, ten years before.

His evaluation of globalists at that time had been starkly realistic. All of them claimed to be globalist, and, at least in general intent, they were that. But for a large proportion of them—Angelists, for example, as well as the historically frozen Eastern Orthodox, the Chinese, the Japanese, the Jewish community—their globalism was at most a regionalism, if not a provincialism, that they yearned to establish on a global scale or, at least, to place in a secure and dominant position.

A few others—New Agers and Mega-Religionists—had elaborated global outlooks but lacked any obvious means for establishing those outlooks globally within the concrete order of things. Their sustaining hope and strategy was that they might piggyback a ride to the ultimate success of their ambitions.

A restricted number of those globalists, Internationalists and Trans-nationalists, did have within their grasp the means—government and corporate institutions, organizational capability, financial sinews, social standing, drive and inspiration—with which to network the society of nations. But, as was clear again in Davos in 1990, the farthest that these were capable of reaching was what one member of the Davos congress called "global localization."

For both Transnationalist and Internationalist were products of Western capitalist democracy and therefore dependent on that democratic egalitarianism for the legroom they needed in order to succeed in their transnationalist/internationalist ventures. They could not lift their eyes beyond the towers of the sociopolitical institutions and structures inherent in democratic egalitarianism. Globalism in its purity—a geopolitical structure—requires that greater overview.

Nothing therefore had changed in John Paul's initial classification. The "movers and shakers" present at Davos were almost exclusively transnationalist or internationalist in bent of mind and intent of will and choice of means to their preferred goals. The other claimant globalists had not really mattered geopolitically then, nor did they ten years later.

In his classification of his contemporaries begun ten years before, John Paul could ultimately classify only one of them as a genuine geopolitician, a man with a mentality, an intention, an organization and an overview that were geopolitical. This was Mikhail Gorbachev. He arrived on the world stage a few years after John Paul, but immediately assumed top place among contemporary globalists in John Paul's critical assessment.

This initial choice of Gorbachev was confirmed by one predominant characteristic of all the multiple discussions and proceedings and conclusions of the Davos congress: Although Mikhail Gorbachev was not present in the congress halls, he was invisibly and effectively there throughout. For the meat and substance of all discussions, and the overhanging assumptions of the common mind manifest in all the delegates, had been conditioned—one could say predetermined—by the geopolitical strategy and tactics of that one man, the Soviet president.

This invisible domination of Transnationalists and Internationalists by Gorbachev in the Davos discussions was highlighted by the presence of the newly chosen leaders from the East European countries, the former Soviet satellites: East Germany's Prime Minister Hans Modrow; Czechoslovakia's President Vaclav Havel, Finance Minister Vaclav Klaus, Prime Minister Marian Calfa and Deputy Prime Minister Valtr Komarek; Yugoslavia's Prime Minister Ante Markovic; Bulgaria's Prime Minister Andrei Lukanov; Hungary's Deputy Prime Minister Peter Medgyessey;

and Poland's President Wojciech Jaruzelski. As a sign of a complete reversal of things past and a new orientation to the sea change, Solidarity's veteran Adam Michnik was present; he even had a very fruitful breakfast meeting with the man who kept him in jail for six years, Jaruzelski. "If we do not adapt the people who led the old system into the transformation we are making, we would have to fight them," Michnik commented.

These newly chosen officials represented a potential new market of 113.5 million people. Mikhail Gorbachev had made their presence here possible.

An even more evident influence of the Soviet president on the thought processes and methods of procedure in the minds of this company of capitalism's greats at Davos was clear in what the London *Economist* described as "the very strong sense at Davos of the centre of gravity of Europe moving east, of the European Community becoming the foundation of a larger and all-embracing East and West."

The very idea that the East—meaning at least some of the former Soviet satellites, if not the USSR itself—should be considered a candidate for membership in the contemplated Europe of 1992 + was once an unmentionable subject in Western political and financial circles. Mikhail Gorbachev brought that outcast idea back abruptly into the light of day in 1988 and 1989. "Europe from the Atlantic to the Urals" is the common home of East and West—this was his assertion. Now, less than a year later, the dyed-in-the-wool "Europeanizers" had accepted the idea and proposal. Why?

Quite simply because in the intervening time, the master player had shifted some geopolitical building blocks, rejected others, placed still others in a new configuration. He had "liberated" the Eastern European satellites, liquidated the Berlin Wall, allowed local Communist parties to declare themselves independent of Moscow's CP—even to change their name and stop calling themselves Communists. He had allowed free elections in the Soviet Union; put Fidel Castro and Daniel Ortega on notice that he was cutting the leash and they would be on their own, more or less; allowed massive Jewish emigration from the Soviet Union; and even tolerated the beginning of autonomy and independence in the three Baltic States.

Thus, from the beginning there glistened on the horizon of the minds united at Davos a near-future possibility of a powerful new bloc of twenty-five European nations (some 500 million people). This was regarded as the inner circle of the future structure of nations. "If the Soviets go ahead with reforms," stated West Germany's Economic Minister Haussmann, "we should guarantee they are part of the European space." That would be an enlargement of that inner circle—a second circle concentric with the first. Mr. Gorbachev, one can be sure, felt and still feels quite confident that he can satisfy the West's demand for reforms. Besides, he along with the other leaders now could see the outlines of their Grand Design for a new world order. And that was the object of John Paul's closest attention and scrutiny.

For John Paul, there were two facts about that Grand Design of the Western nations that indicated the watershed character of this decade of the nineties and the historic importance of the Davos congress in February 1990. First, it is carefully gridded on reality. Second, it will be largely the supreme achievement of Mikhail Gorbachev.

There is, first, the reasoned and humanly well-balanced grid on which its planners have laid out what appears to them to be the feasible evolution and realization of their Grand Design in successive concentric circles.

Despite some ineffectual objections from East Germany's Hans Modrow, and some doomsday reactions of a few U.S. investment bankers attending Davos, it was assumed by the vast majority that, come the end of 1990, the two Germanys would have achieved the political and economic unity of one Germany. Mikhail Gorbachev had made it known before Davos that he had no real objections to German reunification—"if pursued with care." German reunification was taken for granted. Monetary union might even precede that reunification; but united once again the two Germanys will be. And that Germany will be integrated into the European community.

Everyone admitted that in this European community, the leading socioeconomic force—the critical mass—will be a reunified Germany. It will be a "European Germany" in a strongly "Germany-colored" Europe. For no one could dispute the giant economic stature of Germany.

Nor could John Paul or Mikhail Gorbachev cavil at the sentiments of the Germans. "We are not an island," Helmut Kohl said, "we're not in a corner of Europe. We're in the heart of Europe." Wolfgang Berghoffer, mayor of East Germany's Dresden, went even further in his remarks. "We [East Germans] were standing on a moral threshold, and someone had to break out and say: This [unification] is the way." Furthermore, "the two German states have a responsibility for the process of democratization" in the East European nations.

But integration of a reunified Germany into Western Europe is only one major segment of the new circle. A second and necessary one is the integration of the former East European Soviet satellites into that Europe. They must become working parts of the new "European economic space," part and parcel of the "new European architecture." Their accession to that integration, all agreed, must be facilitated; they all need safety nets in order to palliate the effects of their economic reform from centralized to market economies.

Market economics must be introduced. The East Europeans must give Western creditors guarantees of effective use of foreign capital and create "real money" through monetary reform. Comecon, the former—and miserably failed—Soviet answer to the European Common Market of the West, must be reformed: in effect, abolished. Mikhail Gorbachev had acquiesced in this, too. The East Europeans must be helped to undertake this rapid economic reform of Central and Eastern Europe without destructive social upheaval. Investments and credits must flow to the Central and Eastern European states according as the new form of their association with Western Europe is worked out. Already in Davos, everyone knew that on March 19, the day after the East German election, there would be a three-week conference of European political and business leaders to discuss economic cooperation and technological exchange between Eastern and Western Europe. "Building the European space"—this was what they called it at Davos.

The human balance in the achievement of this first circle in the plan was enhanced by the apparent absence of the old competing ideologies that created the dreadful "East-West" coordinate John Paul deplored. "The old European notions of right and left just don't fit what is happening in our region now," Adam Michnik stated. "Not only is socialism dead, but the language of that kind of politics is dead. What remains are values, not notions of right and left."

For John Paul's consolation, too, there is the fact that his beloved Poland had become an economic and political laboratory, and the preconditional sine qua non for economic recovery in the East European nations, so that they could stabilize their political situation. No one saw the Red Army as destabilizing; only economic catastrophe could now destabilize. Poland had demonstrated that. That was Poland's present and near-future importance.

The second circle of the nations' Grand Design involved Mikhail Gorbachev's USSR. The USSR, in Gorbachev's pregnant phrase, "stands on the edge of the abyss" of economic death, wholesale anarchy and possibly the death throes of a horrible war. This did not need to happen, the USSR participants at Davos assured everyone. "We'll climb out of this abyss by ourselves, but we need help from you," Vitali Korotich asserted. But "nations can die of solitude." The USSR under Mikhail Gorbachev must find some bridge between the Soviet centralized economy and the normal market economy. That is the essence of Gorbachev's *perestroika*.

But that *perestroika* depended on the new political configuration of the USSR. There must be and will be a certain disaggregation of various parts—the Baltic States, certain Soviet republics. Even to Georgia and Armenia some form of autonomy within a Soviet/Russian federation will have to be conceded. All this would have to go hand in hand with *perestroika*. And the progress of *perestroika* depended on closer association with the European circle of Western and Eastern European nations. The ultimate aim must be a "Europe from the Atlantic to the Urals" and over to Vladivostok on the Sea of Japan. The greater European economic space!

Already, Gorbachev had taken his geopolitical dispositions. He had agreed to remove 400 medium-sized missiles from Soviet Asia; China and Japan could feel more secure. He had guaranteed a withdrawal of 200,000 troops from the Far East. He forces were, in bulk, out of Afghanistan; and he was pressuring the Vietnamese out of Cambodia. He was in the process of reducing his Pacific fleet by a third and withdrawing his forces based at Cam Ranh Bay, Vietnam, and all over Asia. The Southeast Asian "tigers," Thailand and Singapore, together with South Korea and Taiwan, could breathe easier. He was working on the West-hating North Koreans to desist from their threat to South Korea.

With all the pawns at his fingertips, he was free to move them, reconfigure them, relocate them, reconstruct them, in line with his geopolitical intentions and goals.

He still benefited from the diplomatic connivance of the United States. For Americans, as for the majority of Davos participants, Mikhail Gorbachev must be helped. There would be no strident clamor from the U.S. that the Soviets get out of the Baltic States immediately, or abandon Afghanistan's puppet government. Not even when the Soviets crudely violated the conditions of the already signed INF medium-range-missile treaty would there be any great brouhaha. At the Votkinsk missile plant, when the violations took place and American technicians moved in to verify the violation, the Soviet guards drew their sidearms and threatened the Americans. There would be violations and confrontations of this kind on March 9 and 10, 1990. But there would be no public denunciation of those gross violations.

"I don't want to do something that's going just to inadvertently affect the peaceful evolution of a self-determined Lithuania," President Bush said. If he violently protested the Votkinsk outrage, "would that contribute to the peaceful evolution, or is it better to take a couple of shots for being underemotional?"

The same attitude was manifest in Secretary of Defense Richard Cheney's announcement of troop withdrawals from South Korea. It was the U.S. effort to back up Gorbachev's "softening" of North Korea's bellicose behavior vis-à-vis South Korea. Secretary of State James Baker openly endorsed South Africa's ANC (African National Congress), and had accepted the PLO (Palestine Liberation Organization) of Yasir Arafat as fully representative of the Palestinians. Both the ANC and the PLO are clients of Mr. Gorbachev.

Thus, being able to count on the patience and forbearance of the U.S. administration, and being still the master of the fate of the Eastern and Central European states, Mikhail Gorbachev could push for the ultimate (and not very far-off) integration of his reconstructed USSR into the "greater European economic space." His geopolitical acumen was clear, and his goals were obvious.

At Davos, of course, the participants already contemplated the third circle of the Grand Design, the one that included North America. All agreed that while the decade of the nineties will be the "decade of Europe," the twenty-first century will see the emergence of the "Pacific Rim" as a potent member of the great grid. For the Asia/Pacific countries were already bent on capitalizing on the "new European economic space." Of course, as West Germany's Helmut Haussmann said, the European nations will compete with North America and "Pacific Rim" economies. But the new Europeans must integrate with the economic grid of the Asia/Pacific nations. In other words, the twenty-first century will not be a "European century" or a "Pacific Rim century." The term "geopolitical" was rather rarely used at Davos, but it is the only term adequate enough to cover that third circle (along with the first and second circles) of the Grand Design. The twenty-first century will be the century of the Geopolitical Earth.

At Davos, for the first time, a representative group of the society of nations did peek beyond the traditional limits of international politics and transnational globalism, just long enough to etch the bare outlines of a geopolitical world to come—the new world order, the world of the Grand Design of the nations. And as Helmut Kohl stated soundly, the new Europe must have as its goal the grand vision expressed by Thomas Jefferson: "Life, liberty, and the pursuit of happiness."

When the delegates to the Davos congress departed from that mountaintop, all were aware of the proximate steps that would be shortly taken toward their stated goal. After the March 19 talks on the economic and technological integration of Eastern and Western Europe, there would follow the all-important Conference of European Security at Helsinki in June. There the candidacy of the Eastern European states would be ratified, and the concrete lines worked out for the integration of the USSR into the "greater European space."

Sometime before or shortly after that June meeting—Mikhail Gorbachev had been given the option to choose the exact date according to his political convenience—there would be a summit meeting of Gorbachev and President George Bush. Among other things, both leaders hoped to ratify and sign two important treaties concerning strategic missiles and conventional forces.

In the autumn, the "two-plus-four" process would take place. The two Germanys would formally agree to be reunified, to become one political unit once again. Then they would sit down with the four original Allies —the United States, France, Britain and the USSR—who had separated them in 1945 and hammer out a peace treaty, thus setting post–World War II Germany on its feet again as a sovereign state. And thus the onetime political dwarf of Europe would assume a stature commensurate with the giant proportions of its economic sinews; and the socioeconomic heart of Europe would start beating again.

All would be in place and geared for the next few steps toward the projected Europe of 1992+, the "greater European space." As John Paul had sensed all along, so now he perceived the quasi-inevitability of all this; and along that road to this point, and down that road from the autumn of 1990 onward, he could see the emerging forms of his only two geopolitical contenders: the Western capitalists with their "greater European space" and the USSR of Mikhail Gorbachev.

Officially, of course, the "Europeans" and Gorbachev were seeking integration, both, supposedly, within the Grand Design devised by the capitalist West. In actual fact, and insofar as realism prevailed, nobody ever believed that Mikhail Gorbachev had ceased or would ever cease to cherish and promote his own Grand Design, the Leninist-Marxist plan. In that plan, the Leninist-Marxist ideal would finally prevail over Western capitalism. The real competition between that Leninist-Marxist design and Western capitalism would be a silent, almost underground thing until the crucial moment arrived for a naked and open declaration of intent on his part. Antonio Gramsci would be Gorbachev's patron saint during that first step. For Gorbachevism, as John Paul could see, was Gramscian tactics transposed onto the geopolitical plane by Gorbachev. In the slow evolution of the "greater European space," the fundamental supposition and theme of Marxization would be all-pervasive.

. . .

The third contender in the competition will be John Paul II himself. He will not compete, as the other two do, in the fields of economics and finance, nor for that matter in the field of raw politics. His weapons are those of the spirit, in the area of men's wills and minds. Even there, his actions will be confined to exhortation, to advisement, to discussion and argument. He will move in churchly surroundings and along the avenues of diplomacy. On the strength of his developed ties with government circles, he will be au courant with the twists and turns of all major events, will even be able to intervene by way of advice, of warning, of positive suggestion. For already he has entrée to the inner councils, and his influence is enormous, but he will remain within those limits.

For he is not the originator or the developer, but merely the Servant of the Grand Design he claims is of God. He has already put all nations on notice as to why their most elaborate plans for a "greater European space," for the "common European house from the Atlantic to the Urals," and for the totally "new world order" will not and cannot succeed.

The Grand Designs of his two fellow contenders are built, as he stated to the United Nations Assembly, on "certain premises which reduce the meaning of life to the many material and economic factors—the demands of production, the market, consumption, accumulation of riches, and to the demands of the growing bureaucracy with which an attempt is made to regulate these very processes." Within the scope of those designs, man is subordinated to one single conception and sphere of values, and "sensitivity to the spiritual dimension of human existence is diminished to a greater or a lesser extent."

Instead of the former sinful structures he excoriated in the "East-West" coordinate of tension, there will be, he maintains, a series of new sinful structures. They, like the sinful structures born along the hateful "East-West" and "North-South" coordinates of the past forty-five years, will be created out of greed, pride, power-seeking and an exclusivist reliance on man-based values, inspired and motivated by the nowadays commonly held persuasion that man can go it alone into the darkness of a quite unknown future.

For Europe in particular, John Paul has almost pronounced a lament.

Europe, in the millennium endgame, has an importance and a centrality out of all proportion to its present economic status, its natural resources and its military power. Economically, it is dwarfed by the

United States and Japan. It has manifestly fewer natural resources than the U.S.A., the USSR, Africa or Brazil. Militarily, it depends completely for its security on the United States. Yet no Transnationalist or Internationalist has hesitated to make Europe the starting site for digging the foundations and raising the initial structures of the intended world order.

What Europe has that makes it a focal point in modern history and development is its tradition. It was the cradle and the luxuriant garden of what is called Western civilization. From Europe came the philosophy, the law, the literature and the science that have gone into the makeup of our modernity. Europe's influence is still enormous in its potential. Besides all that, for over forty-five years Europe has been divided in two, the Eastern half housing an ideology and a sociopolitical system that constantly threatened the rest of the world.

Precisely because of Europe's powerful tradition and its sharing half its territory with the "evil empire" of the Soviets, it is the logical crucible in which the lethal contention between the West and the Soviets has to be resolved, if it is to be resolved peacefully. From the Soviet point of view, also, Europe had inversely the same function. If the victory of Leninist Marxism was to come, it had to come first in Europe, all of Europe, from the Atlantic to the Urals. But seventy-three years of Soviet effort failed in this respect. Just one half of Europe, bolstered economically and protected militarily by the United States, outstripped the USSR and by the eighties was beginning to flex muscles that prefigured the girth of a coming superpower. Gorbachev the geopolitician saw all that and made his known decisions. Few commentators have alluded to Gorbachev's chief nightmare: that he would wake up and find himself faced with a new superpower in the West, at his back Communist China and across the seas the U.S.A., all three far superior economically to the USSR and militarily strong enough to make war an act of suicide for Leninist Marxism. If nothing else, the leadership of world Marxism would pass to the Chinese—a sacrilegious violation of a deep-held Leninist-Marxist principle and belief.

But the rising Western Europe was the focal point. There he had to begin. Western Europe, Europe as a whole, really, became for him the building block it already had become for Western capitalism.

In these circumstances, John Paul's lament is understandable. Europe's origins, its rise to power, its contributions to civilization, its glories, all were marinated in Roman Christianity. In fact, Europe became Europe under the close tutelage of the Roman popes. Its tradition was thoroughly Christian. "Europe," Hilaire Belloc wrote, "was the Faith. The Faith was Europe." That tradition of profound moral, spiritual and intellectual excellence was built on the power and according to the laws of Europe's Christian origins.

Now that, in the Gorbachev era, Europe was going to be renewed and, at least in the intention of its renewers, to become one again, surely the tradition that made its great strength would be the basis of renewal, would come to the fore, reassert itself? It was a vain hope, if John Paul or anybody else ever really cherished it. There was absolutely no sign of such a renewal, no revival of the genuine tradition of Europe.

John Paul could not find any sign of such a renewal of Europe. If it had begun, it would have begun, he said, "in the hearts of individuals, above all in the hearts of Christians." But it has not begun there. Europe's "culture is in crisis," he continued, and "its common values are slipping into the oblivion of past history." Europe is no longer the Faith, and the Faith is no longer Europe. The current Grand Design for the new world order is going to be built, according to transnationalist and internationalist plans, within the first circle of the "greater European economic space."

It is concerned with the material conditions of man's life and habitat, and with the "human values" needed to ensure its pleasantness, exclusive of Christianity's moral law, deriving none of its motivations from Christian beliefs and incorporating none of the practices Christianity has always regarded as essential and obligatory for men and women.

Briefly and graphically put, nowhere in the intricate plans for the new or the renewed Europe is the God of Christians affirmed, adored and cultivated. The planned Europe is godless, just as, already, large segments of Europe's population over wide areas are godless and religionless.

Many observers surmised, on the election of the Polish Pope in 1978, that the first thing Papa Wojtyla would do—possibly the only or the chief thing—would be to attempt to revive Catholicism in Europe. Such would be expected from a Pole of Catholic Poland. They expected a crusade on John Paul's part. There was none. Instead he launched his papal career in a totally different direction. At first it was misunderstood, then it was explained away; now finally it has begun to dawn on all that this is a geopolitician-pope, that all along he has been walking on a geopolitical plane, with geopolitical goals in mind.

This is why John Paul never undertook a crusade for the re-Christianization of Europe, any more than he tackled a real reform of his decadent Church structure. In his analysis, the die had been cast in both instances. Europe was beyond the reach of re-Christianization by the normal means. Reform of his Church could not be achieved by the customary ecclesiastical means. He tackled neither.

What is difficult for many to understand is his reason for not tackling those problems head-on. For the reason is, as should be expected, geo-political. That is difficult enough for many of his contemporaries, for the simple reason that few people think geopolitically or understand such implications. An added layer of difficulty is added by the distinctly Polish and Roman Catholic character of John Paul's geopolitical outlook.

For nearly two centuries, Catholic Poles were denied all participation in national politics. The Polish nation did not exist; the Polish people existed as a function of other nations, and their fortunes were tied to geopolitical factors. Besides, as a nation, Poles had—literally for centuries—identified their national politics with the georeligion of Roman Catholicism, specifically tying Poland inextricably with two elements of that georeligion: the universalism of the Roman Pontiff, and the universal queenship of Mary, the Mother of Jesus. One emphatic trait in Wojtyla's mentor, Stefan Cardinal Wyszynski, was that universal Marianism. Mary figured as a georeligious and therefore as a geopolitical fact for Poles.

This was the meaning of the Pacts of Polishness, and more specifically of the vow of "national servitude to Mary" that Wyszynski organized in the sixties. This was reality for Poles, for Wyszynski, for Wojtyla—political reality, geopolitical reality.

And no wonder! Resourceless, held prisoner by the most organized totalitarian power the world has ever known, cast off and unaided by the only other political powers—in the West—that could have helped her, Poland had successfully confronted that Soviet power: confronted it, struggled with it and finally defeated it, becoming, as Adam Michnik said, the laboratory for the other Soviet satellite nations, none of which had been able to deal with Leninist Marxism except in total submission. The Polish mind, in fact, has had two major coordinates for a very long time: the national power of Russia and the geopolitical power Poles ascribe to Mary. For Poles, the fate and fortune of the world depended on which of these two powers prevailed.

Coming to the papacy, Wojtyla brought that peculiarly Polish orientation. As Pope, he found himself the recipient and consignee of the message of Fatima, which again—but with very specific details—was couched in terms that reproduced the double orientation. Commenting on the Davos mentality, the mentality of the Transnationalists and Internationalists as reflected at that congress of February 1990, John Paul said ironically, "At last, the powers of the West have oriented their minds and energies toward the East—if only now they acknowledged the role of Mary!" Mikhail Gorbachev had ensured that new orientation of Western minds by his geopolitical moves. The plans for the new world order of Western Europe and the United States depended on the evolution within the Soviet orbit.

But the essence and the important details of the Fatima message displayed that same orientation: World peace or world catastrophe was described in terms of Mary and of Russia. The reform or the mortal deficiency of the Roman Catholic institutional organization was also described by the Fatima message in terms of Mary and of Russia. In fact, the message emphasized, successful reform of that institutional organization as well as world peace depended absolutely on the Marian factor.

To John Paul's mind, this was tantamount to saying that reform of his Roman Catholic institution was impossible outside the Fatima framework of events—as was world peace.

Hence his lament for Europe: Europe in its classical extent, "from the Atlantic to the Urals." Quite clearly, in the minds of its most ardent exponents at Davos, the Europe of their dreams and projections is not a "Europe of the Faith." Their new Europe is summed up as the "greater economic space of Europe." Helmut Kohl at Davos defined its scope and purpose: to achieve what he called the Jeffersonian goal. But no one would ascribe to Thomas Jefferson and his early-American compatriots the interpretation Kohl and his fellow Europeanizers put on those fundamental words "life, liberty and the pursuit of happiness." Nor would those Europeanizers choose the Jeffersonian interpretation. For they have their own interpretation, and it has no tincture of Christianity in it, not even a breath of the vague deism and skeletal Christianity professed by the Virginia gentleman.

On the lips of moderns such as the builders of Europe, the pursuit of life is the pursuit of a greater GNP and all the goods it can purchase, liberty is the freedom to do what one wishes, happiness is a condition of living protected against poverty, in a clean environment, with adequate medical coverage and access to the labor-saving and pleasure-making products of an ever more sophisticated technology. In principle, Leninist Marxism promises all those things and much more. In practice, democratic capitalism delivers them to hundreds of thousands more people than Leninist Marxism ever did. In this, Leninist Marxism failed utterly.

Within some months, the populations of the Eastern European satellites voted with their feet in favor of those goals of life, liberty and the pursuit of happiness. No more and no less. To join in the development already far advanced in the Western half of Europe and in the United States. While Americans, even in the late twentieth century, are still trying to make up their minds as to whether "a nation so conceived and so dedicated can long endure," their contemporary Transnationalists and Internationalists have decided that the greatest sociopolitical venture ever devised by man—the new world order—can indeed long endure.

John Paul's summary judgment about the Grand Design of Transnationalists and Internationalists is perforce negative. The design cannot succeed, according to him, but must and will end in catastrophe. He has two main reasons for this judgment.

The design is built on the presumption that we ourselves are the authors of our destiny. Man is exalted. The God-Man is repudiated; and with him, the idea of man's fallenness is rejected. Evil is a matter of malfunctioning structures, not in any real way a basic inclination of man. Behind the godless and un-Christian design of Transnationalist and Internationalist there stands man as a Nietzschean figure, a Superman. If it were so, in the age of Superman there would no longer be any reason to believe in Christian morality, individual liberty, and equality before the law. Attachment to civil rights, to the dignity and welfare and political worth of the individual, would become illusory and pointless.

Superman replaces the God-Man, Jesus Christ, Superman as man-god. Culture loses its very heart, which is religion, with its worship of the divine and its observance of God's laws against human-originated evil. Thereby politics as a function of culture loses its equilibrium because it has lost the source of its human decency. G. K. Chesterton was correct when he asserted that when man ceases to believe in God, most likely man will believe in nothing.

John Paul's second reason—the more cogent one for him, personally —is drawn from the Fatima message. That message predicts that a catastrophic change will shortly shatter any plans or designs that men may have established. This is the era of the Fatima "or." Men have abandoned religion. God does not intend to let human affairs go on for a long time in that fashion, because this is his world—he created it for his glory, he made it possible for all men to attain the Heaven of his glory, by sending his only son, Jesus Christ, to expiate the punishment due men for their sins.

This is why John Paul is waiting. God must first intervene, before John Paul's major ministry to all men can start.

In Papa Wojtyla's outlook, therefore, the Grand Design of which he is the nominated Servant is the design of divine providence to recall men to the values that derive only from belief, from religion and from divine revelation. His is an unpleasant message and, for the moment, a thankless job. He has to warn his contemporaries of his conviction that human catastrophe on a world scale—according to his information—is impending.

He has to admit that he, like everybody else, is in the dark as to when it will occur, although he does know some of the horrific details of that worldwide catastrophe. He knows also that it will not come without prior warning, but that only those already renewed in heart—and that would probably be a minority—will recognize it for what it is and make preparations for the tribulations that will follow.

He also knows that these will start unexpectedly and be accompanied by overall confusion of minds and darkening of human understanding, and will result in the shattering of any plans for a "greater European space" and the mega-market plans for "greater Europe" and the "Pacific Rim." It will be the death and entombment of Leninist Marxism and the effective liquidation of the long—centuries-long—war that the forces of this civilized world have waged against the Church Christ founded and the religious belief of that Church. The battle between the Gospel and the anti-Gospel will be over. The other two major contenders in the millennium endgame will be eliminated.

From all the indications he has, John Paul expects the beginning of this Fatima event to start where the millennium endgame started: in the area of Central and Eastern Europe. This aspect of Papa Wojtyla's mind is steeped in a rich symbolism that has escaped many observers: The advent of a Slavic Pope holding the Petrine Keys of authority. The fated role of Poland, Mary's dedicated domain and Romanist in its vitals, as the point man in the shattering of the Iron Curtain. The emergence of Mikhail Gorbachev from the murderous Gulag of the Leninist-Marxist Party-State—even the apparently coincidental presence of that birthmark on the Soviet president's forehead, so reminiscent of the Mark of the fratricidal Cain.

All that comes by way of suffering, of hardship, of severe dislocation and destruction in the affairs of men will be but preparation for the plan of divine providence: preparation and the negative side of the Grand Design. About that Grand Design in its positive lines, John Paul knows only that his function will be as its Servant; that his years of preparation as one of the world's leaders, as a voice and a figure that have received international recognition, will culminate in the apostolic ministrations he must perform in a very different world from the world of the millennium endgame, and among nations that no longer rely on themselves to build on earth a City of Man.

Coda:
The Protocol
of Salvation

34. The Judas Complex

Judas Iscariot will be eternally known as the man who betrayed Jesus Christ to his enemies. In at least twenty languages, his name is a synonym for "traitor." To think of Judas, or to mention his name, is to evoke the image of the whole-cloth traitor. The traitor prototype. Yet there is no good reason for supposing that when he was originally called by Jesus to be one of his own special intimates—one of the foundational Apostles —Judas was already up to treachery; that he was any less enthusiastically devoted to Jesus, any less worthy of that call, or any less determined to follow Jesus to the end than the eleven others chosen by Jesus at the same time he chose Judas. Nor can we suppose that Jesus withheld from Judas any of the special divine graces he conferred on the others.

Similarly today, when obviously there has been gross betrayal of the Roman Catholic Church on an alarmingly wide scale by bishops, prelates and priests of the Church, there is no good reason for supposing that any particular bishops, prelates, officials or priests guilty of that betrayal started off with any less good intentions or less devotion to the Church than those who have not betrayed their calling. Neither can we suppose that those now engaged in betrayal have been denied the divine graces that are summarily necessary for the worthy discharge of ecclesiastical and ecclesial duties.

Judas must have shared completely in the charism of an Apostle, a chief pastor, thus prefiguring—as did all Twelve Apostles—what we call today the bishops of the Church. Living with Jesus day and night, traveling with him, hearing his words and seeing his actions, collaborating with him in his work, sent out by him with a mandate to preach the kingdom of God, to cure the sick, to exorcise demons, to exercise his authority, to rely on spiritual weapons and supernatural means, Judas cannot have started off as more worldly, more cowardly, less enlightened than the other members of that special group.

Yet Judas, and Judas only, out of that select group schooled by Jesus himself, shattered the group's unity. He alone did betray Jesus. He alone set himself up as antihero among those twelve men and the few hundred other disciples and followers who, with Jesus, were living participants in the tense drama of salvation in which Jesus as hero played out God's eternal plan from his birth to the climax in crucifixion—for which Judas was directly responsible—and resurrection, which, in the end, Judas decided not to accept and share. But Judas was no "breakaway." He did not intend to shatter the unity of the group, or to ruin Jesus and the Twelve. Judas was something classical: the antihero who insisted on implementing his own plan for Jesus and the others (in which, of course, he would play a major and self-fulfilling part). He could, he thought, reconcile Jesus and his enemies. He could, by decent compromise, ensure Jesus' success in the world by compacting with the world's leaders.

The same remarks, with due regard to Church development, can be applied to bishops and prelates and their assistant officials in the Church today: They are called to live intimately with Jesus through the fullness of the priesthood that is theirs by their episcopal consecration, to exercise his spiritual authority; and, relying on the power and grace of his Spirit, to be pastors of souls, curing, exorcising, preaching, reconciling; to follow the plan of salvation that Jesus clearly indicated when he established Peter as head of his Church and as his personal representative in the "one, true fold" in which the actual salvation of individual souls can be effectively secured.

But, in a way eerily reminiscent of the error Judas committed, some bishops and prelates and their assistant officials have set themselves up as anti-Church within the Church. They do not want to leave the Church. They are not intending "breakaways." They do not intend to shatter the unity of the Church. They do not intend to obliterate the Church, but just to make it over to their own plan; it is, by now, trivial in their minds that their plan is irreconcilable with God's plan as revealed through the present-day successor of Peter and his teaching authority. For after the manner of Judas' own spiritual myopia, they no longer believe in the Catholic doctrine of the papal magisterium, no more than the Traitor believed any longer that Jesus was divine. They are convinced that they can reconcile that Church and its enemies by "decent compromise," that they really understand what is going on, and that they can ensure the success of Christ's Church by compacting with this world's leaders. But in their devoted creation of the anti-Church within the Church—from the Vatican chancery down to the level of parish life —they have successfully shattered the unity of the Church, done away, in fact, with the once flourishing union of bishops with the Roman Pontiff, and gravely debilitated the entire Roman Catholic institutional organization.

The enormity of this error and its almost boring and repetitive similarity with the error of Judas—in other words, the Judas syndrome of modern Churchmen—becomes very apparent when you examine the Traitor's behavior. Judas did finally betray Jesus. But it is important to note the "good" intentions with which he started down the crooked road that ended in the Field of Blood, where he died suffocated by the noose around his neck and cruelly killed by the evisceration of his belly.

The personal outline of Judas in the pages of the New Testament is dim on all points—except for his awful treachery of the beloved Lord. Understandably, the writers would not, could not, remark anything good or even interesting about Judas, except his treachery. In the light of Jesus' resurrection and the subsequent descent of the Holy Spirit on the remaining Apostles, all that mattered in the eyes of the New Testament writers was that gross treachery, and all they could express for the Traitor was utter contempt and abhorrence. There is perhaps no parallel in the New Testament record to that total and merciless condemnation of Judas. "He got the same offer from Jesus as we all did": Peter must have spat out those syllables with a grating harshness when addressing all Jesus' followers in the Upper Room at Pentecost. "He was one of us. Yet he guided the mob who laid hands on Jesus. And now he has got what he asked for—a field spattered with his own entrails, and his own special torment in Hellfire." There is no hint of forgiveness, no trace even of regret. Perhaps this was because Judas had committed the one sin Jesus said was unpardonable, the sin against the Holy Spirit.

This total rejection of Judas has inclined Christians to see him in a bad light from the beginning of his association with Jesus, as a kind of infiltrator admitted by Jesus to the intimacy of his special people, because, so to speak, somebody had to betray the Lord. But in all logic, this cannot have been the true story of Judas. From a divine and a human point of view, Judas must have appeared initially as one of the more promising candidates for leadership in Christ's future Church. Judas was the only public official of Jesus' group, in a manner of speaking. He was more trusted than the others; to him Jesus confided the keeping and the management of whatever funds were collected by the group for "out-of-pocket" expenses and, therefore, any and all "business" dealings during their travels.

The facts of life were that a group of hale and hearty young men in their prime, who were not regularly employed gainfully and who were continually on the move, had to have a common "purse" for food, for lodging, for road tolls, for taxation, for incidentals: clothes, charitable contributions, support of their families, repair and maintenance of their fishing equipment. Most of them were fishermen, who retained their equipment right through their association with Jesus until well after the Resurrection.

There is no exaggeration in describing Judas as the only official among the group. In the eyes of the other Apostles also, Judas was considered to hold high office. For they may have appeared as a ragtag group to some of their contemporaries, but we today know that they were destined to found an organization that would absorb the whole known world and create a new thousand-year civilization.

We cannot reasonably doubt that Judas started off with great enthusiasm and devotion to Jesus, and with full trust and confidence in Jesus' ultimate success. We know that, for the other companions, until well after the Resurrection, success meant a political restoration of the Kingdom of Israel, with the Apostles occupying twelve thrones of jurisdiction and judgment. Judas cannot have thought differently or hoped for less. He and they even squabbled about which of them would be the greatest in authority. Two of them had their mothers buttonhole Jesus and try to secure them two prime positions around the kingly throne they figured Jesus would occupy when he ruled Israel and the world. For of course, Jesus would eventually be King.

Here is where disillusionment set in for Judas. More in touch with practical affairs than the others, more alive to the politics of his land, he could only grow in disillusionment each time Jesus repudiated attempt after attempt to crown him leader and king. There were more than two such occasions; each time, Jesus sounded those very unworldly sentiments of suffering and death. Further, each time the intermittent clashes with the Hierosolymite authorities dug a deeper gap between Jesus and the political ascendancy of Israel—now concentrated in the Jerusalem council of state, the Sanhedrin—the sense of disillusionment in Judas would grow that much deeper.

Remark that at any given moment Judas could have left Jesus and "walked with him no more," as many indeed did. But no, Judas wanted to stay. He believed, after his own fashion, in Jesus and his group and their ideals. He just wanted Jesus and the others to conform to political and social realities, to follow his plan, not whatever plans Jesus may have had. We can be sure that the last thing he thought of doing was quitting the group.

But he had formed his own ideas about the sensible way Jesus should go about seizing supreme power. Now, in the heady atmosphere of collaboration with the authorities, he saw his way opening out to vistas of greatness, a chief position in the future Kingdom of Israel, once the Romans were driven out and the local Jewish powers-that-were, with the help of Jesus, utterly defeated the hated Romans. Even when Jesus told him plainly and frankly during that last Passover meal that, yes, he knew it was Judas who would betray him, that made no dent in Judas' resolution. He probably did not understand the use of the word "betray" by Jesus. Many times in the past, he had "betrayed" Jesus in the sense that he had done the opposite of Jesus' express will, and things had always turned out just fine. That compromise plan still seemed the best to Judas. The ultimate blindness closed in on his soul like a steel trapdoor. "Satan," the Gospel says, "entered his heart." Judas was now under the control of the one personality who stood to lose most by any success Jesus might have. And Judas could, without any scruple and always fully persuaded that his plan was fine, go and find the Temple authorities, his "high-level contacts," and pinpoint the place where Jesus would be at a certain hour, and identify Jesus to the armed force sent out to bring him in, bound and manacled like a hunted animal.

Every single event that followed on Judas' decision was made possible and evoked directly by that act of malfeasance on the part of Judas, the chosen Apostle of Jesus and his trusted official. All was Judas' responsibility. The terrible agony in Gethsemane; the violence done to Jesus at his arrest and at his mock trials during the night; the hours of imprisonment and abuse by Roman soldiers; the crowning with thorns and the scornful mocking of his person, which we can be sure violated his dignity in every possible way; his arraignment before Pilate and Herod; his scourging; the painful, agonizing path to Golgotha; the searing pain of crucifixion, followed by three hours of death agony, hours divided into weakening efforts not to suffocate, and not to be overwhelmed by the cruelty of the nails pinning his wrists and feet to the cross. All this as well as the final result: the death of Jesus.

All of it, evil and sacrilegious beyond human telling, was a direct consequence of that Judas complex. While the ultimate result of Judas' choice was gross betrayal and treachery, his specific sin was compromise —what really seemed to him a wise and prudent compromise given the otherwise impossible situation into which Jesus had boxed himself and his loyal group by his violent attacks on the status quo and by his refusal to meet Jewish authorities halfway in order to satisfy the needs and questions of men who, after all, were in a position to know what they were talking about when it came to the national cause and the continued existence of Judaism. They were, after all, the Keepers of the Flame.

For Jesus and his doctrine must have been classified in Judas' practical and worldly-wise mind as utterly unsuitable to the social consensus and political mentality of his day. Actually, it was both unsuitable and unacceptable. Unacceptable to the point of provoking its adversaries to a political assassination. It was, after all, a matter of state security and national survival.

This, then, is the essence of the Judas complex: the compromise of one's basic principles in order to fit in with the modes of thought and behavior that the world regards as necessary for its vital interests. The principle of that special group was Jesus—his physical existence, his authority, his teaching. Judas had been persuaded by his tempters and corrupters that all that Jesus stood for had to be modified by a decent and sensible compromise.

This provides us with a sure norm by which we can identify the members of the anti-Church now sitting foursquare within the Roman Catholic institutional organization. While the last twenty years of that organization's history is littered with compromises and hundreds of misfeasances by Churchmen, we must seek out and identify the major compromises that can be accurately described as acts of genuine malfeasance in high ecclesiastical and ecclesial office.

An act of malfeasance has been aptly described as "the doing by a public official, under color of authority of his office, of something that is unwarranted, that he contracted not to do, and that is legally unjustified and positively wrongful or contrary to law," according to Webster.

Both "misfeasance" and "malfeasance" are used to describe abuse of office. The appreciable difference between the terms seems to lie in the extent and effect of the abuse. Misfeasance seems to be particular and limited. For instance, using the authority of one's office in obtaining incidental pleasures. Malfeasance subverts the office itself, converting it into something totally different from and contrary to what the office was meant to be.

A survey of the past twenty-five years of Roman Catholic history leads one to the conclusion that the greatest single act of malfeasance in high ecclesiastical and ecclesial office has been the tolerance and propagation of confusion about key beliefs among the Catholic rank and file, this tolerated confusion being a direct result of a tolerated dissidence by Catholic theologians and bishops concerning those same key beliefs. For to tolerate confusion is to propagate confusion. A primary and fundamental duty of every ecclesiastical office and the ecclesial responsibility attached to all offices in the Church comprise the clear, unmistakable teaching and enforcement of the basic rules and fundamental beliefs the Church holds and declares to be necessary for eternal salvation. There can be no compromise on both points: teaching and enforcement. If Roman Catholics have any rights in the Church, they have a primary right to receive such unequivocal teaching and to be the subjects of such forthright and unhesitating enforcement.

Furthermore, it is relatively easy to identify the four key areas in which ecclesiastics and ecclesial members have tolerated and propagated the maleficent confusion that affects Roman Catholics today. These areas are: the Eucharist, the oneness and trueness of the Roman Catholic Church, the Petrine Office of the Bishop of Rome, and the morality of human reproductive activity.

When you talk of the Eucharist, you are talking about the Roman Mass, which has been and still is the central act of worship for Roman Catholics. The value of the Mass for Catholics is twofold. A Mass, in Catholic belief, presents the real live Sacrifice of the body and the blood and physical life of Jesus consummated on Calvary. It is not a commemoration of that sacrifice, nor a reenactment after the fashion of a historical drama, nor a symbolic performance.

Therein lies the mystery of the Mass. When a Roman Mass is said to be valid, it is believed to achieve that mysterious presentation of Christ's sacrifice of his bodily life. It has validity; and Roman Catholics can then literally adore their Savior under the physical appearance of bread and wine.

In the Roman Church, this mystery was celebrated in the Roman Mass, a liturgical ceremony that attained its traditional form in the early Middle Ages, was confirmed as perpetual law in 1570 by Pope Pius V, and was recognized again by the Council of Trent in that same century. It remained the same in all details, except for the addition or substitution of single prayers and invocations, until the mid-1960s.

At that time, a momentous change sanctioned by Vatican officials took place: That traditional Roman Mass was removed, and a new form, known as the Novus Ordo or the Conciliar Mass, was substituted for it by order of Pope Paul VI, on March 26, 1970. By 1974, this Novus Ordo, in vernacular translations, had been spread by decree all over the Church Universal. The traditional Roman Mass was never forbidden, never abrogated, and never declared illegal, by any competent Roman official. But, all over the Church, there was an active and sometimes a violent policy of suppressing any trace of the traditional Roman Mass.

For a number of years, there was an official pretense on the part of

Roman authorities and many bishops that this Novus Ordo merely implemented the recommendations of the Second Vatican Council. But nowadays that pretense has fallen away. It now is undeniable that the Novus Ordo in its various forms violates the explicit precepts of the Vatican Council concerning the changes in the Roman Mass.

Such violation and departure from the explicit will of the Council would be bad enough. What has done untold damage to the Eucharist, belief and doctrine, is the fact that, without some special care, not indicated in the official text and instructions of the Novus Ordo, the ceremony of the Novus Ordo does not ensure its validity: i.e., that it achieves that presentation of Christ's Sacrifice on Calvary. As a general fact, nowadays throughout the Church such special care is rare. Consequently, the celebration of the Novus Ordo does not always result in a valid Mass. Indirectly, this result can be seen mirrored in the overall lack of sacramental reverence for the Eucharist among the clergy and the laity. For the Novus Ordo, which aims to be a communal spectacle composed of communal actions, has removed all due emphasis on the presence of the Sacrifice to the presence of the congregation praying and gesturing. The Roman Mass was a "vertical" act of worship. The Novus Ordo is strictly "horizontal."

Of course, this attempted destruction of the traditional Roman Mass and the inadequate formulas of the Novus Ordo were part and parcel of the hijacking of the Second Vatican Council by the anti-Church members, who have successfully used that Council's ambiguous and general statements to devise a method of dismantling the specifically Roman Catholic character both of the Mass and of other basic Roman Catholic elements—beliefs and practices. In the wake of their success with the Novus Ordo and the consequent diminishment of the priest as official celebrant in the presentation of Christ's Sacrifice on Calvary, the anti-Church members are logically proposing the priestly ordination of women, the use of altar girls for altar boys, of Eucharistic ministers, male and female, instead of the priest. It is a single integral plan to reduce specifically Roman Catholic worship and practice to such a low common denominator that any non-Catholic can participate and not feel in an alien atmosphere.

But the total result has been confusion. There thus has arisen among the clergy and the people various groups that refuse the Novus Ordo and insist on maintaining the traditional Roman Mass. At first, the anti-Church thought that these would fade away with time. But time has only increased their importance, their preponderance and their number. Many, many more millions of Roman Catholics than Catholic officialdom will admit are in severe doubt as to the religious value of the Novus Ordo. Roman authorities themselves under the anti-Church influence did their best, by ecclesiastical punishment, by ostracism, even by outright lies, to do away completely with the traditional Roman rite. "The traditional Roman Mass has been forbidden by the Pope"; "The Roman Mass has been officially abolished and abrogated"; "The Novus Ordo is the very same as the traditional Latin Mass, only modernized"—such were and still are some of the deceptions and lies used.

None of all this resolved anything. In the meantime, attendance at the Novus Ordo liturgy dropped drastically throughout the Church. The local habits of the clergy and of the bishops and the people made it quite clear to Rome that belief in the Real Presence of Jesus at the Novus Ordo celebration was strictly on the wane.

The general confusion grows only greater with every year, because Roman authorities now give the traditional Mass their grudging approval and because the vagaries of the Novus Ordo in its various vernacular forms throughout the world are such—ludicrous, unseemly, naturalistic, even sacrilegious—that a tiny note of alarm is sounding in the Church.

But now the anti-Church animosity—really a species of hatred—for the traditional Roman Mass is so great, while the obstinacy of the traditionalists has become a proven fact of Roman Catholic life, that only the supreme teaching authority of the Church as embodied personally in the Holy Father as head of the Church can, in a solemn, infallible statement, set the clergy and the people aright. Such a statement is lacking. Meanwhile, the members of the Church continue fractionating and dividing and doubting and deserting the practice of a sacramental life.

The present Holy Father has done a little in this regard. He did grant an indult that facilitated the introduction of the traditional Roman rite into the dioceses of his Church. But the opposition to his recommendations—that is all the Pope made, recommendations—successfully stifled all the traditionalist attempts to take advantage of this perfectly legal means of reintroducing the lost traditional Roman rite. His Holiness is quite aware of what has happened to the sacramental life of the Church. In an extraordinary passage in a letter he wrote in 1980 to all the bishops of his Church, he apologized and asked forgiveness from God, in the name of all his bishops, "for everything which, for whatever reason, impatience or negligence, and also through the at times partial, one-sided and erroneous application of the directives of the Second Vatican Council, may have caused scandal and disturbance concerning the interpretation of the doctrine and the veneration of this great Sacrament" of the Eucharist.

This is the nearest John Paul II has dared to approach a recognition of the gross damage done to the sacramental life of his Church and of the anti-Church's destruction of the Roman Catholic Mass.

The second vital Roman Catholic belief about which confusion reigns and is daily nourished concerns the oneness and trueness of the Roman Catholic Church. The essence of the confusion is this: Since the Second Vatican Council, and because of one of its official documents concerning religious liberty, the persuasion is now commonly abroad among bishops, theologians, priests and laity that membership in the Roman Catholic Church is not essential for salvation; that there are many equivalent roads to Heaven—non-Catholic and non-Christian; that everyone must be granted a moral and religious equivalence as regards the attainment of eternal salvation; even, according to some, that one can be saved without benefiting from the sacrifice that Jesus made of his life. Jesus, in other words, is (for some Roman Catholics) one Savior, and there are other saviors—Buddha, Mohammed, Abraham, even Martin Luther King. That the Roman Catholic Church is the one and the true Church in which and through which exclusively eternal salvation can be achieved—this is now in severe doubt and wrapped in confusion.

There has thus grown up, due to the febrile attention of the anti-Church, an entire panoply of ecumenical "gatherings," "contracts," "celebrations," "liturgies," "documents of agreement," the keynote idea of these being that "we are all sons of God" and "brothers in the human family," so we all set out on "our common pilgrimage," nobody claiming to be solely right (or the one, true Church of Christ) and nobody declared to be wrong.

By an obvious misreading of yet another text from the Second Vatican Council documents, it is declared that the "people of God" includes the Roman Catholic Church but also many, many others who are not and will never be (because they don't want to be) Roman Catholic. In most of the dioceses of Europe, North America and Australia, for instance, any attitude other than the new "ecumenical" attitude will effectively close all doors.

The confusion among the Catholic faithful is enormous under these circumstances. Because the Vatican Council document on religious liberty condemns any attempt to force anybody to adopt a religious belief against his will, it is assumed and understood thereby that any human being has an innate right to choose and believe in a false religion. This is tantamount to saying that anyone has an innate right to be religiously in error. This is not only false as a religious proposition; it is a contradiction in terms for anyone who is supposed to believe in the one, true Church of Christ. For if the proposition is true, then no religion is right, no religion is wrong; in fact, there is no way that a human being can arrive at religious truth.

Nothing has contributed more effectively to the decadence of Roman Catholic religious unity and identity than the pervasiveness of the idea that suddenly, as of the mid-1960s, Roman Catholics found out that they as Catholics belong to "the general mainstream of religious feeling and belief among all men and women." Likewise, nothing has contributed more effectively to the confusion of the Catholic rank and file. For when they see and hear their prelates and their priests acting and talking as if there were no specifically Catholic uniqueness and truth, immediately their logical instinct is to regard the moral laws of the Church and its dogmas as optional. ("If others are not required to believe those dogmas and obey those laws, why should I?") There thus arise the "cafeteria" Catholics, with a pick-and-choose attitude to Roman Catholic dogma and moral law. They insist on remaining in the Church and calling themselves Catholic, but stoutly maintain that they need not believe this, that or the other dogma, need not observe this, that or the other moral law. Their numbers teem in the Catholic Church today and include single individuals and organized groups.

The confusion in this matter continues unabated. Most of the initiatives for the new "ecumenism" and most of the theorizing about it and the false idea of religious liberty have come from Roman Catholic prelates and their theologians, and from minor diocesan officials who engage in an ecumenical network organized at the diocesan level and implemented at the parish level.

There has not yet been a very clear and unmistakable statement by bishops, followed by faithful enforcement of the fundamental Roman Catholic belief that this Church is the one and the true Church founded by Christ, to which all men and women must belong if they are to be saved from eternal damnation. Nor have the Roman authorities made any ostensible effort to rectify this grave deficiency in the bishops of the Church.

The relationship of bishops to the Bishop of Rome as Pope and as personal Vicar of Christ is the third heading under which confusion has been allowed to develop. Catholic dogma says that each bishop is the legitimate chief pastor of his diocese, provided he be in communion with

the Pope: that is to say, that he hold the same beliefs and moral laws as
the Pope and that he be subject to the jurisdiction of the Pope. The
Pope, as universal pastor of the Church, is also pastor of each diocese in
his own right. All the bishops of the Church, about four thousand in
actual number, together with the Pope, constitute the college or assembly of apostles, and they can legislate with infallibility for the Church
Universal as members of that college headed by the Pope.

But Roman Catholic doctrine holds that the Pope by himself can do
all that this college can do doctrinally and in jurisdiction and in moral
discipline; the college of bishops can do nothing without the collaboration and headship of the Pope.

There are, therefore, two distinct relationships: one between each
bishop individually and the Pope; another between the Pope and all the
bishops as a body. And this relationship is called the collegiality of the
Church.

Again by dint of skillful but incorrect reading of texts from the documents of the Second Vatican Council, the persuasion has been nourished by prelates and theologians that a second form of collegiality exists
between the bishops of one country. Thus, it is claimed that the national
conference of Catholic bishops in a country can legislate in doctrine and
discipline quite apart from what the Pope may think, approve or disap-
prove, and that they can do this infallibly: that is, they will not err in
what they propose for belief and moral practice.

No national conference of bishops has as yet had the courage or the
gall to come out with a blanket statement to that effect. But already,
Catholics have noted over a twenty-year period how their national conferences of bishops have legislated both doctrine and discipline in direct
contradiction to the known teaching of the Pope. Needless to say, more
than one theologian has proposed theological arguments to bolster this
heretical independence of bishops' conferences.

The idea of the "national Catholic Church"—American, Canadian,
French, Brazilian, and so on—has been born. It is not merely an idea; it
is the guiding principle of many diocesan activities that have the blessing
of the bishops. Bishops and their activist clerics and layfolk are thinking
along these lines; they have not as yet had the courage to come out
frankly and in bold terms. But we must be careful not to mistake the
purpose of such a slowly emerging "national Church." The ultimate goal
in the minds of those who nourish the idea and promote it actively and
concretely is not merely to solve local problems—for instance, of American priests who want to get married or of homosexuals who demand
homosexual rights or of Latin American Marxists and their North Amer-

ican imitators who claim the right to espouse Marxism and still be called Roman Catholics. In the minds of the purveyors of this new collegiality among the bishops of any one national conference of bishops, there stands as ultimate objective the liquidation of absolute papal control over the dogma and moral discipline in the Church.

In their minds, the truly Catholic Church, no longer called Roman, would consist of a gaggle of "national Churches," bound together by sentiment and association, always reverential toward the so-called "venerable See of Rome and their brother Bishop" but free in their autonomy to be "mature brother bishops" of the "venerable Bishop of Rome," and thus be free to arrange the "national" affairs of their Church merely according to the "local culture."

Obviously, such a liquidation of the Petrine Office could only be effected with the consent of its occupant; and the easiest way in which that could happen would be the election to the throne of Peter of a papal candidate who, prior to his election, is known as favoring such a liquidation. Domination of a papal Conclave by that sort of mind would be a prerequisite for success in this epoch-making venture. For epoch-making it is: to transform the almost two-thousand-year-old tradition of the Roman Catholic Church by ending officially and once and for all the papal primacy such as it has evolved over the centuries and has been asserted by every ecumenical council of the Church, including the Second Vatican Council.

The failure of the Roman authorities to call down national conferences of bishops on matters in which those conferences have transgressed the papal will and decision: This is what has slowly but surely commenced to ingrain the idea in local Catholic communities that their national conference of bishops indeed does have the last word in dogma and moral discipline. But confusion arises because there are sufficient voices protesting that the will and authority of the Pope are supreme. Again, the lack of enforcement on Rome's part is only fomenting the confusion.

The fourth vital issue is a complex one and concerns the reproductive faculties of men and women. The statistics here are horrendous. Under the chief headings of contraception, abortion, homosexuality, premarital sexuality and the modern techniques dealing with reproduction, reliable figures assure us that a great majority of Catholics simply do not accept and a greater majority entertain severe doubts about the traditional Roman Catholic teaching on these five issues. Some particular figures—

say, those for priests who directly counsel their flock in an un-Catholic sense—are appalling. The confusion, where there is confusion, arises because the Pope insists on the traditional laws concerning these issues, whereas in every community of Catholics there are the theologians, priests and layfolk teachers in Catholic institutions who flatly contradict that traditional teaching. Proper enforcement on the part of the local bishops and of Rome would strip any such theologian or teacher of his right to teach and preach to Catholics. There is no such enforcement, either from Rome or from the bishops.

It seems obvious that all those prelates and priests who have gone along with the de-Catholicizing of people's belief and moral behavior do believe that they are making the Church more relevant, more practical, more in tune with the modern mind, more understandable and, therefore, acceptable. The parallel with the Judas complex seems complete.

For those who constitute the anti-Church are convinced that their plan is the one that is good for the Church as they conceive the Church to be. The example of the anti-Church attitude to the Eucharist carries frightening signals for the believer's mind. For the believer, the Church, in its spiritual reality, is the Mystical Body of Christ, which is made up of all those who are spiritually united with Christ by his divine grace. This Mystical Body can have, on this earth, only one tangible and visible form: the Roman Catholic institutional organization. The parallel between the betrayal of Jesus as a living, tangible, visible man by Judas, and the betrayal of the Church by the members of the anti-Church instills a horror in the believer while enlightening him as to the reality of the danger in which the Roman Catholic institutional organization is caught in the late twentieth century. Judas' betrayal of Jesus concerned primarily the physical body of Jesus; it implied several concomitant betrayals.

Judas, for example, felt no particular imperative to participate in the Last Supper—he got out on the first pretext, in order to proceed with his own plan. He did not partake in the Eucharist, of Christ's Body and Blood, as did the other Apostles. He had found nothing significant in Christ's promise of these as the sacrificial means of salvation and membership in his Church. Precisely one major act of malfeasance by the anti-Church indicates a disinterest in that Eucharist as the sacrificial Body and Blood of Christ offered at the immemorial Mass. Replacing that once central Roman Catholic focus with their own wild imaginings, the anti-Church have a vagarious ceremonial, simmering with interest in a "common meal" and relying for its effect on the paraphernalia of a hastily put-together "living theater" and the organized "togetherness" of a social gathering. Disinterest—amounting to betrayal—in the Eucharist is the common element between Judas and the anti-Church.

At this point of rejoining the Judas complex in the anti-Church, we come up against what St. Paul calls "the mystery of iniquity." Judas is the prime example. At the Last Supper, Jesus was quite frank: "It would have been better for that man [his traitor] never to have been born." But Jesus must have known from eternity and, therefore, from the moment that he personally called Judas to be one of his special Apostles that this man would surely betray him. Yet he picked him out. He trusted him. He gave him the only public office in that select group of followers. If we approach this fact from our human point of view, we will meet only with brain-twisting problems. The mystery—God's point of view—will always remain opaque to us, but we can accept it in faith.

Paul used that phrase "the mystery of iniquity" when writing to the Thessalonians about the universal apostasy that will precede the appearance of the anti-Christ, in the last days before the end of all human time. Before those terrible events of the final end, Paul tells his faithful, they will be faced with the fact that, contrary to human expectation, iniquity—the specific attack of Lucifer on the followers of Jesus—will operate on a grand scale. Jesus himself, speaking of those last days, echoed the same note, warning his followers that the servants of that iniquity would do to them exactly as they would do to him, so that even the just would succumb if God didn't shorten those days of their sufferings. Jesus' Church would be treated as Jesus had been treated by his enemies.

It is not fanciful but frighteningly impressive to realize that the Judas complex in Churchmen has already led the Church into a condition that reproduces the sufferings imposed on Jesus through the treachery of Judas.

The agony of doubt and fear Jesus underwent in Gethsemane Garden is paralleled by the Gethsemane of doubt and fear that dissident theologians have created in the Church. The neglect and contempt of Judas for partaking in what actually was a sacred event, the Last Supper, is reproduced in the multiple ways that the anti-Church has effectively diminished the sacramental importance of the Eucharist—indeed, the very reality of the Eucharist as the Body and Blood of Christ.

The imprisonment, torture, scourging and crucifixion of Jesus—direct results of Judas' treachery—have been and still are today reproduced in the bodies of millions who have been betrayed by Churchmen into the hands of cruel governments, in Europe, in Asia, in Latin America, in Africa. More especially, priests and prelates in those places have submitted to indescribable tortures precisely because they embody Christ's official Church and minister to his Mystical Body.

The desertion of Christ by the Apostles once Christ was arrested finds its mystical parallel in today's Churchmen: They deny they know him as the Son of God, or even that they know him or stand with him; and many good Churchmen, orthodox in belief, pure of life, flee from any reaction, any strong reaction, to the destruction of Christ's Church by the anti-Church, thus becoming responsible for the damage they could have prevented by putting themselves and their interests in second position, resisting the anti-Church on the parish and diocesan level.

A peculiar piece of desecration of Christ's Church is being committed by the anti-Church in its fomenting of the feminist movement among female religious. Jesus, in his sufferings, had at least the consolation of knowing that the women among his followers did not scatter like scared rabbits, nor did they betray him. They stayed with him to the bitter end of Calvary. Today, the women's movement in the Church, certainly allowed and in some cases encouraged by the anti-Church, is bent on desecrating the Body of the Church in the Sacrament, in the sacred vows of religion, in the precious functions of priest, pastor and teacher. All this can be traced to the Judas complex, part of the mystery of iniquity that is now operating in high gear throughout the Roman Catholic institutional organization.

Such an overall manifestation of the once latent power of that iniquity, now rampant within the Church and directly the doing of the anti-Church, surely orients the mind to at least the beginnings, if not the actual beginning, of that universal apostasy among believers that St. Paul explicitly foretells and insists is the direct prelude to the climactic arrival of the Man of Destiny, the anti-Christ.

35. The Triple Weakness

The overall deterioration of the Roman Catholic institutional structure has now gone so far, indeed with each passing year proceeds at such a sustained pace; and Pope John Paul II and his papal bureaucracy have been pushed or have retreated into such ineffectual isolation from the day-to-day governance of the Church Universal, that now three dreadful outcomes are possible. Any of them could—probably would—entail the final disintegration of this Roman Catholic institutional organization as we have known it, and as men and women have known it for over five hundred years.

The day that a sizable body of Roman Catholics, clergy and laity, become convinced—rightly or wrongly—that the then occupant of the apostolic throne of Peter is not, perhaps never was, a validly elected pope, that day the presently continuous piece-by-piece deterioration of the organizational structure will be quickened into a muffled collapse of the entire organization. The already schism-split and heresy-ridden Roman Catholic body will then be a headless thing, a complicated machine exploding in all directions into fragments, because its secure casing and capstone cover were shattered.

For the only tangible guarantee Roman Catholics have that a man has truly become Pope is the legal guarantee of valid election in a legal Conclave of legal cardinals. Their faith then assures them that through this man and his predecessors they are in historical relationship with Jesus Christ, who founded the Church, and in supernatural relationship with Christ as he now is in the Heaven of God's glory. The legality—or validity, to use the ecclesiastical term—of a papal election depends on the exact observance, in the presence of witnesses, of the various visible and controllable procedures laid down in the rules for papal elections.

The final outcome of the election—a validly elected pope—is attained only with the freely pronounced *Accepto* of the Pope-elect. This is why Cardinal Laurenti, who became Pope-elect at the Conclave of February 1922, could never be regarded as Pope: He did freely decline to accept the pontificate, having been validly elected by the due majority. No one has to accept the Petrine Office. A pope-elect who refuses to accept is not obliged to explain why he has refused it, just as a pope who resigns the office is not obliged to explain why he has resigned.

What does the term "freely" mean when we say that the Pope-elect must freely accept or reject his election to the pontificate?

Take, for example, the Conclave of 1903, which produced as Pope Pius X Giuseppe Melchiorre Cardinal Sarto. But Sarto was not the prime choice of those sixty-two Cardinal Electors. After one voting session and scrutiny of the votes, on August 1, the first day of the Conclave, it was clear that the required majority (twenty-nine in this instance; Sarto got only five votes in that session) went to Italian-born Mariano Cardinal Rampolla del Tindaro. Rampolla, if allowed, would have pronounced the required *Accepto*, would therefore have become Pope automatically.

But he was not allowed to accept the pontificate. At that time, Emperor Franz Joseph of Austria had the privilege from the Vatican of vetoing any pope-elect he did not fancy. Rampolla he did not fancy— but the majority of Cardinal Electors never found out in their lifetime why it was so. The ostensible reason given for the Emperor's veto was Rampolla's record of political opposition to Austria and his support of France. So, on August 2, the Polish-born Jan Cardinal Puzyna of Austria-Hungary stood up in the Conclave and announced the Emperor's veto on Rampolla.

Rampolla and the other Cardinal Electors bowed to the Austrian veto, because he and all the cardinals knew exactly what damage the persnickety Franz Joseph could cause the Churchmen in Central Europe, where the domains of the Austro-Hungarian empire stretched. In that sense, Rampolla's *Non accepto* was free. He and the other cardinals freely accepted the existence of that veto. But insofar as the Emperor's veto impeded the cardinals' having the pope they freely chose, and impeded Rampolla from acceding to their overwhelming wish, neither they nor he was free. Yet no one then or since would hold that Rampolla was the real Pope, that Sarto—the Pope-elect produced by a later session of voting and scrutiny—was not validly Pope.

It was only in subsequent years that the true motive for Franz Joseph's veto was revealed. The Emperor was privy to a very closely held secret: Cardinal Rampolla had joined the Lodge of Freemasons. Without any doubt, the Emperor had the right to veto a papal candidate he did not fancy. Rampolla and the Electors bowed to the exercise of that privilege. But an entirely different situation would arise if a pope-elect were prevented from accepting the papacy by someone who had no right to do so, someone who threatened ruin and death to a pope-elect's reputation and family and person if he accepted his election as pope. Such a threat would be unjust, would be an undue limitation on the freedom of the Cardinal Electors. In that instance, the Pope-Elect would be in no way free. Unjust force and pressure would rob him of his freedom and would rob the Church of its validly elected Pope.

But very tortuous questions can thus arise. Nowadays, for instance, there is no state power or individual to whom the Holy See has granted a formal veto power on popes-elect. There is, however, a different category of persons outside the Conclave that the Holy See recognizes as having a legitimate interest in the actual identity of the new Pope. The Cardinal Electors entering a Conclave today are aware of which papal candidate is persona non grata to which interested outside party. Veto it is not, in the old formal sense; yet the likes and dislikes of such outside parties are certainly taken into account. And, therefore, at least theoretically, the situation can arise in which a duly elected candidate for the pontificate is vetoed.

In such a case—and it is not as theoretical as it would sound—very puzzling questions would emerge concerning the election of a second pope-elect in the same Conclave. Those questionings could blossom into a persuasion that the second election was invalid, that indeed the freedom of the Electors had been unduly manacled, and that the Church had been hoodwinked, and that the valid Pope-Elect had been sidetracked.

If such a persuasion was shared by a sizable body of Roman Catholics, the consequences could be dire for Church unity.

The same catastrophe of disintegration would desolate the Roman Catholic institutional organization—this is the second dreadful possibility—if a sizable body of Roman Catholic clergy and laity became convinced, rightly or wrongly, that the then occupant of the Throne of Peter was elected quite validly but over time had become heretical, and was actually collaborating, actively or passively, in the piece-by-piece dismemberment of the sacred Petrine Office and its ministerial organization. For a pope who became a heretic would cease to be pope.

In such a situation, the principal cause of disintegration would be the lack of any authoritative voice in the Church structure by which Catholics would be assured authoritatively that their Pope had or had not fallen into heresy. For there is no official mechanism within the structure of the Church that is authorized to pass judgment on pope and papacy. Indeed, the Church's official code of ecclesiastical law, canon law, expressly denies to anyone the right or duty of passing official judgment on pope or papacy.

Only once so far in this century did a situation arise when a pope, Paul VI, did contemplate and take the first steps along a course of action that some of his closest advisers throught would have entailed certain heresy. This arose because of the way in which Paul VI originally proposed to change the age-old and all-important ceremony of the Roman Mass. His first version of a new Mass ceremony, those advisers argued, if ever it had been imposed and enforced throughout the Church Universal, would effectively have done away with those elements of the ceremony that were and still today are dogmatically essential to the successful confection of the Sacrifice of Jesus Christ on the cross of his death. At least two cardinals, Ottaviani and Bacci, made it clear privately to Pope Paul VI and publicly to third parties that if he went ahead with his plans for the new Mass ceremony, they would not hesitate to denounce him publicly to the whole Church as a heretic and as deposed from the Throne of Peter. They were prepared to denounce his new Mass ceremony as reeking of heresy. The faithful would thereby have been released from all allegiance and obedience to Pope Paul VI. He would have ceased to be pope.

In the event, Pope Paul, under such a dire threat from two prestigious cardinals, retreated from his original proposal; and the Church was spared a harrowing experience. But it is to be noted that neither Ottaviani nor Bacci nor any of the other Churchmen involved had any juridical right to make the threat or to carry it out. The mere threat frightened Paul VI into retreat; by modifying his first version of the new Mass in order to eliminate the most glaringly offensive elements of his original text, and by counterthreatening Cardinal Ottaviani with deprivation of the Sacraments, he escaped official censure at the hands of his Vatican colleagues. That 1967 crisis was kept under Vatican wraps.

Thus a great searing and divisive rift could split Church members, some siding with the Pope, others declaring him invalidated by his alleged heresy. Inevitably, at least two Church bodies would emerge, each contesting the other, each claiming to be orthodox. Whether an attempt to elect a new (and supposedly orthodox) pope would be made by those who believed the original Pope to be heretical, or whether solid segments of the Catholic body would detach themselves from obedience to the accused Pope, the effect—disintegration—would be a wholesale loss of faith in the papacy, resulting in abandonment of Catholic religious practice and observance of Catholic moral precepts, which would be followed by the adoption of the "cafeteria" religion John Paul II has derided, the "pick-and-choose" Catholicism of many millions of Catholics today in North America and throughout the Western world.

There is one other possible development within the Roman Catholic body that, if unchecked, could shatter its unity of structure. Briefly, this is the Conclave election of a papal candidate whose policy would be to dissolve the unity and change the structure of the Roman Catholic Church by simply abandoning the exercise of the Petrine Office and privilege on which the structural unity of the Church is built as a visible body and by disassociating the approximately four thousand bishops of the Church from their collegial submission to the papacy—the principle on which they have been, up to now, structured. All this would mean a new function for the Bishop of Rome, and not the traditional one; it would also entail a new relationship of all bishops, including the Bishop of Rome, to each other. If anyone doubts seriously that such an eventuality could come about, let him remember that no one would have seriously speculated during the forties and fifties that a pope in the sixties would attempt to do away effectively with the elements that guaranteed the central happening of the Roman Mass; namely, the reenactment or re-presentation of Christ's Sacrifice on Calvary. Yet that, according to reliable sources, is precisely what happened.

There is a second reason why no one should consider farfetched the third possibility outlined above. A serious consideration of the present situation with dispassionate eyes very quickly reveals the grim fact of Roman Catholic life today: On the universal level of parish and diocese, and on the superior level of papacy and papal ministry, we will find present all the dispositive elements required and sufficient to bring this dire development to fruition. Indeed, we will find these elements have already been working intensively and extensively.

On the level of parish and diocese, and rife among bishops, priests, nuns and lay people, we will find an unshakable persuasion that before the Second Vatican Council there was one Roman Catholic Church—the "pre-Conciliar Church"; but that since that Council, the pre-Conciliar Church has ceased to exist, and its place has been taken by the "Conciliar Church," animated by the "spirit of Vatican II" and no longer called the "Roman Catholic Church" but instead called either, in the biblical words, the "people of God" or simply, vaguely, the "Church."

We will find that the two "Churches" are radically different in the minds of bishop, priest, nun and lay person. Different on four capital points. The "Conciliar Church" lays no claim to exclusive possession of the means of eternal salvation. Non-Catholics as such and non-Christians as such can make equal claims to have the means of salvation within their own religion—or "way of life," if they happen to be religionless. For all of us—Catholics, non-Catholics and non-Christians—are just pilgrims to the same goal, although approaching it by different roads. Second, in the Conciliar Church, the source of religious enlightenment, guidance and authority is the local "community of faith." Correct beliefs and correct moral practice no longer come from a hierarchic body of bishops submissive to the central teaching authority of one man, the Bishop of Rome. Third, the worldwide clusters of "communities of faith" have as their prime function to cooperate with "mankind" in building and assuring the success of world peace and world reform in the use of earth's resources so as to eliminate economic oppression and political imperialism. Fourth, the former Roman Catholic Church rules of moral behavior about life issues—conception, marriage, death, sexuality— must be brought into fraternal alignment with the outlook, desires and practices of the world at large. Otherwise, how can members of the Church claim to have opened up to their human brothers and sisters?

Now, these radical differences between the two "Churches" are seen as the prime fruits of the Second Vatican Council, which is endlessly quoted in order to justify them. The horrible fact is that the documents of that Council can be quoted to support these differences. For those documents are pockmarked with ambiguities in matters of faith, and in at least two of them, there are statements that, prima facie, seem irreconcilable with the constant teaching of the Roman Catholic Church and its popes up to the reign of Pope John XXIII and the opening of his Council.

On the level of papacy and papal ministerial organization, we find elements that foment, protect and give free rein to the aberrant "spirit of Vatican II" rife on the parish and diocese levels. We find that two popes, Paul VI and John Paul II, did not exercise their supreme teaching privilege and authority in order to prevent the birth of the "spirit of Vatican II"; or, once it started to flourish, refused to take the bull by the horns in the one way they and only they could do. For quite a long time now, Roman Catholics have needed a statement issuing from the personal power and privilege of the Pope, from his *ex cathedra* infallibility, once and for all and without ambiguity telling all Catholics and all Christians and, for that matter, the entire world which of the two "Churches" is the orthodox one, which represents the Roman Catholic Church, the one and true Church vindicated by so many popes and so many martyrs and so many saints. Needed, in other words, is the authoritative interpretation of the Second Vatican Council's official documents.

But a papal statement cannot be mere words. The Church has been responding with words, and its atmosphere has been thick with documents and programs and reports, every year since the end of the Second Vatican Council. There must be reenforcement of Catholic laws by means of the traditional sanctions known to all of us: excommunication, expulsion from official positions, name-by-name condemnation of the people—prelates, priests, theologians, nuns, lay people—who refuse to accept the papal statements.

Both popes have refused to do this. Their neglect to do so has been excused or explained away by an attempt to maintain that they are preoccupied with more immediate or more important issues. But in the growing and spreading "spirit of Vatican II," there blossom the baneful flowers of destruction for the Roman Catholic institutional organization. Its protection is the vital element in the Petrine Office both these pontiffs swore to defend as personal representatives of Christ.

This is why the accusation of malfeasance in high office has been hurled against both pontiffs. They were judged as collaborating in the lethal endgame of those who intend to encompass the liquidation of the papacy and of the Roman Catholic institutional organization.

Unchecked and unhindered, the development will go as follows: With the slow leavening of the bishops everywhere by the "spirit of Vatican II," with no countervailing stance adopted by papal Rome, it is inevitable that what we now can see clearly in a restricted number of cardinals will permeate a greater and greater number. There is very little doubt in anybody's mind that cardinals such as Joseph Bernardin of Chicago, Basil Hume of Westminster, Godfried Danneels of Belgium, Paulo Evaristo Arns of São Paulo, Roger Etchegeray of France, are partisans of "the spirit of Vatican II."

There are, to be sure, cardinals alive today who, together with more cardinals yet to be created by Pope John Paul II, will elect the pope who succeeds him. All will come into the next Conclave from a Church structure in which they have functioned for at least twenty-five years and where they not only did not curb or combat or even correct the aberrancies of the "spirit of Vatican II," but fomented it passively (by doing nothing) or actively (because they shared that same "spirit"). They will come from dioceses where the vast majority of bishops will know nothing and will want to know nothing that doesn't cohere with the "spirit of Vatican II." The parishes and dioceses behind them are already thoroughly leavened by that same "spirit."

Barring a last-minute miracle, their choice of papal candidate will be one of their number, whose papal policy will be to crown and confirm the official existence of the "spirit of Vatican II."

Such a cardinal validly elected as pope will have as a principle of action what Popes Paul VI and John Paul II apparently adopted as a temporary expedient: not to exercise the now outmoded Petrine privilege of office. Paul VI promulgated the documents of the Second Vatican Council and sat back while the Church was devastated by the impact of the bastardization employed both by his Vatican officials and by his bishops throughout the Church. John Paul II has again and again sanctified the Council documents with papal assurances that they now hold the norm for Catholic belief and behavior.

Between those two pontiffs, Paul VI and John Paul II, on the one hand, and the next pope, elected after John Paul II dies, there will be this difference. That new pope's deficiency in his high office will be the result of a conviction that the original papal and Petrine Office as practiced by the Roman popes up to the last third of the twentieth century was really nothing more than a time-conditioned result of cultural modes extending way back hundreds of years; and that now is the time to downgrade its importance in order to free the "spirit of Vatican II" to mold the Church in an image that will suit the progressive mind of a new and far different age.

Roman Catholics will then have the spectacle of a pope validly elected who cuts the entire visible body of the Church loose from the traditional unity and the papacy-oriented apostolic structure that the Church has hitherto always believed and taught was divinely established.

The shudder that will shake the Roman Catholic body in that day will be the shudder of its death agony. For its pains will be from within itself, orchestrated by its leaders and its members. No outside enemy will have brought this about. Many will accept the new regime. Many will resist. All will be fragmented. There will be no one on earth to hold the fractionating members of the visible Roman Catholic body together as a living compact organization. Men will then be able to ask for the first time in the history of the Church: Where is the visible body of the Church Christ founded? But there will be none visible. The Church Christ founded will be in the same condition as on the day that the Apostle Philip encountered the Ethiopian official on the road from Jerusalem to Gaza and, finding that this man had received the grace to believe in Jesus, baptized him at a wayside well. After that Philip disappeared, and the official continued on his way. But now he was a living member of the Church of Christ, a participant in the Mystical Body of Christ, as surely as any Christian of a thousand years later who was baptized in one of Europe's cathedral baptisteries and had his name registered as an official member of the visible Church structure to be found everywhere around the cathedral.

But for that Ethiopian official there was no visible Church structure. Actually, by that simple ceremony of entering the wayside stream with the Apostle Philip and accepting baptism in the name of the Father, the Son and the Holy Spirit, that official had joined an underground, the nascent Christian underground, against which already the first pogroms had been launched by the resident Jewish authorities headed by a fiery rabbinical zealot named Saul of Tarsus, who, in the words of the same chapter of the Acts of the Apostles that tells of the Ethiopian's baptism, "wreaked havoc on the Church, entering into every house, and dragging men and women out and throwing them into prison."

For however or wherever the Church founded by Christ survives and lives on, it is sure that it will live on; the whole brute strength of Hell will not prevail against it. And the successor of Peter, whoever he is during those dire days, will finally be converted and will, as Jesus foretold after his resurrection, restore and bring back to spiritual strength the faith of his bishops and people in the Church of Christ.

36. Scenario: The Consistory

It was the first time and, although no one there quite realized it, the last time these particular 153 men would assemble together in the second-floor auditorium of the Nervi Hall of Audiences in Rome and sit down together facing Papa Valeska: a small sea of cardinalitial blood purple wreathing the hemicircle of tiers undulating and spiraling down around the narrow dais where that lone white-robed figure sat as a gleaming and immovable rock on which all waves could fall, falter, break and dissolve into receding rivulets of foam. Not for nothing had Christ anciently renamed Simon as Peter.

The Pope's peremptory, tight-lipped summons to his Consistory—"I wish to speak with all my cardinals privately"—had made no bureaucratic distinction between active and retired cardinals, and no legalistic distinction between voting (under eighty years of age) and nonvoting cardinals (over eighty). "Neither bureaucracy nor legalism has any place in my Consistory." Every cardinal was to come. And in full-dress regalia. They had all come. Whatever their motives might have been—sense of duty, curiosity, fear, hope, force of habit, devotion, ambition, opportunism, love—none of the cardinals boycotted Valeska's Consistory.

This was surprising, seeing that no precise information was available about *what* the Holy Father had in mind; and the usually informative in-house Vatican sources could honestly supply only a sincere "Nobody knows" to all the discreet inquiries made beforehand. All anyone knew was what the papal summons said: "This Consistory will be under the protection of the Precious Blood of Our Savior guaranteeing the Keys of the Kingdom." This appeared to many as the typical language of "Rome" when speaking of subjects as wide-ranging as Peter's Pence, the Vatican budget deficit, papal teaching about the Holy Trinity or in-vitro fertilization techniques. The major world media had described the forthcoming Consistory with the stock explanation that "an imminent reorganization of Vatican finances is expected, " or "consistories have a long and ancient history in the Church of Rome." The consensus among the anti-Church partisans was definitely minimalist. "Probably another semipublic meditation on the Blessed Virgin according to the Pope's personal devotion" —that was the most pitying guess about the subject on the Holy Father's mind. The soundest reaction came from retired nonagenarian Luis Cardinal Silva, who, with crackling bones, had risen from his invalid's bed in Valparaiso, Chile, muttering to his horrified but helpless nurses: "This is it! I've got to go! It's an ending or it's a beginning. I've got to be there! At last that young man is going to do something! Maybe!"

So, on this July 1, the feast day of the Most Precious Blood of Jesus, just two days after the feast day of Sts. Peter and Paul, the Founding Apostles of the Pope's Roman See, all Valeska's cardinals were present. But from the very moment of their arrival at the Nervi Hall, it was clear that this Consistory was not going to resemble any Consistory in living memory.

First of all, security was at its tightest. The approaches to the Nervi were guarded by Italian police armed with automatic weapons. Around the main doors of the hall, a detachment of stalwart Swiss Guards formed a gauntlet of security through which those entering passed in single file. Without proper documents, Sts. Peter and Paul themselves would not have been admitted past those two checkpoints.

Inside, there was a novelty. The lobbies, the elevators and the stairs were manned by what seemed to be a small army of uniformed and bemedaled military men. True, they carried no visible sidearms. But each one wore a sword, and their seriousness and gravity and formal manners suggested men under strict orders. Upstairs in the auditorium, each cardinal was escorted to his place, where a small printed bulletin carrying the golden embossment of the Crossed Keys and Tiara informed him that the Holy Father would address his cardinals at 9:00 A.M. The television and radio booths were occupied by those same military types, as was the back landing of the auditorium.

Of course, the cardinals recognized (some more quickly than others) the uniforms and insignia of the Sovereign Order of the Knights of Malta. That solemnizing fact—you couldn't but be impressed by the formality created by the Knights—together with the bareness of the bulletin notice, induced a quietude among the cardinals in which a low whispering was their loudest sound even before Valeska had entered.

The audience of cardinals had been even further muted into quietude by the way Papa Valeska had entered and opened the proceedings. He had been escorted into the auditorium promptly at 8:55 A.M. without fanfare, without any preceding warning except what that bulletin announced. He carried a single folder, did not look to right or left, took his seat, opened the folder, fingered a few pages thoughtfully, took out a ballpoint pen to make a note or two, put down the pen, and looked up for the first time at his audience. All present realized there was to be no opening hymn to the Holy Spirit, no formal introduction of the Holy Father. Papa Valeska could have been the chairman of the board, come to deliver an annual report.

Only a few popes—and those in modern times—have ever had to face an audience of over one hundred cardinals; and Papa Valeska was the first pope in history who sat down facing 153 of them. He knew them all, of course: about half of them better than the others, and about a dozen quite intimately. With some he had had deeply satisfying conversations, with others more than one head-on collision, with still others a prickly relationship made possible only because of an implicitly accepted cold distance between him and them. He was loved by some, not loved but all the same respected by some, and cordially disliked by some. Only a few had gone on record as hating him. He never had any real difficulty with those; he knew where he stood with them.

But with about half a dozen he always felt profoundly uneasy: those who never violated any rules of conventional respect, papal protocol and ordinary civility but who behind an artful mask of good behavior—even of ecclesiastical bonhomie—could not wait to see his pontificate over and done with. That form of contempt hurt Valeska profoundly.

"May Jesus be praised," Papa Valeska started, his voice low-toned, his pace deliberate. He glanced at his notes, reading a text he obviously knew very well, because he continually lifted his eyes to look at the cardinals while continuing uninterruptedly with his flow of words.

"Those were the first words I addressed to the Church and the world on the night of my election. May they be fulfilled in us today at this Consistory." His whole manner bespoke some terrible deliberacy of mind; and the hint of that maintained the tension in his listeners.

"What I have to say to you today will not take much time. We will be short in words but hopefully long and deep in our understanding.

"There can be no genuine doubt in anybody's mind about two aspects of the Church Universal today." The closed-circuit television cameras panned over the faces of the cardinals, all of them, willy-nilly, hanging on what this one man, the Pope, had to say.

"Since the end of the Second Vatican Council in 1965, there has been a radical change effected in liturgy, theology, piety, morals and ecclesial government—in barely thirty years!" Valeska himself could feel the sudden tension among whole groups of cardinals at these words. He went on calmly. "The Roman Catholic institutional organization of the forties and fifties of this century resembled the Roman Catholic institutional organization of the 1500s—even that of the 1300s—far more closely than the current 'Conciliar Church' resembles that of the forties and fifties. So great a chasm of difference in such a short time! So violently rapid a change!

"Second, throughout every region and in every department of Roman Catholic life today there is an inescapable and continuous slippage into disorder, disunity, confusion, unfaith and open apostasy. It is a rampant decadence everywhere, sparing nobody and no element—seminaries, diocesan and Roman chanceries, religious orders, male and female, schools, colleges, universities, families, our liturgy, our theology, our morality, our devotions, our missions in Africa and Asia, our personal standards. Everything about us has been affected by this slippage.

"At the beginning of my pontificate, in full recognition of these two

vital aspects, my general policy was one of waiting, of patience, of forbearance, of encouragement. The gargantuan changeover consequent
on the Second Vatican Council had, I reasoned, produced a temporary
imbalance. Church members, both clergy and laity, would in time recover their Roman Catholic balance, I argued with myself. There would
be a turnaround, I forecast, a moment when the organization would be
set aright again. I was sure of it.

"Above all, I was thinking of you, Venerable Brothers. You form my
papal subsidiarity; through you, I am supposed to guide and govern the
Church. That action of rebalancing matters in the Church must, therefore, come primarily from you, under my papal authority, and thus filter
down the ranks and echelons of the hierarchy to the level of the ordinary
clergy and the people.

"This was my understanding. That was my policy. This understanding
was inaccurate. That policy was faulty. There has been no turnaround,
no sign of any rebalancing. I know it. You know it.

"Look at what we together have wrought—this 'Conciliar Church' of
ours. Look at it in the broad view, not concentrating on the individual
debilitating agencies now corroding its vitals. Leave all details aside, and
see the big picture.

"In our laissez-faire management, we have nourished an institutional
organization of people and material which every year becomes less and
less recognizable as Roman Catholic. Overall, the pressure on us has
been to fuse with the ever-changing backgrounds of human cultures; to
accept the modern attitude that, in the words of one neopagan philosopher, 'Our brains are stargates, our bodies cells of mystery' to be ex-
plored, to thus attain 'citizenship in a world larger than our aspirations,
more complex than all our dreams.' In sum, to mix into the world around
us to the point of invisibility for Catholicism.

"This is what we have wrought. This is our 'Conciliar Church' today.
Look, please, in the mirror I am holding up for us all to gaze in, for you
as my bishops and prelates, for me as your Pope, so that once, just this
once, we acknowledge the truth of our situation to ourselves and to our
God.

"In the Gospel of the love of Jesus Christ, there is one terrible scene
that has struck fear into my soul. Share it with me, because it concerns
you as my bishops and me as your Pope." Valeska pulled a small copy of
the New Testament from his pocket, and stood up while rummaging
through the pages. "It's described in Luke . . . yes, Luke . . . here it is!"
By this time he had strolled to one end of the dais.

"So! It was the night before he died . . . the Last Supper . . . all the disciples around him"—scanning the text as he spoke. "The traitor Judas had left the Supper Room: Satan, Luke says, had entered into Judas' heart, even though he was one of the Twelve Apostles, and he leaves on the nefarious business of betraying the Lord Jesus." Valeska raised his eyes and looked at the cardinals nearest him. "Even though he was one of the Twelve Apostles." He repeated the words with a look of astonishment on his face.

Scanning the Gospel text again: "Then our Lord consecrated the bread and the wine . . . all the Apostles received it from his hands . . . and then they had a dispute—the Apostles—as to which of them was really the greatest. . . . Jesus rebuked them, assuring them that they all would be important personages in his Kingdom . . . then, answering their question about who would be or was the leader and the greatest among them, he indicated Simon Peter and . . . yes, here he speaks to them all, putting Simon Peter first: 'Simon, Simon, look. Satan has desired to sieve all of you like wheat.' Jesus says that to all of the Apostles listening to him, just as Jesus now says it to all of you listening to me." Now Valeska was looking around the tiers.

"All of you. Satan wanted to separate you all away from the golden grain, the Bread of Life, turn you into worthless chaff, have you thrown into the fires of the eternal furnace." There was no sound from that audience. One Eminence wet his lips. Another Eminence ran his index finger around his collar to free it from the perspiration on his neck.

Valeska looked down at his text. " 'But,' Jesus went on, now speaking exclusively to Simon Peter, 'I have prayed for you.' " Valeska's voice slowed and thickened with feeling. " 'I have prayed for you that you not lose your faith.' " Valeska choked on those last three words. He stood there, head bowed, for some seconds; then, laying his little New Testament on the counter, he sank slowly to his knees. This action produced consternation among the cardinals.

Most of them did not know what to do. Here and there around the tiers, a sprinkling of figures rose to their feet, scarlet exclamation points. Then one after the other, and in twos and threes, the generality stood up. About forty or fifty remained frozen in their seats, shooting glares—nervous, resentful, questioning—at each other. Those standing could not kneel. Those sitting could not bring themselves to stand once they had obviously refused to imitate the generality. Frankevic, the papal secretary, and an irascible papal aide, Father O'Donnell, viewing the event on closed-circuit television upstairs in Valeska's study, quickly scribbled down the names of the seated cardinals.

"The idiots," O'Donnell said in his nervy way. "They've shown their hand!"

"No, Father Joe." Frankevic was smiling grimly. "They were caught off balance. He caught them. Their hatred was stronger than their prudence. Evil will out!"

Valeska found his voice. "Those words, Venerable Brothers, are addressed to me, not to you. For I am Peter today." The words came out of that bowed kneeling figure as if marinated in some deep inner anguish. "The Lord Jesus prayed for me that I not lose my faith." There was a slight pause. "I have a confession to make, Venerable Brothers, and a pardon to ask." The image of kneeling Pope and listening cardinals coming to Frankevic and O'Donnell on the closed circuit might as well have been a still photograph in color, and not a live transmission, so immobile were all the figures for about twenty seconds. No standing cardinal swayed on his feet. No seated cardinal stirred.

"Satan, the Enemy, tried to sieve me like chaff, whether in India or in Italy or in the U.S.A. or in Africa or in Latin America or back home here beside the Tomb of the Apostles. He sieved me. He shook me. He confused me. He led me to commit errors of practical judgment. He made me deaf to the protests of the faithful. He made me vulnerable to the half-lies, the wheedling half-truths, the pleas of hypocrites, the soft talk of those who hated me as Peter's successor.

"*Mea culpa! Mea culpa! Mea maxima culpa!*" Valeska struck his breast with his fist. "It was my own fault. It was my weakness. It was my own fault, my own fault." The voice trailed away into the silence of a few moments. Then, not abruptly, but slowly, he rose to his feet, one hand grazing across his eyes to brush away the tears that blinded him, and muttered almost inaudibly, "At times, only tears . . . only tears, Lord, will suffice . . . only tears."

He started walking back to his chair at the center of the dais, his voice picking up more firmness and volume. "Saint Luke goes on with the rest of the Lord's words to Simon Peter. 'When you, Simon, return once more to the faith, you will restore the strength of faith to your brothers.' " He paused and turned his head, craning around to look up at the cardinals. "Please sit down!" He waited while the standing cardinals took their seats; but he could not see the stony looks of disapproval, anger and threat that some of those cardinals threw at those who had remained seated. Everyone concentrated now on Valeska.

He had stopped walking by then, and turned to face his audience. "No matter what the personal sins and failings of Peter's successors, they remain Peter's successors, sole possessors on earth of the Keys of the Kingdom, who are solely ensured against any misuse of those keys by the blood of Our Lord Jesus.

"The Keys of this Blood." Valeska repeated the phrase, letting his voice linger over each syllable. "The Keys of this Blood." He was regaining his composure and a greater control over his thoughts and delivery.

"My own conscience, and the intelligence available to me as universal pastor, has driven me, willy-nilly, to adopt a plan—I know it will be called the Papal Plan in the popular media—for at least facing the dire situation in which the institutional organization finds itself today."

He walked the short distance to his chair and sat down, turning several pages of his notes until he reached the place he was seeking. "That dire situation throws one grave question in my face: How much longer must I wait? How low can I allow our condition to sink? How low is too low?"

Valeska stood up and closed his folder. "Unless I wish to betray my papal oath, I have to take action. I have to say: This is far enough, low enough. At this point, we fight. Hence"—he looked for a long few moments at the folder, then began again—"hence, the Papal Plan.

"Here in Rome, there will be six new Congregations, all of them granted an interim existence, each one possessing absolute powers, all of them reporting directly to me. Each one will supervise one area of Church structure that needs drastic and immediate reform: Bishops, Religious Orders, Priests, Ecumenism, Diocesan Organizations, the Mass. Besides being endowed with absolute powers of excommunication, suspension and interdict, these interim Congregations will have at their disposal three organizations, two already familiar—the Legionnaires of Christ and the Personal Prelature commonly called the Opus Dei—and a third, which has already been established and exists on a worldwide basis but hitherto has remained in total secret.

"These Congregations will supersede any existing Roman Congregation—for instance, the present Congregations for Religious and for Bishops will cease to function until further notice.

"Now, exhaustive lists have been compiled. Let me just read you the main ones. There are, first of all, five important ones: cardinals, bishops, priests, seminary professors and theologians. Those whose names appear on those lists have a common fate: They will be automatically retired, stripped of any canonical authorization to function, and left free to pursue life as they see fit.

"There is, then, a second series of lists, covering such changes as the transfer of certain cardinals, the abolition of certain religious orders and congregations, both of men and of women, parishes and dioceses placed under interdict until priests, bishops, and layfolk return to Catholic practice.

"It has required a Herculean labor on the part of my collaborators to assemble the names of thousands of retired priests, retired bishops and retired theologians who will immediately replace those who are forcibly retired by papal decree.

"You will discover, in time, that there is a series of particular papal decrees. The principal ones should be mentioned here. There has been in the past and there will be in the future one official Roman Rite of the Mass. For the foreseeable future, there will be two officially sanctioned variations of that sacred Roman Rite: the traditional one that flourished for over a thousand years before the Council of Trent gave it a special cachet; and the Novus Ordo of Pope Paul VI, which, in a reformed state, is also authorized. Both will be said in Latin, as the Second Vatican Council decreed, except for vernacular prayers said by the people. The Pauline Novus Ordo will be purified of its suspect parts, the validating words of Consecration restored to it and, completely purged from it, Luther's additions. Performance of either Mass is decided not by a popular vote but by direct orders from the Holy See. All ecclesiastical sanctions launched against the so-called Traditionalist movements and leaders are hereby revoked. Anyway, most of them were null and void from the beginning.

"Another decree suspends all activities of the Justice and Peace Commission and all offices for ecumenism throughout the Church; and still another decree forbids any further use of both the infamous RENEW program and the RCIA program. These have to be suppressed as un-Catholic.

"There is already established a papal commission for a reexamination of the documents of the Second Vatican Council; its decrees will give the authentic interpretation of those documents, once and for all. I myself will be issuing a series of papal decrees about religious liberty, about the one, true Church as the only means of salvation, and about papal infallibility.

"A special *Motu Proprio* of mine will suspend all meetings and activities of all Bishops' Conferences, local and regional. This whole initiative of Bishops' Conferences has proved to be a seedbed of heresy, schism and theological error; and it has been one of the chief instruments in the hands of the anti-Church partisans in their quest to depapalize the Roman Catholic institutional organization.

"Lastly, there is the question of correcting and reformulating the attitude of the Roman Catholic worldwide organization and institution to the modern world. Unfortunately, what the Second Vatican Council stated in this regard was modeled on what Pope Paul VI formulated. Unfortunately, that Pontiff's formulation was fashioned for him by men of the Vatican and men and women outside the Vatican who had one aim and one aim only: to liquidate the essence of Catholicism and make our human organization of this Church the handmaiden of total secularization of Roman Catholicism. This attitude—already widespread and accepted by bishops, priests, religious and layfolk—must be purged from the Church.

"Your Eminences will be the first to receive all the relevant documents of my Papal Plan. But for the moment, the preceding explanations will suffice.

"Venerable Brothers, all I have outlined may sound like strong medicine. If you think that, you think accurately. It is strong medicine for the virulent disease slowly eating the vitals of the Church Universal."

Valeska was now gathering his papers into the folder. The cardinals were very quiet, most of them still under the impact of the Pontiff's words, some of them trying to answer the all-important question: What changes does this new attitude of this Pope augur in this Pope's foreign policy? One or two felt like asking the question in the silence that followed Valeska's abrupt ending, but they thought better of it.

"Leave them hanging in that wind, Holy Father," Frankevic said under his breath up in the study. "Let them swing a little in the winds of doubt and uncertainty."

The same thought was on Valeska's mind, but he thought better of it. About to turn on his heel and depart, he stopped. "I should perhaps add two further points, very briefly," he said. He put down his folder and folded his arms.

"I would remind Your Eminences that, as Pope, I hold the Keys of this Sacred Blood, and that the Holy See can wait and wait and wait and wait. For as long as is necessary. If I depart this life, when I depart this life, my successor here will wait and wait and wait. What power on earth can wait like that? Which of Your Eminences or of my bishops can wait as long as that? The strength of those Keys will never weaken. The perfection of that Blood will never be diluted.

"I am now proceeding to the Basilica. I expect all of you to join me there in silent prayer." Before his audience had realized what was happening, he had traversed the distance between his place on the dais and the exit, and was disappearing between four security men.

Some twenty minutes later, the last of Their Eminences straggled into the Basilica by the main doors and were motioned reverentially but firmly by security guards to travel up all 630 feet of the nave toward the central place of the Basilica, where the 449-foot-long transept crosses the nave. There the High Altar stands facing east beneath Bernini's all-bronze

canopy. In front of the altar is the circular marble balustrade and staircase leading down to an ancient chapel that holds the bronze sarcopha-
gus of Simon Peter. This whole section of the Basilica is called the
Confession of St. Peter, because the band of Greek and Latin inscrip-
tions running around the upper walls there records Simon Peter's confession: "You are Christ, the Son of the Living God. . . ."

Even from the main doors and up that enormous nave, the entering
cardinals could see the white-robed figure: Frozen by the distance, it
seemed dimly to be draped on the balustrade because of the whiteness
of that beautiful marble. Actually, Papa Valeska was kneeling there, his
cupped hands, fingers intertwined with a Rosary, resting on the balustrade, his eyes fixed on Canova's kneeling statue of Pope Pius VI, who,
the most recent pope to be kidnapped, was taken into exile, held prisoner
for four years by the dictators of the French Republic, and died in a
miserable barracks room of the citadel of Valence, France, in 1802, far
from the Tomb of the Apostles.

The moment Valeska had entered the Basilica, all security walkie-
talkies rattled with the red-alert code: "The dove is loose! The dove is
loose!" A cordon of security guards appeared as if by magic and ringed
around the Confession, surrounding Valeska. All exit and entry points
of the Basilica were barred and heavily guarded.

Three jeeploads of armed carabinieri tore at breakneck speed across
St. Peter's Square and screeched to a halt outside the main doors of the
Basilica. The command helicopter appeared, slowly circling above the
Basilica, the sharpshooters balancing at its doors and watching with
readied weapons. Plainclothes police, male and female, circulated
among the people caught in the Basilica by the security emergency.
Behind the cordon, the chance pilgrims and visitors, speaking a babel of
languages, gathered quickly, eyeing this unannounced event and wondering what was happening.

For some of the cardinals, the walk up that nave was the longest walk
of their lives. They knew that place quite well, knew all the hoary memories clinging to its walls. The also knew this Pope. They had learned to
expect two things from him: a deluge of well-chosen words and a panoply
of gestures heavily laden with symbolism. They had just had one half
hour's deluge of those words. Now surely must come the symbolism in
gesture.

One by one, or in small groups, some with muttered complaints, some
wearing a quiet but obvious air of resentment, one or two with barely
suppressed small supercilious smiles, the cardinals arrived at the Confession; and eventually all but a dozen sank gingerly and awkwardly to their
knees on the marble intarsia around the balustrade. That holdout dozen

bunched together to one side, carrying on a staccato conversation in whispers. They had gone along, noblesse oblige, with the farce of the so-called Consistory. Stone-faced security officers informed them they could not leave the Basilica or exit from the security cordon. They were prisoners; but they had no obligation and certainly no intention of follow-ing the lead of this Polish Bishop, as if they were nothing more than a bunch of junior seminarians flocking docilely on the heels of their spiri-tual director.

But they especially, as well as some others, were severely shaken by old and cranky Luis Cardinal Silva. They could not take their eyes off him. He was ludicrous, and he was a reproach to them. Silva was last in. He made his way slowly, laboriously, agonizingly, pausing every two or three steps, glaring at the cardinals in his way, breathing heavily and talking to himself, eventually reaching the balustrade. He could not kneel down. So he leaned his aching frame on the balustrade to Valeska's right and buried his face in his hands. Silva was crying quietly, un-ashamedly, as if he were totally alone, as only an old man can do with an inviolable sense of privacy.

Frankevic arrived at the tail end of all of them. He stood at the very back, inside the cordon, keeping his eyes on that motionless white-robed kneeling figure surrounded by a ragged hemicircle sea of purple. After a while, as the minutes passed, the secretary relaxed, staring pointedly at the standing cardinals as if each one of them was an unhealthy excres-cence, and praying. Surely some of these Eminences will get the Holy Father's message and meaning—this was his prayer. But his attention was mainly held by the kneeling cardinals.

He noted any and all of their movements, and where their heads turned, and who signaled to whom and what they were signaling. Yes, Frankevic concluded, at least some of them were slowly putting it all together, letting their surroundings and what they had just been told by Valeska sink into their spirits.

There was no escape from the significance of their surroundings: The kneeling statue of that worthy but worldly Pope whose physical beauty was ruined by hardship and whose pride was humbled by imprisonment and death in the contemptuous hands of his mortal enemies. The flick-ering lights of the ninety-five lamps that burn night and day around the entrance to the Tomb of the Apostles. The four massive ninety-five-foot-long bronze pillars, containing the bones of 31,000 ancient Roman mar-tyrs and sustaining the 700-ton weight of Bernini's canopy, brooding over the majesty of the High Altar. Above it all, the band of black lettering in Greek and Latin running around the upper walls and announcing Christ's momentous supreme choice in answer to Peter's confession of faith: "You are Peter. Upon this rock, I will build my Church. And the Gates of Hell will not prevail against it. . . ."

But after some ten minutes, Frankevic began to worry: How would or could all this be ended decorously, fittingly? He need not have worried.

Eventually, the silent posture of Pope and cardinals affected the onlookers behind the cordon of security guards. It was a group of German pilgrims who first broke into a softly sung version of the old Catholic hymn "Salve Regina," the medieval world's universally known and loved canticle of praise and supplication to the Virgin Mary. As they sang, more and more voices joined in. But in the vast expanse of the Basilica, the chant remained a thin piping chorus of voices wafting up into the ample spaces of that huge nave, echoing in the spanning dome and dying away in gently receding waves of appeal and hope and painful expectation.

When the last few notes were still simmering in all ears, it was the old weeping Chilean who took the initiative. To everybody's surprise, and to the horror of the few very formal-minded cardinals present, Silva tapped Valeska lightly on the shoulder with a knobby, bony finger. The sequence of events that followed could have been conceived by an expert choreographer.

In the eyes of the onlookers, the actions and expressions of Pope and cardinal were so unusual and spontaneous that they passed in front of the pilgrims and visitors like a series of sharply defined segments in a filmed drama, a series of slow-motion images designed to convey a spiritual vision and message.

Silva tapping the Pontiff's shoulder . . . Valeska craning around, smiling, listening to the old man . . . Silva's bulging eyes and moving lips . . . Valeska shaking his head, still smiling . . . Silva nodding vigorously, his mouth open in protest, every line of his gaunt, parchment-like face wreathed in vehemence . . . Valeska rising slowly and turning around to face the cardinals . . . Silva trying to kneel down, but instead falling with a little cry, like a thrown bundle of scarlet robes, at Valeska's feet, his lips touching the instep of Valeska's right shoe, one hand fumbling desperately for Valeska's hand as the Pope stretched it down to help him . . . Silva seizing it and kissing the Fisherman's Ring on the fourth finger . . . some Vatican aides rushing with shocked faces to pick the old man up and carry him away between them. . . .

After that, what happened etched itself even more graphically in onlookers' memories: Cardinals rising slowly to their feet. Some standing and looking around. Some moving forward immediately to kneel and kiss Valeska's instep and ring. Others, once on their feet, whispering and gesticulating with colleagues, shooting half-frightened glances in Valeska's direction. Other cardinals standing by themselves, at a total loss. Many lining up in a rough queue in order to perform that double obeisance. Many others backing away as from a dangerous situation, in groups of fives and sevens, eventually piercing the security cordon and leaving the scene with stiffly closed mouths and hooded eyes. They wanted no truck with this act of theater, or with this Pope's real character, now plainly known to them. Now their attitude was a matter of public record too. Why not? All was clear and in the light of day, for their colleagues, for Valeska, for the people.

Throughout it all, Valeska stood mute, motionless, a look of deep tiredness veiling his face, apparently not seeing anyone or anything in particular, withdrawn into some invisible sanctum of his own, some holy of holies, not even reacting as each cardinal held his hand momentarily, kissed it, kissed his instep, and withdrew. Some few gave a quick upward glance at his face, then looked away and departed. Valeska was oblivious to all this, apparently. He did not know how many came forward, and how many turned their backs on him. But Frankevic was assiduously counting and identifying the recalcitrants—actually forty-six of them, and not one surprise among them.

Eventually, it came to an end. Only Valeska remained, his back to the balustrade, Frankevic and Vatican aides standing to one side. The Pope motioned to the officials standing by. He walked over to the marble staircase and disappeared slowly down into the crypt below, as the great bells of St. Peter's starting tolling out the noon Angelus in their inimitable ocean-deep tones. The security cordon drew near, surrounding the High Altar and the balustrade. Other security officers persuaded most of the onlookers to move on.

Frankevic stood apart, tears of joy and frustration blinding him. At least, he reasoned, all was clear now. Friend and foe were on notice. Even if His Holiness had failed to rally all his cardinals, as he had failed in the past to rally all his bishops; and even if his pontificate was reckoned a failure on the human scale; still, ambiguity had been dispelled. Frankevic remembered the sense, but not the exact words, of a desperate plea and prayer made by the Greek warrior Ajax, forced to fight superior odds on a darkened plain:

> Father in Heaven,
> Deliver us from this darkness.
> And make our skies clear.
> If we must die,
> Let us die in the Light.

Index

About the Author

Malachi Martin, eminent theologian, expert on the Catholic Church, former Jesuit and professor at the Vatican's Pontifical Biblical Institute, is the author of the national best-sellers *Vatican, The Final Conclave, Hostage to the Devil* and *The Jesuits*. He was trained in theology at Louvain. There he received his doctorates in Semitic Languages, Archaeology and Oriental History. He subsequently studied at Oxford and at Hebrew University in Jerusalem. From 1958 to 1964 he served in Rome, where he was a close associate of the renowned Jesuit cardinal Augustin Bea and Pope John XXIII. He now lives in New York City.